NOVELS
for Students

Advisors

Erik France: Adjunct Instructor of English, Macomb Community College, Warren, Michigan. B.A. and M.S.L.S. from University of North Carolina, Chapel Hill; Ph.D. from Temple University.

Kate Hamill: Grade 12 English Teacher, Catonsville High School, Catonsville, Maryland.

Joseph McGeary: English Teacher, Germantown Friends School, Philadelphia, Pennsylvania. Ph.D. in English from Duke University.

Timothy Showalter: English Department Chair, Franklin High School, Reisterstown, Maryland. Certified teacher by the Maryland State Department of Education. Member of the National Council of Teachers of English.

Amy Spade Silverman: English Department Chair, Kehillah Jewish High School, Palo Alto, California. Member of National Council of Teachers of English (NCTE), Teachers and Writers, and NCTE Opinion Panel. Exam Reader, Advanced Placement Literature and Composition. Poet, published in *North American Review, Nimrod,* and *Michigan Quarterly Review,* among other publications.

Jody Stefansson: Director of Boswell Library and Study Center and Upper School Learning Specialist, Polytechnic School, Pasadena, California. Board member, Children's Literature Council of Southern California. Member of American Library Association, Association of Independent School Librarians, and Association of Educational Therapists.

Laura Jean Waters: Certified School Library Media Specialist, Wilton High School, Wilton, Connecticut. B.A. from Fordham University; M.A. from Fairfield University.

NOVELS for Students

**Presenting Analysis, Context, and Criticism
on Commonly Studied Novels**

VOLUME 37

Sara Constantakis, Project Editor

Foreword by Anne Devereaux Jordan

GALE
CENGAGE Learning™

Detroit • New York • San Francisco • New Haven, Conn • Waterville, Maine • London

Novels for Students, Volume 37

Project Editor: Sara Constantakis

Rights Acquisition and Management: Margaret Chamberlain-Gaston, Jackie Jones

Composition: Evi Abou-El-Seoud

Manufacturing: Rhonda Dover

Imaging: John Watkins

Product Design: Pamela A. E. Galbreath, Jennifer Wahi

Content Conversion: Katrina Coach

Product Manager: Meggin Condino

For product information and technology assistance, contact us at
Gale Customer Support, 1-800-877-4253.
For permission to use material from this text or product,
submit all requests online at **www.cengage.com/permissions**.
Further permissions questions can be emailed to
permissionrequest@cengage.com

While every effort has been made to ensure the reliability of the information presented in this publication, Gale, a part of Cengage Learning, does not guarantee the accuracy of the data contained herein. Gale accepts no payment for listing; and inclusion in the publication of any organization, agency, institution, publication, service, or individual does not imply endorsement of the editors or publisher. Errors brought to the attention of the publisher and verified to the satisfaction of the publisher will be corrected in future editions.

Gale
27500 Drake Rd.
Farmington Hills, MI, 48331-3535

ISBN-13: 978-1-4144-6700-9
ISBN-10: 1-4144-6700-1

ISSN 1094-3552

This title is also available as an e-book.
ISBN-13: 978-1-4144-7366-6
ISBN-10: 1-4144-7366-4
Contact your Gale, a part of Cengage Learning sales representative for ordering information.

Printed in Mexico
1 2 3 4 5 6 7 15 14 13 12 11

Table of Contents

The Informed Dialogue: Interacting with Literature

When we pick up a book, we usually do so with the anticipation of pleasure. We hope that by entering the time and place of the novel and sharing the thoughts and actions of the characters, we will find enjoyment. Unfortunately, this is often not the case; we are disappointed. But we should ask, has the author failed us, or have we failed the author?

We establish a dialogue with the author, the book, and with ourselves when we read. Consciously and unconsciously, we ask questions: "Why did the author write this book?" "Why did the author choose that time, place, or character?" "How did the author achieve that effect?" "Why did the character act that way?" "Would I act in the same way?" The answers we receive depend upon how much information about literature in general and about that book specifically we ourselves bring to our reading.

Young children have limited life and literary experiences. Being young, children frequently do not know how to go about exploring a book, nor sometimes, even know the questions to ask of a book. The books they read help them answer questions, the author often coming right out and *telling* young readers the things they are learning or are expected to learn. The perennial classic, *The Little Engine That Could, tells* its readers that, among other things, it is good to help others and brings happiness:

"Hurray, hurray," cried the funny little clown and all the dolls and toys. "The good little boys and girls in the city will be happy because you helped us, kind, Little Blue Engine."

In picture books, messages are often blatant and simple, the dialogue between the author and reader one-sided. Young children are concerned with the end result of a book—the enjoyment gained, the lesson learned—rather than with how that result was obtained. As we grow older and read further, however, we question more. We come to expect that the world within the book will closely mirror the concerns of our world, and that the author will *show* these through the events, descriptions, and conversations within the story, rather than *telling* of them. We are now expected to do the interpreting, carry on our share of the dialogue with the book and author, and glean not only the author's message, but comprehend how that message and the overall affect of the book were achieved. Sometimes, however, we need help to do these things. *Novels for Students* provides that help.

A novel is made up of many parts interacting to create a coherent whole. In reading a novel, the more obvious features can be easily spotted—theme, characters, plot—but we may overlook the more subtle elements that greatly influence how the novel is perceived by the reader: viewpoint, mood and tone, symbolism, or the use of humor. By focusing on both the obvious and more subtle literary elements within a novel,

Novels for Students aids readers in both analyzing for message and in determining how and why that message is communicated. In the discussion on Harper Lee's *To Kill a Mockingbird* (Vol. 2), for example, the mockingbird as a symbol of innocence is dealt with, among other things, as is the importance of Lee's use of humor which "enlivens a serious plot, adds depth to the characterization, and creates a sense of familiarity and universality." The reader comes to understand the internal elements of each novel discussed—as well as the external influences that help shape it.

"The desire to write greatly," Harold Bloom of Yale University says, "is the desire to be elsewhere, in a time and place of one's own, in an originality that must compound with inheritance, with an anxiety of influence." A writer seeks to create a unique world within a story, but although it is unique, it is not disconnected from our own world. It speaks to us *because* of what the writer brings to the writing from our world: how he or she was raised and educated; his or her likes and dislikes; the events occurring in the real world at the time of the writing, and while the author was growing up. When we know what an author has brought to his or her work, we gain a greater insight into both the "originality" (the world of the book), and the things that "compound" it. This insight enables us to question that created world and find answers more readily. By informing ourselves, we are able to establish a more effective dialogue with both book and author.

Novels for Students, in addition to providing a plot summary and descriptive list of characters—to remind readers of what they have read—also explores the external influences that shaped each book. Each entry includes a discussion of the author's background, and the historical context in which the novel was written. It is vital to know, for instance, that when Ray Bradbury was writing *Fahrenheit 451* (Vol. 1), the threat of Nazi domination had recently ended in Europe, and the McCarthy hearings were taking place in Washington, D.C. This information goes far in answering the question, "Why did he write a story of oppressive government control and book burning?" Similarly, it is important to know that Harper Lee, author of

To Kill a Mockingbird, was born and raised in Monroeville, Alabama, and that her father was a lawyer. Readers can now see why she chose the south as a setting for her novel—it is the place with which she was most familiar—and start to comprehend her characters and their actions.

Novels for Students helps readers find the answers they seek when they establish a dialogue with a particular novel. It also aids in the posing of questions by providing the opinions and interpretations of various critics and reviewers, broadening that dialogue. Some reviewers of *To Kill A Mockingbird,* for example, "faulted the novel's climax as melodramatic." This statement leads readers to ask, "Is it, indeed, melodramatic?" "If not, why did some reviewers see it as such?" "If it is, why did Lee choose to make it melodramatic?" "Is melodrama ever justified?" By being spurred to ask these questions, readers not only learn more about the book and its writer, but about the nature of writing itself.

The literature included for discussion in *Novels for Students* has been chosen because it has something vital to say to us. *Of Mice and Men, Catch-22, The Joy Luck Club, My Antonia, A Separate Peace* and the other novels here speak of life and modern sensibility. In addition to their individual, specific messages of prejudice, power, love or hate, living and dying, however, they and all great literature also share a common intent. They force us to *think*—about life, literature, and about others, not just about ourselves. They pry us from the narrow confines of our minds and thrust us outward to confront the world of books and the larger, real world we all share. *Novels for Students* helps us in this confrontation by providing the means of enriching our conversation with literature and the world, by creating an *informed* dialogue, one that brings true pleasure to the personal act of reading.

Sources

Harold Bloom, *The Western Canon, The Books and School of the Ages,* Riverhead Books, 1994.

Watty Piper, *The Little Engine That Could,* Platt & Munk, 1930.

Anne Devereaux Jordan
Senior Editor, TALL (Teaching and Learning Literature)

Introduction

Purpose of the Book

The purpose of *Novels for Students* (*NfS*) is to provide readers with a guide to understanding, enjoying, and studying novels by giving them easy access to information about the work. Part of Gale's "For Students" Literature line, *NfS* is specifically designed to meet the curricular needs of high school and undergraduate college students and their teachers, as well as the interests of general readers and researchers considering specific novels. While each volume contains entries on "classic" novels frequently studied in classrooms, there are also entries containing hard-to-find information on contemporary novels, including works by multicultural, international, and women novelists. Entries profiling film versions of novels not only diversify the study of novels but support alternate learning styles, media literacy, and film studies curricula as well.

The information covered in each entry includes an introduction to the novel and the novel's author; a plot summary, to help readers unravel and understand the events in a novel; descriptions of important characters, including explanation of a given character's role in the novel as well as discussion about that character's relationship to other characters in the novel; analysis of important themes in the novel; and an explanation of important literary techniques and movements as they are demonstrated in the novel.

In addition to this material, which helps the readers analyze the novel itself, students are also provided with important information on the literary and historical background informing each work. This includes a historical context essay, a box comparing the time or place the novel was written to modern Western culture, a critical essay, and excerpts from critical essays on the novel. A unique feature of *NfS* is a specially commissioned critical essay on each novel, targeted toward the student reader.

The "literature to film" entries on novels vary slightly in form, providing background on film technique and comparison to the original, literary version of the work. These entries open with an introduction to the film, which leads directly into the plot summary. The summary highlights plot changes from the novel, key cinematic moments, and/or examples of key film techniques. As in standard entries, there are character profiles (noting omissions or additions, and identifying the actors), analysis of themes and how they are illustrated in the film, and an explanation of the cinematic style and structure of the film. A cultural context section notes any time period or setting differences from that of the original work, as well as cultural differences between the time in which the original work was written and the time in which the film adaptation was made. A film entry concludes with a critical overview and critical essays on the film.

To further help today's student in studying and enjoying each novel or film, information on media adaptations is provided (if available), as well as suggestions for works of fiction, nonfiction, or film on similar themes and topics. Classroom aids include ideas for research papers and lists of critical and reference sources that provide additional material on the novel. Film entries also highlight signature film techniques demonstrated, and suggest media literacy activities and prompts to use during or after viewing a film.

Selection Criteria

The titles for each volume of *NfS* are selected by surveying numerous sources on notable literary works and analyzing course curricula for various schools, school districts, and states. Some of the sources surveyed include: high school and undergraduate literature anthologies and textbooks; lists of award-winners, and recommended titles, including the Young Adult Library Services Association (YALSA) list of best books for young adults. Films are selected both for the literary importance of the original work and the merits of the adaptation (including official awards and widespread public recognition).

Input solicited from our expert advisory board—consisting of educators and librarians—guides us to maintain a mix of "classic" and contemporary literary works, a mix of challenging and engaging works (including genre titles that are commonly studied) appropriate for different age levels, and a mix of international, multicultural and women authors. These advisors also consult on each volume's entry list, advising on which titles are most studied, most appropriate, and meet the broadest interests across secondary (grades 7–12) curricula and undergraduate literature studies.

How Each Entry Is Organized

Each entry, or chapter, in *NfS* focuses on one novel. Each entry heading lists the full name of the novel, the author's name, and the date of the novel's publication. The following elements are contained in each entry:

Introduction: a brief overview of the novel which provides information about its first appearance, its literary standing, any controversies surrounding the work, and major conflicts or themes within the work. Film entries identify the original novel and provide

understanding of the film's reception and reputation, along with that of the director.

Author Biography: in novel entries, this section includes basic facts about the author's life, and focuses on events and times in the author's life that inspired the novel in question.

Plot Summary: a factual description of the major events in the novel. Lengthy summaries are broken down with subheads. Plot summaries of films are used to uncover plot differences from the original novel, and to note the use of certain film angles or other techniques.

Characters: an alphabetical listing of major characters in the novel. Each character name is followed by a brief to an extensive description of the character's role in the novel, as well as discussion of the character's actions, relationships, and possible motivation. In film entries, omissions or changes to the cast of characters of the film adaptation are mentioned here, and the actors' names—and any awards they may have received—are also included.

Characters are listed alphabetically by last name. If a character is unnamed—for instance, the narrator in *Invisible Man*—the character is listed as "The Narrator" and alphabetized as "Narrator." If a character's first name is the only one given, the name will appear alphabetically by that name.

Variant names are also included for each character. Thus, the full name "Jean Louise Finch" would head the listing for the narrator of *To Kill a Mockingbird*, but listed in a separate cross-reference would be the nickname "Scout Finch."

Themes: a thorough overview of how the major topics, themes, and issues are addressed within the novel. Each theme discussed appears in a separate subhead. While the key themes often remain the same or similar when a novel is adapted into a film, film entries demonstrate how the themes are conveyed cinematically, along with any changes in the portrayal of the themes.

Style: this section addresses important style elements of the novel, such as setting, point of view, and narration; important literary devices used, such as imagery, foreshadowing, symbolism; and, if applicable, genres to which the work might have belonged, such as Gothicism or Romanticism. Literary terms are explained within the entry but can also be found in the Glossary. Film entries cover how the director conveyed the meaning, message, and mood of the work using film in comparison to the author's use of language, literary device, etc., in the original work.

Historical Context: in novel entries, this section outlines the social, political, and cultural climate in which the author lived and the novel was created. This section may include descriptions of related historical events, pertinent aspects of daily life in the culture, and the artistic and literary sensibilities of the time in which the work was written. If the novel is a historical work, information regarding the time in which the novel is set is also included. Each section is broken down with helpful subheads. Film entries contain a similar Cultural Context section because the film adaptation might explore an entirely different time period or culture than the original work, and may also be influenced by the traditions and views of a time period much different than that of the original author.

Critical Overview: this section provides background on the critical reputation of the novel or film, including bannings or any other public controversies surrounding the work. For older works, this section includes a history of how the novel or film was first received and how perceptions of it may have changed over the years; for more recent novels, direct quotes from early reviews may also be included.

Criticism: an essay commissioned by *NfS* which specifically deals with the novel or film and is written specifically for the student audience, as well as excerpts from previously published criticism on the work (if available).

Sources: an alphabetical list of critical material used in compiling the entry, with full bibliographical information.

Further Reading: an alphabetical list of other critical sources which may prove useful for the student. It includes full bibliographical information and a brief annotation.

Suggested Search Terms: a list of search terms and phrases to jumpstart students' further information seeking. Terms include not just titles and author names but also terms and topics related to the historical and literary context of the works.

In addition, each novel entry contains the following highlighted sections, set apart from the main text as sidebars:

Media Adaptations: if available, a list of audiobooks and important film and television adaptations of the novel, including source information. The list also includes stage adaptations, musical adaptations, etc.

Topics for Further Study: a list of potential study questions or research topics dealing with the novel. This section includes questions related to other disciplines the student may be studying, such as American history, world history, science, math, government, business, geography, economics, psychology, etc.

Compare and Contrast: an "at-a-glance" comparison of the cultural and historical differences between the author's time and culture and late twentieth century or early twenty-first century Western culture. This box includes pertinent parallels between the major scientific, political, and cultural movements of the time or place the novel was written, the time or place the novel was set (if a historical work), and modern Western culture. Works written after the mid-1970s may not have this box.

What Do I Read Next?: a list of works that might give a reader points of entry into a classic work (e.g., YA or multicultural titles) and/or complement the featured novel or serve as a contrast to it. This includes works by the same author and others, works from various genres, YA works, and works from various cultures and eras.

The film entries provide sidebars more targeted to the study of film, including:

Film Technique: a listing and explanation of four to six key techniques used in the film, including shot styles, use of transitions, lighting, sound or music, etc.

Read, Watch, Write: media literacy prompts and/or suggestions for viewing log prompts.

What Do I See Next?: a list of films based on the same or similar works or of films similar in directing style, technique, etc.

Other Features

NfS includes "The Informed Dialogue: Interacting with Literature," a foreword by Anne Devereaux Jordan, Senior Editor for *Teaching and Learning Literature* (*TALL*), and a founder of the Children's Literature Association. This essay provides an enlightening look at how readers interact with literature and how *Novels for Students* can help teachers show students how to enrich their own reading experiences.

A Cumulative Author/Title Index lists the authors and titles covered in each volume of the *NfS* series.

A Cumulative Nationality/Ethnicity Index breaks down the authors and titles covered in each volume of the *NfS* series by nationality and ethnicity.

A Subject/Theme Index, specific to each volume, provides easy reference for users who may be studying a particular subject or theme rather than a single work. Significant subjects, from events to broad themes, are included.

Each entry may include illustrations, including photo of the author, stills from film adaptations, maps, and/or photos of key historical events, if available.

Citing Novels for Students

When writing papers, students who quote directly from any volume of *NfS* may use the following general forms. These examples are based on MLA style; teachers may request that students adhere to a different style, so the following examples may be adapted as needed.

When citing text from *NfS* that is not attributed to a particular author (i.e., the Themes, Style, Historical Context sections, etc.), the following format should be used in the bibliography section:

"Night." *Novels for Students*. Ed. Marie Rose Napierkowski. Vol. 4. Detroit: Gale, 1998. 234–35.

When quoting the specially commissioned essay from *NfS* (usually the first piece under the "Criticism" subhead), the following format should be used:

Miller, Tyrus. Critical Essay on "*Winesburg, Ohio.*" *Novels for Students*. Ed. Marie Rose Napierkowski. Vol. 4. Detroit: Gale, 1998. 335–39.

When quoting a journal or newspaper essay that is reprinted in a volume of *NfS*, the following form may be used:

Malak, Amin. "Margaret Atwood's *The Handmaid's Tale* and the Dystopian Tradition." *Canadian Literature* 112 (Spring 1987): 9–16. Excerpted and reprinted in *Novels for Students*. Vol. 4. Ed. Marie Rose Napierkowski. Detroit: Gale, 1998. 133–36.

When quoting material reprinted from a book that appears in a volume of *NfS*, the following form may be used:

Adams, Timothy Dow. "Richard Wright: 'Wearing the Mask.'" In *Telling Lies in Modern American Autobiography*. University of North Carolina Press, 1990. 69–83. Excerpted and reprinted in *Novels for Students*. Vol. 1. Ed. Diane Telgen. Detroit: Gale, 1997. 59–61.

We Welcome Your Suggestions

The editorial staff of *Novels for Students* welcomes your comments and ideas. Readers who wish to suggest novels to appear in future volumes, or who have other suggestions, are cordially invited to contact the editor. You may contact the editor via e-mail at: **ForStudentsEditors@cengage.com.** Or write to the editor at:

Editor, *Novels for Students*
Gale
27500 Drake Road
Farmington Hills, MI 48331-3535

Literary Chronology

1797: Mary Wollstonecraft Shelley is born on August 30 in Somers Town, London, England.

1818: Mary Wollstonecraft Shelley's novel *Frankenstein* is published.

1835: Mark Twain is born Samuel Langhorne Clemens on November 30 in Florida, Missouri.

1843: Henry James is born on April 15 in New York City.

1851: Mary Wollstonecraft Shelley dies of a brain tumor on February 1 in London, England.

1862: Edith Wharton is born on January 24 in New York City.

1886: Henry James's *The Bostonians* is published.

1894: Mark Twain's *Pudd'nhead Wilson* is published.

1902: John Steinbeck is born on February 27 in Salinas, California.

1910: Mark Twain dies on April 21 in Redding, Connecticut.

1916: Henry James dies of complications from a stroke on February 28 in London, England.

1916: Shirley Jackson is born on December 14 in San Francisco.

1920: Edith Wharton's novel *The Age of Innocence* is published.

1921: Edith Wharton is awarded the Pulitzer Prize for Literature.

1931: The film *Frankenstein* is released.

1931: Toni Morrison is born on February 18 in Lorain, Ohio.

1932: Vidiadhar Surajprasad Naipaul (V. S. Naipaul) is born on August 17 in Chaguanas, Trinidad.

1937: Edith Wharton dies of a stroke on August 11 in Paris, France.

1940: Bharati Mukherjee is born on July 27 in Calcutta, India.

1942: John Steinbeck's *The Moon Is Down* is published.

1946: William Timothy O'Brien is born on October 1 in Austin, Minnesota.

1954: Louis Sachar is born on March 20 in East Meadow, New York.

1954: Louise Erdrich is born on June 7 in Little Falls, Minnesota.

1956: Fae Myenne Ng is born on December 2 in San Francisco, California.

1959: Shirley Jackson's *The Haunting of Hill House* is published.

1962: John Steinbeck is awarded the Nobel Prize for Literature.

1965: Shirley Jackson dies of heart failure on August 8 in Bennington, Vermont.

1968: John Steinbeck dies of a heart attack on December 20 in New York City.

1969: Edwidge Danticat is born in Port-au-Prince, Haiti.

1978: Tim O'Brien's *Going after Cacciato* is published.

1979: V. S. Naipaul's *A Bend in the River* is published.

1981: Toni Morrison's *Tar Baby* is published.

1986: Louise Erdrich's *The Beet Queen* is published.

1988: Toni Morrison is awarded the Pulitzer Prize for Fiction.

1989: Bharati Mukherjee's *Jasmine* is published.

1993: Fae Myenne Ng's *Bone* is published.

1993: The film *The Age of Innocence* is released.

1993: The film *The Age of Innocence* wins an Academy Award for Best Costume Design.

1993: Toni Morrison is awarded the Nobel Prize for Literature.

1994: Edwidge Danticat's *Breath, Eyes, Memory* is published.

1998: Louis Sachar's *Holes* is published.

2001: V. S. Naipaul is awarded the Nobel Prize for Literature.

Acknowledgments

The editors wish to thank the copyright holders of the excerpted criticism included in this volume and the permissions managers of many book and magazine publishing companies for assisting us in securing reproduction rights. We are also grateful to the staffs of the Detroit Public Library, the Library of Congress, the University of Detroit Mercy Library, Wayne State University Purdy/Kresge Library Complex, and the University of Michigan Libraries for making their resources available to us. Following is a list of the copyright holders who have granted us permission to reproduce material in this volume of *NfS*. Every effort has been made to trace copyright, but if omissions have been made, please let us know.

COPYRIGHTED EXCERPTS IN *NfS*, VOLUME 37, WERE REPRODUCED FROM THE FOLLOWING PERIODICALS:

Style, v. 35, Summer, 2001. Copyright © *Style,* 2001. All rights reserved. Reproduced by permission of the publisher and the author.—*College Literature*, v. 22, Feb. 1995. Copyright © 1995 by West Chester University. Reproduced by permission.—*College Literature*, v. 23, Oct. 1996. Copyright © 1996 by West Chester University. Reproduced by permission. Reprinted by permission.—*American Book Review*, v. 31, Nov./Dec. 2009. Copyright © 2009 by *The American Book Review*. Reproduced by permission.—*American Literature*, v. 50, Jan. 1979. Copyright © 1979 by Duke University Press. Reprinted by permission.—*Research in African Literature*, v. 31, Spring 2000. Copyright © 2000 by Indiana University Press.Reproduced by permission.—*Belles Lettres*, v. 10, Fall 1994. Reproduced by permission.—*Public Integrity*, Spring 2007. Copyright © 2007 by M.E. Sharpe Inc. Reprinted by permission.—*Dissent*, Summer 2002. Copyright © 2002 by the University of Pennsylvania Press. Reprinted by permission.—*Texas Studies in Literature and Language*, v. 40, Summer 1998. Copyright © 1998 by the University of Texas Press. Reprinted by permission.—*Variety*, v. 100, Dec 1931. Copyright © by *Variety*. Reprinted by permission.—*MELUS*, v. 24, Winter 1999. Copyright *MELUS: The Society for the Study of Multi-Ethnic Literature of the United States,* 1999. Reproduced by permission.—*MELUS*, v. 29, Summer 2004. Copyright © 2004 by *MELUS*. Reprinted by permission.—*Publishers Weekly*, v. 241, Jan. 24, 1994. Copyright © 1994 by *Publishers Weekly*. Reprinted by permission.—*Publishers Weekly*, v. 245, 1998. Copyright © 1998 by Reed Publishing USA. Reproduced from *Publishers Weekly,* published by the Bowker Magazine Group of Cahners Publishing Co., a division of Reed Publishing USA, by permission.—*National Women's studies Association Journal*, 11:1. Copyright © 1999 by *NWSA Journal*.Reprinted with permission of the Johns Hopkins University Press.—*Critique*, v. 41, Fall 1999. Copyright © 1999. All rights reserved. Reproduced by permission of Taylor & Francis Group, www.informaworld. com, conveyed through Copyright Clearance Center.—*American Studies International*, v. 35, Oct. 1997. Copyright © Mid-American Studies Association, 1997. Reprinted by permission of the publisher and the author.—*Studies in American Fiction*, v. 27, Spring 1999. Copyright © 1999 North-eastern University. Reproduced by permission.— *Film Criticism*, v. 33, 2008, pp. 77. Reprinted by permission.—*Children's Literature in Education*, v. 33, Sept. 2002. Copyright © 2002 by Springer. Reprinted by permission of Springer Science and Business Media—*Journal of Popular Film and Television*, v. 30, Fall 2002. Reprinted by permission of Taylor & Francis Group, www.informaworld. com, conveyed with permission of Copyright Clearance Center.—*Magpies*, v. 15, March 2000. Copyright © *Magpies Magazine* 2000.Reproduced by permission.—*Explicator*, v. 53, Spring 1995. Reprinted by permission of Taylor & Francis Group, www.informaworld.com, conveyed by Copyright Clearance Center.—*Studies in Contemporary Fiction*, v. 39, Summer 1998, pp. 341-53. Reprinted by permission of Taylor & Francis Group, www.informaworld.com—*Commentary*, November 2008, by permission; copyright © 2008 by Commentary, Inc.—*Journalism History*, v. 23, Spring 1997. Copyright © 1997 by *Journalism History*. Reprinted by permission.—*Texas Studies in Literature and Language*, v. 44, Winter 2002. Copyright © 2002 by the University of Texas Press. Reprinted by permission.—*Library Journal*, v. 18, Jan. 1993. Copyright © 1993 by *Library Journal*. Reprinted by permission.—*London Guardian*, Mar 20, 1999. Copyright © 1999 by Guardian Publications Ltd. Reproduced by permission of Guardian News Service, LTD.—*Twentieth Century Literature*, v. 42, Winter 1996. Copyright © 1996 by *Twentieth Century Literature*. Reprinted by permission.

COPYRIGHTED EXCERPTS IN *NfS*, VOLUME 37, WERE REPRODUCED FROM THE FOLLOWING BOOKS:

Newman, Judie. From *American Horror Fiction: From Brockden Brown to Stephen King*, Macmillan, 1990. Copyright © 1990 by Palgrave MacMillan. Reproduced by Palgrave MacMillan.—Friedman, Lenemaja. *Shirley Jackson*. Copyright © 1975 Gale, a part of Cengage Learning, Inc. Reproduced by permission. www.cengage.com/permissions.

Contributors

Susan K. Andersen: Andersen is a writer and teacher with a Ph.D. in English. Entry on *A Bend in the River*. Original essay on *A Bend in the River*.

Bryan Aubrey: Aubrey holds a Ph.D. in English. Entries on *Bone* and *The Moon Is Down*. Original essays on *Bone* and *The Moon Is Down*.

Cynthia A. Bily: Bily, a mother, teaches English at Macomb Community College in Michigan. Entry on *Holes*. Original essay on *Holes*.

Catherine Dominic: Dominic is a novelist and a freelance writer and editor. Entry on *Pudd'nhead Wilson*. Original essay on *Pudd'nhead Wilson*.

Donald G. Evans: Evans is a novelist, journalist, and instructor of writing. Entry on *Jasmine*. Original essay on *Jasmine*.

Charlotte M. Freeman: Freeman is a writer, editor, and former academic living in small-town Montana. Entry on *Going after Cacciato*. Original essay on *Going after Cacciato*.

Michael Allen Holmes: Holmes is a writer and editor. Entry on *The Bostonians*. Original essay on *The Bostonians*.

David Kelly: Kelly is a college instructor of creative writing and literature. Entries on *The Age of Innocence* and *Frankenstein*. Original essays on *The Age of Innocence* and *Frankenstein*.

Kathy Wilson Peacock: Wilson Peacock is a writer and editor. Entry on *The Beet Queen*. Original essay on *The Beet Queen*.

Rachel Porter: Porter is a freelance writer and editor who holds a bachelor of arts degree in English literature. Entry on *Tar Baby*. Original essay on *Tar Baby*.

Bradley A. Skeen: Skeen is a classicist. Entry on *The Haunting of Hill House*. Original essay on *The Haunting of Hill House*.

Kelly Winters: Winters is a freelance writer and has written for a wide variety of academic and educational publishers. Entry on *Breath, Eyes, Memory*. Original essay on *Breath, Eyes, Memory*.

The Age of Innocence

1993

Critics and audiences were surprised in 1993 to find that Martin Scorsese, the director best known for such gritty, contemporary urban dramas as *Mean Streets*, *Taxi Driver*, and *Goodfellas*, had chosen to direct a film adaptation of Edith Wharton's 1920 tragicomedy of manners, *The Age of Innocence*. Wharton's novel deals with repressed feelings among society's upper ranks in New York in the 1870s, while Scorsese's most common themes involved machismo and violence—for instance, 1991's *Cape Fear*, featuring frequent Scorsese collaborator Robert De Niro as a psychotic murderer and rapist. The resulting film ended up on many critics' ten-best lists at the end of the year, and it was nominated for several Academy Awards.

Scorsese, who had been given the book by coscreenwriter Jay Cocks, found an emotional connection with Wharton's close and careful examination of social rituals, and his expert control of cameras and actors helped bring Wharton's writing alive for many viewers who otherwise might not have read her novel. The basic story, about a man who is engaged to marry one woman but finds himself falling in love with another, is familiar to any age, but Scorsese uses it, as Wharton did, to comment on the ways in which one can be imprisoned within a society of almost endless wealth. In the hands of stars Michelle Pfeiffer, Daniel Day-Lewis, and Winona Ryder, along with a strong supporting cast, *The Age of Innocence* brings out

what the Gilded Age and the modern world have in common.

PLOT SUMMARY

The Situation

The Age of Innocence opens with a title card that says "New York City, the 1870s." After establishing that the setting is at an opera (Charles Gounod's *Faust*, which premiered in Paris in 1859 and was new to New York at the time), the camera focuses on a boutonniere on a man's tuxedo coat, pulling back to reveal that it belongs to Newland Archer. Archer is seated in his club's box at the opera house, among other men in similar clothes. Sillerton Jackson, later revealed to be a gossip, notices Madame Olenska in the Welland box while he is scanning the audience with his opera glasses, and he makes a suggestive comment.

Archer goes over to the Welland box and talks to his fiancée, May Welland. He wants to announce their engagement, but she mentions her mother's opposition. May introduces Archer to her cousin, Madame Ellen Olenska, but she already knows Archer from childhood.

After the opera ends, all of the people leave for the annual opera ball at the Beaufort mansion. Scorsese's camera takes in the formalities of the ball. Archer hurries to the Beaufort house to quickly announce his engagement, to direct gossip away from Madame Olenska. Archer, the narrator explains, privately questioned conformity, though publicly he upheld family and tradition. He counted on May to be his moral guide.

Later, May and Archer go to Mrs. Manson Mingott to announce their engagement. In addition to being May's grandmother, she is one of the most famous and well-connected women in New York society. Mrs. Mingott is pleased that the Archer family will be joined with the Welland family, since they are two of the most prominent families in the city. As they leave her house, the camera draws back to show her five-story, block-wide mansion, surrounded by the undeveloped flat land in all directions that was New York north of Central Park at that time.

Sillerton Jackson dines with Archer, his mother, and his sister, who are too shy to venture into society themselves. They gossip about the Beauforts, but then the talk changes to Madame Olenska. Archer defends her divorce when the others make disparaging remarks about it.

Later, when the men are alone smoking cigars, they discuss how the family secretary took Madame Olenska away from the womanizing Count Olenski. Jackson is scandalized, but Archer still defends her.

Mrs. Mingott sends out invitations to all of the society families in New York to come to a dinner to meet the Countess Olenska. The dinner is a failure, however, when everyone declines her invitation. The Welland family is disgraced. Archer goes to the van der Luydens, one of the most powerful society families, to explain that Larry Lefferts has caused society to turn against the Wellands. When Lefferts's wife suspects him of bad behavior, Archer explains, Larry usually starts rumors about someone else, to deflect attention. Mr. van der Luyden, seeing the slight as an injustice, offers to invite Countess Olenska to their own party for a visiting duke the following week, to present her to society.

Madame Olenska arrives late for the dinner, flouting social rules. She is uncomfortable until Archer comes to sit with her. Before he leaves, Madame Olenska invites Archer to her home the following day.

Archer arrives early and looks over her modern and primitive art pieces. As they talk, she invites him to sit near her and offers him a cigarette, and they both smoke. Discussing her difficulty fitting into society, she wells up with tears, and Archer puts his hand on hers. She withdraws slowly.

That night, passing his usual florist, Archer sends flowers to May, as he always does, and then sends another bouquet to Madame Olenska.

The Affair

Casually, Archer tells May that he sent flowers to Madame Olenska. May is surprised, since her cousin mentioned flowers from several people but never mentioned receiving any from him.

Archer is assigned by his superior at his law firm, Mr. Letterblair, to consult with Countess Olenska about her divorce. He is apprehensive, but he is told to try to steer her away from pursuing a divorce from Count Olenski because the scandal with the Count's secretary might be dragged up.

Archer visits Madame Olenska and suggests that she could be hurt by the Count's accusations in a divorce, even if the accusations are unfounded. She notices that he uses the word

FILM
TECHNIQUE

- As is customary for a Martin Scorsese picture, the camera is very seldom still in *The Age of Innocence*. Even in scenes where the actors are standing or sitting still, the camera is usually moving around them, examining their faces, objects in the room, or objects outside the window. In enclosed areas, where the camera could not be mounted to a stable track, Scorsese makes use of the Steadicam. The Steadicam is an invention introduced in 1976 to help camera operators stabilize the film's image and provide smooth motion. This device allows camera operators to move around the actors with hand-held cameras without capturing the natural unevenness of human motion that would result in bumps and bounces on the film.

- Scorsese also makes use of the 360-degree tracking effect, in which the camera, mounted on a track on the floor, circles around its subjects. One conspicuous scene that uses this type of shot is the lunch at the Mingott estate, after Archer has refrained from approaching Madame Olenska as she stands by the ocean. As polite conversation carries on, the camera moves around the table, taking in each speaker while Archer suppresses his anguish.

- Several times in this film, Scorsese ends a scene using the irising effect that was popular with films of the silent era, particularly in the films of early director D. W. Griffith. With this technique, the camera's lens can be seen closing, creating a circle of darkness that contracts around the scene, usually closing entirely to black the screen out. When Archer and Madame Olenska meet in the balcony during the play, for instance, about forty-eight minutes into the film, Scorsese uses the irising effect to close out the talk of the others in their box just as Archer is closing out the chatter of everyone

but her. The reverse effect is used to show how intensely Mrs. Mingott's attention is focused on May's wedding ring before the circle opens up, showing the rest of the room.

- Because this film involves a world of almost unimaginable wealth, Scorsese uses a rich color palette, especially in the opening scenes. The opera house is lined with a deep, velvety red and trimmed with gold, and those two colors carry over to the following scene, in the Beaufort mansion. Most of the indoor scenes have dark backgrounds and include some form of dark red and gold, colors associated with royalty.

- Scorsese ends a few scenes with a color fade. Though most film audiences are familiar with the "fade to black," this film fills the screen with bright colors, to show the emotions that are arising out of the dark backgrounds. When Madame Olenska opens the bouquet of yellow roses from Archer, for instance, the camera shows a look of satisfaction on her face before the screen fades to yellow. When the camera shows Madame Olenska while the narrator discusses how her family suffered a social "eradication," she turns to the camera and the scene fades to red.

- In presenting a society in which emotions are not openly discussed, the film resorts to close-up shots of objects, faces, and gestures. The close-up focuses the viewer's attention on details without commenting on them. Scorsese uses many close-ups in this film, from the gloves and food given to party guests to the tentative touch of hands that gives unexpressed hope to Archer and Ellen Olenska. The frequent, fluid movement from standard shots to close-ups is a sign of the film's storytelling artistry.

"if," uncertain about the truth about the Count's claims, about her innocence. Since the Count is in Europe and she is in America, Archer tells her to leave the situation alone. She agrees to do as he advises.

At the theater, watching a melodrama about two lovers parting, Archer is stricken with emotion. Regina Beaufort calls him up to the box where Countess Olenska sits off to the side, by herself. She mentions the yellow roses he sent, wondering if the man in the play might send yellow roses to his lover. She also mentions that May is away for her annual trip to Florida.

The next day, Archer tries to send Countess Olenska more yellow roses, but they are not available. She does not answer his letters, and he feels rejected, but after a few days she sends him a letter saying she is staying at a house upstate. Archer goes there and finds her alone. For a moment, as they talk, he imagines her coming and putting her arms around him. He sees Julius Beaufort approaching the house and is jealous. Everyone assumes that Beaufort, a womanizer, is involved with Madame Olenska, though his appearance at the upstate house turns out to be only for a real estate matter.

Archer goes to St. Augustine, Florida, to be with May. As she talks, he tunes her voice out, but then he implores her to marry him soon. She says that she has felt since the became engaged that he is interested in someone else. Archer assures her that he has no other lovers. "There is no one between us," he tells her.

Archer goes to Mrs. Mingott to ask her to support an early marriage. Mrs. Mingott tells him about the possibility that Madame Olenska might reunite with her husband, joking that Archer should have married her instead of May. On the way to the door, he takes Madame Olenska aside and asks with urgency when they can see each other.

At her house that night, he eventually admits his feelings for Madame Olenska. She angrily accuses him for being the one to tell her to forget about divorce. He points out that he is still free and that she can be, too, and they kiss. When she breaks away from him, she explains how he has helped her fit into society, describing her fear that an affair with him will take away the goodness in him. While she talks, Archer bends down and kisses her foot.

The Marriage

A telegram from May announces to Countess Olenska that her parents have agreed to move the wedding up. The Countess does not attend the wedding. On their honeymoon in Europe, Archer notices that May is increasingly traditional, making decisions about their lives based on social standing. He looks back on his relationship with Countess Olenska as "the madness" and an "experiment."

Back in New York, they visit Mrs. Mingott. She sends for Madame Olenska, who has been staying with her, only to find that she has left the house. Mrs. Mingott sends Archer to find her. Although it has been a year and a half since they last saw each other, the sight of her, with the sunlit water behind her, stirs up the old feelings. He tells himself that he will go to her only if she turns around before a passing boat reaches the lighthouse; when the boat goes by, he returns to the house and says that he could not find her.

The Wellands are invited to visit the Blenkers, the family that Madame Olenska is staying with. Knowing where she lives, Archer goes to the home to find her, but she has gone to Boston. He lies to the young Blenker girl to find out where she will be in Boston and goes there to find her. When they meet, Archer finds out that Count Olenski's secretary has been sent to America to offer her money to return to the Count.

Archer and Madame Olenska have lunch together and are very open about their feelings for each other. Madame Olenska takes hold of Archer's hand and then leaves.

In a montage of a windy day, with men holding on to their bowler hats, Archer is approached by Rivière. He is the secretary sent to America by the Count to bring the Countess home, but Archer met him during his honeymoon in Europe without realizing his connection to the family. At Archer's office, Rivière explains that he does not really think that Madame Olenska should return to Europe with him, and he asks Archer to use his influence to keep her in America.

At a dinner party, there is talk about the depressed economy destroying Beaufort's business. When Archer hears that Beaufort's failing business will affect Madame Olenska, he flies into a rage at the implication that she is Beaufort's mistress. He has revealed his feelings for her needlessly: she will be affected because she has invested her money with Beaufort.

A message comes that Mrs. Mingott has had a stroke. Archer and May race to see her, only to find out that she is still in fine health. The family is coming to be with her, and when Archer volunteers to meet Countess Olenska's train, May becomes suspicious. In the carriage from the train station, Archer and Olenska kiss. Archer suggests that he wants her with him, but she dismisses his idea, saying that there is no place in the world where they can be together. Archer leaves the carriage before it arrives back at Mrs. Mingott's house.

The Exposure
Sitting in front of the fire with May, Archer reads a book about Japan. He stares at May and thinks about the possibility of her death.

Archer and Countess Olenska meet at a museum. She offers to spend the night with him once before returning to her husband. They agree to meet a few nights later.

The night of the meeting, Archer goes to May while she is at the opera and takes her to a room outside. Just as he is about to confess, she interrupts to tell him that Madame Olenska, having received money from Mrs. Mingott so that she will not have to return to her husband, is leaving for Europe, financially independent. May shows him the letter from Olenska, explaining that she is leaving and cannot be stopped.

Soon, Archer and May give their first society dinner—a farewell dinner for Madame Olenska. Archer assumes that everyone at the dinner knows of his and the Countess's feelings and is there to support his wife in suppressing him. At the end of the evening, Madame Olenska refuses his offer to walk her out to her carriage, choosing to go with her family.

The night of the party, Archer talks to May, expressing his wish to travel on his own. She refuses to let him go by himself, but she does not think she can travel with him because, she reveals, she is pregnant. Although it was confirmed just that day, she told Madame Olenska that she was pregnant two weeks earlier, which explains why she refused to meet with Archer the day they had planned.

The Ensuing Years
The narrator gives a summary of the future of the Archer family: the birth of Theodore and other children and their various career paths, engagements, and marriages. When May dies, Archer, now fifty-seven, honestly mourns her.

His son Theodore phones from Chicago to invite Archer to join him on a trip to Europe. In Paris, Ted tells him that he has arranged to meet with Madame Olenska. Archer is rattled but agrees to go with him. As they walk through the park to go meet the Countess, Ted explains that he knows his father almost threw away his entire life for her but did not; he learned it from May, the day before she died.

Outside Countess Olenska's apartment building, Archer sits on a bench and declines to enter. He looks up at her window and imagines her at the lake, when she did not turn to see him and he did not go to her. Then he stands up and walks away.

CHARACTERS

Newland Archer
Newland Archer is a young lawyer from one of New York's most prominent families. He is played by celebrated British actor Daniel Day-Lewis. He has every had every social advantage and a good education. Outwardly, he seeks to uphold the prevailing social order, but deep inside, he has a subversive streak that encourages him to rebel against society.

At the beginning of the film, the element that keeps Archer socially respectable is his fiancée, May Welland. "May Welland," the narrator explains, "represented for Archer all that was best in their world, all that he honored, and she anchored him to it." He wants their engagement to be announced even before hearing how people gossip about Madame Olenska, though once he realizes he can help her socially he has the announcement made immediately. In general, Archer views May as a well-meaning person who is not bright enough to chafe under the artificial constraints of society.

In Ellen Olenska, Archer sees a reflection of his own self-image. When the social world rejects her for her nonconformity, Madame Olenska stands up for herself. She is willing to divorce her husband to earn her freedom, even if it means a loss of social standing. He starts falling in love with her when she shows her vulnerability, breaking down into tears, empathizing with her as she feels the pressure of social opinion.

Though he has never been a social outcast, he can easily imagine himself to be one.

It is when he finds himself falling for Madame Olenska that Archer pushes the most to marry May, to stop himself from committing a social transgression. After they are married, though, he keeps thinking of Olenska, who is now related to him. He makes up reasons to see her alone and plans to run away with her, but May knows him too well by that point. She stops their affair before it begins. Years later, when their son Ted tries to take him to meet Madame Olenska, he says that his mother told him Archer had given up his affair because she had asked him to. Archer mutters, "She never asked," indicating that his fidelity was to the social order, and not to May.

Ted Archer

Theodore Archer, called Ted, is the first son of Newland and May. In Wharton's novel, this character is named Dallas. It is May's pregnancy with him that makes Madame Olenska agree to leave the country and makes Archer give up the idea of pursuing her. As an adult, played by Robert Sean Leonard, Ted convinces his aging father to accompany him on a trip to Europe. In Paris, he casually mentions that he has arranged a meeting with Madame Olenska, knowing from his mother that she is the true love of his father's life. When Archer balks at meeting her again, Ted is light-hearted. He does not force the issue, but he goes to meet her himself.

Julius Beaufort

Beaufort is played by Stuart Wilson. He is a banker and a romancer of women, in spite of his marriage to Regina Beaufort. Archer becomes jealous of him when he sees Beaufort approaching the house in the country where Madame Olenska is supposed to be living alone. He later flies into a rage when he is told that Madame Olenska will probably need money after Beaufort goes bankrupt, accusing the speaker of implying that she is Beaufort's kept woman. It is clear that Beaufort would like to have Madame Olenska as his mistress, though he is not successful.

Julius Beaufort functions as a dark mirror image of Newland Archer. As Archer finds himself falling for Madame Olenska, he has Beaufort to look to, to remind him of just how ugly it is to be a womanizer.

Regina Beaufort

The wife of Julius Beaufort, she is also a niece of Mrs. Mingott. In the novel, her appeal to Mrs. Mingott to procure a loan for her husband when his business fails is what causes her aunt to have a stroke, though the film presents her stroke as a false alarm.

Sillerton Jackson

Played by Alec McCowen, Jackson is identified early in the film as a man who knows all of the society gossip and lives to spread it around. He gains prestige in this society by spreading malicious stories, surrounding himself with like-minded people who value the naughty thrill of rumor-mongering. Early in the film, Jackson stands out as a the embodiment of society's threat to Ellen Olenska, telling stories about her life in Europe that might or might not be true, but that are not talked about openly.

Larry Lefferts

Lawrence Lefferts, played by Richard E. Grants, is introduced by the narrator as "New York's foremost authority on form," a grand distinction that is put in perspective in the next sentence, which characterizes his opinions about shoe styles. When the Wellands' party to welcome Madame Olenska is ignored by the socially prominent, Archer takes the issue to the van der Luydens, explaining that he is sure Lefferts has pursued a campaign against her just to distract his own wife's suspicious about his behavior. Though Lefferts knows what is and is not socially acceptable, the word of long-established society figures like the van der Luydens can overrule his understanding of what is proper.

Mrs. Manson Mingott

Mrs. Mingott, played by Miriam Margolis, is the widow of Manson Mingott, the mother of May Welland, and the aunt of Regina Beaufort. Wharton's novel gives her first name as "Catherine," though that is never used in the film (she follows the custom of the time of using "Mrs." with her husband's first name). She is the respected matriarch of the family, a woman of such significant social standing that Archer and May feel obliged to immediately bring the news to her when they announce their engagement. Her own social power is not enough, however, to bring people to the party to welcome Madame Olenska to New York once she has been deemed socially toxic.

Madame Olenska lives with Mrs. Mingott for a while in New York. When she leaves the country, it is because Mrs. Mingott, at May's urging, has given her the money she needs to return to Europe.

Ellen Olenska

Madame Olenska, the cousin of May Welland, is played by Michelle Pfeiffer, a casting choice that some critics objected to: the Ellen Olenska of Wharton's novel is dark and mysterious, while Pfeiffer is pale and plays the part with timidity. In the film she is referred to as "Madame Olenska," "Countess Olenska," and "Ellen," depending on who is talking about her, but the narrator of Wharton's novel generally calls her Madame Olenska.

Madame Olenska comes into the film as an unknown quantity. The narrator and the visual design scheme of the film have been used to show that New York society runs by a strict code, but Madame Olenska has been outside that society and therefore is not part of the code. At first, this means that the worst is assumed of her. She is a member of the Welland family, though, and so May, her mother, her grandmother, and her fiancé Newland Archer do what they can to get her accepted, such as talking to social trendsetters like the van der Luydens on her behalf. As she begins to make inroads in New York, she considers formally divorcing the womanizing Polish count to whom she is married, but Archer talks her out of it, fearing what a divorce would do to her reputation, even though it would free her for him to marry.

After Archer's marriage to May, Madame Olenska goes out of her way to avoid Archer, knowing that their mutual attraction can only hurt her cousin and destroy Archer. Eventually, she agrees to accept money from Mrs. Mingott and leave the country, but Archer convinces her to spend one night with him before going. When she hears about May's pregnancy, however, she refuses to break up their marriage, and she leaves without even talking to him. Though her character's motives are kept uncertain throughout the film and Scorsese leaves viewers to wonder if she is willing to steal Archer from her cousin, Madame Olenska turns out to be driven by honor.

Rivière

Archer meets Monsieur Rivière, played by Jonathan Pryce, when he and May are touring Europe after their marriage. Later, Rivière comes to him in New York and explains that he was the secretary who helped Madame Olenska run away from her marriage. He has been sent to America to convince Olenska to return to her husband, but he tells Archer confidentially that he does not think that she should.

Louisa van der Luyden

Mrs. van der Luyden and her husband are among the oldest and most well-established social figures in New York. When Archer tells the couple that Larry Lefferts is unfairly trying to block Madame Olenska from entering society, their sense of justice is offended. They make a point of inviting Olenska to their upcoming party, knowing that people will welcome her if they see that the van der Luydens welcome her.

Henry van der Luyden

Henry van der Luyden is one half of a socially prominent couple that has even more influence than the respected Mrs. Mingott. The Welland family comes to talk to the van der Luydens on the behalf of Madame Olenska, with Newland Archer, who is not married into the family yet, making the case like a lawyer about why the social world is treating Olenska unfairly. Henry van der Luyden weighs Archer's argument and decides to intercede on Madame Olenska's behalf.

May Welland

Twenty-one-year-old May is Newland Archer's fiancée, played by Winona Ryder. She is part of a socially prominent family, and her grandmother, Mrs. Mingott, is one of the most respected and powerful matrons in town. One of the things that Archer likes about her is that she lacks the imagination to be socially rebellious, and he can therefore count on his upcoming marriage to May to keep him out of trouble. At first, she welcomes his involvement with her cousin, Madame Olenska, encouraging him when he sends her flowers. When he finds himself romantically tempted by her cousin, Archer pressures May to marry him sooner than planned. May, thinking that he is interested in his old flame, identified in the novel as Mrs. Rushworth, offers to release him from their engagement. The film does not hint as strongly as Wharton's book that May might just obtain her mother's approval for the marriage to keep him from straying.

At the beginning of the film, May seems sweet but naïve. She has no aspirations other than to be a dutiful wife. Archer's affair with her cousin brings out a hard and defensive side in her, however. She fights for her marriage without seeming to fight. When Archer tries to tell her about his love for another woman, May interrupts him, and when he tries to make plans to leave the country, to pursue Madame Olenska, she stops him with news of her pregnancy. In each case, it is clear that May knows what he is going to reveal but feels that such a revelation would be bad for their marriage. Even more than cunning, though, she turns out to have been surprisingly dishonest, telling Madame Olenska that she is pregnant weeks before this is confirmed so that she will leave the Archers alone. Years later, she dies from pneumonia contracted while nursing her son Bill. "She died," the narrator says, "thinking the world a good place, full of loving and harmonious households like her own." On her deathbed, she tells her son Ted that she knows that Madame Olenska was the love of Archer's life, something that she never discussed with Archer himself.

Mrs. Welland

Mrs. Welland, played by film veteran Geraldine Chaplin, is May's mother. For the first half of the film, she is an obstacle to the marriage between Newland Archer and her daughter, refusing to give her consent. He considers eloping to get around her restrictions, but May will not do such a thing.

THEMES

Aristocracy

The term *aristocracy* comes from a Greek word, pronounced similarly, meaning rule of the best. Literally, it refers to a government that is controlled by a small privileged class. In common usage, however, it has come to refer to the privileged sector of any society, whether they are political rulers or not.

The Archers, the Wellands, and the other families that populate *The Age of Innocence* certainly embody the concept of American aristocracy. For one thing, they are in control of enormous wealth, and that wealth gives them power. Still, wealth is not enough, in itself, to gain one admission into this social set. As Madame Olenska finds

out when she returns from Europe, there are unrecorded codes of behavior that can gain one admission to or exclusion from this group, even if one is born into it, as she was. The film identifies Lawrence Lefferts as having studied the rules of this society, but it also shows how a very powerful person, such as Louisa or Henry van der Luyden, can change these rules if they want.

Conformity

In some cultures, innovation is rewarded. The Darwinian concept of "survival of the fittest," when applied to society, implies that success depends on showing superior talents. The New York society culture presented in this film, however, is populated with powerful people who can generally do what they want. They have the means to travel the world and acquire whatever interests them. The one thing that keeps the egos of the rich and powerful in check is the social pressure to conform.

The film gives viewers a visual tour of the trappings of wealth, starting with the layers upon layers of the opera house and on through mansions, stables, and gardens. During the Archers' honeymoon, viewers are given a glimpse into the lives of wealthy Europeans, who provide the model for the American upper class, with families that have retained their social position for generations, even centuries. Scorsese examines the lives of the rich with a microscope, knowing, as they know, that they cannot deviate from the standards without losing their social standing.

The film gives two parallel examples of nonconformity in this society. Throughout the film, Scorsese's camera sweeps over portraits and landscapes on the walls of homes that are considered safe to display. Early in the film, at the Beaufort mansion's Crimson Drawing Room, Archer looks over *The Return of Spring*, a painting of some nudes, which the narrator says that Julius Beaufort "had the audacity to hang in plain sight"—he is pushing the edges of conformity, but has not gone far enough to be ostracized. Later, however, when Archer is waiting at Madame Olenska's house for her, he looks over some impressionist artworks that help identify Olenska as being too wild and unconventional for the New York social world.

Obsession

Although Wharton's novel and Scorsese's movie are both interested in the behaviors of a certain

READ, WATCH, WRITE

- Edith Wharton is referred to by the Web site *A Lit Chick* as the "gossip girl of the Gilded Age." Create a short film about some behavior in your community and add a narrative soundtrack over it, explaining the social significance of the behavior in the way that the narrator of *The Age of Innocence* does.

- Read a young-adult contemporary tale about a romantic triangle, such as Elizabeth Scott's *The Unwritten Rule* or Susan Colasanti's *Something Like Fate*. Make a list of five or more things the characters do in the novel that you think correspond closely to the things the actors do in *The Age of Innocence*. Read excerpts from the novel for your class as you show the relevant scenes from the film to show that behavior is constant although times change.

- Henry James was an American author who wrote about the upper class at the time when Wharton set this novel. Read his book, *The Europeans: A Sketch*, about an American woman like Madame Olenska who returns after living in Europe. Using the James book as a guide, write a scene from the European honeymoon of Archer and May that shows

an additional site they might have visited and what they would have done there. Include illustrations that show a possible setting for the scene.

- A formal waltz is used to open the ball at the Beaufort mansion. Research this style of waltz; teach the moves to ten or more of your classmates and try to reproduce the choreography from the film.

- This film focuses intensely on the subtle emotional problems of its central characters. Make these characters more exciting by writing a short graphic story (that is, in comic book or graphic novel form) about either Newland Archer or Ellen Olenska. At the end of the story, write an explanation to explain why your character is the same person depicted in *The Age of Innocence*.

- Do you think that the time you are living in now will be remembered as an "age of innocence"? Assign students to two different groups to argue the "yes" and "no" positions before the class. Use examples from popular culture or from past cultures to prove your point.

---

class of people at a certain period in American history, they are both held together by the story of Newland Archer's obsession with Ellen Olenska. His interest in her has actually begun before the start of the film. He sees her in her cousin May's box at the opera and immediately feels compelled to go over to where she is, pausing, stunned, when she offers her hand. She mentions their past together. He kissed her once, she tells him, when they were children, though she dismisses the seriousness of this by noting that she was actually in love with his cousin Vandie, "the one who never looked at me."

Throughout the film, Archer's obsession with her grows. He arranges times for them to

meet for innocent reasons, probably even convincing himself that he has no plans. Each time they meet, though, he is more fascinated by her, even though he knows that they cannot be together without bringing tragic consequences down on both of them. He tries to move his wedding to May forward, to force himself to lose interest in Madame Olenska, but his marriage does little to quench his obsession with her. He ends up lying in order to create occasions for them to be together, and when he goes to the Blenker's farmhouse to see her, he inhales her scent on her parasol and looks enchanted to have this small contact with her, only to find out that it is not hers after all.

© *Moviestore collection Ltd | Alamy*

In the end, after Archer has broken off any contact with Madame Olenska and has raised his family, he is still unable to face her. The film raises the question of whether he was only obsessed with a pretty woman or truly in love.

Innocence

The "innocence" of the title can be taken two ways. For one thing, Archer and Madame Olenska remain innocent because they both take steps to stop their romance before it goes too far. Even though they plan to spend the night together, the news of May's pregnancy makes each of them reconsider. Madame Olenska accepts her aunt's money and moves away to Europe, and Archer, who had originally planned to follow her, remains innocent by staying by his wife's side.

Wharton also uses "innocence" in the sense of being naïveté. For all of their worldliness, their travels and purchases and parties, the people depicted in this novel are quite childlike in their view of the world. They think that they can know what people are all about through gossip and hearsay, and that love is an inconvenience that can be controlled with enough willpower. Their social position has given them a sense of their own importance that Scorsese and Wharton present as almost quaint.

STYLE

Soundtrack

Scorsese fills the background of this film with a lush soundtrack of orchestral music, matching music popular at the time. The opening scenes set the tone for this, as the characters attend a grand opera that would have been new to them. After Archer leaves the opera, though, the music on the soundtrack continues throughout almost every scene for the rest of the film.

Scorsese eases audiences into this style of music by following the opera scene with a ball at the Beauforts' house, with the orchestral rendition of a waltz by Johann Strauss wafting through every room until Archer reaches the ballroom: there, the music is the background for a formal dance. Similar music continues from then on, though it is not part of the story.

The characters are constantly involved with the arts, but they do not attend any more musical events, so the music they hear does not become confused with the music on the soundtrack.

Elmer Bernstein, an award-winning Hollywood composer for hundreds of motion pictures, was nominated for the Academy Award for Best Original Score for *The Age of Innocence*, one of fourteen such nominations over his fifty-year career.

Narration

Narration is often used to fill in plot points that cannot be made clear by presenting the story on screen. In the case of *The Age of Innocence*, the narrator does fill in some plot details for viewers, but more often, she is explaining subtleties about the society the characters inhabit. Wharton's novel is so dense in its explanation of this social setting that it would be virtually impossible to adapt it all to the screen, and the wording used by her narrator was so exact and specific that the filmmakers decided that large pieces of her narration should be included in the film exactly as Wharton wrote it.

Unlike narrators of other films adapted from classic novels, Joanne Woodward does not use a sophisticated or genteel voice. She speaks plainly. This reflects the kind of narrative voice that Wharton used in the book. It is an outsider's voice, looking back with curiosity at the social world of the 1870s from the perspective of the 1920s. Although the narrator knows the rules of the society being shown better than the characters themselves, she has more in common with the viewers than with the characters.

CULTURAL CONTEXT

Films of the 1990s

In the 1990s, the film world, like the world in general, still felt the residual effects of the cultural changes of the late 1960s. That period is remembered as a time when the counterculture ascended to overtake the mainstream culture, a cultural shift that was confirmed when the antiwar movement of the 1960s succeeded and the United States withdrew from the Vietnam war in 1973, soon followed by the resignation of the unpopular President Richard Nixon in 1974. It was an era that made the majority stop and question traditional values. Much good came

of this social upheaval, as those who had been kept on the margins of social involvement joined movements to have their rights recognized. The civil rights movement for African Americans, the women's liberation movement, the American Indian movement, and the gay rights movement took form as these social groups, and others, found their voice in the 1960s and 1970s.

Just as social values were being redefined, the 1970s introduced a new generation of filmmakers to the general public: a small group that since then has been dubbed the American new wave. The directors of this generation generally found their start in small independent productions and brought nontraditional values to their projects. Director Francis Ford Coppola, for example, shot to international fame with a sympathetic look at organized crime in *The Godfather* in 1972. Hal Ashby released a string of movies that questioned social conventions, including *Harold and Maude* in 1971, *The Last Detail* in 1973, *Shampoo* in 1975, and the anti-Vietnam film *Coming Home* in 1978. Brian De Palma spun off his own style of horror film from the works of Alfred Hitchcock with *Carrie* in 1976 and *The Fury* in 1978. Steven Spielberg began the 1970s directing television shows; he moved quickly through one acclaimed television movie and a small independent feature (*Alice Doesn't Live Here Anymore*) before directing one of the biggest box-office blockbusters in history, *Jaws*, in 1975. George Lucas, similarly, went from directing the quirky, character-driven *American Graffiti* in 1973 to the start of one of the most lucrative franchises in film history, *Star Wars*, in 1977. Martin Scorsese showed some indication of his directorial skill with the low-budget exploitation film *Boxcar Bertha* in 1973 and then broke out as a talented artist with *Mean Streets* in 1973.

In the 1980s, the new wave directors became the Hollywood mainstream, as the rebels who had fought to redefine the social order during the previous decades were incorporated into the establishment. During the administration of Ronald Reagan (1981–1989) and on into the presidential administration of Reagan's vice president, George H. W. Bush (1989–1993), films followed society in trying to establish a new relationship with traditional values. They backed away from using the rich as villains, going for a more subtle view of families where wealth was present but not a defining factor, in

© *Photos 12 | Alamy*

films such as *Kramer vs. Kramer* in 1979, *Baby Boom* in 1987, and *Hannah and Her Sisters* in 1988. William J. Palmer dubs these films "Yuppie Texts" in his book *The Films of the Eighties*, playing off of the acronym for young urban professionals popular around that time. As the 1980s ended, films like *Wall Street* (1987) and *Bright Lights, Big City* (1988) looked at society's newfound fixation with the dark side of wealth. When *The Age of Innocence* was released in 1993, the rich were social models again in a way they had not been since the counterculture 1960s.

The Postwar Generation of 1920

When Edith Wharton published *The Age of Innocence* in 1920, the world was reeling from the international devastation wrought by the Great War, which is now known as World War I. The war, which ended officially in November 1918, was referred to by British politician David Lloyd George when it was over with the hope that future generations would look back on it as "the war to end all wars." It is easy to see why people around the world might have taken George's phrase to heart, as World War I

represented a level of military conflict that had never been seen before. The scope of the war was immense, involving more than 100 countries across five continents. In all, eight and a half million men were killed and another twenty-one million were wounded. These grand statistics, however, do not indicate the psychological effect of the first war of the modern era. Advanced techniques in warfare ranged from the airplane, which could drop tons of explosives onto targets virtually anywhere, to the use of chemical weapons, such as mustard gas, which caused bleeding in the lungs and led to near-instant drowning.

Veterans returned from the war having seen horrors that they could never have imagined. In literature, a generation of writers that came to be called the Lost Generation reflected the disillusionment that was felt all over the world as a result of World War I. Those writers, including Ernest Hemingway, F. Scott Fitzgerald, John Dos Passos, and T. S. Eliot, tried to reflect the sense of despair that had overcome an entire generation of intellectuals. At the time that the Lost Generation was starting to publish works about the hopelessness of their time, Wharton was looking back fifty years, to a time when the children of affluence felt that social pressure was the worst thing they faced, calling it the age of innocence.

CRITICAL OVERVIEW

Critics generally approached this film with mixed feelings. It is considered a surprising, ambitious achievement for director Martin Scorsese, but most found it to fall short of its mark. Most critical responses fall between Jonathan Rosenbaum of the *Chicago Reader*, who praises it as an "ambitious and sumptuous" film but ultimately declares it "a noble failure," and Vincent Canby of the *New York Times*, who declares, "*The Age of Innocence* isn't perfect, but it's a robust gamble that pays off."

Many of the critics who were impressed with this film expressed admiration for the way it avoided the coldness of other adaptations of literary classics, especially those produced by Ismail Merchant and James Ivory, starting with their adaptation of Henry James's *The Europeans* in 1979. "As you'd expect from Scorsese, it's no waxworks wannabe classic," Michael Wilmington states in the *Chicago Tribune*. "It has a pulse, a volatile current." Desson Howe of the *Washington Post* notes the treatments of the past given in film by "the stuffy Merchant-Ivory team" before declaring, "What a sublime pleasure it is . . . to experience *The Age of Innocence* through the eyes of Martin Scorsese." He explains his pleasure in it: "Instead of *Masterpiece Theatre*–style fawning, he fills this movie with visual flow, masterful cinematography and assured direction. There's an alert, thinking presence behind the camera."

Still, there were critics who found that Scorsese's good intentions could not overcome the flaws in his approach. In the *Nation*, Stuart Klawans writes that Scorsese treats his rich socialites too respectfully, as if they really are the superior beings that they seem to think they are. "He's deferential," Klawans says, "as if those stiffs from Fifth Avenue were somehow better than a boy from Elizabeth Street"—a reference to the tough hustlers of Scorsese's first film, *Mean Streets*. "The style becomes as repressed as the characters themselves and is

then capped by a further repression of the lead actors." After airing his complaints, though, Klawans admits, "None of this means that *The Age of Innocence* is a failure. In a sense, Scorsese has reached the stage at which there can be no complete failures, since everything he makes has relevance to his career."

Owen Gleiberman, in *Entertainment Weekly*, gives the film an overall grade of *B+*, claiming that, for all its artistry, "*The Age of Innocence* isn't entirely successful." He feels that there are too many meetings between Archer and Madame Olenska after their original breakup, giving the last half of the film a fragmented feeling. "Scorsese and coscreenwriter Jay Cocks would have been wise to drop a few of the later incidents and linger more over the dramatic texture," Gleiberman explains, "As it is, the second half of *The Age of Innocence* comes at us in so many bits and pieces that it fails to achieve the overwhelming sense of loss that is the story's driving emotion."

Despite almost universal approval for Martin Scorsese's daring in taking on a project so far out of his customary field, and for his artistic achievements for the material, he was not even nominated for a best director Academy Award, nor was the picture nominated for best picture. However, *Time* magazine declared it the best picture of 1993, beating out *Schindler's List*, which won the best picture award from the Academy that year. The only Academy Award won by the picture was for best costume design. The two leads, Daniel Day-Lewis and Michelle Pfeiffer, were not even nominated, though Winona Ryder was nominated for best supporting actress. At the Golden Globes, Scorsese and Pfeiffer were nominated, and Ryder won. Scorsese and Pfeiffer did receive the Elvira Notari Prize at the Venice Film Festival.

CRITICISM

David Kelly

Kelly is an instructor of literature and creative writing. In the following essay, he discusses why The Age of Innocence *fits perfectly with Martin Scorsese's body of films.*

Whenever the 1993 version of the film *The Age of Innocence* is discussed, the discussion almost always comes around to what an unusual piece it is in the canon of Martin Scorsese films. Sometimes this is noted as a complaint against

WHAT DO I SEE NEXT?

- In 1993, the year that *The Age of Innocence* was released, Columbia Pictures also released an adaptation of Kazuo Ishiguro's novel *The Remains of the Day*. Though that story, about an English butler who does not realize that the end of his lifestyle is approaching, takes place in the 1950s, it has the quiet tone of a classic book adaptation. Nominated for eight Academy Awards but winning none, it stars Anthony Hopkins, Emma Thompson, Christopher Reeve, and Hugh Grant. The DVD was released in 2001 by Columbia.

- Director Wayne Wang's adaptation of Amy Tan's novel *The Joy Luck Club* was also released in 1993. The film explores the impositions of cultural expectations among Chinese and Chinese American families throughout the twentieth century. It was released on DVD by Buena Vista Home Entertainment in 2002.

- Edith Wharton is often associated with her peer, E. M. Forster. Forster's 1910 novel *Howard's End*, about the shifting of class relations at the turn of the century, was adapted to film in 1992, winning awards for best actress (Emma Thompson), adapted screenplay, and set direction. It stars Anthony Hopkins, Vanessa Redgrave, and Helena Bonham Carter. Columbia Pictures released the DVD in 1999.

- Scorsese once again left his comfort zone of gangster films in 1997 with *Kundun*, the story about the childhood of the Dalai Lama. The film stars several actors playing the central character at various parts in his life, including Tenzin Thuthob Tsarong, the grand-nephew of the real Dalai Lama. Beautifully filmed, it was loved by critics and ignored by audiences. It was released on DVD by Walt Disney Video in 1998.

- The same New York society that is the focus of *The Age of Innocence* is on display in the 2000 adaptation of Edith Wharton's earlier novel, *The House of Mirth*. Starring Gillian Anderson, Dan Akroyd, and Laura Linney, this mannered period piece, directed by Terrance Davies, was released on DVD in 2001 by Sony Pictures.

- *The Age of Innocence* was actually filmed once earlier. The 1934 RKO Pictures version of *The Age of Innocence* features Irene Dunne, John Boles, and Julie Hayden. It was directed by Phillip Moeller. Victor Heerman wrote the script, adapted from a play by Margaret Barnes. Although it is not currently available on DVD, this version does appear on television periodically.

- When he was preparing *The Age of Innocence*, Scorsese watched Orson Welles's *The Magnificent Ambersons*, which some critics consider to be the greatest film by one of the world's greatest directors. It begins in 1873 and follows a wealthy family's decline. Starring Joseph Cotton, Tim Holt, and Anne Baxter, this film is not available on DVD; the VHS version was released by Turner Home Video in 1996.

- The artistic precision on display in the art direction of this film is rivaled in *The Girl With the Pearl Earring*, directed by Peter Webber. It is the story of seventeenth-century Dutch painter Johannes Vermeer, played by Colin Firth, and his obsession with the maid in his household, played by Scarlett Johansson. The film's real star, however, is its visual style, modeled on Vermeer's paintings. The 2004 film is available on DVD from Lions Gate Pictures.

Scorsese for venturing beyond the bounds of his expertise, considered to be the narrow world of male aggression, characterized by his 1980

biography *Raging Bull*, which is cited as often for its beautiful cinematography as for its gut-wrenching violence. Usually, though, the film is

> HER TRANSGRESSION—MARRYING A POLISH
> COUNT AND THEN RUNNING AWAY FROM HIM, BACK
> TO NEW YORK, WHERE SHE INTENDS TO PURSUE A
> DIVORCE—JUST HAPPENS TO INVOLVE SEXUALITY,
> MAKING IT HARD FOR ARCHER TO TELL LOVE FROM
> LUST FROM SOCIAL REBELLION."

noted as a compliment to Scorsese's versatility. Either way, the basic premise is faulty, based on an assumption that Scorsese is a director of action.

This misconception was more understandable back when *The Age of Innocence* was released. At that time, Scorsese's reputation stood on the likes of *Taxi Driver*, *Goodfellas*, *Raging Bull*, and *Cape Fear*, while more diverse works like *Kundun*, *The Aviator*, *Bringing Out the Dead*, and his documentaries about the Rolling Stones and Bob Dylan were still in the future. Early Scorsese had its share of quirky character studies, of course—the feminist road picture *Alice Doesn't Live Here Anymore*, the retro musical *New York, New York*, and the low-budget comedy *After Hours*—but it has taken until the twenty-first century for critics to accept that the director who came to prominence with *Mean Streets* is a versatile craftsman who uses violence to make a point when he wants to but does not use it exclusively.

Not quite as common but still to be found on occasion is the critic who will stand behind the idea that *The Age of Innocence* fits into Scorsese's career arc just fine. Newland Archer, the film's protagonist, may be subdued in a way that most memorable Scorsese characters are not, but he has antisocial tendencies that are only slightly hidden below the surface of his tightly strung façade. He is not as extreme as the desperately alienated characters that actor Robert De Niro played into Scorsese powerhouses such as *Taxi Driver* and *The King of Comedy*, but he is clearly on the same continuum.

Scorsese himself found nothing remarkable about his decision to bring this novel to the screen. In his book on Scorsese's career, Roger

Ebert puts the film in his "masterpieces" section, and he quotes the director about what could have attracted him to a novel about social conformity a hundred years past:

> What has always stuck in my head is the brutality under the manners.... In the subculture I was around when I grew up in Little Italy, when somebody was killed, there was a finality to it. It was done by the hands of a friend. And in a funny way, it was almost like ritualistic slaughter, a sacrifice. But New York society in the 1870s didn't have that. It was so cold-blooded. I don't know which is preferable.

Scorsese saw the genteel society Edith Wharton wrote about in 1920 as being no better, or perhaps even a little worse, than the world he had dealt with so many times before. The prospect of death may energize gangster movies with a primal fear, but to the characters in *The Age of Innocence*, the prospect of being "rubbed out" socially can be just as frightening.

The film's true connection to Scorsese's other films is in the understated struggle between its central characters and their society. It happens again and again in Scorsese's works. Sometimes, the focus is on an individual who was born in his environment but never actually felt a perfect fit, such as Harvey Keitel's Charlie in *Mean Streets* or Henry Hill in *Goodfellas*. Sometimes the protagonist is new to a closed culture, like Howard Hughes, who assumes that his money should allow him unimpeded entry to Hollywood in *The Aviator*, or Jake LaMotta, who thought brute strength could eventually raise him up to respectability in *Raging Bull*. Sometimes, as with Leonardo DiCaprio's undercover agent in *The Departed*, the protagonist is someone who is made to look at his society as an outsider would.

Newland Archer of *The Age of Innocence* has a desire to escape from his society's stringent tribal laws. He is established early on as someone who can sense the limitations of the social order, and part of him chafes against them. The other part of him, however, relies on his fiancée May, whom he reads as an unimaginative traditionalist who can anchor him before his rebellious spirit does some harm. Ellen Olenska flirts with him from the moment she sees him, holding out a demanding hand for Archer to kiss and reminding him immediately that he once did kiss her when they were children, back when such things were small and trivial. Her appeal rests on more than just sexuality, however. She arrives in the

© *Photos 12 | Alamy*

picture already branded an outcast. Her transgression—marrying a Polish count and then running away from him, back to New York, where she intends to pursue a divorce—just happens to involve sexuality, making it hard for Archer to tell love from lust from social rebellion.

All of the signs indicate that society has unfairly branded Madame Olenska a troublemaker because she falls outside its narrow limits. When Archer comes to know her better, however, it becomes clearer that she actually *is* a troublemaker, at least as far as the New York social order is concerned. She smokes and flirts, and Scorsese keeps her just distant enough from the film's narrative thread to prevent viewers from having any clarity about whether her tears are genuine marks of suffering or an instinctive appeal to Archer's chivalric nature. In her first scene in the film, at the opera, Madame Olenska points to the crowd at the opera house—the cream of the New York social world, assembled—and reduces their power and might to the play of children by pointing out that she sees them as she remembers them, "dressed in knickerbockers and pantalettes." She mocks

the entire social order. The point of the film, like any Scorsese film, is to see just how brash the main character is willing to be.

Archer calls off the affair when he finds out that May, now his wife, is pregnant. He also finds out that Madame Olenska abandoned the affair weeks earlier when May claimed to be pregnant, though it was not necessarily true at that time. They have edged toward rebellion, but May has upped the ante: it is no longer about the shallow old gossips who have been holding the social order together for generations but about the continuation of the species. Perhaps Archer could withstand the shunning that he would get for leaving his wife, and perhaps he could not, but that pressure is nothing that he is willing to leave to his son, and so he stays with May and has child after respectable child with her.

The Age of Innocence is not a Martin Scorsese film because it deals with an individual fighting society: that can be said about practically any film, if viewed from the right angle. What makes it a natural for Scorsese is the fact that Newland Archer never even finds out how much he is aching to rebel. By taking audiences so deeply into Archer's world, as Wharton does in her novel, Scorsese makes that world a formidable opponent. It is not an open battle Archer is involved in but a subtle one, a battle for his soul. Perhaps it is because he seems so weak and the social order so overwhelming that critics have read *The Age of Innocence* as presenting a reverse of Scorsese's traditional ethos, but it is the battle itself that plants this film solidly on the common Scorsese turf.

Source: David Kelly, Critical Essay on *The Age of Innocence*, in *Novels for Students*, Gale, Cengage Learning, 2011.

Sarah Kozloff

In the following excerpt, Kozloff maintains that, as in the book, the film's complexity stems from its narrative technique.

II. THE FILM

...The recent adaptation of *The Age of Innocence* (there were earlier versions in 1924 and 1934) was released in 1993 by Columbia Pictures, directed by Martin Scorsese from a script he co-wrote with Jay Cocks. The film was budgeted at $30 million, a sum that bought years of careful research into the time period, lush production design that strove to recreate each detail accurately, and a cast headed by Daniel Day-Lewis, Michelle Pfeiffer, and Winona Ryder. This too is a richly layered text, full of allusions to other period movies (Scorsese and Cocks have published a list of the films by Visconti, Truffaut, Welles, Wyler, Minnelli, and others that inspired them [168–771]) and so carefully thought out that each painting included in the set design deliberately reflects upon the characters or their situation.

Moreover, like the book, the film's complexity stems from its narrative technique. This film departs from the Classical Hollywood style that hides all signs of discourse and pretends to record autonomous, spontaneous action. Contrary to most adaptations, where it seems that the film-makers' primary goal was to dramatize the story events, Scorsese makes no effort to move away from novelistic discourse. Instead, Scorsese and Cocks recreate the novel's narrative structure through extensive use of a voice-over narrator. While other adaptations have also found narration useful—including several of Scorsese's and Cock's models, e.g., *Barry Lyndon, The Magnificent Ambersons, Madame Bovary, Jules and Jim*—in point of fact I know of no other film

that has used such extensive voice-over by a female third person narrator.

Gavin Smith's valuable interview of Martin Scorsese in *Film Comment* about *The Age of Innocence* provides insight into the director's intentions:

You've used first-person voiceover in a number of your films but never third-person, which is more unusual. Did you see the narrator (Joanne Woodward) as an autonomous character?

I wanted to give the audience the impression of the feelings I had when I read the book. Literally as is, Edith Wharton. It's a narrator who's very tricky, who's presenting the story in this way to teach you a lesson.

Did you have a discussion about how you conceived the narrator?

Never did. The first time that came up was from the studio. Columbia Pictures asked, "Who's the narrator?" I said, "Who cares? The narrator's telling the story."

Is the camera in complicity with the narrator?

I think in certain scenes, like the dinner scene, absolutely. Using what may seem to be obvious voiceover narration with the imagery—people said, "You don't need the voiceover." Well maybe not, but I preferred it. [. . .]

You never considered making it without a voiceover.

Oh never, I love that idea of a female voice, taking us through, very nicely, and setting us up for the fall. That's the whole thing. You get to trust the voice and then she does you in [laughs], like he gets done in. I thought that was wonderful. I can't lose that aspect of it.

Is it that the narrator withholds what she knows about May or doesn't realize it at first?

I think she withholds. Maybe. It's part of the lesson that's to be learned (18–19).

In the case of this film, the director is complicitous with the novelist, his camera conspires with the soundtrack, the "male gaze" is in league with the female voice. (David Thomson's article, "The Director as Raging Bull: Why Can't a Woman be More Like a Photograph," demonstrates that this is an unusual stance for Scorsese.) Moreover, just as in the novel, Scorsese uses his narrative structure to manipulate the dispersal of information so as to set Archer and the viewer up for the twist at the end.

Nearly all of the voice-over lines are taken straight from the novel, sometimes compressed and rearranged, but faithfully replicating the words and tone of the omniscient social satirist. She introduces many of the secondary characters: Larry Lefferts, Sillerton Jackson, the Van der Luyden's, Mrs. Manson Mingott, Julius Beaufort. For instance, about Beaufort she remarks: "Now Julius Beaufort's secret was the way he carried things off. He could arrive casually at his own party as if he were another guest and might also leave early for a more modest but comforting address in the East 30s. Beaufort was intrepid in his business, but in his personal affairs, absolutely audacious." Her narration provides explanations of off-screen events, such as how Archer and May end up honeymooning in the Patroon's cottage. And like a wise anthropologist, she explains the meaning of the arbitrary signs through which this society communicates— the gravity of the snub when the circle initially declines to attend the party to meet Ellen; the rebuking lesson that the Van der Luyden's give by inviting Ellen to their compensatory dinner with the Duke of St. Austrey; Ellen's unconsciousness of her blunder at arriving at this dinner rather late. This removed, omniscient perspective also influences the visuals, so that the camera habitually functions in complicity with the narrator, both during scenes when she is speaking and during moments when she recedes.

Perhaps the most obvious way of having a film visually illustrate superiority and omniscience is to place the camera in "impossible" positions, particularly bird's-eye view shots. A director such as Howard Hawks, who is striving for an invisible style, never uses high angle compositions, and a much more self-reflexive filmmaker like Hitchcock uses them sparingly but for memorable effect: Alicia collapsing on the parquet floor in *Notorious*; Roger Thornhill running through the United Nations plaza in *North by Northwest*; the seagulls looking down on their destruction in *The Birds*. *The Age of Innocence*, however, turns to overhead shots again and again: Regina Beaufort getting into her carriage outside of the opera house; the "B" emblazoned on the floor of the Beaufort's ballroom; the Van der Luyden's ornate dinner table; May's farewell banquet for Ellen; the tableau of May resting her head on Newland's knee after she's told him of her pregnancy, with her purple dress spreading on the ground like blood. And though their angle is not as perpendicular, other noteworthy

long shots emphasize the camera's physical remove from the level and perspective of the characters: the view of Mrs. Manson Mingott's house alone in the inaccessible wilderness near Central Park; the shot of the lanterns going out on the Parisian boulevard as the honeymooners drive away; the ending long shot of Archer sitting in the French courtyard outside of Ellen's apartment. Such high angle and long shots function as visual correlatives of the narrator's superior knowledge and wry perspective.

Equally important is the camera's movement through space. As the narrator describes places and people, the camera moves as if under her control, capturing Lefferts or Beaufort—in slow motion—as she introduces them, dollying over the lavish table as she recounts the preparations for a feast. (Diegetic sound is also under her control, of course, fading out when the narrator addresses the viewers.) Generally the images correspond closely with the verbal narration, but on occasion the camera provides another level of commentary. For example, at Mrs. Manson Mingott's house the narrator placidly remarks:

> For now, she [Mrs. Mingott] was content simply for life and fashion to flow northwards to her door and to anticipate eagerly the union of Newland Archer with her granddaughter, May. In them, two of New York's best families would finally and momentously be joined.

Meanwhile, the camera independently saunters up the staircase surveying the paintings hung along the walls, ending on a picture of two savage Indians scalping a white woman. Actually, Michael Ballhaus, the cinematographer, who earlier worked on many bitterly ironic films directed by the German director Rainer Werner Fassbinder, moves the camera incessantly, even in the sequences without voice-over. "I'm your guide through this vanished world," the camera seems to say. "Look over here now."

Verbally and visually the film also flaunts temporal manipulation, showcasing the narrator's god-like ability to summarize and condense, to pick and choose moments in time. Dissolves and narration are used to cover days (such as the kitchen preparations for Mrs. Mingott's party for Ellen, which evaporate when Ellen is snubbed); months (the transformation of the Beaufort ballroom from draped and quiet to festive and bustling with partygoers), or years (Archer's family life over the course of his marriage to May). Because of its use of verbal narration, this film, like a novel, has command of all the subtleties of verb tenses, and can move about in time with both freedom and precision.

Power and control are also foregrounded through the camera's ability to focus the viewers attention, to thrust details into our faces. Scorsese and his editor, Thelma Schoonmaker, do this habitually throughout the film, through cuts, close ups, irises, and lighting. The camera picks out for us details of the opera goers' finery, the fancy food and china, the after-dinner cigars and brandy. Look at how elaborate and costly these little accoutrements are! Look at how wealthy and self-satisfied these people are! Through close-ups and lighting the filmmakers highlight precisely which words we should notice in the numerous notes and invitations exchanged throughout the story.

As we saw above, the novel supplements the narrator's superior perspective with an intimate rendition of Archer's feelings. Recreating this dynamic, the movie frequently ties the viewers' perceptions to Archer's. This connection is blatant in two sequences illustrating his fantasies— we viewers see played out on the screen his desire for Ellen to come up behind him and put her arms around him in the Patroon's cottage, and we share his dazzled vision of Ellen turning around on the pier with a welcoming, loving smile at the very end. Other effects are tied to his consciousness, including an expressionistic use of color. The script confirms that the red wipe over a shot of Ellen on the word "eradication" is meant as Archer's mindscreen of how savagely Old New York is snubbing her. Similarly, the sequence of Ellen receiving and arranging the yellow roses, which itself fades into yellow, is Archer's mental fantasy of her taking pleasure in his gift. Clearly when all the scenery in his library becomes suffused with a red glow at the farewell banquet, the color is a projection of Archer's inner turmoil.

More ambiguous are the point of view shots. Some are certainly meant to record Archer's perceptions. Significantly, all the shots of May looking her most insipid are marked as Archer's POV. Yet some cases are less easily defined. When Gavin Smith questioned him on this topic, Scorsese replied:

> Maybe it's a mixture. To mix all this together may not be the right thing to do, but I don't know what's right and what's wrong, really, when I'm making a movie. I think you make your own set of rules for each one in terms of the subjectivity of the piece. In fact, the ball

sequence begins with the narrator explaining who people are, but ends subjectively: May looks up into the camera and who's standing there? It's Archer. But you could look back at it and it could be Archer's point of view looking at everyone at the ball. (Smith 19)

The intermixing of objective and subjective focalization is so fluid that even sequences ostensibly shot from an "unmarked" point of view can also be inflected by Archer's feelings. For instance, three dissolves are used to show Archer taking off Ellen's glove in the carriage; surely this conveys his erotic rapture, not the narrator's. And Scorsese has described how carefully he shot May's standing up just as she is about to cross the room to Newland and tell him of her pregnancy and her triumph: for this simple movement Scorsese decided to use three separate close-ups and subtle slow motion. Scorsese explained, "I think he'll never forget that moment the rest of his life. He'll play it back many times. When she gets up, I thought we should play it back like a memory" (Smith 15). So as the event occurs, viewers see it through the lens of Archer's future memory.

In the film *The Age of Innocence* the score contributes to the complex interplay between cool irony and subjective passion. Scorsese gave the composer, Elmer Bernstein, rather contradictory instructions. He wanted "a score that evoked a period but was not part of it—music that summoned a particular place and time, but that existed out of time. [. . . ,] something sharp and poignant and a little ironic, music that was absolutely unsentimental and without nostalgia" (Scorsese and Cocks, liner notes). The score has moments that are quite ironic, particularly in its use of source music. During the Beaufort's ball, for example, "The Radetzky March," by Johann Strauss, blares out with a self-satisfied fatuousness. Yet the main love theme played under the credits and repeating throughout is as passionate as can be.

Much of my discussion so far has indicated how innovatively Scorsese has found ways to follow Wharton's blueprint. But for all his boldness in using this narrator (many reviewers objected to the voice-over as uncinematic), one must recognize that Scorsese also held back from giving her the authority she might have. Joanne Woodward may not have been the best casting choice: she conveys intelligence and integrity, but her voice, very flat and marked by traces of her birthplace in Georgia, is thus devoid of the upper-class breeding and cosmopolitanism elan implied by lines such as, "It was widely known in New York, but never acknowledged, that Americans want to get away from amusement even more quickly than they want to get to it." Moreover, if one wants to convey that the narrator is telling the entire story, then the voice should be used to envelope the diegesis; we should hear her both at the beginning and the end of the film. Yet the first sequence of the film at the opera house, recounting Newland's first meeting with Ellen, transpires without accompaniment; the narrator doesn't come in until she describes Mrs. Beaufort's habits: "It invariably happened, as everything happened in those days, in the same way. As usual, Mrs. Julius Beaufort appeared just before the Jewel Song, and again as usual, rose at the end of the third act and disappeared." (Examination of the shooting script reveals that the original intention was to play the opening scene as a pre-credit sequence, then pause for the Main Titles, and then return via narration to the story world. Perhaps the structure was altered during editing because the Main Titles, a lush montage of roses blooming under lace designed by Saul and Elaine Bass, was too showy to be delayed.) Instead of the voice authorizing the camera, the camera envelopes the voice.

Moreover, in another respect Scorsese made a significant departure from the novel. It is very important to Wharton that May, the virginal maiden, be blond, and Ellen, the exotic temptress, be dark. The traditional symbolism of their coloring falls into Wharton's focus on Archer's—and the readers'—underestimation of May and unthinking acceptance of inherited conventions. By casting the fair-haired Michelle Pfeiffer as Ellen and the dark Winona Ryder as May, however, Scorsese would seem to have lost this element, unless the cultural stereotyping that Wharton critiques has something in common with the functioning of the Hollywood star system? After all, viewers approaching this film come with expectations about Day-Lewis, Pfeiffer, and Ryder from their previous films. We may expect Day-Lewis to be the brave, active hero that he played in *Last of the Mohicans*; we may associate Pfeiffer with the sexuality of her roles in *Batman*, *The Fabulous Baker Boys*, and *Dangerous Liaisons*; we may think of Ryder as the sulky contemporary teenager of *Heathers* or *Beetlejuice*. But all of the principals give richly nuanced performances with Day-Lewis playing a man who weeps at melodramas and who ultimately does not take decisive action, just as Pfeiffer, for all her sultry eroticism, embodies a woman who grimly insists that morality is superior to romantic self-fulfillment, and Ryder shocks us with her steely resolve. Despite the change in hair-coloring, Scorsese too uses the audience's expectations and presumptions to teach us, in Wharton's words, that, "Everything may be labeled—but everyone is not" (61).

Perhaps inadvertently, the film's publicity also worked to set filmgoers up for a fall. The widely-used publicity photograph taken by Philip Caruso of Pfeiffer and Day-Lewis passionately embracing is accurate in that, yes, the film is surely about their passion, but fundamentally misleading in that the text does not lead to a love affair, and actually forces us to question whether such fulfillment would be desirable. Similarly, the extensive pre-release magazine publicity about the expensive production design, the fetishism over the china and the costumes, invited viewers to drool over this world of upper class privilege and luxury. Yet surely one of Wharton's and Scorsese's points is that this society is flawed by narrowness and hypocrisy. As Leo Braudy wrote in another context, this film "lures its audience into a seemingly familiar world, filled with reassuring stereotypes of character, action and plot. But the world may actually be not so lulling, and, in some cases, acquiescence in convention will turn out to be bad judgment or even a moral flaw" (617).

I believe the film is serious and effective in getting across this moral lesson. In the final analysis, however, the movie of *The Age of Innocence* is less pointed in its criticism and social awareness than the novel. Although the novel itself provides none of the stark realism and unblinking focus on the class structure of its lumpen near-contemporary, Dreiser's *An American Tragedy* (1925), one of its strands is to ponder Old New York from the vantage point of post-WWI modernity. This leitmotif is woven throughout the book in small references to the technological and cultural changes that are to come. Moreover, the engagement of these characters in history is emphasized by key passages towards the end. As Pamela Knights remarks, "There can be few readers who would predict Theodore Roosevelt as Archer's compensation for Ellen Olenska," yet by bringing Theodore Roosevelt into Archer's library to call him into public service in the closing pages, Wharton emphasizes that Archer's decision to sacrifice his passion and personal fulfillment to be loyal to his wife and family also leads him to contribute meaningfully to the welfare of his city and community (42). Edith Wharton's interest in social activism was neither shallow nor theoretical; she herself had worked tirelessly and successfully to alleviate the suffering of thousands of the orphaned, the sick, and the homeless who flooded France during the War. Scorsese and Cocks, however, omit all mention of Archer's political and philanthropic activities in the narrator's summation of his married life, and overall the 1920 versus 1870 contrast is muted in the film. "The setting's important," Scorsese told Cocks, "only to show why this love is impossible" (Scorsese and Cocks xiii). Scorsese's emphasis turned to the universal, tragic poignancy of the unhappy love story.

In this sense his beautiful, complex film has something in common with the abstraction and idealization of Sir Joshua Reynolds's portrait....

Source: Sarah Kozloff, "Complicity in *The Age of Innocence*," in *Style*, Vol. 35, No. 2, Summer 2001, pp. 270–91.

Richard Grenier

In the following excerpt, Grenier comments that Scorsese's film version of The Age of Innocence *is scrupulously faithful, but gone from it are the elaborate descriptions of household interiors that are a staple of all Edith Wharton's works and that have led some critics to call her "the poet of interior decoration."*

...Although Scorsese's film version of *The Age of Innocence* is scrupulously faithful, gone from it are the elaborate descriptions of household interiors that are a staple of all Edith Wharton's works and that have led some critics to call her "the poet of interior decoration."

Gone also, inevitably, is Mrs. Wharton's predilection for defining her characters by their material possessions. Thus, in the novel, we are meant to feel the attraction of Countess Olenska by her "small slender tables of dark wood, a delicate little Greek bronze in the chimney piece, and a stretch of red damask nailed on the discolored wallpaper behind a couple of Italian-looking pictures in old frames." We learn that the Countess has two Jacqueminot roses in a slender vase, and that her tea is served "with two handleless Japanese cups and little covered

> WHETHER OR NOT THIS IS AN UPLIFTING PROCESS TO CONTEMPLATE, MARTIN SCORSESE LEAVES IT UP TO THE SPECTATOR TO DECIDE."

dishes." A character who has been eliminated from the screenplay is the young Countess's eccentric aunt, who brought her up in Europe after the death of her parents and appears in New York "in a wild dishevelment of stripes and fringes and floating scarves."

Mrs. Wharton makes quite a point of her contention that in the 1870's, before the ostentatious nouveaux riches "invaders" came to dominate New York society, a certain old-fashioned tackiness was the accepted social rule, and to follow too rapidly the latest ladies' fashions from Paris was thought to be vulgar. Thus, New York's Academy of Music, where the novel's opening scene takes place, is described as having shabby red and gold boxes, and the grandest New York ladies of the period, although they order the latest dresses from Paris promptly enough, are reported as leaving them to "mellow" in their delivery boxes for some two years, after which it becomes proper and in good taste to wear them. Most such satirical comments from the novel are gone from the film—although a few are preserved in the voice-over passages read by Joanne Woodward. In general, the novel's decor has been decidedly upgraded, with wardrobes, grand homes, and even the opera house being of the utmost luxury and opulence.

Nevertheless, most of Edith Wharton's attitudes are conveyed, and the heart of *The Age of Innocence* is present almost in full: the love story between Newland Archer and Countess Olenska with all its ins and outs, and a nearly complete cast of characters, including May Welland's entire family, Archer's entire family, several other "prominent" families, a complement of wits and dandies, and an obnoxious upstart financier named Julius Beaufort, who Mrs. Wharton denied was supposed to be a Jew (but who has been assumed to represent the age's celebrated Jewish financier, August Belmont). The older members of New York society are played by an excellent cast of largely British actors—this in accordance with Edith Wharton's reiterated insistence that in her period such people spoke with purely English accents. Fortunately, Newland Archer, Countess Olenska, and most of the younger members of the cast sound American.

Should Newland Archer have run off with Countess Olenska? Martin Scorsese sticks with Edith Wharton, and has emphasized in interviews that he has done his level best to "follow the book." He is prepared to accept her judgment. But what is her judgment?

This, as it happens, is a matter of some dispute. The Columbia trustees, in overruling the Pulitzer Prize jury in 1921, doubtless thought that Newland Archer had done the "wholesome" thing. But in the next decade, the influential critic Edmund Wilson rushed forward to contest that view. *The Age of Innocence*, Wilson insisted, conveys an "active resentment against the pusillanimity" of provincial New York, as well as a special complaint against the "timid American male"—Newland Archer—"who has let the lady down." According to Wilson, it was the "last irony" of *The Age of Innocence* that Newland Archer should become reconciled to the stifling moral values of Old New York.

Similarly today, watching the new film and quite in its grip, the novelist John Updike reported (in the *New Yorker*) feeling a distinct uncertainty as to how it was going to turn out:

> There was, for me, a momentary ambiguity at the end of Scorsese's film. . . . It seemed possible that Hollywood might exercise its prerogative and . . . have Archer do what any red-blooded widower would do, that is, take the ascenseur, give his hostess a hug, and spend the rest of his life with Michelle Pfeiffer.

But Updike went further. Even in Edith Wharton's novel, he wrote, Archer seems "merely perverse." And he asked, "In reworking Wharton, how tied should the workers be to the cruel overseer within her who denied her characters happiness after bringing them tantalizingly close to it?"

In his Pulitzer Prize-winning biography of Edith Wharton (1985), R. W. B. Lewis of Yale gives a direct rebuttal to all such "romantic" readings of Mrs. Wharton. For her, writes Lewis, "there was no genuine and honorable and emotionally fulfilling alternative to the social order . . . Society was the domain of the values that counted most—loyalty, decency,

honesty, fidelity, and the adherence to moral commitment."

For all Edith Wharton's ambivalence about Old New York, the weight of evidence is on Lewis's side. In fact, in the preliminary outline for *The Age of Innocence* which Mrs. Wharton sent to her American publishers (under the working title Old New York), her hero, Archer, does indeed run off with Countess Olenska—and the venture ends in failure. The two meet in Florida where they spend a few mad weeks, after which Archer remorsefully returns to his wife and conventional life in New York, and Countess Olenska to Paris. In further outlines, Mrs. Wharton even had Archer break his engagement to May Welland and actually marry Ellen Olenska, but that too fails to work out. So, in Mrs. Wharton's eyes, whether Newland Archer could find happiness with Countess Olenska was not an open question.

One does not need to describe Mrs. Wharton's moral standards in quite the glowing terms used by R. W. B. Lewis to appreciate that in her work no feverish dashing-off to find romance somewhere over the horizon, or illicit passion of any sort, ever brings happiness. This is even true of an unpublished erotic story, "Beatrice Palmato," which she composed at about the same time she was writing *The Age of Innocence*. Mrs. Wharton was quite proud of this highly explicit work, and boasted about it to her friends. Yet it, too, is shot through with darkness. Beatrice's older sister, who has earlier been seduced by their "half-Levantine" father, kills herself, their mother goes insane, tries to kill her husband, and dies in a lunatic asylum; and the eponymous Beatrice, who has been having regular sexual relations with her father from the age of twelve, also kills herself.

It was only in the half-finished *The Buccaneers* that Edith Wharton planned to have her social-climbing American heiress, Nan St. George, run off with a former officer of the Guards and find true happiness—in South Africa. As she declared cheerfully in her outline for the unwritten final passages of *The Buccaneers*, she meant, perhaps for the first time in her career, to show the triumph of "love, deep and abiding love." And this is just what the novel does in the version completed for Mrs. Wharton and just published, with highly feminist, upbeat alterations, by Marion Mainwaring. "Yet one wonders, given Mrs. Wharton's acidulous temperament, and, especially, the way she altered her plan for *The Age of Innocence*, if this "deep and abiding love" would indeed have found fruition had she finished the novel herself.

Perhaps the last word on this matter should be given to the novelist Louis Auchincloss, himself a (much later) product of the New York aristocratic world and one who is generally quite critical of Mrs. Wharton's "grotesque" (his word) caricatures of American life. To Auchincloss, *The Age of Innocence* expresses a "sense of apology" for the contempt in which Edith Wharton had held the New York of her early years. This book, writes Auchincloss, conveys absolutely no feeling that, in giving up the dream of love, "Archer has condemned himself and the Countess to an unrewarding life of frustration. The author is absorbed in the beauty of rules and forms even when they stamp out spontaneity." In the novel, Countess Olenska tells Archer: "It was you who made me understand that under the dullness there are things so fine and sensitive and delicate that even those I most cared for in my other life look cheap in comparison." Auchincloss glosses: "This is the climax of the message: that under the thick glass of convention blooms the fine, fragile flower of patient suffering and denial. To drop out of society is as vulgar as to predominate; one must endure and properly smile."

Henry James, the most distinguished of Edith Wharton's American literary friends, wrote of her work: "We move in an air purged at a stroke of the old sentimental and romantic values." Many years later, as if mindful of Mrs. Wharton's challenge to these values, W. H. Auden was to write: "About three-quarters of modern literature is concerned with one subject, the love between a man and a woman, and assumes that falling in love is the most important and valuable experience that can happen to a human being."

If there is a significant difference between Edith Wharton's *The Age of Innocence* and Martin Scorsese's extraordinary movie, it stems from the fact that, for all the feminist lectures we have had to endure on the virtues of seeking fulfillment outside of man-woman relationships," our disposition toward romantic love is still so powerful that it tends to condition our expectations of any narrative art—perhaps above all our expectations of movies. Through the remarkable performances of Michelle Pfeiffer

and Daniel Day-Lewis, *The Age of Innocence*, on screen, builds a romantic momentum that seems absolutely to demand fulfillment.

But it was never Edith Wharton's intention to provide this fulfillment. She herself had a conventional, virtually sexless, and certainly passionless marriage to the neurotic socialite Teddy Wharton. Her one experience with fierce, passionate love occurred ten years before she was to write *The Age of Innocence*, and that it was a humiliating episode her abject letters to her lover now bear witness. With Edith Wharton, love never conquers all. Society's moral conventions conquer all.

Whether or not this is an uplifting process to contemplate, Martin Scorsese leaves it up to the spectator to decide. For Scorsese, who almost alone among American directors has concerned himself with moral dilemmas within tight social groups (most famously, of course, the Mafia), and with the equivocal demands of order, tradition, respect, loyalty, and the fulfilling of commitments, understands this difficult truth about Edith Wharton, and honors it to the letter.

Source: Richard Grenier, "*The Age of Innocence*," in *Commentary*, Vol. 96, No. 6, December 1993, pp. 48–53.

SOURCES

Canby, Vincent, "The Age of Innocence: Grand Passions and Good Manners," in *New York Times*, September 17, 1993, p. 1.

Ebert, Roger, *Scorsese by Ebert*, University of Chicago Press, 2008, p. 287.

Gleiberman, Owen, "The Age of Innocence," in *Entertainment Weekly*, September 17, 1993, http://www.ew.com/ew/article/0,,308064,00.html (accessed October 11, 2010).

Howe, Desson, "The Age of Innocence," in *Washington Post*, September 17, 1993, http://www.washingtonpost.com/wp-srv/style/longterm/movies/videos/theageofinnocencepghowe_a0aff3.htm (accessed October 11, 2010).

Klawans, Stuart, "The Age of Innocence," in *Nation*, Vol. 257, No. 10, October 4, 1993, pp. 364–66.

Palmer, William J., "The Yuppie Texts," in *The Films of the Eighties*, Southern Illinois University Press, 1993, pp. 280–307.

Rosenbaum, Jonathan, "The Age of Innocence," in *Chicago Reader*, http://www.chicagoreader.com/chicago/the-age-of-innocence/Film?oid = 1054994 (accessed October 11, 2010).

Scorsese, Martin, and Jay Cocks, *The Age of Innocence*, Columbia Pictures, 1993.

Wilmington, Michael, "*The Age of Innocence*: Martin Scorsese's Lush Romance Seethes With Suppressed Passion," in *Chicago Tribune*, September 17, 1983.

"World War I Casualty and Death Tables," in *The Great War and the Shaping of the Twentieth Century*, Public Broadcasting System, http://www.pbs.org/greatwar/resources/casdeath_pop.html (accessed October 24, 2010).

FURTHER READING

Lee, A. Robert, "Watching Manners: Martin Scorsese's *The Age of Innocence*, and Edith Wharton's *The Age of Innocence*," in *The Classic Novel from Page to Screen*, edited by Robert Giddings and Erica Sheen, Manchester University Press, 2000, pp. 163–88.

> Lee's study focuses on the changes Scorsese made to the source material for *The Age of Innocence*, finding his adaptation to be an excellent one.

Scorsese, Martin, "*The Age of Innocence*—A Personal Journey," in *Scorsese on Scorsese*, edited by Ian Christie and David Thompson, Faber and Faber, 2003, pp. 176–97.

> Scorsese tells of his involvement in the making of this film, from the time it was proposed by writer Jay Cocks in 1980 through the scripting, casting, and shooting processes.

Scorsese, Martin, and Jay Cocks, "*The Age of Innocence*": A Portrait of the Film Based on the Novel by Edith Wharton*, edited by Robin Standefer, Newmarket Press, 1993.

> The shooting script of the film is available in paperback form by itself, but this deluxe edition, with production photographs by Philip J. Caruso, includes the script plus many photographs from the 1800s that inspired specific set and costume designs.

Updike, John, "Archer's Way," in *Edith Wharton's The Age of Innocence*, edited by Harold Bloom, Chelsea House Publishers, 2005, pp. 133–40.

> Although it does not mention the film version, this study, by one of America's greatest writers, is rich with background information about Wharton and the process of producing the novel.

SUGGESTED SEARCH TERMS

Edith Wharton

Wharton AND Martin Scorsese

Scorsese AND Michelle Pfeiffer

Scorsese AND Jay Cocks

The Age of Innocence AND Daniel Day-Lewis

Edith Wharton AND film

Age of Innocence AND Michael Ballhaus

Scorsese AND Gilded Age

New York AND 1870s

Edith Wharton AND manners

The Beet Queen

LOUISE ERDRICH
1986

Louise Erdrich's novel *The Beet Queen*, first published in 1986, features a sweeping plot told from multiple viewpoints over many decades. Set in the fictional town of Argus, North Dakota, beginning in 1932, the story involves the interconnected lives of Mary Adare, her brother Karl, her cousin Sita, the half-Chippewa Celestine James, and Celestine's daughter Dot, who ultimately becomes the Beet Queen of the title in the 1970s. Argus, the nearby Turtle Mountain Chippewa reservation, and its sprawling multigenerational families are featured in many of Erdrich's other works, including *Love Medicine* (1984), a novelistic collection of interrelated stories; *Tracks* (1988), a novel focusing on the lives of the Chippewa from 1912 to 1924; *The Bingo Palace* (1994); and *Tales of Burning Love* (1996). All the works stand on their own and focus on specific characters but feature a certain amount of the sort of interrelational overlap common to rural communities. *The Beet Queen* depicts nontraditional interpretations of family prompted by Mary and Karl's dramatic abandonment by their destitute mother. While the novel dwells less on Native American themes than many of Erdrich's other works, critics have admired its evocative language and rich use of symbolism.

AUTHOR BIOGRAPHY

Erdrich was born in Little Falls, Minnesota, on June 7, 1954, to a Chippewa mother and a German American father. She grew up in North Dakota as

Louise Erdrich (*AP Images*)

a member of the Turtle Mountain Band of Chippewa Indians, where her parents taught at a Bureau of Indian Affairs school. (The Chippewa are also called the Ojibwa or Ojibwe.) Erdrich graduated from Dartmouth College in 1976 and received her master's degree in creative writing from Johns Hopkins University in 1979. She found success as a writer shortly thereafter; her story "The World's Greatest Fisherman" won the prestigious Nelson Algren Prize for short fiction in 1982. Another story, "Fleur," first published in *Esquire* magazine in 1986—concerning the character of Fleur Pillager, who also appears in *The Beet Queen*—received the O. Henry Award in 1987. *Love Medicine*, her first novel, met with resounding success, garnering an American Book Award and a National Book Critics Circle Award, among other honors.

Erdrich first met her future husband, the writer and anthropologist Michael Dorris, while she was an undergraduate at Dartmouth and he was a professor. In 1981, following a long-distance courtship, the couple married and began collaborating on fiction. Dorris contributed

much input to Erdrich's early published works, but they did not share joint authorship until the publication of *The Crown of Columbus* in 1991, a novel about a Navajo academic and her exasperating colleague, who are both researching Christopher Columbus and have vastly divergent opinions on his legacy.

Erdrich and Dorris had three children together and also raised three children adopted by Dorris before they were married. One adopted son suffered from fetal alcohol syndrome, a common affliction in Native American communities, which prompted Dorris to publish *The Broken Cord: A Family's Ongoing Struggle with Fetal Alcohol Syndrome* in 1989, for which Erdrich wrote the preface. Dorris struggled with depression for much of their marriage, which was compounded by the death of another of their sons in 1991. A third son accused Dorris of child abuse and Erdrich of negligent complicity in 1995. The couple later divorced, and in 1997, Dorris committed suicide.

Erdrich has continued to publish well-received novels, including *The Antelope Wife* (1998), a World Fantasy Award winner, as well as *The Last Report on the Miracles at Little No Horse* (2001), *The Master Butchers Singing Club* (2003), and *The Plague of Doves* (2008). Two other novels, *Four Souls* (2004) and *The Painted Drum* (2005), find Erdrich continuing the stories of Fleur Pillager and the Ojibwe Indians of North Dakota. In addition to her novels, Erdrich has published children's fiction and collections of poetry. For many years, she and her sister have owned and run the independent Birchbark Books in Minneapolis.

PLOT SUMMARY

Chapter 1

The Beet Queen opens in 1932 with eleven-year-old Mary Adare hopping off a freight train with her thirteen-year-old brother Karl in Argus, North Dakota. But Karl becomes distracted by a branch of a flowering tree, and a dog chases him back to the boxcar. Mary continues on to the butcher shop owned by her aunt Fritzie and uncle Pete Kozka, where they live with their daughter Sita.

Several months earlier, Mary and Karl's father, Mr. Ober, died in a grain-elevator accident that may have been suicide. Their mother,

Adelaide Adare, was Mr. Ober's mistress, and she and her children lived in a house that belonged to him. His death has rendered them homeless, and they move to a boardinghouse in Minneapolis, where Adelaide soon gives birth to another baby boy. The landlady evicts them after Adelaide steals a piece of her silver. At a church festival, Adelaide flies off with a stunt pilot named Omar, abandoning all three of her children. Mary hands over the baby to a man who takes him home for his wife to feed, and they never see him again.

In Argus, Aunt Fritzie and Uncle Pete welcome Mary the best they can, but Sita is incensed. She cannot stand sharing her clothes and bedroom with dull, dumpy Mary. To repay the Kozkas for their kindness, Mary gives them her mother's locked blue velvet box, which she believes contains a valuable garnet necklace, but which they find contains only a pawn ticket. Sita gloats, but Mary promises to make herself useful so she will never be homeless again.

Following his return to the train, that night, Karl has a brief homosexual encounter with a drifter. Later, he jumps out of the moving boxcar.

Chapter 2

Sita narrates her version of Mary's first days at the butcher shop. She grows infuriated when her father gives Mary a cow's diamond—the lens from a cow's eye—that he had promised Sita as her inheritance. Insult is added to injury when Mary steals Sita's best friend, Celestine James, a half-Chippewa girl who is also orphaned and lives with her half brother Russell Kashpaw.

During her first winter at St. Catherine's, Mary smacks her head against the ice on the playground, resulting in a cracked indentation that the nuns believe is the image of Jesus Christ. Mary becomes a temporary celebrity, but she thinks the mark looks like her lost brother Karl.

In a brief third-person episode, the baby's story is recounted. Martin and Catherine Miller's newborn baby has recently died. When Martin returns from the orphans' picnic with Adelaide's abandoned infant, Catherine feeds him willingly. Several days later, they read a newspaper article that offers a reward for information on the whereabouts of the baby boy whose mother fled with Omar. They realize the baby is theirs to keep and name him Jude, after the patron saint of lost causes.

Chapter 3

In jumping out of the moving boxcar, Karl has broken both feet. Fleur Pillager, a shaman-like nomadic Chippewa woman who travels the countryside pulling a railroad cart, rescues him. She secures his feet in homemade plaster casts and erects a makeshift sweat lodge to break his fever. When he is well enough, she leaves him at a church. The sisters at the church send him back to the Minneapolis orphanage where his mother abandoned him. A year later, he enters the seminary.

Mary receives a postcard from her mother, who is living in Jacksonville, Florida, with Omar. Mary sends a return postcard, telling Adelaide all three of her children are dead. The postcard reaches Omar after a plane crash in which both he and Adelaide have been seriously injured.

Chapter 4

Mary's life in Argus settles into a routine: Celestine is her best friend, and Sita continues to resent her. She enjoys working at the butcher shop and has become an integral part of it. She briefly becomes infatuated with Russell Kashpaw, but he rebuffs her advances, and she exhibits no interest in men after that. When Fritzie's health falters, she and Pete move to Arizona and leave Mary to run the butcher shop. Sita moves to Fargo to chase her dream of becoming a model for a department store.

Karl has left the seminary and has become a traveling salesman. He returns to the orphans' picnic where his mother abandoned him years ago and confronts a teenaged seminarian, whom he recognizes as his long lost brother. Karl is seized by an intense dislike of the boy and insults him, causing the boy to proclaim that Karl is the devil.

Chapter 5

By 1950, Sita's career as a department store model has fizzled, love has eluded her, and her looks are fading. Mary forwards to Sita a letter from Catherine Miller confessing that she and her husband have raised Adelaide's abandoned baby and have not told him the truth of his origins. Catherine offers Mary the opportunity to do so at Jude's ordination as a deacon, which will take place shortly at the cathedral in St. Paul.

Jimmy Bohl, a coarse-mannered owner of a bar called the Poopdeck near Argus, proposes to

Sita. To stall his advances, she tells him that she must travel to Minneapolis for her cousin's ordination, which she intends to disrupt by announcing his illegitimacy. Her first stop in the city is an exclusive department store, where she is shocked to discover that what passes for fashion in Fargo is hopelessly out of style in the big city. At the ordination service, she does not recognize Jude among the many young men and leaves without confronting him. She finds the shop where Adelaide had pawned her garnet necklace years earlier and retrieves it.

Back in Fargo, she drafts a letter to Catherine Miller but never sends it. Sita marries Jimmy, and at the reception, his friends kidnap her, drive her up to the Indian reservation, and abandon her.

Chapter 6

Karl meets Wallace Pfef at a farmer's convention in Minneapolis and mentions that his sister lives in Wallace's hometown of Argus. They share a tryst—Wallace's first—and afterward Karl injures himself while jumping up and down on the hotel's bed. Wallace is Karl's only visitor in the hospital. Upon Wallace's return to Argus, he hatches a plan to transform the town into the sugar-beet capital of the country.

Chapter 7

Russell Kashpaw returns from Korea, a war hero twice over, his body scarred terribly. Sita, having divorced Jimmy and receiving the Poopdeck in the settlement, prepares for the grand opening of her high-class Chez Sita restaurant venture. Celestine, Russell, and Mary grudgingly attend, but when all the cooks come down with food poisoning, Sita persuades them to take over cooking duties in the kitchen. The health inspector, Louis Tappe, promptly shuts the restaurant down; shortly thereafter, he becomes Sita's second husband. They live in Jimmy's old house—the biggest house in Blue Mound.

One night when Celestine is alone in the butcher shop, Karl appears and introduces himself as Mary's brother. They are simultaneously attracted and repulsed by each other; they give in to their carnal desires. Afterward, he sells her a knife.

Two weeks later, Karl shows up at Celestine's house, and their affair continues uneasily. Karl and Mary have a brusque reunion that ends with Mary tossing a can of oysters at his head. Both Mary and Russell disapprove of Celestine's

relationship with Karl, and they break up just as Celestine realizes she is pregnant. Russell returns to the reservation to wait out Celestine's pregnancy.

Chapter 8

Karl shows up one afternoon in Sita's backyard. She is convinced he has come to rob her house, especially when she discovers that the New Testament he is carrying has Celestine's name inside it. She calls the police, but as she sits down to lunch with Karl and Louis, she descends into madness, convinced that Karl is being sucked into the ground. She spews nonsensical pronouncements about judgment and death.

Russell suffers a debilitating stroke in his icefishing cabin, and Celestine discovers him. He survives, but he is permanently incapacitated.

Chapter 9

Wallace has hidden his sexuality by telling people that his fiancée died many years ago. In the absence of a family life, he has thrown himself into the community life of Argus. From the Rotary Club to the Knights of Columbus, he is an organizer and civic leader who is proud to have revived the local economy by developing the sugar-beet industry. However, his heart still aches for Karl.

Before he took up with Celestine, Karl spent two weeks at Wallace's house in Argus, during which they resumed their affair. Wallace was heartbroken when he discovered that Karl left him for Celestine. But when Celestine gives birth in Wallace's living room, on account of a blizzard that prevents her from making it to the hospital, Wallace instantly falls in love with the baby, whom Celestine names Wallacette in his honor. Mary immediately nicknames the baby Dot.

Shortly after Dot's birth, Celestine and Karl are married, although their relationship is loveless. Karl returns to the road, occasionally sending strange gifts to Dot. Celestine loves Dot and enjoys motherhood, but Dot proves to be a difficult and demanding child.

Chapter 10

Mary feels a kinship with Dot's fierce personality and insatiable appetite and admits that she indulges the girl. Their relationship is so close that Mary often usurps Celestine's authority, much to Celestine's annoyance. Dot does not get along well with others and frequently gets in fights with her classmates. Mary avenges Dot's punishment at school by trapping a teacher inside a toy box, an event that prompts Celestine to stop speaking to Mary for months.

Dot romanticizes her father, whom she has never known. When Karl sends her a motorized wheelchair, she is crushed by her mother's insistence that they give it to the mute and paralyzed Russell, who lives on the reservation with his brother and Fleur Pillager.

Louis has Sita committed to a mental institution because she refused to speak for four months. The psychiatrists believe that Louis encouraged Sita's behavior by taking copious notes on her condition and responding to her written demands. Her first night in the institution terrifies her; her roommate is an elderly woman who claims to be a cannibal. The next morning she makes her way to a telephone and screams out loud for Louis to rescue her.

Chapter 11

The butcher shop is damaged in a fire, and Mary moves into Celestine's house while it is being repaired. Celestine becomes infuriated with how Mary marginalizes her relationship with her own daughter and encourages Dot's bad behavior. Dot is thrilled to have been chosen to play Joseph in the school Christmas pageant, but Celestine is livid that Mary has signed up to bring her atrocious Jell-O salad.

Dot's scene in the play goes horribly awry, and she escapes into the cold December night in embarrassment. Later, Celestine admits to Mary that as a joke she brought to the potluck a Jell-O salad made with nuts and bolts. Mary is hurt by the admission, and Celestine realizes that the evening had been equally important to Mary.

A brief scene with Adelaide and Omar reveals that they now live in a house full of birds. She is given to rages in which she smashes things, with a resigned Omar making sure she does not hurt herself.

Chapter 12

In the years since he brought the sugar beet to Argus, Wallace has prospered and enjoyed being a part of Dot's life. He understands that Mary and Celestine dote on Dot too much, and as a result she tortures them with her bad ways. He sees the girl as a combination of Celestine's and Mary's worst traits but fearless in a way he finds admirable. Wallace volunteers to throw a party for Dot's eleventh birthday. He even invites Sita

and Louis, who have never had children of their own and have remained estranged from Celestine and Mary. Mary ruins the festive spirit by organizing events like a drill sergeant. To retaliate, Wallace plies the teetotalling Mary with a very stiff drink. She becomes unusually animated and sets in motion a chain of events that culminates in the birthday cake being flung into Sita's face. Mary collapses into a drunken catatonic state, and Dot considers the party a great success.

Several years later, Karl meets Celestine and Dot at a restaurant. Dot has become a dismissive, surly teenager who dresses provocatively. Karl is selling record players now and wants to know if Dot will listen to some records if he sends them. She responds rudely, finally realizing that her father is a complete stranger who has had nothing to do with her life.

Chapter 13

Mary has become an oddly dressed woman obsessed with the occult and afterlife. Based on one of Celestine's dreams, Mary is convinced that Sita is dying and determines that the two of them must go take care of her. Meanwhile, Wallace plans Argus's first Beet Festival, an idea he hatches for the sole purpose of crowning Dot the Beet Queen, an event he believes will boost the troubled girl's self-esteem and prove how beautiful she is.

Mary and Celestine arrive at Sita's house unannounced. Indeed, she is dying and addicted to her dead husband's pain medication to boot. Sita sleeps on the pool table in the basement and keeps her dead husband's pills in the toilet tank. She is as inhospitable to them as ever; Sita exchanges harsh words with Mary, who beans her in the head with a brick, causing a terrible gash. Celestine finds and mails Sita's ancient letter to Catherine Miller.

The morning of the Beet Festival, Mary and Celestine leave to run errands. Sita painstakingly dresses herself, fastens Adelaide's garnet necklace around her neck, downs the rest of her pain pills, and dies while waiting for Mary and Celestine to pick her up. Not willing to leave Sita sprawled against the bushes in front of the house and not willing to miss Dot's moment as a Beet Princess, they stuff Sita's body into the butcher shop's refrigerated van and drive into town, right down the parade route. At the festival, which takes place on an extremely hot day during a serious drought, they leave Sita's body in the truck.

Also part of the Beet Festival parade is Russell Kashpaw, who is being honored as North Dakota's most decorated war hero. He is precariously perched on a float, where he suffers dehydration and hallucinates about his dead sister.

Chapter 14

Wallace recounts Dot's bad behavior: She smokes, writes compulsively in her diaries, and stays out late. She is vengeful, paranoid, shoplifts, and hangs out with the wrong crowd. Thus, he attaches great importance to the Beet Festival and his chance to show Dot how much he loves her by having fixed the vote that will crown her the Beet Queen. Dot, however, is humiliated by the ugly dress she is forced to wear and the insults hurled at her by the other princesses, who let her know the vote has been fixed. Dot finally takes matters into her own hands. Looking like a "stopped tornado," she hunts down Wallace, who is taking a turn in the dunk tank. She dunks him with the first of her three perfect pitches, leaving him flailing in the water.

Meanwhile, Jude Miller, now Father Miller, arrives by train in Argus the day of the Beet Festival, having received Sita's 20-year-old letter telling him of his family origins. He makes his way to Kozka's House of Meats, but it is closed on account of the festival.

Chapter 15

Karl realizes his life as a traveling salesman has been hollow and has left him with nothing. His brief reunion with Mary ended badly, and he abandoned Wallace because of his need to be loved. He returns to Argus for the Beet Festival, having received a newspaper clipping from Celestine announcing Dot as a finalist for Beet Queen. He is proud of her and would like to reestablish family ties. In the parking lot, he spots Sita in the butcher shop van and joins her for a minute to take refuge from the heat. He has no idea she is dead. From there he witnesses Dot dunk Wallace and runs to his rescue.

Chapter 16

During the ceremony to crown the Beet Queen, Dot is so angry that she can no longer contain herself. She runs off toward the idling airplane, which will write the queen's name in the sky. She tells the pilot to take off. When they are airborne,

she becomes quite sick but is able to fire the silver-iodide cartridges to seed the clouds in hopes of bringing rain to drought-parched Argus. By the time the plane lands an hour later, Dot is ecstatic to be on solid ground. The only person waiting for her in the grandstand is her mother. Later that night, the rain comes.

CHARACTERS

Adelaide Adare

Adelaide Adare is Karl, Mary, and Jude's mother. As a kept woman, she is devastated when her married lover, Mr. Ober, commits suicide in the depths of the Great Depression. She despises her dowdy sister Fritzie and longs to have a glamorous, carefree life. She is beautiful but talentless and has no way to support her children. Thus, she abandons all of them, including her unnamed infant son, at an orphans' picnic near Minneapolis, when she climbs into a stunt airplane with Omar the Great. She remains with Omar, becoming part of his act until she is severely injured in an accident. They live surrounded by birds, symbols of her emotional fragility; she occasionally suffers fits of rage in which she smashes things and Omar must prevent her from injuring herself. Twice she reaches out to Mary, once with a postcard and years later by sending her a sewing machine. Sita idolizes her aunt Adelaide because she is beautiful and leads a romantic life, but Mary and Karl hate her for abandoning them.

Dot Adare

Wallacette "Dot" Adare is the daughter of Celestine James and Karl Adare. As a child, she idolizes her father despite his absence because he sends her exotic gifts from the road, such as a motorized wheelchair. Dot is a headstrong, willful, angry child who rebels against her mother and often sides with her aunt Mary. She is athletic, fearless, tomboyish, suspicious, and rebellious. She is built sturdily, like her mother, and is cast as Joseph instead of Mary in the school play. Wallace Pfef is her closest father figure; he loves her unconditionally, but she turns against him when she finds out he rigged the contest to make her the Beet Queen. He describes her as an amalgam of her family members' most unflattering characteristics: "Mary's stubborn, abrupt ways, Sita's vanity, Celestine's occasional cruelties, Karl's lack of responsibility." Her escape at the book's end mirrors her grandmother's flight with Omar. But instead of disappearing forever, she performs the valuable service of seeding the clouds, which bring much-needed rain to Argus.

Karl Adare

Karl Adare is Mary's older brother. He is a sensitive youth who becomes transfixed by a flowering tree upon arriving in Argus. He is chased by a dog back to the boxcar and thus separated from Mary. On the train, he has his first homosexual experience, after which he leaps out of the moving boxcar. He is nursed back to health thanks to Fleur Pillager's knowledge of Native American medicine. Karl spends the rest of his youth at a Minneapolis orphanage and seminary, where he has sexual liaisons with both priests and tramps. Embittered by the experience, he becomes a traveling salesman in an effort to escape his past and to avoid having relationships. He has an affair at a convention with Wallace Pfef and tells him his sister lives in Argus. He eventually winds up back in Argus, resuming his affair with Wallace briefly before taking up with Celestine James and impregnating her. Shortly after Dot is born, Karl marries Celestine but returns to the road permanently. He visits Dot only once, when she is a teenager. On the day of the Beet Festival, he returns to Argus to see Dot crowned Beet Queen, suddenly realizing how hollow his life has been and wanting to resume his relationship with Wallace.

Mary Adare

Mary Adare arrives in Argus in 1932 as an eleven-year-old girl and grows up to run Kozka's House of Meats. She is Karl's younger sister, Sita's cousin, Celestine James's friend and later sister-in-law, and Dot's aunt. Much of the novel revolves around Mary, who as a child is plain looking, hard working, and unsentimental. Mary never marries or has a relationship with a man. Instead, Celestine and Dot become her surrogate family. She has an antagonistic relationship with Sita that extends even beyond Sita's death. Mary is authoritative and meddlesome, and frequently usurps Celestine's position as Dot's mother, a habit begun with her renaming the girl upon her birth. Mary dresses cheaply and oddly and becomes increasingly superstitious the older she gets. She can be abrasive, such as when she wreaks havoc at Dot's birthday party, but is capable of running the butcher shop almost single-handedly. She never reconciles with Karl, who abandoned her as soon as they reached Argus.

Jimmy Bohl

Jimmy Bohl is Sita's first husband. He owns a tavern outside of Argus called the Poopdeck until the divorce.

Celestine James

Celestine James is a half-Chippewa Native American who is initially Sita's best friend and then becomes Mary's best friend. Her parents are dead, and she lives with her half brother, Russell Kashpaw. Growing to six feet tall, she works at the butcher shop with Mary for most of her adult life. She never has an emotionally significant relationship with a man; her fling with Karl Adare lasts only several weeks—just long enough for her to get pregnant with Dot. She expects little from Karl, even after marrying him, and gets less in return. She is an enthusiastic mother and loves Dot but has a hard time relating to her. She becomes exasperated with Mary for interfering in her relationship with Dot, yet she realizes their lives are inextricably bound. Celestine is quiet yet self-assured enough to subsist as a single mother in an era in which such a thing is frowned upon.

Russell Kashpaw

Russell Kashpaw is Celestine's half brother. He is a full-blooded Chippewa, and as a high-school student he is a star football player. He becomes North Dakota's most decorated war hero for his service in World War II and Korea, although his wounds leave him scarred and debilitated. He spurns Mary's brief romantic advances and never marries. He lives with Celestine in Argus, but when she becomes pregnant by Karl, he retreats to the reservation because he disapproves of the relationship. While ice fishing one afternoon, he has a stroke that leaves him permanently immobilized. He nearly succumbs to heatstroke during the Beet Festival parade, and Dot is the only one who notices he is about to topple off his wheelchair.

Fritzie Kozka

Fritzie Kozka is Adelaide Adare's sister. She disapproves of Adelaide's lifestyle and takes Mary in without a second thought. She is hard working and appreciates how Mary helps out with the butcher shop, unlike her own daughter.

When Fritzie's health begins to fail, she and her husband leave the butcher shop in Mary's care and move to the Southwest.

Pete Kozka

Pete Kozka is Fritzie's husband. He welcomes Mary into the family and gives her the cow's diamond that he had promised Sita as her inheritance, an event that causes Sita much mental anguish.

Sita Kozka

Sita Kozka is Fritzie and Pete's daughter and Mary's cousin. She is a pretty and vain girl who instantly dislikes Mary for usurping her place at home. Sita becomes jealous of the friendship between Mary and Celestine, and her jealousy and vanity stay with her throughout her life. As a young woman, she moves to Fargo, North Dakota, to become a department-store model and believes that this makes her more successful than those who remained in Argus. Eventually, she marries the coarse Jimmy Bohl, who owns a tavern. When they divorce, she tries to open her own upscale restaurant and fails miserably. She ends up marrying the health inspector, Louis Tappe, and living in the largest house in Blue Mound. When Karl Adare turns up in their backyard, she insists that he is trying to rob them and suffers a nervous breakdown. Her mental health deteriorates to the point that she stops speaking, and Louis has her committed to a mental institution, where she miraculously recovers overnight. Mary and Celestine come to take care of her when she is widowed and dying of cancer. She is addicted to pain pills and can no longer take care of herself yet resents their intrusion. When Mary hits her on the head with a brick, the pain becomes unbearable, and she intentionally overdoses on painkillers while waiting for Mary and Celestine to pick her up for the Beet Festival.

Catherine Miller

Catherine Miller is devastated by the death of her infant son. When her husband brings home Adelaide's abandoned baby to feed, she readily complies. She and her husband are honest people who want to do the right thing. She attempts to contact the baby's family, and she raises the boy as her own. She names him Jude after the patron saint of lost causes. By all accounts she is a good mother who is proud that her son has devoted his life to the church. She sends a letter to the Kozkas in an honest attempt to allow his blood relatives to contact him.

Jude Miller

Jude Miller is the youngest of Adelaide Adare's children. When she abandons him at the orphans' picnic, Mary hands him over to a man who says his wife will feed him. The man and his wife, Martin and Catherine Miller, have just lost their infant son; they feel secure in raising him as their own when Adelaide, whom they have identified from an item in the newspaper, fails to appear. As a seminary student, Jude has a distasteful encounter with his brother Karl—unbeknownst to him—in which Karl, visiting a picnic at the orphanage where he was abandoned, recognizes the boy and tells him that he is evil.

Jude is to become a deacon, and his mother sends a letter to the Kozkas telling them of the date and time of his ordination. Sita receives the letter from Mary and travels to Minneapolis for the ceremony but does not confront him. At the end of the novel, Jude, having discovered that he is adopted and his blood relations live in Argus, arrives in town via train on the day of the Beet Festival.

Martin Miller

Martin Miller is Catherine Miller's husband. He urges Mary to hand over her infant brother after Adelaide abandons them at the orphans' picnic. He knows his wife will be able to feed the baby, and he also hopes the baby's arrival will help ease the pain of having lost their own infant recently. He has no intention of returning the boy to Mary, and he proves to be a good father.

Mr. Ober

Mr. Ober was Adelaide's lover and the father of her three children, although he was married to someone else. He paid for her house and car. When he commits suicide, purportedly because he has lost his fortune in the Great Depression, she is left with nothing.

Omar

Omar the Great is a stunt pilot who literally whisks Adelaide off her feet and thus facilitates the abandonment of her children. Together they form a team and travel a circuit throughout the country. Omar appears to love her dearly, despite her fragile mental nature.

Wallace Pfef

Wallace Pfef is the brains behind Argus's transformation into the beet capital of North Dakota and is a civic leader who organizes many community events. He is a bachelor and a closeted homosexual whose first affair is with Karl Adare. Wallace falls in love with Karl when Karl returns to Argus and is crushed when he takes up with Celestine instead. Wallace helps deliver Dot in his living room when Celestine goes into labor during a blizzard. She names the baby Wallacette in his honor. From the beginning, he loves the girl despite her difficult constitution and because of her fearlessness. He throws birthday parties for her and celebrates the important events in her life. When she falls in with the wrong crowd and becomes an angry, rebellious teenager, he concocts the Beet Festival solely as a means of crowning her the Beet Queen. He believes that such validation of her beauty will make her happy and rigs the vote to make her the winner. He is crushed—literally— when Dot dunks him at the festival, whereupon he is rescued by Karl.

Fleur Pillager

Fleur Pillager is a nomadic Chippewa woman who discovers Karl after he has jumped off the train. She sets his broken feet in homemade casts and erects a sweat lodge to break his fever. While he recuperates, she perches him on top of her jerry-rigged railroad cart, which she pulls by strapping a horse collar around her neck. She is a figure of some local renown who travels from town to town, collecting and selling odds and ends and never speaking much. Later in the novel, Fleur becomes Russell's caretaker on the reservation and is none too welcoming when Dot, Celestine, and Mary come to deliver the motorized wheelchair.

Louis Tappe

Louis Tappe is Sita's second husband. He is the health inspector who shuts down Chez Sita. He takes nitroglycerin tablets for his heart and dies young.

THEMES

Abandonment

The Beet Queen commences with Adelaide's abandonment of her three children, and this pattern of abandonment is repeated throughout the book by various characters. In fact, Adelaide's abandonment, in the form of taking off with Omar the Great in his airplane, was precipitated by her abandonment by Mr. Ober, the father of her three children and her sole means of support. Though Mr. Ober dies in a grain-loading accident that may or may not have been suicide, his death effectively strands Adelaide, leaving her with nothing.

Adelaide's abandonment is followed closely by two more abandonments: when Mary hands over her baby brother to a stranger and when Karl strands Mary alone in Argus. The trend continues over the short and long term. Karl is found by Fleur Pillager, who possibly saves his life before dumping him at the door of the orphanage. As a sensitive boy, Karl is wounded immeasurably by his mother's abandonment and never learns to develop healthy relationships. He abandons Wallace, Celestine, and Dot—not to mention Mary—by maintaining his nomadic existence as a traveling salesman, which makes it easy to spurn commitment of any sort.

A more subtle string of abandonments peppers the narrative as well. Russell, North Dakota's most decorated war hero, who has put himself in harm's way repeatedly and has the scars to prove it, is left paralyzed and forgotten on the Chippewa reservation, abandoned by the country he served so honorably. Sita, on her wedding night, is kidnapped by her new husband's brothers and abandoned at a bar on the reservation. In fact, Sita suffers the most esoteric forms of abandonment in the novel. As a girl, she feels abandoned by Adelaide, whom she idolizes for her beauty and glamour. She tries to rectify this situation by keeping the sewing machine Adelaide intended for Mary and by tracking down the pawned garnet necklace and keeping it for herself. When Mary quickly inserts herself into the Kozka household and receives Pete's cow's diamond, Sita feels betrayed—the token was her inheritance, her father had told her. Then Mary steals Celestine's friendship, causing a permanent rift. When Sita attempts to abandon Argus, she fails, eventually coming back to marry after her beauty has abandoned her and success has proven elusive. Ultimately, Sita is abandoned by her own sanity. The sight of Karl in her backyard proves too much for her delicate constitution. She spends time in a mental institution and never regains enough strength to function effectively. In the end, she dies alone

TOPICS FOR FURTHER STUDY

- Research the practice of cloud seeding and devise a flow chart using a graphics or word processing program that depicts the process.

- Research a local festival that takes place where you live. Write a report on who founded it, when and why, and what it celebrates. Discuss the traditions of the festival and how they relate to your community.

- Find out about the Turtle Mountain Band of Chippewa Indians and write a report on where they live, how many members they have, and what traditions distinguish them from other Chippewa/Ojibwe bands. Conclude by discussing the benefits and drawbacks of living on an Indian reservation.

- As part of her interest in the occult, Mary reads numerous books by a man who called himself Cheiro. Cheiro's book *Palmistry for All*, first published in 1916, is available online at Project Gutenberg. Read Chapter 2, "The Line of Head or the Indications of the Mentality," and analyze your own hands. Write an essay on whether you believe Cheiro's ideas have any merit and to what degree the lines in your hands correspond to the traits they are supposed to identify in your life to date.

- Louis has Sita institutionalized because she refuses to speak. Research selective mutism, and in an essay, give three examples of Sita's behavior from the book that correspond with the profile of people who are usually diagnosed with the disorder. Given how the condition usually manifests in patients, do you think Sita's remarkable recovery is realistic? Why or why not?

- Joseph Bruchac's memoir *Bowman's Store: A Journey to Myself* (2001), appropriate for young adults, tells of the author's hardscrabble youth growing up in the Adirondack region of upstate New York during the 1950s and 1960s, unaware of his Abenaki roots but drawn to the stories of the First Peoples. His perseverance and immersion in his Native heritage represent a counterpoint to Dot's deep-seated anger and lack of interest in her cultural heritage. Read the memoir and then start a journal, just as the young "Sonny" Bruchac did, to describe your feelings about your ethnic heritage. Write separate entries on how you relate to your ethnicity, how your parents relate to their ethnicity, and whether you think your ethnicity is important.

---

and is abandoned one final time at the Beet Festival, expired and propped up in an air-conditioned van while everyone turns their attention to Dot's defining moment.

The damage wrought by these abandonments becomes concentrated in Dot, whose fury at those who love her is disproportionate to their crimes against her. It seems almost as if she is the embodiment of the anger Mary and Karl have suppressed their entire lives. Eventually, Dot abandons them all at the crucial moment—as she is about to be crowned the Beet Queen—by reenacting her grandmother's disappearance into the clouds. Her safe return, in which she is met by her mother, who has never abandoned her, marks the triumph of family over abandonment.

Family

The theme of family in *The Beet Queen* is explored through Erdrich's depiction of families of origin versus families of choice. A family of origin is the family into which a person is born; in the novel, the Adare family is the main family of origin. Its implosion becomes the basis for the events of the story. Like swirling cosmic dust that eventually coalesces into a new planet, the characters become caught in each other's orbits and form families of choice that are not dependent on blood ties. The term "family of choice"

Fresh beets (*kiboka* | *Shutterstock.com*)

derives from the gay and lesbian community, whose members, often shunned by their families of origin, band together to form meaningful social networks that function much like families but without the legal definition. While Wallace, Celestine, Mary, and Dot do not consciously form a family of choice, it is what they effectively become. Wallace, especially, loves Dot as much as a father, and it is he, not her real father, who provides the love, support, and birthday parties that are in keeping with the role of a father. His love for her is so encompassing that he dreams up the Beet Festival solely as a way to shower Dot with the type of attention he believes will raise her self-esteem and make her happy. While Mary is Dot's true aunt, the fact is almost incidental given that Mary and Karl want nothing to do with each other. Adelaide's attempt to reconnect with her family is rebuffed by Mary, who sends a postcard announcing the deaths of Adelaide's three children, a gesture in which Mary symbolically kills her family of origin.

Celestine and Mary—especially when Mary comes to live with Celestine and Dot temporarily—act almost as an old, bickering married couple.

They argue over how to raise Dot, and their familiarity sometimes breeds contempt, especially in Celestine, who abhors both Mary's cooking and her superstitious ideas. Both women lead celibate lives, and once their only remaining family of origin members leave Argus (when Sita decamps to Fargo and Russell leaves for the reservation), they have only each other to rely on. Together they run the butcher shop and raise Dot. Ultimately, Sita's life beyond her family of origin disintegrates. Her first marriage ends in divorce and her second produces no children. Alone and ailing, she is forced into Celestine and Mary's ad hoc family when the two women arrive unannounced in Blue Mound and disrupt her sad existence. Sita is infuriated by their attempts to reclaim her as family and escapes Mary's clutches by downing the rest of Louis's pain pills and dying.

Jude Miller, the youngest member of the Adare family, avoids the dysfunctional melodrama that envelops the citizens of Argus. But he does not even know the truth about his family of origin. As a member of the Millers' family of choice, Jude is possibly the only character who grows up well adjusted and happy. When he learns the truth about his family of origin, he travels to Argus to meet them. As such, he is the only member of the Adare family who seeks to embrace his or her family of origin.

STYLE

Multiple Points of View

Erdrich employs multiple-perspective narration in *The Beet Queen*. Several characters narrate chapters in the first person, and these are augmented with chapters told from a third-person omniscient viewpoint. Mary, Karl, Celestine, Wallace, Sita, and Dot all narrate certain events from their perspectives, allowing the reader insight into each character's state of mind. For instance, the reader learns that, upon Adelaide's disappearance, Mary's first emotion was "satisfaction.... For once she had played no favorites between Karl and me, but left us both." Such steely resolve will prove to be one of Mary's hallmarks. Insight into Sita's prissy character comes through an early chapter she narrates, in which she reveals more about herself than her cousin when she relates her take on how Mary came to Argus:

> Mary wasn't really an orphan, although she played on that for sympathy.... I really thought that Mary just ran away from her mother because she could not appreciate Adelaide's style. It's not everyone who understands how to use their good looks to the best advantage.

Karl narrates his thoughts as he recuperates under the care of the nomadic Fleur Pillager, and his transformation from a sensitive mama's boy into a hardened misanthrope is sharply rendered, much more so than if an omniscient narrator were recounting the action:

> It wasn't long, though, before I tired of weeping and began inventing scenes of my mother that gave me more pleasure. For instance, her suffering when we finally met again and I ignored her, turning a marble cheek. Or the shock with which she tried to comprehend my cruelty.

Only days earlier, Karl had been so distracted by a flowering tree that he only turned aside when chased by a dog. His change of heart reflects a profound shift in character that would be difficult for the reader to decipher had the passage not been narrated by the injured boy himself.

Later in the book, when both Wallace and Celestine have recounted Dot's angry, fiery nature, she confirms it with her own version of events. As she rides on the Beet Princess float with jealous girls who have heard that the fix is in for Dot, Dot tells them, "I'll kill you" and then recognizes that her voice is filled with "stark gloom and depression. I have never felt so desperate." Prior to this, the reader has been told about Dot's vengeful streak by the other characters, but hearing it from Dot's perspective lends events a palpable sense of suspense.

In the dispassionate omniscience of the novel's third-person narration, the reader learns the fate of Adelaide's baby, whom she did not love enough to name. Martin Miller has taken the boy home to his wife, and she names him Jude, for the patron saint of lost causes. Third-person narration seems ideal for this scene. Neither Martin nor Catherine plays a significant role in the plot, so having either tell the story in the first person would not make narrative sense. The third-person style allows the reader to peek into a corner of action that is unknown to the main characters of the story.

Before being mastered by Erdrich, the multiple-narration technique was perfected by William Faulkner in several of his works, especially *As I Lay Dying* (1930), the story of a family transporting the body of its matriarch to a nearby town for burial. Various members of the family—even the dead woman herself—take turns narrating events. Faulkner also employed the device in *The Sound and the Fury* (1929), in which various members of the Compton family tell their version of events from their own perspectives, giving the reader added insight and revealing new information about circumstances. Most of Erdrich's books include alternating first-person points of view and occasional third-person passages; such options give an author a wider palette with which to paint the action of the story.

Imagery

Erdrich's prose style is often called poetic, which is not surprising given that she is also a poet. What this means is that she uses precise language to paint vivid pictures in the reader's mind. These images can be presented in the form of symbols, metaphors, or similes. Taken as a whole, the imagery helps to establish the novel's overall tone.

The imagery is especially vivid in the chapter where Fleur Pillager finds Karl, mends his broken feet, and constructs a sweat lodge to break his fever. Erdrich's concise descriptions help readers envision a scene that is highly unusual and most likely unfamiliar. When Fleur gives Karl whiskey to dull the pain of his broken feet, he says it "went through me like a rope of fire, tangling my guts, lighting a pinpoint of sense in my brain." The image of whiskey as a rope of fire is a simile that imparts a sense of violence to the scene. When Fleur uses her knowledge of Native American medicine to break the fever that has come over Karl, he describes his near hallucination with images referencing nature:

> Animals surrounded the edges of my heat. I saw the eyes of skunks, red marbles, heard the chatter of coons, watched the bitterns land.... In the deepest part of the night, the biggest animal of all came through in a crash of sparks and wheels.

This "biggest animal" is a train, the image itself a metaphor that conveys Karl's sense of disorientation.

Images and symbolism go hand in hand. When Mary envisions her mother falling to her death from Omar's airplane, the image becomes symbolic. Having no idea what really became of her mother, she kills off her mother in a fantasy and allows her to remain dead, even when Adelaide's postcard reaches her at the Kozkas. "All night she fell through the awful cold," Mary says; "she was a candle that gave no warmth. My heart froze. I had no love for her. That is why, by morning, I allowed her to hit the earth."

Imagery is instrumental in depicting Sita's break with reality when Karl visits her in Blue Mound. As he eats lunch in her backyard, Sita watches as "the lawn crept up his oxblood shirt. The grass brushed his chin," until finally "the earth paused before swallowing him entirely, and then, quite suddenly, the rest of him went under." Since the reader knows full well that Karl does not actually become submerged underground, the imagery serves to underscore Sita's mental illness.

In one of the book's final scenes, Erdrich's deft imagery allows the reader a glimpse inside Russell's mind as he is perched on a parade float, helpless and dehydrated, making his way down the street. He sees his dead sister, and she signals him to follow her. This image, coming from the mind of a paralyzed veteran, symbolizes his closeness to death, as does his feeling of "his mind spread out like a lake," a nature-related simile that hints at his body letting go.

HISTORICAL CONTEXT

Barnstorming

Omar the Great, the daredevil pilot who absconds with Adelaide Adare near the beginning of *The Beet Queen*, was a barnstormer, a stunt pilot who performed at public events and gave rides during the early days of flight. Between the world wars, from roughly 1920 to 1940, ex-military pilots bought their own airplanes from the government for just a couple hundred dollars each. In the absence of federal regulations, civil aviation thrived due to its novelty and low cost. Barnstormers would fly over rural areas and drop handbills announcing their upcoming performances. Popular stunts included loop-the-loops, barrel rolls, parachute jumps, and wing walking. Occasionally, barnstormers would band together to form a flying circus, a more formal presentation that was usually promoted to towns ahead of time. For a fee, many pilots would take passengers for a ride, a thrilling prospect in the infancy of flight.

Barnstormers' stunts were dangerous, and many pilots crashed. The Air Commerce Act of 1926 was passed to address this issue, and the legislation outlawed many practices and began to regulate the aviation industry. Famous barnstormers included Lincoln J. Beachey (1887–1915), known as "The Man Who Owned the Sky," who once flew eighty loops in a row and who died while performing a stunt over San Francisco Bay; Charles Lindbergh (1902–1974), who was a barnstormer before he became a commissioned officer in the U.S. Army Air Service; Clyde "Upside Down" Pangborn (1895–1958), who owned the popular Gates Flying Circus; and Florence "Pancho" Barnes (1901–1975), a pioneering female aviator who performed stunt maneuvers in several Hollywood films. Bessie Coleman (1892–1926) was the first female African American pilot and barnstormer; her illustrious career came to an end in Jacksonville, Florida, when her plane went into a tailspin and, not wearing a seatbelt, she fell to her death.

Cloud Seeding

Cloud seeding is the practice of injecting either silver iodide or dry ice, which act as ice nuclei,

COMPARE
&
CONTRAST

- **1930s:** The newly formed Red River Valley Sugarbeet Growers Association represents the interests of Minnesota and North Dakota farmers in negotiations with the American Beet Sugar Company.

  1980s: The cooperative produces nearly 1 million tons of sugarbeets annually on roughly 55,000 acres.

  Today: North Dakota produces 5 million tons of sugar beets annually, about 25 percent of the U.S. output. The state's sugarbeet industry remains concentrated in the Red River valley.

- **1930s:** St. Joseph's Orphanage, run by Benedictine nuns in Minneapolis and St. Paul, houses almost three hundred children during the Great Depression, most of whom have at least one living parent.

  1980s: The former St. John's Orphanage in Fargo, North Dakota, merges with nearby Friendship Village and becomes a residential community called Villa Nazareth. Facilities such as these are more commonly home to individuals with developmental disabilities rather than to orphans, as they have been in generations past.

  Today: Catholic Charities of North Dakota, founded in 1923, has numerous programs to benefit children, including traditional infant adoption, special-needs adoption, and international adoption.

- **1930s:** The North Dakota State Hospital in Jamestown is the state's primary institution for the mentally ill. It practices forced sterilization of patients in accordance with accepted ideas on eugenics.

  1980s: The state hospital celebrates its one-hundredth anniversary in 1985. A nationwide trend toward deinstitutionalization continues to reduce the number of patients it serves.

  Today: Only about two hundred patients reside at the hospital, down from a peak of two thousand in the 1940s, due to the trend toward deinstitutionalization and the rise of community mental-health services.

---

into clouds containing supercooled liquid water. Increasing the ice nuclei in the cloud can generate precipitation. In *The Beet Queen*, Argus is suffering from a severe drought after a season of record-low rainfall, and by the time of the Beet Festival, the fields are burnt to a crisp and the town is desperate. Dot convinces the pilot that she is supposed to ride along during his skywriting flight, and he hands her the flare gun with the silver-iodide cartridges. As they head toward a bank of cumulus clouds, she fires the gun, despite her terror at being whirled around in the air. That night, when the drama of the day has passed, she hears the first raindrops fall outside.

Cloud seeding was developed in 1946 by Vincent Schaefer, who discovered the dry-ice method, and Bernard Vonnegut (brother of novelist Kurt Vonnegut), who discovered the silver-iodide method. Both were employed at the General Electric Research Lab in Schenectady, New York. The first attempts to influence the weather via these methods took place in upstate New York later that year, when they teamed up to seed clouds that proceeded to dump snow over Massachusetts. Since then, cloud seeding has been implemented and researched sporadically. Several U.S. governmental agencies have used it, notably in Operation Popeye, which seeded clouds in North Vietnam from 1967 to 1972 in attempts to extend the monsoon season and thus curtail warfare. The U.S. Bureau of Reclamation's Project Skywater operated from 1964 to 1988 and attempted to influence rainfall in western states. Some ski resorts use cloud seeding to increase snowfall. Most scientists do not believe that cloud seeding can end

Beet fields (*Zbynek Burival | Shutterstock.com*)

sustained droughts, such as the one that afflicts Argus, because during those periods, the types of clouds that can be successfully seeded (those containing supercooled liquid water) are not produced.

The Native American Renaissance

Erdrich is considered a leading author in what the critic Kenneth Lincoln has called the Native American Renaissance, a movement he outlines in his 1983 book of the same name. This renaissance dates back to the publication of N. Scott Momaday's Pulitzer Prize–winning 1968 book *House Made of Dawn*, a fictionalized account of what it was like growing up on a reservation. Beginning around this time, Native American writers enjoyed newfound popularity among a wide range of people who had become interested in the historical plights of Native peoples. Colleges and universities began teaching Native American studies, and members of various tribes took renewed interest in their heritage. Leslie Marmon Silko, Gerald Vizenor, Joy Harjo, James Welch, and Paula Gunn Allen are several of Erdrich's contemporaries who are considered part of the Native American Renaissance. Many

of these writers are university professors who have contributed research and criticism to the field of Native American studies in addition to their novels and fiction. Despite the acknowledged significance of the Native American Renaissance, many of its authors object to the term. Native Americans have a continuous literary and cultural heritage, they point out, and the term "renaissance" connotes the viewpoint of whites who have simply been unaware of Native peoples out of ignorance or spite.

CRITICAL OVERVIEW

Critics have enjoyed *The Beet Queen*. In his review in the *Nation*, Russell Banks considers it a "Dickensian story, an angry comedy about abandonment and survival, pluck and luck (ambition and coincidence), common sense and pretension." Michiko Kakutani, reviewing the novel in the *New York Times Book Review*, calls it "fiercely lyrical" with "passages of shimmering, poetic description; startling sequences of physical and emotional violence, and a cast of characters, at once ordinary and strange like eccentric folk-art figures." Indeed, many critics laud Erdrich's language for its poetic grace. "Keeping short sentences and characteristic pitch sequences," remarks Robert Bly in the *New York Times Book Review* in explaining Erdrich's style, "she adds the original image, the revealing blast of light, and opens a channel that allows dangerous impulses from beneath to flow to the surface." Bly also notes that *The Beet Queen* is a novel about women in which the male characters are marginalized and major events are "pungently visualized, suggesting the stark grotesquerie of Günter Grass." Dorothy Wickenden, in the *New Republic*, notes that "Erdrich's novels have little in the way of traditional plot or character development because her characters have already been marked indelibly by fate." Instead of a fast-paced, thrilling plot, Wickenden concludes, Erdrich offers her readers "a prose style of ringing clarity and lyricism, and a shrewd vision of the pathos and comedy that characterize provincial lives." Linda Simon, a contributor to *Commonweal*, calls it "a poet's novel" in which "the texture of the prose finally is more seductive even than the movement of the plot. It is a novel that throbs, at times, with the intensity of its small vignettes."

One expert who expressed dislike for the book was the noted Native American author Leslie Marmon Silko, who claims in an article for *Impact/Albuquerque Journal* that the setting of *The Beet Queen* is a "pristine world" in which "all misery, suffering, and loss are self-generated, just as conservative Republicans have been telling us for years." Silko objects to Erdrich's depiction of Native American culture in the novel, which, as Erdrich pointed out in an interview with Nancy Feyl Chavkin and Allan Chavkin, published in *Conversations with Louise Erdrich and Michael Dorris*, seems to indicate Silko missed the point of, and misread, the novel. "Silko didn't read the book carefully," Erdrich explains, "she thought the main characters were Chippewa when they were actually depression-era Poles and Germans." Nevertheless, in her review, Silko wonders why Russell Kashpaw was willing to sacrifice so much in war for a country that did not appreciate his culture and people.

Writing in the journal *Ariel*, Susan Meisenhelder sees the book in terms of gender and race, comparing the characters of Sita and Russell as individuals who, "despite the racial gulf that separates the two ... are similarly dehumanized, reduced to objects serving the interests of a society dominated by white males." For Sita, this refers to her preoccupation with her physical beauty, which she believes will grant her professional and marital success. When her beauty fades, she finds herself alone, succumbing to mental delirium and addicted to painkillers. In Russell's case, his strong body brings him success first as an athlete and then as a soldier. When he is used up over the course of two wars, his body is scarred almost beyond recognition, and he is put out to pasture, ending his days paralyzed in a wheelchair.

Several critics have taken issue with the book's ending, in which the characters' paths converge during the Beet Festival. Wickenden calls it "a contrivance, not a natural culmination to the drama." Kakutani asserts that it "smacks of artifice" and "diminishes the impact of what is otherwise a remarkable and luminous novel." But others have focused on Erdrich's deft portrayal of her native North Dakota territory, from the Turtle Mountain Indian Reservation to the farming community of Argus. The characters and places featured in

The Beet Queen and her other novels function as a microcosm—similar to Faulkner's Yoknapatawpha County—that, according to Thomas M. Disch in the *Chicago Tribune*, "unites the archetypal and the arcane, heartland America and borderline schizophrenia."

CRITICISM

Kathy Wilson Peacock

Wilson Peacock is a writer and editor. In the following essay, she discusses Mary's role as a trickster in The Beet Queen.

Louise Erdrich's *The Beet Queen* is an ensemble novel; the story's major characters each take turns narrating events, providing their own takes on the ties that bind them, for better or largely for worse, to Argus, North Dakota. Of these characters, Mary Adare is the center around which the others revolve. Although the narratives of Wallace Pfef, Karl Adare, Celestine James, Dot Adare, and Sita Kozka often relegate Mary to the background, the reader feels her pull, as if the other characters are trying to escape her orbit. It is Mary's appearance in Argus, motherless and impoverished on a bleak day in 1932, that kicks off the events of the book. As cousin of Sita, best friend of Celestine, sister of Karl, and eventually aunt of Dot, Mary and her unsentimental spirit become the foundation for the strained, unloving feelings that underpin the novel's comical set pieces. She tells Adelaide that her children starved; she responds to her long-lost brother's reappearance with physical violence; and she barges unwelcome into Sita's house, hastening Sita's final days. Taken individually, the events of Mary's life are mystifying, never cohering into a thematic whole. Why does she never have a romantic partner? What is the significance of the cracked-ice Jesus formed when her youthful face smacks into the frozen ground? Why do her hands glow mysteriously one night, terrifying the mentally fragile Sita? Are her occult obsessions more than just superstition? These disparate characteristics coalesce when Mary's role in the novel is recast from meddlesome, eccentric spinster to something more primal and literary: Mary is a trickster.

In folklore, a trickster is a character whose irreverent behavior dispenses with rules, wreaking havoc on others and upsetting the balance of situations. The trickster figure is common in Native American myths and in literature of all eras and cultures. Loki, the shapeshifting god of Norse

WHAT DO I READ NEXT?

- *Love Medicine* (1984), considered Louise Erdrich's first novel, is a collection of loosely connected short stories that take place on and around the Chippewa reservation in North Dakota. Like *The Beet Queen*, the collection gives numerous first-person accounts by various narrators, with stories revolving around the brothers Nector and Eli Kashpaw. Dot Adare appears as the fiancée of Gerry Nanapush.

- *A Yellow Raft in Blue Water* (1987), by Michael Dorris, is a novel written when he was married to Erdrich, comprising three first-person narratives of troubled Native American women—a mother, daughter, and grandmother—who live in Montana.

- Maxine Hong Kingston's *Tripmaster Monkey: His Fake Book* (1989) is the story of an Asian American hippie growing up in San Francisco in the 1960s. Wittman Ah Sing exhibits many of the carefree characteristics that Dot Adare does, with Kingston portraying a modern version of a Chinese trickster character in an allegory that encompasses many features of Asian mythology.

- *Ceremony* (1977), by Leslie Marmon Silko, widely hailed as one of the greatest Native American novels ever written, concerns a World War II veteran who returns to the Laguna Pueblo Reservation (of which Silko is a member) scarred by his time as a prisoner of the Japanese but finds renewal in immersing himself in the traditions and mythology of his tribe.

- Erdrich's *Tracks* (1988) takes place on the Chippewa reservation in North Dakota in the years before *The Beet Queen* and tells the story of Fleur Pillager and others through multiple-point-of-view narration. It recounts the story of Celestine's parents, Regina Kashpaw and Dutch James, and depicts the dissolution of Native American culture through technology and greed.

- *The Beet Fields* (2000), by Gary Paulsen, is a semiautobiographical young-adult novel about a sixteen-year-old's transformative summer, during which he runs away from his abusive mother, works on a beet farm in North Dakota, and becomes a roustabout with a traveling carnival.

- In *As I Lay Dying* (1930), William Faulkner employs his signature multiple first-person points of view (fifteen altogether—including the dead woman's) in telling the story of Addie Bundren's body being transported by various members of her family to the town where she wished to be buried.

- *The Sacred Hoop: Recovering the Feminine in American Indian Traditions* (1986), by Paula Gunn Allen, is a collection of essays that explore women's crucial roles in Native traditions.

mythology, is a trickster, as are Coyote and Raven, figures of many Native American traditions. Contemporary examples include Bugs Bunny, Charlie Chaplin's Little Tramp character, and Dr. Seuss's Cat in the Hat. Wittman Ah Sing, the hedonistic Chinese American figure in Maxine Hong Kingston's novel *Tripmaster Monkey*, is a latter-day incarnation of the trickster Monkey King of Chinese mythology. Erdrich pays homage to the Ojibwe trickster character Nanabozho through the character of Nanapush in *Tracks*. As described by Lydia A. Schultz in *College Literature*, Nanabozho "is a mix between a manitou (spirit person) and a human being, a trickster who can take on various physical forms. He is credited with providing the gifts of humor and storytelling to the Ojibwe people." Erdrich's character Gerry Nanapush in *Love Medicine* is associated with Nanabozho through his talent for escaping from prison. Yet these novels differ markedly from *The Beet Queen*

> THESE DISPARATE CHARACTERISTICS COALESCE WHEN MARY'S ROLE IN THE NOVEL IS RECAST FROM MEDDLESOME, ECCENTRIC SPINSTER TO SOMETHING MORE PRIMAL AND LITERARY: MARY IS A TRICKSTER."

in that Native American archetypes and culture are their thematic focus, whereas *The Beet Queen* concerns the Polish-German Kozka-Adare family, who, apart from their relationship with the Chippewa Russell Kashpaw and his half-blood half sister Celestine James, are seemingly oblivious to Native traditions as practiced in their corner of North Dakota. Thus, *The Beet Queen* is not a novel about Native American culture, per se, and in it Erdrich sticks largely to the conventions of Western literature. The exception to this is the chapter in which Fleur Pillager encounters the injured Karl and takes him aboard her stockpiled railroad cart, healing his broken feet and sweating out his fever. Fleur, as Erdrich's readers will know, is a trickster character at the heart of *Tracks*. Her powers are evident during this early chapter of *The Beet Queen*, as the young Karl hardens into a hateful, bitter man just as the paste Fleur shapes around his mangled feet hardens into plaster. She appears briefly later in the novel as Russell's caretaker on the reservation.

Despite downplaying Native culture in *The Beet Queen*, Erdrich infuses Mary with many of the trickster's characteristics, making her an engine for the events that propel the story. According to William J. Hynes and William G. Doty, editors of *Mythical Trickster Figures*, a trickster possesses several of the following characteristics: he or she may be ambiguous, be deceptive or play tricks, be a shape-shifter, disrupt situations, serve as a messenger of the gods, and/or be associated with both the sacred and the profane. Mary fulfills most of these criteria. The young Mary, a plain, hard-working schoolgirl who admires her aunt's facility for accounting, transforms into the brash, brick-tossing butcher who summarily renames her niece over Celestine's objections. In terms of ambiguity, Mary displays little femininity, preferring baggy dresses of cheap fabric and a turban that hides her hair, which leads Celestine to remark that "if you didn't know she was a woman you would never know it."

As for disrupting situations, during one vengeful encounter she traps Dot's teacher inside a toy box; elsewhere she reads people's palms and reports only negative predictions. She moves in with Celestine and Dot temporarily while the butcher shop undergoes repairs and thus disrupts Celestine's tenuous grip on parental authority. Celestine smolders as Mary usurps her maternal role in the run-up to Dot's disastrous school play. As a girl, Mary becomes Argus's messenger of the gods when her head collides with ice on the playground, producing the cracked-ice Jesus dubbed the Manifestation at Argus, with the slide itself becoming an "innocent trajectory of divine glory." But the incident proves to be an isolated one, and Mary's body exhibits unearthly traits only one other time, when she finds her hands inexplicably glowing in the middle of the night "with a dead blue radiance," a circumstance she attributes weakly to the solution with which she has washed the kitchen. The glow scares Sita witless, but Mary only looks at her hands in wonder and shakes them until the light fades. When Mary and Celestine show up at Sita's house, having interpreted Celestine's dream as evidence that Sita is dying (correctly, as it happens, which is possibly another indication of Mary's connection to the gods), Mary feeds her cake that has bugs cooked into it, an inadvertent trick that launches Sita into a tirade. In folklore, the trickster commonly inhabits a realm between the living and the dead. Such a realm materializes in *The Beet Queen* when Mary orchestrates the stuffing of Sita's lifeless body into the butcher-shop truck, not acknowledging said lifelessness when stopped for speeding by the policeman who is Sita's former beau, and leaving her unattended in a parking lot during the Beet Festival.

In her book *Writing Tricksters: Mythic Gambols in American Ethnic Literature*, Jeanne Rosier Smith considers both Karl and Mary to be trickster figures, but she feels that Karl more clearly fills the requirements through his slippery, two-faced nature and the way he flits in and out of people's lives, leaving permanent scars and escaping without a scratch. The pious young Jude recognizes Karl as the devil, without knowing of their fraternal bond. Sita becomes convinced Karl has absconded with Celestine's

Bible and is fixing to lift her own possessions; so strong is his disorienting magnetism that she descends into madness before his very eyes. Smith's case for Karl's trickster identity is strong, and thus she does not flesh out Mary's embodiment of the trickster persona beyond her androgynous appearance, her miraculous playground accident, and her love of the supernatural. But there is more.

Nowhere is Mary's status as a trickster more apparent than during the party Wallace Pfef throws for Dot's eleventh birthday. Mary's inappropriate behavior at Dot's parties is already the stuff of legend: "Children were afraid of Mary's yellow glare, her gravel-bed voice. She organized games with casual but gruesome threats." Her yellow eyes, raspy voice, and knack for scaring children make her sound like a coyote—the traditional trickster figure. As Mary rounds up the guests and marches them into Wallace's house, the "children dragged their feet and looked back with imploring eyes." Wallace attempts to subdue her via a couple shots of strong alcohol, but instead her full trickster power is unleashed. Her smile turns "uncharacteristically dreamy," and then "her eyes changed color, softened from the harsh yellow of two gold coins to a radiant amber," ultimately morphing into "caramel, like sugar coming to a boil." Though she keeps her corporeal form, her eyes exhibit the shape-shifting properties common to tricksters. To complete the coyote metaphor, Mary sets her predatorial sights on Sita, who looks

> like a starved deer. She resembled one. Her cheeks were hollow, her eyes were stark, and her ribs were caved in. She melted back from our attention into the shadows of the upper landing. "Join the party!" hollered Mary, straining in her chair.

Mary then sets in motion a chain of events that propels the flaming pineapple upside-down cake off its spinning cake stand and into Sita's face, creating a commotion of unparalleled proportions. In the midst of Celestine's attempt to calm everyone down, Mary passively observes her masterful disruption, as Wallace recounts: "A statue couldn't have been more motionless. A gaunt and Halloweenish grin was plastered to her face. Her eyes had gone a full black." The party breaks up with Mary's face remaining "a mask of devilish glee," evincing a coyote/trickster-like serenity that prompts Wallace to state

The novel examines family dynamics. (*Nowik / Shutterstock.com*)

that "there was no warmth in her, no generous heart."

Without true supernatural powers, Mary remains an imperfect trickster at best. Smith explains that, in the predominantly white town of Argus, she represents "the fragility of a trickster identity when not grounded in community and tradition." Mary's Polish-German roots are negligible with regard to who she is, and the community as a whole is wrapped up in the postwar spectacle of suburbanization, designed to obliterate cultural differences. Mary, lacking an ancestral identity, searches for her trickster identity in the only places she knows to—books, tarot cards, and Ouija boards. There she finds that identity, however faint, while the march of Midwestern homogenization attempts to snuff out all manner of tricksters and shamans, at best relegating them to the church cloisters. And despite Mary's largely severed family roots, her muted trickster blood flows through the tangled branch that has become fiery, hell-raising Dot. Fearless and angry, Dot takes to the skies and fires the silver-iodide cartridges that bring rain to the forsaken town, her own form of trickster magic for a new era.

Source: Kathy Wilson Peacock, Critical Essay on *The Beet Queen*, in *Novels for Students*, Gale, Cengage Learning, 2011.

"AS IF TO UNDERSCORE THE ELEMENTAL

CONNECTION BETWEEN MARY AND SITA, ERDRICH

SHOWS HOW SITA'S IDENTITY SEEMS TO DIMINISH

AS MARY'S IDENTITY SEEMS TO ENLARGE."

Gary Storhoff

In the following excerpt, Storhoff states that The Beet Queen *examines how families develop interactive bonds through differences.*

In Louise Erdrich's *The Beet Queen*, Mary Adare, having taken over Celestine James's household, develops a new hobby: palmistry. Understandably skeptical, her friend Celestine dismisses palm-reading as meaningless, but Mary, ever concerned that people agree with her, argues forcefully: "Well then answer me this... a child is born with certain lines in its hand. Those lines and no others. How do you explain it?" The scene is a trope for Erdrich's persistent concern throughout her trilogy: how one's family shapes, patterns, or even determines life choices in the future. The "lines," symbolizing patterns of choices and actions the child learns intergenerationally through family conduct, become in Erdrich's novels fundamentally directional. Erdrich's emphasis throughout her work is on the interactive bond that develops between families as they negotiate differences through the systems of stability they tacitly, and usually covertly, create.

In her concern for the operation of family systems, she is close to a relatively new analytic psychological concept created by the Gregory Bateson group in the 1950s, family systems theory, which studies how the individual discovers his or her role within a family unit, and how the family structure perpetuates itself even beyond one's childhood. Systems theory focuses on how families as entities attempt in a collective way to maintain stability and unity—sometimes at the expense of an individual member's happiness. According to family systems theory, what is at stake in family actions and decisions is the long-term coherence and stability of the family system itself, regardless of the individual suffering that may give rise to.

Originally developed as a therapeutic methodology for schizophrenic patients, systems theory is now recognized as having relevance for all families, even exceptionally well-functioning ones. Within the context of this theory, individual behavior has meaning only when studied in relation to the behavior of other family members, especially what theorists call "the family of origin." Unlike traditional psychoanalysis, which explores an individual's unconsciousness, family systems studies the surface interactions of family systems and subsystems. The scientific analogue in this instance is the biological study of ecosystems, with the study of living systems as whole entities. Relations between family members are never casual or incidental, but are organized according to concealed laws and structural patterns, typically hidden from the family members themselves. Those covert structures are in most cases learned from parents, who learned from their parents, and so on. Thus, the self's identity is an unstable product of interactions between entire generations, always subject to the formations of new and different systems at any particular time.

Literature, obviously, provides a laboratory for studying family dynamics and is in fact used by some psychiatrists in providing therapy, called "bibliotherapy." (See Bump). *The Beet Queen*, the second novel in Erdrich's trilogy, is particularly fertile for exploring the intersection of literature and psychological theory: it provides a contrast between a conventional middle-class nuclear family (the Kozkas) and a more dynamically communal notion of family (Celestine); it dramatizes the dynamics of Adare and Kozka family members as they attempt to navigate toward stability (termed "equilibrium" or "homeostasis"); and it depicts a family member (Celestine James) who, though troubled herself, is relatively aware of how she was shaped by her family's past. Finally, through Karl Adare and his daughter Dot, the novel implies a general assessment of family relations and the necessity of a revision of family roles and structures.

The novel begins with the Adares, a profoundly troubled "family of origin" that shatters dramatically but exerts a strong influence on its members long after its demise. Suffering terrific deprivation during the Great Depression, Adelaide attempts to cope with poverty by shutting out her world and admitting only lovers; in exchange for sex, these men give her money and trinkets to which she attributes magical properties. Her family—Adelaide, Mary, Karl, and infant Jude—thus represents a closed family system, one that preserves its equilibrium by excluding the outside world. "We rarely saw anyone else," says Mary. Adelaide simply forecloses the opportunity of the children to evaluate their own family structure by comparing it with other, different family values; the benefit to her, of course, is that her system remains relatively unchanging. Within those unrealistically tight family boundaries, Mary and Adelaide themselves establish a complementary subsystem: Mary's conscientious sense of responsibility sets off and balances Adelaide's irresponsible, seemingly feckless nature. Mary thus becomes the surrogate mother of the family; it is she who attends to basic family functioning, even for Adelaide herself. By making Mary a substitute parent, Adelaide is thus freed to continue her own childish paths.

Yet Adelaide's family boundaries are dangerously impermanent. When Mr. Ober, her lover, dies, Adelaide has nothing, and the family itself begins its precipitous collapse; it is he, ironically, who has ensured the fragile organizing principle—caring in exchange for money—by which the family is unified. He was their only connection to the world, and Mary, being a child, cannot negotiate the real-life demands that the world constantly makes. When he disappears, the destruction of the family follows shortly thereafter. Unsurprisingly, Adelaide follows the same pattern that she has apparently established for herself in life: she exchanges her body for the caretaking of yet another man, this time the pilot Omar who flies away with her. But the costs of her psychic strategies will be paid for in the future with the suffering of her two children, the real focal point of the narrative.

Although both Karl and Mary consciously and unconsciously sever themselves from Adelaide and her irresponsible choices, they covertly reenact her life patterns. In this way, the introjected model learned from their family of origin becomes the controlling factor in their lives; their generational succession gives way to a system of fixed relations that Adelaide herself set in motion. Abandoned by their mother, whose sole purpose was to become essential in a man's life, both Mary and Karl manipulate others to affirm their own centrality in the lives of others.

That pattern is seen most clearly in Mary's narrative. When she joins the Kozka family—a seemingly stable family system with very porous family boundaries (as owners of a butcher shop, they constantly come into contact with other people)—her major challenge, understandably, is to become a part of them, to discover a role for herself within their system. Yet Mary is not satisfied with mere membership in the Kozka family system; as she says, "I planned to be essential to them all, so depended upon that they could never send me off. I did this on purpose." However, Mary's confident sense of her purposiveness masks the largely unconscious strategies she deploys to achieve her inclusion. In short, she intends to become once again a surrogate mother, perpetuating the role she learned with Adelaide. Given her precarious status as "poor cousin," her actions are veiled yet obvious, secretive but conspicuous, designed to manipulate the existing family system in ways Mary herself does not grasp. Ultimately, she must utterly transform the system, yet give the appearance of leaving it intact (if not strengthened) by her presence.

Her very presence in the Kozka family confirms their ideal selves. First, she becomes important evidence to Aunt Fritzie that Adelaide was a "bad sister," and that Fritzie's family, secure in its relative prosperity during the Depression, is unquestionably superior—morally and socially. For daughter Sita, Mary, dressed in her plain hand-me-downs, embodies the poor, unadorned, unattractive cousin, and thus sets off Sita's attractiveness and style in school. Mary thus assists the Kozka family in defining themselves; simply by her disheveled presence she strengthens the stability of their life as a family.

But her primary objective in forging these internal ties must be to ingratiate herself with Uncle Pete, the father. He, as father, the most powerful family insider, must establish an interactive relationship with Mary, the least powerful, the outsider, to ensure the functionality and homeostasis of the Kozka family system. That is, the stability of the Kozka family has been momentarily threatened with the introduction of Mary, a new member; she must be accommodated, now, with a new (or modified) system that will ensure both her acceptance and the relative constancy of the family—and it is essential that Uncle Pete, as the patriarch, participate enthusiastically in her welcome. He must be persuaded to believe that Mary (unattractive, but capable, energetic, practical) is the daughter he really wants, as opposed to Sita, her antithesis (beautiful, charming, but passive and ineffectual). That transaction is accomplished, ironically, at the moment of Mary's worst humiliation, when she reveals the emptiness of Adelaide's heirloom, the blue keepsake box. Mary had saved the locked box as a memory of her mother, its contents—Adelaide's gaudy necklace—to be revealed in a future epiphanic moment. Opening the box in the expectation of paying Pete for his expenses—repeating in an ironic reversal Adelaide's custom of receiving cash for care—Mary discovers its worthlessness and almost bursts into tears. Yet her abjection has its desired effect: Pete, overcome with sympathy, gives her his treasured but worthless heirloom, the "cow's diamond," a hardened lens inside a cow's eye that shines at night. But in surrendering Adelaide's useless "treasure" for Pete's "valued" one, Mary not only tangibly disavows Adelaide but also unexpectedly usurps Sita's role as Pete's natural daughter, because the cow's diamond had earlier been kept as Sita's heirloom. (This unconscious arrangement is completed decades later, when Sita, discovering the pawn ticket for Adelaide's necklace, recovers it from a pawn shop and claims it as her own.) Thus, Mary's misery in discovering Adelaide's empty box accompanies—indeed, precipitates—her installation at the center of family dynamics. The result is a "constructed," as opposed to a "natural," father-daughter relationship, around which the "new" family system begins to crystallize.

Sita, the natural daughter, is the ostensible loser in this covert strategy to readjust the Kozka family-system, a necessity with Mary's introduction to it. It is a truism of family systems theory that any kind of dramatic change in family structure (such as an addition in a birth or adoption, or a loss from death) will have an equal and reciprocal reaction, a "rippling" that will affect every member, but some more than others. This dynamic is borne out in the gradual but certain exclusion of Sita from the family center. As she matures, she hardens in her commitment to materialism and class status—not simply an effect of her supposed character-defect, her snobbishness (the interpretation given by other characters in the novel, including Mary herself), but as a compensatory coping mechanism to deal with her sudden loss of her privileged position: if she cannot have her family's attention as only daughter, she will gain attention as the family's scapegoat. But in this new role, she

actually strengthens the new family center. Just as Mary formerly allowed the family members to define their identities, Sita, through her materialistic and snobbish grasping, now serves that function. For the rest of her life, Sita's characteristic efforts to improve her social standing, her life outside the family circle, provide a symmetrical contrast with Mary's efforts within the family circle and Mary's utter indifference to social standing. As if to underscore the elemental connection between Mary and Sita, Erdrich shows how Sita's identity seems to diminish as Mary's identity seems to enlarge. Sita retreats from her role as daughter, to wife, to divorcee, to failed entrepreneur, to recluse, to insanity, and finally to death at the novel's end. Mary, on the other hand, correspondingly expands her identity, as she occupies the roles of daughter, as "saint" in the village of Argus, as successful heir of the Kozka butcher shop, and finally, and most significantly for Mary, as surrogate mother for her niece Dot.

But like Sita, Mary's personality is also shaped and damaged by her struggle to fulfill transacted roles within family systems. In her role as Adelaide's daughter, she was the responsible, essential family member, the Child-Mother who made sure the family functioned as well as it did. In the Kozka family once again she goes about creating a web of dependence on her choices and action, a web the entire Kozka family helps to spin. Her reward is, of course, security—she will never be sent away again. Yet her attempts to become necessary to all ultimately make her unattractive to all those who are not overly dependent on others. Her effort to control other human beings—learned well in her dealings with Adelaide and in the Kozka family—undermines her ability to contribute generously to other people.

Her destructive behavior ironically brings about what she most fears, rejection. She never marries; she estranges her brother Karl and her best friend Celestine; and she creates an explosive tension within her niece Dot, who oscillates between needing the approval of others (Mary's overt purpose) and rejecting others (the ultimate effect of Mary's manipulations). Mary's psychic dilemma is that in making herself essential to Dot, her putative daughter, she experiences a loss of identity-boundary between herself and Dot, the phenomenon known in family systems theory as "enmeshment." Dot is allowed to experience nothing without Mary's close supervision, a pattern repeated again and again in the novel. The clearest—and most humorous—example of Mary's meddlesomeness is her control of Dot's birthday party: "The children were afraid of her... Mary's yellow glare, her gravel-bed voice. She organized games with casual but gruesome threats, and the children complied like hostages... they played mechanically.... But Mary did not notice this." Her failure to "notice" children, those who could at least potentially need her (including Dot herself), recalls Mary's mother Adelaide's neglect of her own children. Both Mary and Adelaide are blinded by antithetical yet correspondent self-consuming needs. Though separated by decades and thousands of miles, Mary and Adelaide continue to play out their roles in the family of origin. Just as Adelaide ends badly, slipping into irrevocable insanity, Mary isolates herself irretrievably, first from her community and then from her adoptive family.

Karl represents the converse of Mary's condition. Although she is completely enmeshed in the emotions of another, Karl is entirely disengaged and emotionally cut off from others, especially his family. But as Murray Bowen, a leading family systems theorist, notes, "the person who runs away from his family of origin is as emotionally dependent as the one who never leaves home." In the beginning of the novel, Karl is as controlled by the roles learned in his family of origin as is Mary, despite the great distance he deliberately puts between himself and his family.

Karl, however, eventually escapes Adelaide and Mary's fate of self-absorption and isolation, but only by renouncing the destructive family system he learned while a child. As a youngster, Karl is analogous to Adelaide; he avoids any permanent contact (he runs away from the Kozkas), and he shares with her an improvidence and a fascination with fairs, baubles, and whimsy. After Adelaide's desertion, and in violent reaction to a series of subsequent rejections, Karl defends himself against his own vulnerability in adulthood. He becomes a traveling salesman, never settling in one place or selling the same item for any length of time (as exemplified by the weird gifts he continually sends Dot, a symbolic repetition of his mother's obsession with trinkets and toys). Contact with others is limited to brief homosexual encounters and clandestine affairs at sales conventions. He quite self-consciously refuses to engage himself in any relationship, heterosexual or homosexual. Like his mother Adelaide, he chooses only lovers who require nothing more from him than his presence. In more ways than he would like to admit, he is his mother's son.

But his chance meeting at a convention with peculiar Wallace Pfef, farmer and businessman from Argus, North Dakota, jeopardizes his erstwhile disconnectedness. During their time together in the hotel room, Karl senses the potentiality of Wallace's love and his unconscious terror of the possible rejection that accompanies it: "I suddenly had the feeling that had always frightened me, the blackness, the ground I'd stood on giving way, the failing no place ... the awful possibility that he wanted to get to know me." Karl combats his fear of falling into nothingness by physically dramatizing it, insanely somersaulting off his bed and suffering momentary paralysis when he crash-lands. He recognizes that his actions are as futile as his psychological stratagems for protection: "I realized the place I'd landed on was only a flimsy ledge, and there was nothing to stop me if I fell." The sensation of falling represents his fear of the potential loss of a role and of a structure of systems that has heretofore given him a stable but inauthentic and estranged sense of identity....

Source: Gary Storhoff, "Family Systems in Louise Erdrich's *The Beet Queen*," in *Studies in Contemporary Fiction*, Vol. 39, No. 4, Summer 1998, pp. 341–53.

Meldan Tanrisal

In the following excerpt, Tanrisal focuses on the depiction of mother and child relationships in the novels of Louise Erdrich.

... The seeming contradiction between chronological and psychological time in the four novels of Louise Erdrich raises crucial issues for understanding the structure and meaning of the novels. The possibility of misunderstanding these novels grows out of the differences between the order of their publication and the dates of the continuing saga that Erdrich is developing. *Love Medicine* (1984) tells the story of several Chippewa extended families in North Dakota. The novel gives an a chronological and multidimensional account of fifty years, 1934–84, through multiple points of view and voices. In *The Beet Queen* (1986) numerous narrators provide a parallel series of the personal stories of several white

> IN ERDRICH'S NOVELS, WOMEN AND ESPECIALLY MOTHERS BEAR THE ENORMOUS RESPONSIBILITY OF FAMILY RELATIONSHIPS THAT SUSTAIN BOTH INDIVIDUAL AND COMMUNITY, DESPITE THE EXISTING CONFLICTS BETWEEN THEM. THEY ARE POWERFUL WOMEN WHO COUNTERACT DESTRUCTION."

and mixed blood Indian characters in Argus, a small and imaginary town in North Dakota between 1932–72. *Tracks* (1988) presents the history of several Chippewa family members related by two individuals, Nanapush and Pauline, from 1912 to 1924. In *The Bingo Palace* (1994) where the specific years are not stated, the story of the younger generation is again told by different narrators, the children and grandchildren of previous generations.

Louise Erdrich, the popular contemporary writer of German American and Chippewa descent, refers to the genocide of Native Americans by Euroamericans as a "catastrophe" and strongly believes that Native American writers "must tell the stories of contemporary survivors while protecting and celebrating the cores of cultures left in the wake of the catastrophe." Like all Native American writers, Erdrich shares the assumption that history holds the key to understanding contemporary Native American life. She tells the story of her people in a way that demonstrates that storytelling brings historical events and legends into the present. The novelist concentrates on "tracing the connective threads between the cultural past and its expression in the present." And she accomplishes this by centering the novels around the strong matrilineal nature of Native American culture and storytelling. She states her main purpose in writing the award-winning *Love Medicine*, saying, "I wanted to tell a story, so if I told it, that's done."

Covering the period from 1912 to the present day, Erdrich's novels provide a perspective on recent American history. Structurally, they blend into one another as successive generations of Kashpaws, Pillagers, Morriseys, and Lazarres weave their overlapping experiences and joint narratives. In "Life as an Uneasy Compromise," a review of *The Bingo Palace*, Rebecca Adams says: "This is writing deeply rooted in the oral tradition. Time moves beyond its normal linear dimension to a far closer approximation of memory. Recollection is not a matter of mere fact, and eternity lies not in the future, but in the past, in the obscure yet enduring connections that exist between siblings or grandparents."

Within the structure of the novels and stories, the narrators' memories, true or false, form the basis of "the story," yet the veracity of the narrators must always be questioned. Nanapush, one of the two characters who narrate the events in *Tracks*, insists several times that Pauline does not always tell the truth. "She was born a liar, and sure to die one," he claims. However, it is Pauline who reveals that Fleur was raped by three men at the butcher shop in Argus. This brings a new dimension to the story. Although it raises more questions about the father of Fleur's child, to a certain extent it also explains her wild behavior. In *Love Medicine* Henry LaMartine is introduced by an omniscient narrator as a highly disturbed veteran who has recently returned from Vietnam. In the next chapter his brother Lyman talks about their close relationship prior to Henry's joining the army and the change that has come over him leading to his suicide. Thus, Lyman, his brother, brings light to Henry's story. Each character or event is central to an element of the narrative.

Like many of her contemporaries, Erdrich writes metafiction that is concerned as much with exploring the process of storytelling as with the story itself. The system of discourse in her novels is extremely complex and demands close attention. As in *Love Medicine*, which is built layer upon layer, participation is expected in the narrative process. It is like working on a jigsaw puzzle, completing the whole by connecting the pieces. The incidents of the novel are to be thought over, sorted, reinterpreted as new events are related and more of the characters is revealed in order to integrate the story into a coherent whole by recognizing the connections between the characters and events of the narrative. Although Pauline/Leopolda makes the transition through the three novels, other characters appear in only one or two of the books. However, characters are connected in other ways to stories in which they do not appear, in both circular and linear ways. Geneological lines provide one of the means of connection in Erdrich's fictional world, while the recollections, retelling of events by reliable and unreliable narrators, create a different tone structure, a psychological structure for the existence of events that moves toward a mythological reality. The words of the wise Nanapush in *Tracks* sum up Erdrich's task in these novels: "Only looking back there is a pattern.... There is a story to all, never visible while it is happening. Only after, when an old man sits, dreaming and talking in his chair, the design springs clear." As Louis Owens states in *Other Destinies: Understanding the American Indian Novel*, "the knowledge of the inextricable interrelatedness of all things and the need to articulate the patterns of things through stories—both qualities integral to Indian cultures and central to Indian literature—" are emphasized in the book by Nanapush when he says, "I shouldn't have been caused to live so long, shown so much of death, had to squeeze so many stories in the corners of my brain. They're all attached, and once I start there is no end to telling because they're hooked from one side to the other, mouth to tail." Although Nanapush tells endless stories, since they are not told chronologically and history is combined with mythology, the narrative becomes complex and confusing.

More than merely a set of novels with common characters, Erdrich's fictional world illustrates the continuity of native culture. Part of Erdrich's message is that there is a mythological and cultural continuity supplied by two factors: 1) a native tradition of storytelling and retelling the events in the history of people, and 2) the matrilineal nature of the Native American structure. These two factors both inform and elucidate the novels of Erdrich.

Erdrich's narrator in *Tracks* repeatedly emphasizes the importance of the ancient art of storytelling. Ironically, the first example is a male. Nanapush, one of Erdrich's influential characters, loses his wife and children to the flu epidemic, but by telling tribal stories and singing old songs, he gives his culture a chance of continuation: "During the year of my sickness, when I was last one left, I saved myself by starting a story.... I got well by talking. Death could not get a word in edgewise, grew discouraged, and traveled on." Thus storytelling becomes a means of surviving by placing the victim in the tribal world of myth, so he is out of chronological order.

The history of a people's encounters with their enemy and its tragic consequences gives a foundation to these stories: the loss of their lands, the loss of their buffalo, and their dissolution. Combining the historical with the mythological and psychological in their storytelling enables them to endure the hardships of the past as well as the present. Thus, they find refuge in the memories of women which make up a psychological time and create mythological characters like June in order to protect themselves from the hostile world of chronological reality.

Due to the "breakup of ancient orders of life" and the destruction of their family identities by Euroamerican domination, Native Americans need to formulate new concepts of self, family and continuity. Therefore, at the center of American Indian fiction is the attempt to recover an identity and to illustrate the continuity of native culture. In a Native American way of life, tradition is equated with the mother; however, since many traditions have been destroyed, the Native Americans have often become motherless children. It is the storyteller's responsibility to retell stories to remind them of their past and of their identities. Moreover, since they are matrilineal tribes, the duties of women cannot be underestimated.

Native American women have played an important role in the continuity of tribal tradition, both through childbearing and through transmission of cultural values in stories. Even Nanapush in Erdrich's *Tracks* tells about the Chippewas' struggle to preserve their land and culture, upon the loss of his family. He cannot help thinking

> how many times in my life, as my children were born, I wondered what it was like to be a woman, able to invent a human from the extra materials of her own body. In the terrible times, the evils I do not speak of, when the earth swallowed back all it had given me to love, I gave birth in loss. I was like a woman in my suffering, but my children were all delivered into death. It was contrary, backward, but now I had a chance to put things into a proper order.

Now, he is not merely an eye-witness to the events, but by taking on the role of a mother, caring for characters like Fleur and her daughter Lulu, he is able to deliver them into life and to ease his former loss by restoring the natural order. He first cures Fleur who suffers from the epidemic and later the child Lulu's frostbitten feet that the white doctor insists on amputating.

Acting like a mother, he contributes to the survival of his people.

In the Chippewa tradition "the mother is not merely one's biological parent; she's all one's relations (male and female, human and animal, individual and tribal); she is connected to the earth." Thus, women make up the backbone of the family which is of utmost importance to the Native American. As articulated by a character in the film *Country Warriors: A Story of the Crow Tribe*: "Crows measure wealth a little differently than non-Indians.... Wealth is measured by one's relatedness, one's family, and one's clan. To be alone, that would be abject poverty to a Crow." This idea can be applied to other Native American tribes as well. One's ancestors are crucial to the sense of identity and belonging. They provide the foundation of a psychological and mythological life, which provides a defense against the tragedies that take place in historical time. In Erdrich's novels, women and especially mothers bear the enormous responsibility of family relationships that sustain both individual and community, despite the existing conflicts between them. They are powerful women who counteract destruction. Although mothers provide the sense of continuity particularly to the children, these women are not idealized, they have their problems.

Within the complete assemblage of characters in Erdrich's works, mothers of all sorts appear: those who have abandoned their children; those who are extremely possessive; those who are abusive. Nevertheless, even if they abandon their children, they are still important because they exert tremendous power over their children. Even Lulu who is the mother of eight sons each with different fathers is adored by them. Although June dies in the beginning of *Love Medicine*, her presence moves throughout the book, and she guides her son Lipsha in its sequel, *The Bingo Palace*. Having discovered the identity of his mother, Lipsha communicates with her ghost who appears frequently to him and supports him by giving advice and by bringing him luck. Different narrators retell their stories and create psychological time as they turn her into a mythological character.

...Throughout Erdrich's novels many kinds of mothers struggle with their children and their communities. Because of the breakdown of traditional Chippewa structures, many of the characters in Erdrich's novels suffer tremendously—and the mixed-bloods suffer most. They occupy a marginal position because they are unwanted by both cultures and are therefore ultimately led into isolation. They are torn between two worlds. Being unable to reconcile them, must create a new identity. The mother-Leopolda seeks escape in solitude and isolation, while her daughter-Marie tries to reconstruct family and community. Those who are traditional, being unable to turn to their ancient ways, refuse to imitate the white man and to assimilate and are faced with tremendous loss as in the case of Fleur, the mythic mother. In spite of the fact that she loses her land, her children, and becomes a wanderer, she can still perform the functions of a mother. She is the one who restores the little white boy (Karl) in *The Beet Queen*, back to life. She never loses her mysterious mythic powers and people go to her for advice, as her grandson Lipsha who goes to her to ask for a love medicine. Fleur and Marie are two of the many strong women characters in the works of Louise Erdrich who prove how Native American women have contributed to the survival of their people and culture.

In all her novels Erdrich accentuates the sense of a united, bounded community in spite of the existing tensions and discontinuities within it. She is the storyteller and the story is the life of her people. Being a writer from such a multicultural background, Erdrich offers different perspectives using different narrative voices to tell stories and show that despite all the problems they face and all the forces interfering with their continuity, Native American women have been a key element in the survival of the community and identity of their people. In Paula Gunn Allen's words:

> We survive war and conquest. We survive colonization, acculturation, assimilation; we survive beating, rape, starvation, mutilation, sterilization, abandonment, neglect, death of our children, our loved ones, destruction of our land, our homes, our past, and our future. We survive, and we do more than just survive. We bond, we care, we fight, we teach, we nurse, we bear, we feed, we earn, we laugh, we love, we hang in there, no matter what.

The complexity of Erdrich's works arises from her combination of chronological time with psychological, mythical time. The Native American tradition of storytelling and the matrilineal nature of the Native American structure play a major role in the continuity of native culture as illustrated in her novels. Historical time, with its unwanted tragic events, is made endurable by the creation of a mythological time and stories that are populated with mythical women who can sustain and provide protection for the Native American people.

Source: Meldan Tanrisal, "Mother and Child Relationships in the Novels of Louise Erdrich," in *American Studies International*, Vol. 35, No. 3, October 1997, pp. 67–80.

SOURCES

Banks, Russell, "Border Country," Review of *The Beet Queen*, in *Nation*, Vol. 243, No. 14, November 1, 1986, pp. 460–63.

Bly, Robert, "Another World Breaks Through," Review of *The Beet Queen*, in *New York Times Book Review*, August 31, 1986, p. 2.

Boxmeyer, Don, "Bless Our Home," in *St. Paul Pioneer Press*, July 16, 1994, p. 1D.

Chavkin, Allan, and Nancy Feyl Chavkin, "An Interview with Louise Erdrich," in *Conversations with Louise Erdrich and Michael Dorris*, edited by Allan Chavkin and Nancy Feyl Chavkin, University Press of Mississippi, 1994, pp. 220–54.

Disch, Thomas M., "Enthralling Tale: Louise Erdrich's World of Love and Survival," in *Chicago Tribune*, September 4, 1988, pp. 1, 6.

Erdrich, Louise, *The Beet Queen*, Perennial, 2001.

Hynes, William J., and William G. Doty, eds., *Mythical Trickster Figures: Contours, Contexts, and Criticisms*, University of Alabama Press, 1997.

Kakutani, Michiko, Review of *The Beet Queen*, in *New York Times*, August 20, 1986, p. C21.

Meisenhelder, Susan, "Race and Gender in Louise Erdrich's *The Beet Queen*," in *Ariel*, Vol. 25, No. 1, January 1994, pp. 45–57.

"N.D. State Hospital Celebrates 125th Year: Hosts Activities May 5–7," in *NEWS from the North Dakota Department of Human Services*, April 28, 2010, http://www.nd.gov/dhs/info/news/2010/4-28-nd-state-hospital-marks-125-years.pdf (accessed December 1, 2010).

"The Red River Valley Sugarbeet Growers Association," in *Sugarbeet Research & Education Board of Minnesota and North Dakota*, http://www.sbreb.org/brochures/RRVSGA/rrvsga.htm (accessed December 1, 2010).

Schultz, Lydia A., "Fragments and Ojibwe Stories: Narrative Strategies in Louise Erdrich's *Love Medicine*," in *College Literature*, Vol. 18, No. 3, 1991, pp. 80–95.

Silko, Leslie Marmon, "Here's an Odd Artifact for the Fairy-Tale Shelf," in *Impact/Albuquerque Journal*, October 8, 1986, pp. 10–11.

Simon, Linda, "Small Gestures, Large Patterns," Review of *The Beet Queen*, in *Commonweal*, Vol. 113, No. 18, October 24, 1986, pp. 565, 567.

Smith, Jeanne Rosier, "Lonely Tricksters: *The Beet Queen*," in *Writing Tricksters: Mythic Gambols in American Ethnic Literature*, University of California Press, 1997, pp. 86–89.

Wickenden, Dorothy, "Off the Reservation," Review of *The Beet Queen*, in *New Republic*, Vol. 195, No. 14, October 6, 1986, pp. 46–48.

FURTHER READING

Angley, Patricia, "Fleur Pillager: Feminine, Mythic, and Natural Representations in Louise Erdrich's *Tracks*," in *Constructions and Confrontations: Changing Representations of Women and Feminisms, East and West: Selected Essays*, edited by Cristina Bacchilega and Cornelia N. Moore, University of Hawaii Press, 1996, pp. 159–69.

> Angley analyzes Fleur Pillager as a character in *Tracks, The Beet Queen,* and *The Bingo Palace* in terms of the imagery and symbolism Erdrich associates with her, especially as it pertains to Ojibwe/Chippewa mythology.

Beidler, Peter G., and Gay Barton, *A Reader's Guide to the Novels of Louise Erdrich*, rev. ed., University of Missouri Press, 2006.

> This guide covers all of Erdrich's novels from *Love Medicine* to *The Painted Drum*, including *The Beet Queen*. It includes explication of each book, a dictionary of characters, a glossary of Ojibwe terms, and a comprehensive bibliography.

Chavkin, Allan, ed., *The Chippewa Landscape of Louise Erdrich*, University of Alabama Press, 1999.

> This collection of essays on Erdrich's novels focuses on their Native American aspects, analyzing such themes as games of chance and hunting as metaphor. *Love Medicine* and *The Bingo Palace* receive much attention.

Norris, Kathleen, *Dakota: A Spiritual Geography*, Mariner, 2001.

> When Norris, a poet, moved from New York to South Dakota in the 1980s, she underwent a drastic shift in her ideas about time, space, religion, and cultural heritage. This memoir details her acceptance of small town life, with its unique mix of hospitality, eccentric local figures, and distrust of outsiders.

Stookey, Lorena L., *Louise Erdrich: A Critical Companion*, Greenwood Press, 1999.

This volume contains extensive commentary on Erdrich's novels through *The Antelope Wife* (1998) as well as a lengthy bibliography and a biography of Erdrich.

Storhoff, Gary, "Family Systems in Louise Erdrich's *The Beet Queen*," in *Critique: Studies in Contemporary Fiction* Vol. 39, No. 4, Summer 1998, pp. 341–53.

The author analyzes Erdrich's novel in terms of family systems theory, as developed in the 1950s by the British social scientist Gregory Bateson, and its representation of a family of origin and how Mary embodies the idea of enmeshment.

SUGGESTED SEARCH TERMS

The Beet Queen

Louise Erdrich

Native American renaissance

Louise Erdrich AND The Beet Queen

North Dakota AND novel

North Dakota AND Chippewa

family AND abandonment

Great Depression AND North Dakota

Louise Erdrich AND Native American literature

Louise Erdrich AND Michael Dorris

A Bend in the River

V. S. NAIPAUL

1979

After winning the Booker Prize in 1971 for *In a Free State*, V. S. Naipaul was considered an important international author with valuable insights on third-world countries. As a Hindu Indian growing up in Trinidad, Naipaul experienced both colonialism and its end, to note that it was sometimes difficult to say which was worse. In 1975, Naipaul wrote a scathing article on the African dictator Mobutu Sese Seko, titled "A New King for the Congo," which he used as a basis for his 1979 novel *A Bend in the River*. The novel was short-listed for the Booker Prize in Fiction. His ambivalence about postcolonial conditions for former colonies is apparent in *A Bend in the River*, in which independence from Europe has led not to freedom but to tyranny in the rule of the Big Man.

The first-person narrator, Salim, is a Muslim Indian who opens a shop in the European ruins of Stanleyville (now Kisangani), Congo, after independence is gained in the 1960s, only to get embroiled in the African violence there. Salim considers whether he can find his place in Africa, as his family has for centuries, or whether he must leave Africa for the West. Naipaul's dark vision of Africans being unable to join the modern world has led many critics to call him a neocolonialist, or supporter of European colonialism. *A Bend in the River* remains valuable for its brilliant evocation of postcolonial contradictions. A 1989 edition is available from Vintage Press.

V.S. Naipaul (RAVEENDRAN / AFP / Getty Images)

AUTHOR BIOGRAPHY

Sir Vidiadhar Surajprasad Naipaul—known as Sir Vidia Naipaul or V. S. Naipaul—was born on August 17, 1932, as the oldest son to an Indian Brahmin family in Chaguanas, Trinidad and Tobago, a former colony of Great Britain. He was descended from indentured laborers from East India who were cheap labor for the sugar plantations. His father, Seepersad, was a journalist for the Trinidad *Guardian* and wrote short stories that influenced his son's desire to be a writer. Naipaul's father was poor but married into the rich Capildeo family and was often dependent on his wife's family for income. Vidia's brother Shiva Naipaul, his uncle, and a cousin all became published authors.

V. S. Naipaul attended Queen's Royal College, in Trinidad, and then won a scholarship to Oxford, leaving Trinidad in 1950. England became his permanent home. After broadcasting for the BBC *Caribbean Voices* program, in 1955 he married Patricia Hale, an Englishwoman who became a lifelong literary partner. His first novels

were satirical and comical portraits of Trinidad. *The Mystic Masseur* (1957) won the John Llewellyn Rhys Prize in 1958 and was adapted as a film. *Miguel Street* (1959), a collection of short stories, won the 1961 Somerset Maugham Award. *A House for Mr Biswas* (1961) is based on Naipaul's father and his problems with poverty. *Mr Stone and the Knight's Companion* (1963) was set in England and won the Hawthornden Prize.

Naipaul began writing more serious political novels as he witnessed the process of decolonization in poorer countries. *The Mimic Men* (1967) won the W. H. Smith Literary Award; *In a Free State* (1971) won the Booker Prize for Fiction. *Guerrillas* (1975) brought him worldwide fame, and *A Bend in the River* (1979) is often cited as his masterpiece. With fame came controversy, as Naipaul's stance seems to favor the former colonial stability over the turbulence of third-world governments.

In his nonfiction travel books, he criticizes his homeland of India for backwardness in *An Area of Darkness* (1964), *India: A Wounded Civilization* (1977), and *India: A Million Mutinies Now* (1990). His criticisms of Islamic societies in *Among the Believers: An Islamic Journey* (1981) and *Beyond Belief: Islamic Excursions* (1998) have also generated hostile reactions. Other books—*The Middle Passage* (1962) and *The Loss of El Dorado* (1969)—have similarly treated the Caribbean. In his collections of essays, *The Return of Eva Peron* (1980) and *The Writer and the World: Essays* (2002) contain his conservative views on postcolonial politics and writing.

Naipaul was knighted by Queen Elizabeth II of England in 1990 and awarded the Nobel Prize for Literature in 2001. As of 2010, he lives in Wiltshire, England, with his second wife, Nadira Naipaul, a former Pakistani journalist.

PLOT SUMMARY

Part One: The Second Rebellion, Sections 1–5

A Bend in the River chronicles the events of the late 1960s and early 1970s in the former Belgian Congo, which was renamed Zaire, during the dictatorship of Mobutu Sese Seko. Historical places and people are not named directly but are easily recognizable. The story opens during an uneasy peace between rebellions occurring

MEDIA ADAPTATIONS

- *A Bend in the River* by V. S. Naipaul is narrated by Simon Vance in a 2009 unabridged MP3 format available by Blackstone Audio.

after Congolese independence in 1960. The Second Rebellion, at the end of Part One, refers to the brief Maoist uprising under the direction of Pierre Mulele, who was publicly executed by Mobutu in 1968.

The first-person narrator, a young Indian Muslim named Salim, drives his Peugeot from his home on the east African coast to a trading town (Kisangani) on a bend in the great river (Congo). He has bought a shop there in this country (Congo or Zaire), which is far from his own land (Zanzibar), and from Nazruddin, a successful businessman and old friend of his family. The journey toward the middle of Africa is so difficult that Salim often fears he is going in the wrong direction in seeking to start a new life for himself. The roads are broken up, and there are many checkpoints with armed guards whom he must bribe to get through. He finds the town itself half destroyed. The European suburb has been burned, and the bush has grown over the ruins. Nazruddin's shop is in the market square, but the stock has been pilfered by natives who hide in the safety of their villages. Natives and foreigners wait to see if the peace will hold, and when it does, business begins again.

One of Salim's customers is Zabeth, a female sorceress from a fishing village who makes a trip once a month to buy items for her tribe, such as pots and soap. The trip is dangerous, for the river is full of snags, and when the people tie their dugouts to the steamer, they often overturn and drown. From her, Salim hears about the tribal people.

Salim speaks to Zabeth of the Big Man (Mobutu) and envisions the town rebuilt under his stable regime. The mysterious and threatening power of the river and the bush, however, seems to contradict this vision of modernizing the land. In the bush, the natives feel safe because there is magic, with the ancestors watching over them.

Metty, the half-African boy who grew up in Salim's family as a slave, comes from the coast to live with him. Salim's family has been in Africa for centuries, but they live on the eastern coast, among the Asians who settled there from India, Arabia, and Persia (by then called Iran). Although Africa is their adopted home, they are still intruders. Salim comes from a culture that does not think of the passage of time, so he has learned history from European books.

Salim worries about the Arabs' and Indians' future in Africa, as they are minorities in a politically unstable land. He realizes that in terms of the great world, his people have fallen behind. Salim feels trapped between the old and the new. Once conquerors themselves, the Muslims exist as strangers in Africa now, neither native nor European. He has spoken of these things with his boyhood friend, Indar, son of a Punjab moneylender, from the wealthy family in their hometown. Indar is going to a university in England. Salim feels jealous and helpless, because he cannot afford to leave Africa or be educated, but he vows to break away from the old life and stand alone, the only way to the future. He takes Nazruddin's offer and buys the shop to get his start in life, though Nazruddin expects Salim to marry his daughter. Nazruddin is a man of the world with European manners, with trade all over Africa. Salim wants to be like him.

Salim describes the deprivations in the town where he is trying to do business. There is little electricity, and supplies are short. There are European ruins with Latin mottoes. He makes a few friends in town, like Shoba and Mahesh, an Indian couple with a shop. Salim cannot return home because of the uprisings there, which have scattered his family. Metty is sent to him for protection and describes the butchery of their hometown by African rebels. Metty is handsome and flourishes in the new town, becoming popular. He works in Salim's shop, lives in Salim's apartment, and tells him the gossip from the natives.

Zabeth brings her son Ferdinand to Salim for protection as well. At sixteen, Ferdinand leaves his father's tribe in the south and stays with his mother's tribe in the Congo. She wants him to go to school at the lycée (high school) in town, a leftover from colonial days. Metty and Ferdinand become friends, as Ferdinand goes to school in the week and to his mother's village on weekends. Ferdinand is confused by his multiple cultures.

Salim becomes friends with Father Huismans, a Belgian priest who runs the lycée. Father Huismans collects African masks and is enchanted by African culture and art. He is unafraid of traveling to the villages and optimistic about the future of Africa and the return of European culture. The town is suddenly surprised by yet another tribal uprising. This refers to the Second Rebellion of Pierre Mulele, which was brutally put down by Mobutu.

The president's army takes over the town. Metty and Salim hide their money and documents. Ferdinand is hysterical and comes to Salim for protection. The president's white mercenaries shoot one of the president's army officers to terrorize both the army and the people, to scare everyone into submission to the Big Man. The foreigners in town are happy the Big Man can restore peace, though airplanes strafe the bush and kill the village people randomly. Only the Big Man wins in this war. Father Huismans is killed and decapitated. Yet the peace established allows the town to settle down and hope that the Big Man's new Africa will build a modern future. Westerners begin to arrive to help him do this.

Part Two: The New Domain, Sections 6–11

Everyone is taken in by the Big Man's idea of progress for Africa. The town rebuilds and flourishes. Airplanes, the steamer, buses, taxis, telephones, bulldozers, and traffic at the hotel are part of the big boom. The new men of Africa arrive with the flag and the president's photo. They have the authority to take whatever they want, including illegal trafficking in gold and ivory. Mahesh also deals illegally in these commodities, making Salim hide his foreign bank notes for him. Everyone is infected with the desire to make money. Mahesh gets a Bigburger franchise. Salim, however, does not want to stay in the town and becomes restless. His father writes him to urge his marriage to Nazruddin's daughter.

The Big Man builds a compound outside of town called a Domain of the State, with modern buildings where European consultants and visitors can stay. The Domain houses a polytechnic institute where the new men can be educated;

Ferdinand wins a scholarship there. Salim, however, is disenchanted to find the real Africa gone. He reads the dire signs: there is a tension of pretense and instability underneath. He feels further betrayed when he finds out that Metty secretly has an African family somewhere in town. He has lost Metty's confidence and feels alone.

Indar returns from England but seems soured by his experience. He tells Salim that he has learned to turn his back on his tradition and no longer grieves for it. Indar is staying at the Domain as a consultant for the government. He shows Salim around the Domain, and Salim is impressed in spite of himself. He begins to get fantasies of belonging to this group. The Domain people are intellectual and excited about the new Africa. The Big Man's photo is everywhere. He is dressed as a chief in a leopard-skin cap and carrying a stick of office. Salim goes to one of Indar's lectures designed to inspire the young African men. Ferdinand asks if the new men have to give up worship of their ancestral spirits, showing he is having a hard time living in both worlds.

At a Domain party, Salim is enchanted in meeting a white Belgian couple. Raymond is a historian and the Big Man's white man in charge of the Domain. His beautiful wife, Yvette, is much younger than he is. Yvette has style and has made the room romantically dark, with the music of Joan Baez playing in the background. Salim suddenly believes in the new era and falls in love with Yvette. Raymond is busy compiling a book on the Big Man's speeches but comes out to dinner to make pronouncements to the guests. He tells how he met the president and defends his policies. Later Indar reveals to Salim that the president has sent Raymond away, but Raymond has to go on pretending he is his advisor.

Indar confesses that his time in London brought disillusionment. He tried to forget the past and move ahead with the times. He tells of his own rage when he discovered that he was not really prepared to participate in the world outside. In London, he can never catch up, and he is a foreigner. He is in two worlds and master of neither. When he tries to become a diplomat with an interview at India House, he is humiliated and filled with anger. In a sudden insight, he finally understands that London, and therefore civilization, was made by men. It is not a sacred tradition. He too can make things happen and invent his own life. He decides to travel around as a speaker so as to round up the intellectuals of Africa and inspire them to create a new country.

Salim sees Indar and Yvette together a lot, and then one day Indar has to leave. Ferdinand is also going away to the capital, to be part of the administration. Salim sees them off at the steamer. Ferdinand has changed and learned to take on all sides of African culture, old and new. It seems from their goodbye that Indar and Yvette have been intimate. When Indar leaves, Salim and Yvette become lovers. Yvette is a new sort of woman for Salim. She is rich, white, modern, educated, and independent. He feels revitalized, and they see each other every day. On the other hand, he begins to worry about his own moral decay in going with a married woman. He once felt superior to the corruption around him, but now he is becoming part of it.

Salim reads Raymond's historical articles on Africa and is surprised to learn that he gets his material only from newspapers instead of direct observation. He understands that Yvette was once dazzled by him but became aware of her mistake and has taken lovers to avoid boredom. Raymond looks the other way.

Part Three: The Big Man, Sections 12–15

Salim thinks that if he had read Raymond's articles earlier he would have understood Yvette's ambition, as well as her disappointment. He wanted to be transported by love to another world, not involved with her mistake. Now he is trapped. Because of this liaison, he feels closer to the president through Raymond, and he develops a political anxiety. The president's photo keeps getting larger, and there is the cult of the African Madonna, based on the Big Man's peasant mother. Raymond's exile from the capital weighs on Yvette. She loved meeting with the president when they first came to Africa. When she unintentionally insulted the Big Man by speaking out of turn, he refused to receive her anymore. He decided that the white man was an embarrassment and dismissed Raymond. Yvette suffers more than Raymond over the situation. Raymond cannot get a job in America, because his position with the president puts him in a precarious position. The president publishes a book of maxims and forces everyone to buy one. He makes the children march with the books and shout his name.

Salim feels defined by Yvette. He begins to mourn for his old self, but he is addicted to her.

The rich Greek merchant in town sells out, and this is a bad sign. It is part of the ongoing nationalization of business. Salim gets a letter from Nazruddin, who says things are bad in Uganda and he is moving to Canada. Salim feels guilt about his pledge to marry Nazruddin's daughter.

A guard is killed in Salim's town, and the president's attention turns there. The officials harass Metty, then Salim, trying to blackmail them. The people begin rioting against the police. A new Liberation Army insists there will be a purge. Nazruddin writes that he is now in England looking for a refuge. Salim has nowhere to go. Everyone lives in fear, and there are many killings. Raymond becomes depressed, and Yvette and Salim meet less.

During one of their meetings, Salim becomes aware that Yvette is losing interest in him. His pent up frustration explodes, and he beats her up. He feels terrible to be infected with the violence around him. She calls Salim later to see how he is, but it is over between them.

Zabeth tells Salim that Ferdinand will become the local commissioner, and she is afraid for his life, because the Big Man regularly and randomly executes members of his staff. Salim sees Shoba and Mahesh stagnant and unable to leave town. He is afraid he will be like them and writes to Nazruddin, deciding to go to London, where he finally becomes engaged to Kareisha, Nazruddin's daughter. Kareisha is a pharmacist, and she is affectionate to Salim, showing him around. He has no idea what he can do in London for a living. Nazruddin tells Salim his story of what he found in his travels—everyone running away, looking for a safe place. He is unable to do business in the larger world because he is cheated by Westerners, but in London he is content to be a landlord. Africans dream of getting out and making it in the West, but it is an illusion, he says. Kareisha confirms this with Indar's story. Indar lost his business and became depressed when he went to America and found people there rich and out of his league. Now he wants to quit and go home. Salim feels the same way but knows there is no home to go to. He returns to Africa simply to wind up his affairs.

Part Four: Battle, Sections 16–17

Metty is surprised to see Salim return because the government has taken away his business in the Radicalization movement. Citizen Théotime now runs his shop, and Salim will have to work for him. Salim goes to the shop and does all the work while Théotime reads comic books. Salim knows he has to make as much money as he can and get out fast. He begins to deal in illegal gold and ivory, hiding the tusks in his backyard. The town is in a state of war and expects a visit from the president.

Théotime is a problem, always drunk and making scenes. Metty threatens to do something terrible under the pressure of Théotime's constant abuse. He finally cracks and turns Salim in to the police for illegal possession of ivory. The policeman Prosper arrests Salim and puts him in jail. The next day, the president will visit the town to witness an execution there.

Ferdinand, the new commissioner, comes to rescue Salim and helps him to escape on the last steamer out of town. Ferdinand is afraid because no one knows who will be executed. He says they are all waiting to be killed. Metty begs Salim to take him with him, but Salim promises to send him money through Mahesh. Metty is terrified because the Liberation Army has threatened to kill anyone who can read and write. As Salim sails away on the steamer, the water hyacinths cut the attached passenger barge loose, and there are gunshots as the barge with the hapless native Africans disappears in the night.

CHARACTERS

The Big Man

The Big Man is a thinly disguised historical figure, Mobutu Sese Seko (originally Joseph-Désiré Mobutu), who ruled the Congo (Zaire) as a dictator from 1965 to 1997. Like Mobutu, the Big Man wears a leopard-skin hat and carries a staff like an African chief. He creates a semidivine personal cult and brutally puts down insurrections, killing village people to keep them in line. Like Mobutu, the Big Man rules arbitrarily, giving people offices or executing them on whims. He uses whites, like Raymond, and blacks, like Ferdinand, alike, not to better his country but to gain personal power and wealth.

Ferdinand

Ferdinand is an African native, Zabeth's son. She sends him to the high school in the town, and then he wins a scholarship to the polytechnic institute at the Domain, where he is groomed to

be one of the Big Man's new men. After graduation, he goes to the capital to assume an administrative cadetship for the dictator and then is appointed commissioner for the town (Kisangani). He releases Salim from jail right before the arrival of the dictator and helps him escape. Ferdinand is often confused about his culture from making too rapid a leap from village life to Western values. Salim protects Ferdinand during the Simba rebellion, and Ferdinand rewards Salim's kindness by helping him to escape the town. He often wishes he could go back to the bush, but he can never go back.

Father Huismans

Father Huismans is a Belgian priest who runs the Christian school in town and collects African art for a hobby. He explains his views of civilization, which are basically colonial in nature. He believes the mixing of Europeans and Africans is a good thing, and he thinks he can appreciate the native culture by collecting and displaying African masks from trips to the villages. Salim admires the priest's fearless confidence, but his confidence turns out to be naiveté when he is murdered and mutilated for the sacrilege of collecting sacred masks.

Indar

Indar is Salim's Indian Muslim friend from home. His family is rich from the banking trade of Zanzibar. Indar warns the young Salim that they must change with the times. Indar goes to school in England to better himself, but when he cannot get a job there, he comes to Kisangani as a teacher and advisor at the Domain's institute for young African men. Indar feels that, in order to compete, he has to repudiate his past and become westernized. He is a self-made man, but when he loses his business and goes to America, he is further intimidated by the superior wealth and know-how of Westerners. Indar is a double for Salim, playing out the options Salim would have with wealth and position. Indar often articulates Naipaul's philosophy of the necessity for third-world people to become westernized.

Kareisha

Kareisha is Nazruddin's daughter, to whom Salim becomes engaged after his affair with Yvette ends. Kareisha represents the traditional obligations Salim wants to leave behind. Ironically, Kareisha is beautiful and modern, a successful pharmacist. She is mature and understanding, a perfect wife for Salim, if not as glamorous as Yvette. He enjoys Kareisha's soothing attention in London, though he feels inadequate to provide for a family.

Mahesh

Mahesh is an Indian Hindu, one of Salim's close friends. He is of a lower caste than his wife, Shoba, who comes from a rich family. Industrious and full of schemes for making money, he tries selling cameras and getting the Bigburger franchise in town. His philosophy is to ignore the local politics and just continue on, minding his own business. Finally, he turns to illegal trafficking in gold and ivory and influences Salim to do the same. Mahesh is dependent on his wife for his self-image and drive. He is isolated and out of touch with the social forces around him.

Metty

Metty, who goes by his nickname in town, is actually named Ali. His nickname means "half breed," for he is half African and half Indian, one of Salim's family slaves. When the Zanzibar Revolution sees the slaughter of many of the Arabs and Indians there, Metty is sent to Salim in Kisangani for protection. Metty expects to be taken care of, as the Muslim slaves were part of the family. He is popular with the townspeople because of his friendliness and helps Salim in his store and lives with him; meanwhile, he secretly takes a native wife and has a family. Metty is unprotected among the natives and betrays Salim out of fear when the Big Man comes to purge the town. Salim fails to provide for Metty but promises to send him money later.

Nazruddin

Nazruddin is an older Muslim friend of Salim's family and has picked Salim for his future son-in-law. Nazruddin becomes a father figure and a mentor in business to Salim, selling Salim the shop in Kisangani. Nazruddin moves on to Uganda to make a lot of money, only to lose it when Idi Amin forces all Indians out of the country. Nazruddin moves his family to Canada and then London trying to make a go of it, and he sends letters to Salim telling him of conditions on the outside. He is cheated in the West and has no skill for Western business and so settles by becoming a London landlord.

Prosper

Prosper is the local policeman in Kisangani. He usually ignores illegal activities for a bribe, but when the Big Man comes to town, he arrests Salim and puts him in jail for illegal possession of ivory.

Raymond

Raymond is a Belgian professor and historian who serves as an adviser to the Big Man as he tries to modernize the country. Once part of the dictator's entourage, he is exiled with his wife to the Domain at Kisangani. Raymond hopes to be recalled by the Big Man to edit his speeches. He tries to get a job at an American university as an Africanist but is too closely associated with the dictator for anyone to want to hire him. Shutting himself in a room to write irrelevant academic papers in the middle of the Congo while his wife has affairs and the country erupts in rebellion, he pretends to be important.

Salim

Salim is the first-person Muslim Indian narrator and main protagonist, through whose eyes the reader witnesses this period of history in the Congo (roughly the late 1960s to early 1970s). Buying a shop in Kisangani, the former Stanleyville, a Belgian colonial town, he tries to build a business in the midst of political chaos, with rebellions, violence, and poverty all around him. He learns to leave his ordered Muslim life behind on the coast and adjusts to the constant upheavals in the Congo. Originally protected because he is a foreigner, he becomes a target after Radicalization, when the Big Man takes his shop and gives it to Africans. Reduced to illegal trade to get enough money to leave the country, he is found out and arrested for dealing in ivory.

Salim's consciousness records the details of the country's disintegration, from the bush taking over the ruins of European civilization to the racial and cultural tensions between Asians, Africans, and Europeans who all meet at this town on the bend of the river. At first trying to identify with European standards by joining the athletic club and nightlife of the foreigners, Salim soon loses his integrity trying to survive and adapt to the brutal reality. He tries to follow Indar's advice to trample on his ethnic background, but his displacement and disillusionment provide keen insights into the plight of third-world peoples and their disadvantages in the modern world. His personal weaknesses surface when he takes first African lovers and then a white lover in defiance of his traditional Muslim morals and engagement to Nazruddin's daughter.

He avoids his Muslim duties toward both his fiancée and his family slave, Metty, leaving Metty in poverty and unprotected. His pretense at identifying with European culture is exploded in his affair with Yvette. He barely escapes, becoming engaged to Kareisha and leaving the Congo behind.

Shoba

Shoba is the pretty but neurotic wife of Mahesh, marrying beneath her for love and paying for her rash decision by being taken to the interior of Africa, cut off from her family on the east coast. She is loyal to Mahesh and pumps up his ego and self-image, but she worries that her brothers will show up and disfigure her with acid, as they have threatened, for her disobedience to the family. Ironically, she becomes scarred not by her brothers but by a peroxide lightener she puts on her skin. She hides indoors and becomes morbid and depressed.

Théotime

Théotime is a lazy African in Kisangani, a former mechanic who is awarded Salim's shop when the Big Man nationalizes the foreign businesses. Salim is reduced to working for Théotime for wages, while the latter gets drunk and reads comic books.

Yvette

Yvette is the young and beautiful Belgian wife of Raymond, who entertains for him in the Domain with parties for Europeans and foreigners. She takes first Indar as a lover and then Salim. Salim is enchanted with her stylish beauty, education, and independence. She represents a prize to be won, proving his own worth. Yvette likes Salim, perhaps seeing him as an exotic dark man of Africa, rather than as a person. He finally rejects her, ashamed of his weak delusions.

Zabeth

Zabeth is a female sorceress from a nearby village who risks her life to come in a dugout by river, along with her women, to the town to trade for her people. She becomes friends with Salim, telling him the news of the bush. The villagers do not like the Big Man and fight him in occasional uprisings. They hide in their villages protected by the magic of their ancestors. Zabeth gives her son a Western education so that he can progress

in the new regime but regrets her decision, fearing her son will be killed by the Big Man.

THEMES

Alienation

With the eyes of a stranger, the Muslim Indian Salim sees the currents in African politics that displace the people in his Congo town. Most of the main characters feel alienated from their surroundings, as if they don't belong, a sense exacerbated by the violence around them. Salim's family members feel African, but they are neither native nor fully integrated, since they cling to the coast and look east to where they came from, India. Salim is afraid of the African bush and river; he likes to associate with upper-class foreigners, but he feels he has no real place in the town. He is always hoping that the town will be swept into the present, into the greater world, for that is the promise of the Big Man, but that never happens. Metty, the family slave, is a half-breed without standing or money who cannot support his African family. Salim is shocked to find out that Metty has deserted their religion and way of life, and this makes him feel more alone. Indar tries to make it in the outside world by getting an English education, but he is rejected in London on the basis of race: "English boys in English jobs." The Belgian couple, Raymond and Yvette, in turn, are terribly out of place in the Congo, creating a false European atmosphere in the compound that is constantly being reclaimed by that of the jungle.

Self-Identity

Salim knows that there is no future for him in his traditional society. When he looks at his Muslim aunt's narrow domestic routine, he is ashamed, thinking "how petty her concern." He is expected to marry Nazruddin's daughter and carry on as his family always has, but he knows that Africa is changing and that the old life is too small. He is an insecure young man, without education or connections, trying to keep up by reading scientific magazines and identifying with the progressive world of the West. Indar encourages Salim to "trample on the past" and not look back. He tells Salim about his own identity crisis in London, where he discovered that he must invent himself in the modern world like everyone else: "They're all individuals fighting to make their

TOPICS FOR FURTHER STUDY

- Naipaul mentions the colonial oppression of the Congolese but does not go into detail about the history that fuels African rage. Conduct online and print research on the Belgian king Leopold II's enforced labor for rubber production in the Congo, which became a scandal involving millions of Congolese deaths. Then write an essay that considers the following question: do you feel Naipaul has left out an important part of the story, or does he allude to colonial abuse adequate in other ways? Provide examples from Belgian colonial history and from the novel.

- African Americans trace their ancestry to the African diaspora, the global community created by the movement of Africans to other parts of the world first through slavery and then through emigration. Many believe this worldwide dispersal has the potential to renew modern Africa, especially through social and business entrepreneurship. Complete a group project documenting some of the efforts of successful Africans in other parts of the world to foster exchange with and sponsorship in African countries. Create a Wiki showing reputable Web sites, foundations, and collaborations and also presenting articles, comments, and annotations that might be used to inspire readers to follow up with some worthy project for social or educational exchange.

- Films like *Invictus* (2009) try to give hope that African countries can move ahead in terms of racial and economic equality and political justice through greater understanding. In *Invictus*, how does Nelson Mandela use sports to create bridges in a postcolonial world? Compare and contrast Mandela's motives to Mobutu's in the 1996 documentary, *When We Were Kings*, about the boxing championship Mobutu sponsored in Zaire in 1974 between George Foreman and Muhammad Ali. Create a presentation using clips from both films as examples of the use of sports to create common ground between cultures, and have a group discussion on the results.

- Read *First Crossing: Stories about Teen Immigrants* (2007), edited by Donald Gallo, about young people from various countries, like Cambodia, Haiti, Kazakhstan, Mexico, South Korea, and others, who were suddenly transplanted to the United States. *A Bend in the River* similarly uses the stories of Indar's and Nazruddin's immigration to the West to reflect on cultural differences. What are the most common problems among ethnic peoples trying to adjust to a westernized culture? Collect interviews of immigrants in your community, then create a Web site or a video with stories and helpful tips for both immigrants and their communities.

- The acclaimed 2007 documentary *War/Dance* shows three African children in a Ugandan refugee camp using arts to heal the wounds of war. Watch the film and write a paper comparing the film to the work of one or more modern African artists who use art for the same purpose.

---

way." Yvette makes Salim feel modern for a time, but he is aware that he is losing his own self in trying to please her. With nowhere left to go, he seems fated to marry Nazruddin's daughter after all, though there is little possibility of a job in London.

Society

Salim is constantly reflecting on the nature of civilization. He grew up secure within his Indian Muslim world, but the Indians did not keep track of change. Once he began to read European books, his ideas expanded, and he began his comparative study of civilization. The novel thus contrasts the societies of the Africans, the Asians, and the Europeans. From his protocolonial Indo-Arab roots, Salim learns to not identify with slaves or native Africans, though he pities their wrongs. His grandfather once traded slaves, and the Muslims treat slaves as protected children. But these traditional distinctions become blurred in modern African politics. Salim sees "black men assuming the lies of white men." His own society has "fallen behind." Salim is afraid of what he calls "African rage" as he views the European ruins of the town. When the oppression of colonialism comes to an end, the Africans, it seems, can only rise up in ethnic violence. They have not had time to build a working national government, thus paving the way for dictators like the Big Man.

The only way for all the societies to communicate, Naipaul suggests, is through Western civilization as the common coinage, the way of the future. Thus, Salim can become friends with Ferdinand and connect to Raymond and Yvette. He believes in Indar's discovery that, to live in the world, they have to destroy the past, for "civilization is a construct," rather than an accepted given.

Bend in a river *(Charmaine A Harvey | Shutterstock.com)*

Tyranny

With the upheavals and rebellions, Salim thinks of "the miraculous peace of the colonial time, when men could, if they wished, pay little attention to tribal boundaries." Order becomes more important than ideology to him, as it is to Naipaul. Therefore, he and the others continue to put their hope in the Big Man's ability to straighten things out.

Yet the Big Man's tyranny grows throughout the story until, at the end, it cannot be ignored. The dictator is arbitrary in his use of power, suddenly executing members of his staff for no reason. The Big Man is vain, making himself into a little god, with gigantic photos everywhere and his own invented mythology mixing African and Western motifs. Corruption is widespread. Mahesh says, "It isn't that there's no right and wrong here. There's no right." The Big Man creates modern Africa by "by-passing real Africa," strafing the villages with airplanes when he wants to beat the tribes into submission, then charming them by calling them citizens.

STYLE

Anglo-African Literature

During the colonial period, British writers found material in the exotic locations of the empires, especially Africa and India. In *A Bend in the River*, Naipaul, a Trinidadian of Indian descent who moved to England at the age of eighteen, is consciously creating within the legacy of Joseph Conrad's *The Heart of Darkness* (1899), the story of a white man's corruption by the primitive nature of the central African jungle. Salim, too, takes a journey into the heart of Africa, where his ideals become broken and he becomes tainted by the brutality of African violence. Other novels written by Europeans about Africa include H. Rider Haggard's *She* (1886), about an Englishman's search for a white queen in central Africa; John Buchan's *Prester John* (1910), about a Zulu uprising in South Africa; and Isak Dinesen's *Out of Africa* (1937), about colonial life in Kenya. Such novels portray the beauty, the violence, and the mystery of Africa, as well as the friendly or hostile contacts between colonial whites and native Africans. Naipaul has been criticized for aligning himself with colonial authors, especially Conrad.

Travel Literature

Naipaul writes both nonfiction travel books and novels about his travels to third-world countries, often blending fictional and nonfictional techniques. A journalistic piece that Naipaul published on Mobutu in 1975—"A New King for the Congo" in the *New York Review of Books*—furnished the details and outline of what would become the fictional *A Bend in the River*. Famous travel-oriented fiction includes Laurence Sterne's *A Sentimental Journey through France and Italy* (1768), exploring the manners of the French and Italians, and Herman Melville's *Typee: A Peep at Polynesian Life* (1846).

Political Fiction

Works of political fiction describe historical political situations or fictional ones based on known political problems, providing commentary and cautionary tales. Naipaul's *Guerillas* (1975) first made him internationally famous with a story about Caribbean revolutionaries. *A Bend in the River* is based on Joseph Mobuto's takeover of the Congo in 1965. *Uncle Tom's Cabin* (1852), by Harriet Beecher Stowe, is credited with helping to abolish slavery in the United States. *To Kill a Mockingbird* (1960), by Harper Lee, examines racial prejudice in the American South in the 1930s. *Cancer Ward* (1967), by Aleksandr Solzhenitsyn, is a novel about Stalin's purge of Russia, when millions were killed and sent to labor camps.

Postcolonial Fiction

Postcolonial literature deals with issues of decolonization after European colonial rule. Racial inequality and cultural differences are usual themes. Postcolonial fiction chronicles the history of cultural stereotypes and the suffering of people under political subjugation. Naipaul's novel deals with the traumas of the Congo in transitioning from a colonial to an independent nation. Native characters in postcolonial fiction, like Ferdinand, are often torn between traditional values and the demands of the modern world. Other examples of such fictional works include the Colombian Gabriel García Márquez's *One Hundred Years of Solitude* (1967), the British-Indian Salman Rushdie's *Midnight's Children*

(1981), and the Chilean Isabel Allende's *The House of the Spirits* (1982).

HISTORICAL CONTEXT

Arabs and Indians in Africa

Salim is a Muslim Indian from the island of Zanzibar, on the east coast of Africa, which was once part of an Arab empire. Arab traders began colonizing the east African coast around the first century CE. By the year 500, traders from the Persian Gulf, southern India, and Indonesia were also in East Africa. The trading posts became Arab city-states with Muslim rulers. They traded in gold, ivory, slaves, tortoise shell, and rhinoceros horn. Indian traders followed the Arab trading routes and enjoyed great wealth through Zanzibar's trade with the Arab world. These traders would have been Indar's and Salim's ancestors. Indians in Zanzibar were also bankers, as Indar's family was. Poorer Indians came to East Africa in the nineteenth century as British indentured laborers, as Naipaul's family had gone to Trinidad.

The British Empire gained control of Zanzibar in the late nineteenth century. The islands gained independence from Britain in December 1963, but early the next year in the Zanzibar Revolution, thousands of Arabs and Indians were killed in a genocide. This event is related by Metty to Salim when he arrives in Kisangani. In 1972, Idi Amin expelled Asians from Uganda, an event mentioned by Nazruddin to Salim in a letter. Many of these Asians fled, like Nazruddin, to Canada or Britain.

The Belgian Congo

In 1876, the explorer Henry Morton Stanley began to travel the Congo territory, the last part of Africa to be explored because of the wildness of the Congo River, with its 220 miles of waterfalls and rapids. King Leopold II of Belgium annexed the Congo in 1885 as his personal possession, and cruelly worked the natives to generate wealth, a scandal that led to his having to relinquish the area to the Belgian government. The country was known as the Belgian Congo from 1908 to 1960. Although some laborers were paid wages, forced labor was still used in copper, cobalt, diamond, and gold mines, as the government gave private companies a free hand. The Congo was a leading copper, uranium, and

COMPARE
&
CONTRAST

- **1970s:** The government of Zaire (now known as the Democratic Republic of the Congo) is a dictatorship under the authoritative regime of Mobutu Sese Seko, who controls the country from 1965 to 1997.

  Today: The Democratic Republic of the Congo has an elected president and a parliament, who serve under the newest constitution, approved by voters in 2005.

- **1970s:** Ethnic violence is initially suppressed by Mobutu but later erupts in a Tutsi/Hutu conflict, which helps bring about his downfall.

  Today: The violence from the Second Congo War (1998-2004) continues in regional ethnic conflict, claiming thousands of Congolese lives each month through displacement, starvation, and disease.

- **1970s:** Mobutu siphons the country's wealth from the mining of minerals into his own bank account.

  Today: Minerals mined for use in electronic products are produced through military force and human abuse to finance war in Rwanda and the Democratic Republic of the Congo. Western countries call for limiting the use of such "conflict minerals."

---

rubber producer. The colonizers claimed to be civilizing the natives through religion and industry, and they did bring wealth—however poorly distributed—to the Congo, as seen in the ruins left behind in Stanleyville (renamed Kisangani), the town of the novel.

Congolese Independence

After World War II, former African colonies were becoming independent, and Belgium was pressured by the United Nations to liberate the Congo. By 1958, the demands for independence had gained momentum, behind such leaders as Patrice Lumumba and Joseph Kasavubu. Belgium quickly gave the Congo its independence in 1960 to avoid a war, but there had not been enough preparation, as not many Congolese were educated at that time and there were no working coalitions. Kasavubu became the first president, Lumumba the first head of government. Within the first weeks, the Belgians were hastily evacuated, leaving towns like Stanleyville a ghost town, sacked and destroyed by the Congolese.

Mobutu Sese Seko

Joseph-Désiré Mobutu (1930–1997) went to a Catholic boarding school and then into the army,

later becoming a journalist involved in independence politics in the Congo. Mobutu's mother was a hotel maid, a fact made much of by the dictator, who made her into a symbolic African Madonna. A series of rebellions followed Congolese independence. The Simba Rebellion in 1964 (referred to as the Second Rebellion in the book) involved tribesmen who believed they could not be hurt by bullets. They were led by shamans and by Pierre Mulele, a Maoist. The army under the command of Mobutu put down the rebellion, took power, and stabilized the government.

Mobutu renamed the country Zaire and himself Mobutu Sese Seko in the early 1970s, ultimately ruling from 1965 to 1997. He nationalized foreign-owned firms and became a dictator with a personal cult designed to purge the country of its colonial past; he took millions of dollars of the country's wealth for himself while the people starved and the infrastructure collapsed. He was backed by Western powers, especially the United States, because of his anti-Communist stance. He consolidated his power through a number of public executions, one of which is about to happen in Salim's town as he hurriedly leaves.

After the cold war ended, Mobutu lost support in the West. In 1997, he was thrown out by a

Child playing in the African bush (*Lucian Coman* / *Shutterstock.com*)

rebel force led by Laurent-Désiré Kabila, who became president and renamed the country the Democratic Republic of the Congo. Mobutu fled to Morocco and died of cancer that year. Naipaul's novel has been called pessimistic, but the Mobutu regime set the stage for a later, worse tragedy in the Second Congo War, or the Great War of Africa (1998–2004), which was fought among eight African countries and brought about millions of deaths from conflict, starvation, and disease.

CRITICAL OVERVIEW

A Bend in the River (1979) is the climax of Naipaul's middle period of the 1960s and 1970s, the time during which he became known as a serious internationally recognized political writer. He had already won the Booker Prize for *In a Free State* (1971), concerning the violence of modern Africa, and *A Bend in the River* was short-listed for the same prize. Many critics comment on Naipaul's dark view, but they recognize his superior writing and cogent analysis of third-world countries. Through Naipaul's middle period, critics begin to question his conservative stance toward his subject matter, though not as belligerently as with his later travel writing.

Linda R. Anderson, in "Ideas of Identity and Freedom in V. S. Naipaul and Joseph Conrad"— writing in 1978, even before *A Bend in the River* was published—compares the two authors based on Naipaul's praise of Conrad and previous treatment of Africa. Both authors, she comments, show characters imprisoned by their cultures, but Naipaul's books are "full of despair," whereas in Conrad's work there is some hope. In a 1979 review of *A Bend in the River* for the *New York Times Book Review*, Irving Howe notes Naipaul's "cool precision" but does not find him "a 'likable' writer, for he no longer performs and barely troubles to please" with his tale of "a complex entangling vision" of a country struggling for modernity. Howe questions whether a writer can morally limit himself to depicting wretchedness with no resolution. Elaine Campbell, in "A Refinement of Rage: V. S. Naipaul's *A Bend in the River*," notes the author's recurring "shudder of horror over the bush returning to engulf civilization" in his African books. The rage is more evident in *In a Free State* but modified and refined in *A Bend in the River*. Naipaul has admitted that he learned to temper his rage with logic while writing. She suspects the novel will be viewed as "neoimperialistic."

Lynda Prescott, in a 1984 article "Past and Present Darkness: Sources for V. S. Naipaul's *A Bend in the River*," sees Naipaul as continuing the image of African darkness established by Conrad, and confirmed for him by his own trips to Africa, even making Stanleyville, featured in Conrad's story of Kurtz, into the town at the bend of the river. The African rage refers to the madness that visits both colonizers and colonized in their mutual degradation, Prescott points out. Steven Blakemore, in "'An Africa of Words': V. S. Naipaul's *A Bend in the River*," focuses on cultures' self-conscious construction of civilization, with the European invention of history giving them power. He reports that "Salim sees that the European sense of self is linguistic." Naipaul shows that when the Africans similarly try to reinvent themselves with false words, they get "cultural schizophrenia." George Packer, in "V. S. Naipaul's Pursuit of Happiness," notes the controversy surrounding Naipaul's career, reviewing his development as a writer and constant denunciation from the left and concluding that his reputation as a conservative derives from his tragic view of the contradictions of third-world countries. In certain senses, the events of September 11, 2001, and global terrorism seem to have borne out his negative predictions. Packer concludes that Naipaul's rage at what he finds in the third world stems from his own internalized colonial background.

CRITICISM

Susan K. Andersen

Andersen is a writer and teacher with a Ph.D. in English. In the following essay, she considers how A Bend in the River *conveys its pessimistic view of Africa through the narrator's point of view, his interaction with other characters, and imagery.*

Patrick French named his 2008 biography of V. S. Naipaul *The World Is What It Is* after the first line of *A Bend in the River:* "The world is what it is; men who are nothing, who allow themselves to become nothing, have no place in it." This survival-of-the-fittest philosophy, as French points out, is Naipaul's own credo: "His achievement was an act of will, in which every situation and relationship would be subordinated to his ambition." Interestingly, no characters in *A Bend in the River* are able to realize this brutal philosophy of will except the dictator, the Big Man (Mobutu Sese Seko). The dictum, then, is tragically ironic, for none of the African characters are able to find a place in the modern world.

The novel has autobiographical elements, with Indar and Salim together most closely representing Naipaul's own experience. Indar, like Naipaul, is educated in England, but neither Indar, with his education, nor Salim's father-in-law, the talented merchant Nazruddin, can succeed in the outside world. They are disabled by their racial and colonial backgrounds. The novel has been faulted as a pessimistic and racist view of Africa, a modernized version of Conrad's *Heart of Darkness*. Why read it, then?

Even those who do not accept Naipaul's conclusions about the hopeless condition of third-world cultures agree that *A Bend in the River* is a postcolonial classic, vividly demonstrating the violent clash between races and cultures, between tradition and modernism. Bruce Bawer, in "Civilization and V. S. Naipaul," sees *A Bend in the River* as Naipaul's most horrific vision of social chaos. Naipaul accomplishes this vision through the point of view of Salim, his

> EVEN THOSE WHO DO NOT ACCEPT NAIPAUL'S CONCLUSIONS ABOUT THE HOPELESS CONDITION OF THIRD-WORLD CULTURES AGREE THAT *A BEND IN THE RIVER* IS A POSTCOLONIAL CLASSIC, VIVIDLY DEMONSTRATING THE VIOLENT CLASH BETWEEN RACES AND CULTURES, BETWEEN TRADITION AND MODERNISM."

interactions with other characters, and recurring imagery.

The first-person narrator is Salim, a Muslim Indian, and his coming of age in the Congo town parallels his adopted country's coming of age as an independent nation, with as little hope. Through his eyes, readers witness the Big Man's evil transformation of the land, which makes the European colonization, admittedly cruel to the natives, seem like heaven. Peter Hughes, in *V. S. Naipaul*, speaks of the author's documenting "a world devolving through history toward dereliction and loss." Salim's growth is not so much maturation as it is a moral awareness of the corruption going on around him. At first, he witnesses this decadence and begins to slide into it himself. Naipaul's use of a narrator who is a stranger to the area and to African politics is effective because his innocent reporting of details creates the shock of an eyewitness account.

Salim is no moral paragon but a decent person who has grown up in an ordered world. He feels guilty about taking his pleasure with the local native women and worried that he is not a model for Metty, but little by little, he abandons his moral superiority. He begins to see things he would rather sweep under the rug, and he lets them go, following Mahesh's advice to "carry on" and ignore the rest. Salim creates blinders for himself with his strict routine of going to the shop, to the Hellenic Club for squash, and to the nightclubs, mingling only with other foreigners. At first, he only worries about the sporadic violence as driving away business. He feels the foreigners are somehow immune to the local rebellions. Making money, meanwhile, is his only ticket out of town. Nazruddin tells Salim

WHAT DO I READ NEXT?

- Chinua Achebe's *Things Fall Apart* (1959) is an important Nigerian novel describing pre-colonial tribal civilization. The story of Okonkwo of the Ibo tribe and his tragic reaction to colonialism gives an African view of history.

- Joseph Conrad's *Heart of Darkness* (1899) is the underlying text informing Naipaul's *A Bend in the River*. Both stories describe the primitive nature of the Congo and its "darkness," but Conrad's story shows a white man's brutality, while Naipaul shows a black man's (Mobutu's).

- *Out of Africa* (1937) is a memoir by the Danish author Karen von Blixen-Finecke, who wrote as Isak Dinesen, about her colonial coffee farm in Kenya, where she was one of the Europeans living outside Nairobi from 1914 to 1931. Her close relationship with the natives and the breathtaking beauty of the land is preserved in her richly descriptive scenes.

- Wangari Maathai, the Nobel Peace Prize winner of 2004, is the founder of the Green Belt movement in Africa and the first woman Ph.D. in biology from East Africa. Her book *Unbowed: A Memoir* (2007) details her environmental work with the women of Kenya planting trees to reforest the land, though she was jailed several times by the government for her democratic influence.

- Naipaul's *A House for Mr Biswas* (1961) is considered his early masterpiece about life on Trinidad. The story of Mohun Biswas, modeled on Naipaul's father, is a dark comedy about his search for a home, symbolic of the postcolonial search for identity.

- *Child of Dandelions* (2008), by Shenaaz Nanji, is a young-adult novel about the expulsion of Asians from Uganda in 1972. Fifteen-year-old Sabine lives in a wealthy Indian family in Kampala, Uganda. When Idi Amin comes to power, her world falls apart, with her African friend Zena suddenly believing she is the enemy.

---

it is easier to get into the country than to get out: "That is a private fight. Everybody has to find his own way." Salim is set up for failure from the beginning, as he himself realizes there cannot be a new life for him in the crumbling African interior. Dagmar Barnouw, in *Naipaul's Strangers*, mentions that Naipaul focuses his narratives on "diminished people in self-destructing societies."

The Big Man's political regime is never presented directly but only obliquely, through Salim's awareness of local events, gossip, pamphlets, and the terror of the people. The underlying fear and instability are finely registered through the many little seismic movements of his point of view, though he does not follow politics or have an ideology. The town is an explosive mingling of the races and a place of open danger. Salim grows aware of "African rage, the wish to destroy,

regardless of the consequences," in viewing the ruins of European buildings with their statues smashed or defaced and vines growing back over the deserted European suburb. African rage is a constant background threat. "You felt like a ghost," Salim says, "not from the past, but from the future," as though his life has already been lived without him.

Salim tries to keep his hope alive by reading popular science magazines, feeling as though "making something of myself, using all my faculties." He thus identifies with the Western world instead of Africa and his Muslim past. Wimal Dissanayake and Carmen Wickramagamage, in *Self and Colonial Desire*, point out that Naipaul's narratives fashion the self in relation to the third world by identifying with the values of European Enlightenment rationality. They cite Naipaul's essay "Our Universal Civilization," from the *New York Review of Books* issue of January 31, 1991, in which Naipaul tells how he got out of his narrow ethnic background by joining the larger intellectual civilization of the West. This essay still circulates on the Internet, celebrating individual choice, the life of the intellect, and personal achievement. Indar excitedly announces this path of salvation to Salim in view of his trip to London. Indar leaves his tradition behind and tries to invent his own modern identity; yet he is fighting a losing battle, for Westerners are better equipped for the fight.

Indar tries to introduce Salim to current events by taking him to the Domain to meet Raymond and Yvette, European advisers to the Big Man. For a while, Salim tries to join in the hope of Congo modernization, until he reads Raymond's academic papers on African history and realizes Raymond does not know what he is talking about. Raymond gets his information from the slanted newspapers; he does not talk to the people on the street, who are in a panic over the arbitrary nature of the dictator's decrees. Salim has to let go of all the rules he once knew: "In the end we couldn't say where we stood." In this way, Naipaul's message for postcolonial societies seems ambivalent, as Helen Hayward points out in *The Enigma of V. S. Naipaul: Sources and Contexts*. Should they embrace modernity or not? *A Bend in the River* shows the people damned if they do and damned if they do not. Robert D. Hamner, in *V. S. Naipaul*, notes the strong flavor of the absurd as a regular theme in Naipaul, where humans often struggle irrationally against overwhelming odds.

Salim's interactions with other characters reinforce the ambiguity of his position. Father Huismans, for instance, who runs the school, represents the remains of colonialism. He collects African masks, looking at African culture from a collector's point of view, as though it is already dead. Salim admires him, but his murder and mutilation show that old Africa is still very much alive. Salim thinks the priest's death is a message to "be careful … and remember where we were."

Ferdinand, Zabeth's son, is a native from the bush who becomes educated as a new African man, ready to become part of the modern administration. Salim, watching Ferdinand's growth, witnesses how far the African consciousness must come from traditional village life to join the modern world. He admires how Ferdinand "leapt centuries" to assume leadership. Yet at the end, Ferdinand, now a commissioner, admits, "Everything that was given to me was given to me to destroy me. . . . Nowhere is safe now." The white man's culture has not freed the African.

Yvette, Salim's beautiful white lover, teaches him his place in the modern world. He is enchanted seeing her at a party where the songs of Joan Baez play in the background, promising political justice. He feels he is finally being saved in a higher world of beauty and ideals. In reality, he finds himself dominated by a bored white woman and becomes what she wants in order to keep up the illusion that he is worthy to win her. When he perceives that she is dumping him, he beats her up, to be surprised and totally shattered by his violent behavior. She regularly chooses dark-skinned men, it is implied, as a thrill. Salim is humiliated at the loss of his integrity, symbolically playing out colonial submission and then experiencing the African rage at being used. His attempt to identify with the West fails, but he is not able to become part of Africa either.

The backward and impenetrable wildness of Africa is represented in the descriptions of the river, the bush, and the choking river hyacinths: "The river and the forest were like presences, and much more powerful than you. You felt unprotected, an intruder." The Big Man pretends he is going to make the banks of the two-hundred-mile-long Congo River into an industrial park; Salim likes to imagine the land being made small and manageable but knows that the river with its rapids does not respond to human control.

The steamer that goes down the Congo is a decaying remnant of the European civilization. The Africans tie their dugouts to the steamer to sell their wares, and the passenger barge for Africans trails behind. In the last scene, Salim escapes on the steamer for an uncertain future, while the river hyacinths tangle the boats, and the dugouts and barge are set loose. Gunshots are heard, and the natives are understood to be left behind to their bloody fate in the Congo. They have not been able to catch the boat of modernism as a way out of the primitive.

Ranu Samantrai, in "Claiming the Burden: Naipaul's Africa," sees the novel as a continuing apology for European colonialism. The West, Naipaul insists, has evolved as a civilization,

Muslim man *(paul prescott | Shutterstock.com)*

while third-world countries have been mired in their past. Samantrai points out the flaw in Naipaul's logic that has continued to incense other postcolonial writers. The Nigerian author Chinua Achebe, for instance, describes an African civilization before colonialism. Naipaul's vision in *A Bend in the River* on the other hand, alludes to African tradition but denies Africa any civilization of its own, as Samantrai notes. Dissanayake and Wickramagamage point out that Naipaul does not pay attention to alternate realities or scenarios for third-world countries or the contributions they can make. Dagmar Barnouw defends Naipaul's critique of postcolonial societies, saying that the author does not see his fiction as a form of activism, as many postcolonial writers do. He feels it is not his mission to show the way out but merely to record the problems. He "has learned to pose questions that go to the core of cultural (ethnic) plurality," she concludes.

Source: Susan K. Andersen, Critical Essay on *A Bend in the River*, in *Novels for Students*, Gale, Cengage Learning, 2011.

George Packer

In the following essay, Packer traces Naipaul's literary development.

In October 1953, V. S. Naipaul's father died in Port of Spain, Trinidad. He died in disappointment and misery. He had been waiting to see his son, who was finishing a degree at Oxford, and waiting for his own book of stories to find a publisher. All his life he had struggled to be more than a journalist for the Trinidad *Guardian*—to be a writer. V. S. Naipaul had not so much been handed this ambition as become its living extension. "I had always looked upon my life as a continuation of his—a continuation which, I hoped, would also be a fulfillment." To read the letters published recently in *Between Father and Son* is to see where Naipaul got the spareness of his style, right down to the semi-colons.

Naipaul's mother and older sister pleaded with him to come home to Trinidad and take up his family duty. Before his death, his father had asked the same thing, and Naipaul had written from Oxford: "If I did so, I shall die from intellectual starvation." With his father dead, the

> THE TRUTH IS THAT NAIPAUL HAS NO EASILY IDENTIFIABLE POLITICAL VIEWS. THE GREAT IDEOLOGICAL STRUGGLE OF HIS WRITING LIFE, THE COLD WAR, IS TOTALLY IGNORED IN HIS WORK. HE HASN'T CHOSEN SIDES IN COMPETING VISIONS OF HOW MODERN SOCIETIES SHOULD BE ORGANIZED. HE IS PROFOUNDLY SKEPTICAL OF EVERY IDEOLOGY."

pressure to return became intense. "Our family was in distress. I should have done something for them, gone back to them. But, without having become a writer, I couldn't go back." And so for three years Naipaul put his family off. He was living in London, writing occasional scripts for the BBC Caribbean Service, and trying to complete the book that would make him a writer and lift his family out of debt.

Years later, Naipaul would come across a de Chirico painting to which Guillaume Apollinaire had given the title *The Enigma of Arrival*. In his book of the same title, Naipaul wrote, "I felt that in an indirect, poetical way the title referred to something in my own experience." It gave him the idea for a story:

My narrator...would arrive—for a reason I had yet to work out—at that classical port with the walls and gateways like cutouts. He would walk past that muffled figure on the quayside. He would move from that silence and desolation, that blankness, to a gateway or door. He would enter there and be swallowed by the life and noise of a crowded city. (I imagined something like an Indian bazaar scene.) The mission he had come on—family business, study, religious initiation—would give him encounters and adventures. He would enter interiors, of houses and temples. Gradually there would come to him a feeling that he was getting nowhere; he would lose his sense of mission; he would begin to know only that he was lost. His feeling of adventure would give way to panic. He would want to escape, to get back to the quayside and his ship. But he wouldn't know how. I imagined some religious ritual in which, led on by kindly people, he would unwittingly take part and find himself the intended victim. At the moment of crisis he

would come upon a door, open it, and find himself back on the quayside of arrival. He has been saved; the world is as he remembered it. Only one thing is missing now. Above the cut-out walls and buildings there is no mast, no sail. The antique ship has gone. The traveler has lived out his life.

Put this unwritten fantasy alongside the moment when Naipaul chose his vocation over the expectations of his family. It required an immense leap of faith for a young Indian in the grip of "a panic about failing to be what I should be" not to lose his own sense of mission. His letters home, often filled with shame, also display an astonishing assurance: "Look, I am going to be a success as a writer. I know that. I have gambled all my future on that possibility. Do you want to throw your lot with me or don't you?" And yet all his life the enigma of arrival has haunted Naipaul—the sense of living out his life, like the traveler in the unwritten tale, without having achieved his purpose.

The bet paid off. At the end of 1955, he sold his first novel, *The Mystic Masseur*. Half a century and two dozen books later, Naipaul at last has his Nobel Prize.

When the announcement came last fall—after years of rumors, short lists, and steadily avowed indifference from Naipaul himself—an article in *Le Monde Diplomatique* compared the selection to Henry Kissinger's receiving the Nobel Peace Prize. According to Pascale Casanova, Naipaul "disavows his past; he sees himself as an English writer...[He] is contemptuous of the peoples of the South, and he is a mouthpiece for extreme conservative and nationalist views." And, as if that weren't bad enough, "His favorite novelist is Balzac."

Through much of his career, Naipaul has been denounced from the left, especially by partisans of third world countries and cultures, those societies that he's called "half-made." Derek Walcott, a fellow West Indian Nobelist, attacked the author of *The Enigma of Arrival* as racist. And, as his rejection by the left grew, Naipaul became something of a hero to the right, the one dark-skinned writer who could be counted on to tell the third world what it didn't want to hear about itself. The embrace culminated in this country a decade ago with an invitation for Naipaul to speak before the conservative Manhattan Institute. Last fall, when the World Trade Center attacks and Naipaul's Nobel followed each other in rapid succession, the address to the Manhattan Institute circulated on the Internet.

Its title is "Our Universal Civilization," and in an unspoken way, it takes one back to the crucial period when Naipaul defied his family's wishes and stayed in London to become a writer. Naipaul turns seventy this summer, in the same month that his latest work, a collection of his essays called *The Writer and the World*, including the Manhattan Institute address, is to be published. He appears to have reached the end of his career. His most recent novel, *Half a Life*, turning over much-plowed ground, is barely half a book. V. S. Naipaul seems to have said what he has to say. Seen from this vantage point, the course of his work follows an internal logic that was not at all clear before. The decision not to return to Trinidad, the pivotal moment of his literary career, also holds the key to the vision that receives its most explicit expression in "Our Universal Civilization." And Naipaul himself turns out not to be what his shallower critics and admires imagined.

His writing life falls into three phases. First there was an early, comic phase. Working alarmingly hard, he produced four books while still in his twenties, books about Trinidadian Indians and their marginal lives and strivings and futilities, culminating in the great portrait of his father, *A House for Mr. Biswas*. Trinidad hasn't yet become one of the "half-made societies." Naipaul is recording what he knows from childhood, and everything—even the epic-length *Biswas*—comes across as a dense miniature, befitting the scale of the insular world where he would have faced intellectual starvation. The speed of composition betrays what Naipaul would call "a fear of extinction."

Then, knowing that he had come to the end of his childhood material, and riding the confidence of having written a masterpiece, in the early 1960s Naipaul began to travel. The travel began his middle phase, a severe and tragic phase, for the places he traveled to, repeatedly, even obsessively (back to the West Indies where racial revolution was stirring; then to his ancestral India; and finally to newly independent Africa) brought out a new kind of panic in Naipaul. This wasn't the merely personal raw nerves of a young colonial becoming a writer in the imperial center. His travels put politics in his writing, and his panic became a political panic:

The new politics, the curious reliance of men on institutions they were yet working to undermine, the simplicity of beliefs and the hideous simplicity of actions, the corruption of causes, half-made societies that seemed doomed to remain half-made: these were the things that began to preoccupy me. They were not things from which I could detach myself.

Instead of suppressing this political panic in order to write, he wrote directly out of it—beginning with *The Mimic Men* (1967), a lesser-known novel that marks the start of the new phase, and then in the novels from the 1970s that made him an international writer: *In a Free State*, *Guerrillas*, and *A Bend in the River*.

The violence that characterizes these books, physical and emotional, confirms that Naipaul could not easily "detach himself." He had nowhere to go, no position from which to view the world's disorders with equanimity. The Europeans in these books appear to have a free ride in the third world countries where they seek personal or political fulfillment, dabbling in Caribbean revolution or African authenticity, only to find out in brutal, sometimes fatal ways that the late colonial world has turned back on them in nihilistic rage. A group of expatriates in *A Bend in the River*, set in a thinly disguised Zaire under Mobutu, sit in a room listening to Joan Baez songs, and only the narrator, an Indian from the east coast of Africa, entranced though he is by the sound of the voice, knows that "it was make-believe.... You couldn't listen to sweet songs about injustice unless you expected justice and received it much of the time. You couldn't sing songs about the end of the world unless—like the other people in that room, so beautiful with such simple things: African mats on the floor and African hangings on the wall and spears and masks—you felt that the world was going on and you were safe in it. How easy it was, in that room, to make those assumptions!" The narrator's own credo, set down in the opening sentence, is that of a man who lives outside the room, without the luxury of indulgent fantasies: "The world is what it is: men who are nothing, who allow themselves to become nothing, have no place in it."

And so Naipaul's great novels from the middle phase gave him the reputation of a conservative. Not only that: a traitor as well, for a writer with brown skin was not supposed to point out the shams and illusions of third world politics. In fact, there's no use pretending that Naipaul's political panic made him a sympathetic or even fair interpreter of the post-colonial world. Under his scrutiny Africa in particular is prone to dissolving in a singularly powerful mood of menace, fear, and disgust. Naipaul never tells you what country is inducing these feelings; it is, indiscriminately, "Africa." After picking up a couple of African hitchhikers, one of the English expatriates driving through Africa in *In a Free State* (1971), for which Naipaul won the Booker Prize, comments on the "smell of Africa ... It is a smell of rotting vegetation and Africans. One is very much like the other."

Guerrillas (1975), about racial disturbance on a Caribbean island, is even uglier. It ends with a scene in which a mixed-race man of revolutionary delusions sodomizes a white Englishwoman who's taken a passing sexual and political interest in him.

... This is the Naipaul most people think they know. The ruthlessness of observation is matched by the precision of language, as if Naipaul can only represent the source of panic with the at most syntactical control. "The greatest writing is a disturbing vision offered from a position of strength," he once said. "Aspire to that." But the idea of a supreme and cold-hearted detachment is an illusion. Naipaul couldn't enter the experience of his blighted characters as deeply as he does, even in a novel like *Guerrillas*, if he were not writing about rage and despair from the inside.

It was these novels, from the middle phase, that introduced me to Naipaul. I read him before I knew not to like him. I had come back from living in Africa in my early twenties, I was trying to write about it, and Naipaul's ability to evoke the anxiety and disorientation I was feeling presented a model from which a young writer could learn. I couldn't feel close to him as I did to other writers—the ugliness was too much—and I was fairly sure that if I met him I wouldn't like him (Saul Bellow once said that after spending an hour with Naipaul he could skip Yom Kippur that year). But as a master of literary craft and a writer fearlessly dedicated to a vision, Naipaul inspired, and still does. It didn't matter that his vision of Africa was different from mine and in some ways repelled me. It was the intensity of his commitment that mattered.

A Bend in the River is Naipaul's masterpiece, and also the last novel of the middle phase. Its imaginative range is broader than anything

before it. Indians, Europeans, and Africans are all portrayed as individuals caught in the swell of history, trying to realize themselves against their own and the world's limitations. In the middle of the novel there is an extraordinary passage, a monologue filling fifteen pages. Indar, a childhood friend of the narrator—both Indians from the east coast of Africa, meeting again as adults in Mobutu's Zaire—tells the story of how he went down from Oxford to London in search of a career. In the story, he presents himself at India House as a candidate for the Indian diplomatic service and is humiliated by a series of lackeys and time-servers. He leaves in a daze of rage and starts walking along the Thames, playing with a fantasy of going back to his old village life. Then he begins to notice the wrought-iron dolphins on lamp standards along the Embankment, the wrought-iron camels acting as bench supports. And he has an insight:

> I understood that London wasn't simply a place that was there, as people say of mountains, but that it had been made by men, that men had given attention to details as minute as those camels.
>
> I began to understand at the same time that my anguish about being a man adrift was false, that for me that dream of home and security was nothing more than a dream of isolation, anachronistic and stupid and very feeble. I belonged to myself alone. I was going to surrender my manhood to nobody. For someone like me there was only one civilization and one place—London, or a place like it. Every other kind of life was make-believe. Home—what for? To hide? To bow to our great men? For people in our situation, led into slavery, that is the biggest trap of all. We have nothing. We solace ourselves with that idea of the great men of our tribe, the Gandhi and the Nehru, and we castrate ourselves. "Here, take my manhood and invest it for me. Take my manhood and be a greater man yourself, for my sake!" No! I want to be a man myself.

In the middle of his great novel about Africa, Naipaul is suddenly writing the central story of his own life, of his younger self—of that moment when he decided not to return to Trinidad after his father's death. And this would become the constant subject of his third, late phase—an autobiographical phase, an obsessive and, finally, exhausted return to his origins as a writer, in books like *Finding the Center* (1984), *The Enigma of Arrival* (1987), *A Way in the World* (1994), and last year's *Half a Life*. The anxiety has subsided. The fiction has turned inward, and the nonfiction (for Naipaul has been an equally obsessive traveler, writing journalism about the troubled corners of the world well into his seventh decade) has grown more generous—his portraits of static and decaying societies are no less harsh, but individuals trapped within those societies emerge as the true voices of these books.

Then what are we to make of the charge that Naipaul has repudiated his background, that he identifies with the oppressor and despises the oppressed? The truth is that Naipaul has no easily identifiable political views. The great ideological struggle of his writing life, the cold war, is totally ignored in his work. He hasn't chosen sides in competing visions of how modern societies should be organized. He is profoundly skeptical of every ideology. What interests him is the individual, and his fiercest passion has always been for the individual to be free from the dead hand of the given. The closest he's come to expressing something like a vision of the good society is the Manhattan Institute talk. In it, he tells the story of a young Indonesian whom he met years ago, and who was thwarted in his desire to become a poet. Naipaul then describes the "universal civilization" that made room for him, a young Indian from Trinidad, when he was trying to become a writer.

> I would say that it is the civilization that both gave the prompting and the idea of the literary vocation; and also gave the means to fulfill that prompting; the civilization that enables me to make that journey from the periphery to the center; the civilization that links me not only to this audience but also that now not-so-young man in Java whose background was as ritualized as my own, and on whom—as on me—the outer world had worked, and given the ambition to write.

It sounds like utter hubris and the worst sort of solipsism: the "universal civilization" is the one that made room for Naipaul to become a writer. And yet, in one form or another, this is the longing of millions of people the world over—those oppressed and nameless masses whom Naipaul is supposed to despise. It is an idea that his critics take entirely for granted. Looking back over the half-century of his writing life, one can now see that his purpose all along was to give value to that longing. At the end of his talk to the Manhattan Institute, Naipaul suddenly mentions the phrase "the pursuit of happiness." He says: "So much is contained in

it: the idea of the individual, responsibility, choice, the life of the intellect, the idea of vocation and perfectibility and achievement. It is an immense human idea." Naipaul, often accused of making himself over as an Englishman, turns out to be an American.

Source: George Packer, "V.S. Naipaul's Pursuit of Happiness," in *Dissent*, Summer 2002, pp. 85–89.

Ranu Samantrai

In the following excerpt, Samantrai examines the function of imperialistic discourse in A Bend in the River *and describes the novel as "a fictional documentation of the political shift from a colonial to postcolonial Africa."*

In his work on the epistemology of the anthropological endeavor, Johannes Fabian argues that the "West" constructs its relationship with "the Rest" (28) through a notion of time that affirms "difference as *distance*" (16). Fabian is concerned primarily with the notion of modernity, the trope through which the West locates itself and constructs the difference of its racial and cultural others. Inherent in his "Politics of Time," however, is a politics of sexuality that, in addition to creating a teleological history for the triumph of the normative Western subject, also posits a specifically gendered location for the Rest. The epistemology Fabian describes is identical to that which informs the neocolonial vision of V. S. Naipaul, perhaps the most widely read contemporary apologist for European colonialism.

To locate his own writing, Naipaul declares, "I do not write for Indians, who in any case do not read. My work is only possible in a liberal, civilized country. It is not possible in primitive societies" (Hardwick 1). His explanation of the link between personal empowerment, literature, and international relations is a small and perhaps trivial example of the residue of the age of the European empires. But the legitimating discourses of imperialism have proven to be surprisingly intransigent, shaping the relations between West and Rest long after the end of direct military occupation of the colonies. In this essay I intend to investigate terms which derive their salience from the logic that once justified imperialism, and which define the still stable boundaries between the major players in the colonial drama. I shall do so by examining their function in a particular text, Naipaul's *A Bend in the River*, which provides a fictional documentation of the political shift from colonial to postcolonial Africa. I take Naipaul's novel to be a local enactment of the process of constructing a logic that enables an expression of imperialism to appear reasonable, even inevitable, despite the loss of the context of European empires. Hence my analysis of this text belongs in the project defined by Paul Gilroy as the ongoing task of "mapping the changing contours of racist ideologies, the semantic fields in which they operate, their special rhetoric, and their internal fractures, as well as their continuities" (263).

A Bend in the River provides a map for reading the "racial subjectification and subjection" of social agents (Goldberg xii). Naipaul creates racial groupings through the language of gender, which in turn is based upon a developmental paradigm of the masculine as progressive differentiation from the feminine. An unquestioned understanding of time as linear and forward moving allows Naipaul to place his characters on an evolutionary scale of racial and gendered development. *A Bend in the River* thus explains colonial rule and the continuing supremacy of the West as the inevitable consequence of the natural laws of progress. Not surprisingly, the violence of colonialism is also explained away as the exercise of the legitimate and benevolent authority of the father over both mothers and children. In other words, Naipaul creates anew the notion of "modern man," drawing upon the concepts of progress and normative masculinity to shore up a beleaguered ideology of Euro-American supremacy. It is, by now, commonplace to note the inextricability of race and gender in the rhetoric of imperialism. The novelty of *A Bend in the River* lies in Naipaul's deployment of this rhetoric at the moment the colony wins its independence. The novel thus takes on the task of defending the practice of colonialism by demonstrating the continuing veracity of its logic in the postcolonial world.

Modernity, according to Fabian, can be traced to "a succession of attempts to secularize Judeo-Christian Time by generalizing and universalizing it." These attempts, most famously undertaken by social evolutionists, undermined the Judeo-Christian understanding of time as "the medium of sacred history" and eventually replaced "faith in salvation by faith in progress and industry." But the teleology remained essentially the same, for secularized Time still "'accomplished' or brought about things in the course of evolution," thus providing a way to

chart the flow of human history. Anthropology, the discourse through which the West articulates its relationship with the Rest, combined the scheme of developmental stages leading to civilization with "the most celebrated scientific achievement of that period, the comparative method" to generate a hierarchy of cultures on a scale of evolutionary time:

> Anthropology contributed above all to the intellectual justification of the colonial enterprise. It gave to politics and economics—both concerned with human Time—a firm belief in "natural," i.e., evolutionary Time. It promoted a scheme in terms of which not only past cultures, but all living societies were irrevocably placed on a temporal slope, a stream of Time—some upstream, others down-stream. Civilization, evolution, development, acculturation, modernization (and their cousins, industrialization, urbanization) are all terms whose conceptual content derives, in ways that can be specific, from evolutionary Time.

As an inheritor of this epistemological tradition, Naipaul reserves the space of modernity for the European civilization and, despite their obvious presence in the physical present, assigns various stages in the evolutionary past to non-Europeans. Hence, although his protagonist's flight away from the moment of decolonization and toward a safely European town is obviously a wish to recover the past of the European empire, Naipaul represents it as a wish to fall into step with the forward march of progress. Moreover, differences between various races and societies are attributed to their positions in the evolution of civilization. The positions themselves are not contingent upon the relational field of political power, but are fixed by the essence of the race. Thus, in his version of African history Salim, the novel's protagonist, can establish the conquest of the weak by the strong as not only justified but inevitable. Here, for instance, is Salim's explanation of the transfer of power in Africa from Arabs to Europeans:

> For Europe it [advancing into the center of the continent] was one little probe. For the Arabs of central Africa it was their all; the Arabian energy that had pushed them into Africa had died down at its source, and their power was like the light of a star that travels on after the star itself has become dead. Arab power had vanished [. . .].

There is no struggle, no domination or resistance. Arabs lose their "energy" and simply vanish. Europeans, an "intelligent and energetic people," step in to fill the void (23). An underlying logical necessity allows human beings to remain innocent, unimplicated in these shifting relations of power. This passage suggests that natural, universal laws provide a neat order for human history that renders irrelevant questions regarding local oppressions and the historical violence of victory. "The Now and then," says Fabian, "is absorbed by the Always of the rules of the game."

But if the transfer of power is always so easy, so much a part of the inevitable march of progress, why then does this novel determinedly oppose it when Africans are the beneficiaries? Why can decolonization not be viewed as another step forward in the grand march of progress? The tautology established between "Europe" and "modern" forecloses this reading of African independence. The primary groups of actors in Naipaul's Africa—Europeans, Arabs and an adjacent group of Indians, and Africans—each manifest a discrete sexual energy that determines their position on the evolutionary ladder leading to modern man. Africans are the most feminized and the least evolved; not surprisingly, Europeans occupy the pinnacles of both masculinity and development. Arabs fall somewhere in between, but do so because of a curious twist: they are not newcomers to civilization, but are rendered effeminate because their civilizations are too old. In other words, while Africans are pre-oedipal, Arabs are senile, made impotent by their great age. In each case, males are taken to be representatives of the group, their virility serving as the measure of the group's development. Together, the three "races" of Naipaul's Africa form a parable of the colonial encounter that affirms European colonial rule as the only logical order that can govern all fairly.

To accomplish this differentiation of racial energies, Naipaul relies on the notion of the racial zone. Specifically, his Africa is a gendered topos. Implicit in the conflation of geography with people is the idea, common to much European racial theory, of "divinely ordained racial zones" (Banton 10). The dark continent gives birth to its own dark people, and together they represent the force of a past so distant and murky that its physical contemporaneity poses a threat to the light of the modern present. Thus Salim's early hopes of finding Europe and moving forward in the story of progress fade as he drives "deeper into Africa" and encounters the bush. Somehow, simply by looking at the landscape he knows that he is "going in the wrong direction," that the land itself precludes the

possibilities of "a new life." Traveling into the heart of Africa, even in an attempt to meet Europe, necessarily involves traveling backward through temporal zones. Here Salim is very much in the tradition of the colonial explorer who traveled in order to complete his knowledge of history. As one contributor to that tradition put it, "The philosophical traveller, sailing to the ends of the earth, is in fact travelling in time; he is exploring the past; every step he makes is the passage of an age" (Degérando 63).

The land of Africa, here called bush, itself becomes evidence of arrested development, as does its people's putative proximity to a state of nature. Salim describes European and Arab energy as always productive, the energy of beating back the bush to establish the fragile hold of human civilization. He admires Arab power at its height on the African continent: "Once, great explorers and warriors, the Arabs had ruled. They had pushed into the interior and had built towns and planted orchards in the forest." The consequences of their eventual failure are a predictable victory for the enemy of culture: "Their towns had disappeared, swallowed up in bush." Arabs and Europeans establish civil societies by taming their natural surroundings and creating civilizations out of bush. When Salim says that "at the bend in the river there had grown up a European, and not an Arab town," he makes the struggle to civilize Africa a task for foreign races. In his story there is no African civilization. Instead, African takeovers result not from the energy of human beings, but from a precivilized nature that is essentially destructive, the enemy of human endeavor. The power that this nature grants to its creatures is strangely devoid of human will or energy: "The slaves had swamped the masters; the Arabian race of the master had virtually disappeared."

In contrast to this ahistorical African essence of destructive anti-energy, the waxing and waning of the positive energies of Arabs and Europeans shape history. Inheriting from his colonial intellectual predecessors the belief that the "failure to build cities [is] incontrovertible proof of barbarism" (Pagden 70–71), Salim constructs a hierarchy of cultures in terms of complexity of social organization and distance from nature. At the bottom of his ladder, Africans are indistinguishable from the bush, acting as agents of its destructive force. They live in "hidden villages," are defined by tribal membership and isolated in a "safe world, protected from other men by forest and clogged-up waterways." Next on the developmental ladder, Arabs establish the larger, more complex social organizations of towns. They clear and cultivate the bush and link Africa with other parts of the world through trade routes. But as our guide through this mythic history of the African continent points out, the "Arab town [which once existed at the bend in the river] would have been only a little more substantial than the African settlements, and technologically not much more advanced."

Finally, when the Arabs accomplish all they can and run out of energy, Europeans step in to complete the civilizing process. They incorporate Africa into international empires and establish cities, providing in their technology evidence of their advanced evolution and superior virility. Under their rule the continent knows a "miraculous peace": they control the destructive nature of Africa and of "the African personality," allowing men to "pay little attention to tribal boundaries" that thwart the development of individual autonomy and collective accomplishment. European rule makes the continent accessible to explorers, traders, and settlers, all of whom serve the important function, as "agents of Europe," of beating back the hostile bush and bringing it to some degree of civilization. So "for a short while before independence," they succeed in making the African land "part of the present." Again, the narrative suggests that the flow of progress is as smooth and uncontested, with power passing along appropriately from the outdated to the modern, always to those most fit to rule.

In a provocative essay on the psychology of power and resistance during British rule in India, Ashis Nandy has argued that British imperialism invariably used a "homology between sexual and political dominance" to justify itself. Naipaul's conflation of evolutionary and gender hierarchies implies that the sexual energy and character of a race can be mapped over time: the Arab contribution exists in the past; only Europeans are described as currently "an intelligent and energetic people, and at the peak of their powers." Thus colonialism is transformed into a phenomenon of the biological, rather than the political world. And given the inevitability of the biological, objections to the European domination of Africa appear increasingly unreasonable.

If the "probes" of the colonial endeavor are the expression of the peculiar and obviously masculine energy of a race, then it is only logical that the group with superior virility should win. With Arabs and Europeans occupying the male position in this intercourse, Africa becomes the female body upon which they prove their masculine prowess. Africans are never represented in the masculine position; indeed, while Europeans and Arabs have the energy for geographic penetration, Africans are never said to have any energy at all. Rather, they and their continent "swamp" and "swallow" their masters, posing by their destructive, feminine behavior the threat of castration to masculine intruders. In Salim's chronology, then, decolonization is an aberration in the orderly, progressive process of change. The sign of its abnormality is the decay of the European towns as they are reclaimed by the bush. Over and again the refrain is sounded of everything returning to the bush as Africans take over from Europeans. Without the visible presence of modernity in the form of European bodies and technology, there is nothing to prevent the land and its natives from destroying the foreign cultivation of civilization and returning to their natural barbaric state.

For Naipaul, the racial zone is both temporal and gendered: everything touched by Africa and Africans not only returns to bush, but is simultaneously feminized. When the palace built by a "great man of our [the Muslim] community" is taken over by the new nation's army, its occupation by Africans is immediately evident in the "women's washing hung out in the partitioned verandahs upstairs and downstairs." The movement toward the feminine after independence is deliberately encouraged by the nation's new President, who creates his political persona as the true son of Africa by dressing in African garb, addressing his people in a common slang and, most important, by making his mother the representative "poor woman of Africa." The President's mother, who financed her son's education by working as a maid in a hotel catering to Europeans, serves as a symbol of the oppression suffered under colonial rule. Her extreme vulnerability as a poor black woman working for white employers makes her the ideal focal point around which the various peoples of the nation can become one group. The President's pilgrimage to his mother's village to establish a shrine in her honor is simultaneously an attempt "to give sanctity to the bush of Africa." All these gestures of valorization of Africa—its land, historical experience, and people—mark the President as an enemy of the values of modernity.

He chooses the feminine, destructive power of the bush and the female victim of colonial energy as the referent for African identity and unity. In Naipaul's parable of the development of civilization, the President provides proof that African rule can only encourage the continent to descend the evolutionary ladder of gendered development....

Source: Ranu Samantrai, "Claiming the Burden: Naipaul's Africa," in *Research in African Literature*, Vol. 31, No. 1, Spring 2000, pp. 50–62.

Christopher Wise

In the following excerpt, Wise contrasts the views of Chinua Achebe and Naipaul on the subject of modern African history and culture as evinced in Achebe's Things Fall Apart *and Naipaul's* A Bend in the River.

> Works of art can fully embody the *promesse du bonheur* only when they have been uprooted from their native soil and have set out along the path to their own destruction. Proust recognized this. This procedure which today relegates every work of art to the museum, even Picasso's most recent sculpture, is irreversible. It is not solely reprehensible, however, for it presages a situation in which art, having completed its estrangement from human ends, returns to life.
>
> —Adorno, *Prisms*

> In the beginning it is like trampling on a garden. In the end you are just walking on ground. That is the way we have to learn to live now.
>
> —Indar in Naipaul's *A Bend in the River*

INTRODUCTION

The extent of Joseph Conrad's impact on both Chinua Achebe and V. S. Naipaul has been copiously documented by both literary critics and scholars, and even by the authors themselves in numerous occasional writings, interviews, and literary essays. But if Achebe's *Things Fall Apart* contests and negates Conrad's previous negation and distortion of Africa and Africans in *Heart of Darkness*, Naipaul's more recent *A Bend in the River* not only reaffirms Conrad's more pessimistic—if not overtly racialist—perspective on Africans and their history, it also serves as the historical and determinate negation of Achebe's now widely influential (but not conclusive) negation of Conrad's novel. Like the history of the novel in Europe then (or anywhere, for that matter), the history of the novel in Africa involves a basic process of determinate negation in which one literary work often criticizes and complicates another. In other words,

as competing ideologemes or discursive formations that seek (however unsuccessfully) to resolve the contradictions and crises of material necessity within their very formal or generic structures, novels such as Achebe's *Things Fall Apart* and Naipaul's *A Bend in the River* tend to demonstrate not the appropriateness or finality of any one structural variant or "cultural dominant" over another (Achebe's politically engaged realism versus, say, Naipaul's cynical or epic modernism), rather they tend to demonstrate the bewildering complexity of recent history itself within the postcolonial African context.

For this reason among others, the contemporary caricature of Naipaul as postcolonial "mandarin" (i.e., pariah) does not really do justice to his complexity and importance as a writer of the Third World, especially in Rob Nixon's *London Calling: V. S. Naipaul, Post-colonial Mandarin*. Many of the remarks that follow are therefore intended as a dialogical response to critics like Nixon (but also Peter Nazareth, Edward Said, and others), who see only bad faith, cynicism, and "hatchet-jobbing" in the writings of Naipaul. To contest the by-now familiar stigmatization of Naipaul as postcolonial mandarin, I will seek instead to excavate the historical truth-content within Naipaul's controversial novel *A Bend in the River*, thereby dialectically preserving it as a crippled monad of historical truth. More specifically, I will argue that in diametrical opposition to Achebe's appropriation of traditional Igbo folk-culture in *Things Fall Apart*, Naipaul's *A Bend in the River* proposes a wholly different *but no less significant* situational response to the predicament of modern African history and culture: whereas Achebe advocates the reinvestment of semantic richness into the traditional cultures of Africa's past, adopting a hermeneutic position that avoids European and essentializing forms of ethnocentrism, Naipaul paradoxically seeks the regeneration of African society through the systematic destruction or liquidation of its traditional cultures, a strategy that is a hallmark of European modernist aesthetics. Though problematic at best, Naipaul's suggestion that Africans today must deliberately "trample" upon the gardens of their past, eschewing all that is not absolutely modern, is not merely reactionary; it also belies Naipaul's utopian hope for the future redemption of African culture and history....

NAIPAUL AND THE INEVITABILITY OF REIFICATION

Throughout *A Bend in the River*, Naipaul seems to share Adorno's belief in the importance of a self-conscious and autonomous subject [*Gesamt-subjekt*], fully capable of decisive and effective action in an increasingly modernized (and often disorienting) world. For Naipaul, sentimentaliz-ing the past inevitably impedes meaningful praxis in the present. By dwelling upon the lost comforts of pre-colonial, religio-community existence, as the early Achebe does in *Things Fall Apart*, we are rendered impotent when con-fronted with the harsher realities of secularized and modernized society. Hence, while Achebe advocates the preservation and dissemination of traditional folk-wisdom as a cultural remedy for the many problems caused by the moderniza-tion of Africa, Naipaul insists that only by for-getting and "trampling upon" the past may the social problems of the present be confronted and effectively resolved. Like Gayatri Chakravorty Spivak, who has stated her "absolute scorn" for those who seek cultural roots, Naipaul often ridicules as misguided those who attempt to recuperate the lost splendors of the pre-colonial past: "It isn't easy to turn your back on the past," the character Indar states in *A Bend in the River*. "It is something you have to arm yourself for, or grief will ambush and destroy you. That is why I hold onto the image of the garden trampled to the ground—it is a small thing, but it helps."

The views of Indar, which are later adopted by the narrator, Salim, form the principal theme of *A Bend in the River*: Given the cataclysmic changes ushered in by the colonization and industrialization of Africa, the past must be utterly annihilated if a new and better African culture is to emerge. Whereas Achebe seeks in *Things Fall Apart* to synthesize traditional and modern culture, Naipaul is much more pessimis-tic about the value of pre-colonial religious and community life in the modern context, specifi-cally tribal and Indo-Muslim lifestyles in Central and East Africa. Though breathtakingly cynical, and far from adequately developed, Naipaul's neo-modernist prescriptions for the ills of post-colonial Africa may actually be more realistic than the pre-revolutionary prescriptions once offered by Achebe in *Things Fall Apart*. This is in part because Naipaul's pessimism regarding the future of pre-colonial African culture is con-nected to his intuitive cynicism regarding the historical inevitability of reification itself, or of the extent of the commodity form's penetration into the daily lives of modern Africans.

For Naipaul, the reification or "objectifica-tion" of material reality in modern Africa con-curs with the advent of both alienated and historical consciousness, a process aptly illus-trated in the early pages of *A Bend in the River* when the narrator Salim muses over how an ordinary British postage stamp enabled him to detach himself from his local surroundings and consider them "as from a distance":

> Small things can start us off in new ways of thinking, and I was started off by the postage stamps of our area. The British administration gave us beautiful stamps. These stamps depicted local scenes and local things; there was one called "Arab Dhow." It was as though, in those stamps, a foreigner had said, "This is what is most strik-ing about this place." Without that stamp of the dhow I might have taken the dhows for granted. As it was, I learned to look at them.

The reification of Salim's material culture is in this sense prior to his own development as alienated or modernist monad, or even the home-less Hegelian-Lukácsian hero of the novel of real-ism, and it is also prior to his feelings of cultural inferiority as colonialist or manichean subject. In the following paragraph, Salim also tells us that "from an early age [he] developed the habit of looking, detaching [himself] from a familiar scene and trying to consider it from a distance." Even more to the point, Salim adds, "It was from this habit of looking that the idea came to me that as a community we had fallen behind. And that was the beginning of my insecurity."

For Salim, then, the British colonization of East Africa indirectly (but also irrevocably) alters the very coordinates or basic structures of his psychic perception. First, physical objects like the Arab dhow are weirdly estranged from their immediate surroundings: they are experi-enced as reified things that are interpellated into a Cartesian, spatial, and grid-like universe, utterly inconsistent with previous or traditional systems of reference and understanding. The immediate consequence for Salim is that the path is now cleared for the estrangement of the self as well: he now experiences his own lived body as an estranged object or material thing. In other words, Naipaul implies that, for Salim, alienated monadic consciousness is a direct result of reification's encroachment into the realm of the ontological.

Another way of saying this might be that Salim is hopelessly "contaminated" with histor-ical consciousness: he has become, as Baudelaire once put it, a frightened child wandering lost in a "forest of symbols" (Kundera 63). However, as Fredric Jameson has also argued in another context, once the techniques of *ostranenie*, or "strange-making" in the Russian Formalist sense, are applied to the phenomena of social life, the positive result is the "dawning of historical consciousness in general" (*Prison-House* 57). Perhaps as a deliberate response to Achebe's critique of European history in *Things Fall Apart*, especially in the last paragraph of Achebe's novel, Salim bluntly states that "[a]ll I know of our history and the history of the Indian Ocean I have got from books written by Europeans." While Salim tells us that the history of the Europeans is filled with lies and hypocrisy, the more crucial fact remains that it is Europeans who first introduce into Africa the "white mythology" of historical consciousness. In this sense, Salim does not really deliberately reject his native culture, customs, and religious beliefs as much as he is like a man afflicted with a debilitating, if not fatal, foreign illness.

Finally Naipaul suggests that people like Salim cannot hope to escape reification but must instead "submit to it" in order to become effective and autonomous agents in the modernized and historical world. The theme of the necessity of submitting to reification is, in fact, the literal meaning of the opening sentence of Naipaul's novel as well, a seemingly innocuous and contradictory tautology with far-reaching implications: "*The world is what it is; men who are nothing, who allow themselves to become nothing, have no place in it.*" While the first independent clause of this compound-complex sentence seems to suggest a static and anti-historical world-view ("*the world is what it is*"), one must carefully analyze the entire sentence, especially the second independent clause and its relation to the novel's greater theme regarding the necessity of the reification (or the "thingification") of the individual self ("*men who are nothing, who allow themselves to become nothing, have no place in it*"). The deliberate "thingification" of the self, or the effort to become "some-thing" rather than allowing oneself to become "nothing" is for Naipaul a crucial step in leaving behind the often stultifying traditions of the past and entering into the modern world. In opposition to Achebe, Naipaul urges his readers to flee from any nostalgic or misplaced longing for onto-communal social existence. We must rather make "things" of ourselves so that we can effectively act within a world of preexistent things—the world that "is what it is," not necessarily because of its static, eternal, or immutable attributes but because it has become "what it is" in the modern era ....

CONCLUSION

Naipaul's double-edged critique of both traditional African and modern Euro-American culture results primarily from specific economic conditions that are far more urgent than the question of Naipaul's individual (i.e., subjective) orientation or his largely anarchistic political beliefs. At the level of "human history as a whole," *A Bend in the River* seeks to resolve the historical conflict between a waning tribal mode of production in Africa and an increasingly dominant form of Western-style capitalism, which Naipaul characterizes as an inevitable, if not salvific, historical phenomenon. Naipaul suggests then that the only possible solution to the modern crisis of African history is the wholesale liquidation of its traditional cultures, so that a new or "absolutely modern" African culture may come into being. If Naipaul's "solution" is extreme, it nevertheless negatively embodies his utopian hope for the ultimate liberation of Africa from political terror, civil-war, debilitating cynicism, and underdevelopment.

The chief problem with Naipaul's approach is that he too quickly dismisses the cultural products of Africa as dying or hopelessly reified objects rather than, as in Achebe's use of folk-lore in *Things Fall Apart*, cultural artifacts that may contain within them the architectural blueprints for a better or more hopeful future. While African art objects for Naipaul may possess a "magical feeling of power," these aesthetic properties must be eradicated to enable the cultural logic of the Euro-American marketplace to prevail within the so-called "heart of darkness." Quite frankly, Naipaul suggests that African magic and mystery must die for Euro-American capitalism to succeed, a negative truth that also suggests a positive agenda for enemies of neo-colonialism.

Source: Christopher Wise, "The Garden Trampled: or, the Liquidation of African Culture in V.S. Naipaul's *A Bend in the River*," in *College Literature*, Vol. 23, No. 3, October 1996, pp. 58–72.

SOURCES

Anderson, Linda R., "Ideas of Identity and Freedom in V. S. Naipaul and Joseph Conrad," in *English Studies*, Vol. 59, No. 6, December 1978, pp. 510–17.

Barnouw, Dagmar, *Naipaul's Strangers*, Indiana University Press, 2003, pp. 1, 7, 8.

Bawer, Bruce, "Civilization and V. S. Naipaul," in *Hudson Review*, Vol. 55, No. 3, Autumn 2002, pp. 371–84.

Blakemore, Steven, "'An Africa of Words': V. S. Naipaul's *A Bend in the River*," in *South Carolina Review*, Vol. 18, No. 1, 1985, pp. 15–23.

Campbell, Elaine, "A Refinement of Rage: V. S. Naipaul's *A Bend in the River*," in *World Literature Written in English*, Vol. 18, No. 2, 1979, pp. 394–406.

Dissanayake, Wimal, and Carmen Wickramagamage, *Self and Colonial Desire: Travel Writings of V. S. Naipaul*, Peter Lang, 1993, pp. 20, 153–56.

French, Patrick, *The World Is What It Is: The Authorized Biography of V. S. Naipaul*, Vintage, 2009, p. x.

Hamner, Robert D., *V. S. Naipaul*, Twayne, 1973, pp. 88–104.

Hayward, Helen, *The Enigma of V. S. Naipaul: Sources and Contexts*, Palgrave Macmillan, 2002, p. 4.

Howe, Irving, "A Dark Vision," Review of *A Bend in the River*, in *New York Times Book Review*, May 13, 1979, pp. 1, 37.

Hughes, Peter, *V. S. Naipaul*, Routledge, 1988, p. 17.

Naipaul, V. S., "A New King for the Congo," in *New York Review of Books*, Vol. 22, No. 11, June 26, 1975, pp. 19–25.

———, *A Bend in the River*, Vintage, 1989.

Packer, George, "V. S. Naipaul's Pursuit of Happiness," in *Dissent*, Summer 2002, pp. 85–89.

Prescott, Lynda, "Past and Present Darkness: Sources for V. S. Naipaul's *A Bend in the River*," in *Modern Fiction Studies*, Vol. 30, No. 3, Fall 1984, pp. 547–59.

Samantrai, Ranu, "Claiming the Burden: Naipaul's Africa," in *Research in African Literatures*, Vol. 31, No. 1, Spring 2000, pp. 50–62.

FURTHER READING

Busby, Margaret, ed., *Daughters of Africa: An International Anthology of Words and Writing by Women of African Descent*, Random House, 1992.
  Busby has compiled an anthology that features women writers from Africa, the Caribbean, and North and South America, favoring contemporary authors but including Egyptian queens and slave narratives. The book has a scholarly bibliography.

Enriquez, Virgilio G., *From Colonial to Liberation Psychology: The Philippine Experience*, University of Hawaii Press, 2010.
  Applying indigenous Philippine psychology to different areas of Filipino life, such as health,

education, and agriculture, the book is an example of the indigenous social science movement, including a discussion of the impact of colonialism on Filipino psychology.

Gikandi, Simon, ed., *Encyclopedia of African Literature*, Routledge, 2002.
  Information on individual authors and essays on the history, culture, and literary criticism of African works are included in articles written by academic specialists.

Jussawalla, Feroza, ed., *Conversations with V. S. Naipaul*, University Press of Mississippi, 1997.
  This collection of interviews covers thirty-six years' worth of Naipaul's intense and candid opinions about India and third-world countries, for whom he has little patience. The later interviews are warmer and more personal.

Naipaul, V. S., *The Return of Eva Perón*, Alfred A. Knopf, 1980.
  Naipaul's prose essays, commenting on what he calls half-made societies, inspired his fictions. Included is "A New King for the Congo," the 1975 article on Mobutu for the *New York Review of Books* that was the basis for *A Bend in the River*.

Narayan, Uma, *Dislocating Cultures: Identities, Traditions, and Third World Feminism*, Routledge, 1997.
  This postcolonial feminist study shows how women in third-world cultures have been misrepresented by political interests from colonial times till now.

Nzongola-Ntalaja, Georges, *The Congo: From Leopold to Kabila; A People's History*, Zed Books, 2002.
  A Congolese academic provides the history of the Congo and its struggle for democracy from the point of view of its own people.

Walcott, Derek, *Omeros*, Farrar, Straus and Giroux, 1992.
  A black Caribbean Nobel laureate, Walcott presents an epic poem of a modern Odysseus who travels to see the fate and history of postcolonial peoples gathered on Santa Lucia, deprived of their homes and heritage.

SUGGESTED SEARCH TERMS

V. S. Naipaul

V. S. Naipaul AND postcolonial novel

A Bend in the River

Zaire AND Mobutu Sese Seko

Naipaul AND universal civilization

Naipaul AND neocolonialism

Naipaul AND third world

Naipaul AND Africa

Naipaul AND India

Naipaul AND Islam

Bone

FAE MYENNE NG

1993

Bone is the first novel by the Chinese American author Fae Myenne Ng. It was published in 1993 and became a national best seller. The story is set in San Francisco's Chinatown and tells the story of one Chinese American family over two generations. The older generation consists mainly of Mah and Leon Leong, who immigrated separately to the United States many decades ago. The novel is narrated by one of the younger generation, Mah's daughter Leila, who has two sisters, Ona and Nina. When the novel begins, Leila has just returned from a trip to New York, where she married her longtime boyfriend, Mason. She reveals that sometime in the recent past, Ona committed suicide by jumping off the thirteenth floor of one of the housing projects in Chinatown. This is the crucial event around which the novel revolves. Leila and her family try to make sense of Ona's suicide, which has no obvious cause. The novel has an unusual structure in that it is told in reverse chronological order. The narrative begins after Ona's suicide and works its way backward until it reaches the crucial days immediately after and, finally, before this crucial act that devastates the Leong family. As Leila describes her world and her family history, she reveals the hard lives led by Chinese immigrants to San Francisco. She also shows how the American-born younger generation develops different attitudes than those of their parents toward their Chinese origins and the American culture in which they live.

AUTHOR BIOGRAPHY

Fae Myenne Ng (pronounced "Ing") was born in 1956 (some sources say 1957) in San Francisco, California, and she and her brother were raised in that city's Chinatown as second-generation Chinese Americans. Her father had immigrated to the United States in 1940 and worked as a cook. Her mother was a seamstress, and from her, Ng learned how to help sew fashion items. Her parents did not speak English; in the family home, the language spoken was Cantonese.

Ng received a bachelor's degree from the University of California, Berkeley, in 1978 and a master's degree from Columbia University in 1984. She then started working on her novel, supporting herself by working as a waitress, as an editorial assistant, and in other temporary positions. She married the writer Mark Coovelis, whom she later divorced.

In 1989, she moved to Brooklyn, New York. Her first novel, *Bone*, was published in 1993, and it met with critical and popular success. It was a finalist for the 1994 PEN/Faulkner Award and was a national best seller. Ng consequently received the Rome Prize from the American Academy of Arts and Letters and the Lila Wallace–Reader's Digest Writers' Award in 1998. In 2008, Ng published her second novel, *Steer Toward Rock*, which is also about the experiences of Chinese American immigrants and was equally well received, winning the American Book Award. In 2009, Ng received a Guggenheim Fellowship.

Ng has also published short stories in a variety of publications, including *Crescent Review*, *City Lights Review*, *Allure*, *Calyx*, *Harper's*, and *American Voice*. Some of these stories have been reprinted in anthologies, including *Asian American Literature: A Brief Introduction and Anthology* (1996). She also published an essay in the *New Republic* about how her father immigrated from China to the United States in 1940; the account closely resembles the story of Leon Leong in *Bone*.

PLOT SUMMARY

Chapter 1

Set in San Francisco, *Bone* is narrated by Leila, the eldest of three sisters. The others are Ona and Nina. Nina is living in New York, and Leila, on a recent visit to see her, has gotten married to Mason Louie.

Ona has committed suicide by jumping off the thirteenth floor of a building. In chapter 1, Leila searches in Chinatown for her stepfather, Leon, to tell him the news of her marriage. Leon does not live with Leila's mother, Mah, but in a cheap hotel, the San Fran. Leila asks Leon's friend You Thin Toy where Leon might be and finds him in a café owned by Croney Kam; Leon is pleased when she tells him she has married. They run into Leon's friend Jimmy Lowe and then visit Mason after he finishes work at the garage where he is a mechanic. Then she and Mason drop Leon off, and Leila goes to see Mah at her baby clothing store. Leila has to pluck up courage to tell her mother that she has gotten married. Mah is shocked and says nothing at first. Then she is angry that Leila kept it secret and did not have a big ceremony.

Chapter 2

This chapter takes place earlier than chapter 1. After explaining how the family suffered after Ona's suicide, the cause of which is not known, Leila describes her trip to New York with Mason to see Nina. There, while Mason visits an old friend, Leila and Nina eat together in a restaurant. Nina has just returned from a visit to China, the first time she has been there. Leila talks about the quarrels between Mah and Leon. Nina persuades her to marry Mason straightaway, in New York, without a ceremony or banquet, even though that goes against Mah's wishes.

Chapter 3

This chapter takes place two days before Leila's trip to New York. Leila talks on the phone to Mah while Mason and his friend Zeke work on a car. Mah is upset and finds a way to blame Leila for Ona's death. The next day, Mason takes Leila to Redwood City to deliver a car to his cousin, Dale. Zeke and his girlfriend, Diana, follow in another car. Mason tells Leila he wants to marry her. Leila does not give him an answer. Since Ona died, Leila has been living with Mah, but she wonders how long Mason will wait.

Chapter 4

Slightly further back in time, Leila is living with Mah, torn between loyalty to her mother and love for Mason. Mah complains that Leon never completes anything he starts. Leon blames himself for Ona's death, because he did not follow custom and failed to send his father's bones back to China. Nina blames the entire family. Anxious to get away, Leila visits Mason. She wants to escape from the pain associated with Ona's death.

Chapter 5

Leila takes Leon to the Social Security office, so he can start receiving payments. But he does not have the right documents and is sent away. Leila searches in an old suitcase of Leon's for a document that would show his date of birth. Leon always saves papers. She eventually finds a government document issued to Leon at the time of his entry to the United States; it shows his birth date.

Chapter 6

Leila learns from Frank Jow at the Seaman's Union that Leon has gone to sea. Forty days later, Leon is due to return, and Leila is about to pick him up. She and Mason drive up to meet him off the ship in Vallejo. As they drive back to San Francisco, Leon says he does not want to go back to Salmon Alley to live with Mah, who is already cooking dinner for him. He wants to go to the San Fran instead, and they take him there. They invite Zeke to Mah's for dinner as a replacement. When Mah sees that Leon is not coming, she goes to her room, leaving the others to eat dinner.

Chapter 7

One afternoon, Leon asks Mason to take him to the Chinese cemetery where his father, Grandpa Leong, is buried. It is locked, but they crawl through the fence. Leon cannot find the grave, and they are quizzed by a security guard who wants to know how they got in. Later, helped by Mah, Leila tries to get the necessary information from a Chinatown family association. She is told that the grave is one of a number that have recently been moved. Leila recalls the grief Mah felt at Grandpa Leong's death. The ladies at the sewing shop, Soon-ping, Luday, and Miss Tsai, tried to comfort her. The narrative then moves back many years in time to when Mah discovered Grandpa Leong dead. At the funeral, Ona, Nina, and Leila were still children. Back in the present, Leila takes Leon to the cemetery. They find the gravestone for the Leong family. Leon leaves an offering of oranges and a packet of cigarettes.

Chapter 8

For months after Ona's suicide, Mah and Leon quarrel. To help Mah, Nina takes her on a two-week trip to Hong Kong. This leaves Leila free to enjoy more of Mason's company. Leon is relieved, too. He takes the opportunity to repair Mah's sewing machine, which she has not used for years. In a borrowed Mercedes, Mason and Leila pick up Mah and Nina on their return. For an evening everyone seems happy, but then the little altar that Leon has built for Ona's ashes brings back the painful memory of her death.

Chapter 9

In the immediate aftermath of Ona's suicide, which takes place just before the Chinese New Year, Leon blames everyone, while Mah blames herself. Leila tries to examine whether she herself has been at fault. Nina returns for the funeral. They return Ona's dresses to the restaurant where she worked. Everyone they talk to says that Ona seemed fine the night she died. When the New Year holiday comes, those who were close to Ona try to forget their grief. Leon, Mah, Leila, and Mason go out for dinner. After school the next day, Leila talks with Serena Choi, who confesses that she used to harass Ona in high school. Over the next few days, people such as Auntie Wong try to console Leila and share their memories of Ona.

Chapter 10

The day after Ona's suicide, Leila finds it hard to get through her workday. A day or so later, she and Nina clear out Ona's clothes and discuss their quarreling parents. Leon has walked out on Mah, but Mason tracks him down. Everyone is worried, distressed, and feeling guilty. Leila thinks back over her memories of Ona. There is a service at their home, and many people attend.

Chapter 11

Leila is given the news of Ona's death by Miss Lagomarsino at school, where she works, and she goes to the police station. She answers questions put to her by a police officer who has to make a report. She calls Mason and tells him the news. Mason takes her to Mah's shop, where she tells Mah and Leon that Ona is dead. They all return to Mah's apartment, where Ona had been living. Leon goes into a rant, wanting to find someone to blame. He storms out, saying he is going to the police station to find out what happened. Leila calls Nina, who agrees to come home from New York. Leila picks her up at the airport.

Chapter 12

Ten years before Ona's death, Leon discovers that Mah has been having an affair with Tommie Hom. Mah says the affair is over, but Leon is furious and moves out of their apartment. Eventually he moves back in. Over the next few years, Leon takes part in a number of business schemes, none of which succeed. Eventually he launches the Ong & Leong laundry, with his friend Luciano Ong, husband of Rosa Ong. All the family helps out at the laundry, and Ona becomes romantically involved with Osvaldo, Luciano's son. Eventually the laundry fails, and an angry Leon blames Luciano. Leon orders Ona to stop seeing Osvaldo, and there is a fierce quarrel between father and daughter.

Chapter 13

In happier times, Mah and the girls await Leon's return from a voyage. On the first night of his return, Mah cooks an elaborate dinner. Everyone in the family gets along well, but at night Mah complains there is not enough money. She tells him he must go to sea again to serve as a merchant mariner.

Chapter 14

While Mah waits again for Leon's return from Australia, Leila reviews her relationship with Mason. She wants to go and live with him. She recalls how, when she was six, Mah told her she was going to marry Leon. Then Leila recalls what Mah told her about her biological father, Lyman Fu, and how he left Mah not long after their marriage. After he stopped sending Mah money, Tommie Hom gave her a job and taught her how to sew. Back in the present, Leila helps Mah dress for Leon's return that night. At dinner, Leon tells Leila about her father, whom he met in Australia. Leila decides to move in with Mason, confident that her heart will take her in the right direction.

CHARACTERS

Serena Choi

Serena Choi used to harass Ona in high school. After Ona dies, Serena tells Leila that she always wanted to apologize to Ona.

Dale

Dale is Mason's cousin. Mason does not like him because he talks too much like a white person. Dale went to an all-white school and is a computer expert.

Leila Fu

Leila Fu is the narrator of the novel. She is the only daughter of Mah and Lyman Fu and the

half sister of Ona and Nina. She is eight years older than Nina. Leon Leong is her stepfather. Leila works at a school in Chinatown as a community relations specialist. She acts as a liaison between teachers and parents and makes a lot of home visits, mostly to the homes of recent immigrants. Her boyfriend is Mason Louie, and for some time, she is conflicted about whether to live with him or remain at her mother's. She eventually decides to move in with him, and not long after Ona's suicide she marries Mason on a visit to New York to see Nina. She does not tell her mother about the marriage until later, fearing her disapproval, even though Mah likes Mason.

Lyman Fu

Lyman Fu is Leila's father and Mah's ex-husband. He married Mah when they were both young. He took her to Hong Kong, and for a few years they lived well, but then he lost all his money. He took Mah to San Francisco to make a fresh start, but things did not work out for them there. He went to Australia, saying that he would send for her when he was established, but he never did.

Tommie Hom

Tommie Hom owns the sewing shop where Mah works. It was Tommie who offered her a job after her first husband stopped sending her money, and he taught her how to sew. Tommie also owns most of Salmon Alley, where the Leongs live, and he is friends with gangsters. About ten years before Ona's suicide, he had an affair with Mah. The three girls liked him then because he was good-looking, and Leila wanted Mah to leave Leon and marry Tommie.

Frank Jow

Frank Jow is one of Leon's friends. He works at the Seaman's Union.

Croney Kam

Croney Kam is one of Leon's old shipping buddies. He is a fat man who owns the Universal Café, where Leon likes to eat.

Miss Lagomarsino

Miss Lagomarsino is a senior employee at the school where Leila works. She informs Leila of the death of her sister.

Grandpa Leong

Grandpa Leong was not Leon's real father, but he did get Leon into the United States by pretending

Leon was his son. Grandpa Leong worked on an alfalfa farm in Marysville, north of San Francisco, but when he could no longer do the work, he moved to San Francisco and lived his last days in the San Fran, the same place where Leon sometimes lives. Leila remembers that he "looked ancient, like one of the Eight Holy Immortals, a smart old god." Many years later, Leon goes searching for Grandpa Leong's grave and feels guilty that he did not send the bones back to China, according to custom.

Leon Leong

Leon Leong is the husband of Mah, father of Ona and Nina, and stepfather of Leila. In about 1940, at the age of fifteen, he immigrated from China to the United States, as sponsored by Grandpa Leong, who was not Leon's real father, after Leon paid him five thousand dollars. Leon memorized fake information about himself in order to get through his interrogation by immigration officers. For much of his life Leo has been a merchant seaman, although after Nina was born he did not go to sea as often as before. Instead, he worked many different jobs, as cook, busboy, night porter, janitor, and welder, but none of them worked out for very long. He started up a grocery store but was forced to sell it at a loss. Then he set up a laundry with his friend Luciano, but it went broke, and Leon blamed Luciano. Leon thinks the entire family has had bad luck, which he blames in part on his failure to return Grandpa Leong's bones. When Ona commits suicide, he blames everyone. When he is not ranting about his ill luck, he does his best to look after Mah. Although he has a tendency to start projects but not finish them, he is good at fixing things and likes to do things for Mah.

Mah Leong

Mah Leong is the mother of Leila, Ona, and Nina and the wife of Leon Leong. Leon is her second husband. Her first, Lyman Fu, took her from a village in China to Hong Kong and then San Francisco, but he left her after a few years, having fathered Leila. His departure left her feeling bitter. She got a job at Tommie Hom's sewing shop and eventually remarried, to Leon. She married him mainly because he was a U.S. citizen and she would therefore be entitled to a green card (signifying the right to reside permanently in the United States). Mah loves Leon but is frustrated by his sometimes difficult behavior and his failure to establish himself financially. They cannot live

together for long before they fall to quarreling, so Leon often lives elsewhere. By the time of Ona's suicide, Mah has lived in the United States for twenty-five years; she runs a shop that sells baby clothing. She is a hard-working woman who has had a hard life.

Nina Leong

Nina Leong is Leila's younger half sister. She is thin and tall. She moved to New York to become a flight attendant because she wanted to escape the family conflicts. Unlike Leila, who often does not answer back, Nina is outspoken and vents her feelings. After Ona's suicide, Nina takes Mah to Hong Kong to help her recover from the loss. While there, she tells Mah that she had an abortion. Mah and Leon are furious with her. Nina does not tell her parents everything, though; she has a boyfriend called Michael but keeps it a secret, only telling Leila. Leila thinks Nina is lonely. Nina is thinking of taking a job as a tour guide, and when she makes a trip to China, she forms a friendship with one of the guides, a Chinese man named Zhang. When she meets Leila in New York, she persuades Leila to marry Mason straightaway.

Ona Leong

Ona Leong was the middle sister of the three, younger than Leila and older than Nina. She worked as a hostess at a restaurant, but at the age of twenty she committed suicide by jumping off the thirteenth floor of a building. No one knows why she killed herself. The police say she was taking downers, but Leila does not think that is significant. What emerges in the story is that Ona was very good at keeping secrets; she kept her thoughts and emotions to herself much more than her two sisters, according to Leila. No one thought she was depressed. She was always looking forward to the future. Leila thinks she may have felt the need to escape.

Mason Louie

Mason Louie is Leila's boyfriend, whom she later marries. He works as an auto mechanic on foreign cars and wants to set up his own business, perhaps with his friend Zeke. He is young and attractive, with a generous heart, and also competent at his work. Leila never has to worry about him. He is considerate to Leila and also gets along well with Mah and Leon. On one occasion, he takes Leon to the cemetery to look for his father's grave, even though this means he will lose a few hours' pay. Another time he loses an afternoon's pay just to take Leila to Vallejo to meet Leon on his return from sea. Mason was born and raised in Chinatown but feels comfortable going farther afield. He likes to ski at Lake Tahoe and does not care if there are no other Chinese there.

Zeke Louie

Zeke Louie is Mason's oldest friend. They share a name but are not related. Zeke works in a BMW auto repair shop. He has a girlfriend called Diana and is known for his short temper. For many years he had a crush on Nina.

Jimmy Lowe

Jimmy Lowe is an old buddy of Leon's. He has nothing much to do and just hangs around Chinatown with his cronies. He used to be a janitor at a hotel.

Luday

Luday is one of the ladies who works at the sewing shop.

Luciano Ong

Luciano Ong is the husband of Rosa Ong. They are both from Peru and moved to just outside Chinatown in San Francisco. Luciano appears to be very wealthy, driving a big car, and he always has plans to make even more money. He is tall and flashy, wearing eye-catching shirts. He and Leon become friends and go into business together, starting up a laundry that flourishes for a while but then goes bust. Leon blames Luciano for the failure.

Osvaldo Ong

Osvaldo Ong is the son of Luciano and Rosa. He has movie-star good looks, and he becomes romantically involved with Ona. However, Leon dislikes him, and after the laundry business fails, he tells Ona she must break up with him.

Rosa Ong

Rosa Ong is Luciano's wife. When she first arrives in San Francisco, she is employed by Tommie Hom in the sewing shop. Mah teaches her how to sew, and she and Mah become close friends.

Soon-ping

Soon-ping is one of the ladies who works at the sewing shop.

You Thin Toy

You Thin Toy is an old seaman who hangs around Chinatown. He and Leon are old buddies, having known each other since they were teenagers.

Miss Tsai

Miss Tsai is one of the ladies from the sewing shop. Leila thinks that Miss Tsai considers herself better than the others because she comes from Hong Kong.

Auntie Wong

Auntie Wong is an old lady and family friend. Ona thought of her as her godmother. After Ona's suicide, Auntie Wong tells Leila how much she loved the girl.

THEMES

Guilt

After Ona's suicide, almost everyone feels guilty in some way, even though no one really knows why Ona took her own life. Nina thinks the whole family is somehow to blame. Leon, too, tries to blame everyone. In particular, he thinks that Ona's former boyfriend, Osvaldo, must have had something to do with it, although he never suspects that the bullying way in which he, Leon, forced Ona to break up with Osvaldo might have been a contributing factor. Leon also blames himself, thinking that he has brought bad luck on the family by failing to return the remains of his adopted father to China. Mah feels guilty because she thinks her affair with Tommie Hom ten years ago has brought multiple misfortunes in its wake. Even Leila, who is levelheaded and less neurotic than her parents, finds herself reliving all her interactions with Ona, trying to see what she had failed to spot at the time. She feels a "secret guilt," feeling that she must have overlooked something that might have helped avert the tragedy. Leila also feels guilty about something else—the fact that she enjoys a better life than her long-suffering, hard-working mother.

Immigrant Life

Bone takes place almost entirely in San Francisco's Chinatown and gives a picture of the lives of Chinese immigrants over two generations. For the earlier generation, including Mah, Leon, and Leon's old friends who drift around Chinatown,

TOPICS FOR FURTHER STUDY

- Read *American Eyes: New Asian-American Short Stories for Young Adults* (1995), edited by Lori Carlson, which includes ten short stories from a variety of Asian American authors. One of the stories is an excerpt from *Bone*. Many of the stories deal with what it is like growing up Asian in the United States. Take one story you like and compare and contrast it in an essay with the excerpt from *Bone*. Examine them both in terms of theme, style, and voice.

- Research San Francisco's Chinatown and write an entry on your blog that explains to a potential visitor why reading *Bone* before visiting would greatly enrich his or her understanding of the area.

- Using online and traditional research sources, prepare a class presentation on teen suicide. Infuse your presentation with charts that convey statistics, reasons people decide to commit suicide, and methods of suicide prevention commonly used.

- Create an interactive time line of Chinese American history from the 1850s to the present. Include at least fifteen important events. Create links to information about the events you choose for the time line. Give a class presentation in which you explain the time line and explain the most important events.

---

life in the United States has never been easy. It has meant long hours in sweatshops, working in various menial jobs, dealing with poverty and financial uncertainty, and struggling to survive in a wider culture very different from their own. Most of these immigrants, like Mah and Leon, were hard workers who learned how to keep themselves afloat.

Leon is a good example of such an immigrant. He does not speak or understand English well, even though he has been in the country for nearly fifty years. He keeps a bag full of what he calls his "Going-Back-to-China fund," although he is not likely to ever return to the country of his birth. This is in spite of the fact that the United States still seems in many ways like a foreign country to him. Many years ago, he declined the government's confession program, through which immigrants who admitted that they entered the country illegally could receive U.S. citizenship. Leon preferred to leave his false identity intact, but this gives him problems later, when he seeks to claim Social Security and must deal with the government bureaucracy. It is left to Leila to sort through his papers and find a document that will satisfy the Social Security office regarding his age and immigration status. Leon, like almost all immigrants, has a foot in two worlds. When he first came to the United States, he did not intend to stay; he just never left. But later he felt strongly that he wanted to belong to his new country. When Leila sorts through his papers, finding records of all his dealings in America, she comments, "Leon had paid; Leon had earned his rights. American dollars. American time."

Life is different for the younger generation, who were born in the United States. They are more Americanized than their parents. This is sometimes revealed in small details, as when Mah tells Leila not to eat so much American food, saying it is not good for her. Leila does not want to argue with Mah, but she complains to Nina, "How can I tell her my tastes have changed, like everything else?" Nina points out that Mah was not talking only about food. This suggests a conflict between generations over cultural issues. The old ways of doing things no longer appeal to the younger generation. Indeed, Nina felt that her family life in Chinatown was so restrictive that she got as far away from it as she could by moving to New York. Leila remembers the resentment she felt when she had to act as translator for her parents whenever they had to visit government offices to claim disability or on immigration matters. Her life is still bound up with her parents, but in marrying Mason she makes a bold move for her own independence, which also means a further stage in her Americanization. Mason is an example of how life and attitudes have changed over the generations. He has a good job, drives a fast car, is at home beyond the confines of Chinatown, and knows where he is going in life. It looks like Leila and Mason will be able to reach for the American dream, beyond the limitations of Chinatown.

Exterior of a garment shop in San Francisco's Chinatown (Gina Smith | Shutterstock.com)

STYLE

Reverse Narrative Structure

Bone has an unusual narrative structure. Normally an author will tell a story in chronological order; in other words, the events are told for the most part in the order that they happen. In *Bone*, however, Ng tells the story in reverse order. The novel begins some while after Ona's suicide and then moves steadily backward in time. Although unusual, this is not unique. Stephen Sondheim's musical *Merrily We Roll Along* (1981), for example, tells the story in reverse order, a device that was also used for one episode in the popular television comedy series *Seinfeld* in the 1990s. In *Bone*, this unusual structure suggests the underlying idea that one must move backward in time in order to understand the present. As Leila puts it, "Remembering the past gives power to the present."

Metaphorical Title

There are several passages in this novel in which bones are mentioned, and these help to explain

why Ng chose this word for the title of the novel. After Mah has cooked a pigeon for the family, she sits alone in the kitchen sucking on the bones. "Bones are sweeter than you know," she says. In this sense, bones represent the hard life of the immigrant. Nothing can be wasted; they must use all that they have to the fullest.

Bones are also representative of family ancestry and the connections people have to their culture and their past. This is brought out in the references to the bones of Grandpa Leong, which Leon goes in search of in the cemetery. He believes he has failed in his filial duty to arrange for the bones to be sent back to China. Leila comments that, because Leon believed this, he gave to those old bones a certain kind of power. They are "restless bones." Bones therefore represent the power of the past to influence the present.

Bone also suggests the basic structure of something, which is revealed when everything else has been stripped away. This is what Leila does during the course of the novel: she penetrates beyond the surface details to the core of her family's relationships and the possible causes of Ona's suicide. By analysis and introspection, she gets to the essence of things.

HISTORICAL CONTEXT

San Francisco's Chinatown

San Francisco's Chinatown is the oldest and largest Chinatown in the United States. The first Chinese immigrants, who were mostly men, arrived in the mid-nineteenth century in search of work. They soon established Chinatown, an area in San Francisco covering roughly twelve blocks, centered around Portsmouth Plaza, a public square. This is the Portsmouth Square where Leila searches for Leon in chapter 1 of the novel. Chinatown was a largely self-sufficient community, with its own form of government. Chinese immigrants created everything they needed in the form of housing, schools, churches, shops, restaurants, entertainment, Chinese-language newspapers, and the like. Chinatown also included benevolent associations that functioned as social and welfare organizations for Chinese immigrants. (In the novel, Leila goes to the Hoy Sun Ning Yung Benevolent Association when she needs information about family graveyards.) In 1882, the largest benevolent associations formed the

COMPARE
&
CONTRAST

- **1990s:** Chinese American authors receive increasing recognition as major voices in American literature. David Wong Louie's short-story collection *Pangs of Love* receives the 1991 Los Angeles Times First Fiction Award. In the same year, Gish Jen publishes her novel *Typical American* to critical acclaim.

  Today: Chinese American authors continue to enrich American literature. Gish Jen publishes the novels *The Love Wife* (2004) and *World and Town* (2010). Amy Tan publishes her sixth novel, *Saving Fish from Drowning*, in 2005.

- **1990s:** In 1990, the total Chinese American population is 1,645,472, while the Chinese population of San Francisco is 127,140, approximately 18 percent of the city's population. During the 1990s, changes in immigration law

  produce an increase in the number of immigrants from China to the United States.

  Today: According to the 2000 census, there are 2,422,970 Chinese Americans in the United States, representing 0.86 percent of the total population. Some 40 percent of Chinese Americans live in California. People of Chinese birth or descent make up approximately 20 percent of the population of San Francisco.

- **1990s:** Clifton D. Bryant's *Handbook of Death & Dying* reports that a 1998 study concluded that the Chinese American suicide rate was 8.3 per 100,000 people.

  Today: Christine McFadden reports in the *Pacific Citizen* that Asian American women ages 15 to 24 have the highest suicide rates among all ethnic groups.

Chinese Six Companies, headed by Chinese merchants, which represented the voice of the Chinese community to the wider business community in San Francisco. At the time, San Francisco contained the largest Chinese community in the United States. Like much of San Francisco, Chinatown was destroyed by earthquake and fire in 1906 but was soon rebuilt. Even in those days, the uniqueness of San Francisco's Chinatown attracted many visitors, and as the twentieth century wore on, Chinatown became established as a major tourist attraction.

In 1910, the immigration station on Angel Island, in San Francisco Bay, was created. All Chinese immigrants (like Leon Leong in the novel) had to pass through Angel Island and satisfy immigration officials that they had a right to enter California. The process was often slow, and immigrants were sometimes detained for months while their papers were examined. In the novel, Leon Leong and his friend You Thin Toy carefully memorize all the details of their false identities so they can pass the interrogations on Angel Island.

From the beginning, Chinese immigrants faced many forms of discrimination, including California's Anti-Coolie Tax of 1862, which aimed to stop Chinese immigrants from taking jobs that would otherwise be done by white people and to discourage further Chinese immigration to California. In 1882, a federal law, the Chinese Exclusion Act, banned the immigration of Chinese laborers and prevented those Chinese already in the United States from becoming U.S. citizens. The act had the effect of reducing the population of Chinatown during the early decades of the twentieth century. In 1881, the population of Chinatown was twenty-six thousand, but by 1920, it had fallen to eleven thousand. The Chinese Exclusion Act was not repealed until 1943, during World War II, when China was a U.S. ally against Japan. Quotas on Chinese immigration were imposed, however.

In 1949, after the Communist takeover of China, there was an increase in Chinese immigration to the United States, including San Francisco. In 1965, new immigration laws were passed that allowed an increase in immigration from Asia. By

---

Chinese visa in a passport along with Chinese currency *(Alexander Gatsenko / Shutterstock.com)*

1970, quotas for Chinese immigration were twenty thousand a year. By this time, Chinese Americans in San Francisco and elsewhere were becoming more prosperous, and over half of them were employed in white-collar occupations. By the 1990s, the population of San Francisco's Chinatown had climbed to eighty thousand.

CRITICAL OVERVIEW

Bone was received very favorably by reviewers. In *Publishers Weekly*, the novel was hailed as "a believable journey through pain to healing, exposing the emotional scars . . . of its characters as they try to survive." The reviewer also notes how Ng "summons a quiet urgency from simple language" in her descriptions of the settings and of the inner lives of the characters.

In the *New York Times*, Michiko Kakutani was equally complimentary. She notes that "Ng conjures the immigrant world of Mah and Leon with the affectionate knowledge of an insider and the observant unsentimentality of an outsider." Kakutani also

points out how effectively Ng portrays the dogged perseverance of Leila's parents, "built, in equal parts, on naivete and genuine courage." Kakutani concludes by noting, "Blessed with a poet's gift for metaphor and a reporter's eye for detail, Ms. Ng writes with grace, authority and grit."

For Heather Ross Miller, in the *Southern Review*, the novel "shows us Chinese immigrants and their first-generation Chinese-American children in spirited struggles over the best of all possible worlds, American or Old." Miller contrasts Ng's work favorably with "the easy anecdotal musings of Amy Tan." (Tan is the Chinese American author of *The Joy Luck Club* and other novels.) Miller argues that "Ng's haunting book ranges wider and penetrates deeper into the subtexts, dead ends, and labyrinthine interior of the new-American experience." In a review for *Entertainment Weekly*, Margot Mifflin proclaims that Ng "has painted a portrait of an immigrant family whose problems are at once culturally specific and universal." A *Booklist* contributor comments that Ng's "evocation of San Francisco is crisp and vivid, and her take on the generational tug of war . . . is both fresh and moving."

CRITICISM

Bryan Aubrey

Aubrey holds a Ph.D. in English. In the following essay, he discusses the familial and cultural issues that create in many of the characters in Bone *a desire to escape.*

Why did Ona commit suicide? This is the central question that dominates Fae Myenne Ng's exquisitely written novel, *Bone*. The suicide devastated the Leong family, and they all struggle to come to terms with it, sometimes blaming others but also examining themselves. On the night she died, Ona gave no signs of being disturbed. When Leila later talks with people at the restaurant where Ona worked, those who saw her say she was acting normally that night. So there is no obvious reason why Ona decided to end her life. How, then, is the family to understand such an event and even be reconciled to it?

The answer to this question is a complex one that revolves around familial and cultural issues. Ona's parents, Mah and Leon, show little ability to delve into the causes of Ona's suicide. Mah thinks that the suicide is part of her own continuing punishment for having an affair ten years before with Tommie Hom. Leon believes that his failure to return the remains of his adopted father to China has brought bad luck on the entire family. He also wants to blame Ona's boyfriend, Osvaldo.

It is left to Leila, the thoughtful, reflective eldest daughter, to examine in more depth what created this family tragedy, and to honor the way Ona chose to escape from whatever problems she had. The word *escape* is key. The word comes to Leila shortly after she hears of her sister's death: "Escape. What Leon searched for, what Ona needed."

This comment by Leila hints at what is apparent throughout the novel: the Leong family lives in an inward-looking, self-enclosing atmosphere that creates great emotional pressures for everyone in it. Mah and Leon are not happily married and cannot even live together for long periods, although they do appear to need each other. Leon is restless, unable to find stable employment and frequently frustrated by his lack of understanding of American culture. He escapes by going to sea. Something about being on the ocean soothes him, gets his life moving again.

Escape is a key idea for Leila and Nina, too. Nina escapes the claustrophobic family dynamic by moving as far away as she can, to New York.

> **IT IS THE CLASSIC SITUATION IN WHICH SECOND-GENERATION IMMIGRANTS, WHO ARE AMERICAN BORN, FIND THEMSELVES IN CONFLICT WITH THE CULTURE OF THEIR PARENTS, WHO ADHERE TO THE OLD WAYS."**

Unlike Leila and Ona, who exercise more control over their emotions and do not always speak their mind, Nina is able to say what she thinks. When Mah and Leon would quarrel with each other or criticize her, she would yell back. Escape for her was therefore much easier than for the other two.

Leila wants to escape and start to live her own life. She realizes that, in a sense, she is living her parents' lives for them. They are dependent on her—for her efficiency, her greater familiarity with English, and her knowledge of how to deal with government bureaucracies—and this gives her a power over them that makes her uncomfortable. She wants to go to live with her boyfriend Mason but is slow to do so because she does not want to upset Mah by leaving their apartment in Salmon Alley. This is especially true after Ona's death, when Mah asks her to stay with her. Leila does not want to leave Mah alone, but she feels her relationship with Mason pulling her away, and eventually she learns to trust this instinct and act on it.

As for Ona, there were things she needed to escape as well, and hers was the most drastic solution of them all. Leila believes that Ona felt the oppressiveness of the family situation even more than she or Nina did. She comments that Ona "felt stuck. In the family, in Chinatown. Ona was the middle girl and she felt stuck in the middle of all the trouble." Ona had the ability to keep secrets, and she did this better than anyone in her family, according to Nina. Leila thinks Ona learned this ability from their secretive parents. The result was that Leila and Nina got used to not knowing much about Ona's inner life. In addition, Ona appears to have been dependent on her parents and unable to assert herself, unlike her two sisters. Leon was a controlling father who forced Ona to give up her boyfriend Osvaldo, and Leila feels this was a key episode in Ona's life. Ona was disappointed with

WHAT
DO I READ
NEXT?

- *Steer Toward Rock* (2008) is Ng's second novel. Like *Bone*, it is set in San Francisco's Chinatown and examines the fortunes of two generations of Chinese immigrants. In the 1950s, like Leon Leong in *Bone*, Jack Moon Szeto enters San Francisco with fake documents showing him to be the son of Yi-Tung Gold Szeto, a Chinese American who is a U.S. citizen. Jack has to work off his debt by working long hours as a butcher and participating in a sham marriage. He falls in love with the woman concerned, however, and she bears him a child. Complications with Yi-Tung result. Reviewers hailed the novel as a worthy successor to *Bone*.

- *American Born Chinese* (2006) is a graphic novel by Gene Luen Yang, illustrated by Lark Pien. It tells two stories: Jim Wang, a Chinese American middle school student, feels out of place and wants to get on better with the white students; Danny, an American teenager, changes schools rather than be around his Chinese cousin. The book was a finalist for the National Book Award for Young People.

- *The Joy Luck Club* (1989) by Amy Tan, is a best-selling novel about four Chinese American families in San Francisco. Four immigrant mothers and their four American-born daughters share stories about their lives. The success of the book made the general reading

public much more aware of Chinese American literature.

- *Interpreter of Maladies* (1999), a collection of stories by Jhumpa Lahiri, won the Pulitzer Prize for Fiction in 2000. The characters in Lahiri's stories are usually Indian and are often immigrants to the United States, trying to find their way in a new culture. Lahiri herself was born in England to Indian parents but raised from the age of three in the United States.

- *Typical American* (1991) is a novel by Gish Jen, a Chinese American writer. Covering a twenty-year period, the novel tells the story of three Chinese people who enter the United States in 1947 and become U.S. citizens in the 1950s. By the mid-1960s, Ralph Chang, his wife Helen, and his sister Theresa have adapted to life in their new country and become "typical Americans."

- In *American Chinatown: A People's History of Five Neighborhoods* (2009) author Bonnie Tsui visits the four most prominent Chinatowns in the United States, in San Francisco, New York, Los Angeles, and Honolulu; her other visit is to Las Vegas. She gives a vivid account of each neighborhood, focusing on the stories of individuals she meets.

---

her father and also with her mother for failing to intervene on her behalf. In the end, the only form of escape she could envision was jumping off a tall building.

The need to escape felt by all three sisters is symptomatic of something wider than the fact that they live with fractious parents who can be irrational in their beliefs and behavior. It is the classic situation in which second-generation immigrants, who are American born, find themselves in conflict with the culture of their parents, who adhere to the old ways. The Leong family and what

happens to them cannot be understood outside the mixed cultural context, which is really what defines Mah and Leon, both born in China, and the three daughters, all born in California. The three girls are perched uneasily between two worlds, the China of their parents, which they have never seen (until Nina visits it for the first time as part of her work), and the America in which they have grown up. Although they lived within the confines of Chinatown and attended Chinese schools, they learned to speak English, developed a taste for American food, and watched the popular

Gates to San Francisco's Chinatown *(Andy Z. | Shutterstock.com)*

sitcom *I Love Lucy* on television. All that they know of China is what their parents have told them about it. Leila reflects:

> We know so little of the old country. We repeat the names of grandfathers and uncles, but they have always been strangers to us. Family exists only because somebody has a story, and knowing the story connects us to a history.

Leila feels she is lucky to have been born in the United States, and lucky to be a member of the second generation of the family in the country. She has not had to endure the same deprivations and humiliations that Mah and Leon faced in their new land. This is brought home to Leila when she goes through Leon's suitcase full of papers, trying to find some documentation that will satisfy the Social Security office. She finds that Leon has kept almost every scrap of paper that ever came his way, including many rejections—from the army, from employers (he could not speak English well), from landlords (he applied for an apartment in the "wrong" neighborhood, that is, outside of Chinatown). The message the papers convey is that Leon was not wanted in San Francisco beyond the confines of what was available to him

in Chinatown. It is not surprising, perhaps, that, as Leila puts its, Leon "was paranoid about everything outside Chinatown." However hard he tries to understand America and be accepted there, he still thinks like a man from China who speaks a different language and adheres to another culture. He saves all his papers because, in China, he once told Leila, there is a tradition of "honoring paper" in the belief that "all writing was sacred." He tells her that, in Chinatown, in the old days, "All letters, newspapers, and documents were collected and then burned in a special temple, and the sacred ashes were discarded in a secret spot in the bay." He shows her a spot on Beckett Street, in Chinatown, where he could still trace "the faint shadow where a paper receptacle had been attached to the wall." For Leon, these old traditions mean something; for Leila, they are just stories. Although she does acknowledge her cultural inheritance, and she wants to remember it, this does not lessen her need to escape and live her own life.

A scene in which Leila is shown doing just that—escaping—occurs early in the novel (although late in the chronological sequence of events). It takes place a day before Leila visits Nina in New York. She and Mason are delivering a car to Mason's cousin Dale in Redwood City. Significantly, this is one of the few episodes that take place outside of Chinatown, and the images employed all suggest freedom, and they have a very American flavor. Mason has opened the sun roof "and it felt like we were flying." Leila not only likes being with Mason, who is able to make his way in the world outside Chinatown, she also likes "being on the road, moving fast in a nice car," and she is able to relax. As their car "swooped through the hills," she lowered the window, put her head out, "and took a big gulp of wind. I love wind, especially coastal wind with its salt taste." A young couple driving a fast car on a California highway—what could be more American than that? Far from the cramped confines of family and Chinatown, Leila gets a taste of the freedom she craves. Unlike Ona, whose story ends in tragedy, Leila is able to make her escape in a more constructive way.

Source: Bryan Aubrey, Critical Essay on *Bone*, in *Novels for Students*, Gale, Cengage Learning, 2011.

Pin-chia Feng

In the following review, Feng states that what Ng has accomplished in Bone *is a presentation of a Chinatown constructed out of lived experiences.*

As a teacher of Asian American literature in Taiwan, I always include Fae Myenne Ng's *Bone* (1993) in my survey course. *Bone* is an essential Asian American text because its emotionally invested yet unsentimental representation of San Francisco Chinatown allows me to introduce an important aspect of Chinese America to Taiwanese students, who are much in need of novelistic representations that can at once build the foundation for their engagement with quality literary work and enrich their understanding of the historical context of the people of Chinese descent residing on the other side of the Pacific. In addition to its aesthetic quality and significance in terms of historicity, I also feel personally attached to *Bone* since I wrote my first Chinese academic paper on this particular text, in which I analyze the way in which Ng employs what I call a "narrative of absence" to recall personal, familial, and ethnic histories into presence. In a very real sense, this novel helps me gain certain recognition in the field of Asian American studies in the Chinese-speaking world. Before the essay was in print, in fact, I had a short but memorable phone

> WHAT NG HAS ACCOMPLISHED IN *BONE* IS
> A PRESENTATION OF A CHINATOWN CONSTRUCTED
> OUT OF LIVED EXPERIENCES."

conversation with the author herself when I was housesitting for my late advisor Amy Ling, in whose class I first came across the novel. Ng asked for a copy of my paper so that she could present it to her families who had limited understanding of English, and I gladly complied. Hence, my preference for this novel is closely linked with personal memories as well.

Before going into further discussion about pedagogical issues of *Bone*, I would like to give a brief introduction to the development of Asian American studies in Taiwan. The curriculum of American literature in Taiwan has always been mainstream oriented. However, we in Taiwan's academic circle have witnessed the emergence and increasing importance of multicultural and multiethnic studies during the past two decades because of the influence of postcolonial studies and Taiwan's specific ethnic composition. Since the island nation is comprised of various ethnic groups—including Native Taiwanese tribal peoples, the Hakka and the Minnan who crossed the black waters four hundred years ago, the so-called "Mainlanders" who migrated from China to Taiwan around 1949 and their descendants, as well as foreign laborers of all nationalities—ethnic heterogeneity is an undeniable fact of the everyday existence in Taiwan. One of the most important political issues for Taiwanese society today is how to contend with this social heterogeneity. Hence, the multiethnic stratification of Taiwan makes the study of multicultural American literature highly relevant to the local sociopolitical reality. Moreover, because of the particular Asian connection, Asian American studies, especially the study of Chinese American literature, is by far the most developed subfield within this multiethnic and multicultural turn. When it comes to designing a syllabus for an Asian American literature course, therefore, Taiwanese academics tend to include more Chinese American texts than those by authors of other Asian ethnicities.

In terms of pedagogy, what Taiwanese students need most in an introductory course to Asian American literature are the proper historical contexts of the variegated ethnic texts. While monographs on Asian American history are naturally the most direct resources of historical information, I would argue that literary representations of specific ethnic contexts can be more intellectually inspiring and emotionally engaging. In this sense, *Bone* is indispensable to an Asian American literature course because of its emphasis on the importance of remembering Chinese American history. As Ng aptly puts it, "Remembering the past gives power to the present." Despite the fact that the plot of *Bone* centers upon a San Francisco Chinatown family, the scope of the narrative nevertheless goes beyond the confines of a family trauma and becomes a story about a unique urban space, San Francisco Chinatown, and Chinese America. One of the major themes in the novel is the representation of San Francisco Chinatown as a space that is intimately connected with the memory of its residents. Thus, while describing her novel to her parents who cannot read English, Ng openly admits that in writing *Bone* she is paying homage to the first generation of Chinese immigrants: "I tell them that the book celebrates the hard work and living that they endured in order to give future generations a better life. It's always very important to them to know that we appreciate their labor." This sense of filial appreciation and inter-generational connectiveness is what students of Asian American literature should be aware of and one of my foci in teaching this text. Additionally, the literary tradition behind this novel is also an important teaching point. Written by a second-generation Chinese American woman born and raised in Chinatown, *Bone* in fact follows in the train of a long tradition of Chinese American writings about Chinatown, such as Jade Snow Wong's *Fifth Chinese Daughter* (1945), Lin Yu-tang's *Chinatown Family* (1948), C. Y. Lee's *Flower Drum Song* (1957), Maxine Hong Kinston's *Tripmaster Monkey* (1989), and Frank Chin's *Donald Duk* (1991).

Within this particular context of San Francisco Chinatown literature, Ng faces the challenge of representing Chinatown without falling into the entrapment of self-orientalization. She needs to present the oldest and biggest Chinatown in North America as a representative site of Chinese American ethnicity; at the same time, she also needs to handle the persistent question of stereotypes, about how the mainstream society perpetuates an orientalist vision of Chinatown and how to re-envision this special space. What Ng has accomplished in *Bone* is a presentation of a Chinatown constructed out of lived experiences. Thus, Sauling Wong rightly observes that Ng is offering "a viable mode of rehabilitative representation" of Chinatown.

In *Bone*, Ng provides a panorama of San Francisco Chinatown in the most intimate and personal way substantiated by a Proustian insistence on sensory details, such as "the small sounds," and a desire to dig into the hidden layers of the past as the narrative takes on a retrospective trajectory. According to Ng, this retrospective form has a specific origin in ethnic memory: the oldtimers' longing to go "back" to their homes in China and the typical racist slurs flung at Chinese Americans telling them to go "back" to China. The novel is also filled with street names, and the streets are composed of countless shops—butchers and bakers and unseen sweatshops—upon which the livelihood of the community is dependent. With careful reading of these details, students can get familiar with Chinatown as a lived place with many inside and hidden stories.

The past in the novel, however, is always overshadowed by a sense of loss, as exemplified by the way that Grandpa Leong's bones get lost among the common grave. Students should be made aware of the fact that such a loss has its historical origin in discriminatory laws and a sojourner mentality. As such, this displacement after death is a powerful symbol of the disembodiment of first-generation Chinese Americans, especially those who helped build America, in the national discourse. One of Ng's primary objectives in writing *Bone* is to *re-member* Chinatown into a lived space that houses the spirits of the forefathers whose memory is in danger of vanishing.

The students should also learn that a major part of Ng's project in *Bone*, furthermore, is to restore a Chinese American "geography" of Chinatown that has been crowded out by tourist imagination and economic discourse, geography in Edward Said's sense "as a socially constructed and maintained sense of place" that is subject to manipulation and invention. The urgency of Ng's project lies in the fact that Chinatown, overshadowed by the Transamerica Pyramid, is an ethnoscape under siege by the global business flow of the Financial District, the high-class commercial glamour of the Union Square shopping district, and the yuppyish aura of North Beach. Chinatown today has become porous,

> THE WAY LEILA CAN ALSO EMBRACE WHAT IS
> TRADITIONALLY CHINESE ALMOST APPEARS INCON-
> SISTENT BECAUSE OF THE BREADTH AND EXTENT OF
> HER AMERICAN ATTITUDE AT OTHER TIMES."

even though the glass ceilings of race and class still remain intact. It is because of its ambiguous status that Ng needs to invent a counter-memory for Chinatown so that it will be a place of memory instead of just a forgettable urban enclave surrounded by the mainstream economic powers of metropolitan San Francisco. It is also because of her successful rendition of such a counter-memory that *Bone* becomes an essential text to my Asian American literature course.

Source: Pin-chia Feng, "Teaching *Bone:* A Taiwanese Perspective," in *American Book Review*, Vol. 31, No. 1, November/December 2009, pp. 7–8.

Allen Gee

In the following excerpt, Gee asserts that Ng's narrator, Leila's "I," can be viewed as the central personality that governs how particular characters and events appear, consequently establishing the hierarchy.

Bone (1993) is Fae Myenne Ng's first novel, set largely in San Francisco's Chinatown. Its central plot concerns how the members of the Leong family, Mah Leon, Nina, the narrator Leila, and her boyfriend Mason Louie, seek to understand why Ona, the Leongs' middle daughter, is driven to commit suicide. We are informed of the suicide from the first page, then the oldest sister, Leila, recounts events leading to and following the family's tragedy.

The framework is circular. The novel ends at a point in time close to where it begins as Leila explores each distinct possibility, no matter how small, that might have caused the loss of her sister. What I wish to argue, however, is not a single reason for Ona's suicide, or how the characters do or do not reach an understanding of it, but how Leila's central character, as the "I" narrator creates a distinguishable hierarchy based on her attempt to find a center that is neither too Chinese

nor too American, thus informing us of the complexity of her Chinese American consciousness.

This narrative process can be examined using Jacques Derrida's criticism, in particular by applying his fundamental post-structuralist essay, "Structure, Sign and Play in the Discourse of the Human Sciences." Ng's narrator, Leila's "I," can therefore be viewed as the central personality that governs how particular characters and events appear, consequently establishing the hierarchy. Characters and events are linked to one another through this same organizing principle.

I would like to argue that what primarily causes Leila to construct a rationalized hierarchy with herself at the top is that she is a second generation Chinese American, caught between traditional Chinese female submissiveness and middle class American individualism. She understands many traditional Chinese customs and values since she and her parents are Chinese, but having been educated in secular American schools, she also comprehends and conforms to American social mores. One who is neither too Chinese nor too American, in other words, a Chinese American like herself, is valued.

Leila is far from the submissive stereotype when she describes her reaction to her father Leon's buying speakers at a Goodwill store. She states, "I hate it when I get bitchy like that, but once I'm in the mood, I can't stop." She is entirely nonconformist, acting with an American sense of individualism or outspokenness, while in traditional Chinese culture the role of the eldest daughter in a Chinese family would demand that she respond with acceptance or deference to her father's actions. Soon after when Leila takes Leon to the social security office, he says to a clerk, "People be the tell me. I never talk English good. Them tell me." She relates that in response she yells at him, and that it drives her crazy how Leon has to find someone to blame. She says, "This is f. . .d. The way you do things is f. . .d." Not only does she reject traditional behavior once more, but the profanity of her language also disrupts tradition.

Leila's less Chinese character is also revealed by her mother. Speaking of how Leila does not hug or kiss Ona when she is crying, Mah tells her, "Where did you ever learn such meanness?" Mah is imposing traditional Chinese family loyalty while Leila has privileged her own feelings; she has learned such "meanness" or individuality from growing up in America. Likewise, toward the end of the text when Leila discusses her desire to move away from the family's neighborhood of Salmon Alley, she speaks of getting close to Mason and wanting her own life, not wanting to worry about Mah or Leon or anybody else. The stereotype of the dutiful, submissive daughter is disrupted again; Leila clearly forsakes traditional Chinese filial obedience and responsibility for her own individualistic American desires, here for romance or passionate love.

Leila's sensuality and pleasure can also be interpreted as significant movement beyond the submissive images of the Asian woman who exists to gratify male desires. Her "I" narrator is very specific when she tells us about being with Mason the night after her mother brews gingseng tea; she speaks of moving first, that "I kissed the hollow of Mason's throat, I licked his smooth lobe. Mason followed, urgent." The subtext here is that she is the aggressive one, the initiator, unmistakably fulfilling her own needs, displaying an American prioritization of individuality again.

Her "I" narrator also does not hesitate to recount alcohol and drug usage. As Leila sorts through Leon's personal papers, she speaks of drinking Scotch. Later after dropping Mah off at the airport for a trip to Hong Kong, she recounts smoking opium with Mason. Eventually, when Leila describes how she feels upon hearing of Ona's suicide, she compares her mood to snorting heroin. Leila's character clearly refuses the model minority stereotype so frequently associated with Asian Americans.

Leila characterizes the old men with whom Leon, her stepfather, associates at Portsmouth Square. They are called "time wasters," "scraps of dark remnant fabric," "fleabag friends," "Chinatown drift-abouts," and "talkers, wanderers, and time wasters." What Leila's "I" narrator is doing at each place can be interpreted as constructing the old men as Other. She makes judgments about all of the men simply based on their appearance and dehumanizes or devalues the way they live simply because they do not meet her standard of masculine decency.

Her denigration of these old men seems surprising because at another place she refers to her "favorite Genthe photo of two little girls walking down an alley." Since the photograph is a "favorite," this may imply that she has seen the rest of the pictures, which appear in a well known book, *Genthe's Photographs of San Francisco's Chinatown*. The photographs date from 1895 through 1906; they are accompanied by captions and entries about Chinese American history. Leila would know, then, why so many old men in San Francisco's Chinatown are there alone, without women or a structured domestic life, as a result of the former stringent immigration laws which forbade Chinese women entrance into the country. She should understand how the men are products of the bachelor societies that Chinatowns once were in the early nineteen hundreds. But the "I" narrator only expresses disapproval for these men. She devalues the men because she judges them according to an American standard of work or ideal of success, believing that they should be gainfully employed, working conventionally from nine to five.

Leila's bias against what is traditionally Chinese can also be found by examining some of her other characterizations of Chinese men. She describes Zeke Louie, with whom Mason works at a garage, by saying, "He had that build she [Nina] liked—the tight fit of muscle and nerve—but not enough height to carry it off." Then she tells Nina that Zeke Louie is "too Chinatown," and that she would not repeat it, but she does repeat the remark, as part of her narrative, for all of us to read; her bias against short Chinese males is easily recognized.

Leila also narrates as if from another side when she recounts talking to Chinese-speaking parents as part of her job. She works at a school as a bridge between teachers and parents and describes the work as "missionary," and how being inside parents' and their kids' apartments "depresses" her. Not only is there a racial judgment in this case, but also one of class since she has little understanding or patience for the poverty (or the most affordable housing) for a new generation of immigrants. Her feeling like a "missionary" also reveals how she speaks with an American sensibility, as if believing that she represents and should promulgate "the city upon a hill."

Although Leila displays predilections toward American over Chinese behavior, she can readily dismiss others as too American. Leila criticizes Dale, Mason's cousin, for having assimilated entirely into mainstream American society. She comments on Dale's all-white school and his nice house, his successful business, and his smooth English, but indicates that she could never "go with a guy like him." A class bias is immediately evident, as in her attitude toward recent Chinese immigrants, but here there is something problematic about someone who holds a white-collar job for a living. As Americanized as Leila is, Dale is still not Chinese enough for her.

The way Leila can also embrace what is traditionally Chinese almost appears inconsistent because of the breadth and extent of her American attitude at other times. When an ancient lady, Auntie Wong, appears after Ona's death, Leila listens to the woman's long lament "out of respect for her age." Leila also comments that the sound of the woman's dialect makes her want to cry and that it sounds "elegiac." Leila recounts Leon's belief about how his Grandfather Leong's unreturned bones are the cause of Ona's suicide and says the only way to respect this is to "leave it alone." She also expresses the desire to "respect" the traditional here.

Leila seems to value the ability to see simultaneously from the Chinese and from the American point of view. During two other incidents, the "I" narrator defends the traditional Chinese side of an Asian American binary when she disrupts tourists' notions of Chinatown. The morning after a New Year's dinner, Leila provides an insider's view of Chinatown as she walks through the streets. She describes a grocer, Chuck Lee, who is setting out vegetables, waves to a noodle maker, sees the butchers on Stockton Street, and a baker carrying bread. The subtext here is that to Leila Chinatown is not a tourist attraction, but a place where real people work and live: she names them and their occupations. Later she describes a drive through Chinatown in Mason's Camaro:

> Looking out, I thought, So this is what Chinatown looks like from inside those dark Greyhound buses....I felt a small lightening up inside, because I knew, no matter what people saw, no matter how close they looked, our inside story is something entirely different.

Leila can see from both within and without. She privileges those who can best negotiate traditional Asian and American spaces, but although she does not dismiss all that she recognizes as Chinese, she still privileges American values. The resulting hierarchy situates Leon and Mah, who are more traditional Chinese, at a lower level, with Americanized Nina one level higher yet lower than Leila and Mason.

I locate Leon at the bottom because Leila measures him by applying conventional American masculine standards. To a large extent, she ranks him, like the old men she calls "time wasters" in Portsmouth Square, against the mythology of the American success story. Her comments about him almost always lean toward the negative. Early in the text she says he forgets the simplest things, and that his ideas are pretty good, but the problem is he never finishes anything. She also includes her mother's critique of him when she tells about how the lights at Mah's Baby Store are not completely installed, so her mother calls him "a useless thing, a stinking corpse." The litany of remarks against Leon continues as Leila says of searching through his personal documents, "On paper Leon was not the hero." Discussing a trip Mason takes to the cemetery with Leon to help find Grandpa Leong's grave, she blames Leon for their becoming lost. Speaking of how he disassembles and reconstructs Mah's old Singer sewing machine, she questions whether he actually put the machine back together.

Leila remains unsparing in her criticism, refusing to value Leon for almost any reason. She reveals a narrowness of vision when she remembers when Leon almost runs off, trying to leave before Ona's funeral. Without any attempt to understand the escapist nature of his personality, Leila speaks only of his "three-day gamblers' special to Reno" and how he is scheduled to leave immediately. She also does not make any effort to understand Leon's agony over Ona's death, only describing his behavior as "ranting," "noise," and "nonsense." His verbose response to an uncharacteristically Chinese tragedy, suicide, appears to be an enigma to her. Subsequently when Leon leaves in anger, Mason reassures her that Leon will return, and her response is, "What? Like a dog?" This condescending tone is still evident when Leila chronicles his moving back to the Salmon Alley apartment after her mother has an affair with Tommie Hom. She offers him little, if any, sympathy.

Leila actually critiques herself, or her own limited perspective about Leon, when she describes how her mother understands his need to wander or "be lost in new places, new things." Leila can only view Leon by imposing conventional narratives of marriage and five day a week employment despite the fact that she knows how happy he appears after partaking in his different lifestyle, that of a merchant seaman. She remembers how "good, tanned and smiling and relaxed" he looks returning from the ocean. She writes about his coming home at one other time, back when she and Ona were much younger, recalling how he always comes back "a new man," "tanned," and "smelling like the sea." These are among the few spaces where

Leila's narrative appears to release him, if only briefly, from a critical gaze.

But Leila's measurement of Leon by conventional standards reveals how trapped she is by American values, so that he cannot help but disappoint her when she takes a job call at her own workplace for a dishwasher. She says, "I took a chance and sent Leon. I figured, How can he f. . .k up a dishwashing interview?" When reaching the end of the text, the argument can be made that Leila's realization of how her mother loves Leon extracts him from the lowest level of a hierarchy, but I think Leila's devaluation of his character has been so persistent throughout that the reader cannot help viewing him negatively, in spite of her final opinions....

Source: Allen Gee, "Deconstructing a Narrative Hierarchy: Leila Leong's 'I' in Fae Myenne Ng's *Bone*," in *MELUS*, Vol. 29, No. 2, Summer 2004, pp. 129–40.

Thomas W. Kim

In the following excerpt, Kim analyzes Asian American fiction based on Bone *and questions of legitimacy among Chinese-Americans while also examining the concept of authenticity and subjectivation in the novel.*

Some versions of multicultural studies have fostered the assumption that Asian American fiction offers unmediated access to the ethnic experience and "authentic" Asian American identity, without attention to the ways in which ethnicity and authenticity are produced and contested. In *The Ethnic Canon*, David Palumbo-Liu argues that multiculturalism allows students to encounter the Other without challenging their sense of self: "[L]iterary texts are read to solicit particular responses that manage conflict and tension at the same time as they reinforce hegemonic 'structures of feeling.'" But Asian American texts can be read more critically, as sites where "identity" and "authenticity" are investigated as ongoing cultural productions that also entail foreclosures and exclusions. Doris Sommer has argued that some ethnic texts resist readers' assumptions about ethnic identity and experience, placing rhetorical and narrative "obstacles" in the way of easy identification and interpretation: casual intimacy with the ethnic text/writer on the part of some readers effaces cultural difference and obscures historical relations of domination.

Fae Myenne Ng's *Bone* (1993) is one such text: narrative questions are raised but never

> THE QUESTION OF LEGITIMACY SEEMS PARTICULARLY PRESSING FOR CHINESE-AMERICANS, WHOSE HISTORY (LIKE THAT OF OTHER ASIAN AMERICANS) IS MARKED BY LEGAL, POLITICAL, AND GEOGRAPHICAL EXCLUSIONS AND DEMARCATIONS."

answered; the "reason" for Ona's suicide—the central plot question—is never given, and the reader does not get to "know" her, even though the novel is narrated by her sister. *Bone* further frustrates attempts at readerly identification with the characters by questioning the process of identification itself. By depicting the contingent historical and political processes by which Asian American subjects are constituted, the novel challenges the stability and coherence of identity. "Authenticity" is revealed to be a social and political construction; rather than reaffirming notions of self-identity and "respect" for presumably stable and determinate cultural difference(s), the novel enables a critique of hegemonic definitions of legitimacy.

Bone tells the story of a family in San Francisco's Chinatown struggling to understand the suicide of one daughter, Ona. The novel, narrated by her half-sister Leila, describes (in flashback and out of chronological sequence) the investigation of Ona's death, the breakup of the mother and father, and the other sister's suffering masked by apparent indifference. The ruptures in the Leong family force the characters to contend with questions of moral and legal accountability, leading to critiques of their heritage and individual identities. Often characters seek legitimation by turning towards official documents such as the police records detailing Ona's death; the identification papers and letters owned by Leon, the father; and church records of their grandfather Leong's burial. The narrative explores various encounters with state-regulated procedures for legitimation.

The question of legitimacy seems particularly pressing for Chinese-Americans, whose history (like that of other Asian Americans) is marked by legal, political, and geographical exclusions and demarcations. Chinese immigrants began arriving in America in 1849, but by 1882 Congress had passed the Chinese Exclusion Act, which barred entry or re-entry of all Chinese laborers for the next ten years; a series of exclusion laws were in effect until 1943, and even then entry was limited to family members or brides of Chinese-Americans. Only after 1965 were immigration restrictions on Asian Americans lifted. Historians have studied "how immigration officials, judges, and the Chinese interacted" during the exclusion era, and Sucheng Chan argues that "the Chinese did not simply suffer as victims and pawns. Rather, they actively and indefatigably challenged the injustice that the laws represented." Ng's novel reveals how contemporary Chinatown politics and culture have developed from the historical specificity of location, economics, and legislation; the encounter with the "Other" in this ethnic text is also an encounter with a specific history of dominations and resistances. While the narrator, Leila, as well as her husband Mason and her sister Nina (who lives in New York), are somewhat distanced from the older generation by language and by lifestyle, Ng's characters are still partly constituted by the history and effects of Chinese exclusion. Leila and her stepfather Leon in particular must work within legal, political, and familial discourses to establish their identities, their "ancestry," and their cultural place in America, all of which are subject to contingency, and all of which are contested.

By exploring the conventions of socially constructed sites of authenticity, legitimacy, and identity, *Bone* enables a critique of processes of identification/subjectivation. When Leon and Leila visit the social security office to apply for his retirement benefits, Leon encounters the bureaucratic demand for a single, coherent, consistent identity that can be "proven" on paper: "[The interviewer] was polite, and patient. He asked Leon why he had so many aliases? So many different dates of birth? Did he have a passport? A birth certificate? A driver's license?" This request for proof of identity, as an official American citizen eligible for benefits, infuriates Leon, but not because he objects to the state-regulated procedures for legitimation. After all, he does keep a suitcase full of documents; he saves every letter, every certificate, admitting that in America, "paper is more precious than blood." Leon reacts angrily to the polite young man because the papers that originally legitimated him, allowing him into the United States despite strict immigration laws, have now been challenged; as Leila observes, when the social security office does not accept Leon's application, "[i]t was as if all the

years of work didn't count." The "work" Leila refers to here is not only the wage-labor from which Leon will now retire, but the work he has put into constructing an authentic Chinese-American identity.

The literal construction of an identity performed by Leon reveals the conflicts inherent in subjectivation—that is, the ongoing process by which subjectivities are produced and constrained by discourse. In *Bodies That Matter*, Judith Butler writes that "The paradox of subjectivation (assujetissement) is precisely that the subject who would resist [regulatory] norms is itself enabled, if not produced, by such norms." Leon's case can be read as an example of Butler's observation, or its corollary, that the rules or conventions that govern and regulate identity are the same conventions that produce the possibility of resisting regulation. The papers Leon has amassed over the years function to authenticate his presence in the U.S.; as such they constitute his compliance with regulatory norms. At the same time, those papers, full of inconsistencies in date of birth, name, origin, etc., and mixed as they are with other documentation such as letters, photographs, newspaper clippings and even his wife's certificate of marriage to her first husband, represent Leon's defiance of a disciplinary system of identification meant to "fix" him as subject of the state. Leon became a U.S. citizen by lying about his parentage; he is a "paper son," having paid five thousand dollars to use Grandpa Leong's last name, since Leong was already an American citizen, facilitating Leon's entry and legitimation. He multiplies his lies, believing that "If you don't tell the truth, you'll never get caught in a lie."

Leon's dilemma of "situating" himself officially provides a site to negotiate the multiple (and agonistic) discourses that constitute and constrain the self. Leon, Leila, and the family itself serve as nodal points for the sometimes contradictory discourses that trouble the processes of subjectivation—how one comes to be recognized, how one comes to "matter"—in various, contingent locales or situations. Hegemony operates contingently, employing different strategies of interpellation and requiring different responses. It is not an easy task to locate a single, monolithic ideology that produces and delimits subjects even in particular instances or in relation to particular power structures. This version of hegemony requires a re-thinking of identity as contingent itself, recognizing the investment in citation to legitimate or lend authority to any utterance or articulation of identity (provisional though such an articulation may be). At the social security office, Leon is asked to produce his papers, as if identification papers reflect or represent an originary, authentic subject. But, like social security law itself, identity is produced by its citation; in other words, the papers will actually produce Leon. The subject is a subject-effect, materialized by the citation of the "laws" of articulation and identification.

Ng's troubling of identification, I will argue, is simultaneously a troubling of cause-effect relations (as in, which comes first, Leon or his papers). My reading of *Bone* exposes the metaleptic maneuver which establishes a fictive effect of authority, the maneuver by which hegemonies are authorized and identities established. "Metalepsis" is the rhetorical move in which a result, or effect, is seen as a cause. In this case, subjects which are produced or enabled by discourse—by their citation of the performative—are (temporarily) installed as the originary authors of the performative. Ng's text even challenges its own narrative authority to resolve its central questions, most notably the reason for Ona's suicide. The novel, and its narrator, cannot answer for Ona's death; the logic of cause and effect, the metanarratives of moral accountability, are left unfulfilled.

To procure an "affidavit of identification" for Leon, Leila rummages through his suitcase full of documents. Searching for a piece of paper that would certify Leon's status, Leila instead encounters records indicating Leon's failures—records that are useless to the state, in excess of the identity he must prove to the social security office. The letters of rejection she finds construct another version of Leon, one who is "unfit" for the army and "unskilled" for work:

> Maybe Leon should have destroyed these papers. They held a truth about a Leon I wasn't sure I wanted to know. Why did he keep every single letter of rejection? Letters saying "We don't want you" were flat worthless to me. What use was knowing the jobs he didn't get, the opportunities he lost? I sorted through the musty papers, the tattered scraps of yellowed notes, the photos. I kept going; I told myself that the right answer, like the right birthdate, had to be written down somewhere.

Leila rejects the failed Leon (the already-rejected Leon) because she is looking for the version of him that will satisfy the social security office. When she does find the affidavit of identification, which Ng "quotes" in its entirety, she says, "It would do." The affidavit identifies Lai-on Leong as citizen of the United States; this is Leon's false identity, the one he purchased years ago. Leila's search is not for the "right answer," the authentic Leon, except insofar as Leon will be authenticated by the social security office, and has been authenticated by the immigration authorities. Those characteristics of Leon in excess of his official identity constitute, however, a Leon that Leila begins to know.

In *Immigrant Acts* Lisa Lowe argues that the papers in his suitcase are a material trace of the past, the "conversion" from Chinese to American, constantly questioned and rearticulated paradoxically in the present. This Leon—or these Leons—coalesce as Leila begins organizing his papers into various files; she constructs "Leon the family man," "Leon the working man," "Leon, the business schemer." The epistemology of Leon is to catalogue his photos, newspaper clippings, letters, even menus and money into paper files, all meant, in Leila's filing system, to define and lend substance to his biography—to materialize Leon as the product of citation. As Butler writes, "The process of ... sedimentation or what we might call materialization will be a kind of citationality, the acquisition of being through the citing of power, a citing that establishes an originary complicity with power in the formation of the 'I'" (*Bodies That Matter* 15). Leila's initial determination to compose files on Leon, to provide reference material for the various headings "family man" or "working man," indicate her own duplication of the hegemonic impulse to register, classify, categorize, and contain identities. But Leila fails, of course; she becomes frustrated and begins throwing the papers back into the suitcase indiscriminately, finding his "affidavit of identification" accidentally.

The passage describing the papers discovered by Leila as she struggles to locate Leon's "identity" represents the sometimes agonistic, sometimes complicit discourses of familial, labor, racial, and capitalist institutions that interpellate Leon. Photographs of "Leon the working man" pressing laundry, sharpening knives, or making beds on board ship—doing servant work, doing whatever he has to do to earn a wage—seem to conflict with "Leon the business schemer," the entrepreneur with his check stubs and signed IOUs from business partners. Yet this capitalist

Leon is still a working class Leon, whose businesses fail, who keeps a diary of his overtime pay from his job as a fry cook, and whose pawn tickets suggest he sometimes needs "Cash-in-a-Flash." "Leon the working man," the merchant seaman, may come into conflict with the discourse of "the family man," since he is gone from home for weeks at a time, and is photographed "with girls in front of foreign monuments." And yet there are the "aerograms from Mah to Leon at different ports," so that the traveling is part of the family relationship, and indeed the wages earned from the sea voyages help support the family. Race- and class-based interpellations are suggested by a cookbook Leila discovers; she describes a "well-used bilingual cookbook that [she] flipped through quickly: Yorkshire pudding, corned beef with cabbage, kidney pie" which leads her to ask "Had Leon been a houseboy?" Here we imagine Leon as "houseboy" in an English mansion, struggling to make sense of recipes for Yorkshire pudding that is not pudding, and corned beef that has nothing to do with corn. The reference to a language barrier, along with the class distinction and racialized identity implied by the term "houseboy," contribute to Leon's subjectivation/subordination by the intersection of capitalist, nationalist, and racial/ethnic discourses....

Source: Thomas W. Kim, "'For a Paper Son, Paper is Blood': Subjectivation and Authenticity in Fae Myenne Ng's *Bone*," in *MELUS*, Vol. 24, No. 4, Winter 1999, pp. 41–57.

Cherry W. Li

In the following review, Li states that Bone *was written without sensationalism and that Myenne Ng's characters are depicted realistically.*

In sharp contrast to the overdramatized lives of Chinese Americans in Amy Tan's work, Ng's simply written first novel is totally without sensationalism. Yet because her characters are depicted so realistically, the reader cannot but be moved by the hopes, grief, and quarrels of two generations of Chinese Americans in San Francisco's Chinatown. Mah, who has worked hard all her life in garment sweatshops, finally is able to own her baby-clothing store. Her husband, Leon, who used to be a merchant seaman, worked two shifts in ships' laundry rooms to provide for his family. Nevertheless, the family is torn apart after Ona, the middle daughter, jumps from the tallest building in Chinatown. The bones of contention and

bones of inheritance come together in great turmoil as Nina, the youngest daughter, leaves Chinatown for New York City and then Leila, the oldest, marries and moves out to the suburbs. Leon, the paper son to old Leung, fails to keep his promise to take Leung's bones back to China. Thus, a family's tragedy is cast in greater historical context, and the reader is rewarded with a rich reading experience.

Source: Cherry W. Li, "Book Reviews: Fiction," in *Library Journal*, Vol. 118, No. 1, January 1, 1993, p. 166.

SOURCES

Bryant, Clifton D., ed., *Handbook of Death & Dying*, Vol. 1, Sage, 2003, p. 354.

"Chinese American Demographics," in *Améredia*, http://www.ameredia.com/resources/demographics/chinese.html (accessed October 5, 2010).

"Exploring Chinatown's History and Culture...Tours, Museums—San Francisco's Chinatown," in *Sunset*, April 1990, http://findarticles.com/p/articles/mi_m1216/is_n4_v184/ai_8833843/ (accessed October 1, 2010).

"Fae Myenne Ng," in *Voices from the Gaps*, University of Minnesota Web site, http://voices.cla.umn.edu/artistpages/ngFae.php (accessed September 27, 2010).

Kakutani, Michiko, "Building on the Pain of a Past in China," in *New York Times*, January 29, 1993, p. C26.

McFadden, Christine, "The Growing Rate of Depression, Suicide among Asian American Students," in *Pacific Citizen*, http://www.pacificcitizen.org/site/details/tabid/55/selectmoduleid/373/ArticleID/490/reftab/36/Default.aspx?title=The_Growing_Rate_of_Depression,_Suicide_Among_Asian_American_Students (accessed November 10, 2010).

Meng, Ying Ying, "Factsheet: Chinese Americans," in *Wildflowers*, http://www.wildflowers.org/community/Chinese/facts. shtml (accessed October 5, 2010).

Mifflin, Margot, Review of *Bone*, in *Entertainment Weekly*, Vol. 154, January 22, 1993, p. 53.

Miller, Heather Ross, Review of *Bone*, in *Southern Review*, Vol. 29, No. 2, Spring 1993, pp. 420–30.

Ng, Fae Myenne, *Bone*, Hyperion, 2008.

Review of *Bone*, in *Booklist*, Vol. 97, June 1, 2001, p. 1944.

Review of *Bone*, in *Publishers Weekly*, Vol. 239, No. 49, November 9, 1992, p. 71.

"San Francisco Chinatown," in *The Bancroft Library*, http://bancroft.berkeley.edu/collections/chineseinca/sfchinatown.html (accessed October 1, 2010).

FURTHER READING

Barde, Robert Eric, *Immigration at the Golden Gate: Passenger Ships, Exclusion, and Angel Island*, Praeger, 2008.

This book tells the story of Angel Island's Immigration Station, where would-be immigrants to the West Coast were processed. Barde shows that the station was more concerned with keeping people out than letting them in, beginning with the exclusion of Chinese but gradually extending to cover all Asian immigrants.

Chang, Iris, *The Chinese in America: A Narrative History*, Viking, 2003.

This book covers the history of Chinese immigration to the United States, from its beginnings in the mid-nineteenth century to the present day.

Ho, Wendy, *In Her Mother's House: The Politics of Asian American Mother-Daughter Writing*, AltaMira Press, 1999.

Ho discusses mother-daughter relationships in fiction by Asian American writers, including Maxine Hong Kingston, Amy Tan, and Fae Myenne Ng.

Jorae, Wendy Rouse, *The Children of Chinatown: Growing Up Chinese American in San Francisco, 1850–1920*, University of North Carolina Press, 2009.

Jorae shows how early Chinese American families tried to combat official policies of exclusion. American-born children of immigrants made efforts to define themselves as Chinese American rather than Chinese. This book serves as very interesting background reading for understanding *Bone*.

SUGGESTED SEARCH TERMS

Fae Myenne Ng

Fae Myenne Ng AND Bone

San Francisco AND Chinatown

Chinatown

Exclusion Act

Chinese American

Chinese American immigration

paper son

Chinese American literature AND Fae Myenne Ng

Fae Myenne Ng AND interview

The Bostonians

HENRY JAMES

1886

In his 1886 novel *The Bostonians*, the American novelist Henry James offers a nuanced, incisive portrayal of the women's rights movement as it churned and gathered steam in the 1870s. Following the turmoil of the Civil War, many Boston-area intellectuals and reformers turned from the accomplished cause of abolitionism to the new quest for suffrage and other rights for women. James recognized this movement's relevance in a journal entry of April 8, 1883, as cited in Leon Edel's biography *Henry James: The Middle Years, 1882–1895*:

> I wished to write a very *American* tale, a tale very characteristic of our social conditions, and I asked myself what was the most salient and peculiar point in our social life. The answer was: the situation of women, the decline of the sentiment of sex, the agitation on their behalf.

For his novel, James devised a provocative premise: an attractive young woman with an entrancing improvisational style of oration is discovered one evening both by a wealthy feminist aiming to propel the movement into a blazing new era and by a chivalrous, conservative Southerner who, utterly charmed, soon realizes that he is falling in love with her—and wants nothing more than to thwart her potential blossoming as a brilliant prophetess of the women's cause. The attractions, repulsions, and agitations among these three archetypal characters lend palpable tension to a tale filled with psychological and social insight into one of the most significant eras in history,

Henry James *(The Library of Congress)*

when the women of the world's preeminent democracy first articulated the collective demand that the two sexes be treated equally, both in law and in life.

AUTHOR BIOGRAPHY

Henry James, Jr., was born on April 15, 1843, in New York City, the second of five children to Henry James, Sr., and Mary Walsh James. The elder Henry James adopted progressive viewpoints, such as the spiritual brand of utopian socialism expounded by the Swedish theologian Emanuel Swedenborg, and promoted them in books that never proved popular. He was nonetheless profoundly influential in the lives of his children, impressing upon them his acute moral consciousness and intellectual devotion. The oldest child, William, would become a renowned psychologist and philosopher; in William's shadow, the young Henry duly attuned himself to a mode of constant analysis and introspection, absorbing education under various circumstances as, after an early childhood in New York, his family moved around Europe between 1855 and 1860. Shy and taciturn, James had few childhood friends and, in his solitude, turned to books and the workings of his imagination, penning stories and dramas from an early age.

Returning to New England, James suffered at age eighteen an obscure trauma while helping put out a fire, a strain of sorts that he rarely and only vaguely referred to. He would suffer back pains at points in his life but otherwise remained active, and yet he evidently perceived the accident as justifying or legitimizing his isolation and estrangement from society. In light of the absence of evidence that James ever engaged in a romantic relationship (though he would have great love for his cousin Minny Temple, who was afflicted with consumption and died in 1870), some biographers have concluded that the accident affected his ability to perform sexually. Regardless of the actuality, the timing of the incident was itself significant: the Civil War was just getting under way, and while his younger brothers enthusiastically enlisted to fight for the Union, James lingered at home. Meanwhile, buoyed by the family's ample wealth, he strove to establish a literary career, publishing critical reviews and short stories beginning in 1864.

In time, James's restless mind and heart drifted away from his homeland. In traveling and writing in England, France, and Italy in the early 1870s, he discovered that Europe, with a culture that he felt to be nobler and richer when contrasted with utilitarian America, agreed more with his nature. After a year in Paris, he settled permanently in London in 1876. By then he had published several novels, with ensuing publications including *The American* (1877), *The Portrait of a Lady* (1881), and *The Bostonians* (1886), which was first published serially in *Century Monthly* from February 1885 to February 1886. James did not gain wide renown during his lifetime, even with later novels now recognized as masterpieces, like *The Ambassadors* (1903). On the surface, this accorded with his acquired belief that the true artist must forgo happiness or face the dissolution of the creative spirit. Now honored as one of the foremost literary minds of his age and of American history—with the *Henry James Review*, founded in 1980, devoted entirely to his work—he is often referred to simply as "the Master." At the end of James's life, his health deteriorated. He gained British citizenship in 1915 and, after suffering a stroke, died in London on February 28, 1916.

PLOT SUMMARY

Book I

CHAPTERS I–III

As *The Bostonians* opens, Basil Ransom is in Boston visiting Olive Chancellor, a cousin of his, whom he awaits in the drawing room while chatting with Adeline Luna, Olive's older sister. Mrs. Luna wittily, even mockingly, characterizes her radical sister, who enters with distinct coldness. Mrs. Luna exits dramatically for an evening of convivial entertainment.

Basil and Olive present themselves to each other, with Olive's stiff, tragic shyness leading Basil to turn accommodatingly talkative. She had written to Basil to offer her support out of a sense of self-sacrificing duty; Ransom's family was ruined during the Civil War, so he has embarked on a legal career in New York, and his work has presently brought him to Boston. She invites him to dine.

Basil marvels at the many accessories adorning the interior of Olive's cultured apartment. He briefly fancies a partnership with her but realizes she is a fated spinster. They chat amiably over dinner, and Olive invites Basil to a gathering at Miss Birdseye's. Basil is interested in being amused but confesses indifference to societal concerns, which agitates Olive, who during the carriage ride fiercely regrets inviting him.

CHAPTERS IV–IX

Miss Birdseye, whose every trait signals her life's devotion to philanthropy and the cause of women's rights, cordially welcomes Olive, who has come early for a private audience, and Basil. Mrs. Farrinder, the matronly orator who is to address the gathering, arrives, as do Doctor Mary Prance, a physician who rents a room from and cares for Miss Birdseye, and many others.

Not in the mood to give her address, Mrs. Farrinder absorbs herself in conversation with Olive, even asking the ardent young woman to give a speech that evening. Olive professes that she does not have the faculty but that she feels inspired to devote herself as fully as she can to the sacred cause of women. Miss Birdseye suggests Mrs. Farrinder might now speak to the gathering.

A graceful hostess, Miss Birdseye introduces the solitary Basil to Doctor Prance. They get along as outcasts in the room, with both expressing a certain indifference to the cause at hand. Prance tells Basil about many of the guests. In the absence

of opposition, Mrs. Farrinder remains uninspired, so Selah Tarrant, prompted by his wife, suggests that his daughter speak. Doctor Prance retires.

Thinking his Southern perspective might goad Mrs. Farrinder, Olive introduces Basil to her, but Basil shies away from asserting any contrary opinions. Verena Tarrant then presents herself, having recently given an inspirational address in St. Louis, and admiringly flatters Mrs. Farrinder, who yet refuses to speak at all. Thus, Miss Birdseye introduces Verena.

Mr. Tarrant, a mildly theatrical mesmeric healer, serves to calm and prepare his daughter through touch, a scene that irritates Basil. When Verena speaks, her words flow forth in a most natural, honest way, deeply affecting Basil, despite his antipathy to the content of her speech. She ends with a smile, and all are impressed.

Mrs. Farrinder praises Verena's spirit and presence, while Olive is dumbstruck. Basil asks Miss Birdseye to be introduced to Verena, but Olive suddenly asserts that she is unwell and must depart. First she strides toward Verena and intently invites her to visit, while Basil can only smile at her. Olive draws Basil out with her but does not offer him a ride.

CHAPTERS X–XII

Urged by her mother to form an advantageous friendship, Verena visits Olive's house on Charles Street the next day. Although a daughter of a famed abolitionist, Mrs. Tarrant's life amounted to little after she married the phony mesmeric healer Selah, and so she is fully vicariously invested in her daughter's potential success and fame.

Olive gushes upon Verena's arrival, at once revealing her profound affection for the gifted, beautiful young speaker. Recognizing Verena's childlike nature and hopeful of shifting control away from the girl's parents, who appall her, Olive proposes a friendship between them, a union founded on devotion to the cause of women.

Basil happens to arrive then, to Olive's irritation. She neglects to introduce him to Verena, and so he charmingly introduces himself before humorously questioning their cause. Feeling Olive's chagrin, Verena excuses herself. Olive then ignores Basil, who is found by Mrs. Luna, again dressed to go out. He confides his affection for Verena, but Mrs. Luna (whose husband is deceased) boldly seeks to claim him for herself. They speak of Verena's bright future before Mrs. Luna exits with Basil, who is to depart that day for New York.

CHAPTERS XIII–XVI

Certain that Olive represents high society, Mrs. Tarrant encourages her daughter in her newfound alliance. Each young woman admires the other, and Olive lends Verena confidence in her abilities and determination. Selah Tarrant envisions his daughter's name and achievements splashed across the newspapers.

Verena's opinions, such as about Olive, flourish independently of her mother, but they both admire Olive, to whom Mrs. Tarrant pays an uninvited visit—partly to see the fascinating Mrs. Luna. In turn, although wanting to dissociate Verena from her parents as much as possible, Olive pays the Tarrants a visit. Mrs. Tarrant proves boring indeed.

The visit reinforces Olive's belief that she must tear Verena away from her vulgar upbringing; the father's odd influence is surely dispensable. Matthias Pardon's presence conjures in Olive's mind the possible threat of young men's romantic advances toward Verena. Then the purported Harvard students Mr. Gracie and Mr. Burrage drop in to flirt with Verena. Olive finds their shallow interest insulting.

The journalist Pardon, likewise deemed a charlatan, seems infatuated with Verena. Gracie and Burrage profess their interest in the cause and suggest they could stir up an audience at Harvard. They wish Verena to speak, but Olive's hesitation, because of their ulterior romantic motives, leads her to dissuade Verena. Before departing, Olive urges Verena to promise not to marry.

CHAPTERS XVII–XX

Upon next meeting, Verena declares her readiness to make the desired promise. However, now Olive does not want Verena's promise; she hopes that Verena will opt not to marry willingly in the absence of a promise—but Olive also intimates that she "shall die" if Verena marries. Pardon visits Olive, proposing to share in Verena's presentation, but Olive thinks he is after money. She wants no man's support and rejects him.

Verena reveals that Mr. Pardon is seeking her hand in marriage, while Mr. Henry Burrage has been visiting often. Verena wants to know whether Burrage, a rich collector, should be respected. Verena and her mother visit Mr. Burrage, and then, at his behest, Verena brings Olive along. Olive perceives that Burrage, who is at least a good pianist, signifies nothing more than amusement but that, as such, he could be a threat.

Over the winter, Verena comes to stay with Olive. Mrs. Luna and Basil Ransom are gravitating toward each other in New York; Ransom will even tutor Newton, Luna's son. Olive realizes that she herself and Mrs. Farrinder represent incompatible forces and so is glad when the matron leaves Boston to tour the nation. Inviting Selah Tarrant to call, Olive presents him with a check and the demand that he and his wife leave Verena alone for one year.

Verena is content with her current living and financial arrangements, while Mrs. Tarrant, saddened but hopeful, hires a servant. Henry Burrage proposes to Verena but is turned down and returns to New York. Wary of such advances, Olive plans to escort Verena to Europe that summer. Olive and Verena meanwhile read, attend concerts, and visit Miss Birdseye, whom Verena honors in another moving speech.

Book II

CHAPTERS XXI–XXII

In New York, Basil Ransom's circumstances remain shabby; he has proven untalented in his law practice and irrelevant in attempts at writing opinionated articles. Sinking into drink and smoke, he recalls Mrs. Luna upon finding a note from her. When the tutoring had failed, he had stopped giving her attention but now decides he will visit once more.

The serenity of the scene at Mrs. Luna's leads Ransom to the notion of marrying her, to devote himself to writing—a notion soon dispelled. He finds out that Olive and Verena returned from Europe six weeks prior, having met with success at the Women's Convention before departing. Abruptly feeling he must recover something lost, Ransom is rejuvenated.

CHAPTERS XXIII–XXV

Three weeks later, a revived business contact brings Ransom to Boston, where, with a day of leisure, he heads toward Cambridge in search of the Tarrants' residence—passing Olive's without intending to stop. Miss Birdseye exits as he passes, and he escorts her onto a streetcar and speaks her to learn where the Tarrants live.

Verena receives Ransom warmly despite the year and a half since they last spoke, relating her recent travels and advancements. She is piqued upon discovering that the provocative Ransom has bypassed a visit to Olive in search of her. After more pleasantries, she impulsively offers to show him around the Harvard campus.

While walking, Verena recalls the success of the convention. Ransom is forward in antagonizing her and in revealing his personal interest in her. They visit the library and Memorial Hall, with its tribute exhibit to those fallen in the Civil War, which Ransom finds moving. They discuss whether Olive is to find out about Ransom's visit, and Verena is persuaded to lean toward conspiracy.

CHAPTERS XXVI–XXVIII

In New York, Ransom receives a card inviting him to an address by Verena at the Burrage residence. Amidst the high society there, he finds Olive and is greeted coldly. He discerns that Verena has not spoken of his Boston visit. Olive is ushered to a front-row seat, while Basil lingers by the door, where Mrs. Luna finds him.

Mrs. Luna insists that the chivalrous Basil accompany her back into the empty drawing room and converse with her there, even as Verena begins speaking. Irritated and having rashly revealed that he had never before met Mrs. Burrage, Basil, upon hearing a round of applause, at last scorns Mrs. Luna and returns to hear the speech. Mrs. Luna leaves.

Basil is again mesmerized by Verena's voice; her speaking skills and intellectual resources have improved, but he still loathes her cause. Afterward, Verena, escorted by the servile Henry Burrage, happens upon Basil, and while Henry moves about, she and Basil chat insinuatingly about the circumstances. Politely withdrawing when Henry escorts a rich man over, Basil finds Mrs. Burrage and Olive, who reluctantly reveals where the Bostonians are lodging, on Tenth Street.

CHAPTERS XXIX–XXXI

Visiting Olive the next morning, the conniving Mrs. Luna shares her impression that Basil must have been invited by Verena, and the two may have met or corresponded secretly. Refusing to gratify her sister, Olive professes indifference but takes the warning gravely.

While Henry Burrage is driving Verena around, Olive schemes to monopolize her time throughout the day and urge her to leave tomorrow. Upon returning, Verena tells of Burrage's evident marital intentions. Olive asks of Basil, and Verena admits that she invited him and has received a letter from him. Verena agrees to return to Boston the following day. They enjoy their afternoon excursions.

Upon returning to their lodgings on Tenth Street, Verena finds a letter from Basil, and she informs Olive that he wishes to see her the next morning at eleven. After observing Henry and calculating through dinner and the opera, Olive shows Verena the letter she received from Mrs. Burrage imploring Olive to pay a visit tomorrow, to discuss whether Verena might stay longer. For the sake of both meetings, they will stay another day.

CHAPTERS XXXII–XXXIV

At noon, while Basil is still visiting Verena, Olive visits Mrs. Burrage, who eventually requests Olive's support for her son's marriage to Verena. Feigning a lack of personal involvement, Olive commits to nothing but considers that Henry Burrage would be a safer match than others, especially Basil. Hoping the courtship will be in vain, Olive thinks a stay at the Burrages could shield Verena from Basil. At three o'clock, Basil and Verena remain out together.

At Tenth Street, with Olive departing, Basil is entreating Verena to walk about the city. After revealing a dependence on Olive's trust, Verena opts to assert herself and agrees to go out. It is a beautiful April day in Central Park. Basil insists on his conservative opinions, which ultimately Verena cannot reconcile with her view of her life and herself.

While the two rest on a bench in the park, Basil divulges the true depths of his particular brand of hyper-masculine conservatism, and Verena realizes he is surely intractable. Basil believes that she has been led by her parents and Olive to play a part she does not truly believe in. She hastens away, wanting to return unaccompanied. Back at Tenth Street, Verena tells Olive she wishes to stay in New York no longer.

Book III

CHAPTERS XXXV–XXXIX

That summer, Basil travels through Boston and takes a train to Marmion, on Cape Cod, where Verena and Olive are vacationing. Outside his hotel, Basil encounters Dr. Prance; she and the ailing Miss Birdseye are staying with Verena and Olive. The doctor leads Basil to their rented house, where Verena is rehearsing for a grand speech at Boston's Music Hall. Basil bids Dr. Prance good night.

At eleven in the morning, Basil visits the house to find the front door open; in the backyard, he ingratiates himself to Miss Birdseye, who believes him converted to the women's cause. Olive and Verena soon arrive; flustered, Olive retreats inside, and Basil takes Verena on a walk to the water, telling her that his essay is to be published. Fifteen minutes later, Verena returns to tell Olive that Basil has proposed.

Verena tells Olive that she does like Basil, more than any other gentleman yet, and she seems insincere in her rationalizations about why not to flee. Thus, Olive can only wait, wracked with anxiety, to see how the situation will be resolved. Meanwhile, Verena and Basil take daily walks.

Verena comes to believe Basil's charge that the cause is not her heart's desire; she is in love with him. During their walks, Verena yet wonders whether her gift will be for naught, and Basil presses his case, indeed intending to preempt her imminent success. One day as the two return, the dying Miss Birdseye summons them. Miss Birdseye blesses Verena for her involvement in the cause, and Verena commits anew. Basil speaks in a way that is vague to the point of being deceptive, appalling Olive.

The next day, Basil learns from Dr. Prance that Miss Birdseye has died, and he receives a note from Verena forestalling further meetings. He thus travels to Provincetown for a week, and Dr. Prance returns to Boston. Upon returning, Basil meets Verena, who, stricken from grieving, declares a union impossible, but they rent a boat for the day. Meanwhile, although Verena swore herself to the cause anew, in her absence, Olive is contorted with the misery of disillusionment. After a walk, she finds the house silent, but Verena is sitting there in the shameful dark, and they embrace sadly. In the morning, Basil is surprised to learn from Olive that Verena has left for parts untold.

CHAPTERS XL–XLII

At Olive's residence in November, Mrs. Luna, who will return to Europe, receives Basil with antagonism. He is seeking Verena; although she is giving a well-advertised address that evening, the Tarrant residence seems deserted. Matthias Pardon, acting the journalistic vulture, also arrives seeking Verena, agitating Mrs. Luna.

Basil wanders Boston, still determined to thwart Verena. At Music Hall, while crowds gather, Basil bides his time. As the organ starts, he slips down a passage toward the dressing room, but a policeman is guarding the door. The audience rumbles with impatience; the curious Pardon joins the scene. Selah Tarrant tries to calm the crowd. Mr. Filer, Olive's agent, arrives in the hall furious and bangs on the door.

At last, a pale Verena opens the door for Basil, also admitting Mr. Filer. Olive is collapsed upon Mrs. Tarrant's lap. Basil enjoins Verena to flee; the others all beg him to leave her be—at least for this one night, Olive says. As the spectators grow ever angrier, Mr. Filer and Dr. Tarrant leave to appease them. Verena pushes Olive and Mrs. Tarrant out and melts into Basil; she begs him to spare her, to let her speak, but he insists she must not. As they try to leave, Mrs. Tarrant pushes Verena back into the dressing room, and then Mrs. Farrinder strides in to belittle Olive, who rushes to the platform as Mrs. Burrage and her son enter. Basil forces Verena out, and the crowd grows silent for Olive as the two slip away, Verena in tears.

CHARACTERS

Miss Birdseye

When first presented to the reader through the eyes of Basil Ransom, Miss Birdseye is a caricature of an aged philanthropic reformer, "a confused, entangled, inconsequent, discursive old woman," who has somehow remained disconnected from humanity. Basil effectively dupes her about being converted to Verena's views and the women's cause, which allows Miss Birdseye to view his second visit to Boston in a positive light and thus happily give him Verena's address.

Miss Birdseye is considered and treated more favorably by the Bostonians; for Olive, she is a resource of nearly infinite dimensions and had "a kind of aroma of martyrdom," while Verena finds her "a picturesque humanity figure" and delivers a tear-jerking address in her honor at one of her hallmark gatherings. The trip to Marmion allows Miss Birdseye a dignified, even glorious, death, with her dying sentiments precipitating a moral crisis for Verena, who cannot bear the thought of betraying the dying woman and the women's cause.

Henry Burrage

A charming young New Yorker who is acquainted with Verena through Mr. Gracie, Henry Burrage's deceptive posing as a law student is dismissed by the bubbly Verena, who finds the "form" of a law student just as impressive as the reality and "didn't see why it wasn't enough when you made yourself as pleasant as that." Henry Burrage's most attractive quality seems to be his ability to converse intelligently about his collections of antiques and curios; his intellect is deemed mediocre, his character shallow. When his mother invites Verena to New York, he proves admirably doting, fetching dainty snacks and water and profusely praising Verena's abilities.

Mrs. Burrage

The mother of Henry Burrage comes across as the consummate elite New Yorker: socially adept, highly fashionable, and full of a haughty self-confidence rendered practically invulnerable by her unfailing sense of the superiority of her city of residence. Olive imagines that Mrs. Burrage could hardly favor Verena as a match for her son, given the inferior social status of the professionally dubious Selah Tarrant and his itinerant family. Even when Mrs. Burrage invites Verena to New York to speak before her Wednesday Club, Olive considers it hostile territory; the high-society women are imagined to be more than happy to let their husbands perform all the work as well as have all the responsibilities—as long as they are allowed enough cash to amuse themselves. When Mrs.

Burrage realizes the enduring nature of her son's infatuation with Verena, she seeks to prove her burgeoning devotion to the women's cause, in hopes of convincing Olive to support the match. Olive realizes how convenient the Burrage wealth and status might prove, but she nonetheless prefers Verena single. Mrs. Burrage has a glossy, impressive surface, but her philanthropy seems to stem from little more than her devotion to coddling her son and maintaining her enviable social status.

Miss Catching

The young Miss Catching is a librarian at Harvard who is supportive of Verena.

Olive Chancellor

With her name being the novel's opening word and her character developed in greater depth than any other, Olive can be seen as the work's main protagonist and moral center. In light of the deaths of her brothers (in the Civil War) and parents, she is able to live off and liberally draw from her inheritance, which she decides to devote to the cause of women's rights. Described by her sister as a radical who believes "whatever is, is wrong," Olive proves sensitive to the slightest injustices and masculine affronts; "her nature was like a skiff in a stormy sea." She preternaturally senses that Basil represents a danger to her life and goals, and she immediately recognizes the immense value to the women's rights movement represented by Verena. She proceeds to engage in a sort of chess match with Basil, with both their kings fighting for possession of the queen without a color, Verena.

Upon taking charge of and shaping Verena, Olive strives not to hold her too tightly, but Verena's one secret—and thus, in a sense, her one uncensored freedom—her outing with Basil, blossoms into a romance that proves Olive's worst nightmare. When Basil whisks Verena away from Music Hall at the end of the novel, Olive at last makes a first step toward fulfilling the destiny she had foreseen for Verena: ushering the women's rights movement into a new era. James leaves the reader to imagine the degree of success Olive is to obtain.

In contrast to the steady temperaments of the placid, content Verena and the cool, calculating Basil, Olive serves as the novel's dramatic barometer: as Verena moves toward becoming the attractive new mouthpiece of the women's rights movement, Olive is in high spirits, but as

Verena veers toward romance with Basil, Olive cannot escape her agitation. The early narration stresses that Olive is "morbid"—which can refer to being liable to abject emotions as well as affected by disease—going so far as to highlight (but not answer) the essential questions, "Why was she morbid, and why was her morbidness typical?" Critics have noted that Olive is unique among James's characters in being characterized in terms of traits manifested as ailments or symptoms; the text veritably begs the reader to try to diagnose her condition, whether physical or psychological.

Many commentators have concluded that Olive is a portrayal, intentional or not, of a repressed lesbian. This is supported implicitly by the quasi-romantic intensity of her relationship with Verena and her antithetical attitude to men generally and explicitly by the passage describing the "primness" that always accompanied her interactions with men, which prove as sensual as an evening at chapel. However, Olive does find Basil Ransom "very handsome" and finds herself unnerved in a visceral way by his presence. Critics have also noted that intense, even passionate friendships between women were not out of the ordinary in James's era. His own sister, Alice, who spent much of her life coping with a nervous condition, shared a most intimate friendship with a woman named Katharine Loring, which some have taken to be a model for Olive and Verena's rapport. As with Olive's destiny, James leaves her sexual identity open to the individual reader's conception.

Mrs. Farrinder

The reigning matriarch of the women's rights movement, Mrs. Farrinder, "at almost any time, had the air of being introduced by a few remarks"—a narrative swipe at her celebrity-size ego and emotional distance from anyone around her. She is seen as having been intrinsically altered by her uniquely authoritative yet unfulfilled relationship with American society; her upright dignity is founded in the nationwide moral tension that will not be dispelled until the ballot is extended to women. Olive recognizes that Mrs. Farrinder, who perceives Verena as dangerously appealing competition, is the only revolutionary feminist "more concentrated, more determined" than Olive herself. Thus, after Mrs. Farrinder fails to endorse Verena with a letter to the *New York Tribune* before leaving for a nationwide tour, Olive is only too happy to

dismiss her. In the closing scene, Mrs. Farrinder's disdainful remark to Olive is what inspires the latter to take to the stage.

Mr. Filer

Olive's agent, Mr. Filer, storms through the closing scene to impress upon the protagonists the urgency of the situation; a failure to provide any lecture at all would be a financial and public-relations disaster. His name connotes concern with little more than the figures appearing on the papers to be filed away in his office.

Mr. Gracie

Presumably a law student (although his friend is only posing), Mr. Gracie brings Henry Burrage on a social call to the Tarrant household in Cambridge. As Mr. Burrage begins to court Verena, Mr. Gracie fades into the background.

Mrs. Adeline Luna

The elder Chancellor daughter offers a sharp contrast to the younger Olive in almost every respect. Adeline, whose husband is deceased (and left her ample wealth) and who returns from Europe to New York with her son, is concerned primarily with amusing herself, having her ego massaged, and generally taking advantage of life as a woman of independent means. Her habit of parental indulgence spoils Newton rotten. In accord with Mrs. Luna's garrulous nature, her primary function in the narrative is to relay information; after setting the tone of the novel in providing Basil (and the reader) with a backhanded introduction of Olive, she later clues Olive in about the possibility that Basil and Verena, of whom she is jealous, have met and corresponded secretly.

Newton Luna

Although he does not appear in person, Adeline Luna's son affects the narrative when she hires Basil Ransom to be his tutor. The boy is inattentive, destructive, and impossible to teach, and Ransom is driven to resign his position and avoid contact with Mrs. Luna.

Matthias Pardon

A young journalist with prematurely white hair that suggests he should be respected, Pardon generally erases this impression with his prying, profiteering nature. He admires Verena, and her father imagines that a husband with connections in the world of print and publicity would be ideal, but Verena never considers him seriously. He proposes a partnership with Olive in promoting Verena, but Olive forthrightly refuses. Otherwise bold in interfering, Pardon—his name suggesting his habitual mode of apologetic intrusion—reveals ethical qualms only with respect to the demands of the his newspaper's readership, who, though hungry for gossip, would surely not approve of the printing of Mrs. Luna's vulgar insult of Verena.

Dr. Mary J. Prance

Dr. Prance's residence in the basement of Miss Birdseye's home allows her to regularly attend to the aging philanthropist. In both appearance and manner, Prance is somewhat more masculine than feminine, being described as "tough and technical" and "spare, dry, hard, without a curve, an inflection or a grace." Dr. Prance's personal indifference to gendered concepts is evident in her remark that "men and women are all the same to me." With regard to devotion to the cause of women's rights, Prance, being an accomplished doctor, rather thinks that she simply has more important and productive things to do; she can hardly bear to lose precious research time so as to appear at Miss Birdseye's gatherings. With so much of the novel occupied with the polarized battle between Basil and Olive for Verena's future, Dr. Prance's wry, scientific perspective seems to urge the reader to bear in mind the fundamental triviality of all humans' wayward sentimental affections. The real-life surgeon Mary Walker, who boldly styled herself in men's clothing, has been considered a model for Dr. Prance.

Basil Ransom

A distant cousin of Olive's, Basil accepts her invitation to visit while in Boston on business. Upon falling under Verena's spell, he astutely plays the cards dealt by circumstance—availing himself of his one idle day in Boston to call upon her, writing a letter (providing a return address) that enables her to invite him to the talk at the Burrages in New York, and arranging one more rendezvous before she leaves there—so as to conjure reciprocating emotions in Verena. With his tall, lean figure, "magnificent eyes" that are "dark, deep, and glowing," and "leonine" black hair that lends him the air of a statesman, Basil Ransom's chivalric charms indeed prove effective on a number of women. Miss Birdseye holds him in higher esteem than he deserves, Adeline practically throws herself at his feet, and Verena ultimately submits to his advances.

While his foibles are revealed and his antifeminist conservative views come across as obtuse, the narration seems to leave Basil painted in a kinder light than Olive, in particular. While she is typically depicted in compromising emotional throes, Basil is ever confident and laughing off inconveniences and affronts. This illustrates what is revealed in the second chapter: that Olive is one of those "who take things hard," while Basil "took things easy."

In light of Basil's evident victory in the battle for Verena's heart—and despite the narrator's revelation of the tears Verena is thus fated to shed—some critics have contentedly concluded that Basil should be viewed as the novel's hero, rescuing Verena from Olive's neurotic clutches. James's intellectual sympathies do, to an extent, seem to lie with Ransom; James would have perhaps stood behind some of Ransom's broader laments about how, for example, "the masculine tone is passing out of the world." However, few readers, especially in the modern era, can accept Ransom's fundamental belief that "women were essentially inferior to men, and infinitely tiresome" when objecting to their secondary status in a patriarchal world. Beyond his intellectual positions, Ransom can be understood as representing a force—the human desire for romantic love—that overpowers the force of Olive's progressive ideals in the battle for Verena's spirit, without any moral valuation being necessarily assigned to either of these forces as a result of the outcome.

Mrs. Tarrant

Although a daughter of a celebrated abolitionist, Mrs. Tarrant finds her own life amounting to little after she marries the "magnetic" Selah. Humbled by her husband's intermittent failures and their resulting poverty, Mrs. Tarrant comes to feed her sense of self-worth through the admirable qualities and modest achievements of her daughter. She is vexed when, despite Verena's potential glory as a sort of debutante among Boston's elite, Olive insists that the young woman devote all of her time and attention to study and improvement. On the eve of Verena's address at Music Hall, it is Mrs. Tarrant who, having tasted of her daughter's imminent success, is bold enough to characterize Ransom's urgent courtship as "the most horrible, wicked, immoral selfishness I ever heard in my life!"

Selah Tarrant

Verena's father, dubiously titled a doctor, is depicted as having anchored his daughter in the eccentric moral morass of mesmeric healing, utopian communities, and broader spiritualism from which she somehow emerges as a perfectly innocent being. Tarrant himself is revealed by his wife to have been a fraud, because she confesses to having bolstered his career as a medium when "the soft hand of a lost loved one was not so alert as it might have been to visit the circle." His mesmeric healing at least proves adequately successful for him to purchase a house near a loyal patient in Cambridge. It is implied that, where the Tarrants once lived in an alternative community, Cayuga (a stand-in for the real-life Oneida Community), which would have allowed him to engage in the sort of "free unions" his daughter professes to espouse, Selah Tarrant presently enjoys the company of some of the women who seek the sort of mesmerism (which entails the harnessing of magnetic forces) he practices. Olive predicts that she will be able to rid Verena of her father's influence with little more than a sum of money, and indeed, the Tarrants prove amiable to effectively leasing out their daughter.

Verena Tarrant

The inspired and inspiring redhead who sets the soul of Olive Chancellor and the heart of Basil Ransom aflutter, Verena is depicted as bereft of virtually all negative human qualities. To Olive, despite Verena's tainted parentage, nothing "could make her spirit seem less pure." Verena smiles benevolently at everyone; she has no thoughts of social status or self-advancement, nor does she harbor any pride. Outside of the notion of forgiveness, she holds no one accountable for faults that would need to be forgiven.

In accord with the depiction, upon her first visiting Olive, of Verena's naive girlishness and "submissive and unworldly" nature, critics frequently characterize her with some disparagement as merely an empty vessel—someone who happens to have a gift for eloquent oratory but has no conceptions of her own to speak of; she simply imbibes and subconsciously regurgitates whatever she has been told or is told to feel. However, beyond her parents' and Olive's influence, Verena's instinctive moral compass proves a guiding sympathetic force. She is acutely aware of the effects of her behavior on Olive's composure, and she is almost incapable of causing her companion grief. It is this humble willingness to oblige the passions of another that leaves her vulnerable not only to Olive's influence but

also to Basil Ransom's insistent advances. Verena's at last relenting to her irresistible attraction to Basil proves not that she is unprincipled, vacuous, or unfeminist after all but only that she is human.

THEMES

Women's Rights

In accord with his journal comments identifying the crucial contemporary issue that he intended to address in his novel as "the situation of women" and "the agitation on their behalf," James presents a fictionalized portrayal of the burgeoning women's rights movement of 1870s Boston. The degree to which his portrayal does the movement justice has been a matter of much debate. He does not go so far as to outline or describe any specific political platforms or social reforms proposed by Mrs. Farrinder, Miss Birdseye, and their various colleagues, other than the achievement of female suffrage. Verena only vaguely defines success as "causing certain laws to be repealed . . . and others to be enacted." His summary portrayal, then, is less of the women's rights movement itself and more of the spirit of the movement, especially as depicted in the divergent approaches of the established Mrs. Farrinder and the encroaching Olive and Verena and in the characters of all the reformist women.

Olive is driven in her devotion to the movement by thoughts of recompense for all of the wrongs endured by women over the course of history. Her effusive laments are genuinely poignant: "The unhappiness of women! The voice of their silent suffering was always in her ears, the ocean of tears that they had shed from the beginning of time seemed to pour through her own eyes." Verena's oratory presents views that align well with Olive's:

> When I see the dreadful misery of mankind and think of the suffering of which at any hour, at any moment, the world is full, I say that if this is the best they can do by themselves, they had better let us come in a little and see what *we* can do.

In reflecting on the state of the movement during Mrs. Farrinder's absence on tour, Olive realizes that her and Verena's concern for the conditions of women in a broader sense—"the historic unhappiness of women"—is what distinguishes them from Mrs. Farrinder, who "didn't appear to care anything for that, or indeed to

TOPICS FOR FURTHER STUDY

- In a style imitating that of James, write an additional closing chapter for *The Bostonians* either as you think James would have written or as you would wish to conclude the novel yourself. In this new chapter, you may choose to address or resolve the nature of Basil and Verena's fate as a couple, Olive's future within the women's rights movement, and/or the stories of minor characters.

- Read *Another Chapter of The Bostonians* by Celia Whitehead, published in 1887 under the name of Henrietta James, and write a paper analyzing how Whitehead's extension seems to validate, contradict, refute, or amplify the various themes and ideas in James's novel.

- Conduct historical research using online and print sources to write a paper comparing and contrasting one of the following characters from *The Bostonians* with their possible real-life model or counterpart: Verena with Cora Hatch, Olive with Susan B. Anthony, or Basil with Lucius Q. C. Lamar. Provide a short biography of the historical figure, remark on the nature of the critically perceived relationship between the character and the model, and discuss whether differences reflect James's needs or aims with respect to his plot.

- Find a passage in *The Bostonians* featuring both dialogue and portions of narrative commentary reflecting the thoughts of the characters in the scene, and form a group to film a version of the scene. Adapt the text as necessary for the constraints of your scene, and use digital editing equipment to add voice-over narration by the characters in the scene and/or a narrator.

- Think of a time in your life, whether recurring or unique, when you feel or have felt most harmonious in your existence; this could be during a passive experience, like meditation, or an active experience, like an athletic activity such as sport or dance. Write a blog post describing this experience and its importance in your life, and create a collage or Web site using images, photographs, poems, or passages that you associate with this experience, whether to convey to others the sense of it or to view at times to inspire yourself.

- Read *Little Women* (1868) by Louisa May Alcott, which is appropriate for young adults, and write a short essay on whether the novel or certain characters might be considered feminist from Olive's point of view, based on her ideology as presented in *The Bostonians*, as well as from a modern point of view.

know much about history at all" but rather limited her plea to a simple demand for suffrage. The women's rights movement indeed experienced a radicalization of approach like that represented by Olive and Verena, and *The Bostonians* can be read as highlighting this conceptual shift as pivotal in the course of the movement.

If the reader seeks to perceive the spirit of the women's rights movement within the characters themselves, the satirical treatment of Miss Birdseye, Mrs. Farrinder, Olive, and even Verena may be seen to render the movement in a disparaging light. Miss Birdseye is depicted as discombobulated and feeble; Mrs. Farrinder,

who is given no chance to demonstrate her oratorical skills, seems haughty and antiquated; Olive is emotionally unbalanced and obsessive; and Verena, the one attractive figure, can be seen as capriciously demonstrating her indifference to the cause in deserting it for the sake of a man. Verena's speeches are largely filtered through the antithetical perspective of Basil, who, given the last word, dismisses them as sentimental drivel. The negative impression collectively produced by these depictions contributed to the unpopularity of *The Bostonians* in its own time, but modern feminist critics have seen fit to confirm that James's final sentence, which notes Verena's future sadness, is a clear condemnation of Basil Ransom's antifeminist views and redeems the embattled Olive Chancellor as the novel's true protagonist.

Gender Roles

Underlying the ideals of the women's rights movement and, more explicitly, Basil Ransom's responses to it are contrasting conceptions of what is feminine and what is masculine. Olive and Verena make clear their understanding of what masculinity has wrought upon the world: Olive holds the "brutal, blood-stained, ravening race" of men responsible for "ages of oppression" of women, while Verena affirms that men in charge have left society stricken with "poverty, and ignorance, and crime; disease, and wickedness, and wars!" Olive asserts that men care only for their pleasure and cannot be trusted to genuinely support the movement because they are too attached to the status quo. She even says that those who do profess support "are not really men," while "any man that one would look at—with him, as a matter of course, it is war upon us to the knife." Interestingly, then, Olive posits a difference between emasculated (or feminist) men and masculine men while disparaging both; that is, she suggests that the feminist agenda entails the emasculation of the male gender.

Basil Ransom, perceiving the women's agenda likewise, finds historical tragedy in the femininity encroaching upon modern society. Olive's "cushioned feminine nest" leaves him feeling "unhoused and underfed"—as if its excess of "culture" signifies that no virile young man could be sustained by its abstract nourishment. Essential to man's virility is the submissive devotion of women, whose rights are summed up as consisting solely in "a standing claim to the generosity and tenderness of the stronger race." While his Southern chivalry conveniently lends him the appearance of respecting women, he only extends this form of respect when they accord with his "most definite notions about their place in nature, in society." While criticizing the feminine, Basil holds aloft certain vague masculine ideals, such as "the ability to dare and endure, to know and yet not fear reality, to look the world in the face and take it for what it is."

It cannot be forgotten that Basil himself served as a Confederate soldier, an experience that surely instilled in him a belief in the necessity of certain qualities, invariably deemed masculine, for the sake of survival. He is described as sometimes seeming inhabited by the "transmitted spirit of a robust but narrow ancestor," a "swordbearer, with a more primitive conception of manhood than our modern temperament appears to require." This passage can be seen as supporting Olive's contention that a certain degree of emasculation of men is necessary—that the stereotypically masculine martial mode of thought and conduct is completely contradictory to peaceful, civilized society and the fair and equal treatment of men and women alike. Verena's contention that what men lack is "intelligence of the heart" is also validated. From a modern perspective, with the then-unimaginable carnage and destruction of World Wars I and II only generations in the future, Verena's words early in the novel at Miss Birdseye's ring with eerie prescience:

> Wars, always more wars, and always more and more. Blood, blood—the world is drenched with blood! To kill each other, with all sorts of expensive and perfected instruments, that is the most brilliant thing they have been able to invent.

Modernization

The opposition of masculine and feminine conceptions ties into a broader theme about the modernization of America, expressed mostly through Basil Ransom. Beyond his contention that the modern age is beset by "the most damnable feminisation," another lamented aspect of modernity is the blurring of the public and private domains. In a journal entry on *The Bostonians* (quoted in a 1998 essay by Joyce Rowe in *Texas Studies in Literature and Language*), James scorns "the vulgarity and hideousness of . . . the impudent invasion of privacy—the extinction of all conception of privacy."

The notion of disappearing privacy is embodied by the journalist Pardon, who seeks to profit from exposing the private acts and thoughts of esteemed or recognized individuals. A legal right to privacy was not even conceived until 1890, by the future Supreme Court justice Louis Brandeis and a colleague, and it would only gradually be codified under U.S. law. As for Ransom, in accord with his belief that the woman's place is the domestic sphere, he seeks to save Verena from being assimilated by the muddled "public mind" because he believes she is meant "for privacy, for him."

Olive, to the contrary, seeks to persuade Verena to sacrifice her private interests for the sake of the public good. The notion of modernization is further tied to the North and Northern activities, like those of abolitionists and other radical reformers, with Ransom and the South representing the romanticized past. His code of chivalry is distinctly Southern, like his drawl,

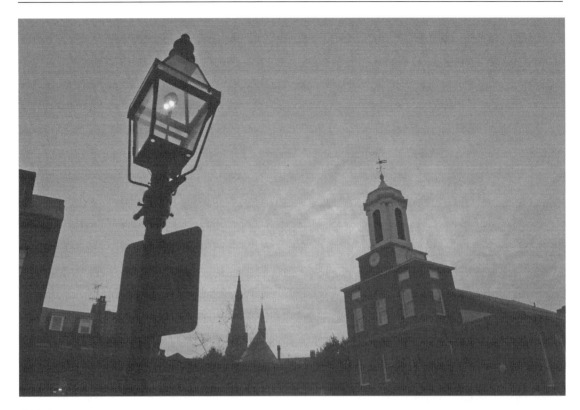

Old Boston *(Chee-Onn Leong | Shutterstock.com)*

and eminently conservative, literally seeking to keep women in their place.

Ransom's condemnations of the modern era are peppered with words evoking these various dichotomies. He finds the times "talkative, querulous, hysterical, maudlin, full of false ideas, of unhealthy germs, of extravagant, dissipated habits." Later echoing himself, he mourns that

> it's a feminine, a nervous, hysterical, chattering, canting age, an age of hollow phrases and false delicacy and exaggerate solicitudes and coddled sensibilities, which, if we don't soon look out, will usher in the reign of mediocrity, of the feeblest and flattest and the most pretentious that has ever been.

The extent to which Ransom has accurately described the end of the nineteenth century—or indeed the twentieth and twenty-first centuries—is for the reader to judge.

STYLE

Realism

James is acknowledged to be a literary realist—a position he effectively articulated in his 1884 essay "The Art of Fiction"—whereby he seeks to portray historically accurate circumstances and psychologically accurate characters rather than idealized or fantastic ones. Nonetheless, the novel is populated by fairly extreme personalities in the fierce feminist Olive, the singularly gifted Verena, and the ultraconservative Basil. As set up to interact with each other, these characters, functioning under absolute terms—with Olive demanding that Verena never marry and Ransom asserting, "if she's mine, she's all mine!"—can thus represent the collision of such absolutes in reality.

As William McMurray affirms in "Pragmatic Realism *The Bostonians*," "Reality in the novel is such that all absolutisms, when tested by experience, either must yield their claims to sanctity or fall in disaster." Thus, Olive's constriction of Verena's options inevitably leads to her need to escape, and Basil's marital constriction of Verena's fulfillment in life will lead to the shedding of many tears. The novel thus communicates a pragmatic realism of open-mindedness; to operate under limited or absolute conceptions of success is to court failure. The ideological impetus behind the realism of James and other writers like William

Dean Howells (whose 1883 novel *A Woman's Reason* supplied the title for Verena's planned lecture) was the recognition that literature, in presenting an accurate portrayal of reality, could play a critical role in influencing the minds of the populace and determining the shape and direction of contemporary life.

Satire

The Bostonians is the only James novel understood to be a satire. By the time he wrote this work, intended to be "a very *American* tale," James was an established expatriate, resident in London from 1876 until the end of his life, and had come to consider himself essentially English. He retained the utmost reverence for the intellectual and moral traditions epitomized by Ralph Waldo Emerson in the 1840s and 1850s, but by the time he returned to visit Massachusetts in the early 1880s, he was no longer charmed.

As Charles R. Anderson notes in "James's Portrait of the Southerner," in correspondence of the time, James described Cambridge as "dry, flat, hot, stale, and odious" and the Boston intelligentsia as overly proud. Anderson concludes, "For James, New England highmindedness had now degenerated into a grotesque comedy"—and James's treatment of the feminist reformers in his novel is indeed boldly comical. Ransom, too, is satirized, but where Ransom spends much of the novel leading the laughter at the reformers, the reader may not be surprised to find Ransom getting the last laugh at the novel's close.

In her essay "Delighting in a Bite: James's Seduction of His Readers in *The Bostonians*," Joan Maxwell suggests an additional target of James's satire: his contemporary audience. One effect of the tradition of publishing novels originally in magazines in serial form was that the novelist would be well aware of the work's early reception, and, especially if readers disapproved or were disappointed, the author would feel pressure to accommodate readers' expectations or preferences in the later chapters. Readers of the era were clear in their desire to have, as Maxwell states, "all issues resolved in the stasis of the myth of the happy marriage." However, such an unconditional preference for happy endings runs counter to James's realist approach, because, without doubt, many of life's dramatic episodes do not have formulaic happy endings. James can be seen, then, as playing a cunning trick on readers of *The Bostonians:* he prefigures

and ultimately supplies the requisite marriage but, with the twist of the final sentence, denies the couple—and his readers—the happiness that they seek.

HISTORICAL CONTEXT

The Women's Rights Movement

A diverse cross-section of historical circumstances and trends are represented in *The Bostonians*. Foremost among these is the women's rights movement of the 1870s, which James depicted with fair historical accuracy, although his characterizations are not especially benevolent. James's satirical style partly explained the novel's poor reception upon its initial serial publication in *Century Monthly*, which had a genteel middle-class readership that generally revered Boston reformist society. After the first installment appeared in February 1885, James's elder brother, William, an accomplished psychologist and scholar, wrote to express his disappointment at perceiving that Henry was surely satirizing Elizabeth Peabody, an abolitionist and women's rights promoter—and the sister-in-law of his literary fellow Nathaniel Hawthorne—in the frail and pathetic character of Miss Birdseye. James denied this, but he undeniably softened his treatment of Miss Birdseye in the later chapters.

Several charismatic figures have been cited as possible inspiration for the character of Verena, including Cora Hatch, Victoria Woodhull, and Anna Dickinson. Hatch was a spiritualist medium who performed in the 1850s and 1860s, as witnessed by James in 1863. Woodhull, a hypnotic speaker who became the first woman to run for president in 1872, published a weekly paper that supported not only women's rights but also free love, spiritualism, and alternative healing methods, like mesmerism.

Anna Dickinson was a Quaker girl from Philadelphia who rose from anonymity to fame in 1863 speaking in support of the Union war effort. Her fervent addresses were consistently described by newspapers as charming, mesmerizing, and even magical. Susan B. Anthony courted Dickinson on behalf of women's rights, with intensely sentimental and even romantic overtones, much in the way that Olive courts Verena in James's novel. Anthony even urged Dickinson, who started supporting women's rights in 1866, not to marry any man. In her essay "Feminist Sources in *The*

COMPARE
&
CONTRAST

- **1870s:** The suffragist, spiritualist, and journalist Victoria Woodhull runs for president in 1872 as the representative of the recently formed Equal Rights Party, although her name is not printed on all ballots and she will be too young, at only thirty-four, at the time of the presidential inauguration.

  1880s: The attorney, educator, and author Belva Lockwood runs for president as the Equal Rights Party candidate in 1884 and 1888. Many of her votes are illegally discounted.

  Today: In 2008, Senator Hillary Clinton, the former first lady, runs a highly competitive campaign against the other leading Democrat, Barack Obama, who wins the party's nomination by a small margin. After his inauguration, Obama names Clinton his secretary of state.

- **1870s:** A financial panic in 1873 sends the nation into an economic depression, slowing the growth of the postwar economy for the remainder of the decade.

  1880s: Behind increases in railroad production and technological inventions and the growth of corporations like Standard Oil, the nation enjoys a time of prosperity and materialism known as the Gilded Age.

  Today: In the wake of the recession of the late 2000s, unemployment remains high, the housing market remains depressed, and the American people remain unsure as to when and how the circumstances will improve.

- **1870s:** Although federal law does not yet provide for female suffrage, women can vote in the territories of Wyoming and Utah.

  1880s: The Edmunds-Tucker Act of 1887 withdraws the franchise from Utah women as part of a broader effort to eliminate polygamy in the state. Women in most states are not able to vote until the passage of the Nineteenth Amendment in 1920.

  Today: With women voters accounting for more than half of ballots cast, and with Hilary Clinton a leading contender in the Democratic primary and Sarah Palin the Republican nominee for vice president, women voters are heavily courted during the 2008 election.

Bostonians," Sara deSaussure Davis quotes the *American Gentlemen's Newspaper* as calling Dickinson "the only pretty, well-shaped, and womanly-looking advocate that progressive ideas ever had for an oratorical champion in this country."

The radicalization of the movement represented in the characters of Olive and Verena, who seek not only suffrage but women's rights in a broader sense, reflects the actual activities of the likes of Anthony and Elizabeth Cady Stanton, who decided to target legal inequalities and double standards in addition to seeking suffrage beginning in 1871. Anthony and Stanton's political vessel was the National Woman Suffrage Association, while divisions and members of the American Woman Suffrage Association sought the vote only. Anthony and Stanton's complementary relationship, with the former organizing and the latter writing and speaking, also loosely reflects Olive and Verena's rapport.

The radical expansion of the aims of the women's rights movement was not an entirely beneficial development. In supporting broader moral issues like temperance, the movement became associated with idealized moral prescriptions intended for all society. This allowed conservative voices to propagate fear of the potential negative consequences of granting women suffrage, and feminists thus suffered setbacks while making few gains through the 1870s and 1880s.

Regionalism
Writing in and about the post–Civil War period, James did not shy away from addressing sectional

Harvard University's Memorial Hall (*Jorge Salcedo | Shutterstock.com*)

differences—although, as he conceded, the only Southerners he knew were ones already transplanted to the North, and so he could not build the character of Basil Ransom from the ground up, so to speak. Critics agree that, where Olive's character is painted with acute and comprehensive detail, Basil—whose portrait was in part inspired by the Mississippi senator Lucius Q. C. Lamar—is more of a patchwork sketch, fully developed in his extreme conservatism, for example, but not in, for example, his domestic habits. Indeed, James's Southerner has a mythical, romanticized aura about him, one that aligns with popular postbellum associations linking the South with conservatism, chivalry, and nostalgia for tradition. Adeline Luna exemplifies these notions in her admiration for Basil, which is founded in his status as an icon of debonair nobility resigned in defeat.

Respecting South and North, the differences highlighted by James go beyond such collective conceptions to also highlight physiological differences. Basil takes Olive's study of German as evidence of "the natural energy of Northerners"; he attributes Dr. Prance's rigidity to "the New England school-system, the Puritan code, the ungenial climate, the absence of chivalry"; and he perceives Miss Catching, with her "refined, anxious expression," to be "in the highest degree a New England type." Verena, similarly, observes during wintertime at the Charles Street house how such ladies as keep society with Olive are "always apparently straining a little, as if they might be too late for something." One might conclude that James is positing that, in the North, the body's need to generate energy to keep warm through the winter months may in part account for Northerners' physical and mental habits, which can contribute to a person's permanent physiology.

A last realm of regional difference depicted by James is that between New York and Boston. His title is intended to refer not to all Bostonians but in particular to Olive and Verena, yet characterizations of the admirable denizens of the "city of reform" are scattered throughout the text. By and large, the people of Boston are considered upstanding and ethically elite. New Yorkers, by contrast—as embodied in Mrs. Burrage—may take inextinguishable pride in their fancier city, but they lag in matters of the intellect and the philanthropic soul.

The Gilded Age

A number of contemporary trends are represented in the persons of Dr. and Mrs. Tarrant. Selah Tarrant's checkered past, with his forays into inauthentic mediumship, utopian communalism, and mesmerism, reflect the influence that spiritualism had in the postbellum era. The turmoil of the Civil War led many to reassess the efficacy of traditional moral codes, medicine, education, and religion. That broad swaths of the population were open to spiritualist notions is reflected in the popularity that allowed Victoria Woodhull, who would later become president of the National Association of Spiritualists, to run for president of the United States.

The Tarrants also embody the negative trends of sensationalism and materialism—hallmarks of the Gilded Age, an era marked by investment in image and luxury that would last until the depression spurred by the Panic of 1893. Selah's modern infatuation with the idea of the Tarrant name appearing in bold letters in the daily newspapers combines with Mrs. Tarrant's desire to gain entry into the heavenly realm of high society to leave the couple perfectly complicit with Olive's generous purchase of their daughter. The precious collections of Henry Burrage and even Olive's sundry "objects that spoke of habits and tastes" are further evidence of broadening societal acceptance of materialism.

CRITICAL OVERVIEW

Controversial and poorly understood upon publication, *The Bostonians* has since inspired an eclectic critical tradition. It remained largely ignored through the early twentieth century, due to initial popular and critical distaste, as well as James's decision not to include the novel in the New York edition of his collected fiction, with twenty-six revised and prefaced volumes appearing between 1907 and 1917.

Critics demonstrating renewed interest in the 1950s and 1960s, as if wary of the looming counterculture explosion of the latter decade, consistently read the novel as, in the words of Charles Anderson in *American Literature* in 1955, "a fable championing the institution of marriage and reaffirming the values of a traditional society in which

the family is central." Many such critics considered the relationship between Olive and Verena decidedly lesbian, unnatural, and criticized by the author. However, the fact that James's sister, Alice, offered a model for such an intense friendship between women surely belies the notion that he meant to condemn them.

Later critics thus qualified the implications of the ending in various ways. Ruth Evelyn Quebe, in her 1981 essay "*The Bostonians:* Some Historical Sources and Their Implications," concludes with regard to Verena's abduction that "Basil's triumph when he steals her away from the feminist movement, a triumph diluted by his vanity and her tears, is nonetheless one of privacy and individual relationships over public life and impersonal organization." In "*The Bostonians:* James's Dystopian View of Social Reform," Robert K. Martin asserts that there is no triumph at all: "The novel offers only defeat, not victory: defeat for Olive's grand plan, defeat for Verena's freedom ... and even defeat in the jaws of victory for Basil." Martin concludes, "A perfected world is for James impossible; and the search for it seems inevitably to lead one to destruction."

Feminist interpretations, in turn, hold that the novel's ending affirms not James's opinions but rather simply the reality faced by contemporary women. In her seminal 1978 reading, Judith Fetterley (as quoted by Alfred Habegger in a 1988 essay in *American Literary Landscapes: The Fiction and the Fact*) praises James for demonstrating

> the central tenets of radical feminism: women will never be free to realize and become themselves until they are free of their need for men, until they know that their basic bonds are with each other, and until they learn to make a primary commitment to each other.

The scrupulous James biographer Leon Edel gives a comprehensive assessment of the *The Bostonians* in *Henry James: The Middle Years, 1882–1895.* His insight into James's sentimental perspective reveals much about the novel's satiric tone. He states that

> *The Bostonians* was the novel in which James wrote out the hidden emotional anguish of the collapse of his old American ties, and he coupled this with a kind of vibrating anger that Boston should be so unfriendly as to let him go.

Edel states that the novel itself "has many fine pages, and much fine writing; and yet a kind of uncontrollable prolixity is everywhere"; it is "a strange instance of a writer of power so possessed by his material that he loses mastery of it."

Edel cites James himself as conceding in a letter to his brother William that the novel was "too diffuse and insistent—far too describing and explaining and expatiating." Edel goes so far as to suggest that "it must be accounted a failure by comparison with James's best work." Nonetheless, in light of the exceedingly high standard that James set for himself, Edel confirms that *The Bostonians* remains "the most considerable American novel of its decade. For all its oppressive detail, there is no other novel of such value and distinction to place on the bookshelf of the late nineteenth century."

CRITICISM

Michael Allen Holmes

Holmes is a writer and editor. In the following essay, he considers how Olive's self-identification as a martyr and the circumstances of her seizing the stage at Music Hall in The Bostonians *suggest that she will succeed in assuming Verena's unfulfilled destiny.*

The majority of commentators on *The Bostonians* have conceived of the novel as a personal fight between Olive Chancellor and Basil Ransom over Verena Tarrant. In the phrasing of Alfred Habegger in a 1969 essay, "The central conflict... is between Olive and Ransom, who struggle for possession of Verena." Robert K. Martin likewise asserts that as Olive and Basil "battle over the soul of Verena... they reduce that soul to a piece of property, available to the stronger claimant." In her essay "Possession and Personality: Spiritualism in *The Bostonians*," Susan Wolstenholme characterizes Verena's father and two admirers as "possessing spirits" who "successively form the center of Verena's energy as she is 'converted' from one to the next."

Olive is arguably never acting out of personal desire but is instead solely functioning as a sworn devotee to the women's rights movement. In this sense, to speak of Olive desiring or possessing Verena is misleading, because her own sentimental concerns have already been superseded by her spiritual devotion, and the final scene will be understood to depict not Olive's failure or defeat but rather her elevation to an almost saintly example of the ideals of her cause.

There is little evidence that Olive is herself spiritual in a religious sense. In the exposition on her uninspiring dates with men, she is said to

> IN VIEW OF WILLIAM JAMES'S ANALYSIS OF THE SAINTLY CHARACTER, THE CONCLUSION OF HENRY JAMES'S NOVEL WOULD SEEM FOREGONE: IT IS OLIVE, NOT VERENA, WHOSE EMOTIONAL EXCITABILITY LEAVES HER PREDISPOSED TO MEET THE ASCETIC DEMANDS THAT SEEMINGLY MUST BE MADE OF THE PROPHETIC NEW VOICE OF THE WOMEN'S RIGHTS MOVEMENT."

attend King's Chapel, a historic Unitarian Universalist church, which suggests that she does not subscribe to any standard Christian dogma. She does profess to "pray heaven every day" that Verena will become a threat to men's "selfishness, to their vested interests, to their immorality," but given the aggressive nature of this hope, the reference to prayer may be merely a manner of expression.

If Olive is to be considered spiritual at all, then, it would seem to be with respect rather to the women's rights movement. The language of the text makes clear the religious intensity of Olive's commitment. In the opening scene, the thought of Basil's Confederate soldierly glory leads to the revelation that "the most secret, the most sacred hope of her nature was that she might some day have such a chance, that she might be a martyr and die for something." The notion of martyrdom is further developed when the narrator notes (with sarcasm) that, for Olive, "the prospect of suffering was always, spiritually speaking, so much cash in her pocket." She has at times imagined "that she had been born to lead a crusade" against the tyranny of men, at whose hands "uncounted millions" of women "had lived only to be tortured, to be crucified." Olive's great belief is that "the day of their delivery had dawned. This was the only sacred cause; this was the great, the just revolution."

Insight into the mindset of the martyr is provided by none other than William James, Henry's older brother, in *The Varieties of Religious Experience* where he asserts in his "Saintliness" lectures that "the highest flights of charity, devotion, trust, patience, bravery to which the wings of human nature have spread themselves have been flown

WHAT DO I READ NEXT?

- James also published *The Princess Casamassima* in 1886, which is often considered alongside *The Bostonians*. It deals with radical politics in the form of an assassination plot.

- As a satire, *The Bostonians* follows in the tradition of the French author Honoré de Balzac, whose work James admired. In *La fille aux yeux d'or* (The Girl with the Golden Eyes), published in 1835, a wealthy heir seeks to seduce a girl who, like Verena Tarrant, gets involved with another woman.

- The Scotsman Thomas Carlyle is said to be Basil Ransom's favorite author; he treats human society's iconic figures in *On Heroes, Hero-Worship, the Heroic in History* (1841).

- Amantine Lucile Dupin, a Frenchwoman who wrote as George Sand, was one of two female novelists regarded by James as a genius. Her novel *Mauprat* (1837) is a romance in which the heroine civilizes, in a feminizing way, the hero.

- The other female novelist James admired was the English author Mary Anne Evans, known as George Eliot. Her masterpiece *Middlemarch* (1871–1872) is a provincial study that addresses, among various themes, women's place in society, marriage, and idealism.

- In *The Master* (2004), Irish writer Colm Toibin offers a fictionalized but realistic portrayal of Henry James's life between 1895 and 1899.

- The title of Verena's undelivered lecture was supplied by the novel *A Woman's Reason* (1883) by James's fellow realist William Dean Howells, a tale that also addresses women's place in society.

- James had great respect for his fellow American novelist Nathaniel Hawthorne, and he was inspired by Hawthorne's *Blithedale Romance* (1852), which treats misogyny and feminism on a communal farm.

- Margaret Atwood's novel *The Handmaid's Tale* (1986), which is appropriate for young adults, is a modern classic feminist tale in which Atwood envisions a misogynist dystopia in which certain women must relinquish their freedom of intimacy.

- The Nobel Prize–winner Toni Morrison's novel *Sula* (1973) depicts how an essential friendship between two girls changes as they become women, with one staying in their hometown to raise a family while the other leaves for college and the city.

---

for religious ideals." Holistic acceptance of religious grace is understood to allow one to ascend to a higher spiritual state in which one is, in effect, psychically and emotionally invincible—in other words, saintly or enlightened. In William James's words, the saintly person is one for whom "spiritual emotions are the habitual centre of the personal energy," and in this vein he delineates four sentimentally saintly characteristics. The foremost encompasses

> a feeling of being in a wider life than that of this world's selfish little interests; and a conviction, not merely intellectual, but as it were sensible, of the existence of an Ideal Power. In Christian saintliness this power is always personified as

God; but abstract moral ideals, civic or patriotic utopias, or inner visions of holiness or right may also be felt as the true lords and enlargers of our life.

This passage accurately describes Olive's spiritual devotion to the women's right movement.

Olive's spiritual stance accordingly colors her perception of and relations with Verena. She believes that Verena is "perfectly uncontaminated, and she would never be touched by evil." Olive calls Verena's gift a "prophetic impulse" and imagines that, like Joan of Arc, the fifteenth-century visionary defender of France, Verena "might have had visits from the saints." Olive proceeds to persuade Verena that she has a mission from heaven, and her convictions about the ingenue's capacities only grow stronger. Verena is said to play the part "of the miraculous," to be "a wonder of wonders," and to have "some divine spark of taste." In Olive's view, "no human origin, however congruous it might superficially appear, would sufficiently account for her." As the narrator reflects, "There were people like that, fresh from the hand of Omnipotence; they were far from common, but their existence was as incontestable as it was beneficent."

Collectively, the religious language strongly suggests that Olive has come to see Verena as something of a female Christ figure, foreordained to be the salvation of the women's rights movement. This conceit of Olive's relates to the second saintly characteristic provided by William James: "a sense of the friendly continuity of the ideal power with our own life, and a willing self-surrender to its control." Previously unsure of her means of devotion, as not yet connected to the women's rights movement in a holistic sense, Olive finds in Verena just this "friendly continuity" that at last allows her to wholeheartedly throw herself into the movement.

As Olive encourages and basks in Verena's glowing potential, she indeed begins to feel "something of the ecstasy of the martyr." This phrase evokes William James's third saintly characteristic: "an immense elation and freedom, as the outlines of the confining selfhood melt down." Already fairly detached from her physical needs—especially in her renunciation of romantic companionship—by this time, Olive has further devised her selfless destiny: her path will be to serve as Verena's guiding spirit, to teach and protect her and channel her energies in the proper directions. As the mythic Christ was obliged to sacrifice his earthly life to save humankind from sin, Olive believes that Verena must forswear marriage—that is, that she must sacrifice her human need for romantic intimacy—in order to fulfill her salvational potential: "Sacredly, brightly single she would remain; her only espousals would be at the altar of a great cause." As Olive herself remarks, "what you and I dream of doing demands of us a kind of priesthood," which, she avers, demands celibacy.

Interestingly, after the lengthy remarks in which Olive communicates this notion, Verena is viscerally impressed with her speaking abilities, asserting, "You would far surpass me if you would let yourself go." The narrator concurs:

When this young lady, after a struggle with the winds and waves of emotion, emerged into the quiet stream of a certain high reasonableness, she presented her most graceful aspect; she had a tone of softness and sympathy, a gentle dignity, a serenity of wisdom.

In such moments, Olive's inherent emotional tension dissipates, and she becomes almost saintly. Her state is aptly described by William James's fourth saintly characteristic: "a shifting of the emotional centre towards loving and harmonious affections." However, only in private does Olive reach this level of internal harmony; in public, she affirms, she loses her composure and falters.

As the novel proceeds, of course, Olive cannot maintain such high spirits because of Basil Ransom's advances on Verena, which she has intuitively dreaded since the evening they first met. When she learns that he and Verena have met in New York and corresponded, Olive is overcome by the fear that the young prophetess, who is "so divinely docile," will be led astray. By this point, it has become apparent that Olive's tensions and agitations are not random or neurotic but rise and fall in direct proportion to the immediacy of the threat of Basil successfully courting Verena.

Many critics yet gauge her agitations as reflecting her sexual repression and/or latent lesbianism, but in accord with her spiritual devotion, Olive's intense emotions seem more palpably tied not to her own egotistical needs but to the needs of the women's movement. She has conceived of Verena's flourishing as essential to the movement's success, and so her mind, both consciously and subconsciously, is ever calculating the possibility that this success will be thwarted, so that she might act to counter any threatening forces. Such calculations are communicated to the reader after her conversation with Mrs. Burrage about supporting a match between Henry and Verena. When her rational mind lacks answers or to verify her conclusions, Olive reads her own agitation or tranquility in order to determine what course of action to take.

In an extended passage particularly relevant to *The Bostonians*, William James delves into habits or aspects of character that might prefigure a state of saintliness:

One mode of emotional excitability is exceedingly important in the composition of the energetic character, from its peculiarly destructive power over inhibitions. I mean what in its lower form is mere irascibility, susceptibility to wrath, the fighting temper; and what in subtler ways manifests itself as impatience, grimness, earnestness, severity of character. Earnestness means willingness to live with energy, though energy bring pain. The pain may be pain to other people or pain to one's self—it makes little difference; for when the strenuous mood is on one, the aim is to break something, no matter whose or what.

Olive Chancellor displays precisely this sort of earnestness in her quest to upend the patriarchal order. William James continues,

The sweetest delights are trampled on with a ferocious pleasure the moment they offer themselves as checks to a cause by which our higher indignations are elicited. It costs then nothing to drop friendships, to renounce long-rooted privileges and possessions, to break with social ties.

Olive appears to derive just such a "ferocious pleasure" in forgoing the sensual side of life—the evenings of entertainment, the intimate company of men or women—in favor of devotion to her cause.

Verena, on the other hand, does not seem to share these saintly traits. Though considered a perfect creature in many ways, she surely lacks the "fighting temper" or "severity of character" William James describes; no matter how much the charming Basil presses his conservative views, she cannot help but respond amiably and brightly. Only when he goes so far as to call her a "preposterous puppet" is she faintly angered, but her instinctive response is not to act on this emotion, which may be felt toward Olive as much as toward Basil, but to retreat. More than once, she tells Olive that she has indeed renounced the idea of marriage—but when Basil finds her again at Marmion, she finally must concede that she has fallen in love with him.

As William James further notes, "The saint finds positive pleasure in sacrifice and asceticism, measuring and expressing as they do the degree of his loyalty to the higher power," and as such, the saintly person cleanses sensual elements from his or her life. As Basil asserts, such inclinations to earnest sacrifice and renunciation of sensual happiness do not seem to be guiding aspects of Verena's nature. She forgoes much in submitting to her education under Olive, but she does not try to deny that she enjoys simple pleasures like a carriage ride, an evening at the opera, or the social attention of men.

In view of William James's analysis of the saintly character, the conclusion of Henry James's

Feminists Elizabeth Cady Stanton and Susan B. Anthony (The Library of Congress)

novel would seem foregone: it is Olive, not Verena, whose emotional excitability leaves her predisposed to meet the ascetic demands that seemingly must be made of the prophetic new voice of the women's rights movement. Indeed, Basil's mere presence at Music Hall evokes Verena's love for him and the haunting dilemma she seems to face: to either renounce the idea of love altogether or to renounce the women's cause. It is only Basil's selfish insistence that she leave that very evening, without speaking—perhaps compounded by Olive's weighty expectation that she never marry—that makes this dilemma an actuality. In the throes of her first love and under the pressure conjured by the several thousand impatient audience members, she is perhaps incapable of imagining forsaking Basil Ransom so as to become a saint of the movement for the present but still hope to someday fall in love again.

In her hesitation, the "divinely docile" Verena is at last swept out of the room by the no-longer-gracious Basil. Then it is Olive, stirred to "inhibition-quenching fury," as William James describes the feeling, by Basil's monstrous intrusion and Mrs. Farrinder's cold rebuke, who at last blazes forth. "Her livid face suddenly glowed" as she rushed to the platform with "indiscriminating defiance," as if "offering herself to be trampled to death and torn to pieces"—ready to die a martyr's death, "like the heroine that she was." Thus does the masterful realist Henry James leave the breathless reader, as well as history itself, to imagine how high Olive will rise and how high the ethic of American equality will be raised.

Source: Michael Allen Holmes, Critical Essay on *The Bostonians*, in *Novels for Students*, Gale, Cengage Learning, 2011.

Joyce A. Rowe

In the following excerpt, Rowe explains how James illustrated in The Bostonians *the power of speech and its place in reshaping the American polity.*

... Many critics have noted that in their common desire to possess the charismatic voice and presence of the lovely platform speaker, Verena Tarrant, Basil and Olive mirror each other. Not only are both ambitious and vengeful, but as cultural kin they have been formed by an antebellum standard of taste and manners which sets them at odds with their coarser-toned contemporaries and is reflected in their sentimental faith in woman's tender and loving nature. Most important for the argument of this essay, however, will be my contention that as male and female complements, the social marginality of each only highlights the underlying gender typicality of their mutual inner emptiness. This lack of being is manifested in the fierce desire (and inability) of each to achieve a public voice of his or her own. These polar twins defend themselves against isolation and the fear of nothingness by displacing it onto their all-or-nothing rivalry to possess an Other—to annex and control Verena's spontaneous power of utterance and the emotional fecundity it promises.

Although some of the strongest recent commentary on the novel has begun to revalue the earlier disparagement of Verena as a significant object of desire and to recognize the importance of her gift, the psychological and cultural ramifications of speaking which pervade the narrative, and which drive Olive's and Basil's reciprocal ideologies, have still to be probed. *The Bostonians* turns on a sexual struggle over speech, silence, and the ambiguities of the public/private dichotomy in America's emerging mass society. As I hope to

> THE IDIOM 'MOTHER-TONGUE' CONDENSES MUCH ABOUT THE UNCONSCIOUS DETERMINANTS OF HOW WE PERCEIVE THE WORLD AND SHAPE IT THROUGH LANGUAGE."

show, James focuses our attention on the significance of the power of speech—who holds it, and under what conditions—and its place among the cultural forces reshaping the American polity.

In some late observations on speech (a 1904 Bryn Mawr commencement address, published as "The Question of our Speech"), James reiterates what was clearly a long-cherished belief in speech's civilizing power. All life, James insists, comes back to speech; it is "the medium through which we communicate with each other; for all life comes back to the question of our relations with each other." The more flexible, delicate, and rich our speech, "the more it promotes and enhances life" and fulfills its great "human and social function."

When Verena Tarrant first claims that her eloquence stems from a source outside her control ("It is not me," she twice insists), she effectively expresses the symbolism of her role as the vessel of speech's generic, generative power. Even as she abandons her Boston audience, she believes in the civilizing potential of discourse for mass democratic life; that she could have tamed the angry and disappointed crowd; that essentially "their nature's fine." Her performances, initiated by a trance-like detachment, are virtual embodiments of the abstract force of language, language released from the stammering inhibitions of personal intention, freed to express its glorious signifying potential. As much as an individual character can, Verena anticipates Saussure's notion of the relation between langue and parole—the abstract structure of discourse and the multitude of individual uses drawn from it. Standing apart from her own gift, she stands for the double nature of language as a force both without and within individual consciousness. In her democratic spontaneity and benevolence ("Verena took life, as yet, simply.... [She] had no vivid sense that she was not as good as any one else"), Verena's future, like that of the democratic crowd she trusts, remains an open, yet dubious, proposition.

For in refusing to identify herself with her public addresses, insisting she is merely a mouthpiece for universal truths, Verena denies herself a responsible civic role. Her cheerful indifference to the source of her ideas points up the easy passage between transcendence and fatuousness. In response to Olive's query as to "where she had got her 'intense realization' of the suffering of women," Verena asks "where Joan of Arc had got her idea of the suffering of France?" The historical naivete which enables Verena to identify her parlor performances with the trials of the Maid of Orleans suggests the vapidity of her claim to speak for "the great sisterhood of women," whom she sentimentally envisions "join[ing] hands, and lift[ing] up their voices above the brutal uproar of the world" to quench "the moan of weakness and suffering" and make the world "a place of love!"

With her beautiful, tantalizing voice and generous, guileless nature, Verena is a kind of idiot savant of language. Indeed, her ability to change her "mind," to alter her values and ideas as she passes from hand to hand (and house to house), points up through caricature the inevitable instability inherent in the "new truths" that Verena seeks to embody. Her ability to reflect the voice of the crowd suggests language's primary function as the demiurge of human socialization—a process that will always defeat the will to control and direct human life through the imposition of fixed and immutable orders of belief. But, by the same token, this process can easily destroy personal integrity which must be won again and again from the flux of the impersonal—the displacements, distortions, and imperceptions endemic to human discourse.

Indeed, it is only toward the novel's end when for the first time Verena begins to experience a new inner force "pushing her to please herself" that she discovers something of the private meaning of love that Basil awakens in her. Verena's real battle lies in the effort to transform herself from a symbol, or mere object of others' desiring, into a woman with enough ego strength to reshape her voice as a medium for self-recognition and the expression of her own personal style of being. James depicts the beginnings of this experience for Verena in bodily terms, as a discomforting new "state of moral tension . . . a sense of being strained and aching" utterly different from her former lecture room frankness,

"her habit of discussing questions, sentiments, moralities . . . her familiarity with the vocabulary of emotion, the mysteries of 'the spiritual life.'"

The narrator's distinction between authentic feeling and the platform enthusiasms which have heretofore shaped Verena's sense of life implies a very different vision of the social order from that which Olive invokes in her "victim *feminism*." For Verena's awakening to what we might call Lacanian jouissance or "libidinal investment" (Miller, 87) as the source of personal identity carries the implication that there are priorities to adult maturity, that authentic civic life is dependent upon a recognition of and respect for the claims and needs of the private self. As the political theorist Jean Bethke Elshtain has argued, only when woman is able to speak about her genuine experiences and concerns can she develop both a collective and an individual public identity (53). To elide the public with the private (exemplified in Verena's emotional transports on the platform) is, paradoxically, to reduce the possibility of a genuine public sphere and thus to flatten the complexity of human relations (101). Ultimately, the sacrifices demanded for the common good have to be judged by the individual well-being they produce.

The novel's insistence on the value of cultivating a private self if social relations among individuals are to thrive flies in the face of the contemporary feminist charge that the personal is political, that private relations will never be successful until public power relations change. This, in fact, is Olive Chancellor's view—and the sadistic cruelty of Ransom's final victory over her demonstrates that James is not unmindful of its merit. Yet Olive's emotional hungers and bodily repressions are the best argument James makes for the imperatives of what, for want of a better term, we deem the private sphere—an arena of social freedom where categorical rigidities and oppositions may be loosened and relaxed. (Indeed, Martha Nussbaum makes the point that James's "commitment to the personal is political" in the sense of "a politics richer in humanity" than the usual ideological abstractions [209, 210].) Olive, for all her love of Verena, denies this to her protege as she denies it to herself. Reversing the current wisdom, through the lens of this novel we might entertain the opposite view: only when men and women acknowledge each other's personal needs and desires will the exclusions and antagonisms of the public sphere dissolve.

D. W. Winnicott has described a portion of the human personality which is always isolate, inviolable, and invulnerable to external reality. Language and sharing in the whole range of cultural activity can soften this isolation, but an element of "incommunicado—sacred and most worthy of preservation" will always remain (Maturational Process, 187). Winnicott believed the task of adolescence is to find "a personal technique for communicating which does not lead to violation of the central self." From this perspective, Olive and Basil's rivalry for control of Verena's voice is suggestive of the cruel parental rivalry for a child's affection that is tantamount to child murder—a plot which seems to have long preoccupied James. (Its moral and psychic horror can be seen in some notable stories, such as "The Author of Beltraffio" and "The Turn of the Screw," as well as *The Princess Casamassima* and *What Maisie Knew*.) To turn Verena into an advocate for one or another side in this gender war—men are responsible for all the cruelties of human history; women are perfectly useless for public life—is not only to absurdly simplify social and historical experience but to deny the individual the freedom to seek his or her own moral development. As Iris Murdoch has put it, we are moral agents before we are anything else, but moral reasoning is difficult to characterize or explain. One must have inner freedom "to see a particular object clearly."

If this vision is to bear fruit for the common good, the subject must be exposed to a continuum of personal and social experience so that judgment and discrimination may develop through the capacity to give and receive love. So Verena's choosing to follow Basil, while a necessary step for her, is also a bitter form of poetic justice which will test her platform claims for women's powers. Unlike Olive, whose feminist separatism drives her to shun Ransom, Verena is now truly in the pit, face to face with a man whose obsessive hatred of her public life denotes his power to both love and destroy her—as well as her reciprocal power over him. The irony in Ransom's need to control Verena ("if she's mine, she's all mine!") is that in policing the boundaries of speech he will stamp Out those very elements of spontaneous feeling he treasures in her, denying her the autonomy which nurtures both intimacy and true civility. Verena's problematic status would seem to mark what is still a central emptiness in our cultural life—the failure to develop a mode of civil discourse flexible enough to acknowledge distinctions among various kinds of experience (private feeling, social existence, political community) and tolerant enough to enable these inevitably entangled skeins of thought and feeling to nourish and sustain one another.

The idiom "mother-tongue" condenses much about the unconscious determinants of how we perceive the world and shape it through language. Wordsworth's belief that the "discipline of love" passes from mother to child and "irradiates and exalts / All objects through all intercourse of sense" is a close approximation of what Freud would later describe as the primary narcissism of the infant/mother bond. Lacan, building on Freud's theories, sees this dyad as initiating the stade du miroir, the creation of the child's (illusory) sense of absolute unity of being through its mirror reflection both literally and metaphorically in the face of the mother. This marks the root stage of intersubjectivity through which psychic reality, "which is primarily the intersubjective world of language" is constructed (Wordsworth, Bk. II, lines 240–60; Wilden, xiii, 200).

Although I do not wish to use Lacan's schema as a template for the novel, certain insights of his have considerable relevance for the connotations of speech that James develops in *The Bostonians*. Lacan's emphasis on the discursive nature of human existence coincides with James's view that "all life comes back to speech." But as a psychoanalytic theorist Lacan's interest, to paraphrase Juliet Mitchell, is in how we come to be linguistically ordered beings in the first place. For Lacan, the child's entrance into the symbolic order of language and the whole structure of gender, law, and culture dependent upon it are determined by the principle of the symbolic father (not the real one). It is the phallic signifier, the third term, that severs the mother/child dyad and moves the child away from the boundless realm of the mother's body and toward acceptance and use of language as symbolic replacement for the "total presence" of primordial being (Wilden, 191). Without this inevitable rupture, posed as the mother's lack—what Wilden calls "a manque etre, a lack which is brought into being" (188) through separation—individual identity cannot develop. It is through language and its analogues that the child creates his or her place in the symbolic order . . . .

Source: Joyce A. Rowe, "'Murder, What a Lovely Voice!': Sex, Speech and the Public/Private in *The Bostonians*," in *Texas Studies in Literature and Language*, Vol. 40, No. 2, Summer 1998, pp. 158–84.

> SHE IS CHARACTERIZED IN THE EARLY CHAP-
> TERS OF THE BOOK AS, AT BEST, AN INEFFECTUAL
> BUSYBODY, AT WORST, A PERNICIOUS VIOLATOR OF
> THE HUMAN HEART."

Daniel H. Heaton

In the following excerpt, Heaton uses James's characterization of Miss Birdseye to show the problem of character disunity in The Bostonians.

One of the key critical problems regarding Henry James's *The Bostonians* has always been the book's apparent lack of structural unity, of focal consistency. James himself seems to have recognized this lack of consistency in a letter of August 25, 1915, to Edmund Gosse concerning the book's omission from the New York Edition of his works:

> The original preparation of that collective and selective series involved really the extremity of labour—all my "earlier" things—of which the Bostonians would have been, if included, one—were so intimately and interestingly revised.... It took such time—*and* such taste—in other words such aesthetic light.... The immediate inclusion of the Bostonians was rather deprecated by the publishers ... and there were reasons for which I also wanted to wait.... Revision of it loomed particularly formidable and time-consuming (for intrinsic reasons).

Critics have, of course, discussed the problem of disunity in the novel at great length, usually citing deficiencies in narration or characterization as the primary flaws. One of the most outstanding examples of inconsistent characterization in the novel, however, James's treatment of the old reformer Miss Birdseye, has, with few exceptions, gone uninvestigated. When Miss Birdseye finds her way into scholarly print at all, too frequently the critic's sole purpose in bringing her into the discussion is to rehash the accusation made by William James that his brother patterned the character on Elizabeth Peabody.

Some critics give the character more attention than that, but classify the portrayal as either strictly positive or strictly negative. A few readers have sensed ambiguity in the portrayal, but have inaccurately found that ambiguity to be consistent throughout the novel.

A close examination of the text reveals that the presentation of Miss Birdseye is by no means a case of consistent ambiguity; rather, she is seen in an almost exclusively negative light in the early chapters of the book, but in an equally consistent positive light in the latter two-thirds of the novel.

In the first fourteen chapters the treatment of Miss Birdseye is consistently satiric; we see her through four distinct points of view—Olive Chancellor's, Basil Ransom's, that of the omniscient narrator, and that of Miss Birdseye herself—and each of these presents an unattractive view of the character. Olive, of course, is sympathetic toward the old reformer, but her pronouncements on Miss Birdseye are mitigated by the fact that Olive herself immediately strikes the reader as unattractive and unreliable. Her first words concerning the character, "Miss Birdseye doesn't give parties. She's an ascetic," are certainly words of praise coming from Olive Chancellor, but what we know of Henry James's view of asceticism and renunciation suggests a strongly negative comment by the author. Similarly, Olive's assertion that "[Miss Birdseye] will never be old. She is the youngest spirit I know" must be taken ironically in light of Ransom's persistent observation that although his cousin is chronologically younger than he, she has nothing to do with youth. And even Olive must admit that Miss Birdseye has not "the smallest sense of the real," and that she "wanted passion, wanted keenness, was capable of the weakest concessions."

The only view of Miss Birdseye through Ransom's eyes at this point is a somewhat editorialized physical description; as would be anticipated from Ransom's prejudiced attitude toward everything Olive has told him Miss Birdseye stands for, this portrait is not flattering:

> She was a little old lady, with an enormous head; that was the first thing Ransom noticed—the vast, fair, protuberant, candid, ungarnished brow, surmounting a pair of weak, kind, tired-looking eyes, and ineffectually balanced in the rear by a cap which had the air of falling backward, and which Miss Birdseye suddenly felt for while she talked, with unsuccessful irrelevant movements. She had a sad, soft, pale face, which (and it was the effect of her whole head) looked as if it had been soaked, blurred, and made vague by exposure to some slow dissolvent. The long practice of philanthropy had not given accent to her features; it had rubbed out their transitions, their meanings. The waves of sympathy, of enthusiasm, had wrought upon them in

the same way in which the waves of time finally modify the surface of old marble busts, gradually washing away their sharpness, their details. In her large countenance her dim little smile scarcely showed. It was a mere sketch of a smile, a kind of installment, or payment on account; it seemed to say that she would smile more if she had time, but that you could see, without this, that she was gentle and easy to beguile.

But Ransom's description flows easily into a much longer treatment of Miss Birdseye—a treatment containing much biographical information which Ransom cannot know—a treatment, in short, which must be attributed to an omniscient narrator. The passage is much too long to present in full, and no condensation of it can do justice to what is a truly remarkable exercise in satire, but a few of the more incriminating details in the passage must be examined. Miss Birdseye is, first of all, at the same time pretentious and totally ineffectual; her pockets are full of assorted papers which have lost any useful purpose they might once have had. She brings no sense of discrimination to her advocacy of causes. Olive has said of her, "She is the woman in the world . . . who has labored most for every wise reform"; the omniscient narrator deletes the adjective, relates her indiscriminate "reformism" to her ineffectuality, and further suggests her essential blindness, in spite of her involvement with social reform, to the true human condition:

> She belonged to any and every league that had been founded for almost any purpose whatever. This did not prevent her being a confused, entangled, inconsequent, discursive old woman, whose charity began at home and ended nowhere, whose credulity kept pace with it, and who knew less about her fellow-creatures, if possible, after fifty years of humanitary zeal, than on the day she had gone into the field to testify against the iniquity of most arrangements.

But beyond these fairly harmless shortcomings, there is in this description a suggestion of a sinister, even noxious side to Miss Birdseye's personality. One indication of this facet is her association with the sterile and stifling imagery in which the reform movement is presented: "In her faded face there was a kind of reflection of ugly lecture lamps; with its habit of an upward angle, it seemed turned toward a public speaker, with an effort of respiration in the thick air in which social reforms are usually discussed." Her material generosity to runaway slaves and European refugees is admitted, but a selfish and even pernicious motive is suggested:

Since the Civil War much of her occupation was gone; for before that her best hours had been spent in fancying that she was helping some Southern slave to escape. It would have been a nice question whether, in her heart of hearts, for the sake of this excitement, she did not sometimes wish the blacks back in bondage. She had suffered in the same way by the relaxation of many European despotisms, for in former years much of the romance of her life had been in smoothing the pillow of exile for banished conspirators.

And finally, she is ironically defended against the rumor that she had once been seduced and abandoned by a Hungarian refugee with the far more damning assertion that she has always been incapable of falling in love: "It was open to grave doubt that she could have entertained a sentiment so personal. She was in love, even in those days, only with causes, and she languished only for emancipations."

Miss Birdseye's personal relationships are, of course, tinged with her characteristic "reformism." She is, for the most part, merely a harmless busybody; when Mary Prance comes upstairs to the gathering at her neighbor's apartment "to see what Miss Birdseye wanted this time," the suggestion is clear that Miss Birdseye frequently "wanted" something from her doctor, that is, wanted to involve Dr. Prance in her own philanthropic interests. When we are allowed to enter Miss Birdseye's own consciousness, however, we become aware that her attempted manipulation of others comes dangerously close to the "Unpardonable Sin" conceived by Hawthorne and believed in quite as much by his literary descendant James. She attributes to Ransom a desire to mingle with the distinguished guests at her party: "He was leaning there in solitude, unacquainted with opportunities which Miss Birdseye felt to be, collectively, of value, and which were really, of course, what strangers came to Boston for." She then acts on that attributed desire by introducing him to Dr. Prance, whom she is simultaneously manipulating: "It would do her good to break up her work now and then." But Miss Birdseye goes even further into Dr. Prance's soul, speculating on the activities within her very *sanctum sanctorum*:

> Miss Birdseye, who was nothing of a sleeper (Mary Prance, precisely, had wanted to treat her for it), had heard her, in the stillness of the small hours, with her open windows (she had fresh air on the brain), sharpening instruments (it was Miss Birdseye's mild belief that she dissected), in a little physiological laboratory which she had set up in her back room, the

> JAMES'S EXPLORATION OF WOMEN WHO STEP
> BEYOND THE CONCERN OF FAMILY LIFE AND WHO
> SEEK LIBERATION IN THE 'WORLD OUTSIDE' BECAME
> ONE OF THE PRINCIPAL THEMES OF HIS FICTION OF
> THE 1880'S."

room which, if she hadn't been a doctor, might have been her "chamber," and perhaps was, even with the dissecting, Miss Birdseye didn't know!

If Miss Birdseye is no Ethan Brand or Madame Merle here, neither can her preoccupation with the thoughts of others be dismissed as totally innocent curiosity. She is characterized in the early chapters of the book as, at best, an ineffectual busybody, at worst, a pernicious violator of the human heart....

Source: Daniel H. Heaton, "The Altered Characterization of Miss Birdseye in Henry James's *The Bostonians*," in *American Literature*, Vol. 50, No. 4, January 1979, pp. 588–604.

Sarah DeSaussure Davis

In the following excerpt, Davis exposes the real-life figures behind the characters of Olive, Basil, and Verena in The Bostonians.

... Just after his return to England James wrote T. S. Perry that "Nothing *lives* in England today but politics." So when James began writing *The Bostonians* in London during the summer of 1884, he would have been justified in feeling that women's rights was a topical subject with a future. He had a powerful sense of the vitality of the movement and its potential influence on society and the individual. From observation of the movement in America he drew the principal characters of his novel: Susan Anthony, Whitelaw Reid, and Anna Dickinson are transmogrified into Olive Chancellor, Basil Ransom, and Verena Tarrant. In *The Bostonians* twenty years of feminist activities are distilled and scrutinized there by the artist's vision.

The striking similarity between the triangle of Anthony-Dickinson-Reid and of Olive-Verena-Basil is easily recognizable, once the historical

facts are known. James altered several important aspects of the historical triangle, however. In probing the relationship of Olive and Verena and the possibilities of a lesbian attachment, James goes beyond what was known or publicly realized about Anthony and Dickinson. As Edel has pointed out, James in all likelihood drew additionally from his observations of the friendship between Kate Loring and Alice James. Yet James's speculation about the potentially lesbian nature of the Dickinson-Anthony relationship was not unreasonable, as Anthony's biographer hints. James also changed the outcome of Reid's proposal to Dickinson. By having Basil carry off Verena in the end (as Reid fails to win Dickinson) James possibly sought to avoid too close a parallel between his real-life sources and his fictional characters. Another reason for the change is that in being false to the actual facts of Dickinson's relation to Reid, James was true to his overall sense of the feminist movement; Ransom's "winning" Verena is symbolically and historically appropriate to the history of the movement at that time.

The story of Verena seems almost an allegory of postwar feminism, and James's vision of the women's rights movement is provocative and historically valid because the most powerful enemy of the movement in the 1870's (and for some time thereafter) was, in fact, post-war reactionary thought and the fear of black votes, best symbolized by the Southerner. Antisuffrage forces were strengthened by the apathy of many women and by the bad publicity resulting from various scandals (such as the Tilton-Beecher affair) and idiosyncratic cults associated with suffrage. The objections of "gentlemen" who believed privilege preferable to rights also added their dead weight; but, as James indicates, those objectors were their own best proof of the reverse of the argument. In Basil's wresting Verena away from the podium, James shows those "gentlemen" willing to use physical force unscrupulously in their attempts to thwart the aims and implied threats of feminism. Verena has the rhetorical ability to persuade but lacks personal conviction and experience. She succumbs to Basil because she is too naive to resist. Her naiveté parallels that of the early feminist movement. Ironically her marriage to Basil will educate her to the experience necessary for integrity as a feminist: "It is to be feared that with the union, so far from brilliant, into which she was about to enter, these [tears] were not the last she was destined to shed." Her period of "education" signals the beginning of the quiescent years of

American and English feminism, from the 1880's until 1890, when feminist activity was renewed on a much stronger basis.

James used more than the outline of Dickinson's story, however. He assimilated numerous details from her life, the lives of those associated with her, and details from the feminist movement. Like Anna Dickinson, Verena has had meteoric, overnight success. Basil Ransom says, "I am told you made an immense sensation...that you leaped into fame." The words used to describe Dickinson's effect on her audiences—magic, charm, mesmerism—are synonyms for those James applies to Verena: "enchanting," "fascinating," "charming," "engaging." The physical beauty of Anna Dickinson recorded by the *American Gentlemen's Newspaper* is, of course, a fundamental part of Verena's charm. James comments, "There had never been a more attractive female speaker before the American public." In fact, Selah Tarrant's prominence in the papers suffers because of the attention given to his "daughter's *physique*" (emphasis James's). Anna Dickinson was originally from Philadelphia, the daughter of a man who died while speaking publicly for abolition. James radically altered Selah into a caricature of a public speaker, but Selah still comes from "down in Pennsylvania."

Dickinson is not the only person whose activities have been translated into *The Bostonians*. In addition to her role in courting Dickinson for the movement and for herself, the beginning of Susan B. Anthony's own speaking career suggests the real-life source for Olive Chancellor's terrible confrontation of the Music Hall audience at the end of the novel. Olive, like Anthony in 1874, risked the hostility and rejection of a public accustomed to the pretty but deceptively pleasant face of a young, beautiful girl. An awareness of Anthony's contemporary reputation—two-sided as it was—adds weight to a more sympathetic view of Olive.

The third member of the real-life triangle that informed the major characters of *The Bostonians*, Whitelaw Reid, bequeathed to Basil Ransom his Southernness. In James's first notes for the novel Ransom was destined to be from the West; but Ransom becomes a Mississippian for the novel. Reid, originally a Westerner from Ohio, spent some time after the Civil War plantation-farming in Alabama and Mississippi. His efforts were evidently not successful; he returned to Xenia, Ohio, and then joined Horace Greeley on the New York *Tribune*. The pattern suggests the post-Civil War actions of Ransom, who like Reid gives up Mississippi plantation life for journalism in New York. Charles Samuels has argued that James changed Ransom's origins from West to South to accord with the hot-blooded virility appropriate to the stereotyped Southerner. But a Westerner would seem equally capable of symbolizing the uncouth "masculinity" of Ransom. Realizing Reid's biographical influence in the evolution of Ransom, one wonders if James was not swayed by a desire to disguise his debts to Reid's life. Too, James wished to draw upon contemporary popular notion about the South and Southern hostility to feminism. In the 1870's, the time of *The Bostonians*, the Southern gentleman epitomized, as a Westerner could not, reactionary objection to feminist goals. After all, Utah and Wyoming were the first states to enact woman suffrage.

Reid's career as a journalist and his use of the *Tribune* to seek personal revenge against Anna Dickinson are reduced to minor themes in the novel. James seems to have combined these two elements with characteristics from the life of the great Boston liberal Wendell Phillips, Dickinson's first important sponsor; the result is Mathias Pardon, the pandering, fey journalist who professes, "I want to work for their [women's] emancipation. I regard it as the great modern question." Like Phillips and Reid, who arranged the political stumping of Dickinson, Pardon "knew Parties who, if they had been present, would want to engage Miss Verena at a high figure for the winter campaign." Like Phillips and Reid, Pardon also sues for the talents of the young orator: "Would Miss Chancellor be willing to divide a—the—well, he might call it the responsibilities? Couldn't they run Miss Verena together?" When Olive refuses his offer, Pardon threatens her with the powers of the "vigilant daily press," which would demand an account from her. Pardon, however, is a pathetic figure lacking any real power or force. The dramatic intensity of Reid's and Phillips's war against Anthony is distilled, of course, into the more personal vendetta of Basil Ransom. James culled too from the newspaper gossip about Reid and Dickinson the popular belief that the only way to silence Dickinson/Verena is "to stop your mouth by kissing you!"

James also assimilated contemporary feminist ideas into the novel. But since he was a novelist, he expresses these themes by scenes of dramatic conflict among the characters rather than political speeches. In Verena's arguments with Basil, James couches the fundamental feminist beliefs of the 1870's: that universities should be open to women; that female political power and suffrage would "usher in the reign of peace"; that assuming the responsibilities for husband and children no longer comprises a career as a matter of course; and that women should have "equal rights, equal opportunities, equal privileges."

James tries to approximate the ideological differences between the two major American feminist groups by opposing the aims of Olive with those of Mrs. Farrinder; though his distinction between the two groups is not particularly accurate in detail, it suggests adequately enough the nature of the split between AWSA and NWSA along conservative and radical lines. More precise is James's observation that feminist activities were entering a new sphere during the 1870's because of the fight against the Fourteenth Amendment. Mrs. Burrage remarks that the movement "has entered into a new phase . . . the domain of practical politics." James carefully avoids dealing specifically with the Negro suffrage amendment, which denied women the vote; however, by pitting Olive and Ransom as antagonists, James suggests the role Southerners played in handicapping women because of their fear of black women voters. Mrs. Burrage and her son are not the only ones who recognize the new domain of politics, of course. Miss Birdseye proclaims that the law book is the feminists' Bible.

Finally, Olive's despair at the end of the novel, her realization that she is giving up her life "to save a sex which, after all, didn't wish to be saved, and which rejected the truth . . . ," evinces the hopelessness appropriate to the mid-1880's, when feminist activities slowed considerably and when James actually began writing *The Bostonians*. Although he did not seem to realize the slow-down when he began the novel, his materials took him to that discovery—historically correct—by the end of the book.

The distinction to be made in analyzing James's use of Anthony and Dickinson is that he was not trying to portray them as people in an historically authentic or complete manner; he was drawing from a brief period of their lives certain facts and characteristics to add to the amalgam of Olive or of Verena as feminists of the American 1870's. Furthermore, his attitude in the novel toward these two characters and his attitude towards the feminist movement are separable. His attitude towards Olive and Verena

(Basil, too, for that matter) changes in the novel, depending on whether the character is acting as a type—Olive, for example, as the rich New England spinster, cultivating romantic illusions about poor shop girls is satirized—or as an individual—Olive wrestling with her desires and tormented by her conscience in making the decision to "free" Verena is portrayed tragically. James said in his notebook that he wanted in *The Bostonians* to write about certain American types, which he does to satirical perfection; but when his characters begin to define their individuality against their "type," James invests them with his own greater interest and illumines them by their own larger humanity. When Olive decides she does not have the right to possess Verena, Olive earns the traditional Jamesian approval.

James's attitude toward the movement is complex and ambivalent; the attitude is revealed only by a thorough analysis of the themes and characterization and is complicated by the slippery irony of the narrative voice. His method, by and large, was reportage, as Oscar Cargill has termed it, and he strives for objectivity by being as satirical of the opponents of the women's movement as of the women's movement itself. The target of James's mordant satire on both sides of the issue is fixed beliefs, codified responses to life—Basil's chivalric code and Olive's political belief—as well as the hypocrisy and moral blindness that result from such codes. Very much like *Huckleberry Finn*, a selection of which was published concurrently with *The Bostonians* in the *Century* (February, 1885), James's satire reveals that these fixed beliefs give rise to frauds who prey upon the weaknesses, false sentiments, and unexamined beliefs of well-intentioned people. Twain's comment notwithstanding—he said he'd rather be condemned to John Bunyan's heaven than have to read *The Bostonians*—the similarities are strong between Selah Tarrant and the Duke and the King. Furthermore, James, like Twain, is consistently suspicious of the group in whatever form. James cannot portray the group behavior of the women's movement without comedy or satire, but as his next two novels, *The Princess Casamassima* and *The Tragic Muse*, reveal, he supports the goals of feminism when they are individually pursued and achieved.

When *The Bostonians* was published in 1884, Boston readers, beginning with William James, reacted quickly against Henry's initially satirical portrait of Miss Birdseye; the prominence of that family name assured Miss Peabody the concern of her fellow Bostonians. No one, including reviewers, however, remarked on the similarity of Verena Tarrant to Anna Dickinson, who had been closely associated with prominent Boston liberals and reformers in the 1860's. Nothing was said of this correlation when the novel came out for several reasons. By 1885 Wendell Phillips had been dead almost a year and Dickinson had dropped from public notice. And, too, the wit present in the characterization of the youthful and resilient Verena probably seemed less offensive than the satire of an old woman whose important activities were behind her. Furthermore, Dickinson was a Philadelphian from an unknown family whose name would not have qualified her for public defense in Boston. Finally, the feminists who might have raised objections to the novel were busy writing their own history and were uninterested in the unflattering picture of women's rights in *The Bostonians*. A lengthy review of the novel in the *Woman's Journal* termed the satire "caricature" and condemned James as untrue to both human nature and to art. The reviewer therefore had a vested interest in not seeing any link between the major figures of the novel and feminists of the 1870's.

A final reason that these parallels attracted little attention is that the novel appeared just after the movement in the United States and England had momentarily peaked. The inactivity lasted from 1884 to 1897; as Ray Strachey states, "the press and public were tired of hearing of it [woman suffrage] . . . a regular Press boycott set in, and the dead period of the movement came on." The public surfeit of women's rights issues which is evident from 1884 to 1890 contributed in a large measure to the poor reception of *The Bostonians*. The average novel reader was uninterested, and the "better sort" were apathetic or antagonistic; the suffragists were writing their own history.

But James had seen and absorbed into *The Bostonians* the public and political as well as psychological aspects of feminism. The two major women figures in the novel are his first political characters: Verena sacrifices her public career for a private life; Olive sacrifices her private life for a public one. James's exploration of women who step beyond the concern of family life and who seek liberation in the "world outside" became one of the principal themes of his fiction of the 1880's.

Women in political affairs during the nineteenth century represented the ultimate conflict between radically opposing values—personal and sexual versus social and political—and focused ideas of crucial artistic interest to James. It is not too much to say that his study of feminism led James to the social issues that provide the themes of his next two major novels: anarchist activities in *The Princess Casamassima* (1885–1886) and the conflict between art and politics in *The Tragic Muse* (1890). James's attention to contemporary affairs perhaps comes as a surprise to those readers whose idea of him is shaped by the late novels; however, in addition to the evidence of the three "social" novels themselves, we have James's own statement to Robert Louis Stevenson in 1888, that he wanted "to leave a multitude of pictures of my time, projecting my small circular frame upon as many different spots as possible." In *The Bostonians* he left more of a picture "of [his] time" than Jamesian criticism has hitherto realized.

Source: Sarah DeSaussure Davis, "Feminist Sources in *The Bostonians*," in *American Literature*, Vol. 50, No. 4, January 1979, pp. 570–88.

SOURCES

Allen, Elizabeth, *A Woman's Place in the Novels of Henry James*, St. Martin's Press, 1984, pp. 83–96.

Anderson, Charles R., "James's Portrait of the Southerner," in *American Literature*, Vol. 27, No. 3, November 1955, pp. 309–31.

Bell, Ian, "The Emersonian Irony of James's Basil Ransom," in *Notes and Queries*, Vol. 233, No. 3, September 1988, pp. 328–30.

Blair, Sara, "Realism, Culture, and the Place of the Literary: Henry James and *The Bostonians*," in *The Cambridge Companion to Henry James*, edited by Jonathan Freedman, Cambridge University Press, 1998, pp. 151–68.

Boudreau, Kristin, "Narrative Sympathy in *The Bostonians*," in *Henry James Review*, Vol. 14, No. 1, Winter 1993, pp. 17–33.

Daugherty, Sarah B., "Henry James, George Sand, and *The Bostonians*: Another Curious Chapter in the History of Literary Feminism," in *Henry James Review*, Vol. 10, No. 1, Winter 1989, pp. 42–49.

Davis, Sara deSaussure, "Feminist Sources in *The Bostonians*," in *American Literature*, Vol. 50, No. 4, January 1979, pp. 570–87.

Edel, Leon, *Henry James: The Middle Years, 1882–1895*, J. B. Lippincott, 1962, pp. 137–46.

Graham, Wendy, *Henry James's Thwarted Love*, Stanford University Press, 1999, pp. 145–76.

Habegger, Alfred, "The Disunity of *The Bostonians*," in *Nineteenth-Century Fiction*, Vol. 24, No. 2, September 1969, pp. 193–209.

———, "Henry James's *Bostonians*, and the Fiction of Democratic Vulgarity," in *American Literary Landscapes: The Fiction and the Fact*, edited by Ian Bell and D. K. Adams, St. Martin's Press, 1989, pp. 102–21.

James, Henry, "The Art of Fiction," in *The Art of Fiction and Other Essays*, Oxford University Press, 1948.

———, *The Bostonians*, Barnes & Noble Classics, 2005.

James, William, *The Varieties of Religious Experience: A Study in Human Nature*, Penguin Books, 1985, pp. 259–84.

Markow-Totevy, Georges, *Henry James*, translated by John Cumming, Minerva, 1969, pp. 1–15.

Martin, Robert K., "*The Bostonians*: James's Dystopian View of Social Reform," in *Mosaic*, Vol. 18, No. 1, Winter 1985, pp. 107–113.

Maxwell, Joan, "Delighting in a Bite: James's Seduction of His Readers in *The Bostonians*," in *Journal of Narrative Technique*, Vol. 18, No. 1, Winter 1988, pp. 18–33.

McMurray, William, "Pragmatic Realism in *The Bostonians*," in *Nineteenth-Century Fiction*, Vol. 16, No. 4, March 1962, pp. 339–44.

Quebe, Ruth Evelyn, "*The Bostonians*: Some Historical Sources and Their Implications," in *Centennial Review*, Vol. 25, No. 1, Winter 1981, pp. 80–100.

Rowe, Joyce A., "'Murder, What a Lovely Voice!': Sex, Speech, and the Public/Private Problem in *The Bostonians*," in *Texas Studies in Literature and Language*, Vol. 40, No. 2, Summer 1998, pp. 158–83.

Sensibar, Judith, "The Politics of Hysteria in *The Bostonians*," in *South Central Review*, Vol. 8, No. 2, Summer 1991, pp. 57–72.

Shaheen, Aaron, "'The Social Dusk of That Mysterious Democracy': Race, Sexology, and the New Woman in Henry James's *The Bostonians*," in *American Transcendental Quarterly*, Vol. 19, No. 4, December 2005, pp. 281–300.

Wolstenholme, Susan, "Possession and Personality: Spiritualism in *The Bostonians*," in *American Literature*, Vol. 49, No. 4, January 1978, pp. 580–91.

FURTHER READING

Daudet, Alphonse, *L'évangéliste*, translated by Mary Neal Sherwood, T. B. Peterson & Brothers, 1883.
    In the Frenchman Daudet's novel, on which James drew as inspiration for *The Bostonians*, a young woman faces a choice between motherhood and the life of a feminist activist.

De Beauvoir, Simone, *The Second Sex*, translated by Constance Borde and Sheila Malovany-Chevallier, Knopf, 2010.
    Simone de Beauvoir's tract, originally published in 1949, addressing the treatment of women throughout history, is considered by many to have laid the foundation for modern feminism.

Douglas, Ann, *The Feminization of American Culture*, Farrar, Straus and Giroux, 1977.
    In this scholarly volume, Douglas treats the reality behind Basil Ransom's claim that America was being feminized.

Wharton, Edith, *The Age of Innocence*, D. Appleton, 1920.
    This novel, which won Wharton the first Pulitzer Prize awarded to a woman, provides a portrait of upper-class New York in the 1870s—the gilded realm of the Burrages of James's novel—through a tangled love story involving a lawyer and two women.

SUGGESTED SEARCH TERMS

Henry James

The Bostonians

The Bostonians AND feminism

The Bostonians AND women's rights movement

women's rights movement AND sexuality

feminism AND lesbian

Henry James AND sexuality

feminism AND utopia

Henry James AND Alice James

William James AND The Bostonians

Henry James AND satire

Henry James AND realism

Breath, Eyes, Memory

When *Breath, Eyes, Memory* was published in 1994, Edwidge Danticat was hailed by *Publishers Weekly* contributor Mallay Charters as "a distinctive new voice with a sensitive insight into Haitian culture." Although there are some similarities between Sophie's story and Danticat's own life, the work is largely fiction, informed by Danticat's own experience. The book was the culmination of many years of writing beginning in Danticat's adolescence, when she wrote a story about coming to America to be with her mother; this story was the seed for the later, much longer work.

Danticat continued work on the novel during her pursuit of a master of fine arts degree in writing at Brown University, where she was given a full scholarship. Written as her master's thesis, the unfinished book was eagerly awaited by Soho Press, which offered Danticat a five thousand dollar advance for it.

Not everyone in the Haitian community approved of the book. In the book, Sophie's mother Martine "tests" her to see if she is still a virgin. Although virginity is highly regarded in Haitian culture, most Haitian Americans no longer follow this "testing" practice, and some felt that Danticat's depiction of it made Haitians seem backward and sexually abusive. Danticat is aware that many people see her as a spokesperson for Haitians but disagrees with the notion. She believes that she is just one person writing about her own experience and

EDWIDGE DANTICAT

1994

Edwidge Danticat (*AP Images*)

that there are many other voices to represent the Haitian experience.

AUTHOR BIOGRAPHY

Edwidge Danticat (pronounced "Edweedj Danticah") was born January 19, 1969, in Port-au-Prince, Haiti, and was separated from her father at age two when he immigrated to the United States to find work. When Danticat was four, her mother also went to the United States. For the next eight years, Danticat and her younger brother Eliab were raised by their father's brother, a minister, who lived with his wife and grandson in a poor section of Port-au-Prince known as Bel Air.

When Danticat was twelve, she moved to Brooklyn, New York, and joined her parents and two new younger brothers. Adjustment to this new family was difficult, and she also had difficulty adjusting at school, because she spoke only Creole and did not know any English. Other students taunted her as a Haitian "boat person," or refugee. She told Mallay Charters in *Publishers Weekly*, "My primary feeling the whole first year was one of loss. Loss of my childhood, and of the people I'd

left behind—and also of being lost. It was like being a baby—learning everything for the first time."

Danticat learned to tell stories from her aunt's grandmother in Bel Air, an old woman whose long hair had coins braided into it. This fascinated the neighborhood children, who fought each other for the privilege of combing it. When people gathered, she told folktales and family stories. "It was call-and-response," Danticat told Charters. "If the audience seemed bored, the story would speed up, and if they were participating, a song would go in. The whole interaction was exciting to me. These cross-generational exchanges didn't happen often, because children were supposed to respect their elders. But when you were telling stories, it was more equal, and fun."

Danticat's cousin, Marie Micheline, taught her to read. She told Renee H. Shea in *Belles Lettres*, "I started school when I was three, and she would read to me when I came home. In 1987 . . . there was a shooting outside her house—where her children were. She had a seizure and died. Since I was away from her, my parents didn't tell me right away. . . . But around that same time, I was having nightmares; somehow I knew."

When Danticat was seven, she wrote stories with a Haitian heroine. For her, writing was not a casual undertaking. "At the time that I started thinking about writing," she told Calvin Wilson in the *Kansas City Star*, "a lot of people who were in jail were writers. They were journalists, they were novelists, and many of them were killed or 'disappeared.' It was a very scary thing to think about." Nevertheless, she kept writing. After she moved to Brooklyn and learned English, she wrote stories for her high school newspaper. One of these articles, about her reunion with her mother at age twelve, eventually expanded to become the novel *Breath, Eyes, Memory*.

Danticat graduated from Barnard College with a degree in French literature in 1990 and worked as a secretary, doing her writing after work in the office. She applied to business schools and creative writing programs. She was accepted by schools in both fields but chose Brown University's creative writing program, which offered her a full scholarship. For her master's thesis, she wrote what would later become *Breath, Eyes, Memory*. After graduating, she sent seventy pages of *Breath, Eyes, Memory* to Soho Press, a small publisher. The press bought the book before it was even completed, sending her notes asking if she was done yet and encouraging her to finish.

Breath, Eyes, Memory and her eight other books have been hailed for their lyrical intensity; vivid descriptions of Haitian places and people; and honest depictions of fear and pain. Danticat won a Granta Regional Award as one of the Twenty Best Young American Novelists for *Breath, Eyes, Memory*, and the 1999 American Book Award for *The Farming of Bones* (1998). Her 2007 memoir *Brother, I'm Dying* won a National Book Critics Circle Award. In 2009, she was awarded a MacArthur Fellows Program grant.

PLOT SUMMARY

Edwidge Danticat's *Breath, Eyes, Memory* begins in Haiti in the early 1980s, when Haiti was ruled by the dictator Jean-Claude "Baby Doc" Duvalier. Widespread poverty, illiteracy, and government-sponsored violence oppress the population, but Danticat's heroine, twelve-year-old Sophie Caco, has led a relatively sheltered life in the small town of Croix-des-Rosets. Although the people of her family have always been poor agricultural laborers, she and her aunt are better off because Sophie's mother, Martine, moved to Brooklyn, New York, when Sophie was two, and she sends money home every month.

Martine's move to Brooklyn was a form of escape, since she was raped at age sixteen by a *Tonton Macoute*, or guerrilla, one of many allowed by the government to kill, torture, and rape anyone he wanted to. This rape resulted in Sophie's birth, but Martine, unable to bear the painful memories, left Haiti—and Sophie—in search of a new life and release from her emotional pain.

The novel opens a few days before Mother's Day, when Sophie has made a card to give to her aunt, Tante Atie, the only mother Sophie knows. She finds out that Martine has finally sent for her and wants her to come to Brooklyn. Sophie is fearful and reluctant to go, but has no choice. Atie tells her that her mother wants the best for her, and that if she becomes educated, she can elevate her whole family. She says that going to the United States will be good for Sophie and everyone else.

On the way to the airport, Sophie and Tante Atie are delayed by a demonstration; they see students fighting soldiers and government officials, an Army truck in flames, and soldiers shooting bullets and tear gas at the demonstrators. They also see a soldier beat a girl's head in with the butt of a gun On the plane, Sophie sits next to a small boy whose father was killed in the demonstration and who has no family left living in Haiti and no luggage.

Adjusting to life in Brooklyn is difficult for Sophie, who is harassed by other students because she is Haitian and does not speak English. For six years, forbidden to date, she spends all her time in the narrow circle of school, home, and church.

When Sophie is eighteen, she falls in love with her neighbor, Joseph, a kind and thoughtful musician who is her mother's age. Aside from Marc, her mother's boyfriend, she does not know any men. "Men were as mysterious to me as white people, who in Haiti we had only known as missionaries," she says.

Although Sophie has not slept with Joseph, her mother suspects that she has, and she makes Sophie lie on the bed while she tests her for virginity. "There are secrets you cannot keep," she tells Sophie, meaning that if Sophie has sex, her mother will know about it. Martine herself was tested in this way, as was Atie, and although it has given her emotional scars, she continues to do it to Sophie every week to make sure she is still a virgin.

Sophie does not tell Joseph about the tests, but she feels deeply shameful about her body and avoids him. He goes away on tour, leaving her lonely and confused. She realizes that if she loses her virginity her mother will stop the invasive testing, so she uses a pestle to break her hymen.

The next time she is tested, she fails. Her mother, disgusted, tells her to get out and go to Joseph, and see what he can do for her.

She goes to Joseph and tells him she wants to get married immediately. They move to Providence, Rhode Island and have a baby, but Sophie is not happy. For the whole first year of their marriage, she feels suicidal and experiences nightmares. Her sexual secret, her memory and experience of testing, and her mother's insistence that sex is filthy and shameful make her unable to enjoy sexual relations with her husband. "[My mother's] nightmares had somehow become my own, so much so that I would wake up some mornings wondering if we hadn't both spent the night dreaming about the same thing: a man with no face, pounding a life into a helpless young girl," she says. Confused, she leaves without telling Joseph where she is going and takes her baby, Brigitte Ife (named for her grandmother), to Haiti.

Sophie's mother does not know that Sophie is in Haiti, or that she is separated from Joseph, but she sends her usual cassette down to Atie and Grandma Ife and mentions that Joseph has called her house looking for Sophie. She is frightened because she also does not know where Sophie is. Atie and Ife encourage Sophie to go home, but she is not ready. Secretly, they ask Martine to come to Haiti and convince Sophie to go back.

Sophie talks to her grandmother about the testing, and her grandmother says she did it to her daughters because it was her duty to safeguard the family's chastity and honor. "I hated the tests," Sophie tells her. "It is the most horrible thing that ever happened to me. When my husband is with me now, it gives me such nightmares that I have to bite my tongue to do it again."

Sophie's mother shows up. Sophie asks her why she put her through the tests if she herself hated them so much. Martine says she did it "because my mother did it to me. I have no greater excuse. I realize standing here that the two greatest pains of my life are very much related. The one good thing about being raped was that it made the testing stop. The testing and the rape. I live both every day."

Eventually, Sophie goes home and calls her husband. They reconcile, and she joins a sexual phobia therapy group, where the therapist says of her mother's rapist, "Your mother never gave him a face. That's why he's a shadow. That's why he can control her. I'm not surprised she's having nightmares.... You will never be able to connect with your husband until you say good-bye to your father." Meanwhile, her mother has become pregnant with Marc's baby. The pregnancy revives all her old fears of rape and violation, and she tells Sophie that when she was pregnant with Sophie, she tried to abort her. She drank "all kinds of herbs, vervain, quinine, and verbena, baby poisons. I tried beating my stomach with wooden spoons. I tried to destroy you, but you wouldn't go away."

The old fears overwhelm Martine, and eventually she kills herself, stabbing herself in the belly seventeen times with a butcher knife. Sophie takes her body back to Haiti, where, at her funeral, Sophie runs into the cane field and beats, attacks,

fights back against the cane and the memory of her mother's rapist.

Her grandmother comes to help her, knowing that this is a cathartic moment and that Sophie is releasing the pain of generations. She tells Sophie, "There is always a place where, if you listen closely in the night, you will hear your mother telling a story and at the end of the tale, she will ask you this question: '*Ou libere?* Are you free, my daughter?... Now, you will know how to answer.'"

CHARACTERS

Tante Atie

Tante Atie, Sophie's aunt, raises her as a mother would. Atie has never married, and she carries the secret of a lost love: Monsieur Augustin, the village schoolteacher, once loved her but married someone else. Illiterate and kind, Atie passes on folklore and family stories to Sophie, telling her that her mother left her in Haiti for a reason, that her mother loves her, but that circumstances out of her control led her to leave Sophie in Haiti for a while. By the end of the book, her friend Louise, who may also be her lover, has taught her to read and write, and she is never without her notebook, in which she copies other writers' poems and writes her own. Despite the fact that she has begun this growth so late in life, she is a much stronger, more self-aware woman.

Martine Caco

Sophie's mother, who is recovering from breast cancer, works as an aide at a nursing home during the day and as a private health care aide at night. She came to the United States when Sophie was two, in an attempt to put Haiti behind her. She is constantly tormented by nightmares of a traumatic event that occurred when she was sixteen: a strange man, wearing a mask, took her into a cane field and brutally raped her. This resulted in Sophie's birth.

Martine was also sexually traumatized by her mother, Grandma Ife, who tested her for virginity until after the rape. Ife meant well when she did this traditional practice, but it resulted in lifelong emotional and sexual scars. Even though Martine hated being tested and knows that it hurt her deeply, she in turn does it to her daughter, Sophie, in a desperate attempt to keep her chaste. She is frightened and disturbed by her daughter's growth into a woman and does all she can to keep her young and away from men. When Sophie becomes interested in a neighbor, Martine is deeply hurt, viewing this as a break in the mother-daughter bond.

Martine has difficulty integrating her Haitian heritage, which both comforts and frightens her, with her new life in America. Still suffering from nightmares brought on by the rape that resulted in Sophie's birth, and from her mother's "testing" of her virginity when she was a girl, she is burdened by fears and sexual anguish. A new pregnancy reminds her of the rape and increases her nightmares, and she eventually seeks escape from her pain by committing suicide.

Sophie Caco

Sophie Caco, the narrator, is twelve years old when the novel begins. She is being raised by her aunt, Tante Atie, in a small Haitian town, because her mother has immigrated to the United States. Born after her mother was raped, she does not know her father, and because her mother left Haiti when Sophie was two, she does not know her mother either. As a child, she imagines her mother as being like the Haitian goddess Erzulie, "the lavish Virgin Mother.... Even though she was far away, she was always with me. I could always count on her, like one counts on the sun coming out at dawn."

In truth, however, her mother is a wounded woman with problems of her own, and Sophie must learn to come to terms with them, as they are handed down to her from past generations. "I come from a place where breath, eyes and memory are one," Sophie says, reflecting on the burden of the past: the emphasis on family honor, chastity, and duty that fall on the women in her family, "a place where you carry your past like the hair on your head."

Throughout the novel, she struggles to come to terms with her family's history of pain and loss, to be comfortable with her body and her sexuality, and to avoid passing on her own and her mother's nightmares to her daughter. In addition, when she moves to Brooklyn, she must decide for herself what parts of her Haitian heritage she wants to keep, and what traditions she wants to drop. In particular, she is frightened and confused by her mother's traditional Haitian practice of testing her to ensure that she is still a virgin, and by her mother's mental and spiritual pain.

The rift between Sophie and her mother widens when she falls in love with Joseph, a neighbor who is much older than she is. Ultimately, she chooses to be with him, asserting her own knowledge of what is good and right for her against inflexible tradition; this move signifies her becoming more Americanized.

Joseph describes Sophie as a "deep, thoughtful person," and she is, describing events in a poetic and vivid way, feeling all her emotions deeply, and reflecting on them in solitude.

Marc Chevalier

Marc is Martine's boyfriend, a prosperous Haitian immigrant and lawyer who helped her get her green card. He lives in a well-to-do neighborhood in Brooklyn. He is very traditionally Haitian in outlook, particularly regarding food, and once drove to Canada because he heard of a good Haitian restaurant there. Martine says of him, "Marc is one of those men who will never recover from not eating his [mother's] cooking. If he could get her out of her grave to make him dinner, he would do it." Apart from his wealth and his interest in food, he is not very clearly drawn; although he is the father of a child Martine conceives later in the book, he seems removed from the horrifying events surrounding her suicide, and only appears again after she is dead.

Brigitte Ife

Brigitte is the infant daughter of Sophie and Joseph, named for Sophie's grandmother. She is a calm child who sleeps peacefully, unlike her mother and grandmother.

Grandma Ife

Ife is Sophie's grandmother, a widow who lives in a Haitian village that is so remote that it can only be reached on foot or by mule. A very traditional woman, she has worn black ever since her husband died. When her daughters, Atie and Martine, were young, she followed the traditional Haitian practice of testing their virginity each week, which resulted in unintentional sexual and emotional scars in both her daughters. She is a storyteller, passing on old folktales, family stories, and healing wisdom. When Sophie asks her about the testing, she explains that a mother is responsible for her daughter's chastity and that, if a girl is not a virgin when she marries, her new husband can shame the entire family and bring bad luck to them. She does not question the practice at all; to her, it is simply an obligation to keep girls "clean." However, when she realizes how much the custom has hurt Sophie, she gives her a statue of the goddess Erzulie and tells her, "My heart, it weeps like a river, for the pain we have caused you."

Joseph

Joseph, Sophie's neighbor, is a jazz musician from Louisiana who is the same age as her mother. He falls in love with Sophie because she seems like a deep, thoughtful person. She also falls in love with him, although her mother has forbidden her to date. Eventually, Joseph becomes Sophie's husband and the father of her child. Like Sophie, he is deep and thoughtful, and this is what attracts her to him; she realizes that he is the kind of man who would be interested in a woman for more than her looks. She chooses wisely, as he is indeed a kind, wise, and loving man. Later in the book, when she leaves him because physical intimacy with him reminds her of her sexual problems, he is understanding, welcomes her back, and encourages her to stay with him and go to therapy to sort things out.

THEMES

Immigrant Life

Throughout the book, Sophie and Martine travel from Haiti to the United States, and back to Haiti. The contrasts between the two settings and cultures are vivid and all-encompassing, and as both women note, it is difficult to find one's way in a foreign country. Both women learn to speak English—which Grandma Ife refers to as "that cling-clang talk," and which Sophie says sounds "like rocks falling in a stream"—but they also continue to speak their own language, Creole. They eat American food because Haitian food reminds them of the emotional pain they endured in Haiti, but at the same time, they long for traditional dishes with ingredients such as cassava, ginger, beans, and rice. Sophie hates her school because it is a French school, and she feels she might as well have stayed in Haiti—but she is also uneasy because American students harass her for being Haitian. Sophie's difficulty with assimilation is also shown by her conflicting attitude toward gender roles: she believes women should be traditionally chaste and sheltered, but talks

TOPICS FOR FURTHER STUDY

- Read about the dictatorship of Jean-Claude "Baby Doc" Duvalier and write an essay in which you explore how his legacy of poverty, illiteracy, and crime is revealed in the scenes of violence in the novel.

- Research the Haitian deities of *voudon*, particularly the goddess Erzulie, and prepare a multimedia presentation describing their importance. Include both visual images of the deities and audio clips of songs and chants in their honor.

- In the eighteenth century, a slave rebellion ended white rule in Haiti. Read about this rebellion, and write a research paper comparing the plight of the slaves in Haiti to that of slaves in the United States during the same period.

- Read Danticat's young-adult novel about a young Haitian immigrant, *Behind the Mountains* (2002), in which Danticat also describes her own immigration. Write an essay comparing the experiences of the fictional Sophie and Celiane with those of Danticat, and explore the choices the author made as she adapted reality to create fiction.

- Using Google Maps or another map application, locate Sophie's hometown of Croix-des-Rosets, Haiti. Prepare a multimedia presentation in which you explain how this town was affected by the 2010 Haiti earthquake.

- Read Frances Temple's young-adult novel *Taste of Salt: A Story of Modern Haiti* (1991), about a teenage boy living under the dictatorship of Jean-Claude Duvalier. Using Inspiration or another diagramming tool, prepare a two-column representation of the similarities and differences between the challenges faced by Sophie in *Breath, Eyes, Memory* and Djo in this novel.

disparagingly of traditional Haitian men, who, she says, will want a woman to stay at home, cooking Haitian food.

Eventually, Sophie becomes Americanized: when she returns to Haiti, a cabdriver is surprised that she speaks Creole so well, and when Martine shows up too, the two of them speak English together without realizing it.

Family Relationships

"The love between a mother and daughter is deeper than the sea," Martine tells Sophie, and generational bonds and conflicts between mothers and daughters are a major theme in the book. Grandma Ife, the matriarch of the clan, followed the traditional Haitian practice of ensuring her daughters' chastity and "tested" them each month to make sure their hymens were still intact. This resulted in lifelong emotional scars for both daughters, particularly Martine, whose sexual guilt, pain, and fear only increased when she was brutally raped at age sixteen. Although Martine knows firsthand how emotionally and physically painful the testing is, she still does it to her daughter Sophie, passing on the family curse of sexual phobias and nightmares. When Sophie finally asks why she did this, Martine says that she has no real explanation or good reason; she did it to Sophie only because it was done to her. Interestingly, although Grandma Ife was also presumably a victim of this practice, she does not seem to be bothered by it, presumably because she has accepted a much more traditional life than either her daughters or Sophie. Sophie realizes that there is a way out of this pain: she manages to exorcise the fear of her mother's rapist, and she vows not to test her daughter or pass on the nightmares and eating disorders that affect both her and her mother. Rather than unthinkingly accepting tradition, she knows that she must shape her own life. She says of her family's emotional pain, "It was up to me to avoid my turn in the fire. It was up to me to make sure that my daughter never slept with ghosts, never lived with nightmares."

Pain

Throughout the book, the female characters suffer from emotional pain that prevents them from living fully, but they seek liberation and in some cases find it. At the beginning of the book, Tante Atie is resigned to being illiterate and unloved, but several years later a friend, who also seems to be her lover, has taught her to read. She carries a notebook everywhere so that she can copy poems and write down her thoughts, and even writes a poem of her own.

Martine also seeks liberation from her pain, but she is unable to do this in a constructive way.

For a while things seem to have improved for her: she's involved with Marc, a good man, and makes enough money to send some home to Haiti every month. Sophie's arrival disturbs her, however, since Sophie resembles her father, the rapist, and Martine is also disturbed by Sophie's growth into a woman and her relationship with a man. When Martine gets pregnant, it reawakens all her memories of the rape, her pregnancy with Sophie, and her mother's sexual testing. Unable to find a cure for her emotional pain, she eventually commits suicide.

Sophie inherits her mother's fear, sexual guilt, and nightmares, but through a therapy group, she is able by the end of the book to move beyond them and to prevent her daughter from inheriting them. She also realizes that her mother, despite her suicide and the testing she inflicted on Sophie, was a strong, capable woman who was simply overwhelmed by circumstance.

STYLE

Point of View

Sophie's story is told in the first person and is largely chronological, although some events are not explained or explored until later in the book, when other events give the explanations more depth and context. Sophie is twelve when the novel begins, and nineteen when it ends; the book is told from the grown Sophie's viewpoint. Danticat skillfully conveys a child's sense of the world in the early chapters and a more mature view in the later ones, where Sophie becomes more aware of the suffering of other women in her family and how it relates to her own emotional pain.

Setting

Set in Haiti and in Brooklyn, the book is steeped in Haitian culture, language, folklore, cuisine, and customs. Danticat's description of Haiti is lush and vivid, filled with colors, smells, and sensory experiences, but with an undercurrent of fear brought on by dangerous political unrest and deep poverty. As a child, however, Sophie is largely sheltered from this fear. The bright colors, tropical tastes and scents, and warmth of Haiti are sharply contrasted with the cold, gray, graffiti-covered, and run-down Brooklyn neighborhood she moves to. In addition, in Haiti she is part of a small-town neighborhood where everyone knows everyone else, and where her grandmother and aunt tell family stories and folktales. In Brooklyn, her life in her mother's small apartment still revolves around Haiti, as her mother shops in Haitian stores, sends money home to Haiti, insists that Sophie stay away from American teenagers, and sends her to a French-speaking school. American students tease her, and because she spends all of her time either at school, church, or home, she does not have any friends and does not know any of her neighbors until, by stealth, she discovers Joseph's name.

Use of Myth and Folklore

Danticat does not directly use myth as a source for her story, but the book is infused with Haitian folklore and the presence of Haitian deities, particularly Erzulie, the goddess whose image is often mingled with that of the Virgin Mary but who is also considered to be beautiful and sexually enticing. Erzulie, "the healer of all women and the desire of all men," who unites and reconciles the chaste and the sexual, embodies one of the major themes of the book: the need for sexual healing that all the female characters experience.

In addition, many folktales are told in the book, often as lessons or as ways of deepening the characters' understanding of real life. Sophie's grandmother tells her that some people have more trouble in their lives than others; this is because, though they do not know it, they are special people, spiritually tall, mighty, and strong, who support the sky on their heads. Sophie's father, the unknown rapist, is compared to a cannibalistic bogeyman known as a *Tonton Macoute*—also a name for the real-life guerrilla vigilantes who roam the countryside killing people.

Symbolism

Several symbols recur throughout the book. Daffodils, which are not native to Haiti, are Martine's favorite flower, because they grow in a place they are not supposed to; after Europeans brought the flowers to Haiti, a vigorous kind of daffodil developed that could withstand the tropical heat. To Sophie and Martine, they are a symbol of resilience and survival, qualities the women need to withstand the sexual and emotional torment they have gone through. Sophie writes a Mother's Day poem for her Tante Atie, comparing her to a daffodil, "limber and strong," and as a child she is upset when Atie insists that she give the poem to her real mother, whom she has not seen since she was a baby. By the end of the book, however, she realizes that the poem applies to her mother, too.

Stories, which, in the book, are always told by women, are a symbol of the connections between generations of women, stretching into the past as well as the future. Late in the book, Sophie says,

> I realized that it was neither my mother nor my Tante Atie who had given all the mother-and-daughter motifs to all the stories they told and all the songs they sang. It was something that was essentially Haitian. Somehow, early on, our song makers and tale weavers had decided that we were all daughters of the land.

HISTORICAL CONTEXT

Literary Heritage of Haiti

Haiti is a country long marked by political unrest and economic depravity as a result of years of dictatorship, government corruption, and a large gap between the wealthy elite in the cities and those living in the poverty-stricken nonindustrial provinces.

Although economically poor, Haiti is a culture rich in its language, folktales, customs, and community. The Haitian people have traditionally looked to their families and friends not only for support but also for forms of entertainment. In a sense, the effects of poverty and illiteracy made the practice of storytelling an important and favorite pastime, allowing this craft to endure throughout the generations, preserving the nation's culture and history.

Haitian literature was not known outside its borders until well into the 1960s, when the civil rights and women's movements pushed for social reforms and gave the Haitian people an impetus to search out and explore their own voices. Still, it was not until the 1990s that Haiti and Haitian literature started to receive the international attention they deserved. As more and more nations began to learn of Haiti's oppression and the violence its people faced under the Duvalier government, the call for information about the country and its people increased. New emerging writers began to meet this demand, describing the horrors as well as the jewels of this besieged nation. These writers, many living in exile from Haiti, created a literature of social consciousness that demanded acknowledgment from the outside world. Their

COMPARE
&
CONTRAST

- **1980s:** Haitian dictator Jean-Claude ("Baby Doc") Duvalier is overthrown in a popular uprising in 1986 after three years of widespread discontent and pressure from U.S. president Ronald Reagan for his resignation.

  Today: After a failed attempt to return to Haiti and run for president in 2004, Duvalier lives in exile in Paris and, in 2010, wins a court ruling in Switzerland that allows him to recover millions he stole from Haiti. In January 2011, he returned inexplicably to Haiti.

- **1980s:** Many talented Haitian intellectuals leave Haiti because of oppression by the Duvalier regime. They write of Haiti as a place of sorrow and suffering.

  Today: French and Canadian publishers come to the forefront in promoting Haitian writers

  who never left the island, such as Lyonel Trouillot, Gary Victor, Yanick Lahens, and Kettly Mars. Danticat emerges as a spokesperson for Haitian literature.

- **1980s:** The HIV/AIDS virus reaches epidemic status in Haiti as rumors spread that Haiti is the source of the deadly virus.

  Today: On January 12, 2010, Haiti suffers immense damage from a massive 7.0 earthquake that kills hundreds of thousands, leaves over one million homeless, and continues to pose health risks in November, 2010, when the nation is dealt another blow by Hurricane Tomas. Cholera is epidemic in the island nation because of a lack of safe drinking water and poor sanitary conditions.

---

writing also served as a mirror in which to look back and examine their own background and culture.

When Haitian-born Edwidge Danticat, the most well known of this new generation of writers, began to record and fictionalize her memories of Haiti, her writings became an extension of the oral tradition of her culture, capturing in print what was natural to her at an early age. Present in Danticat's work is Haiti's painful history but also its uniqueness and beauty.

Political Terror in Haiti

Haiti in the early 1980s was ruled by Jean-Claude "Baby Doc" Duvalier, son of the infamous dictator François "Papa Doc" Duvalier. During Papa Doc's regime, the longest in Haitian history, he executed all political opponents without trial and maintained troops of unpaid volunteers, known as *Tontons Macoutes*, who were given license to torture, rape, and kill people at will. During his rule, the Haitian economy deteriorated and only 10 percent of the population could read. Papa Doc encouraged the

population to believe that he was an accomplished practitioner of *voudon*, or voodoo, and possessed supernatural powers; to rebel against him invited death. After Papa Doc's death in 1971, his son succeeded him, continuing his reign of terror until 1986, when he was overthrown. Even after his overthrow, although the *Tontons Macoutes* were no longer officially condoned, they still terrorized the population.

The *Tontons Macoutes* are central to the book; Sophie was born as a result of one of them raping sixteen-year-old Martine. For the rest of her life, Martine has terrifying dreams of this event, and passes her fear on to Sophie, who is thought to look like the rapist since she does not look like anyone in her family. As a child, Sophie is aware that there is unrest and killing beyond her small town, and she sees it for herself when she is leaving for the United States. Outside the airport, she sees a car in flames, students protesting, and soldiers shooting bullets and tear gas at them. Sophie and Tante Atie watch helplessly as a soldier beats a girl's head in with his gun. On the airplane, Sophie sits next to a small boy whose father has just been killed in the demonstration.

The prevalence of poverty and illiteracy in Haiti is also important in the book. Sophie's aunt Atie, who cannot read, tells her, "We are a family with dirt under our fingernails," meaning that they have always been poor agricultural laborers, and she says that the only way Sophie will improve her life is to become educated. When Atie was small, the whole family had to work in the sugar cane fields, and when Sophie's grandfather died in the field, they had to simply dig a hole, bury him, and move on. Martine also tells her, "Your schooling is the only thing that will make people respect you. If you make something of yourself, we will all succeed."

Traditional Role of Women

In Haiti, traditional belief holds that a woman's place is in the home. When Tante Atie was a girl, Grandma Ife told her that each of her ten fingers had a purpose: "Mothering. Boiling. Loving. Baking. Nursing. Frying. Healing. Washing. Ironing. Scrubbing." Atie wistfully says that she sometimes wished she had been born with six fingers on each hand, so she could have two left over for herself.

Despite the fact that women do so much, they are not valued as much as men in traditional Haitian society. When Sophie returns to Haiti with her baby daughter, she and her grandmother sit at night watching a light moving back and forth on a distant hill. Her grandmother tells her this means someone is having a baby, and the light is the midwife walking back and forth with a lantern in the yard, where a pot of water is boiling. If the baby is a boy, she says, the lantern will be put outside the shack and the father will stay up all night with the baby. Grandma Ife continues, "If it is a girl, the midwife will cut the child's cord and go home. Only the mother will be left in the darkness to hold her child. There will be no lamps, no candles, no more light."

In Haiti, it is, traditionally, important for a girl to remain a virgin until she is married, because her chastity, or lack of it, affects the reputation of the entire family. Because of this, Martine goes to great lengths to keep Sophie away from men, encourages her to dress in conservative clothes that do not show her figure, and does not allow her to date until she is eighteen. As Sophie says, "Men were as mysterious to me as white people, who in Haiti we had only known as missionaries." In addition, Martine follows an old Haitian custom of "testing" Sophie to make sure she is still a virgin. This testing was done to Martine and Atie by Sophie's grandmother, and presumably her grandmother was tested as a girl, too. Although it has caused great emotional pain to every generation, women have continued to do it to their daughters only because, as Martine explains, it was done to them and because they were told it was the right thing to do.

CRITICAL OVERVIEW

Danticat was only twenty-five when *Breath, Eyes, Memory* was published. The book immediately attracted critical notice and acclaim for the clarity and precision of the writing, and its emotional depth. The book was the first novel by a Haitian woman to be published by a major press and to receive wide notice and readership among non-Haitian Americans.

Jim Gladstone writes in the *New York Times Book Review* that the book "achieves an emotional complexity that lifts it out of the realm of the potboiler and into that of poetry," and in *Ms.*, Joan Philpott describes it as "intensely lyrical." Danticat was also compared to African American writer Alice Walker, author of *The Color Purple* and other works. Mary Mackay, a *Publishers Weekly* contributor, writes, "In simple, lyrical prose . . . she makes Sophie's confusion and guilt, her difficult assimilation into American culture and her eventual emotional liberation palpably clear." As Shea notes in *Belles Lettres*, "To read Danticat is to learn about Haiti—the folklore and myth, the traditions, and the history."

On May 22, 1998, Danticat's critical praise was augmented by commercial success, when the book was selected by talk show host Oprah Winfrey for her book club. This catapulted it into the number-one spot on the best-seller lists and led Danticat to do a seventeen-city author tour, as the book sold six hundred thousand copies. Danticat's agent was flooded with requests for interviews, and Danticat was chosen by *Harper's Bazaar* as one of twenty people in their twenties who will make a difference, and she was also named in a *New York Times Magazine* article about thirty creative people under thirty who were expected to do great things.

The novel has continued to sell well, to be taught in high school and college classes, and to draw serious critical attention, particularly from feminist and postcolonial scholars. For example, Donette A. Francis, in a 2004 essay in *Research in African Literatures*, reads the novel as an exploration of "how empires, the postcolonial state, and the patriarchal family have abused, exposed, and compromised the sexed bodies of Caribbean women and girls."

The author's depiction of Haiti and Haitian culture has also interested critics. Danticat's "restructuring of Haitian culture as she creates new myths for new spaces and new ways of living" is the focus of a 2000 essay by Marie-José N'Zengou-Tayo for the journal *MaComère*. In 2004, Katherine M. Thomas examined the novel as the author's "Memories of Home" in the *Kentucky Philological Review*.

CRITICISM

Kelly Winters

Winters is a freelance writer and has written for a wide variety of academic and educational publishers. In the following essay, she discusses the genesis, recurring themes, and critical reception of Breath, Eyes, Memory.

Breath, Eyes, Memory weaves several threads of sexuality, body image, generational bonds and conflicts, the immigrant experience, and the desperate social and political situation in Haiti, to portray a young girl's coming of age and eventual emotional liberation. It was the first book by a Haitian woman to be published in English by a major publisher and to receive wide readership and attention, and because of this, some have seen Danticat as a voice for all Haitian Americans. Danticat has emphatically stressed in many interviews that this view is inaccurate and that she is one voice among many, telling a Random House interviewer, "My greatest hope is that mine becomes one voice in a giant chorus that is trying to understand and express artistically what it's like to be a Haitian immigrant in the United States." However, she is also aware that not everyone is as articulate as she, and she also told the interviewer, "I hope to speak for the individuals who might identify with the stories I tell."

Danticat told *Writers Online* writer Christine Atkins,

> [I hope] that the extraordinary female story tellers I grew up with—the ones that have passed on—will choose to tell their story through my

WHAT DO I READ NEXT?

- Danticat's *Krik? Krak!* (1995) is a collection of short stories set in Haiti. The title comes from a traditional Haitian custom of listeners asking "Krik?" before a story is told. The teller answers, "Krak," and begins the tale.

- Danticat's *The Farming of Bones* (1998) is a novel set during the 1937 mass genocide of Haitians by Dominican dictator Rafael Leónidas Trujillo Molina (known as Trujillo); it vividly shows the brutal existence of workers in the sugar cane fields.

- *Tell My Horse: Voodoo and Life in Haiti and Jamaica* (1990), by African American writer and folklorist Zora Neale Hurston, examines spiritual beliefs in these two countries.

- *Rainy Season: Haiti—Then and Now* (2010), by Amy Wilentz, is a vivid portrait of Haiti since the late 1980s, and provides a clear examination of the parade of dictators and terrorists who have ruled the country since Jean-Claude "Baby Doc" Duvalier. A new introduction by the author discusses the 2010 earthquake.

- *All Souls' Rising* (1996), by Madison Smartt Bell, is a historical epic set during the eighteenth-century slave rebellion that ended white rule in Haiti.

- Diane Wolkstein's *The Magic Orange Tree: And Other Haitian Folktales* (1978) is a collection of Haitian folktales and legends. It features an introduction by Danticat.

- *First Crossing: Stories about Teen Immigrants* (2004) is a collection of stories edited by Don Gallo. Each tells about teens who have come to America from countries as far apart as Cambodia, Mexico and South Korea, their various reasons for coming, and their individual responses to adapting to a new home.

- *Double Stitch: Black Women Write about Mothers and Daughters* (1991), edited by Patricia Bell-Scott, is an anthology of stories by women writers.

> THE EVENTS IN THE BOOK ARE SHAPED BY THE POLITICAL, SOCIAL, AND ECONOMIC CHAOS IN HAITI DURING THE REGIMES OF JEAN-CLAUDE 'BABY DOC' DUVALIER AND HIS SUCCESSORS. DURING DUVALIER'S REGIME, THE ILLITERACY RATE IN HAITI WAS 90 PERCENT, AND THE POPULATION WAS OPPRESSED BY WIDESPREAD POVERTY AND DISEASE."

voice ... for those who have a voice must speak to the present and the past. For we may very well have to be Haiti's last surviving breath, eyes, and memory.

She also told Megan Rooney of the *Brown Daily Herald*, "All my conscious life I have wanted to write. I was persistent, I love writing. I wouldn't be stopped."

Although the book is not factually autobiographical, it is emotionally true to the author's own life. She told the Random House interviewer that one of the most important themes of the book is "migration, the separation of families, and how much that affects the parents and children who live through that experience." Another is the political situation in Haiti—that ordinary people live in fear for their lives and property because of the lawless and armed *Tontons Macoutes*, who roam the countryside raping, pillaging, and killing at will. A third, she noted, is the relationship between mothers and daughters.

The genesis of *Breath, Eyes, Memory* was Danticat's own childhood in Haiti, where she was raised by relatives because her parents had immigrated to the United States when she was very young. When Danticat was twelve, she joined them in Brooklyn. She told Rooney, "It was a big culture shock. I didn't speak English. I was clueless in school. I was getting readjusted to being with my family. And all of this happened when I was on the verge of adolescence."

Sophie attends the Maranatha Bible Institute, a French-English bilingual school where most of the instruction is in French. Surprisingly, she dislikes the school because, as she says, "it was as if I had never left Haiti." Harassed by American students as a "Frenchie," accused of having "HBO—Haitian Body Odor," and accused of carrying the deadly human immunodeficiency virus—HIV, the virus that causes AIDS—because of the high rates of the virus among Haitians, Sophie struggles to find a sense of home in Brooklyn, and to learn English. At first, the lone English words in her mother's Creole conversation—words such as "TV," "building," or "feeling"—"jump out ... like the last kernel in a cooling popcorn machine." Gradually, she learns to read and speak English, although, at first, the words sound heavy and foreign, "like rocks falling in a stream."

Despite her new language, her mother keeps her sheltered, so that for the next six years she lives in a narrow world of school, home, and prayer. Martine, trying to keep her daughter traditionally pure and chaste despite the "loose" American society, forbids her to date until she is eighteen and takes her to work with her. She has no American friends, no Haitian friends, and no knowledge of men. As she says, in a comment that says as much about relations between the races as it does about those between genders, "Men were as mysterious to me as white people, who in Haiti we had only known as missionaries."

Later, after her marriage to an African American musician, Sophie learns more about her new country, travels there, and even attends a therapy group—something unheard of in Haiti. However, she is still pursued by the ghosts of her own and her mother's past in Haiti—the custom of virginity testing, and her mother's rape by a *Macoute*. Before she can become free and truly live her life fully as a Haitian American, she must come to terms with her Haitian heritage and past.

The experiences and daily lives of women in Haiti are largely unknown to most Americans, who are rarely informed about Haitian culture and history. According to Danticat, Haitian women's lives are defined by what Bob Corbett, on the *Haiti Home Page* of the Webster University Web site, calls "the ten fingers of Haitian tradition." According to tradition, each finger on a woman's hand has a purpose: Grandma Ife identifies them for Atie as mothering, boiling, loving, baking, nursing, frying, healing, washing, ironing, and scrubbing. Sophie and Atie both struggle to find space for their own needs and wants in this list of services to others, with varying success. As Corbett notes, the novel is about "the struggle of three individuals to rise above the shaping of their history and to take control of their own lives. It's not a story of much success, but of people in motion."

As Danticat makes clear, a girl's virginity and chastity are highly prized in Haiti, where a young woman's conduct can affect the reputation of her entire family. Danticat told the Random House interviewer that the virginity testing described in the book is not unique to Haiti, and cited the Apocrypha, in which the Virgin Mary is similarly tested for virginity when it becomes apparent that she is pregnant. Danticat stressed the fact that none of the mothers in the book intended the testing to be abusive; they were doing what they believed was best for their daughters and their families, because they wanted their daughters to go farther and do better in life than they had.

Because this custom results in emotional harm, Sophie attends a sexual phobia therapy group so that she can heal. She describes her therapist as "a gorgeous black woman who was an initiated Santeria priestess." When Rena, the therapist, hears that Sophie's mother Martine is pursued by nightmares of the rape that led to Sophie's birth, Rena suggests that, if Martine is uncomfortable with the idea of therapy, she should have an exorcism. This openness to non-Western and non-American modes of healing marks the therapist/priestess as a bridge between the cultures, an integrator. Rena recommends rituals the members of the group can perform to release their fear and pain: burning slips of paper with the names of their abusers written on them, and releasing a green balloon to the sky. Danticat is realistic in depicting the mixed results of these rituals; Sophie feels better after burning her mother's name, but some time later sees the green balloon stuck in a tree—it has not traveled very far from home. However, Rena does offer some advice that ultimately does result in healing, saying about Martine's rape memories and Sophie's phobia of being with her husband:

> Your mother never gave him a face. That's why he's a shadow. That's why he can control her.... You will never be able to connect with your husband until you say good-bye to your father.

She recommends that Martine undergo an exorcism, but Martine commits suicide before she can follow this advice. Sophie, however, ultimately does follow it, revisiting the scene of her mother's rape in the cane fields and experiencing a violent catharsis. Her grandmother and aunt watch, and in the end, acknowledge that she has been liberated from the burden she has carried for so long.

Ann Folwell Stanford comments, in her annotation for New York University's *Literature, Arts and Medicine* database, that the therapy section "barely escapes trendy cliche," but in fact the therapist's use of ritual is highly appropriate for Sophie, whose whole life has been enriched by ritual, symbol, and story. This is a language that Sophie understands, since she was raised with stories of Erzulie and other Haitian deities, and since, in Haiti, even an ordinary bath has ritual elements: at her grandmother's house, they bathe in an outdoor shack using rainwater that has been steeped with healing herbs: "a potpourri of flesh healers: catnip, senna, sarsaparilla, *corrosol*, the petals of blood red hibiscus, forget-me-nots, and daffodils." Ritual is part of everyday life in many other ways, from the use of lanterns to mark the sex of a newborn child, the weekly Mass that people attend, and the endless stories of ancestors, deities, and folk heroes and heroines.

The book ends on a hopeful note. Sophie's baby, Brigitte Ife, is a symbol of the integration of her old and new lives and the potential healing in the generational line of women: the child is untouched, untroubled by nightmares, born in America. At the same time, she resembles Sophie's mother so closely that Grandma Ife, on seeing the girl, is astonished. "'Do you see my granddaughter?' she asked, tracing her thumb across Brigitte's chin. 'The tree has not split one mite. Isn't it a miracle that we can visit with all our kin, simply by looking at this face?'"

Danticat emphasizes this possibility later in the book, when Sophie says, "I looked back at my daughter, who was sleeping peacefully.... The fact that she could sleep meant that she had no nightmares, and maybe, would never become a frightened insomniac like my mother and me." She highlights the idea again when Sophie, after burning her mother's name in the therapy ritual, wisely realizes, "It was up to me to avoid my turn in the fire. It was up to me to make sure that my daughter never slept with ghosts, never lived with nightmares, and never had her name burnt in the fire."

She will succeed in this, the reader knows, because at the end of the book, when she revisits the scene of the rape, she beats and pounds at the cane as if she is possessed. The priest walks toward her, but Grandma Ife stops him, knowing that Sophie must do this. Ife and Tante Atie both call, "*Ou libere?*"—"Are you free?"—a phrase women traditionally use when one has dropped a heavy and dangerous load. Thus, they acknowledge her freedom from the burden that has oppressed her for so long. Before she can answer their question, Grandma Ife puts her fingers over Sophie's lips and tells her, "Now, you will know how to answer," meaning that she is free, and she knows it.

The events in the book are shaped by the political, social, and economic chaos in Haiti during the regimes of Jean-Claude "Baby Doc" Duvalier and his successors. During Duvalier's regime, the illiteracy rate in Haiti was 90 percent, and the population was oppressed by widespread poverty and disease. In addition, ordinary people lived in fear of the *Tontons Macoutes*, formerly the volunteer secret police and death squad of dictator François "Papa Doc" Duvalier. Named for a cannibalistic ogre, a monster from folk tales, the *Macoutes* arbitrarily murdered, raped, and tortured anyone suspected of opposing the regime, or anyone they happened to run into. Sophie's birth is the result of a *Macoute's* rape of her mother, when Martine was sixteen years old, and throughout the book, these figures of terror reappear, shooting students, killing a coal seller, appearing in the market and on a bus Sophie is riding. Sophie herself is a permanent reminder of the power of the *Macoutes*, since she does not resemble anyone in her family, and it is believed that she looks just like the rapist: a physical, daily reminder to Martine of the torture she went through.

Austin Chronicle writer Belinda Acosta described Danticat as a "gifted, compassionate young writer," and noted that one of the most remarkable aspects of Danticat's career is that she "consistently turns out work that is at turns compelling, beautiful, and breathtakingly painful." Atkins remarked in *Writers Online* that the book "traverses between cultures, negotiating an identity constructed in two sharply distinct worlds." The emotional impact of the book was summed up by Mary Mackay, a *Publishers Weekly* contributor, who wrote, "In simple, lyrical prose enriched by an elegiac tone . . . she makes Sophie's confusion and guilt, her difficult assimilation . . . [and her] emotional liberation palpably clear."

Source: Kelly Winters, Critical Essay on *Breath, Eyes, Memory*, in *Novels for Students*, Gale, Cengage Learning, 2011.

Mary Mackay

In the following review, Mackay outlines the pain and struggle of the women in Breath, Eyes, Memory, *and describes the novel as a compelling record of the Haiti that Danticat wishes to be remembered as "a rich landscape of memory."*

Edwidge Danticat dedicates her powerful first novel to "The brave women of Haiti . . . on this shore and other shores. We have stumbled but we will not fall." Such optimism is extraordinary, given the everyday adversity faced by the women whose stories are interwoven with that of Sophie, the narrator.

Grandmother Ife, mother Martine, aunt Atie, and daughter Sophie (and later Sophie's daughter, Brigitte) are rooted as firmly in their native Haitian soil as they are bound to one another, despite the ocean, experiences, and years that separate them. The ties to Haiti, the women's certainty of meeting there at the "very end of each of our journeys," affords their only apparent security. "Somehow, early on, our song makers and tale weavers had decided that we were all daughters of this land," Danticat writes. Structurally, the book reflects the centrality of Haiti: the longest of its four sections takes place there, although covering only a few days in a novel that covers years.

The story begins in Haiti. Through Sophie's 12-year-old eyes, the island seems a paradise of bougainvillea, poincianas, and the unconditional love of Tante Atie. Then Martine, the mother Sophie knew only as a photograph, sends for her from New York City. It seems a mean place that has worn out her mother: "It was as though she had never stopped working in the cane fields after all." Sophie is haunted by the hardships of immigrant life, together with the ghosts from the past and the burdens of womanhood in a hostile world. She describes herself as a frightened insomniac, but somehow survives the test. Her older, jazz-musician husband, Joseph, one of the novel's few male characters and certainly the most loyal and gentle, gives her some strength. She copes through a resilient melange of love, ties to home, and therapy. And when she returns to Haiti as an adult, she senses a sinister edge to the place, represented by the Tonton Macoutes (militiamen), the boat people, and her Tante Atie's bitterness.

"There is always a place where nightmares are passed on through generations like heirlooms," writes Danticat. In this book, one of those places is "testing," part of a "virginity cult, our mothers' obsession with keeping us pure and chaste," in which the mother probes her daughter's vagina (sometime violently) to see if she is still whole. She also listens to her daughter peeing to see if the sound suggests a deflowered, widened passage. Even rape has one positive result: the end of "testing" by an otherwise trusted mother. The invasiveness, pain, and humiliation turn daughter against mother generation after generation, Atie against Ife, Sophie against Martine.

But there is reconciliation, too. As mothers and daughters, the women are bound in love as in hate. A mother may inflict on her daughter the same pain that drove her from her own mother. Why? "I did it because my mother had done it to me. I have no greater excuse." The book is a plea to end these divisive rituals. Mothers indeed long to break the cycle of pain, asking pointedly from beyond the grave, "'Ou libere?' Are you free, my daughter?"

Suffering inflicted by a well-intentioned mother is all the more treacherous in a world where the birth of a girl child is marked by "no lamps, no candles, no more light." Danticat leaves the reader with no illusions as to why the welcome is so dark. As well as "testing," the women in this family endure rape, unwanted pregnancy, and violence that lead to mental illness, nightmares, sexual phobias, bulimia, and self-mutilation. Breast cancer seems almost benign in this context; being unmarried and childless does not.

Sophie wants and seems to be the hope for breaking with painful tradition. Returning to Haiti with her mother's body for burial, she reaches an important understanding: the testing was painful for Martine, too. Doing what she had to do as a Haitian woman, "My mother was as brave as stars at dawn." Sophie breaks free as she madly attacks the sugar cane in the midst of which her father had raped and impregnated her mother. We sense that Sophie—and Brigitte—are finally safe.

Despite all the suffering ("'Can one really die of chagrin?' I asked Tante Atie."), Danticat writes with a light and lyrical touch. Her characterization is vivid, her allusive language richly unembellished. Color (literal as well as linguistic) carries the reader from the daffodil yellow associated with Haiti and Sophie's early days in New York, to the more ominous red with which her mother surrounds herself in interior decoration as in death. Occasionally Danticat devotes too many details to a banal incident or action, but this is a minor criticism for a first novel.

In a personal essay, Danticat calls Haiti a "rich landscape of memory." But she is afraid that female storytellers like herself may be Haiti's last surviving breath, eyes, and memory. In this compelling novel, the reader experiences the Haiti that Danticat fears will be lost.

Source: Mary Mackay, Review of *Breath, Eyes, Memory*, in *Belles Lettres*, Vol. 10, No. 1, Fall 1994, p. 36.

Mary Mackay

In the following review, Mackay describes Danticat's Breath, Eyes, Memory *as a graceful first novel outlining the coming-of-age story of Sophie, the novel's protagonist and narrator, in a world where traditions clash and the beauty of Haiti is inexorably mixed with the burden of sexual trauma, mental brutality, and political terror.*

A distinctive new voice with a sensitive insight into Haitian culture distinguishes this graceful debut novel about a young girl's coming-of-age under difficult circumstances. "I come from a place where breath, eyes and memory are one, a place where you carry your past like the hair on your head," says narrator Sophie Caco, ruminating on the chains of duty and love that bind the courageous women in her family. The burden of being a woman in Haiti, where purity and chastity are a matter of family honor, and where "nightmares are passed on through generations like heirlooms," is Danticat's theme. Born after her mother Martine was raped, Sophie is raised by her Tante Atie in a small town in Haiti. At 12 she joins Martine in New York, while Atie returns to her native village to care for indomitable Grandmother Ife. Neither Sophie nor Martine can escape the weight of the past, resulting in a pattern of insomnia, bulimia, sexual trauma and mental anguish that afflicts both of them and leads inexorably to tragedy. Though her tale is permeated with a haunting sadness, Danticat also imbues it with color and magic, beautifully evoking the pace and character of Creole life, the feel of both village and farm communities, where the omnipresent Tontons Macoute mean daily terror, where voudon rituals and superstitions still dominate even as illiterate inhabitants utilize such 20th-century conveniences as cassettes to correspond with emigres in America. In simple, lyrical prose enriched by an elegiac tone and piquant observations, she makes

Sophie's confusion and guilt, her difficult assimilation into American culture and her eventual emotional liberation palpably clear.

Source: Mary Mackay, Review of *Breath, Eyes, Memory*, in *Publisher's Weekly*, Vol. 241, No. 4, January 24, 1994, p. 39.

SOURCES

"Author Interview: Edwidge Danticat," in *Random House Web site*, http://www.randomhouse.com/catalog/display. pperl?isbn = 9780375705045&view = auqa (accessed August 18, 2010).

Acosta, Belinda, "The Farming of Bones," in *Austin Chronicle*, January 19, 1999.

Atkins, Christine, "Junot Diaz and Edwidge Danticat," in *Writers Online*, Vol. 1, No. 3, Spring 1997, http://www.albany. edu/writers-inst/webpages4/archives/olv1n3.html#diaz (accessed August 18, 2010).

Charters, Mallay, "Edwidge Danticat: A Bitter Legacy Revisited," in *Publishers Weekly*, August 17, 1998, p. 42.

"Cholera Spreading in Haiti," in *UPI.com*, http://www. upi.com/Top_News/World-News/2010/11/10/Cholera-spreading-in-Haiti/UPI-15811289405749/ (accessed November 10, 2010).

Corbett, Bob, Review of *Breath, Eyes, Memory*, in *Haiti Home Page*, Webster University Web site, http://www. webster.edu/~corbetre/haiti/bookreviews/danticat1.htm (accessed August 18, 2010).

Danticat, Edwidge, *Breath, Eyes, Memory*, Vintage, 1994.

Francis, Donette A., "'Silences Too Horrific to Disturb': Writing Sexual Histories in Edwidge Danticat's *Breath, Eyes, Memory*," in *Research in African Literatures*, Vol. 35, No. 2, Summer 2004, pp. 75–90.

Gladstone, Jim, Review of *Breath, Eyes, Memory*, in *New York Times Book Review*, July 10, 1994, p. 24.

Mackay, Mary, Review of *Breath, Eyes, Memory*, in *Publishers Weekly*, January 24, 1994, p. 39.

"1980s Haitian Unrest," in *Global Security.org*, http:// www.globalsecurity.org/military/world/war/haiti-unrest. htm (accessed November 10, 2010).

N'Zengou-Tayo, Marie-José, "Rewriting Folklore: Traditional Beliefs and Popular Culture in Edwidge Danticat's *Breath, Eyes, Memory* and *Krik? Krak!*," in *MaComère*, Vol. 3, 2000, pp. 123–40.

Philpott, Joan, Review of *Breath, Eyes, Memory*, in *Ms.*, March/April 1994, pp. 77–78.

Rooney, Megan, "Danticat MFA '94 Reads from *The Farming of Bones*," in *Brown Daily Herald* (Brown University, Providence, RI), October 5, 1998.

Shea, Renee H., "An Interview between Edwidge Danticat and Renee H. Shea," in *Belles Lettres*, Summer 1995, pp. 12–15.

Stanford, Ann Folwell, Annotation for *Breath, Eyes, Memory*, in *Literature, Arts and Medicine Database*, http://litmed. med.nyu.edu/Annotation?action = view&annid = 1253 (accessed September 4, 2010).

Thomas, Katherine M., "Memories of Home: Edwidge Danticat's *Breath, Eyes, Memory*," in *Kentucky Philological Review*, Vol. 18, 2004, pp. 35–40.

Wilson, Calvin, "Edwidge Danticat's Prose Floats in Realm of Sadness and Eloquence," in *Kansas City Star*, September 22, 1999, p. K0779.

FURTHER READING

Bell, Beverly, *Walking on Fire: Haitian Women's Stories of Survival and Resistance*, Cornell University Press, 2001.
>   An activist, Bell, director of the Center for Economic Justice in Albuquerque, New Mexico, compiled these thirty-eight oral histories during the early 1990s to demonstrate the strength of Haitian women, who are shown to be among the poorest and the bravest women on earth. The foreword is by Danticat.

Chancy, Myriam J. A., *Framing Silence: Revolutionary Novels by Haitian Women*, Rutgers University Press, 1997.
>   Chancy, born in Haiti, examines ideas of identity and culture in work by six novelists, including *Breath, Eyes, Memory*. This was the first full-length study in English of Haitian women's literature.

Danticat, Edwidge, ed., *The Butterfly's Way: Voices from the Haitian Dyaspora in the United States*, Soho, 2001.
>   Eager to not be seen as the sole or primary voice of Haitian American literature, Danticat has energetically supported the work of others. In this collection, she has gathered essays and poems from thirty-three of her contemporaries, demonstrating the rich variety of Haitian American writing.

Mardorossian, Carine M., *Reclaiming Difference: Caribbean Women Rewrite Postcolonialism*, University of Virginia Press, 2005.
>   This volume analyzes novels by four writers— Jean Rhys, Maryse Condé, Edwidge Danticat, and Julia Alvarez—and explores how these writers develop an idea of transculturalism, rather than emphasizing difference. Some sections of this work of postcolonial criticism may be difficult for nonspecialists.

Munro, Martin, ed., *Edwidge Danticat: A Reader's Guide*, University of Virginia Press, 2010.
>   This volume, the first full-length study of Danticat, offers an accessible introduction to her life and work. It includes critical essays by more than a dozen scholars, as well as an interview with Danticat and an extensive bibliography.

SUGGESTED SEARCH TERMS

Breath, Eyes, Memory AND Edwidge Danticat

Duvalier AND Haiti

Edwidge Danticat

Erzuli

Haiti AND Danticat

Haiti AND folklore

Haiti AND voodoo

Haitian diaspora

Haitian literature

Frankenstein

1931 The 1931 film *Frankenstein*, directed by James Whale and starring Boris Karloff, introduced the world to the iconic figure of the Frankenstein monster. The green-faced creature with bolts in his neck, wearing a jacket and stumbling away from torch-bearing peasants, has little in common with the creature depicted in Mary Shelley's 1818 novel, but he has superseded her creation in the popular imagination. Each year at Halloween, variations on Universal Studio's version of the creature show up. Fierce or cuddly, deadly or pathetic, they all draw on the emotional range of Boris Karloff's brilliant, speechless performance.

One reason the film version of the Frankenstein story is so different from Shelley's novel is that it was made in a mass media age, for audiences with little sense of the theological principles that Shelley was exploring. Though it bears the same title, the Universal Studio version of *Frankenstein* is not actually based on Shelley's novel. In the more than one hundred years that passed between the two, there were countless stage adaptations of the novel, each adding a few twists to the story. The film's script, by Francis Edward Faragoh and Garrett Fort, actually credits a 1927 British play by Peggy Webling, a version that included elements that had been added over time.

This movie and *Dracula*, released earlier the same year, established Universal as the premier studio for monster movies and began a franchise, with the sequels *Bride of Frankenstein, Son of*

John Kobal Foundation | Getty Images

Frankenstein, House of Frankenstein and others. It also opened the door for other popular films featuring the Wolfman, the Mummy, the Invisible Man, and the Creature from the Black Lagoon. The film also made Karloff a household name; his portrayal of the monster established new standards for acting in the genre.

PLOT SUMMARY

Prologue

Before the opening credits, the film shows a narrator, who steps out from behind a curtain on a stage, simulating the experience that audiences would have had if they were seeing a live performance in a theater. This narrator is Edward Van Sloan, who will play Dr. Waldman in the film, though here he is out of costume and out of character. He warns audiences of the upsetting and graphic nature of the story they are about to

see and urges those who are squeamish to consider leaving the theater.

Before the Monster

The action of the story opens with the funeral of an unnamed character. The mourners who gather around the grave do not see that they are being observed by Dr. Henry Frankenstein and his assistant, the disfigured hunchback Fritz. When the ceremony is over, the caretaker covers the grave with soil and leaves. Frankenstein and Fritz come out and dig the casket up. "He's just resting," Frankenstein says, with a gleam in his eye, "waiting for a new life to come." They put the casket on a cart and ride off.

They stop at a gallows, where the body of a hanged man still dangles on its noose, and Dr. Frankenstein sends Fritz up to cut the body down. When he is able to examine it, Frankenstein determines that the neck has been broken, rendering the brain no good for his experiment.

FILM TECHNIQUE

- Like many films from the early sound era, *Frankenstein* does not have an alternate track for music while the characters are talking. Music plays over the opening and closing credits, but during the course of the film, the only music that can be heard is music that occurs within story, such as the dance music at the wedding feast. Sound that can be heard by the characters in a film is referred to as *diegetic sound*; sound that is heard only by audiences, such as soundtrack music, is called *nondiegetic sound*.

- The interiors of *Frankenstein* are shot using low-key lighting, and several outdoor scenes occur at night, establishing a sense of gloom and mystery. Whale uses the general dimness to include hot points in the film by putting particular bright spots in the frame. The most notable instances of this are the torch Fritz waves at the monster and the ones that the villagers carry, and the kinetic sparking machines in Dr. Frankenstein's laboratory, as well as the bright flashes of lightning that spontaneously illuminate the school lecture hall and the laboratory. Whale draws attention to the variations in the film's lighting by having Dr. Frankenstein turn off an electric light just before the monster enters for the first time.

- A panning shot is one in which the camera moves smoothly across the scene in one direction. The very first shot of the film is a left-to-right pan at the graveside, showing viewers the mourners, the clergy, and the statue of the Grim Reaper standing behind them before settling on Fritz, whose face is then moved (vertically, not horizontally, as the camera has moved) to reveal the face of Henry Frankenstein. Another notable use of the pan is when Elizabeth, Victor, and Dr. Waldman are at the door of the tower, and Frankenstein shouts down to them. The camera pans very slowly up the tower wall, emphasizing Frankenstein's isolation from his friends.

- The director films several important shots through other things, forcing viewers to focus on items that are beyond whatever is in the foreground. This occurs early, in the graveyard scene, as Fritz and Frankenstein are seen watching through a fence. Later, the creature is seen through the trees as he approaches Little Maria's house and stumbles through the branches to escape after inadvertently harming her. At the film's climax, Whale shows Frankenstein and his creation glaring at one another through the rotating spokes of the mill, highlighting the fear and anger that separate them.

- Most of this film is shot with medium or far shots, showing at least the torso, if not the entire body, of one or more characters. When the monster first appears on screen, however, the film uses a series of close-ups to maximize the shock value of his face. This is a significant moment that is teasingly extended by having his arrival announced by footsteps and having him enter the room backwards. When the monster's face is finally revealed, Whale shows it, then moves in for a tighter close-up, and again for an even tighter close-up.

An establishing shot shows the outside of Goldstadt Medical College, where Dr. Waldman is showing a class the different physical characteristics of a normal and an abnormal brain. After the class leaves, Fritz steals in through a window. He takes the normal brain, but a loud sound frightens him and he drops it on the floor. He grabs the brain marked "abnormal" and leaves.

At the home of Dr. Frankenstein's fiancée, Elizabeth, Victor Moritz enters. Elizabeth has just received her first letter from Frankenstein in four months and is worried about him. Victor says he ran into Frankenstein in the woods a few weeks earlier. They decide to go to talk to Professor Waldman, Frankenstein's old mentor. At his office, Waldman explains that Frankenstein left the university, unhappy that the school could not provide him with the materials he needed for his experiments: human bodies.

At the old watchtower that Frankenstein has turned into his laboratory, it is a rainy night. Frankenstein calls to Fritz, who is up on the roof preparing for the coming experiment, to come down. Fritz is nervous and jumps when a hand drops out from under the sheet on the operating gurney. Frankenstein pulls back the sheet to uncover a human form, with its face still bandaged. Their work is interrupted by a loud knocking at the door. Frankenstein sends Fritz to answer it, and the hunchback, walking with a short cane, takes a long time descending the tower stairs.

At the door are Elizabeth, Victor, and Dr. Waldman. Frankenstein comes to the door to implore them to leave, but when Victor accuses him of being insane, he invites them in to watch the experiment in progress. He seats them in the corner of his laboratory and explains his previous successes in reviving dead animals.

The gurney is raised through the hole in the roof during a fierce lightning storm, until lightning strikes a rod beside it. When it is lowered, they watch, fearing that the experiment is a failure, until Frankenstein notices that the body's hand is moving on its own. "He's alive!" Frankenstein shouts with joy, "Now I know what it feels like to be God." Though this last line captures the philosophical issue at the heart of Mary Shelley's novel, it was removed in 1937 by censors, who considered it too blasphemous. However, it was restored for the DVD release of 1986.

The next scene takes place days later, in the den of Baron Frankenstein, Henry's father. The town burgomaster (a public official similar to a mayor) enters and asks whether Frankenstein and Elizabeth are to be married. The people of the village are already making preparations for the wedding, he explains. Baron Frankenstein leaves to bring his son home from the watchtower laboratory.

In the laboratory, Frankenstein talks with Dr. Waldman about his accomplishment. He gloats about people's opinion that he is insane, but he is visibly shaken when Waldman tells him that the brain stolen from the school was a criminal brain. They hear the creature's heavy footsteps in the hall, and Frankenstein hastens to turn down the lights, explaining that the creature is like a newborn and that his eyes have not learned to focus yet.

The monster enters the room walking backwards. At thirty-one minutes into the film, he turns around, unveiling to audiences for the first time the face that has become iconic in motion picture history.

The Monster's Progress

In the laboratory with Dr. Waldman, the monster obeys Frankenstein's simple commands, backing up and sitting in a chair as told. When the skylight is opened, he withdraws, but then he reaches out like a child, trying to touch the light.

Fritz enters with a blazing torch, and the monster screams and draws back. As he swats at the fire, Fritz whips him, driving him back to his cell. Fritz continues to wave the torch at the monster while Frankenstein, depressed that he might never be able to train the creature to behave, leaves.

Soon, Frankenstein and Waldman, in the laboratory, hear a blood-curdling scream. They race to the cell and find that the monster has killed Fritz. The two doctors struggle to close the cell door before the monster can push his way out. Waldman explains that the monster must be destroyed. They go to the monster with a sedative prepared, but in the struggle to drug him, he gets his hands on Frankenstein's neck and partially strangles him.

Victor arrives with Elizabeth and Baron Frankenstein. Frankenstein meets them in his study, trying to act as if nothing is wrong, but he soon collapses. Dr. Waldman suggests that Baron Frankenstein take his son home to rest. He tells Dr. Frankenstein that he will destroy the creature but will keep the notes about his experiment.

Waldman has the monster strapped to a gurney and is holding a scalpel, prepared to dismember him, when the monster's hand comes up behind him and strangles him. The creature stumbles down the tower stairs and out the door.

At his father's estate, Frankenstein recuperates from his encounter with the monster, a scene that echoes a similar period of calm in Shelley's novel after the monster is thought to have left. Preparations are made for the upcoming wedding. The Baron gives wine to the servants for the celebration, and he talks about providing beer for the entire village. The film cuts to the village, showing dancing in the streets.

Outside of town, a little girl, Little Maria, plays with flowers beside a lake. She is not frightened when the monster approaches, and she asks if he would like to play with her. She is throwing flower-heads into the lake to make them float like boats. The monster is amused by this, but he is also frustrated. Maria runs out of flowers. Looking for something else to float on the water, the monster, smiling, picks the girl up and throws her in. He then runs off into the woods, frightened at what he has done.

Elizabeth, in her bridal dress, explains to Frankenstein that she has experienced a frightening, ominous dream. Victor enters to explain that Waldman is missing and the monster has been sighted at large, so Frankenstein leaves with him, locking Elizabeth in. Soon they hear a clatter in the room, and the servants run to the locked door. The monster, in the room, approaches Elizabeth, and she faints. (In the novel, he murders her.)

Ludwig, Little Maria's father, carries the child's wet and lifeless body through the streets. The music falls silent and the dancing stops as people notice him. He takes her corpse to the burgomaster, who vows that justice will be done.

The villagers, armed with torches, clubs, and farm implements, gather to hunt the monster. They are divided into three groups, to be led by the burgomaster, Ludwig, and Frankenstein. As they search, the monster is seen briefly. Soon, they find a man whom he has mauled. Frankenstein separates from his group and soon finds himself face-to-face with the monster.

The villagers see the monster carrying Frankenstein and pursue him. He goes into a windmill and climbs to the top. Frankenstein escapes his grasp, but the monster chases him outside, onto a balcony, and throws him off. The villagers use their torches to light the wooden windmill on fire. As the flames rise, the monster shrieks in terror. A beam falls from the roof, pinning him in the fire.

The Ending

A group of maids is gathered outside of the bedroom of Henry Frankenstein, giggling. They bring him a glass of the wine that was saved for his wedding. Baron Frankenstein tells them, though, that his son is not well enough. He drinks the wine himself, toasting the potential for a son in the house of Frankenstein, as he pushes the maids back, away from the door, to give Frankenstein and Elizabeth their privacy.

CHARACTERS

The Burgomaster

The burgomaster is a local politician. He is portrayed by Lionel Belmore as a stereotypical civil servant, groveling before the powerful Frankenstein family and trying to gain their favor by bringing a bouquet of flowers for Elizabeth when he visits, cheerfully accepting the baron's verbal abuse. Later in the film, he organizes the posse to search for the monster.

Elizabeth

Shelley's novel offers its readers a much more detailed explanation of Elizabeth Lavenza's background: how she was taken into the Frankenstein home when her mother, the sister of Baron Frankenstein, died, and was raised with her cousin (who is named Victor in the novel, rather than Henry) with the expectation that they would eventually be married. The Elizabeth of the film, played by Mae Clark, is presented as a generic love interest. She worries about Frankenstein, but she also leaves him for months so as not to impede his research. She does not talk about his work at all, leaving the moral and philosophical arguments to others.

Elizabeth becomes important to the film's plot as the time for her marriage to Henry Frankenstein draws closer. As in the book, the wedding day is ruined by the monster. In the novel, however, the monster is intelligent and angry, and it has the ability to speak. It threatens well in advance to disrupt the wedding day, and when Frankenstein marries Elizabeth, it kills her. In the film, the monster sneaks into a room where Elizabeth is preparing for her wedding, leaving after it causes her to faint. The wedding never actually takes place in the film, but the prospect of the wedding lets the story end on a hopeful note.

Baron Frankenstein

Henry Frankenstein's father, played by Frederick Kerr, is a gruff old man, one of the most socially prominent people in his community. He is presented as a somewhat foolish character in the film, wearing a fez and a bow tie and smoking a ridiculously long pipe.

Baron Frankenstein shows little interest in his son's experiments, and unlike his counterpart in Shelley's novel, he has no understanding of the work that Frankenstein is doing. He objects because his son has locked himself away, and he is happy when the wedding to Elizabeth is planned, welcoming the young woman to his family with a wreath of flowers that has been in the Frankenstein family for three generations. To celebrate the upcoming wedding, the baron provides enough beer for the entire town, and the town celebrates. The baron has no comment on the rampaging monster that his son has unleashed. His concerns are relieved when, after the monster has been destroyed, he finds out that the wedding is still on.

Dr. Henry Frankenstein

Frankenstein is played by Colin Clive, whose work had been mostly in theater up to the time of this film. In the film, as in the novel, Frankenstein is a man who is obsessed with the idea of his own scientific abilities. Shelley's novel devotes much more space to establishing Frankenstein's intellectual background and the upbringing that led him to seek out ways to create life in the laboratory. The Dr. Frankenstein of the film, by contrast, is already deep within his experiments when viewers get to know him. His course of action is already determined. In the novel, the doctor's first name is Victor, the name that the film assigns to his best friend.

Viewers might think that Frankenstein is insane when they first view him, side by side with his deranged assistant Fritz, watching a funeral from their hiding place. His enthusiasm about robbing the grave of the recently deceased is notable. Throughout the assembling and animation of his creature, Frankenstein appears to allow his obsession to take control of his rational mind, ignoring his father and the woman he loves. Dr. Waldman's discussion with Elizabeth about why Henry left his position at the college supports this impression of him. The design of his laboratory, mixing bubbling chemical solutions with loud, open electrical currents, highlights the strangeness of his quest.

After first establishing him as a mad scientist, the film goes on to acknowledge some of the thoughtfulness of Shelley's protagonist. In his dialogue with Dr. Waldman after the monster has been reanimated, he calmly explains his success. He makes light of Waldman's fears, feeling that he has contributed to humanity, though his calmness is quickly shaken when he hears about the abnormal brain that Fritz has stolen from the college.

Once Dr. Waldman has agreed to destroy the monster for him, the function of Frankenstein as a character changes. He becomes the film's romantic lead as he focuses on his upcoming wedding to Elizabeth. He becomes a heroic figure, leading the search for the monster, striking out by himself when the rest of his search party is lost. Although the Victor Frankenstein of the novel ends up racked with guilt as the monster strikes out against members of his family, the Henry Frankenstein of the film does not carry his guilt for the monster's actions so heavily. The film's happy ending implies that viewers should be glad that he has survived the monster's attack and that he will soon be married.

Fritz

The character of Fritz, Dr. Frankenstein's hunchbacked assistant, was added for the film. He gives Dr. Frankenstein someone to talk to while preparing the monster, and he provides an antagonist for the monster when the creature is new and innocent. Dwight Frye, the actor who portrays him, has Fritz so stooped under his misshapen back that he walks with a short cane. His deformity gives some insight into why he would torture the creature with a flaming torch: he has found someone less powerful than himself for once. It is a foolish move, however, and the creature easily kills him. In subsequent Frankenstein movies, and in horror movies in general, the physically deformed laboratory assistant has become a standard cliché.

Little Maria

Little Maria, played by Marilyn Harris, represents childhood innocence. She is the first person in the film to not be terrified, or even disturbed, by the monster's features.

Her first scene with her father establishes that Maria is lonely, as the monster is. Her father leaves her alone at their cabin while he goes to town for one of the free drinks that the Frankenstein family is providing to everyone to celebrate the upcoming wedding. Before he goes, she asks him to stay with her; in response, he kisses her and tells her that she has her cat to play with. When the monster arrives, she does not hesitate to take him by the hand and invite him to join her in playing. Just before she hits the water, she shouts that he is hurting her, but he does not understand until too late.

Ludwig

Ludwig, Little Maria's father, is not listed in the film's credits. He leaves her alone at their cabin while he goes to town for the wedding celebration. The film does not show him coming home to find his daughter drowned in the lake, but the long sequence of Ludwig carrying his dead daughter through the festivities in the streets with a haunted look on his face provides one of the film's most horrifying scenes.

The Monster

Boris Karloff became an international star with his nuanced portrayal of the Frankenstein monster. It is a character who has no lines and does not appear until the film is nearly half over. The Universal publicity department intensified the campaign to raise public curiosity about the monster by leaving Karloff's name out of the film's opening credits, putting just a question mark next to "The Monster."

Karloff's performance gives viewers a look at a creature who was born fully grown. He matures before the audience's eyes. At first, he is like a baby, reaching up as if he thinks he can touch the sunlight. He obeys Frankenstein's commands without objection, but Fritz's taunting angers and confuses him, and he strikes out against it. In his scene with Little Maria, viewers can see that he has a gentle side: he is moved by flowers and a child's innocence, and tries to play with her, but his underdeveloped mind, just weeks old, is unable to comprehend the danger of throwing her into the water. After he has drowned her, he panics, realizing that he has done something wrong. In the scene at the windmill, however, he looks at Frankenstein with true anger, conveying the bitterness he feels about his tortured life. In the end, he is still terrified by fire, and his screams as the windmill burns show his vulnerability.

By contrast, the monster in Mary Shelley's novel quickly grows into a rational adult when he is away from the narrative. He explains at great length, with complex language, how he learned language and human customs by observing a family from hiding for untold months. Shelley's monster is motivated by anger at the man who made him and who dooms him to loneliness by refusing to make a mate, but Karloff's creature is an innocent, frightened being who never understands why the world is hunting him.

Victor Moritz

Victor Moritz is Henry Frankenstein's best friend, played in the film by John Boles. He is loosely based on the character of Henry Clerval, who is Frankenstein's childhood friend in the novel. In Shelley's version, Clerval is murdered by the monster while traveling with Frankenstein, but Whale's film has Victor on hand to facilitate discussions about Frankenstein's behavior with Elizabeth and the baron. The film also adds a touch of romantic intrigue when, early on in the film, Victor admits that he is in love with Frankenstein's fiancée, Elizabeth, making her uncomfortable. The romantic triangle that has been hinted at is never brought up again, but the connection helps explain why Victor is around the family while his friend is secluded in his laboratory for months at a time.

Narrator

An unnamed narrator, played by the same actor who plays Dr. Waldman, briefly introduces the movie, warning audiences about its graphic nature.

Doctor Waldman

Dr. Waldman, played by Edward Van Sloan, is a professor at Goldstadt Medical College, which Henry Frankenstein was associated with earlier, before the film's beginning. Like a character of the same name in the novel, he is Frankenstein's mentor at the college. In the film, he provides a scientific and philosophical connection, someone to whom Frankenstein can talk about the morality of creating life, although their discussions barely touch on the depth that Shelley covers in her novel. After stopping the monster when it attacks Frankenstein, Dr. Waldman offers to destroy the creature while its creator recuperates. He is killed because he is distracted by taking scientific notes about the process of destruction instead of paying attention to the creature on the table in front of him.

THEMES

Existence of God

The subtitle of Mary Shelley's *Frankenstein* is "The Modern Prometheus," a reference to the character from classical mythology who stole fire from the god Zeus and gave it to humanity. The implication is that one person could unlock secrets previously unattainable

READ, WATCH, WRITE

- Read Elizabeth Young's *Black Frankenstein: The Making of an American Metaphor*, published by New York University Press in 2008. In it, Young explains how the Frankenstein myth applies to racial divides in modern America. Choose another racial or ethnic group in the United States and write your own explanation explaining how aspects of the Frankenstein story might apply to that group.

- Write a scene in which the childlike monster of the movie is able to talk, explaining his actions. Be sure to explain how his perspective differs from that of the monster in Mary Shelley's novel. Then, watch *Bride of Frankenstein*, the 1935 sequel to this film, and in an essay, compare how your talking monster differs from the one conceived by the filmmakers.

- Popular writer Dean Koontz has updated the Frankenstein story in a series of books (*Prodigal Son*, *City of Nights*, and *Dead and Alive*). Read one book from the Koontz series and create a digital or traditional storyboard for adapting one of the scenes to film, doing it in the way that you think Whale and his cinematographer, Arthur Edeson, would have done it if they were adapting Koontz instead of Shelley in the 1930s.

- This film has no soundtrack. In groups of two or more, compose or choose existing music that you find appropriate for two scenes, one with action and one with quieter discussion. Synchronize your music to the film using a digital video editing program, taking care to emphasize specific gestures with specific musical cues. Play it for your class and then give a brief explanation of why you made the artistic choices you made.

- At the time of its release, the face given to the monster in this film was considered a shocking portrayal of dead tissue brought to life, but hundreds of interpretations of Boris Karloff's makeup have rendered this version benign or even friendly at times. Draw or sculpt a version of the monster that would be considered horrifying in modern times. Keep a written or digital journal (including sketches or photographs) of your thought process and the revisions that you make as your work progresses, and present your journal to your class along with your work.

- Frankenstein is sometimes looked at as a metaphor for teen angst, since the monster rebels against its creator, symbolizing its parent. Write a comparison between the family dynamic portrayed in this film and the family portrayed in your favorite movie drama about a difficult family situation, explaining what the characters in each film have in common.

- Read *Frankenstein: The Graphic Novel*, adapted in 2008 by Classical Comics for the Classic Graphic Novel collection. Suitable for young adults, it includes a glossary, a table of contents, a biography of Shelley, and the novel's origin and history, among other helpful features. It received a starred review from *Library Journal*. Write a review of the graphic novel that compares it with the film. Post it to your blog and invite your classmates and teacher to comment.

---

by humans and make them accessible. This idea is echoed in Whale's film when Dr. Frankenstein exclaims, upon reanimating dead tissue, that he now knows what it feels like to be God. He feels that he has a power that, until then, only God had.

In the novel, Frankenstein's monster functions as a guilty conscience, stealthily showing up after months of lying low, hundreds of miles from where he was last seen. The film also punishes Frankenstein for his blasphemous presumption, but it does so in a quicker, though less gruesome, manner. Colin Clive plays Frankenstein as a man who is racked with guilt from the moment that he first realizes that his monster is dangerous. Elizabeth is not murdered by the monster in the film, but she is threatened. The last half of the film, after the monster comes alive, presents the process of Frankenstein realizing how little like God he is: although he managed to reanimate dead tissue, he has no control of his creation, and he struggles to undo the mistake he has made.

Predestination

One of the most memorable scenes in this film is when Fritz, the assistant, is sent to the medical school to retrieve a brain for the monster and, after dropping the normal brain, ends up bringing Dr. Frankenstein a brain marked "abnormal," which Dr. Waldman earlier described to his students as being that of a murderer. Waldman's later revelation about the brain horrifies Frankenstein, as he instantly understands that the creature's violence is not something that it will grow out of, that it is predestined to live out the behavior of a sociopath. Several of the film's sequels, including *The Ghost of Frankenstein* and the horror comedy *Abbot and Costello Meet Frankenstein* dealt with plans to replace the monster's abnormal brain with another one.

Although this plot twist establishes that the creature is destined to be violent, the plot of the film itself is not so clear about the subject. The creature kills three people in the film. The first two, Fritz and Dr. Waldman, are threatening him when he kills them, so his assault on them can be viewed as self-defense. Throwing Little Maria into the pond could be viewed as the inevitable action of a criminal mind, but he does not act with anger or cunning: in fact, as he runs from the scene of the crime, he appears to be frightened at what he has done. The monster lacks the mental capacity to control the mighty body Frankenstein has given him, but his actions do not seem to be as malicious as those of a born criminal.

Childhood

Working with the situation established in the first half of the film, the creature could have been presented as a person who retains the thoughts that were already firmly planted within its brain. Instead, the filmmakers decided to follow Mary Shelley's conception that the creature is someone who came into existence at the time

Hulton Archive | Getty Images

of Frankenstein's experiment and therefore had to learn about life anew. While Shelley had this learning process occur out of the narrative range, only to have the creature tell Frankenstein all about it later, Whale presented the creature's learning process from its beginning.

When he is first introduced to audiences, the creature is implicitly compared to an infant. He walks backwards, having not yet learned how to walk; the curtains are drawn because his eyes are not yet accustomed to light. When he does see sunlight, he reaches out as a child would, unsure of the range of his power to grasp. He has a primordial terror of fire. Later, when he encounters Little Maria near her home, he is willing to sit down and play a childish game that she has made up to keep herself amused.

Later in the film, Whale implies some of the resentment that drives the creature in Shelley's novel. The creature stumbles into the study where Elizabeth waits, prepared for her wedding, though he leaves without harming her. When he encounters Frankenstein face-to-face in the woods, he has grown; earlier, he obeyed commands, but now he is angry at the man who created him. It is as if the creature has grown into a rebellious adolescent, blaming his father figure, who brought him into the world and therefore caused all of his woes.

STYLE

Grand Guignol

Critics reviewing the film at the time of its release frequently characterized it as *Grand Guignol*. This phrase comes from *La Theatre du Grand Guignol*, a theater in Paris that became famous for producing macabre, graphic stage presentations from 1897 to 1962. Its experiments with the outer boundaries of horror came to define the concept of terror for a generation of budding filmmakers.

At a time when melodrama was the most popular theatrical form, providing audiences with sweet stories about average people who triumph over adversity, the Grand Guignol made its name by focusing on the darker side of life, often with a sardonic twist of humor. Rick Worland, author of *The Horror Film*, provides a list of subjects that were typical of this kind of theater: "The special technical forte, the major 'attraction' of the Grand Guignol, was its realistic presentation of shockingly graphic mutilations, eviscerations, stabbings, beheadings, electrocutions, hangings, rapes, and other atrocious acts performed live on stage." To modern audiences, the events depicted in Frankenstein might not seem to match the terrors presented at the Grand Guignol, but audiences of 1931 found much to be repulsed by, starting with the extremism of Boris Karloff's makeup as the creature, which highlighted the concept of a being made from pieces of corpses, stitched together. One scene, the drowning of Little Maria, was considered so gruesome that censors had it removed from the film, and it was not seen for decades.

German Expressionism

The most notable visual elements in this film—off-kilter camera angles; gloomy, misty settings; and the crowded laboratory, filled with sound and action—are techniques usually associated with German expressionism. Having become popular in German cinema in the 1920s, German expressionism focused on characters who were at intellectual extremes, frequently at or near the point of insanity, surrounded by a cluttered visual world that mirrored their confusion and paranoia. Shadows were frequently worked into the visual scheme to suggest the sinister. The early European films of director Fritz Lang are often categorized as prime examples of the German expressionist style, including *Metropolis* (which takes place in a futuristic city, with a robot woman created to stop a workers' uprising), *M* (about a police hunt for a suspected child molester), and *Dr. Mabuse, the Gambler* (about an insane criminal mastermind who controls people through hypnosis). In the field of horror, F. W. Murnau's groundbreaking silent vampire film *Nosferatu* (1922) is considered a model of future German expressionist films.

CULTURAL CONTEXT

Adaptations of the Novel

Almost immediately after Mary Shelley published the first version of her novel in 1818, people saw the story's basic appeal to popular culture and began adapting it to other media. The first stage version on record was called *Presumption, or the Fate of Frankenstein*, produced at the English Opera House in London in July of 1823. The idea of a scientist dabbling in God's domain drew some protesters, but that did not stop other versions from popping up. By the end of that year, there were two other dramatic adaptations, at the Coburg and the Royalty theaters. There were also several burlesque versions of the story, comedies with titles such as *Frankenstitch* and *Frank-n-stein, or the Modern Promise to Pay*.

Numerous adaptations followed, each adhering to the basic premise of the story but changing it slightly. Fritz, the laboratory assistant, was an early addition, giving Frankenstein someone to discuss his plans with. In general, the looming, powerful presence of Frankenstein's monster proved to be a crowd-pleaser, and so authors writing new adaptations focused on his role, chiseling away at Dr. Frankenstein himself, who had been the undeniable focus of the novel. Different stagings addressed in different ways the problem of ending a play about an immortal creature; he was buried under an avalanche, trapped in a fire, or struck by a thunderbolt.

After the initial rush, stage productions continued, though not at the same pace. There was seldom any time throughout the latter half of the 1800s when some small theatrical company was not putting on its own version of Shelley's story, such as the 1887 production at the Gaiety Theater called *The Model Man*, which starred Nellie Farren as a female Dr. Frankenstein, whose creature was significantly more friendly than most familiar versions, laughing and dancing in a way that audiences rejected.

The most notable stage version of the twentieth century was the one written by Peggy Webling in 1927, which *Frankenstein* director Whale credits as the source material for the movie. Webling was asked to write an adaptation of *Frankenstein* by Hamilton Deane, an actor who had earlier written a stage version of Bram Stoker's novel *Dracula* and enjoyed theatrical success with it. Webling's play toured England for two years before making it to a London stage in 1930. After the success of Tod Browning's film *Dracula* in 1931, Universal Studios bought the rights to Webling's play and immediately adapted it for the Whale film, released by the end of that year.

The Universal adaptation was actually the second film version of the Frankenstein story. In 1910, a short silent version was made for Edison Studios. Thomas Edison, the inventor of the motion picture camera, is sometimes credited as a producer of this film, though historians doubt that he had any particular input into this production. The film, which compacts Shelley's story down to thirteen minutes, stars Charles Ogle as the monster and Augustus Phillips as Dr. Frankenstein. Because it was made before 1920, its copyright has expired and it is in the public domain. This movie can be legally downloaded in its entirety from the Internet.

Popular Entertainment in 1931

Motion pictures became the most prevalent form of popular entertainment in the early 1930s for several reasons. One reason was technology. Until recently, most films had been presented without sound, forcing viewers to imagine the characters' dialogue while music was played, often in synchronization with the action. Various experiments with sound (actors talking) in film took place throughout the 1920s, but film studios were hesitant to commit to any one format until the financially struggling Warner Brothers studio released *The Jazz Singer*, starring Al Jolson, in 1927. The popularity of that film was so overwhelming that studios raced to upgrade their systems, knowing that audiences' tolerance for silent films was over. While audience tastes changed almost overnight after *The Jazz Singer*, movie theaters tried to hold off. There were two prevailing formats for synchronizing sound and film: one, called sound-on-disk, provided a soundtrack on a record disk, while the other format, sound-on-film, put the soundtrack right on the strip of film. Gradually, the sound-on-film format won out, and by 1930 most theater owners wired their theaters with speakers to accommodate the new technology.

Archive Photos | Getty Images

The stock market crash of October 1929, which led to the Great Depression, helped to push movies forward as a prevailing force in popular entertainment. As the unemployment crisis deepened and savings were lost, people found themselves with little money in their budgets for amusements. Films cost much to make, but they could reach massive audiences. Movie tickets rose at the end of the 1920s, as theaters were investing in sound systems, so that the average ticket price in 1929 was between thirty-five and fifty-five cents, but prices decreased during the Depression, bringing the average ticket in 1934 down to twenty-three cents. Compared with other distractions, movies were an affordable bargain. While many industries suffered throughout the Depression, film studios grew. As the competition grew, studios invested heavily in scripts, rights, and special effects, struggling for audience attention.

CRITICAL OVERVIEW

Since the very moment that *Frankenstein* was released into theaters, it has been considered a groundbreaking effort, one of the works that defined the horror genre in cinema. Its release had been promoted by Universal Studios for months, building on the success of the Tod Browning film *Dracula*, also released in 1931, and teasing audiences about what the monster would eventually look like. In *Variety*, a show-business newspaper dedicated to watching industry trends, Alfred Rushford Greason gave unmitigated approval when the film opened in December of 1931. "Looks like a 'Dracula' plus," Greason writes in the paper's signature choppy style, "touching a new peak in horror plays and handled in production with supreme craftsmanship." Greason also notes that "subtle handling of the subject comes in the balance that has been maintained between the real and the supernatural, contrast that heightens the horror punches." After praising the acting of Colin Clive, Boris Karloff, Mae Clark, and John Boles, he also compliments the technical effects, noting that the "photography is splendid and the lighting is the last word in ingenuity."

Also at the time of the film's initial release, Mordaunt Hall wrote, in the *New York Times*, that he observed people at the premier laughing "to cover their true feelings." "No matter what one may say about the melodramatic ideas here, there is no denying that it is far and away the most effective thing of its kind," he notes, pointing out that *Dracula* looked "tame" beside it. His review singles out Colin Clive as Dr. Frankenstein for praise, though more recent critics have found Clive's performance to be almost humorous in its exaggeration.

Frankenstein was a commercial success, grossing more than twelve million dollars, much more than its 250,000 dollar budget. While *Dracula* had been successful in its own right, it was *Frankenstein* that established the standards of the look and feel of the Universal horror film, a standard that was to be copied by its own sequels and by other franchises the studio produced, from the *Mummy* movies of the 1930s to the *Wolf Man* films of the 1940s to the *Creature From the Black Lagoon* films of the 1950s.

As acclaimed as *Frankenstein* has been since its initial release, serious critics prefer its first sequel, 1935's *Bride of Frankenstein*. Radu Florescu captures the general consensus in his 1975 book *In Search of Frankenstein* when he notes that "here was a case where all the elements of filmmaking meshed together to form a nearly perfect feature," listing the story, photography, and music as elements that showed just the right

touch and crediting Whale for the fluidity of camera motion that he had acquired between the two projects. *Bride of Frankenstein* is frequently chosen over the original film on lists of significant movies, such as *Time* magazine's list of "All-Time 100 Movies."

CRITICISM

David Kelly

Kelly is an instructor of creative writing and literature. In the following essay, he examines how Frankenstein*'s two endings serve to complete the transition between Shelley's view of the monster and the one common in popular culture.*

Universal Studios' 1931 film *Frankenstein* uses a few of the same character names as Mary Shelley's novel and the same basic premise, that of a terrifying giant man made of dead flesh. After these and a few incidental details, though, the resemblance ends. Shelley's novel is best approached as a philosophical treatise on the dangers of crossing the line that separates humans from God. It has some narrative motion, in that the action moves around between Italy, Switzerland, and the North Pole, but it shows little sense of or interest in what makes a story gripping. The film, on the other hand, was created to entertain and to please a widely varied public. A part of the film's popular appeal was the way it pretended to show off its literary roots, drawing attention to its relationship to Shelley and the romantic movement in literature.

Because the two versions are so different, it makes little sense that they would be held up for comparison as often as they have been. Fans of Shelley's version look at James Whale's film and wonder why they should be expected to care about a mindless, grunting creature. The filmmakers were going for scares, not ideas, loading the screen with visual gimmicks such as the pointless but interesting electronic devices in the scientist's laboratory in scenes central to the film but nonexistent in the novel. Fans of the film, most of them not readers at all, much less readers of ponderous, idea-driven narratives, are likely to just plod through the novel wondering when each long sentence and paragraph will end. Those in the literary camp want to see the monster express his thoughts about his situation, while fans of the film feel that his struggle can be shown, and shown better, without words.

WHAT DO I SEE NEXT?

- This film spawned several sequels at Universal Studios, which eventually ran out of imagination or innovation and became mere catalogs of horror movie clichés. The first sequel, *Bride of Frankenstein*, is considered to be superior to the original and is often included on lists of the best films ever. Directed by James Whale and starring Colin Clive and Boris Karloff again, it continues moments after this film ends and is closer to Shelley's novel in that the monster talks, insisting that Frankenstein create a mate for him. The DVD was released by Universal in 1999.

- In 1994, Kenneth Branagh directed a more faithful adaptation of the original novel in *Mary Shelley's Frankenstein*, starring Branagh as the doctor and Robert De Niro as the creature. Dark and moody, the film never scored with audiences, though critics praised De Niro's performance. It was released on DVD by Sony Pictures in 1998.

- Mel Brooks gave *Frankenstein* and its sequels a comic skewering with his 1974 film *Young Frankenstein*. Brooks used several of the sets from Whale's original production and filmed in black and white to give the parody a look that matches its source material. It is available on DVD from 20th Century Fox in a 2006 revised edition.

- The 1998 feature film *Gods and Monsters*, starring Ian McKellen and Brendan Fraser, presents a fictionalized account of director James Whale at the end of his life, recalling his early days in Hollywood, how being gay gave him a feeling of alienation that drew him toward sympathetic monsters in his work. It won the Academy Award for best screenplay, and McKellen was nominated for best actor. It was released on DVD by Lions Gate in 2003.

- British studio Hammer Film Productions ushered in a new era of monster films with its 1957 release of *The Curse of Frankenstein*, starring Peter Cushing and Christopher Lee, who would both star in a series of Frankenstein, Dracula, and Mummy films for the studio. It was released on DVD by Warner Home Video in 2002.

- *Shrek*, a 2001 production of Dreamworks Studio, is the story of a green ogre and is a fairy tale of evil and love. Suitable for younger audiences, it has, like *Frankenstein*, been followed by several sequels.

Each version of the Frankenstein monster has its virtues. Shelley's monster is an intellectual. He disappears from the story for a while and then shows up again, having pondered the mystery of his own existence. The conclusion he reaches is that, having been brought forth into a world he did not ask for, he will find his fulfillment only by being paired off with a mate like himself. This forces Dr. Frankenstein to consider whether he should dabble in God's realm once more. He refuses, even at great personal cost, as friends and family are murdered. The monster of the film is iconic in his own right because he taps into a primordial feeling, common to most adults. Most adults remember the childhood awkwardness of figuring out appropriate behavior while surrounded by others who, like the torch-bearing mob in the film, stand ready to punish. Just as Shelley's medium, the novel, is more abstract and cerebral than film, so too her philosophical monster is appropriately more abstract and cerebral. In the end, though, both monsters address universal truths about the human condition.

Shelley's narrative is bent on presenting its story at arm's length, so much so that the action is often discussed well after it happens, sometimes even through dispassionate letters. In contrast, the 1931 film is almost too eager to get its

WITHOUT THE SECOND ENDING, *FRANKENSTEIN* MIGHT HAVE BEEN A GOOD HORROR FILM, BUT WITH IT, THE FILM MAKES A STATEMENT THAT MARY SHELLEY NEVER TOUCHED ON: THE STATEMENT THAT HORROR MOVIES ARE, AFTER ALL, ONLY MAKE-BELIEVE."

audience's emotions involved. This is seen most clearly in the ending the studio tacked on. Even audiences who respect the film's original take on the monster's dilemma—that of finding his way through a world that hates him on sight—have little choice but to throw their hands up and sigh. In the end, the film tries to wipe away the terror it has worked so hard to establish.

Whale's film actually has two endings. The story has a natural conclusion, but that is followed by a stereotypical Hollywood ending that has little to do with the story. The first ending gives viewers the satisfaction of seeing where the film's events would almost inevitably lead. Dr. Frankenstein, who has tried to ignore the monster, leads the hunt for it after the creature has frightened his fiancée and then left when she fainted (a pale shadow of the doctor's pursuit of the monster across the frozen Arctic sea after the creature murders Elizabeth in the novel). In the film, the two meet. The monster overpowers his creator and, hearing the approach of the mob, carries Frankenstein off to an empty windmill. The windmill makes no particular narrative sense, but with its spinning blades and whirring gears, it provides a great visual setting. The monster taking the scientist with him does not make much sense, either—what does he want from him?—but Whale takes great care to show that the monster does have emotions toward Frankenstein when they meet.

Inside the windmill, the doctor tries to escape. The monster obliges, throwing him from the balcony, and his limp body is jackknifed across the windmill's slow-turning blade before falling to the ground. Once the creature has committed the Freudian act of destroying his creator, the villagers step forward and burn the windmill,

surrounding Frankenstein's monster with the thing that has terrified him most throughout his short life: fire.

At this point, the story is complete. Frankenstein has been punished for desecrating corpses and tampering with the line that God has drawn between life and death. The creature is punished for the lives he has taken and for being made with a "criminal brain," akin to being born with original sin on one's soul. Overall, it is a satisfactory ending, much more satisfactory than that of Shelley's novel, which leaves the creature floating off into the Arctic darkness, more a state of mind than a reality.

But this is not really the film's ending. It goes on. Frankenstein has survived the fall. He is taken home to recuperate in the hands of Elizabeth, who has forgiven all. The atmosphere there is festive. Five giggling, pretty maids bring him wine, but they are stopped outside his bedroom by his father, Baron Frankenstein, whose cantankerousness has already provided the film with comic relief. The camera shows Baron Frankenstein and the maids in the foreground, Frankenstein and Elizabeth far behind, clearly played by different actors. Baron Frankenstein jokes about the family wedding custom and toasts the grandson he hopes for. Soon, the whole unpleasant "life from dead tissue" incident will be but a memory for these people.

This ending is a terrible fit to the movie, but it fulfills several functions for the studio. For one thing, it opens the door for a sequel, which eventually came about four years later, with even more aspects of Shelley's novel (such as a talking monster who insists on a mate) woven into it. Mainly, though, it sent audiences out of the theater happy, not concentrating on matters of punishment or death.

Though it serves no narrative purpose, ending the movie with neither Frankenstein nor the creature in the scene is what has given the film its identity. It begins with another scene added in post-production, with actor Edward van Sloan stepping out from behind a curtain and pretentiously giving the audience a warning on the behalf of the producer, "Mr. Carl Laemmle," as if showing this film is dangerous but unavoidable, a social responsibility. Tacking on an ending that has no stars and has little to do with the plot—an ending that is clearly there to lighten the mood and make this film more commercially attractive—has the opposite effect. It sends the

Getty Images

message that nothing serious has gone on, that it can all be waved away at the studio's command.

This ending finalizes the transformation of the Frankenstein story, taking it out of Mary Shelley's hands for good. It is an important step between Shelley's ponderous meditation and the lighthearted cardboard cutouts of the creature that stores tape to their doors each Halloween. Without the second ending, *Frankenstein* might have been a good horror film, but with it, the film makes a statement that Mary Shelley never touched on: the statement that horror movies are, after all, only make-believe.

Source: David Kelly, Critical Essay on *Frankenstein*, in *Novels for Students*, Gale, Cengage Learning, 2011.

Steffen Hantke

In the following essay, Hantke examines Robert Spadoni's book Uncanny Bodies, *which looks at the early history of sound in American cinema, focusing primarily on Tod Browning's* Dracula *and James Whale's* Frankenstein.

Aside from brief excursions into American (and partially German) horror films of the late silent and early sound era, Robert Spadoni's *Uncanny Bodies* deals with a highly limited group of primary texts. Its two introductory chapters trace the early history of sound in American cinema, and the two central chapters of the book are, respectively, devoted to Tod Browning's *Dracula* (1930) and James Whale's *Frankenstein* (1931).

This is not, as one might think, a concession to the canonical status of these two films and their significance for the development and consolidation of the horror film genre. The two films' canonical status is hardly in question. Much—perhaps too much—has already been written about them, their stars, and their directors. And yet canonicity is the central focus of Spadoni as he tackles the question of why, among all possible choices, it has been these two films that have lasted and have even come to define horror film as a genre. It is to the credit of the book that its author manages to find a fresh angle from which to ask that question.

Why have these two films stood the test of time? Spadoni asks this question pointedly against many of the negative assessments that both films—Browning's perhaps more than Whale's—have had to suffer throughout the years. *Dracula*, Spadoni acknowledges, is in fact a notoriously bad film. Stagy and slow, it has acquired a reputation only to be valuable, and watchable, as a piece of high camp, thanks largely to Bela Lugosi's seminal performance as the eponymous Count. While *Frankenstein*'s long-term reputation has fared better than that of *Dracula*, Spadoni marshals quite a few sources, both from the time the film was released and from more contemporary viewers, that point out how rough and tumble especially the film's editing is. Compared to some of Whale's other, even earlier, work, *Frankenstein* seems not quite up to par. As historical documents, both films are still interesting; as horror films, however, they seem to fall behind the more accomplished entries in the genre.

But Spadoni is not out to undercut both films' claim to canonicity. What may come as a surprise to many contemporary viewers, whose perception of the films is, of course, filtered through layer after layer of successive critical and popular opinion, is that they were both considered highly effective machines for scaring their audiences at the time of their release. For someone unwilling to assume a patronizing attitude toward those audiences (what did they know, after all, back there in the dark ages?), this assessment, especially of the creaky, clumsy, plodding *Dracula*, posits a mystery worth puzzling over. Which is exactly what Spadoni is doing: asking a question seriously that has become facile as long as it is asked merely as a rhetorical question. What, indeed, did they know, back there in the dark ages? Good question.

What they—these audiences in 1930, whose perception differs so dramatically from our own—knew was that the merging of sound and image, which we contemporary viewers have come to embrace unthinkingly and unknowingly, is, in fact, not as natural as we might want to believe. Sound, as Spadoni reminds us, only came into pictures in 1927, most notably with Warner Bros.' release of *The Jazz Singer*. For all those who, literally, hadn't "heard anything yet," this was not only a momentous breakthrough but the beginning of a unsettling period of transition. Sound was neither universally embraced as an improvement upon the medium—a position fairly well known, if only through the detour of later

films like *Singin' in the Rain*—nor accepted as a technology that contributed to the realism, the verisimilitude, or mimetic accuracy of cinema.

This was the result of the idiosyncrasies of early sound technologies, which often divorced sound from object and voice from body. But it was also, more generally, the result of an audience response that had been conditioned by preceding technologies—technologies that had taught viewers to suppress the knowledge of the essential artificiality of the medium. When sound entered the picture(s), disrupting these established forms of reception, it brought aspects of cinema to the audience's consciousness that had previously—and have ever since—vanished into patterns of repetition and habituation. During this brief moment of transition, however, the audience grew conscious of the medium itself and learned to be more savvy about its essential artifice.

At the heart of this moment, and of the aesthetics it fostered, was *Dracula*. Browning's film, Spadoni suggests, was particularly suited to explore and exploit the cognitive dissonances that the transition from silent to sound film created because of its monstrous creature's ability to be simultaneously absent and present. In detailed shot-by-shot analyses of scenes from *Dracula*, Spadoni shows how Browning and Lugosi create an interplay of image and sound (and, perhaps equally importantly, of off-screen events and silence) that played on a cinema that, thanks to the introduction of sound, had just become strange and uncanny to its contemporary audience. Much of what later audiences have criticized about the film—from the lack of narrative complexity to the long silences between moments of dialogue—Spadoni reconstructs as audiences at the time must have perceived it: an unsettling spectacle that reflected back on the experience of cinema itself.

Though released only a year after *Dracula*, James Whale's *Frankenstein* already marks a moment in which a horror film transcends the paradigm set by its predecessor and "propelled the horror genre into the mature sound era" (97). Unlike the ghostliness with which *Dracula* permeates Browning's film, Spadoni notes the visual directness, the bluntness, with which Karloff's body, aided by the work of Universal make-up wizard Jack Pierce, dominates the frame. Aggressively visible yet conspicuously mute, this body served as a site for the film's evocation of "the uncanny of early and sound cinema at the same time that it evoked a silent cinema newly estranged by the same" (115).

Readers interested in the transition from silent to sound film will find *Uncanny Bodies* intriguing for its focus specifically on horror films, which, in contrast to, for example, the musical, are not generally considered in this context. For those interested in horror film, the book has even more to offer. Asking readers to consider *Dracula* and *Frankenstein* as two increasingly sophisticated and conceptually distinct responses to the arrival of sound in cinema, Spadoni rehabilitates the films themselves, their makers, and their contemporary audiences. These were not the clunky, creaky, awkward first steps of the genre; filmmakers were not cluelessly fumbling with a new technology; and viewers were hardly the simpletons we like to take them for. Although the book, with its tight argument and detailed background information on the period, is a far cry from a fan's plea for his favorite movies, fans of horror cinema might come away with a new appreciation of a moment in the history of their favorite genre that is largely dismissed as a stepping-stone for better things to come.

Source: Steffen Hantke, "Uncanny Bodies: The Coming of Sound Film and the Origins of the Horror Genre," in *Film Criticism*, Vol. 33, No. 1, 2008, p. 77.

Publishers Weekly

In the following review, a Publishers Weekly *contributor reviews James Curtis's book, which shines some light onto the life and thoughts of* Frankenstein *director James Whale.*

Shortly before his death, film director James Whale admitted that he'd looked in the mirror and realized that he'd launched "this horror" into the world that he couldn't stop. Was he referring to his creation of the classic film *Frankenstein* (1931) or its inferior off-shoots? Was he alluding to his inability (despite succeeding in mainstream genres) to transcend his reputation as a specialist in monster movies? Curtis (*Between Flops: A Biography of Preston Sturges*) narrates in seamless detail how this innovative son of a West Midlands coal man rose from obscurity to acclaim as a British theater and Hollywood director. Trained as a West End actor and stage manager, Whale gained recognition for his rendition of the WWI war drama *Journey's End*. He traveled to Broadway and finally Hollywood to adapt *Journey's End* (1930) to the movies. Curtis charts Whale's triumphs as

well as his failures, lending insight into the convoluted collaborative world of moviemaking in the days of Hays Office censorship. Many of Whale's mainstream films (*Waterloo Bridge*; *One More River*; etc.) disappeared while *Frankenstein* and *The Bride of Frankenstein* never went out of circulation. *Showboat* (1956) marked the pinnacle of Whale's career and was followed by a gradual decline and slide into suicide. One comes away from this quixotic and compelling biography with the feeling that Whale, who was homosexual, not only reinvented the monster movie but also himself, and that his particular genius was often ill appreciated, except in the one genre he disdained.

Source: Review of *James Whale: A New World of Gods and Monsters*, in *Publishers Weekly*, Vol. 245, No. 15, April 13, 1998, p. 60.

Alfred Rushford Greason

In the following review, Greason reports favorably on the movie Frankenstein.

Looks like a *Dracula* plus, touching a new peak in horror plays and handled in production with supreme craftsmanship. Exploitation, which dwells upon the shock angle, is also a punchful asset with hair-raising lobby and newspaper trumpeting.

Appeal is candidly to the morbid side and the screen effect is up to promised specifications. Feminine fans seem to get some sort of emotional kick out of this sublimation of the bed time ghost story done with all the literalness of the camera.

Maximum of stimulating shock is there, but the thing is handled with subtle change of pace and shift of tempo that keeps attention absorbed to a high voltage climax, tricked out with spectacle and dramatic crescendo, after holding the smash shiver on a hair trigger for more than an hour.

Picture starts out with a wallop. Midnight funeral services are in progress on a blasted moor, with the figure of the scientist and his grotesque dwarf assistant hiding at the edge of the cemetery to steal the newly-buried body. Sequence climaxes with the gravedigger sending down the clumping earth upon newly-laid coffin. Shudder No. 1.

Shudder No. 2, hard on its heels is when Frankenstein cuts down his second dead subject from the gallows, presented with plenty of realism. These corpses are to be assembled into a semblance of a human body which Frankenstein seeks to galvanize into life, and to this end the story goes into his laboratory, extemporized in a gruesome mountain setting out of an abandoned mill. But first our scientist must have a brain, which leads to another s[t]ock touch of the creeps, when the dwarf crawls into a medical college dissecting room to steal that necessity. If you think these episodes have exhausted the repertoire of gruesome props they are but preliminaries.

Laboratory sequence detailing the creation of the monster patched up of human odds-and-ends is a smashing bit of theatrical effect, taking place in this eerie setting during a violent mountain storm in the presence of the scientist's sweetheart and others, all frozen with mortal fright.

Series of successive jolts continue through the moment when the monster creeps upon the scientist's waiting bride, probably the prize blood-curdler of the picture, and its final destruction when the infuriated villagers burn down the deserted windmill in which it is a prisoner. Finish is a change from the one first tried, when the scientist also was destroyed. The climax with the surviving Frankenstein (Frankenstein is the creator of the monster, not the monster itself) relieves the tension somewhat at the finale, but that may not be the effect most to be desired.

Subtle handling of the subject comes in the balance that has been maintained between the real and the supernatural, contrast that heightens the horror punches. The figure of the monster is a triumph of effect. It has a face and head of exactly the right distortions to convey a sense of the diabolical, but not enough to destroy the essential touch of monstrous human evil.

In like manner the feeling of horror is not once let go past the point at which it inspires disbelief, where out of excess it would create a feeling of makebelieve. This is the trick that actually makes the picture deliver its high voltage kick. The technique is shrewd manipulation. After each episode of dealing with the weird elements of the story there is a swift twist to the normal people of the drama engaged in their commonplace activities, a contrast emphasizing the next eerie detail.

Playing is perfectly paced. Colin Clive, the cadaverous hero of *Journey's End* (1930), is a happy choice for the scientist driven by a frenzy for knowledge. He plays it with force, but innocent of ranting. Boris Karloff enacts the monster and makes a memorable figure of the bizarre figure with its indescribably terrifying face of demoniacal calm, a fascinating acting bit of mesmerism.

Mae Clarke makes a perfunctory ingenue role charming, and John Boles is satisfying as a family friend, playing with neat elegance a part that loses much with the alternative finale.

Photography is splendid and the lighting the last word in ingenuity, since much of the footage calls for dim or night effect and the manipulation of shadows to intensify the ghostly atmosphere. It took nerve for U[niversal] to do this one and *Dracula* all of which may track back to the gruesomeness in *The Hunchback of Notre Dame*, which was also produced by this company. The audience for this type of film is probably the detective story readers and the mystery yarn radio listeners. Sufficient to insure financial success if these pictures are well made.

Source: Alfred Rushford Greason, Review of *Frankenstein*, in *Variety 100*, December 7, 1931.

SOURCES

Corliss, Richard, and Richard Schickel, "All-Time 100 Movies," in *Time*, http://www.time.com/time/specials/packages/0,28757,1953094,00.html (accessed October 6, 2010).

Dixon, Wheeler Winston, and Gwendolyn Audrey Foster, "The Growth of the Studio System," in *A Short History of Film*, Rutgers University Press, 2008, pp. 89–91.

Florescu, Radu, *In Search of Frankenstein*, New York Graphic Society, 1975, pp. 193–94.

Fort, Garrett, and Francis Edward Faragoh, *Frankenstein: The Legacy Collection*, DVD, Universal Studios, 2004.

Greason, Alfred Rushford, "Frankenstein," in *Variety*, December 7, 1931, http://www.variety.com/index.asp?layout = variety100&content = jump&jump = review&reviewID = VE1117791080&category = 1935&query = Frankenstein + Greason (accessed September 21, 2010).

Hall, Mordaunt, "The Screen: A Man-Made Monster in Grand Guignol," in *New York Times*, December 5, 1931, p. 21.

Hudson, David, "German Expressionism," in *GreenCine*, http://www.greencine.com/static/primers/expressionism1.jsp (accessed October 6, 2010).

"Questions and Answers: Q#19," in *The Picture Show Man*, http://www.pictureshowman.com/questionsandanswers4.cfm#Q19 (accessed October 6, 2010).

Shelley, Mary, *Frankenstein, or The Modern Prometheus: The 1818 Text*, Oxford University Press, 2009.

Worland, Rick, *The Horror Film: An Introduction*, Blackwell Publishing, 2007, p. 36.

FURTHER READING

Curtis, James, *James Whale: A New World of Gods and Monsters*, University of Minnesota Press, 2003.

> After the release of the Academy Award–winning film *Gods and Monsters*, Curtis revised his 1982 biography of the director, adding substantial new material that helps readers understand the perspective he brought to making this film.

Dettman, Bruce, and Michael Bedford, *The Horror Factory: The Horror Films of Universal, 1931–1955*, Gordon Press, 1976.

> This study offers a chronological look at the main Universal Studios franchises—*Dracula*, *Frankenstein*, *The Mummy*, and the *Wolf Man*—and the ways in which the studios writers bound these series together in sequel after sequel, creating a particular artistic film style.

Dixon, Wheeler Winston, "Transferring the Novel's Gothic Sensibilities to the Screen," in *Readings on Frankenstein*, Greenhaven Press, 2000, pp. 115–28.

> This essay gives an overview of the many screen versions of Shelley's novel, from the 1910 Edison film to *The Bride*, with rock musician Sting as Baron Frankenstein in a remake of *Bride of Frankenstein*, and many lesser-known adaptations in between.

Glut, Donald F., *The Frankenstein Archive: Essays on the Monster, the Myth, the Movies, and More*, McFarland, 2002.

> All of the essays in this book were written by Glut, who is an acknowledged expert regarding the cultural phenomenon that has grown from the 1931 movie. His works range in scope, looking at portrayals of Frankenstein's monster in such diverse venues as cartoons, comedies, superhero stories, and pop music.

Hitchcock, Susan Tyler, *Frankenstein: A Cultural History*, W. W. Norton, 2007.

> From the novel to the film to costumes, models, and the use of the word "Frankenstein" as a common reference for unintended consequences, Tyler examines the ways in which this particular story has seeped into the modern consciousness.

Jones, Stephen, *The Illustrated Frankenstein Movie Guide*, Titan Books, 1994.

> Jones has done a comprehensive study of all things related to the movie, including other movies with similar themes. His book, aimed at a commercial audience, includes a brief article about *Frankenstein*, written in 1957 by Boris Karloff.

Soister, John T., *Of Gods and Monsters: A Critical Guide to Universal Studios' Science Fiction, Horror, and Mystery Films, 1929–1939*, McFarland, 2001.

> Though this book does touch upon *Frankenstein*, *Dracula*, and the other well-known films that came out of the Universal stable, its primary interest is in its discussion of the more obscure movies the studio was churning out at the same time.

SUGGESTED SEARCH TERMS

Frankenstein AND James Whale

Frankenstein AND Universal Studios

horror AND Frankenstein

James Whale AND Mary Shelley

James Whale AND Arthur Edeson

Peggy Webling AND Frankenstein

Mary Shelley AND gothic

Dracula AND Frankenstein

horror film AND literature

James Whale AND Carl Laemmle, Jr.

Going after Cacciato

TIM O'BRIEN

1978

Going after Cacciato is a classic of Vietnam War literature. Published in 1978, it won the 1979 National Book Award for fiction. Loosely based on Tim O'Brien's experience as an infantry soldier in Vietnam, the novel follows Paul Berlin, a young soldier who is terrified and confused by his experience in the war. During one long night, Berlin keeps watch in an observation tower beside the South China Sea. The novel takes place in three different narratives with three different time frames that intertwine throughout the novel.

The first thread is the narrative of the observation tower and Berlin's night watch, during which he decides not to wake the soldier who is supposed to relieve him but to keep watch all night over his fellow soldiers. As he keeps watch, Berlin imagines a fantastical story of what might have happened had his fellow soldier, the deserter Cacciato, completed his escape with the squad chasing him all the way to Paris. In between the narrative of Berlin's night in the tower and his imagined narrative of the journey to Paris is his attempt to make sense of the breakdown he suffered when the squad caught up to Cacciato. When the flares went up, Berlin lost control of himself, firing his weapon wildly before blacking out and fouling himself.

Much of the novel concerns Berlin's attempt to reconstruct the chronology of events that constitute his actual experience of the war. It is by imagining an escape from the war that he

Tim O'Brien (AP Images)

manages to construct a coherent narrative for himself of his actual experience in Vietnam, an experience to which he returns through this act of imaginative reconstruction.

AUTHOR BIOGRAPHY

O'Brien was born William Timothy O'Brien on October 1, 1946, in Austin, Minnesota, to William T. O'Brien, an insurance salesman, and Ava E. O'Brien, an elementary school teacher. When he was ten, the family moved from Austin to Worthington, Minnesota. Worthington has about 10,000 inhabitants, a community college, and Lake Okabena and, because of the abundance of poultry farms in the area, is self-proclaimed as the "Turkey Capital" of the United States

O'Brien had a classic midwestern childhood. He played football, golf, and baseball on a team coached by his father, although he admits he was not a good athlete, which set him apart from his

peers. After high school, O'Brien attended Macalester College in St. Paul, Minnesota, where he majored in political science and was the student-body president during his senior year. He graduated Phi Beta Kappa and summa cum laude.

Two weeks after graduation, he received his draft notice. O'Brien was conflicted about the war. Both of his parents had been active participants in World War II, his father in the Pacific theater and his mother in the women's volunteer arm of the U.S. Navy. When O'Brien was drafted, he considered defecting to Canada, but as he wrote in a 1994 essay for the *New York Times* about returning to Vietnam, his parents' service, as well as "the prospect of rejection: by my family, my country, my friends, my hometown" convinced him he had to go. He has on numerous occasions referred to this as an act of cowardice.

O'Brien went to Vietnam in 1969 and served in the U.S. Army Fifth Battalion, 46th Infantry, known as the Americal Division. He was sent into the "Pinkville" area, where, in the spring of 1968, the United States forces massacred an estimated 500 Vietnamese citizens in the village of My Lai, many of them women, children, and infants. When O'Brien was sent over, news of the massacre had not yet become public, and he told D. J. R. Bruckner of the *New York Times* that "we all wondered why the place was so hostile." O'Brien, who was promoted to sergeant during his tour, was wounded by shrapnel from a grenade and was sent home after thirteen months.

After the war, O'Brien pursued a doctorate in political science at Harvard while writing short stories and articles on the side. In 1973, he left Harvard to work for the *Washington Post* and married Anne Weller (they divorced in 1995). In 1973, his memoir *If I Die in a Combat Zone* was published, and in 1975 he published his first novel, *Northern Lights*. In 1975, he won an O'Henry award for "Where Have You Gone Charming Billy?," a short story that appeared in *Redbook* magazine in 1975 and that appears as the "Night March" chapter in *Going after Cacciato*. In 1978, *Going after Cacciato* was published and became the first big success of O'Brien's career. He won the National Book Award in 1978 for the novel, and it has become a classic example of postmodern storytelling technique. After *Going after Cacciato*, O'Brien was able to write full time, and in the following years he published *The Nuclear Age* (1985), *The Things They Carried* (1990), *In the Lake of the Woods* (1994), *Tomcat in Love* (1998), and *July July* (2002). He won the French Prix du Meilleur Livre Étranger in 1990 for *The Things They Carried* and the James Fenimore Cooper Prize for Historical Fiction in 1995 for *In the Lake of the Woods*. As of 2010, he was a distinguished visiting writer at Texas State University in San Marcos, Texas.

MEDIA ADAPTATIONS

- An audio recording of *Going after Cacciato* was released by Harper Audio in 1991.
- The audio recording *Tim O'Brien Discussing His Life and Writing* was released by Macalester College in 1981.

PLOT SUMMARY

Chapter 1: Going after Cacciato

A list of the dead opens the book: Billy Boy Watkins, Frenchie Tucker, Bernie Lynn, Lieutenant Sidney Martin, Pederson, Rudy Chassler, Buff, and Ready Mix. Paul Berlin reports that Cacciato has deserted and plans to walk the 8,600 miles to Paris. The squad is led by Lieutenant Corson, who has been sent to replace Lieutenant Martin after the squad has killed him and covered it up as an accident. They follow Cacciato, who taunts them. On the fourth day, Stink Harris trips over a wire, which he thinks launches a grenade but is only a smoke bomb. Paul Berlin imagines himself going along to Paris. The squad surrounds Cacciato's position, and sends rocket flares up into the sky, where they explode in red and green starbursts that Paul Berlin thinks of as "Cacciato Day."

Chapter 2: The Observation Post

The observation post chapters take place during a single night during which Berlin is on night watch in an observation post on the seashore. Berlin sees Cacciato's face in the full moon and tries to figure out what actually happened on the hillside after the squad sent up the flares. Did they kill Cacciato? Or did he get away and continue his journey to Paris?

Chapter 3: The Road to Paris

There is debate among the squad members about whether following Cacciato over the Laotian border constitutes desertion or not. They hold a vote, and Paul Berlin casts the deciding vote to "keep going" so they can "see what happens." Harold Murphy, who objects to continuing the chase, deserts the squad the next morning and turns back.

Chapter 4: How They Were Organized

Paul Berlin arrives in Vietnam and attempts to orient himself. He worries about his terrible sense of direction and remembers a humiliating experience as an Indian Guide with his father. Finally, he meets the other members of his squad and learns that they are organized less by formal standard operating procedure (SOP) than they are by the informal SOPs of "personalities, specialties of knowledge, and tradition."

Chapter 5: The Observation Post

It is just past midnight, and Paul Berlin is thinking of ways to keep himself awake. First, he looks out at the sea and imagines it both as a safety buffer and as a means of escape. He reassures himself that his thoughts of escape are merely "pretending," only "a way of passing time, which seemed never to pass." He tries to get the chronology of his war experience straight, something he finds difficult in a war that he experiences as fluid and confusing. Finally, he turns toward thoughts of the future, of returning home a bold and confident man whom his father will respect, of going to Paris after the war, and indulging in a fantasy of café life where he will look for "all the things Cacciato would have looked for."

Chapter 6: Detours on the Road to Paris

The squad leaves the jungle and enters a country with open meadows. Stink Harris, enraged by the sight of Cacciato's dropped gum wrapper, loads his gun and leads them along an ever-widening road. Surprised by the sight of a cart harnessed to two water buffalo, Stink opens fire on one of the water buffalo, emptying his automatic weapon in a frenzy. When he is done, the buffalo is dead, and the squad discovers a young girl and two old women in the cart. The girl is Sarkin Aun Wan, and she explains that they are refugees.

Chapter 7: Riding the Road to Paris

Berlin tells Sarkin that the squad intends to chase Cacciato to Paris. She begs to come along, making him feel her legs to demonstrate how strong she is. The Lieutenant says she cannot come, but the matter remains unresolved because Stink Harris captures Cacciato.

Chapter 8: The Observation Post

When it is time to relinquish his watch, Paul Berlin instead leaves the observation post and wades into the sea where he urinates. He thinks of it as "his bravest moment." He observes the observation post and remembers his father telling him that, while war will be terrible, he should look for the good things too. He climbs back into the tower, not waking his replacement, and thinks about Paris.

Chapter 9: How Bernie Lynn Died after Frenchie Tucker

Although Frenchie Tucker is killed immediately after being sent in to search one of the many tunnels in which the Vietcong hid, Bernie Lynn is still alive when they pull him out of the tunnel. Doc immediately administers M&Ms, which the squad recognizes as a sign that Bernie Lynn is dying. Lieutenant Martin enrages them further when he takes a long time figuring out the correct codes and coordinates with which to call in the helicopter. While Doc struggles to get an intravenous line into Bernie Lynn, the ground around them shakes from the force of other squads blowing up tunnels.

Chapter 10: A Hole in the Road to Paris

Cacciato gets away from Stink Harris but leaves him with a nasty bite wound. Cacciato leaves them a map with a warning about a hole in the road, so the squad decides to go across country, which means leaving Sarkin. Sarkin asks Berlin to imagine them in Paris, and then tells him that he will find a way. As the cart is leaving, Paul Berlin admits to a "lapse of imagination," and a gigantic hole opens in the earth, through which they all fall.

Chapter 11: Fire in the Hole

After Jim Pederson is killed, Lieutenant Martin calls in air strikes on the village of Hoi An. The village appears to be empty, but the soldiers call in round after round of white phosphorous, which the soldiers call "Willie Peter," and "HE," a general-purpose high explosive. As the village burns, the entire platoon fires on it.

Chapter 12: The Observation Post

Paul Berlin maintains watch while trying to understand the nature of courage and to discover why he has always been afraid.

Chapter 13: Falling Through a Hole in the Road to Paris

The squad lands in a tunnel, deep beneath the surface. Paul Berlin has an attack of the nervous giggles but recovers, and they discover Li Van Hgoc, a North Vietnamese soldier, in a bunker. He tells them that "the land is your enemy" and that the war is simply the land trying to defend itself. He gives Berlin a tour of the tunnels and through the periscope shows him a group of soldiers peering into a tunnel.

Chapter 14: Upon Almost Winning the Silver Star

When Frenchie Tucker is shot in the tunnel, the squad hears it. Lieutenant Martin insists that someone must go after him, but no one volunteers. Someone suggests sending "the gremlin," Cacciato, and as he is shrugging off his pack to do it, Bernie Tucker goes in, swearing. He is shot immediately, and they pull him out.

Chapter 15: Tunneling Toward Paris

Li Van Hgoc is hospitable, and the tunnels are pleasant, but Lieutenant Corson says that they must leave. Hgoc claims them as his prisoners. They tie Hgoc up and threaten to kill him if he does not tell them where the exit is. He tells them there is no exit. Sarkin tells them that "the way in is the way out," takes Berlin's hand, and leads the squad into the hallway. They invite Hgoc to come, but he refuses. Sarkin leads them through tunnel after tunnel as they try to find a way out.

Chapter 16: Pickup Games

During a long period of silence in the Song Tra Bong region, the squad, let by Lieutenant Martin, plays pickup games of basketball. Paul Berlin likes "the clarity of it. He liked knowing who won, and by how much, and he liked being a winner." As the silence stretches on, the men come down with nervous ailments, and they bicker. They hatch a plan that will lead to Lieutenant Martin's death, and as they cross into a village, Rudy Chassler breaks the silence when he steps on a mine.

Chapter 17: *Light at the End of the Tunnel to Paris*
Sarkin leads the squad upward through tunnels and through a manhole cover into the streets of Mandalay. They check in to the Hotel Minneapolis, where they clean up and sleep in real beds. Sarkin and Berlin "almost make love," and they walk around the streets of Mandalay.

Chapter 18: *Prayers on the Road to Paris*
The squad searches for Cacciato but without conviction. Berlin muses on the photo album that Cacciato carried with him. Sitting in a café with Sarkin, he sees Cacciato pass by dressed as a monk. Sarkin warns Berlin that he must not disturb evening prayers. When Berlin wades into the crowd of monks, they beat him. He wakes with Sarkin tending his wounds, and she tells him Cacciato escaped via the train station.

Chapter 19: *The Observation Post*
While looking out over the South China sea, Berlin anticipates objections to his Paris story and answers his internal critics by insisting that all the practicalities could have been managed and the important thing is that it could have been done.

Chapter 20: *Landing Zone Bravo*
The platoon survives a terrifying flight in a Chinook helicopter under fire. Harold Murphy falls to the floor in fear and is unable to get up. Jim Pederson loses his helmet. The platoon is shoved out into rice paddies while the side gunners continue to fire, accidentally shooting Pederson. Pederson manages to fire back at the retreating helicopter.

Chapter 21: *The Railroad to Paris*
The squad, led by Oscar Johnson, is convinced Cacciato is hiding on the train, so they search every car. While searching, Berlin remembers Lieutenant Martin forcing them to frisk a village of civilians. Berlin and Doc are beset by an enraged crowd, led by the train conductor. Later, they are met by Oscar and Eddie, who have found only Cacciato's empty AWOL bag.

Chapter 22: *Who They Were, or Claimed to Be*
Chapter 22 contains a description of each of the characters that explores the meaning of naming, the ways they named themselves, and the ways they named one another.

Chapter 23: *Asylum on the Road to Paris*
The squad stops in Delhi, where the Lieutenant falls into a passionate affair with Jolly Chand, the proprietress of the Hotel Phoenix. Berlin goes out into the streets, mails a postcard to his parents, and then suffers a bout of homesickness.

Chapter 24: *Calling Home*
While on furlough, the members of the platoon get an opportunity to call home. Each of the soldiers returns from his phone call touched and amazed. While the phone rings and rings in an empty house, Berlin imagines the inside of his home and what he will say to his parents.

Chapter 25: *The Way it Mostly Was*
On a long march to a battle, Lieutenant Martin reflects on the meaning of war, of being a soldier, and on his own leadership. Berlin simply marches.

Chapter 26: *Repose on the Road to Paris*
The squad grows bored and restless in Delhi. There is no sign of Cacciato, and the Lieutenant does not look for him. Doc spots a picture of Cacciato in the paper, at the train station, on his way to Kabul. The Lieutenant refuses to go, so they wait until he has passed out and then take him with them.

Chapter 27: *Flights of Imagination*
On the train to Afghanistan, Berlin begins to remember what happened in Lake Country, named by Doc Peret for the way the bomb craters filled with water. When the train is stopped by snow, the mayor of a small town in the mountains shows them great hospitality.

Chapter 28: *The Observation Post*
Stung by the mayor's refusal to tell his history, Berlin tells himself his own history.

Chapter 29: *Atrocities on the Road to Paris*
They arrive in Tehran, where they are forced to wait out Lieutenant Corson's dysentery. They watch the beheading of a young man. Afterward, they are arrested by the Iranian internal police.

A police captain asks for their passports, and Doc claims that they do not need passports because of an imaginary military treaty. The captain takes them to a nightclub. There, they discuss the nature of war and get very drunk.

Chapter 30: The Observation Post

At eight minutes to four, Berlin continues to muse on the nature of stories, wondering why his fantasy has led him to a beheading in Tehran and why he finds it so difficult to create a coherent account of the war.

Chapter 31: Night March

On a night march early in his war service, Berlin struggles against his own fear and remembers the fate of Billy Boy Watkins, who would have survived the loss of his foot but whose own fear killed him.

Chapter 32: The Observation Post

Berlin eats a can of pears and manages, for the first time, to think of Billy Boy Watkins's death without terror.

Chapter 33: Outlawed on the Road to Paris

The squad is arrested again. After eight days in solitary confinement, Berlin is blindfolded and then reunited with his squad mates in an execution chamber. After several delays, when faced with imminent execution, they all confess to desertion.

Chapter 34: Lake Country

Lieutenant Martin orders the men to search a tunnel, and they refuse. He searches the tunnel himself. While he is underground, Oscar Johnson pulls the pin on a grenade and asks each man to touch it if he agrees that killing the Lieutenant is an act of self defense. He hands the grenade to Berlin and tells him to get Cacciato's approval. The Lieutenant emerges from the tunnel.

Chapter 35: World's Greatest Lake Country

Cacciato fishes in the bomb craters, although they tell him they are not really lakes. Berlin explains the grenade, and Cacciato says he will not do it. Berlin presses Cacciato's hand to the grenade as Cacciato insists he has a nonexistent fish biting his line.

Chapter 36: Flights of Imagination

While the squad prepares for execution, Berlin tries to figure out how to get them out of their fix. He thinks it is going to take a miracle, but then Cacciato's face appears like the moon in the barred window. There are explosions, and the squad runs, following Cacciato, and escapes the prison. There is an American muscle car waiting for them, and Oscar Johnson drives them through a tank ambush and out of Tehran on an open highway. Later, Berlin, driving, remembers what they did to Lieutenant Martin. The squad drives through Turkey, all the way to the sea.

Chapter 37: How the Land Was

Paul Berlin describes the things he has learned about the paddies, hedgerows, trails, villages, and beaches of Vietnam.

Chapter 38: On the Lam to Paris

The squad books passage for Piraeus. When they arrive, the docks are swarming with customs officials. Faced with the defeatism of the squad, Stink Harris jumps ship and swims for shore.

Chapter 39: The Things They Didn't Know

Chapter 39 consists of a catalog of the many things the soldiers did not know, starting with the Vietnamese language and ascending to the reason they are fighting the war. Berlin prevails in his promotion board hearing.

Chapter 40: By a Stretch of the Imagination

The squad passes through the customs agents with no trouble and boards a bus for Zagreb. They miss Stink Harris and hitch a ride with an American girl who so enrages them with her hippie attempts to bond with them that they throw her out of the car at gunpoint, dumping her luggage along with her. They drive through Germany.

Chapter 41: Getting Shot

Berlin remembers when Buff died. Berlin, Eddie Lazzutti, and Cacciato find him face down, in a ditch, dead. Doc calls in the helicopter and prepares the body for evacuation while the squad smokes and talks about Buff. As the helicopter comes in, Berlin climbs down into the ditch to retrieve the big machine gun, while Cacciato retrieves Buff's helmet, which contains what is left of his face.

Chapter 42: The Observation Post
As the sun begins to rise, Berlin thinks that, while the lessons he has learned were hard ones, they were also ordinary ones. While he reconciles himself to another day at war, he wonders what might have been, had they followed Cacciato to Paris.

Chapter 43: The Peace of Paris
The squad arrives in Paris by train in a rainstorm and proceeds to march into the city, single file. They find a hotel, and Sarkin convinces Berlin to leave the squad and move in to an apartment with her. When Berlin asks the Lieutenant for permission, he says to ask Oscar, who is running things now. Paul returns from buying furnishings to find Oscar demanding that the squad move out now.

Chapter 44: The End of the Road to Paris
The authorities have caught up with them, so Oscar leads them out into the streets, where they sleep in a park, but the Lieutenant's health deteriorates, so they go to the apartment. They search in earnest for Cacciato while Sarkin and the Lieutenant refuse to participate. Berlin finds Cacciato and follows him home. In a fantasy sequence that mimics the Paris peace talks, which ended the war, Sarkin lays out her case for peace, after which Berlin takes the microphone and lays out his incompatible case for fulfillment of his duties to the squad.

Chapter 45: The Observation Post
Dawn breaks as Berlin comes to terms with the facts of the war, including Cacciato's fate on the hillside.

Chapter 46: Going after Cacciato
Doc Peret informs Berlin that Sarkin and the Lieutenant are gone. They have left a note saying that they are headed back east, reversing the journey. Oscar Johnson leads their final raid on Cacciato's apartment, and when the moment comes, he forces Berlin to go through the door first. Berlin loses control of himself, firing wildly, and when he wakes up, he is back in Vietnam, in the aftermath of the attack on Cacciato. Cacciato appears to have gotten away.

CHARACTERS

Paul Berlin
Paul Berlin is the protagonist of the novel. A young man sent to Vietnam right out of college, he comes from Fort Dodge, Iowa. Berlin is terrified of the war and on several occasions loses control of himself during combat. Doc Peret diagnoses Berlin as suffering from "the biles," and although he is ashamed, his fellow soldiers are mostly sympathetic. During one long night in an observation post overlooking the South China Sea, Berlin imagines a story in which the deserter Cacciato actually accomplishes his flight to Paris, pursued by the squad. In the process of imagining this fantasy journey to Paris, Berlin also comes to terms with several actual incidents that he has previously been unable to process.

Buff
Buff is short for "Water Buffalo," the nickname he was given because of his size. His given name is Toby, but no one calls him that. Buff is the one who smothers Berlin's laughter when he has a nervous attack of the giggles during the "Night Watch" chapter. Buff dies during a battle in a ditch, where he is found by Cacciato, Eddie Lazzutti, and Berlin. His death is disturbing because he is found face down, and his face remains inside his helmet when they prepare the body for evacuation.

Cacciato
Cacciato is the deserter who leaves the war claiming he is going to walk to Paris. Cacciato is considered a buffoon by the others, who cannot quite figure him out. He is always cheerful but vague, and the other soldiers are not sure that he is not mentally defective. Berlin thinks he seemed to be "blurred and uncolored and bland." He is the only soldier who does not touch the grenade to signal his assent to the death of Lieutenant Martin.

Jolly Chand
Proprietor of the Hotel Phoenix in Delhi, Jolly Chand is a middle-aged woman who once studied at Johns Hopkins University in Baltimore, Maryland. The Lieutenant falls madly in love with her, and she detains them in Delhi. Oscar thinks she's "a phony."

Rudy Chassler
Rudy Chassler is one of the soldiers. He dies in the explosion from a land mine, the sound of

which breaks the long, eerie silence of the Song Tra Bong period.

Lieutenant Corson

After Lieutenant Sidney Martin is killed by his own men, Lieutenant Corson joins the platoon. He is an older man who served in Korea and is rumored to have been demoted at least twice. He has a bad back and a drinking problem. He is often sick with dysentery, although Doc Peret diagnoses the root of the problem as nostalgia. The soldiers love him because "he took no chances, he wasted no lives." He recovers for a time when the squad reaches India and he meets Jolly Chand. Eventually, Corson and Sarkin Aun Wan desert the squad in Paris, leaving a note that they are returning to the east.

Stink Harris

Stink Harris leads the squad as they chase Cacciato, whom he hates for terrifying him with the smoke grenade. Harris is quick to shoot and kills Sarkin Aung Wan's water buffalo in a fit of shooting. He is a mechanic who loves his gun and who comes from a family of four sisters. He befriends Bernie Lynn, who strikes up a correspondence with one of Harris's sisters. When Stink finds a naked picture his sister has sent to Bernie, he feels betrayed. He jumps ship outside of Pireaus, afraid he will be captured, and the squad mourns his loss on the last leg of the trip to Paris.

Li Van Hgoc

Li Van Hgoc is the North Vietnamese soldier the squad encounters at the bottom of the hole in the road to Paris. They pepper him with questions about the war and the enemy, and he replies that "the land is your true enemy." He tells them that the land is merely trying to defend itself. He takes Berlin on a tour of the tunnels and tells the squad that there is no escape, that they are all prisoners of the war.

Oscar Johnson

Oscar Johnson is a soldier who claims to be from Detroit, Michigan, but whose mail goes to Bangor, Maine. He becomes enraged when Lieutenant Martin endangers Bernie Lynn's helicopter rescue by taking a long time to get all the codes and coordinates right. Johnson is the one who comes up with the plan to kill Martin. In Mandalay, a small boy is amazed by Johnson's black skin, and once they arrive in Paris, Oscar Johnson takes up command of the squad.

Eddie Lazzutti

Eddie Lazzutti is never described in much detail, although he accompanies them all the way to Paris. He is Pederson's friend, and he loves to sing. The squad relies on his musical abilities in times of stress.

Bernie Lynn

Bernie Lynn dies after being shot in the throat trying to rescue Frenchie Tucker. He is "a medium-sized, brown haired kid with thin arms and tanned skin and wide-open eyes." He is incredulous after being pulled out of the tunnel, repeating over and over that he could hear when he was shot. He lives long enough to be pulled out of the tunnel and be given M&Ms by Doc Peret.

Lieutenant Sidney Martin

Lieutenant Sidney Martin is a West Point graduate who insists on following standard operating procedure (SOP) in all instances. The squad hates him because they do not feel he has their interests at heart. Formal SOP declared that all tunnels must be searched before being blown up, but because the tunnels were so dangerous, informal SOP was to simply blow them up without a search. The Lieutenant insists that the squad search the tunnels, resulting in the deaths of Frenchie Tucker and Bernie Lynn. The squad votes by touching a grenade to kill Lieutenant Martin, and although the exact scene of his death is never described, we know he dies because Lieutenant Corson comes to replace him.

Harold Murphy

Harold Murphy is a large man, and he takes on the big machine gun after Buff is killed. Although he goes on the initial mission to recapture Cacciato, he objects to following him across the Laotian border because that is desertion. The morning after the vote to follow Cacciato, the soldiers discover that he is gone and presume that he has returned to the war.

Nguyen

Nguyen is the water buffalo that Stink Harris kills. Sarkin's elderly aunts raised him from infancy and mourn him by keening each night around the fire.

Ben Nystrom

Ben Nystrom is one of the soldiers. After consulting with Doc Peret about what is the most effective but least damaging self-inflicted wound, Nystrom shoots himself in the foot. He is evacuated from the war and does not write letters back to the squad.

Jim Pederson
The most religious member of the platoon and a former missionary to Kenya, Pederson hands out postcards of Jesus to Vietnamese civilians. Terrified of flying, he is killed by friendly fire after being shoved out of a Chinook helicopter in the middle of a firefight. Knowing he has been shot by the side gunners of the helicopter that brought them into the battle, Pederson methodically shoots back at the retreating helicopter and at the side gunners who accidentally shot him.

Doc Peret
Doc Peret is the unit medic. He considers himself a scientist and insists on analyzing confusing situations to separate out fact from impression. Doc is an explainer, the one person on the squad who always seems to have an answer for the terrified soldiers. He tends to Billy Boy Watkins after he steps on the land mine and explains to the soldiers that Billy Boy Watkins died of fright, not from his wound. He tells Berlin that his nervous disorder is a result of an "excess of fear biles" and helps him through it. Doc uses M&Ms as "medicine" for soldiers who are overwrought or dying.

Ready Mix
Ready Mix is a sergeant who dies in the highlands after being with the platoon for only twelve days. No one in the platoon knows his given name.

Captain Fahyi Rhallon
Captain Rhallon is a member of the Savak, the Iranian secret police, who arrests the squad in Iran because they do not have passports. He engages in lengthy conversations with them about the nature of war, the role of the soldier, and the role of the state in controlling its civilians. He is an urbane man, yet he very nearly executes the entire squad.

Frenchie Tucker
Frenchie Tucker dies after Lieutenant Martin makes him search a tunnel. He is shot through the nose and dies instantly. After he dies, Berlin notices the contrast between the disarray of his body and the tidiness with which he folded his clothes before entering the tunnel. Bernie Lynn is shot trying to retrieve Frenchie Tucker's body from the tunnel.

Vaught
Vaught is a soldier who catches an infection from shaving the rotting skin off his arm with his bayonet. He is evacuated to Japan and later sends a smiling photo of himself in Japan, missing the arm, which had to be amputated. Lieutenant Corson confuses Vaught and Berlin.

Sarkin Aun Wan
A part-Chinese refugee girl of uncertain age, Sarkin Aun Wan is discovered with her two aunts in a cart drawn by water buffalo. After Stink Harris shoots one of her water buffalo in a fit of violence, she convinces the squad to take her along to Paris. Berlin falls in love with her.

Sarkin Aun Wan's Aunties
The Aunties are two elderly Vietnamese women who rescued Sarkin from the war. They are lost when the squad falls through the hole in the road into the Vietnamese tunnels.

Billy Boy Watkins
Billy Boy Watkins is a member of the unit who steps on a land mine and loses a foot. Despite Doc's efforts, Watkins dies of a heart attack brought on by fright after seeing that his foot has been blown off. Watkins's death, followed as it is by the gruesome spectacle of his body falling from the evacuation helicopter and the subsequent search for it in the rice paddy, terrifies Paul Berlin.

THEMES

Imagination
Imagination, the ability to form ideas, thoughts, and stories independent of one's immediate sensory perception, is a central theme in *Going after Cacciato*. Indeed, the entire storyline in which the squad follows Cacciato to Paris is a figment of Paul Berlin's imagination. Although Berlin first imagines the story of the chase in the first chapter, when he tells the Lieutenant that Cacciato has gone, it is in the second chapter where we first encounter Berlin in the observation post, where he explains to himself that imagining

TOPICS FOR FURTHER STUDY

- Some stories explore how crucial experiences in life are framed with meaning. Watch the documentary film *Operation Homecoming: Writing the Wartime Experience*, in which O'Brien discusses the nature of war stories and how they figure in his own work. Then find a veteran and do a videotaped interview about how that member of the armed services experienced the war. What stories does that soldier tell about his or her experience? What stories would he or she rather not tell? Then research the war in which your interviewee served for visual and historical documentation. Using a program like iMovie, edit the interview and your research materials into an account of that conflict.

- The Vietnam War was famous for many strong photojournalistic images that affected how people in the United Stated viewed the war. Research photographs of the war, and pick three that had an impact. Write an evaluation of that impact, and make a presentation to your class that includes reproductions of the images. Explain the influence of photojournalism on the course of the war and what effect your specific images had on the domestic audience.

- O'Brien has noted that although he was sent to Vietnam right after the My Lai massacre and was deployed to the area in which it took place, because his squad knew nothing of the event, they had "no idea why the place was so hostile." Research the massacre, and write a paper that explains what happened at My Lai, how the story was discovered and published, and what effect it had on the prosecution of the rest of the war.

- The Vietnam War inspired large public protest demonstrations and a body of protest music from folk and rock performers of the day. Research the anti-war movement and the role that popular music played in that movement. Along with several classmates, form a band in which you have both singers and musicians, and learn one of the classic protest songs of the era. Perform the song for your class.

- In *Going after Cacciato*, Paul Berlin frequently turns to the activity he calls "pretending" in order to escape the immediate reality of the war. Write a short story in which your central character, when faced with an immediate reality that he or she cannot quite manage, resorts to fantastical pretense in order to deal with this reality.

- Chris Albani's novella *Song for Sight* (2007) follows a fifteen-year-old boy named My Luck, the leader of a platoon of boy soldiers used to clear mines in an unnamed African war. When My Luck finds himself separated from his platoon, he makes a journey to find them. Read the book, and compare the similarities and differences of My Luck's journey and the one Paul Berlin imagines in *Going after Cacciato*. How do My Luck and Berlin use fantasy and memory to make sense of their war experiences? In what ways are they similar, and in what ways are they different? Write a paper that examines these topics.

"wasn't dreaming and it wasn't pretending. It wasn't crazy. . . . It was a way of asking questions. . . . What happened, and what might have happened?"

Fear is also a kind of imagination, and it is one that plagues Berlin throughout the novel. Although Doc Peret claims that Berlin's problem stems from an overabundance of "fear biles,"

Soldiers in Vietnam war *(Alexander Smulskiy | Shutterstock.com)*

even Berlin knows that this is primarily an imaginary diagnosis, meant to make him feel better about his inability to maintain his focus during battle. Doc also resorts to imaginary medicine when he administers M&M candies to dying soldiers, an act that argues for the importance and influence of imagination in the ways we experience the world. To the dying soldiers, the M&Ms and the serious manner in which they are administered provides real comfort. They feel that something is being done. The soldiers spend much of their time trying to distract themselves and one another from the terrifying reality in which they are trapped. They tell one another stories and jokes, and as the chapter "Who They Were and Who They Claimed to Be" points out, they may very well be telling one another lies, which are another form of story.

It is Berlin's use of imagination as a way to ask questions about what had happened to him in the war, as well as to incorporate the truth of those experiences into his psychic reality, that forms the central theme of the book. In a speech he gave at Stanford University, O'Brien noted

that "as a fiction writer, I do not write just about the world we live in, but I also write about the world we ought to live in, and could, which is a world of imagination." By telling himself the story of what could have happened, as well as by incorporating the incidents that had happened to him into stories, Berlin finds a way, over the course of his night in the observation tower, to accept the reality of his experience without being overwhelmed by it. He uses his imagination not only to define what might have been but to identify what has happened.

Cowardice

Courage and cowardice play themselves out as both individual and collective dilemmas in *Going after Cacciato*. On an individual level, Paul Berlin is terrified of the war. In every firefight, he is overcome, blacks out, and loses control of his bowels. Doc Peret diagnoses this as an "overabundance of fear biles," but Berlin suspects that he is simply a coward. He admits that he went to the war because he was too frightened not to, because he did not want to disappoint his parents and his town, but he feels none of the bravado or anger that mark the actions of the kinds of soldiers one sees in war movies.

On one level, Berlin simply wants to survive the war. On another level, as represented by his elaborate fantasy of following Cacciato to Paris, a fantasy in which he rescues a pretty girl, behaves manfully in combat situations, and even faces an execution squad, Berlin wishes he could act in ways he finds impossible in real life. In a collective sense, the entire squad is engaged in an ongoing examination of what it means to be a coward, for the ultimate act of battlefield cowardice is to go AWOL. Desertion on the battlefield is punishable by death, and one of the central themes of Berlin's fantasy of following Cacciato to Paris is whether the squad is on a mission or has deserted the war. If they are deserters, then they are cowards like Cacciato, but if they are simply on a mission, they are a brave band of soldiers who refuse to give up.

In Tehran, they are nearly executed as deserters, and when they get to Paris, Berlin resists Sarkin Aun Wan's entreaties to leave the squad and the war and to build a life with her. Even though they have arrived in Paris, to leave the squad is to leave the war, something that even in his fantasy life Berlin proves unable to accomplish. By playing out in his imagination the worst act of cowardice a soldier can perform, Berlin discovers that he is unable to flee the war, no matter how much he might want to. O'Brien's portrait of what it means to have courage is essentially negative, his definition of courage seems to be the ability to resist one's own most cowardly impulses. The question of courage versus cowardice is one that runs through all of his novels and provides one of his central artistic tensions.

STYLE

Metafiction
Metafiction is fiction that takes storytelling and the nature of fiction itself as its central subject. That is, metafictional texts not only tell a story but explore the nature of storytelling. Metafictional texts often use this technique to study the relationship between fiction and reality, as O'Brien does in *Going after Cacciato* and in most of his other books. In his 1997 critique of O'Brien's novels, Herzog notes that O'Brien "does this by experimenting with and commenting on narrative

voices, structure, concepts of storytelling, the nature of creating a work of art, the relationships between reality and fiction, the development of an author" and that, as a result, "readers of O'Brien's works are treated to a short course in creative writing."

In *Going after Cacciato*, Paul Berlin spends much of the story thinking about the kinds of war stories he will tell when he gets home and about how those stories will be different from the actual experience he is having. Berlin also spends a lot of time in this novel "pretending" to be somewhere else, pretending that events in the story did not happen, pretending in advance how future events will unfold. While the use of fantasy is a classic technique of realistic fiction, O'Brien uses it in this novel as a metafictional tool in order to foreground the way that narratives do not simply arise organically but are deliberately constructed to produce specific effects.

Berlin uses narrative technique to shape the stories he tells himself about what has actually happened in the war and what might have happened in the war in much the same way that O'Brien uses narrative technique to shape the story of Paul Berlin. O'Brien's use of narratives within narratives highlights his belief, as he stated in a speech at Stanford University, that the purpose of fiction is "getting at the truth when the truth isn't sufficient for the truth." Paul Berlin tells himself stories in the hopes that he can shape his experience of Vietnam, just as O'Brien writes a story about a character who tells himself stories in order to show how the stories we tell ourselves shape the people we become. In this way, the story is metafictional; it is a story about the act and purpose of storytelling as much as it is a story about the Vietnam war.

Autobiographical Fiction
O'Brien is well known for using autobiographical elements in his work. He first wrote a memoir about his experience in Vietnam, *If I Die in a Combat Zone*, and then recast that experience as fiction in three novels: *Northern Lights*, *Going after Cacciato*, and *The Things They Carried*. The experience of the Vietnam veteran also occurs as a motif in his non-war novels—*July, July*; *In the Lake of the Woods*; and *Tomcat in Love*. However, it is important to clarify that, while O'Brien's novels borrow heavily from his personal history, they are fiction and make use of all the art and artifice of the genre.

In *Tim O'Brien*, Herzog recounts an appearance at Wabash College, where O'Brien told a story to a student audience about nearly defecting to Canada the summer he was drafted. O'Brien spoke "with such detail and emotion that the listeners who were unfamiliar with his novels became hooked—emotionally drawn into Tim O'Brien's life." Herzog recounts how those among them who knew the story, which appears as "On the Rainy River" in *The Things They Carried* became anxious, because they knew from previous experience that, as compelling as this story is, and no matter that the protagonist is named Tim O'Brien, the story never happened in real life. It is entirely fictional.

Indeed, O'Brien often uses his writing as a way to illustrate the difference between what he told Herzog he thinks of as the "story-truth" and the "happening-truth" of autobiographical fiction. The former refers to the events in a written story that give it verisimilitude and make a reader believe it, while the latter refers to the truth of the lived experience of authors and characters. Happening-truth "contains the facts of an event, the surface details," whereas story-truth "presents the pain and passion surrounding the experience: what is felt in your [readers'] bowels, and in your gut, and in your heart, and in your throat."

However, O'Brien is also careful in interviews to clarify that, although both Berlin and Tim O'Brien served in Vietnam, one cannot surmise that Tim O'Brien necessarily saw a man die of fright, like Billy Boy Watkins. There is not a one-to-one correspondence between story-truth and happening-truth. What an author of autobiographical fiction does, however, is use the events of his life as a starting place for the creation of fictional stories that can fully express the emotional, psychological, and artistic truth of those experiences.

Point of View: Third-Person Limited

A story uses the third-person point of view when the narrator is separate from the protagonist and narrates the events of the story from outside the protagonist's point of view. You can often identify a third-person story by its use of the pronouns *he*, *she*, and *they*. The narrative point of view in *Going after Cacciato* is considered limited third-person because, for the most part, the narrator is limited to the knowledge that the protagonist, Paul Berlin, possesses.

Although there is ample use of fantasy throughout the novel, even the fantasy sequences are limited by Berlin's imagination. For example, when the squad is facing execution, Berlin cannot figure out a way to get them out of their jam. Paul Berlin, in the observation post, "considered the possibilities. A miracle, he thought. An act of high imagination—daring and lurid and impossible. Yes, a cartoon of the mind," and then he imagined Cacciato's moon-face bursting through the prison walls to rescue them. Even in this moment of deep fantasy, the narration is limited to Paul Berlin's point of view.

Using the third-person limited narrative allows an author the freedom to express a character's thoughts or feelings in more sophisticated language than that which the character might use if describing the situation directly. For instance, when O'Brien describes Paul Berlin's terror during the "Night Watch" chapter, he says that the character was "bundled and tight, and he'd been on his hands and knees, crawling like an insect, an ant escaping a giant's footsteps and thinking nothing, brain flopping like wet cement in a mixer." It is the narrator, not Paul Berlin, who is creating metaphors that are more sophisticated than those a first-person narrator would use in order to describe the inner state of the character. This is the advantage of the third-person limited narrative. It allows the author to limit the reader's knowledge to what the character actually knows, but it also allows an author to describe the experience that character is having in language the character might not use for himself.

Verisimilitude

Verisimilitude and the related concept of mimesis are the terms by which we describe how a work of art imitates and represents the known world. O'Brien noted, in an essay he wrote for the *Atlantic Monthly*, that, while verisimilitude is important "to provide background and physical description and all the rest is of course vital to fiction," it is "vital only insofar as such detail is in the service of a richly imagined story." Because *Going after Cacciato* is a work of metafiction, the issue of verisimilitude is one that is shared by the author and Paul Berlin, the protagonist. Verisimilitude functions on several levels in this novel.

On the one hand, O'Brien is concerned with providing sufficient sensory detail that we can share in Berlin's experience of Vietnam. Knowing that, for Berlin, the war smells of "mud and algae and manure and chlorophyll and decay and mildew" brings the reader into the physical setting with which Berlin struggles. Verisimilitude functions on a second level in Berlin's own struggle to accurately describe for himself the factual reality of his experience in Vietnam. While keeping watch, Berlin notes to himself, "Keeping track wasn't easy. The order of things—chronologies—that was the hard part." One of Berlin's tasks over the course of the novel is to create a story for himself that contains sufficient verisimilitude to allow him to separate what actually happened from what might have happened.

This brings us to the third level upon which verisimilitude operates in this novel. Verisimilitude is crucial even to fantasy because it is the tool the author uses to create the illusion of a coherent world in which the reader can believe. Much of this novel is set in Berlin's fantasy of chasing Cacciato to Paris. At one point, while musing on the story that he has created, Berlin anticipates the skeptics who would doubt that his story is possible. "But he would explain," Berlin thinks. "Carefully, point by point, he would show how these were petty details." Like any good author, Paul Berlin carefully outlines in his head all the details of the big adventure, where they would get money, passports, and transportation. In the end, however, like Tim O'Brien, Berlin insists that it is imagination that is the most important factor. "Wasn't that the critical point?" he asks himself. "It could truly be done."

HISTORICAL CONTEXT

Vietnam War

The U.S. combat involvement in Vietnam began in 1964 with the Gulf of Tonkin Resolution and ended in 1975 with the fall of Saigon. During the cold war, many in Washington were convinced that there was a vast communist conspiracy to take over the world. South Vietnam was seen as a test of the domino theory, the conviction that, if communist forces succeeded in South Vietnam, then other south Asian countries would fall like dominoes. Because Vietnam had been divided into two countries after the French-Indochina war and because North Vietnam's communist government joined the Vietcong rebel forces in their attempt to overthrow the government of South Vietnam, the United States decided it was in the national interest to support the South Vietnamese in repelling communist aggression.

Thus began ten years of war not only in Vietnam but in Laos and Cambodia as well; more than fifty-eight thousand American soldiers were killed, as were millions of Vietnamese, Laotian, and Cambodian citizens. In 1969, in order to fill a shortfall of soldiers for the war, a draft was instituted, and a lottery was held to determine the order by which young men between the ages of nineteen and twenty-five would be required to serve. This coincided with the peak American involvement in the war, the period of the Tet Offensive. After 1969, domestic opposition to the war, fueled in part by revelations of U.S. war crimes like the My Lai massacre, slowly forced the United States to withdraw from Vietnam. It was not until 1975, however, when the North Vietnamese forces took over Saigon and the United States was forced to evacuate its embassy, that troops were entirely withdrawn. The Vietnam war is the only war the United States has ever lost.

My Lai Massacre

On March 16, 1968, the men of Charlie Company, 11th Brigade, Americal Division, under the command of Lieutenant William Calley, entered the village of My Lai with orders to "search and destroy." Instead of searching out enemy fighters and destroying them, the men rounded up all five to seven hundred inhabitants of the village, including old people, women, children, and infants, and brutally murdered them. Later accounts by eyewitnesses included horrifying details about old men being bayoneted, infants being shot, and the rape and murder of at least one girl. A few soldiers refused to take part, including Chief Warrant Officer Hugh Thompson, who landed his helicopter and put himself between Calley's men and the remaining survivors of the village in order to rescue them.

The U.S. forces attempted to cover up the massacre, and it was nearly a year before freelance reporter Seymour Hersh broke the story. He was aided by Ronald Ridenhour, who heard eyewitness reports of the massacre from soldiers who had taken part and who tried unsuccessfully to alert the authorities to what had taken place. When news of the massacre became public, Lieutenant Calley was charged with murder. He was sentenced to life in prison but released on appeal in 1974.

COMPARE
&
CONTRAST

- **1969:** The year 1969 is the heyday of the hippie movement, which has its zenith over August 15–18, when more than 500,000 people converge on the Woodstock Music Festival in Bethel, New York. Huge crowds gather in the rain-soaked fields to watch thirty-two acts, including Richie Havens, Janice Joplin, The Grateful Dead, and Jimi Hendrix. Woodstock also achieves fame as a central event celebrating the hippie ideals of peace, free love, and expanding human consciousness, although it is criticized by those who disapprove of drug use and casual sex.

  1978: By the late 1970s, the peace and love vibe of hippie protest music has morphed into the darker, more angry punk and new-wave movements. These musicians become famous for raging against corporate control of media, economics, and political systems. Elvis Costello appears on *Saturday Night Live* when the Sex Pistols cannot get visas and is banned from the show for playing his protest song about commercial radio, "Radio Radio."

  Today: The legacy of the hippie movement for music is most evident in the tradition of annual music festivals like South by Southwest in Austin, Texas, the Telluride Bluegrass Festival in Colorado, or the New Orleans Jazz Festival. These festivals tend to have strong identities, and many repeat visitors come as much for the values of peace, joy, and human fellowship as for the individual musical acts.

- **1969:** Domestic opposition to the war in Vietnam grows as the fighting escalates. On November 15, 1969, the biggest anti-war demonstration of the era takes place in Washington, DC. Approximately 500,000 people gather on the National Mall in Washington, where speakers, including Senator Edward Kennedy and Dr. Benjamin Spock, address the crowd, urging an end to the war.

  1978: In the middle of the Jimmy Carter presidency, the United States suffers through an energy crisis, and poll numbers reflect that,

for the first time, a majority of Americans no longer believe that the future is going to be as good as the present. This sense of "malaise," as it will come to be known after a speech the president gives the following year, comes to characterize the era for many.

  Today: The anti-war movement of the Vietnam era set the template for subsequent protest movements. Techniques used by protesters of the Vietnam era, including sit-ins, huge public marches, and boycotting corporations that support the war effort, are used by those who object to the wars in Iraq and Afghanistan.

- **1969:** The Vietnamization of the war begins as the newly elected president Richard Nixon orders the U.S. forces to begin handing over prosecution of the war to the South Vietnamese army. The failure of the South Vietnamese forces to cut off the supply routes at the Ho Chi Minh trail is seen as a serious blow to this early attempt to withdraw. The United States continues to send troops to Vietnam for the next four years, although the troop levels continually drop after 1969.

  1978: Vietnam's war with Cambodia heats up, exacerbated by China's entrance into the war. Because it is illegal to leave the Communist regime in Vietnam, over one million people flee the country in small fishing boats. They become known as the "boat people." Estimates of how many boat people die in the exodus vary from fifty to two hundred thousand, in part because some neighboring countries refuse to accept them and even sink boats deliberately. Eventually, many boat people are given asylum in the United States and Europe.

  Today: In 1995, the United States formally re-establishes diplomatic relations with Vietnam, and in 1999, ownership of the U.S. Embassy is returned to the United States. In the years since then, a vital tourist and commercial relationship develops between the two nations. In 2006, President George W. Bush makes a formal diplomatic visit to the nation.

Soldier Cacciato went AWOL from his unit. *(Oleg Zabielin | Shutterstock.com)*

In a 2009 speech reported in the *New York Times*, Calley finally apologized for the massacre, stating, "There is not a day that goes by that I do not feel remorse for what happened that day in My Lai." In 1994, O'Brien returned to the area and wrote in an essay for the *New York Times*,

> I more or less understand what happened that day in March 1968, how it happened, the wickedness that soaks into your blood and heats up and starts to sizzle. I know the boil that precedes butchery. At the same time, however, the men in Alpha Company did not commit murder. We did not turn our machine guns on civilians; we did not cross that conspicuous line between rage and homicide.

Fall of Saigon

As it became clear to citizens of the United States that the Vietnam war was a quagmire, there was still enormous concern that President Richard Nixon negotiate a peace treaty that did not indicate that we had "lost" the war. Nixon had campaigned on a pledge to restore "peace with honor," and the treaty signed on January 27, 1973, was an attempt to do just that. The conditions of the treaty included the return of prisoners of war within sixty days and require that the United States withdraw its troops within the same time period. While the last American troops left Vietnam by March 1973, a diplomatic presence remained in Saigon, the capital of South Vietnam. The government of North Vietnam made clear by its violation of the treaty agreements that it had no intention of allowing the country to remain divided and began to invade the south.

In April 1975, President Gerald Ford, who had been appointed after President Nixon resigned in the face of impeachment charges, ordered that all American personnel and those South Vietnamese who had worked directly for the United States be evacuated from Saigon. In order to prevent panic and out of concern for those Americans still in Saigon, the song "White Christmas" was broadcast in the streets as a coded means of announcing that the evacuation could begin. In the United States, thousands watched in horror as television news cameras captured the often chaotic scenes of evacuation.

A helicopter landing pad was established atop a small tower on the American embassy building, and the scenes of desperate people lining up on the staircase as the helicopters, in a marathon eighteen-hour airlift, evacuated were covered by U.S. television news. South Vietnamese helicopters also took off from other points in Saigon, landing on the U.S. aircraft carriers, although eventually more than one hundred of them were ditched into the South China sea in order to make room for more refugees. Ultimately, not everyone made it, and the last helicopter that was sent into Saigon to retrieve Ambassador Glenn Martin had orders to arrest him if he refused to board. Despite his pleas to rescue more Vietnamese, the evacuation eventually ended amid celebrations that broke out across Saigon as the country was finally united.

CRITICAL OVERVIEW

Going after Cacciato was published in 1978 to both critical and popular acclaim. Richard Freedman in the *New York Times*, writes,

> By turns lurid and lyrical, *Going after Cacciato* combines a surface of realistic war reportage as fine as any ... with a deeper feel—perhaps possible only in fiction—of the surrealistic effect war has on the daydreams and nightmares of the combatants. To call *Going after Cacciato* a novel about war is like calling *Moby Dick* a novel about whales.

The book was the surprise winner of the National Book Award in 1979, beating out both the huge best seller *The World According to Garp* by John Irving and John Cheever's *The Stories of John Cheever*. In their citation, the National Book Foundation states that "O'Brien's landscapes have the breadth and scope of Tolstoy's, and the essential American wonder and innocence of his vision deserves to stand beside that of Stephen Crane." Michiko Kakutani, also of the *New York Times*, finds that *Going after Cacciato*

> was one of the few Vietnam novels to capture that war's hallucinatory mood, the oddly surreal atmosphere produced by jungle warfare, heavy drug use and the moral and political ambiguities of American involvement. In relating the adventures of a deserter and the soldiers who are pursuing him, Mr. O'Brien was able to

use the devices of magical realism to create a novel that evoked both the brutal realities of that war, and the romantic yearnings of young men caught up in a conflict they did not understand.

O'Brien published eight stories before *Going after Cacciato*, six of which made it into the novel. Among them is "Where Have You Gone Charming Billy?" which was originally published in *Redbook* magazine in 1975. It won an O'Henry Prize, an annual award given to the twenty best short stories published in U.S. and Canadian magazines. "Where Have You Gone Charming Billy" appears in *Going after Cacciato* as the "Night March" chapter.

In the intervening years, as Mark A. Heberle notes in his introduction to *A Trauma Artist: Tim O'Brien and the Fiction of Vietnam*, *Going after Cacciato* "has provoked more critical articles and studies than any other literary representation of Vietnam and has probably been more widely read and more frequently taught in schools and universities."

CRITICISM

Charlotte M. Freeman

Freeman is a writer, editor, and former academic living in small-town Montana. In the following essay, she examines how Paul Berlin's quest in Going after Cacciato *to formulate a true war story for himself is a metafictional reflection of our common human impulse toward storytelling.*

War is a perennial subject of fiction precisely because it is so difficult to portray. Although the predominant media image of the warrior, especially post–World War II, is the macho figure played by John Wayne in so many movies, a man stoically unafraid, rallying his troops to serve their country with honor, the soldiers Tim O'Brien portrays are often confused, usually have no idea what they are fighting for, and are simply trying to serve out their time and go home alive. O'Brien has described in many interviews, particularly in those he did with Tobey Herzog, how he went to the war plagued by guilt and shame because he knew that the war was "ill-conceived and morally wrong." He told Herzog that, by joining up, he

> committed an act of unpardonable cowardice and evil. I went to a war that I believed was

WHAT DO I READ NEXT?

- Vietnam occurs as a theme in most of O'Brien's work. *The Things They Carried* (1990) is also considered one of the classics of Vietnam War literature. Written as a series of interlocking chapters, each of which can stand on its own as a short story, the book follows a character named "Tim O'Brien," who is not a direct autobiographical portrait of the author. Nominated for both the Pulitzer Prize and the National Book Critics Circle award, *The Things They Carried* is an exploration of the nature of the truths we tell ourselves and the stories we live by.

- *A Rumor of War* (1977) is Philip Caputo's memoir of his three years serving as a U.S. Marine in Vietnam, with a postscript that incorporates his experience nearly ten years later covering the fall of Saigon as a reporter for the Chicago Tribune. One of the most acclaimed memoirs of the Vietnam experience, the book is intensely personal. Caputo describes his journey from an idealistic twenty-year-old to a veteran of one of America's most ambiguous wars.

- Philip Caputo follows up his memoir and report on the Vietnam war with *10,000 Days of Thunder: A History of the Vietnam War* (2005), a book he wrote especially for young-adult readers. The book covers not only the history of the war and how the United States became involved but also focuses on the many groups affected by the war: U.S. soldiers, the Vietcong, nurses, villagers, and journalists. There are many photographs to humanize the conflict. This book manages to simplify the issues without talking down to its audience.

- Jana Laiz has received critical acclaim for her young-adult novel about two teenage girls, one American and one a Vietnamese refugee, who become friends in *Weeping Under This Same Moon* (2008).

- In *What Is the What* (2007), Dave Eggers tells the story of Valentino Achak Deng, one of Sudan's "Lost Boys." Although Eggers has called his book a novel, it is based on more than 100 hours of interviews with Deng, who is an actual person. Deng was separated from his family as a child, when Arab soldiers destroyed his village. His story contains accounts of the epic cross-country trek that he and the other Lost Boys made to the safety of Sudanese refugee camps, as well as his journey to America.

- Often considered the best account of the Vietnam war, Michael Herr's *Dispatches* (1977) is a memoir of his experience covering the Vietnam war for *Esquire* magazine. Herr garnered acclaim not only for the literary qualities of his prose but for the access he gave to soldiers and veterans whose voices had not been heard before. The book is a brutally honest depiction of a war that was often murky to both the combatants in the field and those at home who wondered what the United States forces were doing there at all.

- Bobbie Ann Mason's novel *In Country* (1985) tells the story of a young girl, Sam Hughes, whose father was killed in the Vietnam war. Sam lives in rural Kentucky with her uncle, Emmett, who seems to be suffering the effects of Agent Orange, a powerful chemical the U.S. Army dropped by the ton on Vietnam in an attempt to kill plants, thus depriving guerrilla fighters of cover. Set in the years just after the war, Mason's portrait of Sam's quest to piece together the truth of how the war has affected them all results in a powerful portrait of the home front.

IT IS BY IMAGINING THE POSSIBILITY THAT

CACCIATO GOT AWAY AND DID THE CRAZY THING HE

SAID HE WOULD DO, WALK ALL THE WAY TO PARIS,

THAT BERLIN BEGINS, OVER THE COURSE OF THE

NOVEL, TO ABSORB THE FACTS OF WHAT HAS

INDEED HAPPENED TO HIM IN VIETNAM."

wrong and participated in it actively. I pulled
the trigger. I was there. And by being there I am
guilty.

O'Brien's characters, including Paul Berlin
in *Going after Cacciato*, struggle with these same
contradictory feelings. Berlin dreams of becoming a hero, of winning the shining Silver Star for
valor, of returning to Iowa a man of substance, a
man of whom his father would be proud. However, he is plagued by terror so complete that he
collapses at several crucial moments in battle,
losing control of his mind and body, and finds
himself unable to remember what happened.
Berlin's challenge in this novel is to construct
several narratives for himself: a war story of the
sort he can tell when he goes home and a true
account he can tell to himself of what has happened in Vietnam. In order to do this, he "imagines" the story of the flight to Paris. Over the
course of one long night watch in a peaceful
observation post on a deserted stretch of the
South China Sea, Berlin uses the imagined
adventure of Cacciato's flight to Paris as a way
to construct a coherent account of the deaths
of his comrades and his factual experience in
the war.

In this way, the book is metafictional. The
story of the book is the story of Berlin's authorship of his own story, or, as Mark A. Heberle
points out in *A Trauma Artist: Tim O'Brien and
the Fiction of Vietnam*, "The increasing metafic-
tionality of O'Brien's novels makes explicit what
was evident as early as *Cacciato* (1979): The
most common subject of O'Brien's writing is
writing itself." While Heberle is interested primarily in how the novels reflect the author's life
story when he claims that, in O'Brien's work,

"the power of the imagination . . . is more than
just a theme—it is a way of redeeming the
author's own life," it is by resorting to the same
mechanism that the character Paul Berlin seeks
to redeem his own life with in *Going after
Cacciato*.

The novel comprises three different narratives in three different time frames. The present
tense of the novel is represented in the ten Observation Post chapters. These chapters take place
over the course of a single night, during which
Berlin decides to take the entire watch. Throughout the night, he imagines the journey to Paris
and considers his war experience thus far. There
are sixteen chapters comprising Berlin's dis-
jointed memories of the war, chapters in which
he tries to construct a narrative that reflects what
"really happened." These chapters revolve
largely around the deaths of his eight companions. The remaining twenty chapters contain
Berlin's imagined narrative of escape, in which
the squad leaves the war and follows Cacciato all
the way to Paris. Berlin is not a writer—during
the course of the novel the only thing we ever see
him write is a postcard, and that occurs in one of
the fantasy chapters. However, readers can
nonetheless consider him an author for he
spends the entire course of the novel as creator
of his own story through three primary activities,
by "pretending," by "remembering," and by
"imagining."

"Pretending" is something Paul Berlin does
when he cannot process the immediate present.
In the first chapter, when they are chasing Cacciato and Doc and the Lieutenant discuss
whether or not to continue the chase, Paul Berlin
retreats into a game of Las Vegas-style solitaire:
"Pretending ways to spend his earnings. . . . Wine
and song on white terraces, fountains blowing
colored water. Pretending was his best trick to
forget the war." When Paul Berlin cannot cope,
he pretends. He is often shown pretending on
marches, as a way to try to contain his own
fear or as a means of passing the time. In the
first observation post chapter, he notes, "Pretending. It wasn't dreaming, it wasn't craziness.
Just a way of passing time, which seemed never
to pass." The night in the observation post happens about halfway through Berlin's tour of
duty, and it is during this night watch that he
looks back on his experiences thus far. His time
in Vietnam has been primarily characterized by
pretending: by pretending he is not there at all,

by pretending that the M&Ms Doc Peret administers are not a sure sign a soldier is about to die. He hopes that, if he pretends hard enough, he can simply get to the other side of his tour. Berlin cannot cope with the reality into which he has been thrust, so, for the first half of his tour, he hides out in his own imagination.

In the first of the Observation Post chapters, Paul Berlin explicitly states to himself that it is "time to consider the possibilities." He thinks of Doc Peret and his insistence on scientific thought and decides that it is time to determine "what part was fact and what part was extension of fact? And how were facts separated from possibilities?" He decides that he must determine "what had really happened and what merely might have happened?" It is by imagining the possibility that Cacciato got away and did the crazy thing he said he would do, walk all the way to Paris, that Berlin begins, over the course of the novel, to absorb the facts of what has indeed happened to him in Vietnam.

Inspired by "the immense powers of his own imagination" and unable still to recall exactly what happened to Cacciato when the squad caught up with him on that hillside, Berlin makes up an elaborate story about how the journey to Paris might have happened. By giving in to the core fantasy of every soldier, the idea that one could simply walk away from the war, and by making it a collective defection, Berlin finds a way to imagine how he might react to all sorts of situations: to meeting a girl who likes him, to encountering a member of the enemy to whom he can speak and communicate, to bonding with his squad mates and sticking together through the stereotypical sorts of wartime adventures that are familiar to him from the movies but that were not reflected at all in his actual experience of the war.

It is by imagining the stories in the fantasy chapters that Berlin manages to accurately remember the events recounted in the sixteen chapters that account for his actual experiences of the war and especially the experience of watching his fellow soldiers die. These are the chapters in which he seeks to determine "what part was fact." The novel opens with a litany of the dead and the declaration that "it was a bad time." Over the course of the observation post chapters, Berlin manages not only to imagine his way through the possibilities of the journey to Paris but to begin straightening out the time line

of events that has characterized his tour thus far, a time line defined by the deaths of Billy Boy Watkins, Frenchie Tucker, Bernie Lynn, Lieutenant Sidney Martin, Pedersen, Rudy Chassler, Buff, and Ready Mix. The most complicated of these deaths is, of course, the death of Lieutenant Sidney Martin, who dies at the hands of his own men. It is not until Berlin has reduced the deaths of each of them to "a few stupid war stories, hackneyed and unprofound" that he can think of his dead fellow soldiers in a calm manner. By the end of his night in the observation post, Berlin has, through the construction of several different sorts of stories, incorporated his war experience into his psyche. By imaginatively escaping the war during a night he spends literally watching over his men, Berlin emerges into the dawn as someone who has overcome a level of psychic damage that has been, up until this point in the war, paralyzing to him.

While critics like Heberle argue that the "subject of O'Brien's writing is writing itself" and that the book is hence metafictional, it can be argued that the subject of O'Brien's writing is actually storytelling. The book clearly uses many of the hallmarks of metafiction in its layered time and story lines and its focus on fictionality, or as Berlin puts it, its project of determining fact from "the extension of fact," but the novel's emphasis on the many ways we tell one another stories aligns it with the old oral tradition out of which the classical war epics of the past arose. Storytelling is our oldest form of knowing, our oldest way of understanding not only ourselves but one another. Through the millennia, soldiers have come home from war, bearing their "hackneyed war stories," each of which is as individual as Berlin's are to him.

One of Paul Berlin's biggest fears is that he is not going to be able to find a socially acceptable way to speak about his war experience. He certainly does not want to tell his family and the people at home that he was reduced to a twitching, giggling, terrified wreck during combat. His terror is the one subject about which he cannot speak, even in the joking way of some soldiers. He cannot gain any coherent hold on what has happened to him until he manages to use "the immense powers of his imagination" to sort out his war experience into the imagined adventure of what might have been had they chased Cacciato to Paris and the factual stories of how his fellow soldiers died. It is storytelling that saves

In the novel, Doc Peret sometimes used M&Ms as medicine to treat overreactive soldiers. (*Pablo Eder /*
Shutterstock.com)

him, and storytelling, or fiction, that O'Brien holds up as the saving grace not just of Berlin but perhaps of us all. We must learn to tell a coherent story about our lives if we are to function in the world at all.

Source: Charlotte M. Freeman, Critical Essay on *Going after Cacciato*, in *Novels for Students*, Gale, Cengage Learning, 2011.

Jack Slay Jr.

In the following essay, Slay discusses Going After Cacciato, *specifically examining the ten observation post chapters and their representation of escape and absurdity in war.*

Tim O'Brien's *Going after Cacciato* (1978) is a labyrinthine narrative of reality and fantasy, of fact and imagination. In portraying these various levels of reality and imagination, O'Brien structures the novel on a three-tiered narrative: the war memories, the Cacciato chapters, and the Observation Post sections. Critical consensus is that Paul Berlin's violent memories of the war constitute the harsh reality of the novel, that

the Observation Post is Berlin's easier but temporary reality, and that the trek to Paris in pursuit of Cacciato is fantasy, an elaborate conjuration of Berlin's mind: However, a close reading of the novel reveals that the Observation Post is as much a fantasy as is the journey to Paris, both creations of Berlin's war-exhausted mind. Consequently, the majority of the novel—the fantasies involving the Post and Cacciato as well as the chaotic remembrances of Berlin's real war experiences—takes place in the few minutes of blind panic that paralyzes Berlin as his patrol ambushes the fleeing Cacciato.

The recollected war stories are a past remembered, spanning from June 3, 1968, Berlin's arrival in Vietnam, to late October and the escape of Cacciato. Primarily, those chapters relate the deaths of Berlin's fellow grunts; they are, consequently, a litany of graphic and violent death. Berlin's narrative, however, is hardly chronological, barely cohesive; it is often hazily remembered, occasionally disorienting and confusing. For example, the novel opens with a death roll:

"IN THE MIDST OF HIS DEEPEST HUMILIATION, AN EMBARRASSMENT CAUSED DIRECTLY BY HIS COWARDICE, BERLIN STEPS BACK INTO THE LINE OF DUTY AND FIRE AND DISMISSES THE OCCASION TO DESERT IN CACCIATO'S FADING FOOTSTEPS. THAT, THEN, IS HIS ULTIMATE ACT OF COURAGE; *THAT*, INDEED, IS PAUL BERLIN'S BRAVEST MOMENT."

It was a bad time. Billy Boy Watkins was dead, and so was Frenchie Tucker. Billy Boy had died of fright . . . and Frenchie Tucker had been shot through the nose. Bernie Lynn and Lieutenant Sidney Martin had died in tunnels. Pederson was dead and Rudy Chassler was dead. Buff was dead. Ready Mix was dead.

Much later, Berlin again reviews the chronology,

[attempting] again to order the known facts. Billy Boy was first. And then . . . who? Then a long blank time along the Song Tra Bong, yes, and then Rudy Chassler, who broke the quiet. And then later Frenchie Tucker, followed in minutes by Bernie Lynn. Then Lake Country . . . where Ready Mix died on a charge toward the mountains. And then Buff. Then Sidney Martin. Then Pederson.

Berlin's memories are products of an exhausted and traumatized psyche; coherence and order are hardly important, if, indeed, possible. Still, though confounding and seemingly random, these memories compose the novel's most truthful and tangible reality.

The going-after-Cacciato chapters, on the other hand, are an imagined future, a world of breathtaking escapes, lucky breaks, and magic realism. Above all, those chapters represent an escape; they are a pretending, a chance for Berlin momentarily to forget the war. The faithful and rigorous chronology presented in those sections counters the haphazard recollection of the war memories. Spanning the months from October 1968 to April 1969, the chapters constitute a fantastic possibility, a time of miracles, of love, and the search for happy endings. For Berlin the imagined chase is "a splendid idea. [. . .] not a dream. Nothing mystical or crazy, just an idea. Just a

possibility." Too, these sections are filled with absurdities, ambiguities, the inexplicable. For instance, every person the patrol encounters—including the South Vietnamese refugee Sarkin Aung Wan, the North Vietnamese Li Van Hgoc imprisoned in a Wonderland of tunnels, and Fahyi Rhallon, a captain of the Savak—speaks perfect English! More curious is how Berlin—whether imagining in the safety of the Observation Post or in the mud and heat of Cacciato's hill—knows that Eisenhower dies in April 1969 when he is creating this scenario in November 1968. Nevertheless, these chapters comprise an escape for Berlin, innocent and complete and, most important to him, filled with courage and composure.

The ten chapters depicting the Observation Post are presented as time present, the immediacy of Berlin's tour of duty, covering the hours between midnight and 6 a.m. in late November 1968. The Post, beside the South China Sea and facing Quang Ngai, is a place where Berlin feels safe, countering not only the chaos of the war memories but also the (moral) confusions that infiltrate the going-after-Cacciato chapters; it is a place where standing another's watch can be his "bravest moment." In fact, it is a complete escape from the war, a place where "if the day went as most days went, there would be nothing but heat and flies and boredom." O'Brien has said that the novel is "structured as a teeter-totter, with the 'Observation Post' chapters as the fulcrum—the present of the book. The teeter-totter swings back and forth between reality—the war experience—and fantasy—the imagined trek to Paris" (McCaffery 139). It is also a place where, for a change, Berlin is in control. Even in the Cacciato sequences, he loses control and is led to absurd, even impossible solutions that still refuse to discover happy endings: falling into Wonderlandish holes, being imprisoned for desertion, escaping Tehran in a souped-up '64 Impala, slipping through a harbor patrol search unchallenged, unnoticed.

The fantastical episodes of the Cacciato chapters, too, closely parallel his real experiences. For example, "A Hole in the Road to Paris," in which the patrol falls into a complex and elaborate tunnel system, is immediately followed by "Fire in the Hole," in which Berlin recollects the destruction of the village Hoi An, where he remembers the patrol shooting into the firebombed village until it becomes "a hole." Likewise, the patrol's quick search of the passengers on the Delhi Express reminds Berlin of the embarrassment, even humiliation, of his body searches conducted on the Vietnamese. The membrane between his reality and his fantasy, Berlin quickly learns, is too thin; his fantasies are continually tainted with "an odd sense of guilt" [that makes] "the whole made-up world [seem] to dissolve [. . .]." That continual interaction between what is real and what is imagined is, as Dean McWilliams points out,

> a flight not only from Vietnam but from responsibility for a mutinous murder [of Lt. Martin] committed there. It also shows that, despite this attempted evasion, the repressed memories haunt the fantasy and finally cause its collapse. The only true hope for moral regeneration occurs after the collapse of the fantasy when Berlin is, perhaps, ready for an honest moral confrontation with his past.

Largely as a result of his guilt, Berlin's imagination falls quickly beyond his control—"Why [couldn't he imagine] pretty things?" he wonders at one point. "Why not a smooth, orderly arc from war to peace?"—and, as a direct consequence, the Observation Post intrudes more and more into his imagined world. Berlin finds himself "partly here, partly there. Hard to tell which was real."

However, as Michael Raymond points out and, surprisingly, most critics overlook, the Observation Post is as unreal, is as much a work of Berlin's imagination as is the search for the runaway Cacciato. Berlin himself makes that clear in the last chapter: "They talked of rumors. An observation post by the sea, easy duty, place to swim and get solid tans and fish for red snapper." It is a fantastic anomaly in the midst of chaos and carnage, "an observation post with nothing to observe. No villages, no roads or vital bridges, no enemy, not a dog or a cat. A teetering old tower by the sea." Ultimately, it is little more than a further, less-elaborate conjuring of Berlin's mind, an oasis as unreal as the pilgrimage to Paris.

The entire novel, then, encapsulates the time in Berlin's mind during the brief moments, even seconds, following his bungling of the ambush of Cacciato. The novel, therefore, can most accurately be read as Berlin's internal debate concerning his courage.

Ernest Hemingway, in his introduction to *Men at War*, states that

a thing is bad only when it is bad. It is bad neither before nor after. Cowardice, as distinguished from panic, is almost always simply a matter of ability to suspend the functions of the imagination. Learning to live completely in the very second of the present minute with no before and no after is the greatest gift a soldier can acquire.

(xxvii)

Going after Cacciato, similarly, is Paul Berlin's moral struggle to live, even survive, in his present moment, to face up to, if not overcome, his repeated cowardice.

In the space of just over five months, Berlin has seen his courage challenged as many times; in each instance he succumbs to his fears, proving himself a coward time and again. During his first battle, he collapses into a fetal position: "Twitching in his hidden little depression, hiding out during the one big battle of the war, he could only lie there, twitching, holding his breath in messy gobs, fingers twitching, legs pulled around his stomach like a shell, but his legs twitching too as the bombers came to bomb the mountains." Later, in a chapter appropriately entitled "Upon Almost Winning the Silver Star," when Lt. Martin asks for a volunteer to search the tunnels, Berlin "stood alone. He felt the walls tight against him. He was careful not to look at anyone." Again and again he forgoes the opportunity for bravery. His ultimate failure, though, both morally and personally, is his complicity in the fragging of Lt. Martin, done more by his complacency than his cowardice. His acquiescence is further compounded by his forcing Cacciato to touch the fragmentation grenade that will be used to murder Lt. Martin. Knowing that he is wrong, Berlin, nonetheless, forces Cacciato—the most innocent of Berlin's comrades—into the patrol's compliancy, needing to share his blame, his guilt. Berlin's final act of cowardice is his blind panic during the ambush on Cacciato's hill, an ambush that concludes with Berlin firing his gun wildly, uncontrollably, and then urinating on himself.

In the midst of all that surrounds Berlin—carnage and guilt, fantasy and manipulation—is the issue of courage. From the beginning of his tour of duty, Berlin has anticipated his possible return in valor: "[. . .] he would," he thinks early in the novel, "step off [the train] boldly, boldly, and he would shake his father's hand and look him in the eye. 'I did okay,' he would say. 'I won some medals.' And his father would nod." He wraps himself in the guise of possible courage, at first hoping to prove himself, and later hoping to manage himself with at least some shred of dignity. His first battle, however, terrifies him; other confrontations—with the enemy, with the land, even with the most inept man in his patrol—prove even worse. Still, Berlin perseveres, reminding himself again and again that

> the issue, of course, was courage. How to behave. Whether to flee or fight or seek an accommodation. The issue was not fearlessness. The issue was how to act wisely in spite of fear. Spitting the deep-running biles: that was true courage. He believed this. And he believed the obvious corollary: the greater a man's fear, the greater his potential courage.

Toward the end of the novel, as the imagined pursuit of Cacciato nears its culmination, Berlin tells Sarkin Aung Wan, during their imagined peace talks, "I fear being thought of as a coward. I fear that even more than cowardice itself." Nonetheless, every day that passes multiplies his fear; every fear, in turn, increases his cowardice. In the end, all realities, all fantasies, all his loosely held notions of courage lead to the ambush on Cacciato's hill, the ultimate test of his mettle.

The first and last chapters are opposite ends of the same scene: the squad's attempted ambush of Cacciato. The chapters are united through a series of echoes and recurrences: For example, in each chapter Doc Peret announces, "'He's gone. [. . .] Split'"; Berlin calms himself by counting; there is the barked order "Go!"; Berlin wets himself in panic; and finally, each chapter is titled "Going after Cacciato." Those two chapters are the only present of the novel; all that falls in between is remembrance and imagination.

Chapter 1 is Paul Berlin's present, the origin of all his recollections and imaginings. Cacciato—"open-faced and naive and plump," a boy "dumb as a bullet [. . .] dumb as a month-old oyster fart [. . .]"—walks away from the war, dumbly determined to traverse the 8,600 miles that separate him from Paris. The Third Squad, under the new command of Lt. Corson, pursues. In the chase, the seeds of Berlin's fantasy are born; always just behind Cacciato, Berlin begins to wonder, to imagine: "Where was it going, where would it end?" Later, just before the ambush, he attempts "to imagine a proper ending" and so originates the slow journey across the continent, his refrain already "Maybe . . . maybe so." The squad's ambush and attempted

capture of the runaway Cacciato (occurring, quite appropriately for a story about the magic and power of creation, on the morning of the seventh day of the pursuit) throws Berlin into yet another seizure of fear and panic.

Chapter 1 concludes with the squad in mid maneuver and Berlin in mid panic; chapter 46 resumes the ambush, bringing us "back to where it started." The last chapter begins as a conclusion to the going-after-Cacciato sequence, the squad—again in ambush formation—bursting into Cacciato's Paris apartment. Amid the confusion of the Paris ambush Berlin is yanked back into his harsh reality, forcibly and unwillingly returning to the jungles of Vietnam, to the original ambush on Cacciato. In blind fear, he fires his rifle wildly, uncontrollably, and in the grip of this unreasoning panic he stains himself with an ultimate humiliation, the obvious sign of his cowardice: "[. . .] there was a floating feeling, then a swelling in his stomach, then a wet releasing feeling." Shortly afterwards, the mission a failure, the squad heads back to the war, "the old order restored" and the fantasy dismissed, marching toward the *rumor* of an observation post.

Though many critics contend that the novel therefore concludes in the past (because we never again see Berlin in his Observation Post by the sea), a closer reading reveals that the last chapter is indeed the present, that in fact everything between the opening and closing chapters—the unordered, chaotic memories and the ordered, controlled fantasies—is the work of Berlin's war-fevered mind. There is, in the end, no escape: for Berlin, less than halfway through his tour of duty, there is only war and then more war.

The forty-four chapters between the first and the last, therefore, are filled with Paul Berlin's instantaneous contemplations on courage and his ultimate attempt to come to terms with his repeated cowardice. He believes that he has failed his squad, his family, his country, and, worse, himself. In those few blind minutes of fear and panic, Berlin cowers in the jungle of Vietnam, his pants wet with his own urine, his rifle firing maniacally, and finally achieves a realization, a sort of mini-catharsis.

In the last minutes of his Paris fantasy, Berlin faces Sarkin across the peace talk table, where she asks him "to step boldly into [his dream], to join your dream and to live it. Do not be deceived by false obligation. You are obliged, by all that is just and good, to pursue only the felicity that you yourself have imagined. Do not let fear stop you." Berlin refuses, however, to step into the fantasy, refuses to succumb to the temptation of desertion. He tells Sarkin, attempting to convince her as much as himself,

> More than any positive sense of obligation, I confess that what dominates is the dread of abandoning all that I hold dear. I am afraid of running away. I am afraid of exile. I fear what might be thought of me by those I love. I fear the loss of their respect. I fear the loss of my own reputation.

Critics' responses to Berlin's final decision vary. James Wilson finds no real resolution: "Even in his imagination, Berlin retreats into official slogans and platitudes, unable to either imaginatively or intellectually transcend the propaganda of his own government." Dennis Vannatta sees the novel concluding with indefiniteness: "There is no reason to believe that flight will not once again become an attractive alternative to Paul." James Griffith discovers a positive outcome: "As for courage [. . .] Paul at least imagines a heroic journey, and in order to complete it, he performs a slight, but real-world, act of bravery: remaining on duty atop the observation post, even through the 'dangerous time' of the 'darkest hours' when attack is most likely."

I, too, see Berlin's final actions as those of a hero, or, at the very least, a potential hero: however, those acts occur not in the Observation Post. Rather, they occur in Berlin's decision to continue, to persevere in spite of his fears. In the midst of his deepest humiliation, an embarrassment caused directly by his cowardice, Berlin steps back into the line of duty and fire and dismisses the occasion to desert in Cacciato's fading footsteps. That, then, is his ultimate act of courage; *that*, indeed, is Paul Berlin's bravest moment.

Source: Jack Slay Jr., "A Rumor of War: Another Look at the Observation Post in Tim O'Brien's *Going After Cacciato*," in *Critique*, Vol. 41, No. 1, Fall 1999, p. 79.

Vera P. Froelich

In the following essay, Froelich highlights the first chapter of Going After Cacciato, *which enumerates those who died or who have been wounded in action, as well as the diseases and misery experienced by a squad to which the protagonist belongs.*

It is generally recognized that Tim O'Brien's *Going After Cacciato*, the winner of the National Book Award for 1978, is most likely the best novel of the Vietnam War, albeit an unusual one in that it innovatively combines experiential realism of war with surrealism, primarily implemented in the fantasy journey of escape by the novel's protagonist, thoughtful and sympathetic soldier Paul Berlin. The first chapter in this novel is of more than usual importance. Designed to be a self-sufficient story (McCaffery 137) and often anthologized as such, this chapter is crucial to the novel in that it not only introduces us to the characters and the situation but also sets the tenor of the novel and reveals its author's view of this war in relation to which all else in the novel must be judged.

In this chapter, the plot of the entire novel is defined: A very young soldier named Cacciato deserts, intending to walk by land to Paris. As his squad—amused but increasingly intrigued, even inspired—follows under orders to capture him, Paul Berlin begins his liberating mind-journey of "going after Cacciato," of escape from, and later also a reexamination of, the reality of war. But what is defined first, in the first two pages to be exact, is this war reality and its cost to the young American soldiers involved. These pages list for us those who have died, in action and otherwise (one through "fragging," we later find), and those who have been maimed, at times through self-injury, underscoring the urgency of the desire to live. These pages also vividly delineate for us the daily miseries and sufferings of this war, from incessant rain and mud to dysentery and rotting flesh, from monotony and hopelessness and fear to a lack of sense of any larger purpose for which lives might be justifiably given, or lost. And the young soldiers undergo all this while being "led" by an ill, alcoholic, misanthropic lieutenant who cannot even remember who among his young charges is who, or who alive and who dead—so much for the nature of military authority in Vietnam.

These beginning pages contain another and quite different image of destruction, which helps to make this somber portrait of the Vietnam War more complete. We are told that Berlin and his squad are using a nearly mined Buddhist pagoda for their housing:

> . . . in shadows was the cross-legged Buddha, smiling from its elevated stone perch. The pagoda was cold. Dank from a month of rain, the place smelled of clays and silicates and dope and old incense. It was a single square room built like a pillbox with stone walls and a flat ceiling that forced the men to stoop or kneel.

Once it might have been a fine house of worship, but now it was junk. Sandbags blocked the windows. Bits of broken pottery lay under chipped pedestals. The buddha's right arm was missing but the smile was intact. Head cocked, the statue seemed interested in the lieutenant's long sigh. (O'Brien)

In this very American novel, which focuses on the American soldiers' experiences, feelings, and minds, and in which Vietnam is presented primarily as merely a terrain and a climate, this image of the pagoda seems to be symbolic of the country of Vietnam at this time. Invaded, desecrated, nearly destroyed, it still endured, sustained by a culture and a spirituality against which the war and the American warriors seem unimportant and small.

Some critics have thought that *Going After Cacciato* is "not an antiwar novel" (Vannatta 246; McCaffery 145), but surely they must be mistaken. If, as many have observed, in this novel O'Brien seems much preoccupied with memory and especially with imagination, probing its power and scope as well as its limitations, it is nevertheless the horror of the wartime situation that gives imagination its urgency, its desperate importance. And if at the end of the novel Paul Berlin finds he must return and resign himself to the war reality, he makes clear to us that he does so not because of "courage" (Bates 278) or principle but because, like his creator, he cannot withstand the societal pressures of family and country and is afraid of the isolation and hardship that opposition to them would impose (322–23)—an understandable but hardly an admirable or a happy ending.

As for O'Brien himself, he has frequently said that war is a complex affair, especially for those who must face it directly, but his prevalent views have become increasingly explicit. For instance, shortly after this novel was published, he said that his main concern in it was "to have readers care about what's right and wrong and about the difficulty of doing right, the difficulty of saying no to a war" (qtd. in Schroeder 146). Several years later, speaking at the Asia Society conference in 1985, he was even more forthright: "Wouldn't all of us admit that a mistake was made in Vietnam? ... we misunderstood Vietnamese history ... and we were shooting anyway" (qtd. in Lomperis 73). Both the novel and its author condemn this war. And it is in this novel's first, crucial chapter that such views are most clearly embodied, molding all the rest.

Source: Vera P. Froelich, "O'Brien's *Going After Cacciato*," in *Explicator*, Vol 53, No. 3, Spring 1995, pp. 181–84.

SOURCES

"Background Note: Vietnam," in *U.S. Department of State: Diplomacy in Action*, http://www.state.gov/r/pa/ei/bgn/4130.htm (accessed September 17, 2010).

Baldick, Chris, "Metafiction," "Third-person Narrative," and "Verisimilitude," in *The Oxford Dictionary of Literary Terms*, Oxford University Press, 2009, pp. 203, 335, 349.

Brogan, Hugh, *The Penguin History of the USA*, new ed., Penguin, 2001, pp. 645-49, 668.

Bruckner, D. J. R., "A Storyteller for the War That Won't End," in *New York Times*, April 3, 1991.

"Ex-Officer Apologizes for Killings at My Lai," in *New York Times*, August 22, 2009.

Freedman, Richard, "A Separate Peace," in *New York Times*, February 12, 1978.

"Final Words: Cronkite's Vietnam Commentary," in *National Public Radio (NPR)*, http://www.npr.org/templates/story/story.php?storyId=106775685 (accessed September 17, 2010).

Heberle, Mark A., *A Trauma Artist: Tim O'Brien and the Fiction of Vietnam*, University of Iowa Press, 2001, pp. 34, 108.

Herzog, Tobey C., *Tim O'Brien*, Twayne's United States Author Series, No. 691, Twayne Publishers, 1997, pp. 1, 5, 14, 29.

Kakutani, Michiko, "Books of the *Times*: Slogging Surreally in the Vietnamese Jungle," in *New York Times*, March 6, 1990.

Linder, Douglas, "An Introduction to the My Lai Courts-Martial," in *Famous American Trials: The My Lai Courts-Martial 1970*, University of Missouri-Kansas City School of Law, http://www.law.umkc.edu/faculty/projects/ftrials/mylai/Myl_intro.html (accessed September 17, 2010).

O'Brien, Tim, *Going after Cacciato*, Broadway, 1999.

———, "Telling Tails," in *Atlantic*, http://www.theatlantic.com/doc/print/200908/tim-obrien-essay (accessed September 17, 2010).

———, "Tim O'Brien Lecture Transcript," in *Writing Vietnam*, http://www.stg.brown.edu/projects/Writing Vietnam/obrien.html (accessed September 17, 2010).

———, "The Vietnam in Me," in *New York Times*, October 2, 1994.

Review of *Going After Cacciato*, in *Random House Academic Resources*, http://www.randomhouse.com/catalog/display.pperl?isbn=9780767904421 (accessed December 17, 2010).

Saturday Night Live 25th Anniversary, DVD, Lions Gate, 2004.

Smith, Patrick A., *Tim O'Brien: A Critical Companion*, Greenwood Press, 2005.

Solotaroff, Theodore, "Memoirs for Memorial Day," in *New York Times*, May 29, 1977, http://www.nytimes.com/books/97/08/10/reviews/caputo-rumor.html (accessed September 17, 2010).

"Vietnam Online," in *American Experience*, Public Broadcasting System (PBS), http://www.pbs.org/wgbh/amex/vietnam/ (accessed September 17, 2010).

"Vietnam War," in *A Dictionary of World History* Oxford University Press, 2007, pp. 674–75.

"Walter Cronkite Dies," in *CBS Evening News with Katie Couric*, July 17, 2009, http://www.cbsnews.com/stories/2009/07/17/eveningnews/main5170556.shtml (accessed September 17, 2010).

FURTHER READING

O'Brien, Tim, *If I Die in a Combat Zone*, Delacorte, 1974.
Published prior to *Going after Cacciato*, *If I Die in a Combat Zone* covers much of the same territory but in an unvarnished, raw, nonfictional form. O'Brien kept detailed notebooks while he was in Vietnam and sent short dispatches back to newspapers in Minnesota, many of which he uses in this account.

O'Brien, Tim, *In the Lake of the Woods*, Penguin Books, 1994.
In the Lake of the Woods is the story of John Wade, a Vietnam veteran who has moved to a small cabin in northern Minnesota to recover after a losing campaign for the U.S. Senate following revelations that he was involved in a massacre like the one at My Lai. He awakes one morning to discover that his wife Kathy is missing. The novel mixes genres, incorporating "interviews" with John and Kathy's friends, news reports of the incident, and John's flashbacks in order to raise questions about what happened to Kathy. The novel posits several possibilities but never directly answers the question.

Peacock, Doug, *Grizzly Years*, Holt, 1996.
Peacock returned from two tours of duty as a medic in Vietnam shattered by the experience. What saved him was a map of Wyoming and Montana, a map he studied while in Vietnam, memorizing the places without roads. When he returned, he headed into these areas, seeking solitude and trying to recover from his experience. What he found was grizzly bears, and over the course of the next decade he studied them denning, feeding, playing, and raising their young. While learning to coexist with these dangerous animals, Peacock began to heal from his Vietnam experience. Despite his lack of formal biology training, Peacock is considered one of the foremost authorities on grizzly behavior and has become one of America's most dedicated defenders of wild spaces and wild animals.

Tram, Dang Thuy, *Last Night I Dreamed of Peace*, Three Rivers Press, 2008.
In 1970, an American military intelligence officer found a tiny diary written by a young Vietnamese doctor. He smuggled it out of the country and translated it before returning it to her family in 2005. Published simultaneously in Vietnam and the United States, this moving diary was written between 1968 and 1970 by Tram, a young, passionate doctor who served on the front lines. The book chronicles the strife she witnessed until the day she was shot by American soldiers at age twenty-seven.

Wolfe, Tobias, *The Barracks Thief*, Harper Perennial, 1984.
Wolfe won the 1895 PEN/Faulkner Award for Fiction for his novel about three soldiers who, while waiting to be shipped out to Vietnam, spend a sweltering afternoon standing guard over an ammunition dump threatened by a forest fire. They discover in each other an unexpected capacity for recklessness and violence. Thrilled by the discovery, they emerge from their common danger filled with confidence in their own manhood only to have their confidence shaken by a series of thefts. Wolfe shifts between the perspectives of both the betrayer and the betrayed, forcing the reader to identify with the positions of both parties.

SUGGESTED SEARCH TERMS

Tim O'Brien

Tim O'Brien AND Vietnam

Tim O'Brien AND interview

Going after Cacciato

Vietnam AND war

metafiction

Fall of Saigon

new journalism AND Vietnam War

Hemingway AND war reporting

postmodernism AND Vietnam War

The Haunting of Hill House

SHIRLEY JACKSON

1959

Shirley Jackson's 1959 novel *The Haunting of Hill House* is an emblematic modern ghost story that resuscitated an abandoned genre and provided a framework for new gothic novels by authors ranging from Joyce Carol Oates to Stephen King. The novel is satirical, subverting the restricted lives of housewives in prefeminist America as much as the gothic genre itself. But to classify the novel simply as horror is to undervalue it as genre fiction, rather than literary fiction, where its complexity and quality more naturally place it. *The Haunting of Hill House* is heavily indebted not only to the gothic tradition—going back to novels like *The Castle of Otranto* (1764) by Horace Walpole—but also to first-wave feminist literature like "The Yellow Wallpaper" (1892), by Charlotte Perkins Gilman, from which Jackson found inspiration for much of her plot and theme, reading the horror-story tradition as an allegory for women's lives in a male-dominated society. *The Haunting of Hill House* also grew out of extensive research that Jackson conducted into the pseudoscientific world of parapsychology. She introduces themes such as ghost hunting, extrasensory perception, and the strange paradoxes investigated by Charles Fort to a mainstream literary audience from their origins in narrow technical literature, enabling them to become mainstays of modern popular literature, film, and television. Jackson's novel is available in a 1996 Penguin Classics paperback edition.

Shirley Jackson (AP Images)

AUTHOR BIOGRAPHY

Jackson was born on December 14, 1916, in San Francisco, California. She always deflected questions from the press about her biography, claiming that it did not matter with regard to her work, and usually claimed that she had been born in 1919 so as to appear younger than her husband, curiously an important point of social conformity in mid-century America. After her family moved to New York, she attended the University of Rochester but completed her degree, and met her husband, Stanley Edgar Hyman, at Syracuse University. Jackson kept her maiden name after marrying in 1940, flouting the name-change convention because she was already a published author. Hyman became an important literary theorist and a professor at Bennington College, in Vermont, where the couple moved.

Within the family, Jackson bore the responsibility of staying at home to raise the children, despite carrying on with an ever-more successful writing career that eclipsed her husband's in importance and income. She published several

novels, dozens of short stories, a play, and various works for children and young adults during the 1950s and was generally considered to be in the first rank of young American writers during her lifetime. Perhaps her best known work is the short story "The Lottery," first published in the *New Yorker* in 1948, which explores the everyday brutality of life through a disturbing small-town ritual. *The Haunting of Hill House*, Jackson's revival of the gothic haunted house story, is her most popular novel. These two stories are unusual for Jackson in dealing with fantastic themes; nevertheless, their popularity, perhaps especially through their film adaptation, eventually led to her being stereotyped as a horror writer of little literary importance. Since about 2000, however, her reputation among scholars has been revived. Several collections of her short stories, including *Just an Ordinary Day*, *The Lottery and Other Stories*, and *Shirley Jackson: Collected Short Stories*, have been published posthumously.

Jackson died on August 8, 1965, at her home in Bennington. She had undergone a mental decline for some time, and it was undoubtedly her mental state that brought about her death, whether the immediate cause was her obesity, her chain-smoking, or her abuse of prescription medications.

PLOT SUMMARY

Chapter 1

The anonymous third-person narrative voice that tells the story begins to lay out the elements of the plot almost at the very beginning of the novel, in a highly expository fashion. The pseudoscientist John Montague "had been looking for an honestly haunted house all his life," and, believing he has found one in Hill House, sets out to study it, inspired by the work of the Society for Psychical Research of a half century before. He searches his newspaper file of old reports of psychic phenomena among people who had witnessed unusual events, on the supposition that something about their nature contributes to observing such events. He finds two such people, Eleanor Vance and an artist who goes by the single name of Theodora. When Montague rents the house for the summer, Mrs. Sanderson, who owns it, insists that her

MEDIA ADAPTATIONS

- In 1963, Nelson Gidding adapted *The Haunting of Hill House* into a screenplay for a film titled *The Haunting*, starring Julie Harris, Claire Bloom, and Richard Johnson and directed by Robert Wise. It was released on DVD in 2003 by Warner Home Video.

- In 1999, *The Haunting* was released by Dream-Works, directed by Jan de Bont, crediting Jackson's novel as its source but with little real connection to the original story. It is available in DVD format.

nephew Luke stay there during the investigation to represent her interests.

Eleanor, who spent eleven years nursing her ill mother, who is now deceased, is eager to accept Montague's invitation as a way of escaping her unpromising domestic situation. Her drive to Hill House is an occasion for the production of wild fairy-tale fantasies on the slightest provocation. When she encounters any strangers, no matter how fleetingly, she is filled with fear and loathing. Eleanor has her last fantasy just before cresting the hill from which she can first see the house, imagining it as a castle from a gothic novel.

Chapter 2

When Eleanor reaches Hill House, she meets the Dudleys, the husband and wife caretakers of the house. She finds them menacing, and their announcement that they will not stay on the property after dark an ominous warning.

When Eleanor sees and actually enters the house, she is seized by a hysterical fear of it, nearly fainting and feeling a strong impulse to flee, which she overcomes. As she settles in, Eleanor recites to herself over and over a line from Shakespeare's *Twelfth Night:* "Journeys end in lovers meeting"; she has impossibly romantic expectations for her sojourn at Hill House. Eleanor imagines she has been swallowed by Hill House the monster and is squirming inside it. Theodora

arrives, and she and Eleanor spend an hour exploring the grounds of the house, meanwhile discovering many similarities between themselves, though it is clear that Eleanor is struggling to play a role rather than exposing her true self. It may be that Theodora is always playing a role.

Chapter 3

When the two women get back to the house around sunset, they meet Luke. He begins to flatter them shamelessly. He explains who he is—"Since we are listing our cast of characters ... my name is Luke Sanderson"—and indicates that Dr. Montague is already inside. They go in for supper. Montague makes a toast to the imminent success of his experiment. But he is forced to admit that he cannot define what success would mean (an unheard-of condition for a scientific experiment) and is reduced to admitting that he is really aiming for a sensationalistic book.

After dinner, Montague begins to outline his idea that Hill House, or any haunted house, is not really haunted by spirits but somehow acquires a character, whether from its inhabitants or from some other source. This manifests itself in an energy that affects future inhabitants. Eleanor revisits a stone-related incident from her childhood, insisting that all that happened was neighbors threw stones at their house—or rather, insist that her mother told the story that way. Finally, Montague tells the full story of Hill House. It was built only a few years after the Civil War by Hugh Crain. His wife died in a carriage crash coming up the drive of the house for the first time. A second wife died in a fall. The house was inherited by one of Crain's daughters, who died of pneumonia in the house; seemingly, the village girl hired to look after her neglected her and let her die. Nevertheless, the house was passed to this companion, and she eventually killed herself there. The companion's cousins, the Sandersons, inherited the house but could not bear to move in, and no renter has ever stayed more than a few days in the house. Montague believes that the sadness of those who died in the house is somehow transferred to the structure and then to any new inhabitants.

Chapter 4

After breakfast, Montague and the others start to explore the house. Montague explains that there are no right angles or other regular architectural features, giving the house a labyrinthine quality. He suggests that the original designer, Crain, intended to create something like the Winchester

House, which is famously full of false doors and stairs that lead nowhere because its builder and owner, Sarah Winchester, believed that such arrangements would fool and confuse the spirits she imagined to follow her around the house. The touring party find a cold spot in the nursery; this is a mainstay of parapsychological lore, supposedly a small space within a room where the temperature is much lower than in the surroundings. The others only notice this cold spot after Montague, the expert in such matters, points it out to them.

That evening, Eleanor wakes up and is called into Theodora's room through their shared bathroom. They hear someone knocking on each of the doors in the hallway and finally, quite thunderously, on Theodora's door. Later, they hear laughter, and then, after a while, Luke and Montague arrive. Montague claims that he saw a dog, or an animal like a dog, running through the halls, and that he and Luke followed it outside but lost track of it. The two men claim not to have heard any knocking. The four of them conclude that this was some kind of supernatural occurrence. Eleanor and Theodora do not consider other possibilities.

Chapter 5

At breakfast the next morning, Montague is quick to liken whatever happened last night to events in famous haunted houses: Ballechin House, Borley Rectory, and Glamis Castle. Montague tells the others that, no matter what they experience, there is unlikely to be a threat of physical, rather than psychological, damage. The three other guests, as usual by now, discuss their situation allegorically, through references to fairy tales and children's games.

After breakfast, they find chalk writing in the hallway: "help Eleanor come home." Eleanor immediately comments, "It's *crazy*." Montague, having finally found, as he presents it, physical evidence of the supernatural, proceeds to erase it. Eleanor suggests that one of the others wrote it, but they all deny it, and Montague points out that none of them could have written it, although this is far from demonstrable.

During the rest of the day, Montague reexamines the cold spot but is unable to register any change inside of it on a thermometer. He also announces that his wife will be joining them on Saturday, in two days. In the afternoon, they discover the same message as in the chalk writing scrawled now in Theodora's room, but in a substance described as red paint or blood, and the same is smeared all over Theodora's clothes. Theodora has remained in Eleanor's room after the haunting of the previous night, and now announces she will have to remain there because her own room has been defiled.

During the after-dinner conversation, Eleanor constantly thinks of how much she now hates, and is disgusted by, Theodora. She reveals that she has an obsessive fear of her personality dissolving in some other larger identity. That night—in what the narrative presents as reality but is most likely a dream—Eleanor hears disturbing noises from Theodora's former room. She holds Theodora's hand, and the room is dark. But then (at the moment when she seems to awaken), Eleanor realizes that she is not holding the other woman's hand and that the room's light is on, as they left it when they went to bed.

Chapter 6

The visitors find a scrapbook that Crain, the builder of Hill House, made for his daughter. It is composed of paraphrases from the Bible and cut-out pictures and his own drawings of hell and heaven and sin—as calculated to frighten her into maintaining her sexual purity (and indeed, she died a spinster). Later, when Eleanor and Theodora are walking the grounds, Theodora comments on the fact that Luke is working on seducing the other woman, which Eleanor seems to be unaware of. After that, the sexual tension seems, to Eleanor at least, to reach a height where the two women are going to blurt out that each loves the other. Then Eleanor has a vision of a ghostly children's picnic. Theodora, in turn, sees something (the reader is never told what) and starts to scream and run back to the house, closely followed by Eleanor. The fact that whatever Theodora saw, she saw while looking back, is emphasized over and over.

Chapter 7

Mrs. Montague arrives, driven by Arthur Parker. She is a spirit medium and begins to use automatic writing—a technique by which a medium allows a spirit to communicate through her in writing—to tell a story (typical of gothic literature) set in a medieval monastery, involving a nun bricked up alive inside a wall. Mrs. Montague takes this to reflect the history of Hill House, built in the 1870s, probably in the New England region. The automatic writing also reproduces the message to Eleanor that was twice written on the walls, which, of course, Mrs. Montague knew of.

Later that night, Luke, Eleanor, and Theodora all stay in Montague's room. There is a repetition of the knocking from a few nights ago; Parker is known to be patrolling around the house throughout the night. This leads to a description of weird sensory disconnects from reality, surreal changes of light and perspective, described from Eleanor's viewpoint, so that it is clear she is becoming detached from reality—to the point that it is no longer entirely accurate to talk about the narrative as a description of objective events, even within the fictional framework of the novel. "Hill House went dancing," as Theodora describes it.

Chapter 8

The next morning, Mrs. Montague and Arthur, who slept downstairs, say that they experienced nothing extraordinary during the night. The narrator's revelations of Eleanor's thoughts show that she is rapidly deteriorating, starting to be unable to perceive the difference between herself and the house. Later, Eleanor tells Theodora that after they leave Hill House, she wants to go home with her, because she's never had anyone to care about before (an admission that she has resented rather than cared about her mother). Theodora outright rejects any such idea. The other characters start to say to Eleanor the same things that she has only said to herself before, demonstrating that she is losing her grip on the difference between interior and external reality. When Eleanor, Theodora, and Luke walk through the grounds, Eleanor—oblivious to what Theodora has told her—goes right on planning to herself how she will move to live with Theodora, something she has earned because her past suffering with her mother gives her the right to happiness now. Yet Eleanor hears the other two plotting against her and mocking her (precisely the way she has supposedly heard ghosts before), and what she hears gradually becomes the house telling her to stay. Eleanor spends the rest of the day spying on the others, and that night, when they all gather after dinner, she again experiences hallucinations, whereby she can perceive what is going on in every part of Hill House, just as one might feel what is happening to the parts of one's own body.

Chapter 9

That night, Eleanor wanders through the house, talking to it, calling it "Mother," and hearing its answers. She stops to knock on Mrs. Montague's door, and she is mistaken for a ghost. When the others notice she is not in her bed, they go as a group to look for her, but Eleanor evades them; she begins to speak of herself in her own mind in the first-person plural, believing that she and the house are becoming a single entity. They finally find her on a precarious staircase in the library, and Luke is able to help her down, after which she seems to return to a more normal way of thinking.

Montague, believing that the house has somehow possessed Eleanor, decides that she has to go away for her own safety. But Eleanor insists that she wants to stay—wants to become the nun bricked up in the wall. Nevertheless, they put Eleanor in her car to drive away. Instead, she decides, as she imagines, to stay with the house by running her car into a tree and killing herself on the grounds. As she heads for the tree, she thinks, "I am really doing it, I am doing this all by myself, now, at last; this is me, I am really really really doing it by myself"—and then an instant after it is too late, "Why am I doing this? Why don't they stop me?"

CHARACTERS

Carrie

Carrie is Eleanor's sister. Her passive-aggressive efforts to prevent Eleanor from using her own car to drive to Hill House set the tone for understanding Eleanor's earlier life. Carrie is aided in this by her unnamed husband.

Mr. Dudley

Dudley is the caretaker of Hill House and serves mostly for comic relief. He also serves the purpose of foreshadowing by suggesting to Eleanor when she arrives at the gate of the house grounds that she would be better off driving away and never coming back.

Mrs. Dudley

The wife of Dudley, the caretaker, acts, at least part-time, as the housekeeper and cook at Hill House. She also functions as comic relief. She goes through precisely the same script about her duties when each guest arrives, while the guests talk around her, ignoring her, among themselves. The narrative effect is reminiscent of set pieces in opera where the singers' lines intersect musically but not logically, melding different conversations together.

Hill House

The house itself is one of the most important characters in the novel. It is an isolated estate in the country and is eighty years old. It has a bizarre, labyrinthine floor plan. In the manuscript of the novel, Jackson made a sketch of the house that is a caricature of a human being, so she indeed conceived of it as a humanlike character. This becomes clear from the first description of the house given in the novel:

> No human eye can isolate the unhappy coincidence of line and place which suggests evil in the face of a house, and yet somehow a maniac juxtaposition, a badly turned angle, some chance meeting of roof and sky, turned Hill House into a place of despair, more frightening because the face of Hill House seemed awake, with a watchfulness from the blank windows and a touch of glee in the eyebrow of a cornice.

Beginning in Chapter 2, the house is specifically identified with Eleanor's mother, through the image of Eleanor squirming inside the house, which inevitably suggests a baby kicking in the womb. The house is accordingly also a double of Eleanor, figuring her ego ideal, the part of her personality that bears the image of her mother. One way of thinking of the plot of the book is as Eleanor being brought into line with this particular part of herself. She increasingly leaves reality to identify with the house. Her thought processes become warped and distorted, like the bizarre layout of the house. By the end of the novel, she kills herself to punish herself for what she sees as her betrayal of her mother. Eleanor's attempt to leave the house is an enactment of her abandonment of her mother, but this time her internalized mother is able to punish her for it.

Just as Eleanor has difficulty differentiating between the processes of gestation and digestion, she and also Theodora, her human double, fear that the house/mother is trying to eat them: "The sense was that it wanted to consume us, take us into itself, make us a part of the house, maybe."

Dr. John Montague

Montague is the prime mover in initiating the plot of *The Haunting of Hill House*. He purports to be a scientist, investigating haunted houses, but this rather leaves him in the position of being a pseudoscientist. He seems to have obtained a Ph.D. in anthropology almost as a cover for his real activities. The narrative voice of the novel exposes him to the reader on the first page: "He was scrupulous about the use of his title because, his investigations being so utterly unscientific, he hoped to borrow an air of respectability, even scholarly authority, from his education." He objects, though ineffectually, to his wife's mediumship because its highly traditional and spiritual character works against the scientific veneer he tries to place over his psychical researches. Early in the novel, after the first knocking incident, the reader may conceive that Montague was knocking and fabricated the story about chasing the dog, with Luke simply going along with the story. One could see this manipulation of the two women as part of Montague's experiment. In Chapter 5, Montague's comparison of the events there with those of other haunted houses expose his hope and belief that his publication about Hill House will create a new famous haunted house.

Mrs. Montague

Mrs. Montague arrives at Hill House on Saturday, the sixth day of the experiment, as chauffeured by Arthur Parker. She is malignantly narcissistic and, aiming to dominate everyone around her, turns every interaction, every bit of conversation, into a power struggle. This renders her a ridiculous comic figure. Figuratively speaking, she has her husband thoroughly beaten into submission. She is also a spirit medium.

Arthur Parker

Parker, the headmaster of a private boys' school, drives Mrs. Montague to Hill House. Their relationship is based around the fact that she likes to dominate and he likes to be dominated. He assists her in her mediumistic activities.

Luke Sanderson

Luke is the nephew and heir of Mrs. Sanderson, who owns Hill House. His aunt insists that he stay at Hill House during the summer to keep an eye on the property. An attractive and outwardly-seeming personable young man, Luke bides his time waiting for his aunt's death and his inheritance by stealing petty cash from her and cheating at cards. His aunt sends him off to Hill House as much to keep him out of mischief as for any other reason. When he meets Eleanor and Theodora, he flatters them and also pretends to take them as ghosts, adding, "These being dead . . . then dead must I be." At first glance, this sounds like another Shakespeare quote, but it is a pastiche, signifying Luke's essential falseness. He is also a poor martini maker. He, alone of all the characters, undergoes a sort of redemption at the end of the novel when he risks his own safety to rescue Eleanor from the staircase in the library. But this, too, may be meant as satire.

Mrs. Sanderson

Mrs. Sanderson owns Hill House. She never enters directly into the story, but she insists that her nephew stay in the house to keep an eye on Montague's party, and at the end of the story, she expresses relief that the rental period passed without mishap to the house, ignoring Eleanor's death.

Theodora

Theodora, a professional, but not especially successful, artist, was chosen to participate in the Hill House summer because she once scored exceptionally well in a test of ESP mental powers based on guessing cards. She generally only uses her first name, and the reader never learns her last name. But Jackson revealed in her marginal notes on the manuscript of her novel (now housed in the National Archives in Washington, as reported by Darryl Hattenhauer in *Shirley Jackson's American Gothic*) that her name was to be Vane. She is, in many senses, a double of Eleanor. At one point, when they have to share a room and Eleanor's clothes, Eleanor calls her a twin. Eleanor, in turn, borrows Theodora's clothes and clearly wants to join together with her. Eleanor's self is fractured and longs to rejoin its different parts, but Theodora rejects her (in contrast to the house, which accepts her). Theodora's fleeing from whatever she sees in Chapter 6 recalls Lot's wife in the biblical book of Genesis (19:26), who was destroyed when she looked back at Sodom. This would suggest that the scene is symbolic, that the horror Theodora runs from is the possibility of feeling homosexual desire. Theodora functions as a representation of Eleanor's id, her desire for freedom and pleasure that she has never been able to exercise.

Eleanor Vance

Eleanor, the main character of *The Haunting of Hill House* is one of the subjects chosen by Montague to participate in his Hill House experiment in light of a report in an old newspaper article describing a mysterious fall of rocks from the sky on her house when she was twelve years old. Eleanor is now thirty-two years old and has spent her whole adult life nursing her mother

through a long physical and mental decline. Thus, she never attended college, has never worked outside of the house, and has not married or had children of her own: "She could not remember ever being truly happy in her adult life." Her mother has recently died. She is anxious to accept Montague's offer because it fits in with her own increasingly grandiose fantasies of her own importance that are part of her paranoia. She believes that she is somehow fated for great things as compensation for what she gave up for her mother, and that Montague's experiment will lead to some success at every level, including, irrationally, romance and adventure. As her expectations become more and more inflated, she also increasingly believes, throughout the book, that she is being persecuted by everyone around her.

Having lived her whole adult life essentially as her mother's servant, Eleanor's personality is stunted. On the one hand, she is afraid to engage with others because she is "afraid of being ineffectual," while, on the other, she constantly engages in fantasies of a very childish type. The narrative voice frequently describes her speech and affect as inadequate or comically insufficient. Montague's invitation appeals to her precisely because it is ridiculous and fantastic. She constantly reinterprets real events in unreal, self-serving ways. Once everyone has arrived at Hill House, Montague takes them aside to have a drink and become acquainted, but in her own imagination, she is undergoing a transformation into a new way of life, and she recasts the people with whom she has only the slightest acquaintance and who, at best, are her coworkers accordingly. She thinks of herself as "an Eleanor, she told herself triumphantly, who belongs, who is talking easily, who is sitting by the fire with her friends." She imagines that coming to Hill House is going to somehow give her the life that she never had.

As soon as she wakes up on her first morning in Hill House, she thinks that, the previous night, all the others were mocking her. Solipsism, the belief that nothing perceived in the real world can be verified as real rather than a dream or delusion, is often a sign of mental illness; Eleanor suggests that she has solipsistic tendencies in regard to distinguishing between the perceived reality of her companions versus the perceived reality of the supposed apparitions of the second night in Hill House: "I could say ... 'All three of you are in my imagination; none of this is real.'" Significantly, this points to the convergence of Eleanor's imagination and the narrative of the novel.

In the reality that Eleanor experienced with her mother, she was never able to form a mature identity and constantly felt under threat of being absorbed or consumed by her mother—in other words, of falling back into an infantile state prior to the differentiation of a fully formed personality. After her mother's death, she both obsessively fears such a collapse and, at the same time, desires it. After her mother dies, she comes to see Hill House as the entity threatening to consume her. The chalk message—"help Eleanor come home"—relates, in the larger plot of the novel, to Eleanor's identification of the house with her mother and her failure to help her mother at the moment of her death, things that none of the others know about, so the logical conclusion is that Eleanor wrote the text. In that case, Eleanor's statement is her admission of her own deteriorating mental condition. She kills herself either to succumb to the threat of being consumed by the house or else to relieve the unbearable anxiety of simultaneously fearing and desiring being engulfed and obliterated: "I could stand ... it if I could only surrender."

Waitress
When Eleanor reaches Hillsdale, the nearest town to Hill House, she stops at the café. The waitress there sees Eleanor in her desperation and hopelessness; but Eleanor seems to identify the waitress with her own past life, believing that she is now on a momentous adventure.

THEMES

The Supernatural
Montague found Eleanor as a subject for his experiment from an account of a supposedly supernatural event in an old newspaper article. The reader is never shown the article but is given a version of events from Eleanor's perspective:

> One day, when she was twelve years old ... showers of stones had fallen on their house, without any warning or any indication of purpose or reason, dropping from the ceilings, rolling loudly down the walls, breaking windows and pattering maddeningly on the roof. The stones continued intermittently for three days, during which time

TOPICS FOR FURTHER STUDY

- Elements of Japanese folk traditions about ghosts are frequently incorporated into modern manga (comics or print cartoons) like *Kekkaishi* and *The Record of a Fallen Vampire* and in anime like *PomPoko* (1994). Follow this lead and design a scene of *The Haunting of Hill House* in manga form using a sketch pad or a digital cartoon creator program.

- Beginning with keywords drawn from the text of *The Haunting of Hill House*, such as spirit medium, Society for Psychical Research, ectoplasm, and planchette, use the Internet to research the history of spiritualism. Then write a paper situating the novel's themes in relationship to that movement.

- Read either *Burnt Offerings* (1973), by Robert Marasco, or *The Shining* (1977), by Stephen King. Write an essay comparing the themes and style of the novel you choose with *The Haunting of Hill House*

- Watch the two film adaptations of *The Haunting of Hill House* and give a multimedia presentation comparing them to the novel, illustrating your points with clips from the films and excerpts from the novel.

- Rewrite a scene from *The Haunting of Hill House* describing events as they would have been recorded by a film crew, filming events from every relevant angle and location.

- Write a research paper describing Eleanor's character and its degeneration from the point of view of the psychological understanding of schizophrenia.

- Choose one of Shirley Jackson's stories that were written for children or young adults, such as *9 Magic Wishes* or *Charles*. Write a review of the short story that evaluates Jackson's strengths and weaknesses as a writer for both adults and children.

Eleanor and her sister were less unnerved by the stones than by the neighbors and sightseers who gathered daily outside the front door.

This is not Jackson's invention but something she found through research. In the early twentieth century, the writer Charles Fort became obsessed with reports of seemingly miraculous events that he believed really happened yet were ignored by the scientific establishment. He documented these in a series of books, of which the earliest was *The Book of the Damned* in 1919. Fort accepted that any story printed in a newspaper was true, and reports many "instances of stones that have been thrown, or that have fallen, upon a small area, from an unseen and undetectable source." He quotes a story from the London *Times* on April 27, 1872:

> From 4 o'clock, Thursday afternoon, until half past eleven, Thursday night, the houses, 56 and 58 Reverdy Road, Bermondsey, were assailed with stones and other missiles coming from an unseen quarter. Two children were injured, every window broken, and several articles of furniture were destroyed. Although there was a strong body of policemen scattered in the neighborhood, they could not trace the direction whence the stones were thrown.

So that no one could think that this was a case of a vandal hiding in woods or other cover and throwing stones, Fort assures the reader that "the direction could not be traced because it never occurred to any one to look upward." He was convinced beforehand that the stones fell from the sky, so for him that was the most, indeed, the only, logical explanation of the news report.

Reading the story as Fort did, it is quite close to Jackson's fiction, and this very text could well have been her inspiration; certainly the general idea of showers of stone from the sky that Fort insisted upon was what Jackson had in mind. The popularity of Fort and his ideas has grown progressively throughout the last century and is now supported by a national magazine, the *Fortean Times*, and an endless number of television shows expounding his ideas or others like them.

Gothicism

The gothic style, especially in novels, arose in the late eighteenth century in reaction to the prevailing style of neoclassicism. In neoclassicism, beauty and life were idealized as ordered and rational; the model to be emulated was the philosophical and aesthetic clarity of classical Athens. The gothic took precisely the opposite tack, featuring interest in the irrational, the cultivation of intense emotion, magic, superstition, and the Middle Ages (hence, *gothic*, after the Goths, Germanic tribes that had destroyed the Western Roman Empire). Although the novel is the typical gothic medium, gothic style can be found in the work of the romantic poets (as in John Keats's "The Eve of St. Agnes"), in art (as with Henry Fuseli), and in architecture that imitates medieval styles and even artificial ruins (like Horace Walpole's villa Strawberry Hill). The gothic style also influenced American writers like Edgar Allan Poe and Nathaniel Hawthorne. Critics of the time classified neoclassicism as enlightened, beautiful, intellectual, literary, and masculine, while the gothic was benighted, grotesque, ignorant, popular, and feminine. Gothic novels take place in decaying castles in dark forests, concern the fate of female protagonists who are constantly threatened, and involve forces of both emotion and the supernatural that are beyond human control. The villain is typically a wizard, or a Catholic priest (the gothic being largely a Protestant phenomenon), from whom the heroine is to be rescued by a dark and brooding Byronic antihero who is hardly less threatening than the villain, even if he is simultaneously attractive. Characters meet their doubles, work out ancient ancestral curses, and encounter demons, ghosts, and vampires.

Never entirely respectable in the eyes of the cultural establishment, the gothic declined throughout the nineteenth and twentieth centuries. In the 1950s, it barely existed above the level of self-parody in Hollywood monster movies and the figure of the mad scientist. But Jackson revitalized this moribund genre with *The Haunting of Hill House*. She used the fact that it was subversive of the predominant culture, particularly in that it celebrated the feminine, to criticize and undermine that culture. Jackson begins (as well as ends) her novel with a powerful evocation of the gothic:

> No live organism can continue for long to exist sanely under conditions of absolute reality; even larks and katydids are supposed, by some, to dream. Hill House, not sane, stood by itself against its hills, holding darkness within; it had stood so for eighty years and might stand for eighty more. Within, walls continued upright, bricks met neatly, floors were firm, and doors were sensibly shut; silence lay steadily against the wood and stone of Hill House, and whatever walked there, walked alone.

This passage also contains the seeds of satire. Gothic piles are meant to be crumbling ruins; Hill House is sensible and well-kept. It is disorder that is supposed to be associated with insanity, but here it is a well-ordered (if uniquely designed) house that will eventually drive Eleanor mad. This begins

Old abandoned haunted mansion *(stephanie Connell | Shutterstock.com)*

to suggest a feminist argument that the overly structured and limited role of women as housewives in 1950s American culture was unhealthy.

But the main object of satire throughout the novel is the gothic itself. The mad scientist is reduced to a simple pseudoscientist. Lesbianism, so threatening in gothic works like Samuel Taylor Coleridge's *Christabel* (1816), is reduced to a vulgar joke. Eleanor perceives Theodora as her double—indeed, she eventually can no longer tell herself apart from Theodora—but the theme is reduced to wish fulfillment. As unappealing as Theodora is as a character, Eleanor's life has been so hollowed out that the other woman seems an attractive ideal. Above all, the theme of the supernatural is reduced to madness. The modern world cannot tolerate a real eruption of the irrational in physical form. This particular reduction is what made the revival of gothic literature spurred by Jackson possible. Even a novel like Stephen King's *The Shining*, in which supernatural elements are accepted within the plot, is essentially a study in psychological breakdown. Jackson states this quite explicitly within the novel: "The menace of the supernatural is that it attacks where modern minds are weakest, where we have abandoned our protective armor of

superstition and have no substitute defense." She seems to refer to the unconscious mind. In earlier ages, perhaps Jackson thought, routine everyday religious practices occupied deep human instincts of fear and self-destructiveness, but as such practices are increasingly abandoned, there is a new propensity toward madness. Given the turn Jackson's own life was taking as and after she wrote *The Haunting of Hill House*, this conclusion may well have been the result of introspection.

STYLE

Unreliable Narrator

The Haunting of Hill House is told by a third-person narrator, one who quickly and decidedly identifies herself with the main character, Eleanor Vance. The reader may be inclined to accept the narrative voice of the novel as presenting the truth. As such, if seemingly impossible supernatural events occur within the narrative, the initial reaction is to accept them as true within the narrative through the willing suspension of disbelief—to accept the reality of the supernatural as a premise of the story. But a slightly more nuanced reading suggests another interpretation. For instance, Eleanor maintains that she feels guilt over the death of her mother, because she slept through her mother's knocking on the wall between their bedrooms for help. But if Eleanor heard the knocking, then she was not asleep, while if she was asleep she would not have heard the knocking, so Eleanor's statement is obviously false, something that she made up and on whose truth the reader cannot rely. Indeed, the reader may be forgiven for speculating that she is lying, perhaps even to herself, to cover up an entirely possible scenario: that she was awake and heard her mother knocking and purposefully did nothing, in the hope her mother would die, and thereafter pretended, even to herself, that she had slept through it. In view of this ambiguity, nothing that Eleanor says or perceives can be simply accepted as true. Given the evident signs of Eleanor's mental illness, such as depression, grandiosity, and fears of persecution, the reader is within one's rights to suspect that all of the supposed supernatural phenomena that depend upon Eleanor's observation are rather delusions and symptoms of her mental illness.

Foreshadowing

Foreshadowing occurs when the author inserts some piece of information that gives a clue about what will happen later in the text. Most likely the foreshadowing will be recognized after the fact and help to give the whole text a greater sense of cohesion and meaning in the reader's memory. Jackson uses foreshadowing frequently through *The Haunting of Hill House* as when Eleanor, driving to the house, passes a dilapidated billboard on which she can scarcely make out two words:

> Dare, one of them read, and another, evil, and she laughed at herself, perceiving how she sought out omens everywhere; the word is daredevil, Eleanor, daredevil drivers, and she slowed her car because she was driving too fast and might reach Hill House too soon.

This passage suggests her grandiosity, that she imagines that she is to become some kind of spiritual champion to 'dare evil,' but it more particularly foreshadows her later suicide by driving into a tree on the Hill House property. The same event is foreshadowed in Montague's introductory speech at Hill House, when he mentions a previous guest of the house who was killed when he was attempting to leave and his horse smashed him against the same tree Eleanor later runs into.

HISTORICAL CONTEXT

Feminism

Jackson's short story "The Lottery" concerns a village that each year picks out a villager at random to be stoned to death by the other villagers. No one ever doubted that the story is allegorical in intent—that it makes a point about the real world through a fable or myth—but the precise meaning of the allegory is not so obvious. Jackson generally did not give interviews or expend much ink explaining her stories. Judy Oppenheimer reports that in *Private Demons: The Life of Shirley Jackson*, how the author mentioned to a reporter who asked about the meaning of "The Lottery" that the story had been banned in South Africa, since there, at least, they understood it. At that time, South Africa officially maintained the apartheid system of racist oppression of the black majority of the country by the minority white population. Jackson surely meant not that "The Lottery" is about racism per se but rather that it is about the many traditional structures in society that are destructive of human freedom and accomplishment.

It is plausible to read *The Haunting of Hill House* as a similar allegory. The main character, Eleanor, had the prospects of her youth for either an education or marriage destroyed in her being forced to become a nurse to her ailing mother. In the course of the story, she is seduced, possessed, driven mad, or at any rate destroyed, as it seems, by Hill House. She becomes part of the house itself. It is not hard to read this as an allegory of the fate of the American housewife in the 1950s, stifled by social convention and powerful new forces, such as mass-market advertising, that tried to ensure that housewives' lives were devoted to their household duties and that they were not enabled to acquire any outside professional or personal identities. Jackson, whose work as a professional writer had to be balanced with the full-time work of a housewife, must have felt this limitation keenly. But she was hardly alone, as the revolt against housewifery became the center-piece of the feminist movement in the 1960s, as led by Betty Friedan's *The Feminine Mystique*. Friedan, too, conceived of the lives of women unable to work outside the home as tending toward mental breakdown.

There are very strong connections between Jackson's novel and Charlotte Gilman's "The Yellow Wallpaper," a nineteenth-century protofeminist

COMPARE & CONTRAST

- **1950s:** Research is commonly conducted into so-called parapsychological phenomena with little prior plausibility, with the results often sensationally reported in the media.

  Today: Parapsychology is still a common subject of investigation despite a complete lack of evidence supporting such phenomena, and the media pays more attention to it than ever, with several cable television networks and innumerable Web sites devoted to ghost hunting and similar subjects. While a history of parapsychology is lacking, a place to start looking at its chronological development is *An Encyclopedia of Claims, Frauds, and Hoaxes of the Occult and Supernatural* by James Randi.

- **1950s:** Women have little economic or social independence, as will be detailed in Betty Friedan's 1963 tome *The Feminine Mystique.*

  Today: Women nominally have the same social and economic opportunities as men, although a pay discrepancy for equal work still exists, and women are less often promoted to positions of high authority in private industry.

- **1950s:** Although small-town America has been declining for fifty years because of changes in the industrial economy, the hopelessness and dread experienced in Hillsdale are taken as exceptional side effects of the evil in Hill House.

  Today: While some small towns have found new identities based on tourism or high-tech industries, many small towns are plagued by crime and drug addiction as a result of economic failure, as described in Nick Reding's 2009 book *Methland: The Death and Life of an American Small Town.*

---

story. Therein, an aristocratic woman is taken to an old mansion in the country for a summer vacation to be locked in the attic, supposedly to cure her of hysteria—essentially, the disease of being of the female gender—but effectively cutting her off from any meaningful self-expression or occupation, even the management of her own house, as her freedom and identity are completely subordinated to her husband, for her own good, of course. She is eventually absorbed into a hallucinatory world within her attic's yellow wallpaper and driven mad, killing her own husband. This story also takes the outward form of a gothic ghost story and may conceivably have served as a model for Jackson's novel.

Psychic Research

Theodora was chosen by Montague because

> she had somehow been able, amused and excited over her own incredible skill, to identify correctly eighteen cards out of twenty, fifteen cards out of twenty, nineteen cards out of twenty, held up by an assistant out of sight and hearing.

This refers to testing for extra-sensory perception, or ESP, with the cards designed for the purpose in the 1930s by Karl Zener and used in experiments in collaboration with J. B. Rhine. The deck of twenty-five cards would have five each bearing the symbols of a circle, a square, a cross, a star, or three wavy lines. The idea of the experiment was to give a more scientific veneer to the spiritual medium—supposedly a person with some natural gift to be able to communicate with spirits, foretell the future, and the like. For this experiment, spirits were dispensed with, in favor of the intended detection of some uncanny ability natural to the person. A test consists of running through a deck of the cards and having the subject guess which symbol is on the next card to be exposed. A score higher than chance (roughly one in five) was interpreted as showing that the subject possessed ESP.

But from a scientific viewpoint, such a conclusion is putting the cart before the horse, so to speak, since a phenomenon would first have to

Face of terror (*Poprugin Aleksey | Shutterstock.com*)

be observed before it could be explained, and ESP is in any case a label rather than an explanation. Just as in the case of spiritualism, an explanation is given, and then evidence is sought to justify it—the opposite of the scientific method. Rhine's original experiments could not detect any difference between, for instance, being able to tell the future (which card would come up next) or telepathy, since the experimenter knew the order of the cards. It also did nothing to control trickery on the part of the experimental subjects. For instance, the first cards that were used for many months of experiments were so thin that the symbol could be seen through the back. The experimenters failed to take into account "card-counting" (commonly used by blackjack players in casinos), or remembering which cards have been seen so as to narrow the choice of which cards could come next. When it was discovered that a subject, like the fictional Theodora, who had a few statistical outliers in card guessing would soon have many more results closer to the statistical average, this

was interpreted not as suggesting that the original high scores were mere accidents that would regress to the mean over time but as evidence that the psychic power supposedly at work became bored and ceased to function. These aspects of the experimenters' approach hopelessly muddled the evidence and made it impossible to ever disprove their theories, violating the scientific principle of falsifiability. Clearly, Jackson had researched Rhine's experiments and had them in mind for the background of Theodora's character. A narcissist like Theodora would be particularly adept at and interested in gaming the system to achieve a result far beyond chance, in order, as she admits, to inflate her own ego.

CRITICAL OVERVIEW

During her lifetime, Jackson was usually considered at the forefront of American writers of her generation, rated with the likes of Bernard Malamud and

Eudora Welty. As late as 1968, her work was included in the anthology *The American Experience: Fiction* (a standard college textbook), alongside the first rank of American authors from Poe to Steinbeck. But for the following generation, her work was dismissed as belonging to simple genres, either the Erma Bombeck type of amusing family stories or the moribund gothic. Recently, Jackson's reputation has benefited from a reevaluation of the gothic as a precursor of the postmodern style. Jackson's work was appraised on this premise in 2003 in Darryl Hattenhauer's *Shirley Jackson's American Gothic*, which generally rehabilitated her within the critical establishment. This new tendency is confirmed in Angela Hague's 2005 essay in *Frontiers*. Jackson's work—and *The Haunting of Hill House* is foremost in this—is now seen as exploiting gothic conventions in the direction of postmodernism. The fantastic element in the gothic becomes a destabilized, irrational world, or, more particularly, a destabilized, irrational character who functions as an unreliable narrator, presenting a world that is fantastic in its idiosyncrasy, highlighting the impossibility of true communication between individual and collective experience. Nevertheless, Jackson's work has had an undeniable influence on genre horror fiction, helping move it in a postmodernist direction. The supreme genre author Stephen King, in his *Danse Macabre*, praises Jackson's novel as perhaps the finest horror story of the second half of the twentieth century and charts its influence on his own work, particularly in the psychologization of horror.

One of Jackson's updating of gothic convention is the reinterpretation of the classic double as a whole character presented as two halves, or two variants, as with Eleanor and Theodora in *The Haunting of Hill House*. It was observed in Jackson's own lifetime that the creation of such characters resulted in apparent lesbian attractions, an implication Jackson herself strongly rejected. Yet there can be little doubt that Eleanor sees at least the possibility of an affair with Theodora, even if Theodora rejects her (not out of the unconventionality of such a relationship in the 1950s but out of personal distaste). This theme is the subject of Colin Haines's 2007 volume *"Frightened by a Word": Shirley Jackson and Lesbian Gothic*, the principal monograph to so far take up the new evaluation of Jackson's work.

CRITICISM

Bradley A. Skeen

Skeen is a classicist. In the following essay, he situates The Haunting of Hill House *within the history of spiritualist literature.*

The earliest human beings lived in small, closely related family groups. Group cohesion—people helping each other—was the most important factor in human survival. Such bands were led by the most senior family members, not only because of the natural dynamics that exist between parents and children but because memories of the old were the only repositories of wisdom and experience. When a member of a band died, he did not cease to be a member of the band; rituals were carried out in his honor. As early as one hundred thousand years ago, burials by *Homo sapiens* and even *Homo neanderthalensis* were accompanied by ritual. The dead were buried with the tools they had used in life (as if, perhaps, they would still need them) and with markers of ritual action such as flowers. By the time human beings were living in permanent settlements during the Neolithic Age, ten thousand years ago, the dead were typically buried in the houses of their families or in nearby cemeteries. Respect for dead ancestors was shown through rituals periodically carried out at the grave sites. By the time written records were kept, the dead were indeed evidently conceived of as continuing to share in the life of the family or clan, periodically visiting the houses of their descendants, where food and other offerings would be set out for them. If these rituals were neglected, it was believed, the dead could take punitive action, just as could living elders who were shown disrespect. Cemeteries or abandoned houses could, if one accepted the existence of the spirits of dead ancestors, become haunted, as the spirits might take vengeance on whomever they encountered since they were no longer receiving the rituals that were their due. The idea of the haunted house occurs already in the second century BCE in the *Mostellaria* (*The Haunted House*), by the Roman playwright Plautus. But the play is a comedy: while Plautus's audience knew what a haunted house was, they also knew it was a silly superstition and could laugh at the foolish characters who believed in it. There has always been a tension in ghost stories between the possibility of accepting them as true, in light of their persuasive logic about family duty and the seeming "proof" that they offer of life after death, and the rational conclusion

WHAT DO I READ NEXT?

- Jackson's *The Witchcraft of Salem Village* (1956) offers a history of the crazed witch-hunting in colonial Salem, Massachusetts, intended for young-adult readers.
- A. B. Mitford's *Tales of Old Japan: Folklore, Fairy Tales, Ghost Stories and Legends of the Samurai* (1893) contains a collection of ghost stories and other tales of the supernatural from a Japanese folk tradition untouched by contact with the West.
- S. T. Joshi's *The Modern Weird Tale* (2001) creates a critical framework for modern horror fiction derived from Jackson's work as a revitalizer of the genre.
- *Shirley Jackson: Essays on the Literary Legacy* (2005), edited by Bernice Murphy, reprints several critical studies of Jackson's work.
- Lenemaja Friedman's *Shirley Jackson* (1975) is the earliest sustained scholarly study of Jackson's works.
- Jackson wrote a large number of short stories based on her experiences as a housewife and mother in the 1950s. They are collected in the anthologies *Life Among the Savages* (1953) and *Raising Demons* (1957).

---

that there are not and cannot be any such things as ghosts.

In the nineteenth century, ghost beliefs underwent a radical transformation. It then seemed to most rational people that there was no room left for ghosts left in a world ruled by science, and that while ghost beliefs might hang on as a peasant superstition for a few generations, the rising tide of education would sooner or later wash them away. But two teenage girls from Upstate New York, the Fox sisters, upended that expectation. As they later explained in their memoirs, they began playing a joke on their parents, making strange sounds (for example, by cracking their toes, as one cracks one's fingers, under their

> JACKSON GOES RIGHT TO THE DISPUTE BETWEEN SCIENCE AND SPIRITUALISM THAT HAS ALWAYS CHARACTERIZED THE SPIRITUALIST MOVEMENT."

---

blankets) and pretending that the sounds were being made by ghosts. This was in the 1840s, when new inventions like the telegraph made it possible for the same news story to run in papers all over the world at the same time; when, for the first time in history, most people in the West were able to read; and when there was a large audience for popular sensationalistic literature. The Fox sisters became a sensation. But a vital element of the story was that scientists investigated the case and could offer no scientific explanation for what was happening. In a world in which many people felt threatened by science, because they did not understand it and because it was rapidly changing every aspect of life in unpredictable and not necessarily beneficial ways, there was a ready audience for the idea that science could not explain everything. This was enough to spark off the new movement of spiritualism, which would be spurred by the upcoming historical coincidence of the Civil War, when suddenly hundreds of thousands of grieving parents would do anything and believe anything in hopes of establishing contact with sons who had died before their time.

Spiritualists concocted a theology out of the religious philosophy of the mystic Emmanuel Swedenborg, among other sources, which held that the dead went to dwell in a paradise called the "summerland," where they would gain enlightenment and from which they could visit the earth as ghosts, to otherwise undergo a series of reincarnations until the experience of the cumulative lives would grant them moral perfection and freedom from the earth. The ritual of the new religion was the séance, in which a medium with the special gift of communicating with the dead could act as a go-between for the dead and the living, hearing, as it might be, the words of a grieving mother, passing them on to her dead son, and then hearing and repeating the response. This was often called the spiritual telegraph, a metaphor that suggested that this was a new and exciting medium of communication, just as the telegraph was. The medium was so called because she (almost all spirit mediums have been women) acted as a substance through which communication between the earthly and spiritual world was conveyed. The main tension in spiritualist literature was always with science: spiritualists claimed that the phenomenon they had discovered was as scientific as any other new discovery, and they dared scientists and skeptics to prove them wrong. Some scientists proved unusually easy to deceive, since in their professional work they do not normally encounter purposeful fraud. Yet there was much literature written exposing spiritualism as fraudulent. Spiritualists were quick to align themselves with progressive political causes like the abolition of slavery and women's suffrage.

The Fox sisters and other mediums were not content to hold private séances but traveled the country (as well as overseas) on lecture tours, filling large theaters with paying audiences. The productions that evolved in these spirit shows will be familiar to modern Americans from viewing any performance of a stage magician, whose standard act evolved from it. The medium would perhaps perform a séance on stage for some members of the audience, perform mentalist tricks like reading sealed letters (which is relatively easily done by a magician through sleight of hand), and then have herself tied up and locked in a cabinet, as if this guaranteed that there could be no trickery in what followed. Then musical instruments and other objects might appear on the stage and seem to fly around and play themselves—as lowered from wires above the stage—which the spiritualist claimed were physical manifestations of the dead from the spiritual world that had come to the earth through a miracle. Next the medium, who had escaped her ropes and chains by the same techniques as magicians like Harry Houdini and emerged from the back of the spirit cabinet, would come onto the stage dressed in a white robe and with white make-up. The audience was supposed to accept this as a manifestation of a ghost before their eyes. A short time after departing the stage, she would make a costume change, just as any actor in a play, retie herself (perhaps with assistance), and then slip back into the cabinet, which would then be opened, in token of the "fact" that she had been tied up the whole time and could not have faked the

"miracles" the audience had seen. It is no wonder, then, that professional magicians, like Harry Houdini and James Randi, have always been the most effective debunkers of spiritualism.

In 1887, the Seybert Commission, a group of scientists employed by the University of Pennsylvania to investigate spiritualist claims, published its report finding no evidence of any unexplainable phenomena in spiritualism, but rather simple fraud. The Society for Psychical Research had been founded in Great Britain in 1882 jointly by spiritualists and skeptics to investigate spiritualism. One of the projects this society undertook was to rent Ballechin House, in Scotland, for the summer of 1899. This house was supposedly haunted (though it seems that this reputation was largely fabricated by the real-estate agents), and the idea was to observe and record any supernatural phenomena. A number of members of the society moved in, including John, Marquess of Bute (the head of the project), Ada Goodrich-Freer, and a number of spirit mediums. A large number of spiritual phenomena were observed, including spirit talking, footsteps heard where no one was walking, and the ghostly apparitions of nuns, along with communication through the Ouija board and other forms of automatic writing supposedly controlled by spirits. But these were only observed by the spirit mediums, who were, of course, paid to perceive evidence of the spirit world. The results were published later that year.

That very report on Ballechin House was Jackson's chief inspiration for *The Haunting of Hill House*, as she acknowledges on the first page of the novel:

> Dr. Montague's intentions with regard to Hill House derived from the methods of the intrepid nineteenth-century ghost hunters; he was going to go and live in Hill House and see what happened there. It was his intention, at first, to follow the example of the anonymous Lady who went to stay at Ballechin House and ran a summer-long house party for skeptics and believers.

Jackson rather brilliantly transforms the unreliable information given by the corrupted mediums in the report into the unreliable narrator Eleanor, whose descent into madness is indexed by her observation and acceptance of spiritualist phenomena.

Jackson goes right to the dispute between science and spiritualism that has always characterized the spiritualist movement. The reader of the novel is never obliged to accept the reality of any supernatural event, even within the framework of the fictional narrative. Indeed, at the very beginning of the novel, the narrator exposes Montague as a pseudoscientist who only wishes to use his scientific credentials to legitimize the entirely unscientific investigation he undertakes. A scientist would take any unusual observations made at Hill House and use them to formulate a hypothesis or provisional explanation. He would then conduct an experiment that would try to prove that hypothesis false. If several experiments failed to falsify the hypothesis, and if the original phenomenon could be repeated by himself and by other researchers, he would then formulate a theory offering the simplest and most logical explanation of the observed data. In fact, no spiritual or ghostly phenomenon has ever been observed that cannot be explained by either the limitations of human perception or conscious human fraud. But because Montague is essentially a pseudoscientist, he follows an entirely backward procedure. He begins with the theory that ghosts exist and attempts to find or interpret evidence to support it. This makes falsification, the most important element in science, impossible, since any evidence that he observes can be interpreted to fit the theory.

Source: Bradley A. Skeen, Critical Essay on *The Haunting of Hill House*, in *Novels for Students*, Gale, Cengage Learning, 2011.

Steven Jay Schneider

In the following excerpt, Schneider compares and contrasts the novel The Haunting of Hill House *with each of the two films adapted from it.*

Acclaimed American novelist and short story writer Shirley Jackson (1916–65) in 1959 published *The Haunting of Hill House*, a book that through the decades has been widely praised as one of the most frightening tales ever committed to paper. Three years later, director Robert Wise chose this story as the one he would adapt for the big screen to honor the memory of his one-time mentor, Val Lewton (auteurist producer of a number of atmospheric, suspenseful, and highly successful B-grade horror pictures for RKO in the 1940s). MGM, to whom Wise owed a film under a previous contract, obtained the rights to Jackson's novel, Nelson Gidding wrote the screenplay, and, because of budgetary constraints, the production was funded through the studio's overseas arm with a largely British cast and crew. The result, *The Haunting* (1963), is

> CLEARLY, A GREAT DEAL OF THOUGHT AND EFFORT WENT INTO HOW BEST TO SIMPLIFY (AND SO HOPEFULLY INTENSIFY) ELEMENTS OF JACKSON'S NARRATIVE."

considered by a great many scholars, aficionados, and casual fans of the genre to be one of the scariest movies of all time—if not the scariest. Tellingly, the word most often employed to describe Wise's film is "effective" (Jeremy Dyson, for example, uses it three times on the very first page of his essay on *The Haunting* [228]). And the impressive fidelity it bears to its literary source material has come to be taken as an unquestionable assumption in most discussions of the film.

In 1999, after the wave of self-reflexive, Gen-X-targeted "neo-stalker" movies (including *Scream* [1997], *I Know What You Did Last Summer* [1998], and *Halloween H20* [1998]) initiated a return to box-office popularity of the horror genre, DreamWorks Pictures released a special effects-laden, $80 million version of *The Haunting*, directed by Jan DeBont (*Speed* [1994], *Speed 2* [1997]), following a great deal of anticipation and fanfare. Fresh off the abysmal response to Gus Van Sant's nearly shot-for-shot remake of the Alfred Hitchcock classic *Psycho* the previous year, many critics and potential viewers were skeptical of the chances for success of a film that had already been done nearly perfectly before. Unlike the case with Van Sant's *Psycho*, however, this new *Haunting* was in no sense intended as an homage to the original version of the film: The DVD commentary makes no mention of Wise's picture, and executive producer Steven Spielberg felt it necessary to "travel the road not taken by Wise to deliver the goods for modern audiences" (Jensen 22). Harvey Roy Greenberg's provocative thesis concerning the "intensely rivalrous spirit" inhabiting *Always*, Spielberg's 1990 remake of Victor Fleming's *A Guy Named Joe* (1943)—namely, that "an unconscious, oedipally driven competitiveness comprises the dark side of Spielberg's intense admiration for the original and its director" (120)—here receives additional and independent support, with Wise standing in for Fleming, and Jackson's crisp novel subbing for Dalton Trumbo's meandering screenplay.

In pursuit of such a dubious goal, and because Wise's *Haunting* is so faithful to Jackson's novel, the original plot was altered by screenwriter David Self to such an extent that what audiences finally saw bore little resemblance to either of the story's previous incarnations. But despite winding up as a film that betrays the spirit (pun intended) of its literary and cinematic precursors, the 1999 *Haunting* still bears traces of both its adapted and remade status. Although not sufficiently innovative or distinctive to be placed in Robert Eberwein's category of the "apparent remake whose status as a remake is denied by the director" (30)—the example Eberwein gives is Coppola's *The Conversation* (1974) and Antonioni's *Blow-Up* (1966)—DeBont's film nevertheless qualifies as an "unacknowledged, disguised remake." Greenberg, summarizing the work of Michael B. Druxman, explains that remakes of this type undertake "major alterations ... in time, setting, gender, or ... genre. The audience is deliberately uninformed about the switches" (126). Complicating matters further in this particular case is the fact that the remake in question disguises itself even more by eschewing in large measure the originally adapted source material.

For reasons I will speculate on below, DeBont's picture—despite a massive publicity campaign and the presence of two of Hollywood's most recognizable stars (Liam Neeson and Catherine Zeta Jones) in major roles—struggled mightily to just break even at the box office, and was derided by reviewers for, among other things, its reliance on computer-generated imagery, spectacle, and supernatural explanation at the expense of psychological realism, suspense, and ambiguity. Taken together, these three texts provide an ideal case study for examining a number of the possibilities, complexities, and difficulties involved in literary-cinematic adaptation. By holding the two film versions of *The Haunting* up against Jackson's novel, we can go a long way toward determining where and how each of them managed—or else failed—to provide audiovisual analogues for the innovative literary techniques that Jackson employed to horrify her readers.

Although *The Haunting of Hill House* can be summarized briefly and without much difficulty, the extreme uncanniness of Jackson's story can only be experienced firsthand—that is, by reading it oneself. After some cryptic remarks to open the novel ("Hill House, not sane, stood by itself against its hills, holding darkness within"), each of the four main characters (the human ones, at least) is introduced by an omniscient narrator. First we meet Dr. John Montague, an anthropologist who "had been looking for an honestly haunted house all his life" and who has arranged an experiment for himself and two women with documented paranormal abilities to "go and live at Hill House and see what happened there." Accompanying Montague are Eleanor Vance, thirty-two years old, friendless, and "ever since her first memory ... waiting for something like Hill House"; Theodora ("that was as much name as she used"), an artist, psychic, and—it is strongly suggested—a lesbian; and Luke Sanderson, the immature future owner of Hill House, sent there by his aunt. Jackson then shifts gears, placing us for an extended period of time directly inside the mind of Eleanor, who leaves the small room she has been subletting from her sister ever since their mother—a cruel invalid whom Eleanor took care of for eleven years—passed away to make the trip to Hill House. From this point, Eleanor becomes the story's unlikely protagonist ("unlikely" because she is only moderately sympathetic and in no sense heroic); almost everything that transpires in the house is focalized through her, and Jackson spends more time detailing Eleanor's thoughts, fears, and insecurities than she does describing the external activities of everyone else (save for the house itself) combined.

On her arrival at Hill House, Eleanor meets the others and quickly develops a bond with the liberated Theo, as well as a secret crush on Luke. Dr. Montague goes over the troubled history of the house, which was built by a strange man named Hugh Cram eighty years earlier as a country home for his wife and two young daughters. But Hill House "was a sad house almost from the beginning"—Crain's first wife was killed in a carriage accident on the driveway, and his second died from a mysterious fall (a third lost her battle to consumption). After Crain's own death, his eldest daughter became the primary resident of Hill House and lived there as a recluse (save for a lone female companion) until contracting pneumonia and dying there an elderly woman. The companion was accused by many townspeople of neglecting old Miss Cram during her illness; she eventually hanged herself from a turret on the house's tower. Ever since then, Hill House has been empty, "'Nothing in it touched, nothing used, nothing here wanted by anyone any more, just sitting here thinking.'—'And waiting,' Eleanor said. 'And waiting,' the doctor confirmed." As Eleanor and her companions quickly find out, the geography of Hill House bears a strong, strange resemblance to its creator: "'Hugh Crain … made his house to suit his mind. Angles which you assume are the right angles you are accustomed to, and have every right to expect are true, are actually a fraction of a degree off in one direction or another.' … 'It is'—and his [the doctor's] voice was saddened—'a masterpiece of architectural misdirection.'"

After a peaceful night's sleep, inexplicable and vaguely threatening events begin to take place with increasing regularity and with Eleanor at the center of them all: loud, relentless bangings on the door to her and Theo's room; a message inviting/instructing her to "COME HOME" written on the wall; children's voices whispering her name. Psychologically isolating herself from the others, Eleanor eventually comes to believe that Hill House is her true abode: She hears her dead mother calling for her, dances with a statue of Hugh Cram, and climbs to the top of a rickety old staircase, where she has to be rescued by Luke. Fearing for her physical and mental safety, Dr. Montague finally dismisses Eleanor from Hill House, despite her pleas ("'I really wasn't afraid. I'm fine now. I was happy.... I don't want to go away from here'") and demands ("'You can't just make me go,' she said wildly. 'You brought me here'"). Eventually, Eleanor realizes that there is nothing she can say to make Dr. Montague change his mind. Waving goodbye to the group, she pulls away in her car, but rather than drive off she presses her foot down hard on the accelerator and crashes straight into the huge tree at the base of the driveway: "'They can't turn me out or shut me out or laugh at me or hide from me; I won't go, and Hill House belongs to me.'" These are Eleanor's last words.

In the following sections, I look closely at how the *Hauntings* of Wise and DeBont compare and contrast with *The Haunting of Hill House* linguistically, stylistically, and thematically. With this larger task in mind, it would help to identify the major deviations in plot from book to films. As mentioned, Wise's *Haunting* is a great deal more loyal to the original text than is DeBont's. But this must not be mistaken for the claim that Nelson Gidding's screenplay is a mere transcription of the novel: Clearly, a great deal of thought and effort went into how best to simplify (and so hopefully intensify) elements of Jackson's narrative.

Some of the most obvious plot differences between the novel and the 1963 film are as follows: (1) The back story is simplified in the film: Hugh Grain now has only two wives, not three, and just one daughter, not two. Also, Wise gives us our history lesson immediately after the opening title sequence: An unidentified speaker (who we soon discover is Dr. John "Markway" [Richard Johnson]) provides voice-over narration to accompany what we can only assume is an objective/omniscient montage of Crain's first wife dying in a carriage crash, of his daughter Abigail spending most of her life inside Hill House's nursery (an extraordinary temporal ellipsis is achieved here via special effects as Abigail's face transforms from child to adult to elderly woman without any apparent cuts), and of old Miss Crain's female companion committing suicide in the tower. By way of contrast, Jackson's Dr. Montague does not share his knowledge of Hill House's dark past until much later. Dr. Montague, "round and rosy and bearded" in the book, becomes a slim, clean-shaven, and decidedly romantic figure in the film. This enables Dr. Markway to take Luke's (Russ Tamblyn) place as the object of Eleanor's (Julie Harris) affection, with the result that their scenes together operate on multiple discursive levels: They converse not only as scientist-subject, teacher-pupil, and doctor-patient, but as potential lovers. Markway is far more responsive to Eleanor's not-so-subtle advances than is Luke in the novel. This nod to generic convention renders Eleanor a more sympathetic figure, as her psychological deterioration after Mrs. Markway's (Lois Maxwell) arrival on the scene is, if not justified, at least understandable and certainly conceivable.

There are three additional differences: Dr. Markway's wife plays a much smaller role in Wise's film than does Dr. Montague's wife in the book, and the latter spouse's hypermasculine (though quite possibly asexual) friend Arthur does not appear in the film at all. The reduction and omission of characters stand as a definite improvement over Jackson's novel, as the mere presence of this pair of annoying, skeptical, and stock personalities undercuts whatever tension Jackson has created, along with our feeling that

Dr. Markway, Eleanor, Theo, and Luke are all alone in a completely alien environment. Theo's relationship with Eleanor, in the book extremely ambivalent, is here rendered in somewhat (though not entirely) more straightforward terms. On the one hand, Jackson's Theo, although probably gay, expresses only a mild attraction toward Eleanor, and by the end of the novel seems to be hitting it off quite well with Luke. Wise's Theo (Claire Bloom), in contrast, makes a number of fairly obvious passes at Eleanor and evinces a strong negative reaction toward Luke. Going in the other direction, Theo's insensitivity, if not outright cruelty, toward Eleanor becomes manifest as *The Haunting of Hill House* proceeds ("I don't understand. ...Do you always go where you're not wanted?"); in the 1963 film, Theo only becomes angry in response to Eleanor's own expressions of jealousy and animosity. Finally, Eleanor's last moments alive are handled quite differently by Jackson and Wise. In *The Haunting of Hill House*, Eleanor's death drive is, at least until the "unending, crashing second before the car hurled into the tree," an indisputably self-willed—perhaps even suicidal—act: "I am really doing it, she thought, turning the wheel. ... I am really doing it, I am doing this all by myself, now, at last; this is me, I am really really really doing it by myself." Gidding and Wise, almost certainly under pressure to rule out suicide as a possible motive for their protagonist's demise, make it clear that Eleanor is not trying to kill herself, that the wheel of her car is being controlled by an outside force that she cannot resist, despite her strongest efforts.

Having already noted that the 1999 *Haunting* self-consciously works to separate itself from its literary and cinematic forbears, I restrict myself to a quick sketch of some of the major plot differences effected by DeBont and Self. In the most recent *Haunting*, Dr. David Marrow (Neeson, who, like Johnson, cuts a dashing figure, but no matter: this Eleanor doesn't have a crush on anyone, save perhaps the already-dead Hugh Grain) brings his subjects to Hill House under false pretenses, telling them that they are there to participate in an experiment on sleep disorders. Dr. Marrow also takes two assistants with him, although a convenient "accident" arranged by the house forces the pair to leave after a single evening (which raises the obvious question: Why introduce them as characters in the first place?). One of the biggest differences between the book and the 1999 film is the fact that DeBont's Eleanor (Lili Taylor) is given no

internal monologue, thereby denying the audience direct access to her mind. But perhaps the most obvious change is the manner in which the novel's back story is altered and extended so as to connect with the main narrative. As Eleanor discovers (in an unlikely nod to the detective/mystery genre), Hugh Crain achieved his great wealth by exploiting the labor of young children, depositing the ashes of those who died under his rule in the house's massive fire pit. Big Daddy Crain is the unambiguous ghost that threatens the sanity and lives of those who reside at Hill House, and even in death he stalks the children whose souls are trapped in purgatory.

Finally, three differences that correspond to those mentioned above: Dr. Montague's wife, whose role is reduced in Wise's *Haunting*, is left out of DeBont's version altogether; Theo's (Zeta Jones) lesbianism, here explicitly coded in terms of bisexual preference, is left unexplored after her first scene; and Eleanor's death now takes place inside the house—though self-willed once again (as in the novel), her motive this time is not suicide but sacrifice (for the children of Hill House, whose souls are freed from purgatory once Eleanor succeeds in sending Hugh Grain to hell) ....

Source: Steven Jay Schneider, "Thrice-told Tales: *The Haunting*, from Novel to Film ...to Film," in *Journal of Popular Film and Television*, Vol. 30, No. 3, Fall 2002, pp. 166–78.

Judie Newman

In the following excerpt, Newman applies "feminist psychoanalytic theory" to a reading of The Haunting of Hill House, *exploring the ways in which both "the pleasures and the terrors of the text" derive from Jackson's treatment of the mother-daughter relationship in the novel.*

One of the most enduring mysteries of horror fiction consists in its exploitation of the attractions of fear Why, one may ask, should a reader seek out the experience of being terrified, particularly by horror fiction, which adds abhorrence, loathing and physical repulsion to the purer emotions of terror evoked by the supernatural tale? For H. P. Lovecraft the answer lay in the human fear of the unknown. Freud, however, developed a different hypothesis, describing the experience of the 'uncanny' (*unheimlich*) as that class of the frightening which leads back to what is known of old and long-familiar. Observing that *heimlich* (familiar, homely) is the opposite of *unheimlich*, Freud recognises the temptation to equate the uncanny with fear of the unknown. Yet he noted that *heimlich* also means 'concealed,' 'private,' 'secret,' as the home is an area withdrawn from the eyes of strangers. In Freud's argument, therefore, the experience of the uncanny arises either when primitive animistic beliefs, previously surmounted, seem once more to be confirmed (Shirley Jackson's 'The Lottery' is a case in point) or when infantile complexes, formerly repressed, are revived (a theory which brings *The Haunting of Hill House* into sharp focus). For Freud, various forms of ego disturbance involve regression to a period when the ego had not marked itself off sharply from the external world and from other people. In the context of a discussion of ghosts and doubles, Freud cites Otto Rank's description of the double as originally an insurance against the destruction of the ego, an energetic denial of the power of death. (In this sense the 'immortal soul' may be considered as the first double of the body.) The idea of doubling as preservation against extinction therefore springs from the unbounded self-love of the child. When this stage of primitive narcissism is surmounted, however, the double reverses its aspect, and, from being an assurance of immortality, becomes the uncanny harbinger of death and a thing of terror. Since Freud considered art as an organised activity of sublimation, providing the reader with pleasures 'under wraps,' it is tempting to argue that the horror tale actively eliminates and exorcises our fears by allowing them to be relegated to the imaginary realm of fiction. Rosemary Jackson, however, has indicated the case for the fantastic as a potentially subversive reversal of cultural formation, disruptive of conventional distinctions between the real and the unreal. Arguably, although Shirley Jackson builds her horrors on the basis of the *heimlich* and of repressed infantile complexes, in the process she subverts the Freudian paradigm, both of art as sublimation, and in broader psychoanalytic terms. In this connection, new developments in psychoanalytic theory offer fresh insights into Jackson's work.

Recent feminist psychoanalytic theorists have set out to revise the Freudian account of psychosexual differences, which bases gender, anatomically, on possession or lack of the phallus. In the Freudian paradigm, the male achieves adulthood by passing through the Oedipus complex, which fear of castration by the father induces him to

> THOUGH SHE SWIFTLY REVISES THIS DAYDREAM OF MOTHER-DAUGHTER REUNION, INTO A MORE CONVENTIONAL FANTASY OF COURTSHIP BY A HANDSOME PRINCE, SHE REMAINS MUCH PREOCCUPIED WITH IMAGES OF PROTECTED SPACES AND MAGIC ENCLOSURES, OF A HOME IN WHICH *SHE* COULD BE MOTHERED AND GREETED AS A LONG-LOST CHILD."

overcome. Fear facilitates acceptance of the incest prohibition, promoting the formation of the superego, which thereafter polices desire in accordance with adult social norms. In a parallel development, the female discovers the lack of the phallus, sees herself as castrated, recognises her mother as similarly inferior, and therefore abandons her attachment to the mother to form the Oedipal relation with the father, which is the necessary precursor of adult heterosexual relationships—always the Freudian goal. Feminist analysts, however, have shifted the focus from the Oedipal to the pre-Oedipal stage, tracing the influence of gender on identity to the dynamics of the mother-infant bond. Nancy Chodorow in *The Reproduction of Mothering* offers a persuasive analysis of early infant development in these terms. Because children first experience the social and cognitive world as continuous with themselves, the mother is not seen as a separate person with separate interests. In this brief period of immunity from individuality, the experience of fusion with the mother, of mother as world, is both seductive and terrifying. Unity is bliss; yet it entails total dependence and loss of self. In contrast the father does not pose the original threat to basic ego integrity, and is perceived from the beginning as separate. Thus, the male fear of women may originate as terror of maternal omnipotence in consequence of the early dependence on the mother, and may be generalised to all women (in images such as the witch, the vampire and the Terrible Mother) since it is tied up with the assertion of gender. Boys define themselves as masculine by difference from, not by relation to, their mothers. Girls, however, in defining themselves as female, experience themselves as resembling their mothers, so that the experience of attachment fuses with the process of identity formation. Girls therefore learn to see themselves as partially continuous with their mothers, whereas boys learn very early about difference and separateness. Male development therefore entails more emphatic individuation, and more defensive firming of experienced ego boundaries, whereas women persist in defining themselves relationally, creating fluid, permeable ego boundaries, and locating their sense of self in the ability to make and maintain affiliations. Female gender identity is therefore threatened by separation, and shaped throughout life by the fluctuations of symbiosis and detachment from the mother. Girls may also fear maternal omnipotence and struggle to free themselves, idealising the father as their most available ally. Daughterly individuation may be inhibited by paternal absence and by over-closeness to mothers, who tend to view their daughters as extensions of themselves. Conversely, coldness on the mother's part may prevent the loosening of the emotional bond because of the unappeased nature of the child's love. In maturity women may form close personal relationships with other women to recapture some aspects of the fractured mother-daughter bond. Alternatively they may reproduce the primary attachment, by themselves bearing children, thus initiating the cycle once more, as the exclusive symbiotic relation of the mother's own infancy is re-created. Mothering therefore involves a double identification for women in which they take both parts of the pre-Oedipal relation, as mother and as child. Fictions of development reflect this psychological structure. Recent reformulations of the female *Bildungsroman* have drawn attention to the frequency with which such fictions end in deaths (Maggie Tulliver, Rachel Vinrace, Edna Pontellier) understandable less as developmental failures than as refusals to accept an adulthood which denies female desires and values. In addition, a persistent, if recessive, narrative concern with the story of mothers and daughters often exists in the background to a dominant romance or courtship plot.

An exploration of *The Haunting of Hill House* in the light of feminist psychoanalytic theory reveals that the source of both the pleasures and the terrors of the text springs from the dynamics of the mother-daughter relation with its attendant motifs of psychic annihilation, reabsorption by the mother, vexed individuation, dissolution of individual ego boundaries, terror of separation and the attempted reproduction of the

symbiotic bond through close female friendship. Eleanor Vance, the central protagonist, is mother-dominated. On her father's death the adolescent Eleanor was associated with an outbreak of poltergeist activity, in which her family home was repeatedly showered with stones. The event invites comparison with 'The Lottery,' in which the victim of the stoning, Tessie Hutchinson, is not only a mother, but a mother who sees her daughter as so much an extension of herself that she attempts to improve her own chances of survival by involving Eva in the fatal draw. Eleanor clearly resented her recently dead mother, whom she nursed for eleven years: 'the only person in the world she genuinely hated, now that her mother was dead, was her sister.' Initially her excursion to Hill House to participate in Dr Montague's study of psychic phenomena appears as an opportunity for psychological liberation, the first steps towards autonomy. The trip begins with a small act of assertion against the mother-image. When Eleanor's sister refuses to allow her to use their shared car ('I am sure Mother would have agreed with me, Eleanor'—), Eleanor reacts by simply stealing it, in the process knocking over an angry old woman who is clearly associated with the 'cross old lady' whom she had nursed for so long. Once *en route* Eleanor is haunted by the refrain 'Journeys end in lovers meeting,' suggesting (as the *carpe diem* theme of the song confirms) that Eleanor's goal is the realisation of heterosexual desires.

Eleanor's fantasies on the journey, however, imply that her primary emotional relation remains with her mother. In imagination she dreams up several 'homes,' based on houses on her route. In the first, 'a little dainty old lady took care of me,' bringing trays of tea and wine 'for my health's sake.' The fantasy reveals just how much Eleanor herself wishes to be mothered. In the preceding period, as nurse to a sick mother, Eleanor may be said to have 'mothered' her own mother, losing her youth in the process. A second fantasy centres upon a hollow square of poisonous oleanders, which seem to Eleanor to be 'guarding something.' Since the oleanders enclose only an empty centre, Eleanor promptly supplies a mother to occupy it, constructing an enthralling fairy world in which 'the queen waits, weeping, for the princess to return.' Though she swiftly revises this daydream of mother-daughter reunion, into a more conventional fantasy of courtship by a handsome prince, she remains much preoccupied with images of protected spaces and magic enclosures, of a home in which *she* could be mothered and greeted as a long-lost child. A subsequent incident reinforces this impression. Pausing for lunch, Eleanor observes a little girl who refuses to drink her milk because it is not in the familiar cup, patterned with stars, which she uses at home. Despite maternal persuasion, the child resists, forcing her mother to yield. The small tableau emphasises both the child's potential independence and resistance to the mother, and the attractions of the familiar home world, here associated with mother's milk and starry containment. Eleanor empathises with the little girl's narcissistic desires: 'insist on your cup of stars; once they have trapped you into being like everyone else you will never see your cup of stars again.' Eleanor's final fantasy home, a cottage hidden behind oleanders, 'buried in a garden,' is entirely secluded from the world. Taken together, her fantasies suggest her ambivalent individuation and the lure of a magic mother-world. They form a striking contrast to the reality of Hillsdale, a tangled mess of dirty houses and crooked streets. For all its ugliness, however, Eleanor deliberately delays there over coffee. Despite her reiterated refrain 'In delay there lies no plenty,' Eleanor is not quite so eager to reach her goal and realise her desires as she thinks. Another scene of enforced delay, negotiating with a surly caretaker at the gates of Hill House, further retards her progress. The emphasis here on locked gates, guards against entry, a tortuous access road, and the general difficulty in locating the house reinforces the impression of its desirability as *heimlich*, secret, a home kept away from the eyes of others.

Entry to this protected enclave provokes, however, a response which underlines the consonance of the familiar and the uncanny: childish terror. Afraid that she will cry 'like a child sobbing and wailing,' tiptoeing around apprehensively, Eleanor feels like 'a small creature swallowed whole by a monster' which 'feels my tiny little movements inside.' The intra-uterine fantasy immediately associates Hill House with an engulfing mother. Eleanor's fellow guest, Theo, reacts in opposite terms, characterising the two women as Babes in the Woods (abandoned by parents) and comparing the experience to the first day at boarding-school or camp. The vulnerable continuity between fear of engulfment and fear of separation is indicated in the women's response to the threat. Reminiscing about their childhoods, they eagerly associate themselves through fancied family resemblances, until Theo announces that theirs is an indissoluble relationship: 'Would you let them separate us

now? Now that we've found out we're cousins?' Yet on the arrival of the remaining guests, Luke and Dr Montague, Theo's assertion of female strength through attachment is swiftly replaced as the four establish their identities, in playfully exaggerated form, through separation and differentiation: 'You are Theodora because *I* am Eleanor'; 'I have no beard so *he* must be Dr Montague.' Fantasy selves are then elaborated. Luke introduces himself as a bullfighter; Eleanor poses as an artist's model, living an 'abandoned' life while moving from garret to garret; Theo describes herself as a lord's daughter, masquerading as an ordinary mortal in the clothes of her maid, in order to escape a parental plot of forced marriage. Interestingly, though both women characterise themselves as homeless, Eleanor converts homelessness into an image of abandonment, Theo into active escape from an oppressive parent by asserting a different identity. For Eleanor, however, identity remains elusive. In envisaging herself as an artist's model she acquiesces in a self-image created by a controlling other . . . .

Source: Judie Newman, "Shirley Jackson and the Reproduction of Mothering: *The Haunting of Hill House*," in *American Horror Fiction: From Brockden Brown to Stephen King*, Macmillan, 1990, pp. 120–34.

Lenemaja Friedman

In the following essay, Friedman provides an overview of Jackson's work, highlighting the unusual characteristics of her fiction as well as her unique literary style.

I. PRINCIPLES OF AND FOR A WRITER

Among Miss Jackson's non-fiction works are the essays about the craft of writing. These are significant to this study in that they embody the principles around which Miss Jackson formed her own works. Each rule is one that applies to her own stories. Three of the lectures, presented earlier at college and writers' conferences, are included in the anthology *Come Along With Me*. Of these, "Experience and Fiction" later appeared in the January 1969, issue of the *Writer*. As the title implies, all experience counts for something; the writer regards the events of his life as a potential source for stories. These events may have to be manipulated and shaped, for true experiences as such seldom make good fiction. Along with this realization, she indicates several specific truths about fiction writing: " . . . no scene and no character can be allowed to wander off by itself; there must be some furthering of the story in every sentence, and even the most fleeting background characters must partake of the story in some way; they must be characters peculiar to *this* story and no other."

Miss Jackson practices what she preaches, for her background characters are individuals. Mr. and Mrs. Dudley in *The Haunting of Hill House* are good examples, for they appear as eccentric as the old house of which they are caretakers. In the short story form, following this advice is more difficult, but such characters as the housekeeper in "The Rock" and the storekeepers in "Home," "Renegade," and "The Summer People"—who are sources of important advice or information—show that Miss Jackson uses her characters to advantage. They are also appropriate to the surroundings in which she places them.

A second point Miss Jackson makes is that "people in stories are called characters because that is what they are. They are not real people. Therefore the writer should not try to transfer real people literally to his pages of fiction. He does not need pages and pages of description. A person in a story is identified through small things—little gestures, turns of speech, automatic reactions . . . ." (209). In the same way, Mrs. Dudley is remembered for her automatic responses to the visitors at Hill House. It should be noted that, even in the autobiographical family tales, the characters and events are heightened and shaped to conform to Miss Jackson's purposes.

Thereafter, Miss Jackson gives several instances of experiences she used in the process of creating stories. One of these is her account of how she happened to write *The Haunting of Hill House*; another is the family interview with the income-tax man, which she turned into a short story; and another involved the night that all of the family, including herself, became ill with the grippe, one of her funniest stories. This particular lecture ends with her acknowledgment of a letter from a lady in Indiana who wanted to earn some extra money. The lady, who asked where Miss Jackson got her ideas for stories and stated that she, herself, could "never make up anything good," had apparently never considered shaping her own experiences.

Another of Miss Jackson's favorite lectures is entitled "Biography of a Story," and it was given in conjunction with a reading of "The Lottery." She presents a history of the famous short story and then a detailed account of the

> BECAUSE HER STYLE IS ADMIRABLY SUITED TO THE PURPOSES OF THE STORYTELLER: SHE DOES NOT WRITE LONG, UNWIELDY SENTENCES CLUTTERED WITH ABSTRACT NOUNS OR LONG METAPHORICAL PASSAGES OF DESCRIPTION; HER THOUGHTS AND SENTIMENTS ARE NOT MUDDIED THROUGH ENDLESS PHILOSOPHICAL MEANDERINGS; THERE IS NO ATTEMPT AT AFFECTATION OR FUSSINESS."

public reactions to it, including excerpts of letters from all over the world. The third of the lectures included in the anthology, "Notes for a Young Writer," was originally intended as a stimulus for her daughter Sally; but she again cites principles exhibited in her own works. Among the "do's" and "don't's" she warns: the reader will willingly suspend disbelief for a time, but he will not suspend reason: a story is an uneasy bargain with the reader. The author's objective is to play fair and to keep the reader interested—his role is to keep reading. The writer has the right to assume that the reader will accept the story on the author's terms, but the story must have a surface tension that can be stretched but not shattered.

The story should move as naturally and easily as possible without any unnecessary side trips. The writer must *always* make the duller parts of his story work for him: "the necessary passage of time, the necessary movement must not stop the story dead, but must push it forward" (245). The writer must describe only what is necessary; his "coloring words, particularly adjectives and adverbs, must be used where they will do the most good." As has been observed previously, she, herself, uses adjectives sparingly and makes excellent use of strong nouns and verbs.) "Inanimate objects," she states, "are best described in use or motion" (246). The writer must use a great deal of economy in written speech, and he must spend time listening to people talking, noting the patterns of speech reflected in the speaking. A writer's characters must be consistent—in speech and action. Also, the would-be writer must remember that he is living in a world of people, and he must think in terms of concrete rather than abstract nouns.

He must realize that the beginning and ending of a story belong together and that the ending is implicit in the beginning. For instance, the first line of "The Beautiful Stranger," which reads: "What might be called the first intimation of strangeness occurred at the railroad station," foreshadows the ending in which Margaret has lost all sense of reality and no longer knows where she is. But even "The Lottery," which begins with a pleasant summer day, shows traces of tension within a few lines; and the reader (looking back) can see that the ending, surprise though it may be, has been adequately planned from the beginning.

A portrait artist selects his materials carefully; he mixes here, blends there, and focuses always on the evolving subject on his canvas; and what he chooses to include in his scheme tells much about him as an individual. In the same way, Miss Jackson has chosen to include the specific subjects that are the most meaningful to her as an artist, and her themes and the characters of her special world represent evil cloaked in seeming good; prejudice and hypocrisy; the character whose mind escapes the bounds of reality; the suspense and terror of the helpless protagonist-victim; and loneliness and frustration.

II. CHARACTERISTICS

The subjects she has *ignored* in presenting her material, however, may also be significant in revealing the characteristics of her work. For example, the major characters in her stories are rarely elderly; they tend to be young, often teenagers or persons in early middle age. In *Road Through the Wall*, the focus is on the fourteen- and fifteen-year-olds of Pepper Street; in *Hangsaman*, the schizoid Natalie is seventeen and just entering college; in *The Bird's Nest*, the multiple personality of Elizabeth is in her early twenties; in *The Haunting of Hill House*, the psychic researchers are in their late twenties and early thirties; in *The Sundial*, although Mrs. Halloran is a main character, the younger persons in the household receive equal emphasis—Gloria, Maryjane, Julia, Arabella, and the ten-year-old Fancy who is to become Mrs. Halloran's heir; in *We Have Always Lived in the Castle*, Merricat is eighteen and Constance is twenty-eight. In the

short stories, also, except for those cases of kind, harmless-looking grandmothers with benevolent exteriors and warped interiors, most of the protagonist are "youngish."

One sees these people most often in isolation; and, aside from the instances of social interaction that reveal prejudice, one observes them in their loneliness. They are single people; and discounting the brief glimpse into the unhappy married state of the families of *Road Through the Wall*, Miss Jackson does not deal with marital relationships. Her heroines are unmarried; and, while the early-"thirtyish" ladies in her stories may suffer from sexual frustrations (about which nothing is said), no one in all of the stories has a love affair. One finds in them no love scenes and no sexual deviates; in fact, Miss Jackson avoids sex altogether.

The characters are often concerned, instead, with establishing their own identity. The teenagers on Pepper Street in *Road Through the Wall* are vying for attention and recognition, and rivalry also exists among the families—the Robertses, the Martins, and the Donalds—because each wants to be important in the eyes of the community. In *Hangsaman*, Natalie struggles with her insecurities; she wants to be appreciated for what she is, but the resultant Tony-Natalie conflict almost destroys her. In *The Bird's Nest*, the multiple personalities of Elizabeth fight for control until she at last becomes well and discovers who she is, thereby making friends with the past. Eleanor's stay at Hill House involves the process of seeking her own identity and her desperate need to belong somewhere; and the narrative ends with her desire to join the spirits of the house. Mrs. Halloran in *The Sundial*, after playing foully for her supremacy in the household, seeks to establish herself as a queen. Her desire is to reign over the family, but each of the other characters strives to maintain his own dignity and pride. Merricat eliminates her family, outmaneuvers Charles, and becomes her sister's protectress before she feels secure and free to be herself, not realizing that they are now doomed.

As stated previously, the Jackson world is set apart from the usual world. In the psychological stories, the reader is carried through the convolutions of the protagonist's mind—a detour from normal everyday events. In *We Have Always Lived in the Castle*, the isolation is both physical and mental. The Blackwoods are isolated from the rest of the community, but Merricat with her psychotic nature is also isolated from the normal understanding of others. The remaining novels, too, involve groups that are outside the pale of ordinary living; for example, *The Road Through the Wall* has its own milieu in Pepper Street, which the reader sees, on the one hand, as typical, but, on the other, as the very special environment of a closed society. The would-be survivors in the Halloran mansion cling together as they prepare to live in the new world, since they alone seem to have been chosen to see it; and Dr. Montague's people, isolated in Hill House, experience contact with the spirit world.

Because few close, meaningful relationships exist among her fictional people, her characters experience no deep emotions except those of fear and anxiety; no strong love; no strong anger, jealousy, or hate. The most violent moments of hatred are found in *The Bird's Nest* when two of the multiple personalities of Elizabeth battle in one scene to dominate each other and in *We Have Always Lived in the Castle* in which Merricat has in the past hated her family and now vaguely (in a psychotic state) hates the villagers, who are on the periphery of the scene. She hates and fears Charles, but the moment that the object of her hatred is removed, she is in a euphoric state, knowing that she is safe, that no outside forces will take Constance away from her. Her relationship with Constance is closer than that of any other characters; and, because they feel secure in each other, Constance and Merricat are prepared to withstand the terrors of the outside world. The vague hatred that other characters feel appears often in the form of prejudice, like that of the villagers for the Blackwoods or of the Pepper Street families for the one Jewish family on the block. This hatred is a chronic illness in a society in which there is more hate than love.

Miss Jackson avoids ugliness or grisly realistic details of unpleasantness. When death occurs, which is seldom, it happens offstage as in *Road Through the Wall*, or is disposed of in a sentence or two as in *The Haunting of Hill House* when Eleanor crashes into the tree and as in *The Sundial* when Orianna Halloran is found lying at the bottom of the stairs. The body is carried off to rest beside the sundial on the lawn, but no unpleasant details are given. At the end of "The Lottery," the reader discovers with horror what is about to happen; but the story ends with the casting of the first stones. Miss Jackson prefers to leave the sordid details to the reader's imagination.

Again one notes that there is a lack of religion or of reference to God in Miss Jackson's work: the characters struggle against loneliness, insanity, or the hatred of others, but they never call upon God for aid. God is nonexistent. Even in *The Sundial* the would-be voyagers do not see or anticipate a supernatural being. Mrs. Halloran is to be supreme ruler, and she does not intend to take orders from anyone. Fanny's father acts as a comic-ominous being who hovers about somewhere in space but has no specific authority. Only the domain of spirits manifests itself in the presence of ghosts. Beyond this manifestation, the hereafter is a big nothing, which, if not polluted already, will soon be so by contact with humans.

Many of Miss Jackson's people, the villains, lack sensitivity and an awareness of the needs of others; and, because of this lack, they intentionally or unintentionally inflict pain. Since these people are not grotesques but ordinary human beings, the discovery of evil beneath the seeming good is especially terrifying, as in "The Lottery." The outward grotesques are those characters who have ceased to function normally, having been trapped in a world of shadows, such as Mrs. Montague in "Island," or Elizabeth in *The Bird's Nest*; but they are in most cases sympathetic if vulnerable persons.

Because Miss Jackson does not concentrate on love, on sexual relationships, or on broad social problems, her fiction differs from the popular, usual fictional fare of the day; nor does her work have any kinship to the so-called modern Gothic novels. Instead, her sphere is that of the individual involved in good and evil; therefore, her work resembles more that of a modern Hawthorne or Edgar Allan Poe. Her family tales, so different from the rest of her work, revolve around the humor that arises from the problems of daily living; and they resemble other such family chronicles as Jean Kerr's *Please Don't Eat the Daisies* or the stories of Betty MacDonald.

III. ACHIEVEMENT

Delightful as Miss Jackson's humor is, and touches of it are found throughout her fiction, it is not for the family chronicles that she will be remembered although the story "Charles" has become a favorite with anthologists. Her most effective tale is still "The Lottery"; but, even if she had not written "The Lottery," she would still be an important writer. Her greatest strengths are in the expert handling of humor, mystery, ambiguity, and suspense. Her wit and imagination have created off-beat and original stories. Her characters are authentic, if often strange, people;

and, as the critics point out, her prose style is excellent. Why? Because her style is admirably suited to the purposes of the storyteller: she does not write long, unwieldy sentences cluttered with abstract nouns or long metaphorical passages of description; her thoughts and sentiments are not muddied through endless philosophical meanderings; there is no attempt at affectation or fussiness. Instead, she chooses a simple, unadorned direct, clear manner of speaking to her reader. Her lines flow evenly, smoothly, and have a distinct rhythm. She shows a meticulousness in word choice and a deft manipulation of words; she has a poet's ear. She has, also, an excellent sense of timing with a punch line, but more often, her sense of fun creeps into the lines and takes the reader by surprise. Her wit and imagination add sparkle to her prose.

Miss Jackson is not, however, a major writer; and the reason she will not be considered one is that she saw herself primarily as an entertainer, as an expert storyteller and craftsman. She has insights to share with her readers; but her handling of the material—the surprise twists, the preoccupation with mystery and fantasy, her avoidance of strong passions, her versatility, and her sense of sheer fun—may not be the attributes of the more serious writer who wishes to come to grips with the strong passions of ordinary people in a workaday world, who prefers to deal directly with the essential problems of love, death, war, disease, poverty, and insanity in its most ugly aspects. Even with "The Lottery" one wonders if Miss Jackson may have chosen the situation for its shock value. The message is, nevertheless, effective; and the story is superb, regardless of the intent of the author. Despite the lack of critical attention, her books continue to be popular with those people who are sensitive, imaginative, and fun-loving; and perhaps, in the long run, that popularity will be what counts.

Source: Lenemaja Friedman, "Overview," in *Shirley Jackson*, Twayne Publishers 1975, pp. 155–61.

SOURCES

Barrows, Marjorie W., et al., eds., *The American Experience: Fiction*, Macmillan, 1968.

Buescher, John B., *The Other Side of Salvation: Spiritualism and the Nineteenth-Century Religious Experience*, Skinner House, 2004.

Carrington, Hereward, *The Physical Phenomena of Spiritualism, Fraudulent and Genuine*, 2nd ed., Small, Maynard, 1908.

Clery, Emma J., "The Genesis of 'Gothic' Fiction," in *The Cambridge Companion to Gothic Fiction*, edited by Jerrold E. Hogle, Cambridge University Press, 2002, pp. 21–39.

Davenport-Hines, Richard, *Gothic: Four Hundred Years of Excess, Horror, Evil, and Ruin*, North Point, 1999.

Friedan, Betty, *The Feminine Mystique*, Norton, 1963.

Fort, Charles, *The Book of the Damned*, Boni and Liveright, 1919, pp. 167–68.

Gilman, Charlotte Perkins, *The Yellow Wallpaper and Other Stories*, Oxford University Press, 1997, pp. 3–20.

Goodrich-Freer, Ada, and John Patrick Crichton-Stuart Bute, eds., *The Alleged Haunting of B—— House*, George Redway, 1899, http://www.archive.org/stream/alleged haunting00butegoog#page/n6/mode/1up (accessed September 22, 2010).

Hague, Angela, "'A Faithful Anatomy of Our Times': Reassessing Shirley Jackson," in *Frontiers: A Journal of Women Studies*, Vol. 26, No. 2, 2005, pp. 73–96.

Haines, Colin, *"Frightened by a Word": Shirley Jackson and Lesbian Gothic*, Uppsala Universitet, 2007.

Hattenhauer Darryl, *Shirley Jackson's American Gothic*, State University of New York Press, 2003, pp. 155–73.

Houdini, Harry, *A Magician among the Spirits*, Harper & Brothers, 1924.

Jackson, Shirley, *The Haunting of Hill House*, in *Shirley Jackson: Novels and Stories*, edited by Joyce Carol Oates, Library of America, 2010, pp. 241–417.

Kilgour, Maggie, *The Rise of the Gothic Novel*, Routledge, 1995.

King, Stephen, *Danse Macabre*, Berkley Books, 1987, pp. 267–82.

Oppenheimer, Judy, *Private Demons: The Life of Shirley Jackson*, Putnam, 1988.

Preliminary Report of the Commission Appointed by The University of Pennsylvania to Investigate Modern Spiritualism in Accordance with the Request of the Late Henry Seybert, Seybert Commission, University of Pennsylvania, J. B. Lippincott, 1887.

Randi, James, *An Encyclopedia of Claims, Frauds, and Hoaxes of the Occult and Supernatural*, St. Martin's Press, 1997.

Rhine, J. B., *New Frontiers of the Mind: The Story of the Duke Experiments*, Farrar & Rinehart, 1937.

Williams, Anne, *Art of Darkness: A Poetics of Gothic*, University of Chicago Press, 1995.

FURTHER READING

Bleiler, E. F., ed., *Three Gothic Novels*, Dover, 1966.
This text contains the complete text of three of the earliest and most influential gothic novels: Horace Walpole's *The Castle of Otranto*, William Beckford's *Vathek*, and John Polidori's *The Vampyre*, as well as a gothic fragment by Lord Byron.

Hall, Joan Wylie, *Shirley Jackson: A Study of the Short Fiction*, Twayne, 1993.
This work studies Jackson's short stories, a corpus much larger than that of her novels and, at one time, one taken more seriously.

Jackson, Shirley, *The Bad Children*, Dramatic Publishing, 1959.
This is a musical play based on the story of Hansel and Gretel. The score is by Allan Jay Friedman.

Jackson, Shirley, *The Lottery and Other Stories*, Modern Library, 2000.
This collection of short stories contains "The Lottery," often considered to be Jackson's most important work.

Oates, Joyce Carol, *A Bloodsmoor Romance*, Dutton, 1982.

Oates is one of Jackson's staunchest supporters in the literary community. This novel is one of her own efforts in the gothic genre.

Reinsch, Paul N., *A Critical Bibliography of Shirley Jackson, American Writer (1919–1965): Reviews, Criticism, Adaptations*, Edwin Mellen, 2001.
This is the standard reference work for the publication history of Jackson's works and their adaptations.

SUGGESTED SEARCH TERMS

Shirley Jackson

The Haunting of Hill House

gothic literature

parapsychology

unreliable narrator

gothic AND Shirley Jackson

Shirley Jackson AND novel

Shirley Jackson AND feminism

Shirley Jackson AND postmodernism

Holes

LOUIS SACHAR

1998

Holes, published in 1998, has become one of the most frequently taught young-adult novels in American middle and high schools. It was the first book to win both the National Book Award for Young People's Literature (1998) and the Newbery Medal (1999), which recognizes the most distinguished contribution to American children's literature; as of 2010, no other book had captured both awards. *Holes* has been adapted as both a film and a stage play, and has sold more than five million copies in at least fifteen languages, including English, Spanish, Japanese, and Chinese.

The story deals with Stanley Yelnats, a fifteen-year-old boy who is sent to Camp Green Lake, a boot camp for wayward boys, for a crime he did not commit. At the camp, boys spend hours each day in the hot Texas sun, digging large holes in the desert in a program that is supposed to build character. As the novel tells what happens to Stanley there, it weaves in tall tales featuring the ancestors of several of the present-day characters. *Holes* is striking for its humor, and also for its insightful portrayal of young men who need a second chance, of the power of friendship, and of the importance of family.

AUTHOR BIOGRAPHY

Sachar was born in East Meadow, New York, on March 20, 1954. An only child, he moved with his parents to Orange County, California, when

Louis Sachar *(© AF archive / Alamy)*

he was nine years old, and graduated from high school there. He was a strong student, good at math and excited about reading and writing. He spent one year at Antioch College in Yellow Springs, Ohio, but when his father died, he transferred to the University of California at Berkeley to be nearer to his mother. At one point in his college career, Sachar needed three credits to satisfy a requirement, and he signed up to be a teacher's aide because it looked like an easy way to complete the credits. He had no particular interest in teaching or in young people when he began, but he took to the children quickly, and they liked him. Sachar began writing a series of humorous stories about schoolchildren, naming the characters after kids at the school where he worked. Shortly after graduating from college, he learned that his first book, *Sideways Stories from Wayside School* (1978), had been accepted for publication.

By this time, Sachar was enrolled in law school at the University of California at San Francisco. He completed his law degree in 1980 and began practicing law part-time in 1981, but he continued writing, and tried to decide which way his career path would take him. In 1983, he visited Texas as part of a promotional tour for his second book, and met Clara Askew, a school counselor, whom he married in 1985. The couple have one child, a daughter named Sherre, born in 1987. They spent their early years as a couple in San Francisco; Carla continued to work in education, and her husband quit his law practice to write full-time. His fourth novel, *There's a*

Boy in the Girls' Bathroom (1987), won several awards, and established Sachar as an important writer of humorous and insightful books about middle-school-aged misfits. He has written several books for children, including five books in the Wayside School series and eight novels about a third-grade boy named Marvin Redpost.

In 1990, the Sachar family moved to Austin, Texas, where they lived as of 2010. It was there, faced with the relentless Texas heat, that Sachar wrote his most important novel, and his first one for young adults, *Holes*, in 1998. The book enjoyed great critical and popular success, winning both the National Book Award and the Newbery Medal. Sachar followed the novel with two sequels and a film version, for which he wrote the screenplay. Between 2000 and 2009, much of Sachar's time was consumed with projects related to *Holes*, but 2010 saw the publication of *The Cardturner*, a young-adult novel about a teen who gets involved in one of Sachar's favorite hobbies: playing bridge.

PLOT SUMMARY

Chapters 1–6

Holes opens with a description of Camp Green Lake, a dried-up lake bed in Texas with little shade. The narrator addresses the reader directly, explaining that the one shady spot—a hammock between two trees—belongs to the Warden, and warning readers to beware of rattlesnakes, scorpions and, especially, the dreaded yellow-spotted lizards, whose bite is always fatal. It is not until the second chapter that the protagonist, Stanley Yelnats V, is introduced. Stanley, the narrator explains, was given a choice by a judge: go to jail or go to Camp Green Lake. Stanley is an unpopular, overweight middle-school kid who comes from an unlucky but optimistic family. They trace their bad luck to Stanley's "no-good-dirty-rotten-pig-stealing-great-great-grandfather," who brought a curse down on the family generations ago. Now, Stanley's inventor father is unable to find any success, and Stanley has been sent to Camp Green Lake for eighteen months for a crime he did not commit.

The story moves back and forth between the past and the present, introducing Stanley's ancestors and their fates. But the focus in these chapters is on Stanley's arrival at Camp Green Lake after a long bus ride across a barren

MEDIA ADAPTATIONS

- *Holes* was adapted as a film starring Shia LaBeouf and Sigourney Weaver, with the screenplay by Sachar. It was released by Walt Disney Pictures in 2003 and is distributed on DVD.

- Listening Library produced an unabridged audio edition of *Holes* in 2006. Read by Kerry Bever, it is available on CD or as an MP3 download.

landscape. The first person he meets there is Mr. Sir, who issues him two sets of orange clothing, a towel, and a canteen, and tells him how he will spend his time at the camp: every day he must dig a hole five feet deep and five feet across. When his hole is completed each day, his work is done and he may relax any way he chooses. Stanley is assigned to D tent, and introduced to his counselor, Mr. Pendanski. He also meets the six other boys who live in D tent, including Armpit, X-Ray, and Zero, as they return from digging. After a shower and dinner, Stanley lies down on his cot, thinking of the day not long before when, as he was walking home from school, a pair of sneakers fell out of the sky and hit him on the head. The sneakers turned out to be a pair donated for a homeless shelter fund raiser, and Stanley was sent to Camp Green Lake as punishment for stealing them.

Chapters 7–9

On Stanley's first day at Camp Green Lake, he rises at 4:30, has breakfast, and heads out with the others to dig his first hole. He sees that the area around the camp is covered with holes and with mounds of the dirt that came out of the holes. Each camper is shown where to dig each day, with the added warning that "anything interesting or unusual" must be given to the authorities. However, the boys are made to understand that they are not looking for anything in particular; they dig holes simply to build character. Stanley begins to dig in the hard earth,

and blisters form on his hands almost immediately. Mr. Sir brings the boys water partway through the day, and when he takes a break, Stanley can see that he is digging much more slowly than the others. As the day goes on, the sun becomes hotter, and Stanley's blisters burst and re-form. Zero, a skinny quiet boy, is the first to finish, and all the rest of the boys finish well before Stanley does. With his last bit of strength, Stanley climbs out of the hole, spits into it, and walks back to camp.

He takes a shower, using his allotted four minutes of water, and heads to the recreation room, where the boys can watch a broken TV, play with broken games, or just hang out. Stanley writes a letter to his mother, lying about the fun he is having at camp. Zero, who rarely speaks and whom everyone else ignores because he is quiet and strange, asks Stanley if the shoes he found had red *X*'s on the back, but only stares when Stanley tells him that they did. The boys head off to dinner.

Interwoven with Stanley's first day is the story of his great-great-grandfather Elya Yelnats, who lived in Latvia. As a teenager, he fell in love with Myra Menke. To win her, he needed to beat out a pig farmer who also wanted to marry her, and who could offer Myra's family a fat pig in exchange for her hand. Elya turned to Madame Zeroni, an Egyptian, for advice. She gave him a baby pig and instructed him to carry it to the top of a mountain every day and let it drink from a stream there. By Myra's fifteenth birthday, the pig would be the fattest pig around, and he could win Myra's hand. Then, he was to carry Madame Zeroni to the top of the mountain and let her drink from the stream. If he failed to do this, he and his descendants would be cursed. On Myra's birthday, each man brought a pig, and the two pigs were found to weigh exactly the same amount. Myra, who was rather stupid and unable to decide which man to marry, asked them to pick a number between one and ten. Disgusted, Elya walked away.

He signed on as a deck hand, and came to America to start over, forgetting that he had promised to carry Madame Zeroni up the mountain. He settled in America, learned English, got married and tried to be a farmer, but lightning kept striking his barn and wiping out his crops. He searched for Madame Zeroni's son, supposedly settled in America, so that he could somehow settle his debt to the family, but never found him. In a few years his son, the first Stanley Yelnats, was born.

Chapters 10–15

Stanley digs his second hole, which proves to be much harder than the first because of his sore muscles and torn-up hands. X-Ray urges Stanley to give him anything "interesting" he might find, so X-Ray can turn it in and get a day off as a reward; Stanley agrees, wanting to fit in with the more experienced boys. That night, Mr. Pendanski, whom the boys call "Mom," leads the boys in a discussion about their future when they leave Camp Green Lake. He tries to make the boys accept responsibility for the misdeeds that got them sent to the camp, and to think about what they like to do. He belittles Zero, calling him "not completely worthless," earning Zero's angry stare.

As the days pass, the digging gets easier. One day, Stanley does find something interesting in his hole, a gold tube with a heart and the letters *K* and *B* engraved on it. He gives it to X-Ray, and encourages him to wait until the following morning to turn it in, so he will get more of the day off as a reward. X-Ray rewards Stanley with a more favored place in the line for water, and Stanley, who never had friends at school, begins to feel more accepted by the others. The next morning, X-Ray shows the tube to Mr. Pendanski, who summons the Warden to see it. The Warden turns out to be Mrs. Walker, a tall red-haired woman, who is excited by the find and sets all the boys to digging near X-Ray's hole. Only Stanley knows exactly where he was digging the day before, when the tube was actually found, and knows that today's dig is far away.

Chapters 16–22

After a few more days, the Warden becomes discouraged because the boys do not find anything else of interest. Stanley gets a letter from his mother, which tells him that his father's experiments with ways to recycle old sneakers are creating an awful stink. As Stanley is writing back to her, Zero confesses that he does not know how to read and asks Stanley to teach him. But Stanley does not have the energy, and refuses.

One day, one of the boys steals Mr. Sir's bag of sunflower seeds from the water truck, and as they are passing it around Stanley drops it. He accepts the blame for stealing the bag, and is taken to see the Warden for his punishment.

The Warden is not interested in Mr. Sir's sunflower seeds, and takes from her makeup bag a special nail polish made with rattlesnake venom; she scratches Mr. Sir's face with it, raising horrible welts. When Stanley is taken back to his hole by the furious Mr. Sir, he finds that Zero, the fastest digger of the group, has almost finished it for him. The two boys agree that Stanley will teach Zero to read in exchange for help with digging his holes. That night, thinking about the Warden and her makeup bag, Stanley realizes that the gold tube he found was part of a lipstick case. Remembering that his great-grandfather Stanley Yelnats, who had made a fortune in the stock market, had once been robbed in the desert by the outlaw Kissin' Kate Barlow, he wonders if the lipstick case could have been hers.

Chapters 23–28

Now the narrator flashes back one hundred and ten years, to a time when Green Lake was actually a lake. Miss Katherine Barlow was a schoolteacher, famous for her beauty and her spiced peaches. The richest man in town was stupid and arrogant Trout Walker. Walker expected to marry Miss Katherine, but she had no interest in him. Instead, she favored Sam, an African American man who sold sweet onions that had the power to cure illness. Sam had a little rowboat and an old donkey, Mary Lou. He was strong and smart, and he helped Miss Katherine make repairs on her schoolhouse in exchange for jars of spiced peaches. One day, the two were seen kissing. Drunk and angry, Trout Walker led an angry mob who burned down the school and killed Sam and Mary Lou. Miss Katherine became the outlaw Kissin' Kate Barlow, who left a lipstick imprint of a kiss on the foreheads of all the men she killed. And no rain fell on Green Lake for the next one hundred ten years. Twenty years after Sam's death, Kate returned to Green Lake, now a ghost town. Trout Walker and his wife found her, and demanded at gunpoint that she tell them where she had buried her loot. She walked them out to the center of the dried-up lake bed, but before she could tell them anything, she was bitten by a yellow-spotted lizard and died, laughing.

Back at Camp Green Lake, Mr. Sir's face swells horribly, and he takes out his pain and anger on Stanley, pouring his share of water on the ground instead of into his canteen. Stanley begins teaching Zero to read, beginning with the alphabet and then teaching him to write his name. Zero tells Stanley that his real name is not Zero, but Hector Zeroni.

Chapters 29–36

The weather gets hotter and more humid at Camp Green Lake, making the digging even harder. One day, a flash of lightning in the distance makes a rock formation look like a giant thumb, and Stanley remembers the family legend that his great-grandfather, after being robbed but not killed by Kissin' Kate Barlow, "found refuge on God's thumb." After forty-five days of digging, Stanley is leaner and stronger than he has ever been, but the other boys begin to resent the help he is getting from Zero, and the harmony among the white, black, and Hispanic boys begins to dissolve. During a fistfight, Zero comes to Stanley's aid, and nearly strangles another boy. Mr. Pendanski hears about the reading lessons and mocks Zero for being too stupid to learn anything. At the end of his rope, Zero hits Mr. Pendanski in the face with his shovel, and runs away across the lake. No one chases him; they know he will have to come back soon for water. But he does not come back. After a few days, the Warden has all of Zero's files destroyed so there will be no record of him, and another boy is brought in to fill his place.

Stanley cannot forget Zero, and feels guilty that he did not try to help him. A few days later, on impulse, he steals Mr. Sir's truck, but not knowing how to drive, he promptly drives the truck into one of the holes. Like Zero, he takes off. After hours of walking, he comes across an upside-down boat, the *Mary Lou*, and finds Zero hiding beneath it. Zero has stayed alive by eating from a cache of canning jars filled with what he calls "Sploosh," a sweet mush that tastes faintly of peaches. Zero refuses to go back to camp, so the two boys head toward the rock formation that resembles a thumb, taking the last four jars of Sploosh with them. Zero has been eating the Sploosh for days, and his stomach begins to cramp painfully, but he and Stanley manage to reach the steep mountains.

Chapters 37–42

The boys move closer and closer to the Big Thumb, climbing as they go. Finally they come to patches of weeds and swarms of bugs and realize they must be near water. But Zero's strength is gone; he can go no further. Stanley picks him up and carries him up the mountain until they reach a flat, muddy area. Digging for water, Stanley discovers that they are in a field of onions. The story flashes back to Sam and his donkey Mary Lou, and the first time Sam's onion tonic made a sick child well. Zero slowly regains his strength as he eats the onions, and he tells Stanley about his childhood.

Zero and his mother were homeless, and they often survived by stealing what they needed. In fact, it was Zero who stole the sneakers from the homeless shelter, not being able to read the sign that identified them as valuable shoes from a celebrity athlete. When the commotion started over the missing shoes, he went outside and set them on top of a parked car; he was arrested the next day when he stole another pair of shoes from a store. The shoes that Stanley was accused of stealing had, apparently, fallen off the car and onto Stanley's head when the car went over an overpass. Now the boys are alone on top of a mountain, with nothing to eat but onions, but Stanley feels glad for all he has been through and for the friend he has gained. And he develops a plan, asking Zero if he would like to "dig one more hole."

Chapters 43–50

The boys hike down the mountain, and Zero tells the rest of his story. He remembers standing in a crib in a yellow room before he and his mother became homeless, and he remembers that he used to wait for her in a playground structure during the day while she went off in search of food. One day, she did not come back, and he lived alone in the park for more than a month, sleeping in the playscape. The boys make their way back toward camp, and after the diggers leave for the day, the two go to the hole where Stanley found the lipstick tube. Digging through the night, they find a suitcase buried in the hole. They begin to climb out, but are surprised by the Warden shining a flashlight on them and thanking them for finding the suitcase. Mr. Sir and Mr. Pendanski arrive, but the adults are prevented from taking the case by the discovery that, along with the boys, there are several of the deadly yellow-spotted lizards. The Warden, who says she spent every weekend and holiday digging holes with her parents when she was a child, decides she can wait a little longer for the lizards to kill the boys, if it means she will finally have the suitcase. After the boys are dead, they can easily be buried in one of the holes.

As everyone waits to see what will happen next, the adults reveal that an attorney has come to the camp that day to get Stanley released; they know it will be difficult to make up a believable story about Stanley's running away and being bitten by the lizards. When the sun comes up, the attorney comes back and finds them all gathered around the hole. The Warden accuses the boys of sneaking into her cabin and stealing her suitcase, but Zero astonishes everyone when he shows that the suitcase has Stanley's name on it. The lizards move off, the boys crawl out of the hole, and Stanley and Zero are released into the attorney's custody, taking the suitcase with them.

Again, the novel flashes back to Sam the onion man. Two men from the town of Green Lake headed to the mountains to hunt rattlesnakes one day, and Sam gave them bottles of onion juice to drink before they went. The juice, he said, would protect them from yellow-spotted lizards, which "don't like onion blood."

Suddenly, things begin to look up. Stanley's father has successfully invented a product to eliminate stinky feet—a product that smells like spiced peaches. Rain falls on Green Lake. The suitcase, which was stolen from Stanley Yelnats by Kissin' Kate Barlow, is filled with jewelry and financial documents worth almost two million dollars. Zero is reunited with his mother. It may or may not all be due to Elya Yelnats's great-great-grandson Stanley having carried Madame Zeroni's great-great-great-grandson up a mountain.

CHARACTERS

Armpit

Armpit, whose given name is Theodore, is one of the campers in D tent. Armpit is tall, African American, and, after X-Ray, the second most senior boy in Group D. Armpit generally follows X-Ray's lead, befriending Stanley or turning on him when X-Ray does. He is tough, an unemotional survivor, but seems genuinely glad when Stanley and Zero turn up alive.

Katherine Barlow

Miss Katherine Barlow is a beautiful schoolteacher in the nineteenth-century town of Green Lake. She is good-hearted and generous, and famous for her canned spiced peaches. Every man in town, including the wealthy Trout Walker, wants to marry her, but she is in love with the African American onion peddler Sam. Flouting the law that prohibits romantic relationships across racial lines, Katherine and Sam kiss, and are seen by one of the townspeople. When a gang of angry white men kills Sam and burns down the schoolhouse, Katherine Barlow becomes the outlaw Kissin' Kate Barlow. Many people suspect that she has cursed the town of Green Lake because, after Sam dies, rain stops falling in the area and the lake becomes a desert. For twenty years, she roams the West, robbing men and killing many of them. Those she kills she marks with the lipstick imprint of a kiss on their foreheads. Kissin' Kate is a successful robber, accumulating a great hoard of loot. She retires to a quiet cabin in Green Lake, by then a ghost town. But Trout Walker and his wife track her down, demanding the loot. Before she can tell them where she has buried it, she is bitten by a yellow-spotted lizard and dies, laughing. More than one hundred years later, Zero avoids death in the desert when he finds the last remaining jars of her spiced peaches, naming the substance "Sploosh."

Caveman

See Stanley Yelnats V

Derrick Dunne

Derrick Dunne is a bully who tormented Stanley every day at school. No one believed Stanley's accusations, because Derrick was much smaller than Stanley.

Kissin' Kate

See Katherine Barlow

Mary Lou

Mary Lou is the beloved donkey of Sam the onion peddler, and the namesake of his little boat.

Mom

See Mr. Pendanski

Myra Menke

Fourteen-year-old Myra Menke is the pretty but stupid Latvian girl who Stanley's great-great-grandfather Elya Yelnats falls in love with when he is fifteen. She is spoiled and delicate and useless, but Elya can see only her beauty, so he tries to win her hand in marriage. Myra's father agrees to give Myra to the man who offers the biggest pig, but on the appointed day, the pigs presented by Elya and his rival are equal in weight. Myra, not caring whom she marries, tells the men to each pick a number; Elya finally realizes she is stupid and indifferent, and walks away.

Mr. Pendanski

Mr. Pendanski is the counselor for Group D at Camp Lake Green. He sometimes acts kindly toward the boys, earning him the nickname "Mom," but he is also stern. He refuses to use the boys' nicknames because he wants to prepare them for how they will be received when they leave Camp Green Lake, and he leads a discussion to help them articulate their dreams for the future. But he is merciless to Zero, repeatedly calling him stupid and worthless. When he does this out where the boys are digging on a particularly hot day, Zero is finally pushed to hit Mr. Pendanski in the face with his shovel and run away. After Zero has been missing for a few days, Mr. Pendanski erases his file from Camp Green Lakes computers so there will be no record of his having ever been there.

Sam

Sam is an African American man who sells onions and an onion tonic in nineteenth-century Green Lake. With his donkey, Mary Lou, he delivers onions from a secret field across the lake, and his onions and tonic are said to cure diseases that medicine cannot touch. Sam is also handy with tools, and he fixes up the schoolhouse where Miss Katherine Barlow, the white schoolteacher, works. Sam is well liked by the people of Green Lake, but when he is seen kissing Miss Katherine, a line has been crossed. A gang of men come to lynch him, and Sam and Katherine try to escape across the lake in his boat, the *Mary Lou*. Sam is shot and killed out on the lake, and the boat sinks after Katherine is rescued from it.

Mr. Sir

Mr. Sir is the director of Camp Green Lake, second-in-command to the Warden. As the novel opens, he has recently given up smoking, and he chews on sunflower seeds to help him avoid cigarettes. He wears sunglasses and a cowboy hat and has a rattlesnake tattooed on his arm. He greets Stanley when he arrives at the camp, runs through the rules with him, and utters what will become a refrain for him: "This isn't a Girl Scout Camp." Mr. Sir is tough but fair, until the boys steal and spill his bag of sunflower seeds. Stanley takes the blame for the theft,

and Mr. Sir delivers him to be punished by the Warden. But the Warden instead punishes Mr. Sir for wasting her time, scratching his face with her special nail polish made from rattlesnake venom. His face swells up painfully, and for the next several weeks he turns against Stanley, refusing to give him water when he brings it to the others. Mr. Sir is the one delivering water the day Stanley steals the truck and tries to get away, driving into a hole instead.

Squid

Squid is one of the boys in Group D at Camp Green Lake. Early in the book, he makes fun of Stanley for writing a letter to his mother. At the end, however, as Stanley is about to leave Camp Green Lake, Squid gives Stanley his mother's phone number and asks him to phone and tell her he is sorry for his past mistakes.

Stanley's mother

Stanley's mother is patient and kind, and continually optimistic. When Stanley or his father good-naturedly blame their bad luck on the curse brought down on their heads by the misdeeds of Stanley's "no-good-dirty-rotten-pig-stealing-great-great-grandfather," Stanley's mother, who does not believe in the curse, reminds them that Stanley Yelnats once made a fortune investing in the stock market. Stanley's mother is a full-time homemaker, and puts up with her husband's smelly experiments and repeated failures. Stanley, her only child, lies to her about conditions at Green Lake Camp, pretending it is a fun recreation spot, so she will not worry about him there.

Charles "Trout" Walker

Charles Walker, nicknamed "Trout," is the son of the richest man in the county surrounding nineteenth-century Green Lake. He has earned the nickname "Trout" because his feet always smell like dead fish. Trout attends the evening adult classes taught by Miss Katherine Barlow, but he comes only to flirt with her or to make stupid jokes; he has no interest in learning. When Miss Katherine rejects Trout and chooses Sam instead, Trout leads the mob that burns the school and kills Sam. Twenty years later, he and his wife attempt to force Kissin' Kate to turn over her stolen loot, but all they learn is that it is buried somewhere in the desert. At the end of the book, it is made clear the Trout Walker is the grandfather or great-grandfather of the Warden, Ms. Walker, and that his descendants have spent their lives digging holes, looking for buried loot.

Ms. Walker
See The Warden

The Warden
The Warden is Ms. Walker, a tall red-haired woman who runs Camp Green Lake. She is strict and humorless, and neither the boys nor the staff members ever dare cross her. In fact, when Stanley first arrives at Camp Green Lake, Mr. Pendanski teaches him the camp's only rule: "Don't upset the Warden." She does not yell, but speaks her commands in a quiet, gentle voice, and even says, "Thank you"; still, when she tells Mr. Pendanski to refill the boys' canteens, he knows that she expects him to do it without questioning her authority. When Mr. Sir wastes her time with his complaint about his spilled sunflower seeds, she scratches his face with nail polish made with rattlesnake venom. She pokes Armpit with her pitchfork for taking a bathroom break, making three small puncture wounds in his chest. And when it appears that Zero has run away and probably died in the desert, she has no qualms about ordering his files destroyed so there will be no record of his having ever been at the camp. It is the Warden who has come up with the plan to have the boys dig holes to build character, with the warning that anything they dig up must be reported to her. After Stanley and Zero find the buried suitcase, the Warden reveals that she has been looking for it her entire life, that she grew up watching her parents "dig holes, every weekend and holiday." As she grew older, she dug, too, "even on Christmas." She is willing to watch the boys be killed by the yellow-spotted lizards if it means she will finally have the treasure. The thought that she could be so close to having the suitcase and still not get it—or even get to see inside it—is terrible for her.

X-Ray
X-Ray is the de facto leader of the boys in Group D. X-Ray's given name is Rex, but only Mr. Pendanski calls him that at Camp Green Lake. He has the nickname "X-Ray" because he wears thick glasses and still sees poorly. A large, tough African American boy, X-Ray determines how the boys line up when it is time for their water breaks, and he intimidates Stanley into letting him be the one who claims credit for finding the

gold tube. Still, he looks after Stanley once Stanley has earned his trust, and the younger boy starts to feel for the first time that he has friends. But when X-Ray comes to see it as unfair that Zero helps Stanley dig his holes every day, he expresses his displeasure in racial terms, accusing the white Stanley of making the African American Zero his slave, and later mockingly insists Stanley stand at the front of the line for water since he feels he is better than the others. This taunting leads to a fight that ultimately leads to Zero striking Mr. Pendanski and running away.

Elya Yelnats
Elya Yelnats is Stanley's "dirty-rotten-pig-stealing-great-great-grandfather." As a fifteen-year-old boy in Latvia, he falls in love with Myra Menke, a beautiful but stupid girl. Myra's father has agreed that she will marry the man who brings him the fattest pig on Myra's fifteenth birthday. Elya consults his friend Madame Zeroni, who gives him a small pig and instructs him to carry it up the mountain each day to a special stream, until it grows fat and he grows strong. In exchange for the advice and the pig, he promises to carry Madame Zeroni up the mountain as well. He follows her advice and presents Myra Menke's father with a pig exactly as large as his rival's, and Myra decides to have the men pick a number to win her hand. Instead, Elya leaves for America to start over, forgetting his promise to Madame Zeroni. He marries, and fathers Stanley Yelnats, but he and his descendants are cursed to endure constant bad luck because of his forgotten promise.

Stanley Yelnats
The first Stanley Yelnats, Elya's son and the protagonist's great-grandfather, at first seemed to be proof that the family was not truly cursed. Stanley Yelnats made a fortune in the stock market. On his way west, however, he was robbed of his fortune by the outlaw Kissin' Kate Barlow. Kissin' Kate did not kill him, but left him stranded in the desert.

Stanley Yelnats II
Stanley Yelnats II is Stanley's father, an inventor who tries and tries but never succeeds, but who keeps his spirits high. He has recently been trying to invent something to make sneakers stop smelling, but all he has managed to do is stink up the family's apartment and get them

threatened with eviction. On the day after Stanley carries Zero up the mountain, strengthened by Katherine Barlow's spiced peaches, Stanley's father invents a peach-scented product that stops foot odor. It is his first successful product. With the money Stanley V ultimately gets from the contents of the buried suitcase, he buys his family a new house with a laboratory for his father.

Stanley Yelnats V

Stanley Yelnats V is a white, overweight, unpopular middle-school boy, and the main character of the novel. Although he is well loved at home, he is bullied at school, and he seems to be followed by bad luck that makes his inability to stand up for himself even worse. Walking home from school one day, he is suddenly hit on the head by a pair of sneakers that seem to have fallen from the sky. No one believes this version of the events, and he is sentenced to Camp Green Lake for the theft. At the camp he is assigned to Group D with other boys who have committed crimes. From the beginning, Stanley struggles to fit in with this new group of tough, cynical young men, but when he accidentally bumps into a boy from another tent, he earns the nickname "Caveman" and some grudging respect as a good fighter. At first, Stanley's low expectations for his own life serve him well; the digging, the blisters, the four-minute showers, and the bad food are no more than he expects, so although he suffers, he does not rebel. As the days go by, Stanley becomes physically and mentally stronger. He does what he can to get along: he lets X-Ray take the credit for digging up a gold tube, he takes the blame for spilling Mr. Sir's sunflower seeds, and he learns to keep his mouth shut and do what the adults tell him. He keeps his promise to his mother and writes her a letter every week, but he lies to make the camp seem like fun. And he tells no one when he figures out what the gold tube is, and when he remembers where it was actually found.

It takes Stanley a while to realize that although Zero cannot read, he is actually quite smart. When Stanley begins to think for himself where Zero is concerned, and goes out of his way to teach Zero to read, he makes his first real friend. Later, when Zero runs away and seems to be in danger, Stanley is the only one to take action to save him: he tries to steal a truck, but ends up following Zero across the desert on foot. He finds Zero, and the two boys make their way to a rock formation that Stanley calls God's Thumb, where his great-grandfather may have taken refuge decades before. Zero becomes ill, and Stanley uses his muscles and his brain to get them both to safety. He carries Zero up the mountain, finds water and digs for it, uncovers the onions, and makes a plan for finding Kissin' Kate Barlow's hidden loot. The boys find the buried suitcase—and a nest full of poisonous lizards. When it appears that Stanley has a chance to be rescued and taken away from Green Lake Camp by the attorney who appears suddenly, he will not leave Zero behind, so the attorney is forced to look into Zero's case as well. Stanley is rewarded for his loyalty and intelligence with a suitcase full of treasure, a new home for his family, the restoration of his honor, and a new best friend.

Zero

Zero is a small, quiet African American boy at Camp Green Lake, one of the boys in Group D. He has a long skinny neck and wild blond hair, and he almost never speaks. The other boys pay him little attention, thinking that he is "one weird dude," but Mr. Pendanski taunts Zero mercilessly, making fun of him for being stupid and worthless. In fact, Zero is naturally intelligent and quite good at math, but as the reader learns later, he has had little formal education because he and his mother were homeless for many years. He has never heard of *Sesame Street* or common nursery rhymes, and he cannot read or write. He does have one useful skill, however: he loves to dig, and is by far the fastest hole-digger at Camp Green Lake.

Slowly, Zero and Stanley become friends. The first time Zero asks Stanley to teach him to read, Stanley rejects him, and goes over to join the more popular boys. But he does begin to give Zero reading lessons in exchange for help digging holes, and Zero learns quickly. When Stanley gets into a fistfight one day, Zero jumps in to defend his friend, although he is much smaller than the other boys. Stanley repays this loyalty when he runs off to find Zero in the desert. Together, the boys learn to work together, and so save their lives. It is Zero who finds the upturned boat and the Sploosh, and who reads the name "Stanley Yelnats" on the once-buried suitcase, and it is Stanley who finds the water and the onions, and who carries Zero to the top of the mountain. As they hike, Zero tells Stanley about his past: his dim memory of a yellow bedroom, his years of homelessness, how he and his mother used to steal to survive, how he was arrested for stealing a pair of shoes. He confesses that he was the one who stole the shoes the Stanley was convicted of stealing, and reveals that his real name is Hector Zeroni. (Neither he nor Stanley realizes that he is the direct descendant of Madame Zeroni, or that the two friends have fulfilled Stanley's ancestor's promise and ended the curse.) In the end, Zero is rewarded for his perseverance, his loyalty and his courage in the way fairy-tale heroes are rewarded: he becomes rich and is reunited with his mother.

Hector Zeroni
See Zero

Madame Zeroni
Madame Zeroni is an old Egyptian woman who lives at the edge of the Latvian town where Elya Yelnats lives. She has dark, exotic looks and only one foot, and she has a store of old stories that Elya loves to listen to. She tries to help Elya win Myra's hand, advising him to carry a pig up the mountain each day and then present the pig to Myra's father. In exchange, she makes Elya promise to carry her up the mountain as well and let her drink from a stream there and sing to her. When Elya forgets to do this part of his task, she curses him and his descendants for all eternity.

THEMES

Friendship
The most important lesson Stanley Yelnats learns in *Holes* is the power of friendship. It is not a lesson he learns grudgingly; he yearns for friendship, although he may not be able to articulate that feeling. Before he came to Camp Green Lake, he was continually bullied at school. Although his parents were loving and attentive, "He didn't have any friends at home," and as he rides the bus to Camp Green Lake he thinks, "Maybe he'd make some friends." Of course, to have a friend one must be a friend, and Stanley has had little or no practice at this. When Zero first asks Stanley to teach him to read, he refuses. Zero is generally thought of as worthless and weird, and Stanley desperately wants to fit in with the boys in Group D. He decides that, after a long day of digging, he had better "save his energy for the people who

counted" instead of wasting it on Zero. The narrator comments that it is not only Stanley's muscles that have gotten tougher through all the digging—"His heart had hardened as well."

Over time, though, Stanley learns how to be a friend. At first, when he does seemingly selfless things like turning over the gold tube to X-Ray or taking the blame for stealing the sunflower seeds, he is only doing them to gain acceptance; he expects to gain more than he gives up in these transactions. But when he begins to teach Zero to read, he is taking his first steps toward kindness, and that kindness is quickly repaid when Zero jumps in to defend Stanley during a fistfight. After Zero runs away, Stanley realizes that he should have coached Zero without asking for anything in return. When he sets out to save Zero, risking his own safety, it is out of friendship only, not for any gain. The two boys survive physical hardship in the desert and in the mountains through trust and cooperation—through friendship. If Zero did not share the Sploosh, if Stanley did not share the water and onions, they would starve. If Stanley had not taught Zero to read, Zero would not be able to identify the suitcase's owner. And if Stanley did not insist that he would not leave Camp Green Lake without Zero, Zero would surely be harmed. Both boys, who through no fault of their own, have spent their lives depending only on themselves, learn about friendship, and they are rewarded with money, security, and love.

Ancestry
A common theme in literature is the idea that future generations continue to pay for the mistakes that people make. This idea, that children continue to pay for the mistakes of their ancestors, runs throughout *Holes*. In Stanley's family, there is the curse laid upon Stanley's "no-good-dirty-rotten-pig-stealing-great-great-grandfather," Elya Yelnats, who failed to fulfill his promise to Madame Zeroni. Ever since Elya sailed to America, bad luck has followed the family. Elya was a hard-working farmer, but lightning kept striking his crops before he could harvest them; Stanley Yelnats made a fortune in the stock market, but had it all stolen by Kissin' Kate Barlow; Stanley's father fails repeatedly to invent something useful and profitable; Stanley is bullied at school and has the bad luck to be caught with a valuable pair of sneakers that fall out of the sky and hit him on the head. Although the Yelnats clan works hard and remains cheerfully optimistic, they seem to have

TOPICS FOR FURTHER STUDY

- After watching the film version of *Holes*, write an essay in which you compare how Stanley is portrayed in the book and in the film. Do the differences change how you perceive Stanley and what he goes through? You may wish to examine another character instead, for example, Sam the onion man or Mr. Pendanski.

- Using characters from the history of your school or your town, write a folk tale or a tall tale. If the resources are available, adapt the tale into a short video, and post it on YouTube or on your school's Web site.

- The novel *Holes* reveals some of the background of what Stanley, Zero, and the Warden were doing before they all met at Camp Green Lake. Choose another character—perhaps one of the other boys in Group D, or Zero's mother, or Mr. Sir or Mr. Pendanski—and write a five-minute monologue in that character's own voice, explaining what she or he was doing before appearing "on stage" in this novel. Read or recite your speech to your class.

- Read the young-adult novel, *Hoppergrass*, by Chris Carlton Brown. Fifteen-year-old Browser gets sent to the Hill, an institution for troubled teens. Create a chart that compares the characters in *Holes* with the characters in *Hoppergrass*. Provide an explanation of why you think each set of characters is a match.

- Using Gliffy.com or another diagramming program, create a map of Camp Green Lake and the surrounding area. In another color or another layer, make a map of the same area as it appeared before the rains stopped.

- Visit the online bulletin board that Scholastic, the publisher of *Holes*, has created for kids to discuss the novel, and read several of the discussion threads. Post a comment on one interesting thread. With a group, come up with a new question that you believe will generate a lot of responses. Write a report in which you describe your process for brainstorming and choosing a question, and summarize the online responses.

---

been "doomed for all of eternity" by the curse. When Stanley fulfills Elya's promise by carrying Zero up a mountain, the curse is broken, and the new line of good luck extends backwards through the generations. Stanley finds the buried treasure, his father has his first success as an inventor, and Stanley the First's wealth is recovered.

The curse can be broken because Zero is also part of a long line. He is a direct descendant of Madame Zeroni, the dark-skinned Egyptian woman who somehow made her way to Latvia. They share the same wide mouth (as does Zero's mother), and Madame Zeroni's eyes "seemed to expand" when she looked intensely at someone, just as Zero's do when Mr. Pendanski taunts him. Across the generations, Zero's family and Stanley's are connected

by the song that Stanley learned from his father and Zero's mother learned from her grandmother: "*If only, if only.*"

Even the Warden is bound to her fate through her family tree. She is descended from Charles "Trout" Walker, the man who led the mob attack on Sam and the school, and the man who watched Kissin' Kate die before she could reveal where she had buried her loot. Apparently, his descendants have been digging holes ever since. The Warden remembers that her parents dug every weekend and holiday when she was a child, and that she joined them when she was old enough. This knowledge makes the Warden seem a bit more sympathetic; after all, the forces of family and destiny are powerful in this novel.

The boys dug 5x5 holes all over the lake bed. *(IgorXIII | Shutterstock.com)*

Race Relations

Race is an important element in the story, always underlying the action although it is seldom discussed directly. Stanley, like many people his age, is less conscious of race than his elders might be. When he meets Squid and X-Ray for the first time, for example, "their faces were so dirty that it took Stanley a moment to notice that one kid was white and the other black." After that comment, Stanley does not take much notice of their color. When he meets the other boys in tent D, their race and color are not identified by the narrator, and it may take readers several chapters to realize that Zero, with his "wild frizzy blond hair that stuck out in all directions," is black. In fact, although the boys of Group D are unusually diverse—three of them are African American, three are white, and one is Hispanic—they almost never discuss race. As Stanley observes, "On the lake they were all the same reddish brown color—the color of dirt." There is the possibility of racial tension when X-Ray and the others complain about Zero's helping Stanley dig his holes, and one of the boys taunts Stanley by calling Zero his "slave," but it

is just part of the normal bad-mouthing that goes on among them, and within seconds they have moved on from calling Stanley a slave-master to saying that he thinks he is better than all of them. For the boys, race is not a divisive factor. And the only way Stanley and Zero survive in the desert is by working together, sharing everything equally.

But in the town of Green Lake a century before, race was much more prominent. Sam the onion man was respected because of his ability to cure illnesses, and generally liked because of his charm, but he was not allowed to attend the school because he was not an equal member of the society. Sam, an African American, is killed because he and Miss Katherine, a white woman, fall in love. As the sheriff explains, "It's against the law for a Negro to kiss a white woman." Katherine declares, "We're all equal under the eyes of God," and while the readers are meant to agree with her, the townspeople do not. Twice, people of Green Lake tell Miss Katherine, "God will punish you," and she does suffer the pain of losing Sam. But the town is also punished for its intolerance when the rains stop falling, the lake dries up, and the entire town disappears.

STYLE

Flashback

Holes relies heavily on flashbacks, or scenes depicting events that happened before the beginning of the main story. How Stanley Yelnats V is sent to and emerges triumphant from Camp Green Lake is the main narrative in the novel, occupying the story's "present." But in order for readers to understand the implications and the causes of Stanley's story, Sachar also tells several stories from the past: Elya Yelnats's quest to marry Myra Menke and his unfulfilled promise to Madame Zeroni in Latvia; Stanley Yelnats the First's success in the stock market and his subsequent robbery and stranding in the desert; Katherine Barlow's story of love, loss, and revenge; and Hector Zeroni's story of his life as a homeless petty thief. Sachar tells Stanley's story in roughly chronological order, from the time he arrives in Camp Green Lake to the end, with a small flashback to explain how he found the valuable sneakers falling from the sky. But the other flashbacks come in as the narrator feels compelled to give background information, often called exposition, without regard for chronology. Thus, readers do not learn until Chapter 49, after Stanley and Zero have left Camp Green Lake, that the secret to keeping yellow-spotted lizards from biting is to consume a lot of onions—something Sam the onion seller knew all along.

If Sachar or his narrator had told all of the pieces of the various narratives in chronological order, from the early days in Latvia to the day a year and a half after Stanley and Zero uncovered the buried suitcase, readers would have been denied delightful surprises. They would know as soon as the boys find the field of onions that eating them will be protection from the lizards. They would know before Stanley finds the shoes that Zero is the one who stole them. And they would know right away when Stanley's father invents his successful peach-scented odor remover, instead of learning about it when Stanley does. By using flashbacks, the novelist is able to parcel out information as he pleases, juxtaposing elements to highlight—or conceal—connections.

Tall Tale

While much of the material in *Holes* is realistic—sometimes grimly so—there are also elements of magic or fantasy. The story of Elya Yelnats in Latvia sounds very much like a typical fairy-tale or folk tale, with a suitor given a challenge by the father of his intended bride, a special stream on top of a mountain, and a curse laid on Elya and all his descendants by a one-legged Gypsy woman. Generations later, one of Elya's descendants breaks the curse and is rewarded with riches. A particularly American kind of folk tale is the tall tale. Tall tales are presented by straight-faced narrators, as humorous but factual, as the stories of Elya and of Katherine Barlow are, and although they contain elements of magic or exaggeration, their narrators seem unaware of these elements. The borderlands between settled land and wilderness in North America were especially fertile ground for the development of these stories, with larger-than-life heroes including Davy Crockett, "King of the Wild Frontier"; Pecos Bill, who tamed the Wild West by lassoing and then riding a tornado; and the superhuman lumberjack Paul Bunyan, whose blue ox was named Babe. These stories captured the imagination of people who thought of the frontier as a wild place where anything could happen, but also as a place that American heroes could tame.

Holes is set in Texas, which, in the days of Kissin' Kate Barlow, was a rough-and-tumble place. Although Katherine Barlow starts out as a mild and pretty schoolteacher, when Sam is killed, she instantly changes into Kissin' Kate, "one of the most feared outlaws in all the West," with the power to control even the rain. Although she is, within the world of the novel, a real person (as Davy Crockett was), she also becomes a legend, with exaggerated stories of her exploits reaching down through the generations to Stanley. Stanley's mother has apparently never believed in the curse or the story of Elya, but Sachar strongly suggests the truth of the story, and points out that "the reader might find it interesting" that the curse—the generations of bad luck that have followed the Yelnats family, despite their good hearts and hard work—ceases to have power over the family the day after Stanley carries Zero up the mountain. By the end of the novel, Stanley's mother may not believe in magic or in curses, but the reader surely does.

COMPARE & CONTRAST

- **1880s:** The U.S. Supreme Court upholds the rights of states to prohibit interracial romantic relationships in the 1883 case *Pace v. Alabama*. However, interracial sex or marriage, called miscegenation, is not a crime punishable by death.

  1990s: No states have laws prohibiting relationships between people of different races.

  Today: The Pew Research Center reports that 14.8 percent of couples married in the United States in 2008 were interracial or across ethnic lines, the highest percentage ever recorded.

- **1880s:** There is no separate juvenile justice system in the United States. Children and adults are tried and sentenced in the same courts, and face the same punishments.

  1990s: Alternative detention facilities for juvenile offenders, often called "boot camp

  detention facilities," are operating in each of the fifty United States.

  Today: Following the 2006 death of a boy in a Florida boot camp detention facility, such facilities are banned in that state, and many other facilities across the United States have been closed.

- **1880s:** As the narrator points out, there are no telephones to help spread the word that Katherine Barlow and Sam the onion man have been seen kissing.

  1990s: Land line phones are found in nearly every home and building in the United States. The Attorney General uses the phone in the Warden's office to call his own office.

  Today: According to the Federal Communications Commission, there are more than 270 million cell phone subscribers in the United States.

HISTORICAL CONTEXT

Young Adult Literature in the 1990s

Holes is an example of the literature often called young-adult fiction, or adolescent fiction. Young-adult fiction typically has main characters who are in their teens, and these books are written for—or marketed toward—readers of a similar age. The books may have elements of fantasy or science fiction, but their protagonists and their conflicts are portrayed realistically. Scholars who study young-adult literature, including Michael Cart and others, often refer to S. E. Hinton's *The Outsiders* (1967) as one of the earliest young-adult novels (though others argue for other earlier works, even reaching back as far as Mark Twain's *Huckleberry Finn*, 1884). Before *The Outsiders* and the work of Hinton's contemporaries, including Robert Lipsyte and Robert Cormier, books for young teens tended toward adventure stories, science fiction,

and stories of sports heroes, rather than realistic novels about the kinds of problems teens actually face in their lives.

By the 1970s, young-adult literature was well defined, at least by publishers and marketers. Writers sometimes resisted being labeled young-adult authors, fearing that the label would limit their ability to attract adult readers and serious critical attention. Still, a well-defined readership of young people aged twelve to eighteen years old was established, and for nearly all of the decade, young-adult fiction focused on pessimistic portrayals of teens suffering the effects of drug abuse, divorce, depression, friends' suicides, and other traumas. As Cart points out, the 1980s saw a turning away from this gloom with the rise of paperback series novels such as the "Sweet Valley High" series. Although many excellent writers were producing young-adult literature during this period, including Gary Paulsen, Jerry Spinelli,

A juvenile correctional facility *(idiz | Shutterstock.com)*

and Cynthia Voigt, the period from the late 1970s through the 1980s is seen as a dull spot in the history of young-adult literature. In an *Orana* essay, critic Mary Owen attributes this to publishers seeming "to want quantity over quality," and observes that "the genre was at risk of dying out."

The middle of the 1990s, however, saw a new energy and a widening readership, what Owen calls "a resurgence and reinvention" of young-adult literature as well as an appeal to readers ranging from as young as twelve to as old as twenty-five. Part of the credit for this expanding audience goes to Philip Pullman's series "His Dark Materials," beginning in 1995, and to J. K. Rowling and her "Harry Potter" series, which first appeared in 1997. Both series were quickly adopted by adults as well as by children—in fact, the Harry Potter books were so popular among adult readers that some of the novels were published in separate editions with cover art deemed more suitable for adults to walk around with. This expanded audience, according to Cart, "freed authors to tackle more serious subjects and to introduce more complex characters and

considerations of ambiguity." Authors were also freed to use a wider variety of narrative techniques. To recognize the high quality of this new age of young-adult fiction, the presenters of the National Book Award established a new category, Young People's Fiction, in 1996, and gave the first award to Victor Martinez for *Parrot in the Oven: Mi Vida.*

Holes, published in 1998, is a prime example of the work coming out of what Cart calls a new "golden age" of young-adult literature. The novel features a teen-aged protagonist, and its characters face real-life issues, including homelessness, poverty, abandonment, and bullying. But like many books of its period, *Holes* is optimistic and hopeful about its characters' chances for a good life. The novel achieved great popularity among young readers, even outside the influence of the classroom, driven in part by the increasing use of the Internet in the late 1990s. The novel's publisher, Scholastic, maintains a *Holes* discussion board online and also has on the Web site an interview with the author based on questions submitted by readers; Sachar also has an active Web site, and there are pages dedicated to him and to the novel on social media sites. But the success of *Holes* is based on quality as well as popularity, as was demonstrated when the book became the third to win the National Book Award for Young People's Literature in 1998.

novel as a positive view of a young man's maturation, arguing that, "while *Holes* may, on the surface, appear to champion a kinder and gentler version of masculinity, on the level of the subconscious, it champions a ... version of boyhood attempting to distance itself from ... all things feminine."

CRITICAL OVERVIEW

Holes, Sachar's first young-adult novel after several successful novels for children, was an immediate critical and popular success. Roger Sutton, reviewing the book for *Horn Book*, called it "exceptionally funny, and heart-rending," declaring that "we haven't seen a book with this much plot, so suspensefully and expertly deployed, in too long a time." In *School Library Journal*, Alison Follos called the novel "captivating," "compelling," and "a brilliant achievement." Bill Ott, reviewing *Holes* for *Booklist*, was virtually alone in giving the novel only lukewarm praise, observing that the plot's "mismatched parts don't add up to a coherent whole, but they do deliver a fair share of entertaining and sometimes compelling moments." The novel won the Newbery Medal, the National Book Award, and the *Boston Globe—Horn Book* Award, and was chosen a Best Book of the Year by *Publishers Weekly*, a Best Book for Young Adults by the American Library Association, and a Notable Children's Book of the Year by the *New York Times Book Review*. Interest in the book increased in a second wave in 2003, when the Disney Studios film version of *Holes* was released. The novel has sold millions of copies, and has been adopted for classroom use in middle schools across the country.

Holes has also been analyzed by scholars. Stephanie Yearwood examined the novel's "ontological issues of being and nothingness" in a 2002 essay for *ALAN Review* titled "Popular Postmodernism for Young Adult Readers: *Walk Two Moons, Holes,* and *Monster*." The same year, Pat Pinsent published an essay in *Children's Literature in Education* in which she observed that the novel includes many fairy-tale elements and "like many fairy tales, it conveys a sense that Fate and Fortune are at work in ensuring the happy ending." Annette Wannamaker, in a 2006 essay for *Children's Literature in Education*, challenges the common view of the

CRITICISM

Cynthia A. Bily

Bily, a mother, teaches English at Macomb Community College in Michigan. In the following essay, she examines the roles of mothers in Holes, *and discusses criticism as a conversation, in which different readers thinking carefully come to very different conclusions.*

Critics agree that *Holes* is a *bildungsroman*, a story of a boy—Stanley Yelnats—becoming a man, alongside his new best friend, Zero. As commonly happens in stories like this, Stanley and Zero are separated from their families and cast adrift in an unforgiving world of physical and mental hardship. The boys must learn to care for one another, to work together, and to display the courage to show weakness in front of each other if they are to survive. Often, at the end of one of these rite-of-passage novels, the hero goes forth to have a career, to marry, to explore new territory. But Stanley and Zero are in their middle teens. Their reward for success is safety, wealth, and reunion with their mothers.

Stanley, the main character of *Holes* comes from a two-parent family. His father is a dreamer, an inventor who never manages to invent anything useful, a cheerful optimist who shrugs off his failures by nodding to the family curse. Stanley's mother is the more level-headed parent. She doesn't believe in curses, and she repeatedly points out that Stanley Yelnats actually did make a fortune in the stock market. Stanley's mother is loving and kind, and she does not nag. She calmly accepts the fact that her husband, the family breadwinner, is unable to earn enough to keep the family comfortable, and laughs off the fact that they might be evicted from their apartment. The simple reality is that she believes in her husband and son, perhaps naively. When Stanley's trial date is approaching, she tells him, "You don't need a lawyer.... Just tell the truth," but the truth does not help Stanley avoid Camp Green Lake. Once Stanley

WHAT DO I READ NEXT?

- *Stanley Yelnats' Survival Guide to Camp Green Lake* (2003) is Sachar's unusual sequel to *Holes*. Narrated by Stanley himself, it offers advice to readers who have been sentenced to spend time at Camp Green Lake, based on new anecdotes from Stanley's time there with Armpit, X-Ray, Zigzag, and the others.

- In a more conventional sequel, *Small Steps* (2008), Sachar follows Armpit and X-Ray, now released from Camp Green Lake, as they try to rebuild their lives.

- In April Henry's *Shock Point* (2006), sixteen-year-old Cassie is sent to a harsh Mexican prison camp for troubled teens to keep her from revealing her stepfather's illegal activities. How she survives the brutal prison and makes her way home to Oregon makes for a thrilling novel.

- Wendelin Van Draanen's *Runaway* (2006) is the story of twelve-year-old Holly, a homeless city girl who keeps a poetry journal as she struggles to find food and shelter and a warm bath.

- Barbara Hayes has collected sixty-eight *Folk Tales and Fables of the World* (2007), beautifully illustrated by Robert Ingpen. The stories come from Africa, Asia, the Americas, Europe, and the Middle East.

- In *True Notebooks: A Writer's Year at Juvenile Hall* (2004), Mark Salzman describes the year he spent teaching a creative writing class in a Los Angeles detention facility for teenage boys who were awaiting trial for serious and violent crimes. The boys' humanity is made vivid through the author's storytelling and through excerpts from their own writing.

- Walter Dean Myers's 2010 novel, *Lockdown*, relates the story of a fourteen-year-old boy who tells, in first-person narration, about his struggle to finish his sentence and then face his future.

- Roger Smith and Marsha McIntosh examine the juvenile justice systems of the United States and Canada in this 2007 nonfiction book, *Youth in Prison*, written specifically for a teen audience.

---

is at the camp, he keeps his promise to write to her every week, but now he does not bother with the truth. Instead, to keep her from worrying, he invents details about swimming in the lake and rock climbing.

One thing Stanley learns at Camp Green Lake is the difference between what his parents can do for him and what they can't. His mother, he sees quickly, no longer needs absolute truth-telling from him; he is becoming a man and is able to make distinctions himself between being truthful and being kind. As he forms friendships for the first time, he sees that other young men can be his allies against bullies like Derrick Dunne; his cheerful and oblivious parents seem not to know about the bullying Stanley faced at school, but when Stanley dreams about Derrick,

he dreams that the boys from D group confront the bully in Stanley's defense. By the time Stanley and Zero are climbing the mountain, half-delirious with thirst and food poisoning and weariness, he does not fantasize about his parents coming to find him but instead worries about how hard it would be for them to learn of his death. Through the rest of the boys' time on the mountain, Stanley acts as an independent agent, planning and executing their survival, but his thoughts never stray far from his anchor, his parents. It is finally the thought of escaping and living the rest of his life as a fugitive, unable to contact them, that leads Stanley to the decision to try to dig up Kissin' Kate's treasure. And at what seems like Stanley's darkest hour—when he is caught between the Warden and the yellow-

> **FOR SQUID, HIS MOTHER IS HIS ONLY LINK WITH HOME, WITH THE PERSON HE USED TO BE AND THE PERSON HE WILL BECOME—WITH ALAN. IN ORDER TO BECOME A GOOD AND DECENT MAN, HE MUST MAKE THINGS RIGHT WITH HER."**

spotted lizards and is prepared to die—he chooses what the last image in his brain will be, "his mother's face."

In many ways. Zero's childhood was quite unlike Stanley's, but for most of it he did have his mother (he has apparently never had a father in his life). "I remember standing in a crib," he says, "with my mother singing to me. She held my wrists and made my hands clap together. She used to sing that song to me." Zero's sweet memories of his mother's singing, his yellow bedroom, his imaginary stuffed giraffe, his mother's prize for selling the most Girl Scout cookies, have lingered with him even through the horror of living alone for a month in a playground and then being sent to Camp Green Lake, where he is known to the other boys as "one weird dude" and to Mr. Pendanski as "not completely worthless." To the rest of the world, Zero is easy to forget because he has no family. "He had nobody," Mr. Pendanski says. "He was nobody." He even mentions the heart-breaking detail that, during his time alone, he occasionally sneaked into the homeless shelter to sleep, but he had to find someone to pretend to be his mother in order to get in. The last image in the novel, however, is of Zero and his real mother; Zero, now Hector again, has used part of his share of the treasure to "hire a team of private investigators" to find her. She fluffs his hair, she looks tired and world-weary, but she smiles the Zeroni wide-mouthed smile, and her song to her son is a song of encouragement and independence: "Be strong my weary wolf, turn around boldly. / Fly high, my baby bird."

Many of the characters in the novel do not have mothers in their lives. Elya Yelnats does not appear to have parents at all, at the ripe age of fifteen, and Myra Menke is under the influence of her father, but no mother is mentioned.

The closest thing Elya has to a mother is Madame Zeroni; "He had become friends with her, though she was quite a bit older than him." The woman is in fact someone's mother—she has a son in America. Elya prefers sitting with Madame Zeroni and listening to her stories to hanging out with the other boys in the village, and she is the one he turns to when he needs advice. Elya's two biggest mistakes arise out of his trying to be his own man, and behaving independently of Madame Zeroni: he ignores her advice to stay away from the empty-headed Myra Menke, and he forgets his promise to carry her up the mountain. And as fifteen-year-old boys have learned the hard way for generations, it's always best to listen to your mother. Elya's punishment is a curse dooming his descendants for eternity.

Mothers do not play a prominent role in the story of nineteenth-century Green Lake, although there are children at Miss Katherine Barlow's school. The teacher herself never mentions parents, and neither does Sam. Trout Walker is "the son of the richest man in the county" and surely has a mother, but she does not appear. The only mother clearly identified is Mrs. Gladys Tennyson, who comes running out into the street in her nightgown and robe to thank Sam for the onion tonic that saved her daughter Rebecca's life.

The boys in D Tent are separated from their homes, and not much is said about their mothers. They know that Stanley writes letters to his mother, and that she writes to him, but there is no evidence that they write similar letters. Still, they feel a lack. The Warden is obviously no substitute for a mother's attention, so the boys take to calling Mr. Pendanski "Mom." "If it makes you feel better to call me Mom," he says, "go ahead and call me Mom." Clearly it make the boys feel better in some way, because they all use that nickname for Mr. Pendanski. Just how poor a substitute for a mother Mr. Pendanski represents is revealed when he gathers the boys in a circle and tries to talk with them about their futures. Some of his ideas about personal responsibility make sense, although he expresses them in weak pop-psychology phrases, but his lack of respect for the boys and his real contempt for Zero undercut any motherliness he might otherwise exhibit. He tries, but there is no substitute for a mother.

Other than Stanley and Zero, Squid is the only character who reveals that he misses his mother. One night, Stanley is awakened by a sound that turns out to be Squid crying quietly into his pillow. Squid is embarrassed about it, in the way that young men are often embarrassed about crying in front of each other, and he insists that he is fine, that the sniffling is due to allergies. When Stanley asks Squid the next morning if he is all right, Squid reveals who it is that is foremost in his mind: "What are you, my mother?" The two boys have little contact after that; each keeps mostly to himself. Squid is aware that Stanley writes to his own mother and receives letters back from her, and he makes fun of their correspondence. But near the end of the novel, when Stanley is about to leave Camp Green Lake with Ms. Morengo, Squid approaches Stanley to ask a favor: "Call my mom for me, okay? Tell her ... Tell her I said I was sorry. Tell her *Alan* said he was sorry." For Squid, his mother is his only link with home, with the person he used to be and the person he will become—with Alan. In order to become a good and decent man, he must make things right with her.

In *Holes*, the mother-child bond is important even as young men begin to grow up and take steps toward independence The mothers who appear in the novel are important to the success of their children and teens. Stanley's mother is an anchor while he is at Camp Green Lake, his tie to home (his father does not seem to write letters); in writing lies to her about the fun he is having at camp, he focuses on the positive, he looks forward to the future, and he shows compassion for someone other than himself. Zero had a hard life during the years he and his mother were homeless, but he felt loved, and his deepest wish is to be reunited with her. Even Squid shows his first evidence of caring about another person when he asks Stanley to contact his mother on his behalf. The boys who do not have evident connections with their mothers seem less ready to face the future as responsible, capable adults after Camp Green Lake.

The scholar Annette Wannamaker, who specializes in studying how children's books deal with the idea of masculinity, sees *Holes* quite differently. To Wannamaker, the novel demonstrates the truth of "psychoanalytic theories that assert that men must, symbolically, separate themselves from their mothers or from an identification with their mothers." As she reads it, the Warden represents all that makes women

dangerous to men, and when Stanley works to escape the dangers posed by the Warden, he is working to define and refine his sense of himself as a man. In order to step into their new roles as mature young men, Stanley and Zero must, in Wannamaker's words, "vanquish the domineering woman (and mother figure) that is the Warden." This means not only escaping from the Warden, but escaping from the influence of their mothers.

This is only a brief summary of a complex and fascinating argument. One thing it illustrates is how interesting it can be when people read novels—or other texts—carefully and thoughtfully and try to make sense of them. Because we cannot help being ourselves, because we each bring different personal and educational backgrounds to everything we do, because we are interested in different things and attracted to different ideas, the world of literary criticism at its best is like a big conversation among passionate, respectful friends. When critics write essays—or when students write critical papers—they do not believe themselves to be speaking The Truth from on high; instead, they intend to say smart things in a rational way, encouraging a reader to say, "Yes, this is a reasonable way to read this text." Their fondest wish is that the next thing that reader will say is, "But have you thought about it this way? Here's another way to look at it." Wannamaker is certainly right that grown men need to stand on their own two feet, and not rely on their mothers—or their fathers—to steer them through the challenges of being good people. But Stanley and Zero and Squid and Elya are still teenagers, still being formed, and they still need their mothers.

Miss Katherine Barlow, who loves and loses Sam the onion seller, never has a chance to become a mother. Sam's death transforms her into Kissin' Kate Barlow, "one of the most feared outlaws in all the West," and she spends the next twenty years alone, missing Sam, and robbing and killing other men. Ms. Trout, the Warden, is also childless, loveless, friendless. She has become so consumed by her inherited quest to find the buried loot that she has had no time for human companionship. In the end, she loses her business and then her land, and disappears from view. Childless women in this novel have nothing to leave behind but small remnants of their lives: half a lipstick tube, sixteen jars of

Dry lake bed in Texas *(Heather A Craig | Shutterstock.com)*

spiced peaches, a fortune in stocks and bonds, and the lasting effects of their anger and bitterness. If Katherine and Sam had been permitted to marry and have children, and if the Warden had been raised to value people more than money, Camp Green Lake would never have existed.

In the end, Stanley and Zero are rewarded for their courage, intelligence, and loyalty; they escape from danger, and they become rich. But they are still teenage boys, not ready to set up their own empires and live independently as kings. Instead, each boy, now a young man, uses his treasure to build security with his family—with his mother.

Source: Cynthia A. Bily, Critical Essay on *Holes*, in *Novels for Students*, Gale, Cengage Learning, 2011.

Pat Pinsent

In the following excerpt, Pinsent maintains that Holes *is an impressive example of how the themes and motifs of one of the oldest genres, the fairy tale, live on in contemporary children's fiction, and thus provide authors with an alternative to "gritty realism" as a means of presenting to young readers the harshest of topics and environments.*

If ever there was a literary genre that continues to live 'happily ever after,' it is the fairy tale. Traditional stories carry on appearing in a variety of forms, their elements sometimes updated to avoid strictures about race and gender stereotyping or to attract a contemporary audience. Another sign of the vitality of the genre, however, is the way in which many children's authors find that incorporating aspects of fairy tale into a text is an effective means of tackling twenty-first-century issues. A book that does just this is *Holes* by the American writer, Louis Sachar (US, 1998; UK, 2000).

There have been many attempts to define fairy tale. For the purposes of my discussion, I am regarding magic as a key characteristic of the fairy tale genre. J. R. R. Tolkien ('On Fairy Stories,' in *Tree and Leaf*, 1964/1976) says, 'A "fairy-story" is one which touches on or uses Faerie, whatever its own main purpose may be.... Faerie itself may perhaps most nearly be

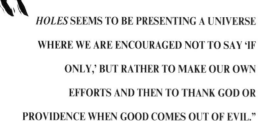

HOLES SEEMS TO BE PRESENTING A UNIVERSE WHERE WE ARE ENCOURAGED NOT TO SAY 'IF ONLY,' BUT RATHER TO MAKE OUR OWN EFFORTS AND THEN TO THANK GOD OR PROVIDENCE WHEN GOOD COMES OUT OF EVIL."

translated by Magic—but it is magic of a peculiar mood and power' (p. 17). The *Larousse Dictionary of World Folklore* (1995, p. 285) defines magic as 'the attempts of humankind to bend spiritual and natural forces to its own will.'

In fairy stories, magical objects range from potions to talismans, while there are countless instances of magic words that must be spoken in a particular way. Fairy tales tend to be populated by characters such as princes, princesses, fairy godmothers, ogres, wicked stepmothers, witches, and talking animals, and are often characterised by repeated motifs and recurrent themes featuring the eventual success of younger sons or the rejects of society. They often have happy endings, not infrequently brought about by what Tolkien describes as a 'eucatastrophe...a sudden joyous turn' (1964/1976).

It might seem perverse to describe *Holes*, set in a bleak, inhospitable landscape in contemporary America, as a fairy tale, but it has many qualities in common with the genre and, like the traditional tales, has much to say about human nature and relationships. Louis Sachar has written a number of currently popular works for younger readers, including a series of stories featuring 'Wayside' School. More cognate to *Holes* is *The Boy Who Lost His Face* (1989), in which David, feeling guilty for his part in an attack on an old lady, interprets a series of personal misadventures as resulting from a curse she has put on him. When he is finally reconciled with her, he learns that the so-called curse was no more than angry words, and no one but himself was responsible for these minor disasters . . . .

FAIRY TALE QUALITIES OF *HOLES*

Even though *Holes* could be regarded as falling entirely within the mode of realism, in that none of its events actually transcends possibility, it seems to me that it is more illuminating to describe the book as a fairy tale, partly because it possesses so many elements of the genre, but also since, like many fairy tales, it conveys a sense that Fate and Fortune are at work in ensuring the happy ending.

There is no shortage of magic objects that serve to ensure that the protagonist survives and inherits the fortune that is rightfully his. Such objects are also revealed as having a provenance that, if not totally supernatural, at least defies probability. The peach liquor, which preserves the lives of the boys on their journey across the baking-hot plain, derives from the bottled peaches for which Kate Barlow, in her schoolmistress days, won prizes at the town fair and with which Sam, her lover, an onion seller, had filled his boat before it was capsized by the more powerful boat of Trout Walker when Sam was killed. Other magic objects are the two halves of the lipstick case owned by Kate Barlow; one of these is found by Stanley in a hole, the other is already familiar to him because it belongs to his family. Magic formulae are not lacking either, from the curse that ruined Elya, to the song that Elya should have sung to the old woman on the mountain in Latvia but that, much later, his great-great-grandson sings to her great-great-great-grandson, Zero.

The characters of fairy tales tend frequently to follow certain predefined roles and are often related to each other. In this text, both Stanley and Zero are only sons, and their family relationships are foregrounded, while inheritance, of both curse and treasure, is a central theme. Both still bear the surnames of their ancestors, who were the characters of the original 'folk tale,' while the reverberative and non-naturalistic aspects of naming are emphasised by the fact that Stanley, like all male members of his family after Elya, has a first name that mirrors his surname. (Elya's own name only uses four letters of the surname, perhaps appropriate to his reduced circumstances!) Additionally, Stanley and Zero are certainly underdogs, the kind of characters most likely to be the recipients of magic favours. Supporting characters also have roles that recall the fairy tale. Contemporary America may not provide traditional royalty, but an extravagantly rewarded baseball player is surely the next best thing to a king. Other traditional roles are performed by Madame Zeroni, who is something of a fairy godmother, while Trout Walker is an ogre, and his descendant, the warden, is certainly a Witch—her nail polish poisons anyone she scratches. This polarisation of good and evil characters is also very characteristic of the fairy tale. At the culmination of the story, Stanley's final triumph reveals him as ultimately a kind of prince.

One of the most obvious features of fairy tales is the use of repeated motifs. In *Holes*, the most obvious of these is displayed in the proliferation of holes of many kinds: the holes that the boys have to dig in the desert; the hole in which they shelter under the boat; the holes in the hammock where the warden, Ms. Walker, reposes; the holes where the lizards and rattlesnakes hide; and even the repeated 'ooos . . .' in the song: 'He cries to the moo-oo-oon.' Particularly significant is the name given to Hector Zeroni, Zero; as Stanley muses as he sees the other boy learning to write his name:

> Zero Zero Zero Zero Zero Zero Zero . . .
>
> In a way, it made him sad. He couldn't help but think that a hundred times zero was still nothing.

Many people think of Zero's mind being as empty as his name, and his apparent nothingness is emphasised by the hole in cyberspace into which Zero's records have fallen, together with the fact that 'no one cares for Hector Zeroni.' The irony that his first name has so heroic a quality may be lost on the young reader, but is surely part of Sachar's intention.

Perhaps the most significant holes are those that are deliberately left in the narrative. The short final section, Part Three, is titled 'Filling in the holes.'

Sachar also supplies repeated formulae, similar to the fairy tale 'once upon a time' or 'they all lived happily ever after,' in his repetition of phrases such as 'No-good-dirty-rotten-pig-stealing-great-great-grandfather.' This device recalls the kind of repetition of phrases so characteristic of oral narratives in general (cf. W. Ong, *Orality and Literacy*, 1982, p. 23).

On a structural level, fairy tales are often characterised by a polarisation between what may be termed Fate, as indicated by the characters' situations and the bad things that happen to them without their deliberate intent, and Fortune, at work in the good things, such as the positive coincidences and the 'eucatastrophe.' To cite some instances from traditional tales: it is Fate that Cinderella is oppressed, Fortune that her godmother comes and that she marries the prince. It is Fate that Hansel and Gretel are twice left out to die in the forest because of the poverty of their family, and that they land up at the witch's house where Hansel is nearly eaten. It is Fortune, however, that a kindly Duck eventually appears to conduct them home after they have defeated the witch by their own resourcefulness.

Fate and Fortune are often inextricably linked: without Fate, Fortune would be impossible. In both *Rapunzel* and *Rumpelstiltskin*, for instance, the characters need to be afflicted by what appears to be bad destiny or a punishment for a fault not their own (Fate) in order for them to achieve their eventual triumph (Fortune).

Fate and Fortune are just as intertwined in *Holes* as in traditional tales. By the action of Fate (the dropping of the trainers), Stanley is sent to the desert, which is the place where he needs to be in order to recapture his family's Fortune. Because of the tyranny of those in charge at the Camp, particularly the warden, he and Zero go away to the only place where they can find the peach juice sploosh (finally also the agent that defeats the smell and brings fortune to Stanley's father) and the onions (which defeat the yellow lizards). It is also Fate that has led Zero to be in the camp at the same time as Stanley, but Fortune that brings them together. In particular, Fortune would be useless if their characters were not who and what they are. Not only are they the descendants of people involved in what in effect is the original folk tale, but they are also benevolent, brave, and intelligent boys. . . .

CONCLUSION

At the end of the book, in parallel with the fairy tale ending, Sachar raises doubts in the reader's mind as to whether the story contains any magic elements after all: 'Stanley's mother insists that there never was a curse. She even doubts whether Stanley's great-great-grandfather really stole a pig.' This recalls a comparable scene in *The Boy Who Lost His Face*, where the old woman denies having any supernatural power:

> 'But no, I did not put a curse on him,' she continued. She turned to David. 'When you and your compatriots attacked me, one of them said something like, "Watch out, the witch might put a curse on you." So I made up a curse. I don't even remember what I said.'

In *Holes*, however, Sachar lends weight to the magic explanation by following the expression of the mother's doubts by the audience-aware statement: 'The reader might find it interesting, however, that Stanley's father invented his cure for foot odor the day after the great-great-grandson of Elya Yelnats carried the great-great-great-grandson of Madame Zeroni up the mountain.' This is followed by a description of the 'sparkling jewels,' then undercut by the devaluing note: 'But the jewels were of poor quality, worth no more than twenty thousand dollars.' Yet another reversal follows, as the papers in the hidden suitcase turn out to be worth much more: 'After legal fees and taxes, Stanley and Zero each received less than a million dollars. But not a lot less.'

Sachar's technique here recalls the way in which the oral storyteller plays with an audience, raising expectation only to dash it and then to raise it again. The actual final note of the book is provided by the song, here sung by the grandmother of Hector Zeroni, who recalls it from when her own grandmother, the original Madame Zeroni, sang it to her when she was a little girl. She seems almost to personify the original perpetrator of the curse and thus to guarantee that its effects no longer apply by in effect giving a blessing. This is surely ratified by the verse of the song, which she sings and with which Sachar finishes the book. In the first verse, which Stanley has learnt from his mother and sings to Zero, the woodpecker on the tree sighs 'If only,' because the bark on the tree is too hard, while at the foot of the tree a hungry wolf cries out the same words to the moon. But the second verse counteracts this melancholy mood by giving words of encouragement to both woodpecker and wolf:

> Be strong my weary wolf, turn around boldly.
> Fly high, my baby bird,
> My angel, my only.

Perhaps the final message of the book is to live positively, as Stanley and Zero have done throughout, not to regret being placed in undeserved evil situations but to live with hope and integrity within them. This message resembles that of many fairy tales. *Holes* seems to be presenting a universe where we are encouraged not to say 'If only,' but rather to make our own efforts and then to thank God or providence when good comes out of evil.

Source: Pat Pinsent, "Fate and Fortune in a Modern Fairy Tale: Louis Sachar's *Holes*," in *Children's Literature in Education*, Vol. 33, No. 3, September 2002, pp. 203—12.

Helen Purdie

In the following review, Purdie states that Sachar wanted to create a character that readers would really care about and who would inspire readers to become better people.

> *'If you take a bad boy and make him dig a hole every day in the hot sun, it will turn him into a good boy.'*

If it hadn't been for his *no-good-dirty-rotten-pig-stealing-great-great-grandfather* Stanley Yelnats wouldn't have been at Camp Green Lake Juvenile Correctional Facility testing the truth of this belief. It is because of the curse placed on his pig-stealing ancestor by a one-legged gypsy, that an innocent Stanley finds himself in this parched expanse, the home of rattlesnakes, scorpions and the dreaded, deadly poisonous yellow-spotted lizards.

There is no lake at Camp Green Lake and nothing is green. The Warden is a sinister woman who paints her nails with rattlesnake venom. Mr. Sir is a sadistic supervisor, creatively vicious and fond of withholding much-needed water rations. Each day Stanley and his 'D' Tent companions (all nicknamed—Stanley's bulk earns him the sobriquet, 'Caveman') are driven out into the unbelievably hot expanse of what was once the largest lake in Texas. There they are allocated an area and it is only as each boy completes digging his five feet wide and five feet deep hole that he is allowed to go back to their tent. In these appalling conditions, soft city-bred Stanley wilts. The only respite he has is when he teaches Zero to read in return for Zero's labour—a fortuitous relationship as things turn out.

When Stanley finds a gold object in his hole it becomes obvious that the Warden has a specific purpose in making them suffer a seemingly-pointless punishment. And when Zero flees the camp, timid Stanley makes the bravest decision of his life.

This funny, poignant 'Boys Own Adventure' is the winner of the 1999 Newbery Medal. It is a tale of violence, of pointless cruelty, of bullying and misplaced justice. Stanley is a victim, bullied at school and by fate. His innocence is disarming: he chooses Camp Green Lake over gaol because, being from a poor family he has never been to camp, and even looks forward to the experience. His letters home to his family reflect his anxiety that they not be worried, and his natural kindness leads him to help Zero. His ancestor's legacy is a dreadful one, but Stanley's honesty and resilience change his destiny.

A parallel story tells the tale of Stanley's great-great-grandfather and of Kissin' Kate Barlow, who robbed him, thus plunging the family into poverty. It is when these two stories intersect that the detective work starts and serendipity begins. The reader has as much fun working out the family connections as in deciding what on earth spiced peaches, onions and deadly yellow-spotted lizards have to do with the plot. (Everything, as it turns out.)

The writing is simple enough to appeal to upper primary readers, but the book's black humour widens the reading age considerably, and the folkloric elements add an extra dimension. In America the book [*Holes*] has been deservedly popular as a read-aloud, climbing up the best-seller lists, and it has held particular appeal for boys who are reluctant readers. Sinister baddies and huge doses of suspense spiced with magic realism is a compelling combination. The book is often paired in popularity with the *Harry Potter* series; perhaps it is that in both cases the hero is an ordinary boy with an innate goodness and optimism. The delightful conclusion will have the readers celebrating while mourning the end of an excellent reading experience.

In his Newbery Medal acceptance speech, Sachar said that he began writing about the *oppressive Texan heat* and the characters and plot grew out of that subject. This is obvious; reading the book during the hottest summer Brisbane has known was not a good idea. Indeed, so evocative is the writing about Stanley's ordeals that the reader constantly feels the need to clutch at a glass of iced water. Sachar also wanted to create a character that readers would really care about. We do, Mr. Sachar, we do. His other ambition, that Stanley would inspire readers to become better people should also be fulfilled.

Source: Helen Purdie, Review of *Holes*, in *Magpies*, Vol. 15, No. 1, March 2000, pp. 8–9.

SOURCES

Cart, Michael, "From Insider to Outsider: The Evolution of Young Adult Literature," in *Voices from the Middle*, Vol. 9, No. 2, December 2001, pp. 95–97.

Follos, Alison, Review of *Holes*, in *School Library Journal*, Vol. 44, No. 9, September 1998, p. 210.

Genachowski, Julius, "Statement before the U.S. Senate Committee on Commerce, Science and Transportation, Hearing on 'Rethinking the Children's Television Act for a Digital Media Age,'" in *Federal Communications Commission Web site*, July 22, 2009, p. 2, http://hraunfoss.fcc.gov/edocs_public/attachmatch/DOC-292170A1.pdf (accessed October 1, 2010).

"Juvenile Justice History," in *Center on Juvenile and Criminal Justice*, http://www.cjcj.org/juvenile/justice/juvenile/justice/history/0 (accessed October 1, 2010).

Ott, Bill, Review of *Holes*, in *Booklist*, Vol. 94, No. 19–20, June 1, 1998, p. 1750.

Owen, Mary, "Developing a Love of Reading: Why Young Adult Literature Is Important," in *Orana*, Vol. 39, No. 1, March 2003, http://www.alia.org.au/publishing/orana/39.1/owen.html (accessed October 2, 2010).

"*Pace v. Alabama*, 106 U.S. 583 (1883)," in *Justia.com: U.S. Supreme Court Center*, http://supreme.justia.com/us/106/583/case.html (accessed October 1, 2010).

Passel, Jeffrey S., Wendy Wang, and Paul Taylor, "Marrying Out," in *Pew Research Center*, June 4, 2010, http://pewresearch.org/pubs/1616/american-marriage-interracial-interethnic (accessed October 1, 2010).

Pinsent, Pat, "Fate and Fortune in a Modern Fairy Tale: Louis Sachar's *Holes*," in *Children's Literature in Education*, Vol. 33, No. 3, September 2002, pp. 203–12.

Sachar, Louis, *Holes*, Farrar, Straus, and Giroux, 1998.

Sutton, Roger, Review of *Holes*, in *Horn Book*, Vol. 74, No. 5, September/October 1998, p. 593.

Wannamaker, Annette, "Reading in the Gaps and Lacks: (De)Constructing Masculinity in Louis Sachar's *Holes*," in *Children's Literature in Education*, Vol. 37, No. 1, March 2006, pp. 15–33.

Yearwood, Stephanie, "Popular Postmodernism for Young Adult Readers: *Walk Two Moons, Holes*, and *Monster*," in *ALAN Review*, Vol. 29, No. 3, Spring/Summer 2002, pp. 50–53.

FURTHER READING

Greene, Meg, *Louis Sachar*, Rosen, 2004.
    This biography, written for middle-school readers, includes an interview with Sachar, a chapter dedicated to *Holes*, and excerpts from *School Library Journal* reviews of other novels by Sachar.

The Newbery and Caldecott Medal Books, 1986–2000: A Comprehensive Guide to the Winners, American Library Association, 2001.

   In a section dedicated to *Holes*, this book gathers two reviews, a transcript of Sachar's Newbery Medal acceptance speech, and a biography of the author. Three introductory essays analyze trends in young-adult literature and in the selection of award winners.

Marcus, Leonard S., *Funny Business: Conversations with Writers of Comedy*, Candlewick Press, 2009.

   Marcus interviews thirteen writers of humorous books for young readers, including Sachar, Judy Blume, Beverly Cleary, and Christopher Paul Curtis.

Sachar, Sherre, and Carla Sachar, "Louis Sachar," in *Horn Book*, Vol. 75, No. 4, July/August 1999, pp. 418–22.

   In this two-part article, Sachar's twelve-year-old daughter, Sherre, and his wife, Carla, describe what it is like to live with the author, and how he balances being famous with being a normal member of a family.

Szalavitz, Maia, *Help at Any Cost: How the Troubled-Teen Industry Cons Parents and Hurts Kids*, Riverhead, 2006.

   This nonfiction book examines various treatment programs for troubled teens, including boot camps in wilderness settings that are intended to rehabilitate strong-willed teens by breaking their spirits. Szalavitz cites research demonstrating that these highly profitable programs are destructive to the teens they are intended to help.

York, Phyllis, David York, and Ted Wachtel, *Toughlove*, Doubleday, 1982.

   After the Yorks decided not to post bail for their troubled daughter after her arrest, they began a movement of parents, adjudicators, and educators that became known as Toughlove. This movement, based on the idea that the best way to deal with destructive behavior begins with simply not tolerating it, led to the creation of family support groups and residential boot camps for defiant teens.

SUGGESTED SEARCH TERMS

Louis Sachar

Sachar AND Holes

Stanley Yelnats

Holes AND LaBeouf

Sachar AND Newbery

YA literature AND Sachar

juvenile corrections facilities

juvenile justice AND Sachar

Sachar AND awards

Jasmine

BHARATI MUKHERJEE
1989

Bharati Mukherjee's *Jasmine*, the story of a widowed Punjabi peasant reinventing herself in America, entered the literary landscape in 1989. The same year, Salman Rushdie published *Satanic Verses*. Rushdie, also an Indian writer, received international attention for his novel when a *fatwa* (an Islamic legal judgment) was issued against him. The fatwa essentially proclaimed it a righteous act for any Muslim to murder Rushdie. Michelle Cliff's *No Telephone to Heaven*, Jill Ker Conway's *The Road to Coorain*, Tsitsi Dangarembga's *Nervous Condition*, Jamaica Kincaid's *A Small Place*, and Amitav Ghosh's *The Shadow Lines* were all published during this period. Each of these writers works in the genre of postcolonial literature. Although there is considerable debate over the term "postcolonial," in a very general sense, it refers to the time following the establishment of independence in a former colony, such as India, which was a colony of Great Britain until the mid-twentieth century. The sheer extent and duration of the European empires and their disintegration after World War II have led to widespread interest in postcolonial literature.

Partly because of the abundance of such postcolonial works, some critics suggested *Jasmine* was part of a fad. The *New York Times Book Review*, however, named it one of the year's best works. It is available at bookstores and online in a 1999 Grove Press paperback edition.

Bharati Mukherjee (AP Images)

Mukherjee's time as a student at the University of Iowa's acclaimed master of fine arts program, the Writers' Workshop, almost certainly informed the setting of *Jasmine*. Iowa City is a small college town, and the state as a whole is 95 percent farmland. In the 1980s, when *Jasmine* is set, many family farmers on the outskirts of Iowa City faced the same dilemma as Darrel Lutz, a character in *Jasmine*. The hard life of farming coupled with tough economic times persuaded many farmers to sell out to large corporate farms or to nonagricultural corporations. Other farmers struggled on, determined to save the farm their parents and grandparents had built up, as well as to preserve this unique way of life.

AUTHOR BIOGRAPHY

Mukherjee was born on July 27, 1940, into an elite level of society in Calcutta, India. A Bengali Brahmin (a high caste, or social grouping), Mukherjee grew up in a house cluttered with extended family, forty to forty-five people by her own count. In a 1993 interview with Runar Vignission in *Journal*

of the South Pacific Association for Commonwealth Literature and Language Studies, Mukherjee said she "had to drop inside books as a way of escaping crowds."

Mukherjee was educated as a proper Indian girl of a good family: she spoke Bengali her first three years, then entered English schools in Britain and Switzerland. She returned to India in 1951 and attended the Loretto School, run by Irish nuns. She subsequently studied at universities in Calcutta and Baroda, where she earned a master's degree in English and Indian culture. She immigrated to the United States in 1962 to attend, on scholarship, the Writers' Workshop at the University of Iowa. There, she earned her master of fine arts degree in fiction writing, and subsequently a doctorate in English and comparative literature. She also met and married writer Clark Blaise, thus avoiding a traditional Hindu marriage, to an Indian nuclear physicist, that had been arranged in India by her father. Mukherjee and Blaise have two children. They have collaborated on several writing projects.

Mukherjee left Iowa for Wisconsin in 1964, where she taught at the University of Wisconsin and Marquette University. In 1966, she and Blaise moved to Montreal, Quebec, Canada, and took positions at McGill University. Her first novel, *The Tiger's Daughter*, was published in 1972. In 1973, she received a Canada Arts Council Award. After the publication of her novel *Wife* in 1975 and her nonfiction title *Days and Nights in Calcutta* (with Blaise) in 1977, she was awarded a Guggenheim Foundation grant. Mukherjee and her husband grew unhappy in Montreal, though, and they left their positions to move to New York in 1980. She taught at a variety of institutions throughout the 1980s.

In 1988, Mukherjee became an American citizen, and also published her most critically acclaimed work, *The Middleman and Other Stories*. The short story collection won the 1988 National Book Critics Circle Award for Fiction. *Jasmine* was published to highly favorable reviews in 1989. On the strength of her work, she was offered the position of distinguished professor at the University of California at Berkeley in 1989, which she accepted.

Jasmine represented Mukherjee's return to the novel form. It had been fourteen years since the publication of *Wife*, her last novel. The *New York Times Book Review* listed *Jasmine* as one of the best of 1989.

In the years after the publication of *Jasmine*, Mukherjee published an additional four novels, including *The Tree Bride* in 2004. She has written seven novels, three short story collections, and five nonfiction titles. Her work often thematically explores the exile and the immigrant experience, as well as the role of women in both India and the United States.

Though Mukherjee has been a citizen of India, Canada, and the United States, she clearly identifies herself as American. In "American Dreamer," an essay published in 1997 in *Mother Jones*, she writes

> I choose to describe myself on my own terms, as an American, rather than as an Asian American. Why it is that hyphenation is imposed only on nonwhite Americans? Rejecting hyphenation is my refusal to categorize the cultural landscape into a center and its peripheries; it is to demand that the American nation deliver the promises of its dream and its Constitution to all its citizens equally.

PLOT SUMMARY

Jasmine, the title character and narrator of Bharati Mukherjee's novel, was born around 1965 in a rural Indian village called Hasnapur. She tells her story as a twenty-four-year-old pregnant widow, living in Iowa with her disabled lover, Bud Ripplemeyer. It takes two months in Iowa to relate the most recently developing events. During that time, Jasmine also relates biographical events that span the distance between her Punjabi birth and her American adult life. These past biographical events inform the action set in Iowa. Her odyssey encompasses five distinct settings, two murders, at least one rape, a maiming, a suicide, and three love affairs. Throughout the course of the novel, the title character's identity, along with her name, changes and changes again: from Jyoti to Jasmine to Jazzy to Jassy to Jase to Jane. In chronological order, Jasmine moves from Hasnapur, Punjab, to Fowlers Key, Florida (near Tampa); Flushing, New York; Manhattan, New York; and Baden, Iowa. Finally, as the novel ends, she is off to California.

Chapters 1–5

The novel's opening phrase, "lifetimes ago," sets in motion its major motif, or theme: the re-creation of one's self. Jasmine is seven years old. Under a banyan tree in Hasnapur, an astrologer forecasts her eventual widowhood and exile. Given the traditional Hindu belief in the accuracy of such astrological forecasts, this is a grave moment in the young girl's life. It foreshadows her first husband's death and even her move to the isolated Iowa farm town of Baden.

The action shifts, at the end of the first chapter, into the more recent past. The twenty-four-year-old Jasmine currently lives in Baden. The next four chapters provide details about her current situation. It is late May during a dry season, which is significant because the farm community relies on good harvests. Bud, her partner, became wheelchair-bound some time after the onset of their relationship. Bud wants Jasmine to marry him and wants to have a child with Jasmine. To accomplish this, Jasmine has been artificially inseminated with the help of fertility doctor Dong-jin Kwang (sometimes called Dick Kwang) and is now pregnant. A neighbor boy, Darrel Lutz, struggles to run his family's farm, which he inherited after his father's sudden death a year before. Darrel entertains the idea of selling off the farm to golf-course developers, but Bud, the town's banker and thus a powerful figure to the independent farmers, forbids it. Bud has close, though sometimes strained, ties with all the farmers. Though change—technological, social, and sexual—seems inevitable, Bud resists it. Du, Jasmine and Bud's adopted Vietnamese son, a teenager, represents this change. He comes from an entirely different culture than his classmates, who are the children of Iowa farmers.

Jasmine describes her introduction to Bud and their courtship, introduces her would-be mother-in-law, Mother Ripplemeyer, and Bud's ex-wife Karin. She hints at sexual tension between her and Du, and between her and Darrel. When Jasmine makes love to the wheelchair-bound Bud, it illustrates the reversal of sexual power in her new life. Desire and control remain closely related throughout the novel. Du's glimpse of the lovemaking adds another dimension to the sexual politics: there are those in control, those who are helpless, and those bystanders waiting to become part of the action. This resonates with ideas later chronicled about Indian notions of love and marriage.

In these early chapters, the narrator, Jasmine, alludes to more distant events. These hint at important people and events: her childhood friend Vimla, her Manhattan employers Taylor and Wylie, and their child and her charge, Duff. These allusions begin to create the more complicated and full circumstances of the story, but the story remains sketchy until later, when the narrator gives each its own full treatment.

Chapters 6–10

In chapter 6, Jasmine dips back in time to her birth. She was born during a bountiful harvest year, which for a male would have signified enormous luck. Jasmine, however, was the fifth daughter (the seventh of nine children) in a poor family. What little money there was would go to the older daughters. She seems destined, since she will have no dowry, to remain unmarried, a grim prospect in a male-dominated society. A dowry is money or property brought by a bride to a husband at their wedding.

Jasmine's childhood in Hasnapur is humble, maybe even impoverished. Her family had been forced to move there from Lahore after their village was sacked by Muslims during the Partition Riots. This historical event, like others in the novel, is rendered true to actual events. The Partition Riots of 1947 were a consequence of the attempt to create separate Hindu and Muslim states. More than two hundred thousand people died as Hindus fled their homes in Pakistan and Muslims theirs in India. Her father, who wore fancy clothes despite having no money, clung to nostalgic notions of his past life. Like so many Indians, he exchanged relative wealth for squalor. In Lahore, the family lived in a big stucco house with porticoes and gardens. In Hasnapur, they live in mud huts. Jasmine, of course, never knew Lahore. She distinguishes herself during her Hasnapur childhood as beautiful and exceptionally smart, none of which seems to matter, given that she is a poor girl. Her first teacher, Masterji, and her mother, Mataji, lobby for her right to stay in school. With her mother and teacher's backing, Jasmine is allowed to stay in school six years, twice as long as the average girl.

Jasmine fends off a mad dog with a staff, in a scene filled with underlying meaning about the young woman's power to effect the trajectory of her life. This relates to one of the novel's philosophical questions: Does free will exist? Pitaji, Jasmine's father, gets killed by a bull a short time later.

Chapters 11–15

Jasmine eavesdrops on the impassioned arguments of her brother and their friends: they speak of political and social turmoil in their homeland.

She hears the voice of Prakash, whom she soon after marries.

Jasmine lives with Prakash Vijh in a two-bedroom apartment, a break from the tradition of living with relatives. Prakash is studying to be an engineer, and he works several demeaning jobs to earn money. Jasmine and Prakash plot their move to the United States and a "real life." Their dreams of opening an electronics store are fueled by a letter from Prakash's old teacher Professorji, who pronounces America a land of vast opportunity and riches. Prakash's efforts result in acceptance to a technical college in Florida. They decide that Prakash will move to Florida to begin his studies, and Jasmine will follow in a few years. She is just seventeen years old. On the brink of Prakash's departure, Sukhwinder, a political terrorist from her brother's circle of acquaintances, plants a bomb. Prakash dies, thus fulfilling the astrologer's prophecy of widowhood for Jasmine.

Chapters 16–20

Jasmine goes to America alone. She secures illegal immigration papers and journeys across the sea. She plans to kill herself on a makeshift pyre of Prakash's clothes. Eventually, she lands, alone, in a desolate Florida coast town. After docking, Half-Face, the deformed captain of the *Gulf Shuttle*, drives Jasmine to a seedy hotel called Flamingo Court, where he rapes her. Jasmine uses a knife given to her by another crew member to kill her rapist. She burns the suitcase filled with her late husband's American suit and her bloody sari.

As the narrative moves back to the most present past, Mary Webb, an Iowa acquaintance, talks to Jasmine of her past lives. She is part of a network of women who believe in literal rebirth. Mary, for instance, believes she once was an Australian aborigine. Mary's guru, Ma Leela, inhabits the body of a battered Canadian wife. The placement of this chapter is important: it raises the issue of literal rebirth just as Jasmine begins to tell her story of figurative rebirth in America.

Shifting once again to the period after Jasmine's rape, she recalls how Lillian Gordon, an elderly Quaker woman, rescues Jasmine and nurtures her back to health in an informal halfway house. Three Kanjobal women also stay there. Lillian teaches Jasmine American mannerisms to protect her against possible arrest and deportation. Lillian puts Jasmine on a Greyhound bus, destined for the New York home of Prakash's former teacher.

Jasmine stays five months in the Flushing apartment of Professorji, his wife Nirmala, and his two elderly parents. A pseudo-Indian culture has been recreated in their neighborhood, particularly in their apartment building, where thirty-two of fifty families are Indian. Here, Jasmine is expected to live the life of an Indian widow. Professorji's family watches Indian movies and television, eats Indian food, and socializes with other Indians of a similar class. This life disappoints, even depresses, Jasmine, who is without money or a green card. Professorji finances and arranges for Jasmine's forged green card.

Chapters 21–26

Through Lillian's daughter, Kate Gordon-Feldstein, Jasmine obtains work as an au pair for a young professional couple, Taylor and Wylie. She cares for their daughter Duff, and for the first time in her life, she earns a paycheck. Taylor and Wylie treat Jasmine with respect and love. Though there are minor tensions, Jasmine settles into a safe, happy existence. She eventually takes on extra work, making what seems to her to be fantastical amounts of money. Jasmine, the caregiver, learns from her charge: "I was learning about the stores, the neighborhood, shopping, from [Duff]." Jasmine feels that she is part of the family, and maybe a little in love with Taylor, who also might be a little in love with her. In the summer of her second year with the Hayeses, Wylie leaves to be with another man, Stuart Eschelman. Jasmine and Taylor become even closer, acting very much like a family. Finally, at a park, Taylor declares his love, but seconds later, seconds from the realization of Jasmine's American bliss, Prakash's killer appears. Jasmine, in fear, makes the immediate decision to move to Iowa, the place she knows to be the home of Duff's birth mother.

The Iowa narrative goes back to Jasmine's first autumn, about a year after her move to Iowa. Two days before Christmas, Harlan Kroener comes to their home looking for Bud. Jasmine has a chance to alert police, but she fails to understand what is happening. Harlan shoots Bud twice in the back with a rifle and then kills himself.

During this first year in Iowa, Jasmine encounters tension with Bud's ex-wife Karin. Jasmine still thinks about Manhattan. She remembers her final days there; she and Taylor consummated their love before she left for Iowa. She explains, "Iowa was a state where miracles still happened." Duff was born there, and her birth allowed her mother to attend college (the Hayeses paid for it as part of the deal to adopt Duff), and thus gave Jasmine the opportunity to break out of Flushing.

In Baden, Jasmine receives a postcard from Taylor saying that he and Duff are on their way to Iowa. Though this turns out to be a false alarm (several similar postcards follow), the novel's tension revolves around this impending visit. Will Jasmine stay with Bud or leave with Taylor?

Darrel invites Jasmine over to his house. He is in a strange mood. He has prepared, poorly, an Indian dish. He begs Jasmine to run away with him to New Mexico to run a Radio Shack. Jasmine flees and, once home, calls Karin to convey her fears for Darrel's sanity. Du, meanwhile, plots to leave Iowa, to find his sister in California.

Karin goes with Jasmine to Darrel's to see if they can help, but when they arrive, Darrel is hard at work on the hog house. Jasmine lies to Bud about Du's trip, saying that it is temporary and that he will be back for school. Bud works out a loan for Darrel, but it is too late: he has hanged himself above the hogs.

Finally, Taylor and Duff show up. Though Jasmine is torn between her former family, her life in Iowa, and her obligation to Bud, she goes off with Taylor and Duff.

CHARACTERS

Arvind-prar

Jasmine's brother also inherits the responsibility of caring for his large family upon his father's death. He quits technical college in Jullundhar, sells the family farm, and opens a scooter repair shop. His political activism brings Jasmine in contact with her future first husband, as well as her husband's killer. He is given no character traits that distinguish him from his brother.

Astrologer

Under a banyan tree, he tells the young Jasmine her fate of widowhood and exile.

Sant Bhindranwale

Sant Bhindranwale is the leader of all fanatics and can be found at the Golden Temple.

Dida

Jasmine's maternal grandmother aggressively supports traditional Indian values. Dida opposes

Jasmine's efforts to extend her formal education. When Jasmine is thirteen, Dida unsuccessfully tries to arrange a marriage with a Ludhiana widower. In reference to Jasmine's bleak prospects, she says, "You're going to wear out your sandals getting rid of this one."

Stuart Eschelman

Stuart, an economist, has an affair with Wylie Hayes. Eventually, it breaks up their comfortable family and allows Taylor to pursue Jasmine. He is tall, extremely thin, and pleasant.

Lillian Gordon

The kind Quaker lady rescues Jasmine from a road just east of Fowlers Key, Florida. She lives in a wooden house on stilts and runs a sort of halfway house for refugee women. Three Kanjobal women who lost their husbands and children to an army massacre stay in her daughter's old bedroom. She earns a name as the facilitator of ordinariness by coaching Jasmine on being American: the clothes, the walk, the attitude. Lillian continues to be Jasmine's benefactor, sending money and gifts long after her departure. She is arrested for harboring undocumented immigrants.

Kate Gordon-Feldstein

The photographer daughter of Lillian Gordon, Kate puts Jasmine in touch with her friends Taylor and Wylie Hayes.

Half-Face

Half-Face is the deformed captain of the *Gulf Shuttle*. He drives Jasmine to a seedy hotel called Flamingo Court, where he rapes her.

Hari-prar

Jasmine's brother also inherits the responsibility of caring for his large family upon his father's death. He quits technical college in Jullundhar, sells the family farm, and opens a scooter repair shop. His political activism brings Jasmine in contact with her future first husband, as well as his killer. He is given no character traits that distinguish him from his brother.

Duff Hayes

Duff is the adopted daughter of Taylor and Wylie. Jasmine is hired to be Duff's au pair. Through Duff, Jasmine learns about their Manhattan neighborhood. She sleeps with Duff at night. During this time, Jasmine, largely because of her attachment to Duff, develops a sense of family. Duff's birth

mother accepted the price of tuition at Iowa State University as a kind of adoption fee. Jasmine eventually moves to Iowa because she knows it as Duff's birthplace.

Taylor Hayes

Taylor, a Columbia University physics professor, falls in love with Jasmine while she is working as the au pair (nanny) for his daughter. When his wife Wylie leaves Taylor for another man, he expresses his love to Jasmine. Eventually he drives to Iowa and convinces her to go with him to California. He is in his early thirties, with crooked teeth and a blonde beard. He speaks convincingly to Jasmine of a person's ability to create change. His advice to Jasmine to pull down the imaginary shades and block out the evil world beyond is a recurring image.

Wylie Hayes

A tall, thin, serious woman, Wylie leaves her husband Taylor in favor of her lover, Stuart Eschelman. This creates an opportunity for Taylor to pursue Jasmine. Wylie is in her early thirties and is a book editor for a Park Avenue publisher.

Mr. Jagtiani

Mr. Jagtiani is Prakash's boss at Jagtiani and Son Electrical Goods. He forces Prakash to adjust the accounting books to hide his illegal income.

Karin

Bud's ex-wife remains in Iowa after her husband leaves her for Jasmine. She answers phones for a Suicide Hot Line, the existence of which shows the desperation and tension in dry farm communities like Baden. She lives in the house Bud built.

Harlan Kroener

Harlan expresses his sense of betrayal toward Bud with two rifle shots to the banker's back. His dramatic action represents the frustration, anger, and helplessness of the Baden farmers. He kills himself just after shooting Bud.

Dick Kwang

See Dong-jin Kwang

Dong-jin Kwang

Dong-jin Kwang is a fertility doctor who artificially inseminates Jasmine so that she can have Bud's child.

Orrin Lacey

An advisor to Bud, Orrin suggests ways to solve Darrel's problem of what to do with the farm.

Ma Leela

Ma Leela is Mary Webb's thirty-six-year-old guru.

Carol Lutz

Carol, a neighbor of the Ripplemeyers, moved to California after her husband's death. When she returns to sell the farm after her son Darrel's death, she blames Bud for the tragedy.

Darrel Lutz

Darrel struggles to manage the thousand-acre, 150-hog farm he inherited from his father Gene. Just twenty-three years old and alone, Darrel variably thinks about modernizing the farm and selling it off to a golf course developer. Bud, Darrel's neighbor, a family friend, and the town's banker, appeals to his sense of tradition. Some community members, including Bud, consider it almost sacrilegious to give up farmland for nonagricultural uses. Darrel, a shy young man, secretly longs for Jasmine. With an awkward presentation of poorly prepared Indian food, Darrel declares his love and lays out all his desperate plans. Jasmine rejects him, and shortly afterwards, Darrel hangs himself above his hog pit. The hogs chew his feet to stumps.

Gene Lutz

Gene is Darrel's deceased father. He choked to death on a piece of Mexican food one year before the novel begins, during a vacation with his wife.

Masterji

An elderly teacher in Hasnapur, Masterji advocates Jasmine's continued education. He loves America and has a nephew in California. A gang of boys humiliate and kill Masterji in front of the schoolchildren.

Mataji

Jasmine's mother, Mataji, begs Pitaji to let their daughter study English books. Her pleas help Jasmine stay in school six years instead of the customary three for girls.

Nirmala

Nirmala is Professorji's nineteen-year-old wife. She works in a sari store.

Pitaji

Jasmine's father, Pitaji, remains nostalgic for Lahore, the village in which his family lived before the Partition Riots, right up until his death. He lived in relative prosperity in Lahore before being forced to move to Hasnapur. He is gored from behind by a bull in a country lane.

Potatoes-babu

Potatoes-babu is Vimla's father.

Bud Ripplemeyer

Bud hires Jasmine to work in his bank, a family business started by his father, and soon after leaves his wife to be with her. Bud is the pillar of Baden, Iowa, a small farm town experiencing a drought. He wields the power to lend farmers money. As a result, he creates some resentment, particularly from Harlan Kroener, who cripples him with two rifle shots in the back. Bud wants Jasmine to marry him, especially now that she carries their unborn child. He is twice Jasmine's age, and an avid Cardinals baseball fan.

Mother Ripplemeyer

The seventy-six-year-old Mother Ripplemeyer gets Jasmine a job at her son Bud's bank. Bud is one of her nine children. Jasmine compares Mother Ripplemeyer favorably with Lillian Gordon as a representation of kindness.

Vern Ripplemeyer

Vern, Bud's father, is dead before the start of the novel.

Scott

Scott is Du's friend.

Vancouver Sing

A land prospector, Vancouver Sing buys Jasmine's family farm in Hasnapur and some of the neighbors' land as well. He attended agriculture school in Canada. It is rumored by the village's political activists that his newly acquired land is being used as a haven for drug pushers and gunmen.

Mr. Skola

Mr. Skola is Du's teacher.

Sukhwinder

A political extremist, Sukhwinder, or Sukkhi, kills Prakash in an Indian sari shop. He turns up later in a Manhattan park as a hot dog vendor. His threatening presence drives Jasmine away from an idyllic American life in New York to Iowa.

Sukkhi

See Sukhwinder

Du Thien

The adopted son of Jasmine and Bud, Du came from a large family in Saigon, Vietnam. He survived refugee camp, and therefore shares with Jasmine memories of torture, violence, and a fight for life. Jasmine and Bud adopted Du when he was fourteen, three years prior to the start of the novel. He is called Yogi in school. Du hoards things and experiments with electronics. He feels unloved by Bud. As the novel ends, Du leaves Iowa to find his only living sister, the one who fed him live worms and lizards and crabs to keep him alive in the detention camp.

Professorji Devinder Vadhera

Prakash's benefactor and teacher during the first year of technical school, Professorji provides housing for Jasmine during her five months in Flushing, New York. Professorji fueled Prakash's dreams of American riches. He lent Prakash money to bolster his efforts at procuring an education. He preceded Prakash to America and, in his letters back to India, exaggerated the vast potential for riches and employment in the country. Professorji poses as a professor at Queen's College, but he really works as an importer and sorter of human hair.

Jasmine Vijh

Jasmine, born Jyoti, is a beautiful, smart, dowryless girl born eighteen years after the Partition Riots in a makeshift birthing hut in Hasnapur, Jullundhar District, Punjab, India. She is the fifth daughter, the seventh of nine children. An astrologer tells the young Jasmine's fate of widowhood and alienation, and both predictions come true. She attends school twice as long as most Indian girls and impresses her teachers with her intelligence. Jyoti's name and identity change and change. Her grandma names her Jyoti, meaning "light." Prakash, her Indian husband, who is killed by a terrorist bomb, calls her Jasmine. Lillian Gordon calls her Jazzy, Taylor calls her Jase, and Bud Ripplemeyer calls her Jane. Jasmine originally shares Prakash's dream of an American life of prosperity. After his murder, she travels abroad to burn herself on his pyre. Upon landing in America, Half-Face, the captain of the boat that carried her over, rapes her. She then kills him. Lillian saves

Jasmine, coaches her in how to seem more American, and sends her to Flushing, New York. There, she spends five oppressive months with Professorji, an Indian immigrant, and his family. From there, she goes to Manhattan to be the au pair for a young girl, Duff. She falls in love with her employer, Taylor, who eventually entices her to run away to California with him. In Iowa, she is Bud's lover Jane, a caregiver to a disabled man. She becomes pregnant through artificial insemination. Du, their adopted teenaged child, also flees to California.

Jyoti Vijh

See Jasmine Vijh

Prakash Vijh

Prakash marries Jasmine two weeks after they first meet. He is twenty-four and she is fifteen at the time. She had already fallen in love with his voice, overheard while he speaks with her brothers. She is called Jyoti until Prakash gives her a new name and identity, Jasmine. Prakash lost his parents when he was ten. A modern man, Prakash rents a two-bedroom apartment rather than live with his family. He studies engineering and works several demeaning jobs in pursuit of his dream to move to America. Just prior to leaving India to attend Florida's International Institute of Technology, Prakash is killed by a bomb. Sukhwinder, a Sikh extremist, probably intended the bomb for Jasmine. Jasmine's American dreams die, for a time, with Prakash.

Vimla

Jasmine's rich childhood friend, Vimla has the fanciest wedding in their village. Her husband dies of typhoid when she is twenty-one, and a year later, she burns herself to death. Her suicide, or *sati*, illustrates the culture's gender politics: a widow's future seems endlessly gloomy.

Dr. Mary Webb

Mary Webb is part of a group of women who believe in past lives. In one past life, she was an Australian aborigine.

THEMES

Rebirth

The major theme of rebirth plays out literally and figuratively in *Jasmine*. (When something happens literally, it actually happens and is not simply

TOPICS FOR FURTHER STUDY

- When Mary and Jasmine meet for lunch at the University Club, they discuss reincarnation. Using reputable Internet sites, research the idea of reincarnation in major world religions. Create a poster and make a presentation to your class describing reincarnation and detailing how at least three different religions or sects view reincarnation.

- Postcolonialism, a term often associated with Mukherjee's work, is a critical theory that examines the ways former colonies, such as India, have internalized or discarded the values, culture, language, and politics of their former colonial masters. Read *Postcolonialism: A Very Short Introduction* (2003) by Robert J. C. Young and published by Oxford University Press. What connections can you draw between Young's descriptions of postcolonialism and Mukherjee's work? Write an essay summarizing your findings.

- Jasmine's childhood friend Vimla burns herself after her husband's death. This act is called *sati* or *suttee*. Define suttee and discuss its cultural, historical, and religious origins. In addition, read current articles from world newspapers available online about wife-burning and dowries in India. With a small group of classmates, use the information you have found to create a documentary film using video editing software such as Vegas or Final Cut. Present your work to your classmates.

- Prakash and Jasmine, in plotting their move to the United States, confront problems getting their green cards or visas—the certificates of lawful permanent residency in the United States. Later, in Flushing, Jasmine again worries about procuring her green card, even

equates it with freedom. Imagine that you are a modern-day citizen of India. Research the requirements you would have to meet in order to legally make a permanent move to the United States. What obstacles might you encounter? Prepare a list of items you would have to obtain and steps you would have to take to make such a move, and explain, in a class presentation, why you chose the items on the list.

- In literature and film, farmers are often stereotyped as being rather simple, sometimes crude, people. In Darrel Lutz we see a more complicated portrait of the farmer: a young, hard-working person who must understand sophisticated technology and high financing. With a small group of your classmates, research the modern American farm. How big are farms in the twenty-first century, on average? How many family farms remain? How much do farms cost to run, and what is the average profit a small farmer can expect? Using the information you find, create a blog in which members of your group post essays concerning modern farming. In addition, post photographs, graphs, illustrations, and videos concerning farming, as well as informative links for your readers.

- The book *American Eyes: New Asian-American Short Stories for Young Adults* (1995), edited by Lori Carlson, is a collection of ten stories about the immigrant experience, told through the eyes of young adults. Read this book and imagine the experiences of the young people portrayed. Select one short story to adapt as a play. With a small group of friends, perform the play for your class.

---

a figure of speech; figurative language, on the other hand, is used for a certain effect. Figurative language might exaggerate, embellish, or help the reader understand otherwise difficult-to-grasp concepts.) The opening line, "lifetimes ago," hints

at all the transformations the title character has undergone. Mukherjee consistently highlights this transformation, making authorial connections between the fictional action and its significance as a subject under investigation. The narrator says, "There are no harmless, compassionate ways to remake oneself." Later, she says, "I picked [Sam] up and held him. Truly I had been reborn."

Jasmine undergoes life transformations, or metaphorical rebirths. Mary Webb shares with Jasmine her belief in literal rebirth, or reincarnation. Mary claims to have been an Australian aborigine in a past life. When channeling this past life, she speaks tribal languages. Ma Leela, Mary's guru, inhabits the body of a battered wife who has become suicidal. Mary has presumably confided in Jasmine because she is Hindu, and Mary understands that Hindus keep revisiting the world. Jasmine confirms this: "Yes, I am sure that I have been reborn several times, and that yes, some lives I can recall vividly."

This incident further blurs the distinction between the figurative and the literal. Jasmine never gets into details of these rebirths. When Jasmine, the narrator, considers the concept of an eternal soul, she thinks of distinct stages of her present twenty-four-year-old-life: her youth in Hasnapur, her blissful time in Manhattan, her life in Baden, Iowa. Are these the figurative past lives she means to tell Mary about, or does she mean, on a literal level, that she believes her soul has been reborn after the body's death? The text remains ambiguous.

This melding of literal and figurative underlines the importance of the metaphors. Mukherjee implies that the experience of a person's self-reinvention is so powerful as to be real.

Identity

Tied to the theme of rebirth is the theme of identity. This is the most persistent motif in *Jasmine*, infiltrating every aspect of the story. The most obvious manifestation of identity comes in the title character's name.

When Jyoti marries Prakash, a modern Indian man, she becomes Jasmine. Lillian Gordon calls her Jazzy, Taylor names her Jase, and Bud Ripplemeyer calls her Jane. With each name comes a new identity, a rebirth of sorts, complete with new personality traits.

The narrator says, "I shuttled between two identities." Other characters and Jasmine herself even speak of these splinter personalities in the third person, as if they really did exist independently. She says, "Jyoti of Hasnapur was not Jasmine."

Prakash says, "You are Jasmine now. You can't jump into wells." Prakash characterizes Jyoti

as feudal. Prakash wants Jasmine to call him by his first name, rather than the pronoun used in traditional address between women and men. This identity helps create a semblance of equality between husband and wife in the male-dominated society.

Jasmine seems to like most the name Taylor gave her. "Jase was a woman who bought herself spangled heels and silk chartreuse pants." Indeed, each of Jasmine's identities has distinct characteristics. "Jyoti would have saved. . . . Jasmine lived for the future, for Vijh & Wife. Jase went to the movies and lived for today."

The theme of identity also pertains to place. Jasmine's name, her identity, changes with each locale. The notable exception to this is in Flushing, New York, where the narrator's name is never mentioned. Whereas Jasmine forged a distinctive identity in every other place, the Flushing apartment building filled with Punjabis did not represent a significant change.

Free Will

Hinduism and Western notions of self-reliance oppose each other in this debate. Believers in predestination accept the idea that a higher power designs all events. Believers in free will think that each person has the power to change the course of events. In the opening chapter, the astrologer accurately predicts Jasmine's fate of widowhood and exile. This seems to support predestination, which is sometimes loosely referred to as fate. As the novel ends, however, Jasmine boldly decides to change her life, to exert free will, stating, "Adventure, risk, transformation: the frontier is pushing indoors through uncaulked windows. Watch me re-position the stars, I whisper to the astrologer who floats cross-legged above my kitchen stove."

Jasmine's childhood is a time when she seeks to break free from her inherited circumstances. In one dramatic scene, Jasmine kills a mad dog with a staff. A Westerner would surely credit Jasmine for having saved her own life. Dida, however, knows God willed it to happen that way.

The scenes in which Jasmine's partners are assaulted heighten the debate. Prakash, an Indian, is killed by a bomb. As he is dying, a voice shouts, "The girl's alive. This is fate." Later, Dida claims that God, displeased with Prakash and Jasmine's modern ways, sent Sukkhi to murder him. Jasmine, even at this early stage of her development, has an uneasy relationship with fate. She says, "If God sent Sukkhi to kill my husband, then I renounce

A Punjabi village in India. Jasmine*'s title character, a widowed Punjabi peasant, creates a new life for herself in the United States.* (© Hulton-Deutsch Collection / Corbis)

God. I spit on God." Before Bud is shot, he tries to covertly communicate his grave situation to Jasmine, but she doesn't understand that Harlan Kroener is about to shoot her partner, and she cannot process any of the signals. In retrospect, she realizes that her son Du or Bud's ex-wife Karin would surely have summoned the sheriff and stopped the assault. In other words, an act of free will would have changed Bud's fate.

Jasmine clearly exerts free will in her decision to join Taylor and Duff on their trip to California. Earlier in the novel, Jasmine and Taylor disagree about that very topic. The narrator takes a humble position, though she poses her thoughts as questions, leaving the issue unresolved. "The scale of Brahma is vast, as vast as space in the universe. Why shouldn't our lives be infinitesimal? Aren't all lives, viewed that way, equally small?" Taylor believes that Jasmine's take on the subject is a formula for "total fatalism."

Gender

Sex and power are closely linked in Jasmine's life. As a Punjabi peasant woman, Jasmine would have a servile relationship to men. She would be expected, in her homeland, to make herself useful to the male society. We see this even in her relationship to Prakash, a modern Indian man. There is never a thought that Jasmine will pursue an education, get work, and in that way help the couple realize their dreams. Rather, her role is to support Prakash's education and work. Jasmine carries this attitude with her to America, where she spends five months in Flushing living the life that Professorji plots for her. She even kisses his feet when he agrees to help her get a green card. Jasmine says, "I have had a husband for each of the women I have been. Prakash for Jasmine. Taylor for Jase. Bud for Jane. Half-Face for Kali."

However, Mukherjee depicts sex as being an act that somehow shifts the power balance.

Prakash encourages a free exchange of ideas with Jasmine. He is nine years older than her, however, and always demonstrates superiority in reasoning. Mukherjee juxtaposes a scene in which Jasmine is defeated intellectually with a scene of the couple in the throes of sex. Prakash says, "Jasmine . . . help me be a better person."

Taylor, another sensitive and liberal man, pays Jasmine's salary. He provides her food and shelter. Though he promotes equality, Jasmine cannot treat him as anything but a superior—until the night when they consummate their relationship. "I am leading Taylor to a bed as wide as a subcontinent," she says. "I am laying my cheek on his warm cheek, I am closing his eyes with my caregiving fingertips, I am tucking the mosquito netting tight under his and Wylie's king-sized mattress." Here, again, Jasmine wrestles the power away from her male counterpart: she is actively doing things, not having them done to her.

Bud, despite his disability, manages to be the head of the household and a leader in the community. When it comes to sex, however, Jasmine is entirely in charge. She says, "It shames Bud that now, for sex, I must do all the work, all the moving, that I will always be on top."

With sex comes power and with power, violence. Half-Face rapes Jasmine on her first day in America. He surely will rape her again. She might not survive his brutality. She kills him not out of revenge, it seems, but rather fear.

STYLE

Setting and Chronology

In this novel, the time, place, and culture of the action constantly shift. The narrator tells of events that happened in the past, but not in chronological order. Some events happened in a distant past, some in a more recent past. The reader understands the order of events partly in relation to place. Events in Hasnapur, Punjab, happened during Jasmine's childhood, and references to Lahore indicate events that happened before her birth. When the setting shifts to Florida, the reader knows the action is set during Jasmine's first weeks in America. Scenes in Flushing precede scenes in Manhattan, and scenes in Manhattan come before those in Iowa.

Why does the narrative timeline shift back and forth? There is a sense of urgency in the Iowa scenes because Jasmine's life is moving forward, possibly in the direction of monumental change. The past events are critical to the reader's understanding of Jasmine's dilemma, but they are not as urgent. The narrative strategy, then, is to maintain this sense of urgency through the Iowa story line, while working in all the important people, places, and things from prior times.

Foreshadowing

This device, used in literature to create expectations or set up an explanation of later developments, is used frequently in *Jasmine*. The astrologer's forecast of Jasmine's widowhood and exile operates in this way. It alerts the reader to future events. Viewed in hindsight, Prakash's death seems linked to this prediction. Were it not for foreshadowing, however, the reader would not make the connection between the theme of fate and the death.

In other instances, foreshadowing is used to build tension. Jasmine says, "That day I found the biggest staff ever, stuck in a wreath of thorny bush. I had to crawl on stony ground, and of course thorns bloodied my arms, but the moment my fist closed over the head of the staff, I felt a buzz of power." The strong imagery and language—the blood, the thorns, the fist—clue the reader into the importance of this scene. The reader wonders what she is going to do with that staff—the staff with which she will later kill the mad dog.

The knife that Jasmine receives from the crew member has a similar role. The playwright Anton Chekhov famously expressed the principle that if a gun appears early on in a story, it must go off before the story is over. In other words, the elements of a story should all play a role, and in the case of a gun or knife, they prime the reader to expect danger and violence. Jasmine's knife goes off, so to speak, when she kills Half-Face.

Symbolism

A symbol is something that suggests or stands for something else without losing its original identity. In literature, symbols combine their literal meaning with the suggestion of an abstract concept. Mukherjee uses symbols to help readers understand a complex fabric of ideas.

Jasmine grasps a drowned dog in a stench-filled river, and as she does, it breaks in two. The reader accepts the literal action, the breaking apart of the dog. Given Mukherjee's treatment of the theme of identity, the reader must also associate the broken body with the splitting apart of life.

The dog becomes two parts from one, just as Jyoti splits into Jasmine and Jyoti.

One symbol repeats itself throughout the novel. The narrator explains that, when a pitcher breaks, the air inside is the same as outside. The author returns to this symbol when Vimla sets herself on fire, and again in a discussion of Jasmine's father:

> Lahore visionaries, Lahore women, Lahore ghazals: my father lived in a bunker. Fact is, there was a difference. My father was right to notice it, and to let it set a standard. But that pitcher is broken. It is the same air this side as that. He'll never see Lahore again and I never have. Only a fool would let it rule his life.

Another, more subtle symbol is the small crack in the television set at the Flamingo Court hotel room. A reader detects symbols because of their placement and importance in the context of a scene. The highly charged rape scene, on Jasmine's first day in America, shows an ugly, imperfect aspect of the country. The television represents a medium of Hollywood fantasies and fables. The crack in the television, then, can be read as a crack in the American dream. That Jasmine's head causes the crack lends even more power to the symbol.

HISTORICAL CONTEXT

Violence and the 1947 Partition of India

As a stipulation of achieving independence from Great Britain in 1947, India was partitioned into the largely Hindu country of India and the largely Muslim country of Pakistan. Violence broke out in response to the partition in 1947, in what have come to be known as the Partition Riots. More than two hundred thousand people died as Hindus fled their homes in Pakistan and Muslims fled theirs in India. The state of Punjab was a scene of much violence, as it was divided between India and the newly created Pakistan. Many Hindus fleeing the area that became Pakistan settled in Punjab.

Although Jasmine was born around 1965, some 18 years after the Partition Riots, the riots had a profound affect on her life.

Jasmine's family, like many Hindus at the time, were among those who left the area that became Pakistan, leaving behind relative riches in exchange for squalor during the Partition Riots. It was a time of violence and upheaval. Families abandoned not only material wealth but established roots. The Muslim-Hindu religious divide

continues to be a source of tension in India. The *CIA: World Factbook* cites the 2001 Indian census, which describes the population as 80.5 percent Hindu, 13.4 percent Muslim, 2.3 percent Christian, 1.9 percent Sikh, and 1.8 percent other religious groups.

The Sikhs and the Downing of Flight 182

The Sikhs are a religious group that made up about 1.9 percent of India's population in 2001. After India gained independence in 1947, virtually all Sikhs wound up on the Indian side of Punjab. They have a social identity separate from other Punjabis. The new Punjabi-speaking state of Punjab, established in 1966, had a Sikh majority. In *Jasmine*, there would have been tensions between Sukhwinder, the Sikh extremist, and Prakash Vijh.

Mukherjee herself was deeply affected by Sikh extremism in 1985, when a Sikh terrorist planted a bomb in Air India flight 182, en route from Montreal to Bombay. When the bomb exploded, the aircraft was in Irish airspace. It crashed into the ocean with the loss of all 329 people on board. Of these, nearly all were either Canadian citizens of Indian descent or Indians.

Mukherjee explored grief and anger over the event most fully in her 1988 short story "The Management of Grief," a story included in the collection *The Middleman and Other Stories*. Indeed, several Mukherjee's stories and novels written after the 1985 event touch on Sikh violence.

The Green Revolution

Punjab, like many Indian states, cherishes its own subnational identity, including its own language. Punjab is largely agricultural, much like Iowa. The majority of India's wheat is grown in Punjab. During Jasmine's childhood, rapid technological advancement was being made in the agricultural sector. She says,

> When I was a child, born in a mud hut without water or electricity, the Green Revolution had just struck Punjab. Bicycles were giving way to scooters and cars, radios to television. I was the last to be born to that kind of submission, that kind of ignorance."

The green revolution of the late 1960s brought some gains in productivity and made the country self-sufficient for grains. Poverty, however, remains a chronic problem in India. According to Daniel Zwerdling, in a 2009 report for National Public Radio's *Morning Edition*, although the Green Revolution held the promise of feeding the subcontinent, many Punjabi farmers have been plunged

COMPARE
&
CONTRAST

- **1980s:** Although outlawed in 1961, the custom of a bride's family paying the bridegroom's family a dowry continues to be practiced throughout the 1980s.

  Today: Dowry abuse, wherein the bride is burned or killed for her dowry money, remains a common crime in India, according to an article by Kalpana Sharma writing in *India Together* in 2002. The India National Crime Records Bureau reveals that in 2008 there were 8,172 reported cases of dowry deaths.

- **1980s:** The Green Revolution, begun in the 1960s and continuing to yield benefits through the 1980s, results in a transformation of agricultural practices in India resulting in greater quantities of food being produced.

  Today: In 2010, U.S. President Barack Obama calls for a second Green Revolution for India through a cooperative effort with the United States to improve weather forecasting and farming technology.

- **1980s:** In 1985, Sikh terrorists explode Air India flight 182 en route from Bombay to Montreal. The crash kills 329 people.

  Today: Post-2001 security measures in airports have largely prevented terrorist attacks using planes. However, in October 2010, packages mailed in Yemen to Chicago-area synagogues are transported via passenger planes and are found to contain bombs.

- **1980s:** Religious violence flares in the Indian state of Punjab, with Sikh separatists committing acts of terror in support of their political causes. Anti-Sikh riots shake the Indian state after Prime Minister Indira Gandhi is assassinated by her Sikh bodyguards.

  Today: Religious violence continues to plague India. Hindu extremists increase attacks against Christians in several Indian states.

into crushing debt as a result of the technological advances of the 1960s and 1970s.

Dowries, Suttee, and Bride Burning

India, during Jasmine's childhood and today, is a male-dominated society. Men hold most of the economic and political power. Dowries have been officially banned, but in reality, the practice of giving them remains a prevalent practice, as reported by Lucy Ash in the *BBC News* in 2003. A dowry is money or property brought by a bride to a husband at their wedding. Essentially, a dowry acts as an incentive package to entice prospective husbands. The debate over the wisdom of dowries is discussed openly in newspapers and in government.

Jasmine entered young womanhood in the late 1970s, when her family would have been expected to offer a dowry to her prospective husband. For somebody like Jasmine, whose little family money would go to the older four daughters, the future seemed grim.

A Hindu wife, indeed, saw her role as subservient to her husband. When Jasmine's friend Vimla burns herself after her husband's death, she is following a now-illegal Hindu practice called *suttee* in which the widow cremates herself on her husband's funeral pyre in order to fulfill her true role as wife. Jasmine intends to follow the same ritual after Prakash's death. She brings his suit to America in order to make a pyre. She says, "I had not given even a day's survival in America a single thought. This was the place I had chosen to die, on the first day, if possible."

An additional troubling trend in India is bride burning and murder by the groom's family in order to keep the dowry but get rid of the wife. Ash, in her 2003 BBC report, tells of women being coerced by their future husbands to increase their dowry; in cases where the marriage has already taken place, brides are sometimes doused in kerosene and set aflame.

Furthermore, according to Ash, providing dowries for girl children has become such a burden that parents are aborting girl fetuses before birth to avoid having to pay dowries in the future. The issue of dowry underscores the position of women in many Indian Hindu families.

CRITICAL OVERVIEW

When Bharati Mukherjee's *Jasmine* was published in 1989, it received generally favorable reviews. Michael Gorra, writing in the *New York Times*, calls *Jasmine* "one of the most suggestive novels we have about what it is to become American." Furthermore, at year's end, the *New York Times* named the book one of the best of 1989. Likewise, in a 1991 review appearing in *Publishers Weekly*, Penny Kaganoff writes that *Jasmine* is a "richly atmospheric, beautifully controlled novel," and Eleanor Wachtel writes in the Canadian news magazine *Maclean's*, "In her powerful depiction of clashing cultures and philosophies, Mukherjee has created an ambitious and impressively compact work."

In the 1993 critical anthology *Bharati Mukherjee: Critical Perspectives*, edited by Emmanuel S. Nelson, *Jasmine* is seen in less generous terms. Debjani Banerjee, in an article titled "In the Presence of History: The Representation of Past and Present Indias in Bharati Mukherjee's Fiction," indicates that Mukherjee fails "to contextualize the historical and political events of India" and is unable to "perceive the complex workings of postcolonial and neocolonial forces." Banerjee articulates a backlash among South Asians to Mukherjee's work. She writes that Mukherjee represents Indians in such a way that implies "one must escape from the disillusionment and treachery of postcolonial history." In sum, Banerjee accuses Mukherjee of "catering to a First World audience while still mining the Third World for fictional material."

Other critics have taken different approaches to *Jasmine*. Carmen Faymonville, in a review published in the *Explicator* in 1997, argues that the novel "relies on frontier myths and narratives of Americanization associated with western locales, mobility, and frontier-hero lifestyles." She further argues that Mukherjee employs references to *Shane*,

a American western novel, to underscore a thematic concern with liberation and morality.

Likewise, in 2009, critic Walter S. H. Lim published "Class, Labor, and Immigrant Subjectivity in Bharati Mukherjee's *Jasmine* and Shirley Geok-lin Lim's *Among the White Moon Faces*." In this essay, Lim sees the character Jasmine as a "late-twentieth century allegory of the pioneering immigrant." He proclaims the novel to be Mukherjee's rejection of "an outmoded medievalism" and argues that "Mukherjee unapologetically affirms her wholehearted embracement of the United States as her preferred homeland."

CRITICISM

Donald G. Evans
Evans is a novelist, journalist, and instructor of writing. In the following essay, he explores the conflict between duty and desire inherent in Jasmine.

Desire is the root of American fairy tales: desire for riches, desire for fame, desire for better this, different that. Duty suppresses desire. Jasmine, the Punjabi heroine and title character of Bharati Mukherjee's novel, debates whether to act according to desire or duty. The Indian consciousness in which she was raised, embodied by Dida, her grandmother, supports duty. In her culture, there is a greater connectedness, a sense that individual acts affect so much more than the individual. The Western consciousness, embodied by her Manhattan employers Taylor and Wylie Hayes, encourages desire. The notion of America as a free country seems, in this mindset, to be an invitation to pursue one's wildest inclinations, with little respect for those left behind.

The novel opens with the phrase, "lifetimes ago." This phrase seems deliberately ironic, recalling the classical fairy tale phrase, "once upon a time." The ensuing scene, in which an astrologer predicts Jasmine's widowhood and exile, frames the discussion of whether fate or free will dictate one's life trajectory. This is the core of existential philosophy: a focus on the conditions humans create for their existence, rather than those created by nature. This relates closely to the idea of desire and duty: does one necessarily follow the prescribed path, or can one make one's own path?

The young Jasmine, because of her religious and cultural background, believes in predestination. She reflects, "Bad times were on their way. I

WHAT DO I READ NEXT?

- In *The Mistress of Spices* (1997), a novel of magic and everyday life by Chitra Banerjee Divakaruni, the heroine, Tilo, forgoes a life of special powers to live and love as an ordinary woman.

- *Teenage Refugees and Immigrants from India Speak Out*, edited by R. Viswanath and published in 1997, is a young-adult nonfiction title featuring teenagers from India who discuss why their families left India and what life has been like for them in the United States.

- *Days and Nights in Calcutta* (1977), by Mukherjee and husband Clark Blaise, is a journal of the couple's 1973 visit to India.

- Jhumpa Lahiri's 2004 novel, *The Namesake*, is the story of a young man, the child of Indian immigrants in the United States, and his struggles in life.

- In *The Holder of the World* (1997), a novel by Mukherjee, a diamond called Tear Drop connects a contemporary woman, Beigh Masters, to a seventeenth-century Puritan woman, Hannah Easton.

- *Blue Jasmine* (2006), by Kashmira Sheth, is a young-adult novel. In it, twelve-year-old Seema moves with her parents and younger sister from India to Iowa City.

- The short stories in *The Middleman and Other Stories* (1988), by Mukherjee, trace the lives of third-world immigrants and their adjustments to becoming Americans.

- In *Wife* (1975), a novel of morals by Mukherjee, Dimple moves to the United States with her husband and becomes torn between Indian and American cultures.

- In *A House for Mr. Biswas* (1961), a novel by V. S. Naipaul, the title character yearns to be something greater than a henpecked sign writer.

- *How I Became a Holy Mother and Other Stories* is a 1981 collection of short stories by Jhabvala Ruth Prawer. Its characters are divided into two essential categories, Seekers and Sufferers.

- *When Heaven and Earth Changed Places* is Le Ly Hayslip's 1989 memoir recounting her childhood in Vietnam, her marriage to an American serviceman, her escape to the United States, the dissolution of her marriage, and her eventual assimilation into the life of an American citizen.

---

was helpless, doomed." Outwardly, however, she whispers to the astrologer, "I don't believe you." That she whispers—rather than says, or states, or shouts—indicates the tentativeness of Jasmine's position as an agent of change. The astrologer plays an all-important role in the novel: he is there, under the banyan tree, as the story opens, and he is there, in Jasmine's thoughts, as the novel ends.

Dida, the grandmother, firmly believes in duty. Dida knows that a girl must marry, that she must bear a son. It is the family's burden, their duty, to ensure that the girl find a husband. To tinker with this tried-and-true formula requires a certain amount of arrogance and, in Dida's mind, disrespect. Her pronouncement, "Some women think they own the world because their husbands are too lazy to beat them," demonstrates her unflinching belief in the social order.

When Jasmine fends off a mad dog with a staff, Dida refuses to credit her granddaughter, claiming, instead, that God did not think her ready for salvation. "Individual effort counts for nothing," she says. Later, Dida explains Prakash's death according to religious beliefs. "God was displeased" that Jasmine did not marry the man Dida chose for her, that she called her husband by his proper name, that they spent money extravagantly, that her husband planned to go abroad. Reward and retribution: God controls it all.

However, Jasmine all along shows an inclination to veer from the prescribed path. She tells her father she wants to be a doctor. This is the first

> THIS IS THE CORE OF EXISTENTIAL
> PHILOSOPHY: A FOCUS ON THE CONDITIONS
> HUMANS CREATE FOR THEIR EXISTENCE, RATHER
> THAN THOSE CREATED BY NATURE."

hint that she harbors Western-like dreams. For Dida, education for a woman seems frivolous, and even dangerous: it defies her future duty.

Jasmine eventually marries a modern Indian man. On the surface, it seems that her life merely represents a breaking of tradition, an exchange of new values for old. Certainly, that is a part of it, but in the deeply ingrained mindset of the Hindu Indian, change puts the whole culture at risk. Who will care for Prakash's uncle, now that his nephew has chosen to live in an apartment?

Rejecting duty in favor of desire is a dangerous business. Mukherjee creates at least three characters who wind up bloody, in part, because they place following their desire before their sense of duty. Prakash gets blown to pieces holding the money that would purchase the clothes in which he would follow his American dreams. Darrel, who made a desperate, futile attempt to follow his desires, hangs limp from an electrical cord, chewed on by the hogs that represent his duty. Bud winds up in a wheelchair, partly because the wife he left—his duty—could not apply her relative wisdom to the task of saving him. (Jasmine thinks that Karin, under the same circumstances, would have understood to call the sheriff and thus stop Harlan Kroener's assault.)

Darrel, like Jasmine, internally debates the value of acting out his desires at the price of neglecting his duty: "Crazy, Darrel wants an Indian princess and a Radio Shack franchise in Santa Fe. Crazy, he's a recruit in some army of white Christian survivalists. Sane, he wants to baby-sit three hundred pound hogs and reinvent the fertilizer/pesticide wheel."

Mukherjee's careful use of imagery and sensory details in Darrel's suicide scene demonstrates the danger of both desire and duty. The fantastical images of far-off galaxies and the pleasantly strong smell of cumin stand in contrast to the word "rawness":

The frail man who is still slowly twisting and twisting from the rafter with an extension cord wrapped around his stiffly angled neck isn't the Darrel, would-be lover, would-be adventurer, who only nights ago in a cumin-scented kitchen, terrorized me with the rawness of wants. This man is an astronaut shamed by the failure of his lift-off. He keeps his bitter face turned away from the galaxies that he'd longed to explore.

Desire, however, does not necessarily end in blood. The danger is always there, but Mukherjee allows for success. Du, Jasmine's adopted Vietnamese son, represents this opportunity. In following his own desire, he betrays Jasmine's sense of duty. In Du's departure scene, he bends over a rifle to kiss Jasmine. The two are fairly close in age, seven years apart, and given their history it's fair to assume an undercurrent of sexual tension. At least, the tenderness goes beyond that normally exchanged between mother and son. The kiss seems to symbolize so much desire, just as the rifle symbolizes so much violence. Mukherjee might be suggesting that it's necessary to pass through violence to fulfill desire.

Make no mistake: Mukherjee's novel supports the Western notion of self-determination and individual initiative. Of all the settings in the novel, only Manhattan allows for the possibility of freedom, which seems closely tied to happiness. Hasnapur is mud huts and arranged marriages and a lifetime of servitude. Prakash and Jasmine experience a certain kind of bliss in plotting their escape from Hasnapur. Florida is economic and sexual shame. Jasmine gets raped and wanders penniless, sure to die if not for the saint-like kindness of Lillian Gordon. Flushing is India all over again, in costly replication. Jasmine lacks the power, financial and otherwise, to purchase her escape. Baden, Iowa, is India with white people, an agricultural community bound, in so many ways, to tradition. Jasmine plays the role of dutiful wife. The postcards Prakash received from his old teacher— "CELEBRATE AMERICA...TRAVEL...THE PERFECT FREEDOM"—seem highly ironic in retrospect.

Manhattan is different, however. It is where Jasmine claims to become an American. "On Claremont Avenue I came closest to the headiness, dizziness, porousness of my days with Prakash. What I feel for Bud is affection. Duty and prudence count. Bud has kept me out of trouble. I don't want trouble. Taylor's car is gobbling up the highways."

The Hayeses, an urban professional couple, represent the antithesis of Dida's stubborn relationship with duty. The Hayeses possess confidence, wit; they seem happy. Their inclination, surely, is to act according to desire. Wylie Hayes, on the surface, seems to live an idyllic life. Her relationship with her husband, Taylor, is an equal partnership; Taylor is smart, caring, and sensitive. She loves her darling daughter Duff. The family has sufficient financial means and meaningful work. However, when she falls in love with Stuart Eschelman, she sees an opportunity to improve upon all that. She chooses to follow her desire and neglect her duty.

It is as natural for Wylie to act out her desires as it is for Jasmine to suppress them. Taylor, though hurt, never seems to begrudge Wylie's decision. Taylor, like Wylie, does not seem to consider it a wife's duty to remain with her loving husband and daughter.

Earlier, Taylor and Jasmine exchange ideas on the subject of free will. Jasmine explains, in Hindu terms, how "a whole life's mission might be to move a flowerpot from one table to another." In the Hindu worldview, all the details of life might be nothing more than God's will to put one person in a given room with one particular flower. Taylor responds angrily to this, saying that a world in which rearranging a particle of dust ranks with discovering relativity is "a formula for total anarchy. Total futility. Total fatalism."

This argument frames Jasmine's ultimate dilemma, whether to remain as caregiver to the crippled Bud Ripplemeyer or run away with the man of her dreams, Taylor Hayes. Jasmine finds safety in her duty to Bud, in being a caregiver. She understands responsibility, such as raising her child there in Iowa, as not only practical but expected. She cannot, however, deny the oppression that comes with the duty. "I am not choosing between men," she says. "I am caught between the promise of America and old-world dutifulness. A caregiver's life is a good life, a worthwhile life. What am I to do?"

The reader should notice the similarities between Wylie's rhetorical question, "What can I do?" and Jasmine's more sincere question, "What am I to do?" Jasmine, of course, chooses to run away with Taylor, to once and for all show that a person can determine her own fate. Jasmine will not end up like Darrel. Earlier, she disagrees with Bud's insistence that Darrel keep up the farm. "What I say is, release Darrel from the land." Jasmine, in the end, releases herself. As Taylor says, "Why not, it's a free country?" In doing so, Jasmine executes all the traditional values held by Dida. She leaves a handicapped lover to fend for

himself. She takes a baby away from his father. She trades security for the unknown.

Mukherjee, in the end, circles back to the astrologer. "It isn't guilt I feel," Jasmine says, "it's relief. I realize I have already stopped thinking of myself as Jane. Adventure, risk, transformation: the frontier is pushing indoors through uncaulked windows. Watch me re-position the stars, I whisper to the astrologer who floats cross-legged above my kitchen stove."

Here, the astrologer, the teller of fate, seems to symbolize old-world duty. The astrologer's position above the stove recalls Vimla's suicide scene. In the Hindu practice called *sati*, or *suttee*, the widow cremates herself on her husband's funeral pyre in order to fulfill her true role as wife. Jasmine intended to follow the same ritual after Prakash's death. She brought his suit to America in order to make a pyre. This practice is based on the idea that a wife's duty to her husband is absolute and eternal. Now, Jasmine mentally has the astrologer hover above the stove, as if to commit a kind of sati himself. The image seems to symbolize a ritual death of duty.

The ending of the novel recalls so many Hollywood endings in which the happy couple rides off into the sunset. "I am out the door and in the potholed and rutted driveway, scrambling ahead of Taylor, greedy with wants and reckless from hope." The tone and language, along with the final word "hope," suggest that Jasmine does not regret her decision to act out her desires. The author draws very little attention to the sorrowful image of an abandoned Bud and focuses instead on the thrill of Jasmine's liberation.

Source: Donald G. Evans, Critical Essay on *Jasmine*, in *Novels for Students*, Gale, Cengage Learning, 2011.

F. Timothy Ruppel

In the following essay, Ruppel suggests that Jasmine *disrupts the traditional narrative process, thematizing narration and identity by illustrating, through the circumstances of Jasmine's character, how identity can be ascribed by outside influences that desire to define her character as known, or as conforming to, their own social, economic, or hierarchicalized mythos.*

> We are the outcasts and deportees, strange pilgrims visiting outlandish shrines, landing at the end of tarmacs, ferried in old army trucks where we are roughly handled and taken to roped-off corners of waiting rooms where surly, barely

> *JASMINE* IS A NOVEL THAT RESISTS CLOSURE
> AND SUGGESTS A STRATEGY OF CONTINUAL
> TRANSFORMATION AS A NECESSARY AND
> HISTORICALLY CONTINGENT ETHIC OF SURVIVAL."

wakened customs guards await their bribes. We are dressed in shreds of national costumes, out of season, the wilted plumage of intercontinental vagabondage. We only ask one thing: to be allowed to land; to pass through; to continue. (Mukherjee)

Who are these "strange pilgrims"? Certainly, we see them infrequently on the evening news when their "vagabondage" becomes intolerable, when their passage can no longer be ignored, when they put spectacular pressure on our borders. Then, these "outcasts and deportees" emerge into a brief visibility beneath Western eyes. Watching TV the other night, I saw Haitian "boat people" crammed on their small, overcrowded crafts off the Florida shore. Through its spokesman, the United States administration reasonably explained its policy of denying these refugees entry, citing a benevolent and humanitarian concern with the possible loss of life. In other words, their "vagabondage" was being treated as an issue of water safety, of laudable nautical rigor, rather than as an issue of political and material conditions. In addition, and due to the interests of electronic brevity, the Haitians had been resolutely fixed into the already known, and therefore available, category of "boat people," a distinction that defined them as a collective identity. As Chandra Mohanty writes, "the idea of abstracting particular places, peoples, and events into generalized categories, laws, and politics is fundamental to any form of ruling."

We are thus insulated from the historical trajectories that set this population in motion, the contradictions and ruptures that have propelled them out of their native culture. This insulation involves a substitution, a metalepsis, where a sociopolitical effect is identified as a cause. As a result, these "strange pilgrims" become the originary cause of scrutiny, interest, or benevolence of a discourse that seeks to situate them in teleological narratives of Western civilization and progress,

rather than as the effects of these same narrative gestures. In this paper, I want to suggest that texts such as Bharati Mukherjee's *Jasmine* attempt to disrupt this even flow of narrative historiography with a counter-discourse that thematizes prior narratives of enforced identity—narratives that through accumulation and repetition seek to define and circumscribe identity as a fixed and available resource, constituted wholly by another's desire. At the same time, *Jasmine* illustrates the inherent difficulty of such an attempt, since Mukherjee's overt critique of debasing stereotypes based on gender and exoticism tends to impede a sustained critique of problematical representations of India.

Although *Jasmine* is a narrative of emergence, I do not wish to assert, in any sense, that this novel relates an immigrant's success story, charting a steady and inevitable progress that culminates in the achievement of an autonomous, unified self. Nor is it a completely realized postcolonial text, since Mukherjee's portrayal of India relies on the trope of the manichean allegory and the demonization of the Sikh community. Rather, *Jasmine* is a novel that resists closure and suggests a strategy of continual transformation as a necessary and historically contingent ethic of survival. This continual remaking of the self invokes "two temporalities: that of oppression, memory, and enforced identity, and that of emergence after the 'break,' the counter memory, and heterogeneous difference" (Radhakrishnan, "Ethnic Identity"). On the one hand, *Jasmine* thematizes narration and identity by bringing into focus how differences are social products of interested desire. At the same time, it offers the symbolic possibility of the emergence of a reinvented, paralogical, heterogeneous "family," based on affinity and multiplicity rather than fixed identity. Thus, I will be reading *Jasmine* as a counter-narrative where "re-inventing ourselves a million times" becomes a reflexive, historically situated strategy for negotiating power.

Discussing narrative history, Frantz Fanon writes that when the colonizer comes to write the history of the colonial encounter "the history which he writes is not the history of the country which he plunders but the history of his own nation . . . ." Such interested productions become, for Lila Abu-Lughod, "the great self-congratulatory literature of the rise of the West, which for so long has shaped our view of the past . . . ." Suggesting that this literature should be "revaluated" and "remade," Abu-Lughod recommends an analysis based on triangulation, or multiple, contradictory points of view. It is just this voice of the excluded and marginalized respondent that feminist, Afro-American, and multicultural studies try to recover. But, at the same time, this voice is seen as a threat to the accomplishments and values of Western culture simply because it has been historically marginalized and may have a different story to tell. In other words, the silent, demarcated subject who is the product of Western and patriarchal historiography built upon theories of synchronous development is again resituated just at the very moment of emergence, at the very moment s/he speaks.

Moreover, as Edward Said suggests, when the postcolonial subjects speak, they are considered by many Western intellectuals to be merely "wailers and whiners," denouncing the evils of colonialism. They are thus implicated in the politics of blame. As Said explains, such a politics proceeds from a willingness to assert that colonialism has ended. Therefore, "any claims about or reparations for its damages and consequences into the present are dismissed as both irrelevant and preposterously arrogant" ("Intellectuals"). The phrase "into the present" is crucial. As I mentioned earlier, the former colonial subject becomes an originary cause, a source of discourse. Instead of being grateful for what "we" have historically done for them, "they" are constituted in the present as a pack of unappreciative whiners. They have declined the invitation, refused the call to step up into a world that is not of their own making. They are then implicated in a failure of recognition that only confirms their essential and underdeveloped nature.

This rhetorical and strategic resituating of the resisting respondent tends to maintain boundaries of exclusion. What is at risk here is the erasure of those traces of resistance that might disrupt the inevitability of the Western narrative of progress and benevolence. These exclusions occlude the complete record of colonialism, even as they resolutely try to define the excesses of colonialism as the product of aberrant individuals, a succession of Kurtzes, rather than as effects of the system that produced them. Such an experience of colonialism does continue into the present, producing an endless ripple of effects. For specific reasons, different in each case, the historical discourse produced by the colonizer created a system of representations (mostly centered around, and justified by, supposed traits of the native) that effaced the possibility of resistance. Resistance to domination was portrayed as an essential misrecognition on the part of the native.

This is the complex of concerns articulated by *Jasmine*: resistance, hierarchical distinctions, and boundaries that exclude and include. In what follows I will be examining these in light of what Chandra Mohanty calls (following Dorothy Smith) "relations of ruling"—a model for cultural analysis that "posits multiple intersections of structures of power and emphasizes the process or form of ruling, not the frozen embodiment of it." In *Jasmine* these concerns, embedded in relations of ruling, reveal themselves through the actions of the religious fundamentalist, Sukhwinder, the rapist, Half-Face, and the seemingly benevolent banker, Bud Ripplemeyer, individuals who continually attempt to place *Jasmine* into prior narratives of desire that would define her as a known, visible, and essential self conforming to one or another of the myths that their narrativized knowledge of her authorizes and legitimizes.

Confronted by the repeated pleas from Bud Ripplemeyer, the father of her unborn child, the narrator of *Jasmine* reflects upon how much he doesn't know about her. In fact, he has studiously avoided such knowledge, since her "genuine foreignness frightens him." Instead, his desire and interest are spurred by his image of "Eastern" women. For her prospective husband, she is "darkness, mystery, inscrutability. The East plunges me into visibility and wisdom." This visibility then involves an identity as an already-known subject. But she knows differently: she has been "many selves" and has "survived hideous times." In contrast to her, Bud lives innocently within "the straight lines and smooth planes of his history."

Two versions of history and narration emerge in the narrator's comments. For Jasmine, history is the discontinuity and rupture produced by material and political events and, as a result, the self becomes plural and contradictory. Her survival depends upon a flexible strategy of appropriation and transformation. For Bud, history is a straight line, a teleological and progressive ordering of existence where the phenomenological world is transparent and the self is unified and autonomous. It is "a history whose perspective on all that precedes it implies an end of time, a completed development" (Foucault). The narrator's displacement of fixed identity and these two views of history provide a point of entry into Mukherjee's *Jasmine*. In the course of the novel, the narrator is Jyoti, Jasmine, Jane, and Jase. Each of her names represents a transitional self as she travels from Hasnapur, India to Baden, Iowa. Rather than a recapitulation of the stereotype of the deceitful, mendacious Asian, these name changes can be seen as a response to the still ongoing effects of colonialism. She must change to survive and to continue her journey. In fact, the narrative structure is that of a journey and passage, a liminal state, which places the third world inside the first world. In the process, the narrator must continually remake herself to avoid the threat posed by enforced identity. She must avoid the limiting boundaries that seek to confine her in traditional and specific gendered roles, both in India and America.

As a village girl from Hasnapur, she is "born to that kind of submission, that expectation of ignorance." Her transformation from Jyoti to Jasmine represents her ability to escape from "a social order that had gone on untouched for thousands of years." This social order can be seen as symptomatic of the relations of ruling I discussed earlier. For Jyoti and the other women of Hasnapur, these relations of ruling involve a submission to the patriarchal order, which demands limited education, arranged marriages, and constant reproduction. These gendered restrictions are also configured along the lines of class and religion in *Jasmine*. Jyoti's expectations as a bride are limited by the fact that she is undowered. Her husband dies in sectarian religious violence. As the fifth daughter of nine children, Jyoti is born into a culture where daughters are a curse, since they must have dowries—which her family is unable to provide. Jyoti's mother, in an effort to spare Jyoti from a history similar to hers, a history of incessant childbearing and beatings, tries to kill her at birth. This is a culture that brings up daughters "to be caring and have no minds of our own." Nevertheless, her mother fights to keep Jyoti in school for six years and to prevent her from being married at the age of eleven to a widowed landlord.

When Jyoti does marry, it is to Prakash Vijh, a city man whose values are those of Gandhi and Nehru. In contrast to the other men of the traditional culture, Prakash does not see marriage as the cultural sanctioning of patriarchal control and enforced obedience. He renames Jyoti as Jasmine, a symbolic break with her feudal past. Yet this break causes Jyoti/Jasmine deep conflict. As a traditional woman she wants to get pregnant immediately to prove her worth and to validate her identity. Indeed, in this society, pregnancy is the only available identity. Jyoti still feels "eclipsed by the Mazbi maid's daughter, who had been married off at eleven, just after me, and already had a miscarriage."

The point to note here, as Jasmine later realizes, is that Prakash does exert a Pygmalion effect on her, since he wanted "to make me a new kind of city woman"—a new woman for his new India. Thus, Prakash is entirely determining Jyoti's new identity. He tells her that it "was up to women to resist." Despite his modern views, Prakash is first defining Jyoti's role in the new political landscape of India, and then he is telling Jyoti how to be this new woman. As such, Prakash exerts a more subtle form of patriarchal control, disguised as benevolence and demanding her active complicity. Jyoti fully recognizes her husband's limitations. She instinctively hides her detergent sales' commissions from Prakash. "For all his talk of us being equal, was he possessive about my working?" she wonders. Indeed, his talk of equality contradicts his belief that a "husband must protect the wife whenever he can." At the same time, Jyoti begins to read, even reading Prakash's repair manuals. Her ability to read and understand technical manuals leads to the turning point in their marriage: the night when they work together, repairing a VCR with an equal division of labor. They dream of opening their own business, Vijh & Vijh. This vision is important in the narrative economy of Jasmine, since it provides the first model of the reconstituted family in the novel.

This possibility is decisively put to an end by the religious fundamentalist, Sukhwinder, who has "unforgiving eyes" and a "flat, authoritative voice." Conveniently forgetting the history of violence that followed Partition, Sukhwinder wants to create the new, separatist state of "Khalistan, the Land of the Pure" for believers who renounce "filth and idolatry." Within this codified economy of sameness, "whorish women" would be kept off the streets. Indeed, "all women are whores," and "'the sari is the sign of the prostitute.'" Sukhwinder thus wishes to uphold the traditional rigid segregation of the sexes and the exclusion of women as a corollary of his religious beliefs. For Sukhwinder, the nation-state is an exclusionary border, an enclave that celebrates the will to sameness in its univocal narrative of historical and human destiny. In her desire for stark narrative contrast, Mukherjee, however, demonizes the entire Sikh community, portraying them solely as violence-crazed fundamentalists. Here, as in her portrayal of the asymmetrical relationship between India and the West, Mukherjee succumbs to those relations of ruling that, at other points, she struggles to dismantle.

Jasmine and Prakash cannot escape the sectarian violence that has spread from the provinces to the city. Prakash is killed by a bomb wired into a radio as his assassin yells "'Prostitutes! Whores!'" The bomb is meant for Jasmine, who becomes a political target because her aspirations pose a threat to the social order built on women's subjection. Like Jasmine's father, and later Professor Devinder Vadhera, Sukhwinder and his cohorts desire to return to an imagined, timeless, and seamless moment that, to them, reflects the natural order. For Jasmine, this political killing means an abrupt end to the dreams of Vijh & Vijh. Instead, she must join her mother in enforced widowhood. As she laments, "I am a widow in the war of feudalisms." In spite of this temporary recognition, however, she is still balanced precariously between Jyoti and Jasmine. Her place, her "mission," is to travel to the United States and commit ritual suicide, suttee, where Prakash intended to go to school. As such, she is still ensnared in the same imaginary relations as her contemporary from the village of Hasnapur, Vimla. When Vimla's husband dies of typhoid, Vimla, although just twenty-two, douses herself with kerosene and flings herself on the stove. "In Hasnapur, Vimla's isn't a sad story."

At this point in the novel, India merely serves as a regressive and repressive background to further Mukherjee's thematic aims. It is a timeless India that is forever feudal, undeveloped, and barbaric, and, hence, still in need of Western guidance. On strictly literary grounds, Mukherjee argues that "I had to give her [Jasmine] a society that was so regressive, traditional, so caste-bound, genderist, that she could discard it" much easier than "a fluid American society" could be discarded ("Interview"). Here, India's stalled backwardness is unfavorably contrasted to the more attractive fluidity of Western society. Following Abdul JanMohamed, we can see that Mukherjee deploys the trope of the manichean allegory in her representation of India, since "the putative superiority of the European" depends upon "the supposed inferiority of the native." As JanMohamed explains, the manichean allegory exerts such a powerful influence, consciously or subconsciously, that "even a writer who is reluctant to acknowledge it and who may indeed be highly critical of

imperialist exploitation is drawn into its vortex." Mukherjee's interests in Jasmine do not include such a critical attitude towards "imperialist exploitation" or the practice of suttee. Instead, her focus remains on the gendered subject in transit from the third world to the first world. For Mukherjee, then, a critique of stereotypes based of gender and exoticism supersedes a critique of imperialist influence in India. In many ways, this omission points to the inherent difficulties involved in avoiding the powerful attraction of the manichean allegory and, again, indicates the pervasive effects of colonialism continuing into the present.

These effects become more apparent in Mukherjee's novel when Jasmine leaves Hasnapur. She joins the dangerous, unstable category of "refugees and mercenaries and guest workers," slipping into "a shadow world" of interchangeable bodies. This floating population only asks to be allowed "to continue," while it journeys, simultaneously and side-by-side, with the tourists and businessmen who travel through legal channels of access and availability. These pilgrims are thus seen and unseen. They are ignored because of their obscene message that colonialism is not over yet. Colonialism has merely shifted into a different register. As Donna Haraway writes, the international economy of electronics and capital has redefined the notion of work. This new worker is "female and feminized," conforming to the twin imperatives of constant vulnerability and availability, as she is thoroughly "exploited as a reserve labor force."

For the refugees, the goal is simply to survive. However, this survival is threatened at the moment of their emergence into visibility. They then become the locus of suspicion and discourse. As a "'visible minority,'" these refugees are enveloped in an "atmosphere of hostility" based upon a whole series of "'crippling assumptions'" ("Interview") that are the product of prior colonialisms, textualities, and cultural myths. These myths then represent and influence behavior towards the native. For Jasmine, these myths of the available and passive Eastern woman create the climate that legitimizes her rape.

Jasmine's journey has taken her from Hasnapur to the United States aboard unregistered aircraft and ships. As an illegal immigrant traveling on a forged passport, she must complete her pilgrimage to Tampa aboard The Gulf Shuttle, a shrimper engaged in "the n[. . .]r-shipping bizness." She ends up in a motel room at the run-down Florida Court with the captain of the trawler,

Half-Face, whose name derives from the loss of an eye, an ear, and half his face in Vietnam, where he served as a demolitions expert. Half-Face, a character "from the underworld of evil," is thus marked by his neocolonialist experience in Southeast Asia, and in this sense is like the young man at the bar later in the novel who reacts to Jasmine's entrance with the remark that "'I know whore power when I see it.'" Recognition and association are immediate: "His next words were in something foreign, but probably Japanese or Thai or Filipino, something bar girls responded to in places where he'd spent his rifle-toting youth." The young man and Half Face, both veterans of the East, respond similarly because Jasmine represents an already known and gendered subject.

With banal conviction, Half-Face tells Jasmine, "You know what's coming, and there ain't nobody here to help you, so my advice is to lie back and enjoy it. Hell, you'll probably like it. I don't get many complaints." For Half-Face, Jyoti's vulnerability is a "'sort of turn-on,'" and his boast implies a prior knowledge/narrative of known Eastern women and an entire history of others who have not complained. In other words, for Half-Face and his cohorts, women have not complained because ultimately they accepted the inevitability of the hierarchical situation and their presumed sexual nature, thus discovering that they "really" liked it after all. In this interested configuration of desire, cause and effect are conflated, and the threat of violence occluded. The myth of the available and passive Eastern woman eliminates any possibility of resistance, any possibility that these women did not "really" like it. For Half-Face, Jyoti is merely "'one prime piece,'" a gendered marking of the body that "cancels out" any other considerations. With mechanical and perfunctory obliviousness, Half-Face drinks, rapes, and then falls asleep. As a consequence of her "personal dishonor," Jasmine considers killing herself as Half-Face snores in the next room.

Occurring at the exact center of the novel, Jasmine's rape signals a crucial moment in her successive transformations and in the formation of her ethics of survival. Instead of killing herself and passively conforming to an identity politics that would define her solely as a victim, she decides instead to kill her attacker. With ritualistic attentiveness, she first thoroughly cleanses her body, and then she purifies her soul through prayer. She has a small knife, given to her by Kingsland, a savvy fellow nomad traveling aboard

The Gulf Shuttle. She first uses it on herself, cutting a strip across her tongue. As Mukherjee explains, Jasmine becomes Kali, the goddess of destruction, since "Kali has her red tongue hanging out" ("Interview"). In addition, this gesture of marking and naming reclaims her body. It is an active intervention in the relations of ruling that provided the justification of her rape and her subsequent conception of herself as a victim.

One further observation here has implications for Jasmine's later desertion of her crippled husband. Mukherjee has remarked that Kali is "the goddess of destruction, but not in a haphazard, random way. She is the destroyer of evil so that that world can be renewed" ("Interview"). As such, this restructuring and renewing function of Jasmine as Kali provides a key to the possibility of a postcolonial politics where resistance to the myths, histories, and narratives of the metropolitan center involves an active thematizing of the structures of enforced identity, and an affirmative transformation that involves appropriating the weapons and technologies that have served to maintain the center. Jasmine's killing of Half-Face involves a reappropriation—a violent sundering and subsequent adapting of the controlling strategies of violence and desire—and the reinscription of active resistance into the patriarchal narrative of vulnerability and availability. She appropriates the knife/phallus, and she penetrates his body. Then, instead of committing suttee—burning the suit of her dead husband and then lying on the fire, the "mission" that controlled her journey to the United States—Jasmine burns Prakash's suit and her Indian clothes in a trash can next to the motel. She breaks the chain of causality, the metalepsis that continually tries to substitute cause for effect in the relations of ruling, the terrible causality that led to her being "raped and raped and raped in boats and cars and motel rooms" on her journey to America. With the killing of Half-Face, Jasmine passes from innocence and enacts a radical break, suggesting a form of resistance that is contingent, disruptive, and strategic. Rather than reifying a past that is continuous and identical with itself, Jasmine suggests a history dislodged from origins and a self fractured from organic wholeness.

As R. Radhakrishnan writes, "[t]he task for radical ethnicity is to thematize and subsequently problematize its entrapment within these binary elaborations with the intent of stepping beyond to find its own adequate language" ("Ethnic Identity"). For Jasmine, this "adequate language" involves the

ability "to adjust, to participate," without succumbing to the desire to hold on to the past and certainty.
To do so would be to become like Professor Vadhera and his family, who recreate an artificially
maintained Indianness. In contrast, Jasmine must
seek to negotiate and resituate, continually, the
horizon of her fears and desires. This process of
constant adjustment propels her to New York,
where she acquires an illegal green card and comes
to work as a domestic in the Hayes household. In
the process, she is again renamed. Like Prakash,
Taylor Hayes acknowledges her liminal state: "Taylor didn't want to change me. He didn't want to
scour and sanitize the foreignness. My being
different . . . didn't scare him." In contrast to her
earlier transformations, she asserts that "I changed
because I wanted to." She thus becomes "Jase, the
prowling adventurer."

But Sukhwinder reappears in New York. To
protect her new family, Jase escapes to Baden,
Iowa. Here again, she changes, exchanging Jase
for Jane. The point to note here is that she is
actively changing her name, rather than passively
accepting a name as she had with Prakash. But
this new role requires a "regression, like going
back to village life, a life of duty and devotion"
("Interview"). Settling in Baden as the wife of Bud
Ripplemeyer, the head of the local bank, would
be the same as remaining in Hasnapur, since
becoming Bud's wife would be merely another
form of enforced identity. As Jane, she only feels
affection for Bud. Crippled by a distraught
farmer whom his bank has foreclosed on, Bud
appeals to her feelings of responsibility to be a
caregiver as she had been in the Hayes family. To
become Mrs. Jane Ripplemeyer, therefore, would
require renouncing her desire to gain control of
her body and destiny.

I began my reading of Jasmine with Jane and
Bud by noting their two different conceptions of
narrative and history, and I want to return to the
connection between these conceptions and the
production of enforced identity through another's
desire. These two contrasting views become apparent when Bud and Jane are driving through
Baden and pass "half-built, half-deserted cinder-
block structures at the edge of town." The "empty
swimming pools and plywood panels in the window frames" remind her of the Florida Coast
motel where she was raped because as constructed
by prior narratives of female identity she could
be imagined as provocatively vulnerable and
available.

Bud reacts differently to the cinder-block structures. Contemplating these undeveloped resources,
Bud "frowns because unproductive projects give
him a pain." In fact, Bud sees these unproductive
resources and can only wonder "who handled their
financing." For Bud then, individuals, resources,
and land are only understandable within an economy of productivity and efficiency. Thus, "Asia
he'd thought of only as a soy-bean market," presumably tended by productive and silent natives.
And, indeed, Bud imagines the natives of his
own region in terms of similar evaluative categories.
A "good man" is one who displays "discipline,
strength, patience, character. Husbandry." To
Bud, individuals like Darryl who do not want to
be tied down by the family farm, who want to make
"something more of his life than fate intended," are
irreducibly "flawed."

Bud Ripplemeyer is like a series of characters
in this novel—Sukhwinder, Professor Vadhera,
and Jyoti's father—who want to preserve a vision
of the past as a pure, uncontested, and originary
terrain. This nostalgia precludes change while it
authorizes relations of ruling that seek to deny the
interested subordination of oppositional voices and
knowledges. Thus, the narrator can easily "wonder
if Bud ever sees the America I do." The answer is
no. Bud's desire manifests itself in the will to possess and to define. Jasmine has learned a different
lesson from history.

Rather than preservation, stasis, and attach-
ments, Mukherjee's novel proposes a counter-narrative that suggests that "transformation" must be
embraced. Such a strategy questions the drive to
essentialize that characterizes Sukhwinder, Half-
Face, and Bud Ripplemeyer. It also suggests a
different relationship between former colonial
partners, a resituating of history that involves a
thematizing of prior myths of enforced identity
and a breaking into a new space, provisional and
based on affinity, not identity. This postcolonial
space is portrayed symbolically as the reconstituted family that emerges at the end of the novel:
Jase is carrying Bud's child, Duff is an adopted
child, and Taylor is emerging from a failed marriage. In addition they are going to California to
be reunited with Du and his sister, victims of
Vietnam's colonial past.

In the reconstituted family, they do not have
the certainty of Bud's straight line of history, but
neither do they have those benevolent assumptions
that authorize exclusions based on fear of immigrants. Here, individuals survive through a flexible

strategy of "scavenging, adaption, and appropriat[ing] technology," not exactly because they want to, but because they must in order to survive. It is not coincidental that the skills of Prakash and Du involve the rewiring of the circuitry of electronic machinery. Yet, this skill can also be turned to destructive ends, since Sukhwinder and his cohorts, the Khalsa Lions, wire bombs into radios. In this sense, an affinity that recognizes difference and contradiction, rather than an affiliation solely based on identity politics, becomes a necessity.

But survival also depends on a recognition of the historical and material forces that set this floating population in motion. As I indicated earlier, such a recognition might have informed Mukherjee's portrayal of India and her understanding of the ideological complexity of suttee. With its title character scarred by history, Mukherjee's *Jasmine* concludes with an image of affiliation through affinity—a hopeful imaging of a postcolonial world where difference is acknowledged and history is reconfigured. Yet, at the same time, this achieved state or topos of the reconstituted family cannot be seen as fixed and realized. Instead, Jasmine wonders how many "more selves" are in her. There are no answers to these questions in *Jasmine*, since any answer would involve a refutation of the novel's ethic of survival, adaptation, and transformation.

"Re-inventing ourselves" may be seen as an active strategy that implies the possibility of resistance and reappropriation through a reconfiguring of the received knowledges that constitute colonial history. As JanMohamed and Lloyd note, such a critical reinterpretation "assert[s] that even the very differences which have always been read as symptoms of inadequacy are capable of being re-read transformatively as indications and figurations of values opposed to the dominant discourse." Thus, this archival work involves a strategy of re-reading the received history of the past, with particular attention to its silences, ruptures, and contradictions. It strives to avoid mistaking effects for causes, and to maintain a critical activity that sees differences as a product of competing discursive fields. Identity is never reducible to one stable and essential position, but is an effect of these discourses and contestations. To think only in terms of the implacable opposition of center to margin is to revalidate the essentializing binary grid of identity. To think in terms of shifting the center, de-centering, is to imagine an ascendancy of the margins, a simple reversal, where "interested" versions of heterogeneity vie for prominence.

A third option is to illuminate the borders where centers and margins rub against each other in often contradictory ways. It is to bring the border into visibility, while resisting the urge to speak for it.

Jasmine examines this play of borders. As such, the novel avoids becoming a simple attack upon identity-based discursive formulas. Instead, it addresses the multiplicity of material forces and discursive regimes that seek to position the gendered subject. Put another way, *Jasmine* examines the doubleness involved in being "always moving and always still," a shifting and multiple identity that is in a state of perpetual transition. This novel presents the possibility of the acceptance of a plural self, one that resists the impulse towards certainty and totalization. In addition, resistance and transgression become viable alternatives, since, as the narrator remarks, "[t]here are no harmless, compassionate ways to remake oneself." Remaking oneself becomes the only possible response to enforced identity and subjugated knowledge.

It is a mistake, I think, to seek agency at the conscious level of enactment. Even when there is a face on the machine—for instance, Half-Face or Bud Ripplemeyer—it is only one of many replaceable faces. The task for the intellectual is to delineate the workings of the machine, the relations of ruling, at its tentacle extension, at the extended point where it is most vulnerable, disputed, and diffused. Such a strategy involves a reappropriation, but also a negotiation, since negotiation recognizes difference as a site of both affinity and contestation. Negotiation is a desire to open up larger spaces in a common field of dialogical interaction. Yet, at the same time, there is the persistent danger noted by R. Radhakrishnan, related to the "profound contradictions that underlie the attempt to theorize change," that "our attempts to change the subject" may be "potentially wrong and repressive, even barbaric" ("Changing Subject"). In other words, there is the real danger of reproducing the very same relations of ruling that we have identified. To some extent, these processes occur in Jasmine.

Rather than locating agency in a unified subject position capable of correctly reading the real, a subject who has somehow "successfully" resisted its interpellation, Mukherjee's Jasmine struggles to articulate another form of knowledge. This negotiated knowledge is a modality of action predicated on a series of shifting subject positions. These temporary roles then become vectors of intersection and intervention, and, because they are temporary and mobile, possibly prevent succumbing to the desire for certainty and completeness. A "role" is not originary, unique, or substantial. In fact, it points to the fictiveness of the gesture towards complete, realized development and continuity. It reveals discontinuity beneath the "role," the mask. Rather than a frozen category, Identity, then, becomes an historically specific strategy: not a "free" subject acting, but an available site for negotiation. Mukherjee has argued that an ability to adapt and appropriate is transformative, establishing the "sense of two-way traffic" ("Interview"). This "two-way traffic" captures the sense of Said's call for "a tremendously energetic attempt to engage with the metropolitan world in a common effort at re-inscribing, re-interpreting and expanding the sites of intensity and the terrain contested with Europe" ("Intellectuals").

No doubt, this "common effort" does not in any way help the Haitian "boat people" that I began this paper with. Nor will it probably help the next floating population of refugees and deportees. The failure lies in the too-easy conflation of cause and effect and the ready availability of abstract categories, so that these people are not seen as the effects of colonialisms "into the present." We can, however, continue to create the conditions where these silent people might speak of a different history. I think Mukherjee's strategy of "re-inventing ourselves" does open up the transformative possibility of not only interrogating these structures of power and knowledge, but also suggesting a historically-situated strategy where borders serve as multiple sites of contestation, transformative rereadings, and affinity. As such, the visible border becomes the site for critical interruption and discontinuity, for rewiring the circuitry.

Source: F. Timothy Ruppel, "'Re-inventing Ourselves a Million Times': Narrative, Desire, Identity, and Bharati Mukherjee's *Jasmine*," in *College Literature*, Vol. 22, No. 1, February 1995, pp. 181–92.

Faymonville, Carmen, Review of *Jasmine*, in *Explicator*, Vol. 56, No. 1, Fall 1997, pp. 53–54.

Gorra, Michael, Review of *Jasmine*, in *New York Times*, September 10, 1989, http://www.nytimes.com.1989/09/10/books/call-it-exile-call-it-immigration.html?scp=1&sq-jasmine+bharati+mukherjee&st=nyt (accessed September 12, 2010).

"India," in the *CIA: World Factbook*, August 19, 2010, https://www.cia.gov/library/publications/the-world-factbook/geos/in.html (accessed September 12, 2010).

Kaganoff, Penny, Review of *Jasmine*, in *Publishers Weekly*, Vol. 238, No. 1, January 18, 1991, p. 55.

Lesser, Wendy, "United States," in *The Oxford Guide to Contemporary Writing*, edited by John Sturrock, Oxford University Press, 1996, pp. 406–31.

Lim, Walter S. H., "Class, Labor and Immigrant Subjectivity in Bharati Mukherjee's *Jasmine* and Shirley Geoklin Lim's *Among the White Moon Faces*," in *Journeys*, Vol. 10, No. 1, June 2009, pp. 4–28.

Mukherjee, Bharati, "American Dreamer," in *Mother Jones*, January/February 1997.

Sharma, Kalpana, "Rooted Custom," in *India Together*, November 2002, http://www.indiatogether.org/opinions/kalpana/dowvict.htm (accessed November 17, 2010).

Smith, William, "Death in the Garden: Indira Gandhi's Assassination Sparks a Fearful Round of Sectarian Violence," in *Time*, Vol. 124, November 12, 1984, pp. 42–48.

Vignission, Runar, "Bharati Mukherjee: An Interview," in *Journal of the South Pacific Association for Commonwealth Literature and Language Studies*, edited by Vijay Mishra, No. 34–35, 1993.

Wachtel, Eleanor, Review of *Jasmine*, in *Maclean's*, Vol. 102, No. 43, October 23, 1989, p. 72.

"Yemen Eyed as Source of Suspicious Packages," in *CBS News.com*, October 29, 2010, http://www.cbsnews.com/stories/2010/10/29/national/main7003589.shtml?tag=stack (accessed November 17, 2010).

Zwerdling, Daniel, "'Green Revolution' Trapping India's Farmers in Debt," in *Morning Edition*, National Public Radio, April 14, 2009, http://www.npr.org/templates/story/story.php?storyId=102944731 (accessed September 12, 2010).

SOURCES

"Air Flight 182," in *CBC News*, June 17, 2010, http://www.cbc.ca/news/airindia (accessed September 12, 2010).

Ash, Lucy, "India's Dowry Deaths," in *BBC News*, July 16, 2003, http://news.bbc.co.uk/2/hi/programmes/crossing_continents/3071963.stm (accessed September 12, 2010).

Banerjee, Debjani, "In the Presence of History: The Representation of Past and Present Indias in Bharati Mukherjee's Fiction," in *Bharati Mukherjee: Critical Perspectives*, edited by Emmanuel S. Nelson, Garland Press, 1993.

FURTHER READING

Chua, C. L., "Passages from India: Migrating to America in the Fiction of V. S. Naipaul and Bharati Mukherjee," in *Reworlding: The Literature of the Indian Diaspora*, edited by Emmanuel S. Nelson, Greenwood Press, 1992, pp. 51–61.

This book discusses Mukherjee's and V. S. Naipaul's portrayal of Indian immigrants in North American, and their struggles to realize the American dream.

Edwards, Bradley, ed., *Conversations with Bharati Mukherjee*, University Press of America, 2009.

Edwards has collected extensive interviews with Mukherjee dating back to her first interview some thirty years ago in this useful anthology.

Kumar, Nagendra, *The Fiction of Bharati Mukherjee*, Atlantic, 2001.

Kumar's study of Mukherjee's fiction includes an investigation of the phases of the writer's life, including expatriation, transition, immigration, and final settlement.

Piciucco, Pier Paolo, ed., *A Companion to Indian Fiction in English*, Atlantic, 2004.

This comprehensive overview of Indian literature in English provides students with not only biographical and critical information concerning Mukherjee but also insight into a substantial number of important Indian writers, both in India and throughout the world.

SUGGESTED SEARCH TERMS

Jasmine AND Bharati Mukherjee

Bharati Mukherjee

Indian literature

immigration

Hindu customs

identity AND immigration

Clark Blaise

Clark Blaise AND Bharati Mukherjee

India Air flight 182

The Middleman and Other Stories

The Moon Is Down

JOHN STEINBECK
1942

The Moon Is Down is a short novel by the twentieth-century American writer John Steinbeck. It was published in March 1942, only a few months after the United States entered World War II. The novel is set in an unnamed small town that has just been swiftly conquered by a small but well-armed invading army. Although it is never explicitly stated, the town is presumed to be in Norway and the invaders the German Nazis. The Germans invaded Norway in just this fashion in April 1940, seven months after World War II began in 1939. In 1942, Norway was still under Nazi occupation, and Steinbeck wrote the novel in order to demonstrate that a free, democratic people, even though outgunned, would eventually rid itself of invaders who live under a nondemocratic system led by a dictator. The hero of the novel is the mayor of the town, who sacrifices his life rather than counsel his people to abandon their resistance. *The Moon Is Down* is notable not only as a war story that correctly foresees the triumph of the Allies in World War II but also for the inspirational effect it had on readers in occupied Europe, where it was eagerly read and distributed, in spite of being banned by the Nazis. *The Moon Is Down* is available in a 1995 Penguin Classics edition.

AUTHOR BIOGRAPHY

Steinbeck was born on February 27, 1902, in Salinas, California. His father, John Ernst Steinbeck II, was a Monterey County official, and his

John Steinbeck (*National Archives and Records Administration*)

mother, Olive Hamilton, was a teacher. Stein-beck enrolled at Stanford University in Palo Alto in 1920 and studied intermittently until 1925, but he left without earning a degree.

In 1925, he moved to New York City, where he tried to make a living as a freelance writer. He also worked briefly as a newspaper reporter before returning to California, where he took various manual jobs but was still determined to pursue his ambition to become a writer. He published his first novel, *Cup of Gold*, in 1929. Two more novels and several short stories followed in the early 1930s before he gained his first popular success with *Tortilla Flat* (1935), which won an award from the California Commonwealth Club for the best novel by a California author. Stein-beck followed this with the novel *Of Mice and Men* (1937) and his masterpiece, *The Grapes of Wrath* (1939), a tale of the exodus of farm families from the Dust Bowl during the Great Depression. The novel won the Pulitzer Prize for Fiction.

During World War II, Steinbeck was a war correspondent for the *New York Herald Tribune*. In 1942, he published *The Moon Is Down* as both a play and a novel. It had a controversial reception in the United States but was well received in Nazi-occupied Europe.

In 1952, he published one of his best-known novels, *East of Eden*, which he had worked on for five years. Set in California's Salinas Valley, the novel follows the fortunes of two families over several generations. The novel met with mixed reviews.

Steinbeck married Carol Henning in 1930, but the marriage did not last. In 1943, Steinbeck married his second wife, Gwyndolyn Conger. The couple had two sons, but the marriage ended in 1948. Steinbeck married Elaine Scott in 1950.

In 1962, Steinbeck was awarded the Nobel Prize for Literature. In 1964, he was awarded the Presidential Medal of Freedom by President Lyndon B. Johnson. Steinbeck died of a heart attack four years later, on December 20, 1968, in New York City.

PLOT SUMMARY

Chapter 1

The Moon Is Down begins on a Sunday morning in an unnamed town and country. The town has been invaded and swiftly conquered. Although it is never stated directly, the town is in Norway, and the invaders are the German Nazis in World War II.

The invasion catches the town by surprise because of the preparatory work done by shop-keeper George Corell, a traitor who wants the invaders to succeed. The small town had only twelve soldiers to defend it; six were killed, three were wounded, and three escaped. The invading force is small but heavily armed.

At eleven o'clock, Colonel Lanser, the commander of the invading army, meets with Mayor Orden, the mayor's wife, and Doctor Winter in the mayor's palace. Accompanying the colonel is Corell. Orden, shocked at Corell's treachery, refuses to speak if Corell remains. Lanser orders Corell to leave. Then he tells the mayor that he wants to get along with the local people. The invaders need the coal from the mine, and they want the people to continue to work in it. The colonel hopes that everything will be orderly and the people will not resist. He appeals to the mayor for his cooperation, but

MEDIA ADAPTATIONS

- A film version of *The Moon Is Down*, directed by Irving Pichel, was released by Twentieth-Century Fox in 1943. Lee J. Cobb starred as Dr. Albert Winter.

the mayor refuses to commit himself. He says he will follow what the people decide.

Chapter 2

Lanser and the five members of his staff set up their headquarters upstairs in the mayor's palace. They are Major Hunter, Captain Bentick, Captain Loft, Lieutenant Prackle, and Lieutenant Tonder.

Hunter is at his drawing board designing a railroad siding. Loft and Hunter discuss the fact that Bentick went out on duty wearing only a fatigue cap, not his helmet. Hunter says it is all right because the people are obedient, but Loft thinks there will be trouble if they do not follow military regulations. Prackle pins up a picture of a pretty girl on the wall, but Loft tells him to take it down because it is not suitable for a military office.

Colonel Lanser enters. Prackle asks him when the war will be over; he is confident they will win. But Lanser says he does not know. Tonder says that after the war he might like to settle in the conquered country, since he likes the land and the people.

Corell enters. Lanser thanks him for his work in preparing for the invasion but warns him he may be in danger. Corell disagrees; he thinks the townspeople are not violent. Corell proposes that he be made mayor but Lanser refuses. He says Orden knows the people better, and Lanser needs to know what the people are thinking. Lanser says he will recommend to his superiors that Corell leave the country.

Loft enters and reports that Captain Bentick has been killed by a miner who objected to being told to go to work.

Chapter 3

In the drawing room of the mayor's palace, Joseph the servant and Annie the cook discuss the situation. Joseph says that Alex Morden, the man who killed Bentick, is to be tried and shot. Annie is indignant and says the people will be angry. Joseph also tells Annie that two of the town's young men have escaped to England and that he does not expect Corell to live long. The people are getting organized.

Mayor Orden and Doctor Winter enter and discuss the upcoming trial. Molly Morden, Alex's wife, enters. She asks the mayor for reassurance that he will not be the one who sentences Alex, even though people are saying he will do so to preserve order. The mayor confirms that he will not sentence her husband.

Lanser enters, and he and Orden speak alone. Lanser says that he regrets what has happened but that he has a job to do. He tries to persuade Orden to pass a sentence of death on Alex, but Orden refuses, saying he has no legal authority to do so. Lanser says that Alex must be shot in order to deter others from violence; the mayor comments that the spirit of the people cannot be permanently held down.

Chapter 4

Snow falls as the trial begins in the palace drawing room. Captain Loft reads an account of the crime and says the military court finds the prisoner guilty of murder and recommends a death sentence. When asked whether he killed the captain, Alex admits that he hit him but does not know that he killed him. He explains that he got angry and that he really intended to hit Loft, who had ordered him to work. He says he is not sorry he did it because he is a free man and does not take orders.

Lanser announces that Alex has been found guilty and that he will be shot immediately. Orden makes a speech in which he supports Alex, saying that Alex was the first to publicly express anger against the invaders. Orden wants the people to know that he is not collaborating with the conquerors.

The firing squad waits outside. Orden tells Alex that his death will unite the people, and the invaders will have no rest. Alex is taken to the town square and shot. Just after the shots are fired, someone shoots through the window of the drawing-room. Prackle is injured in the shoulder. Lansing orders his men to search the town for firearms. Any man who has one is to be taken hostage.

Chapter 5

Months go by. There are acts of sabotage at the mine, which is also bombed by the English. The people are hostile to the invaders and kill them when they have an opportunity. The conquerors can no longer relax, knowing they are surrounded by silent enemies. They become afraid.

Hunter, Prackle, and Tonder are in the drawing room. Prackle and Tonder talk about girls, and Prackle says to Loft that it would be nice if they could go home on leave for a while. Tonder also wants to get away; he hates the people in the town. He says he wants a girl and has noticed a pretty blond girl in town. Prackle tells him to be careful.

Captain Loft enters and reports on another act of sabotage at the mine. He says he shot the man responsible. He has also instituted a new policy: if the men do not produce coal, their families will be given no food. In response to Tonder's questions, Loft insists that the war is almost won and reproaches Tonder for what he interprets as an attitude of doubt. He says the colonel is requesting reinforcements, and Tonder hopes that when and if they come he will be able to go home for a while. He says he dreamed that their Leader was crazy; he starts to laugh in a hysterical way and Loft has to slap him to make him stop.

Chapter 6

In her home, Molly Morden sits in her rocking chair and knits. Annie arrives and tells her that the mayor, the doctor, and two young men, Will and Tom Anders, who are about to escape to England, are coming to Molly's house within the hour.

After Annie leaves there is another knock on the door. This time the visitor is Tonder. He says he means no harm and just wants to talk. Molly is the blond girl he has had his eye on. She tells him he can only stay fifteen minutes. He admits that he just wants her to like him and says he has written a poem about her, which he recites. He then admits that the poem was written by Heinrich Heine. She taunts him by saying she is hungry and will only like him if he brings her two sausages. She says she hates him, but then corrects herself, saying that, like him, she is lonely. Tonder says he wants to look after her; Molly

responds by talking about her dead husband. Tonder leaves but says he will come back.

Annie returns with Will and Tom. The mayor and the doctor arrive. Tom and Will say they plan to escape by taking Corell's boat. They will also take Corell and throw him in the sea. Orden tells them to get the English to send them weapons in the form of dynamite and grenades.

Tonder returns and knocks on the door. The men depart the back way. Molly takes a large pair of scissors and places them inside her dress. Then she lets Tonder in.

Chapter 7

The land is still covered in snow. At night British bombers drop packages of dynamite by parachute all over the countryside. The local people collect them.

Lanser, Loft, and Hunter examine one of the packages. Hunter says it is a simple device, with a one-minute fuse. There is also chocolate inside the packages, to ensure that everyone will look for them, as well as instructions on how to use the dynamite. Lanser says that his orders are to set booby traps and poison the chocolate, but he knows this will not work. He also alludes to the fact that Tonder was killed.

Correll enters and says that the mayor is helping the saboteurs. He advises Lanser to take the mayor hostage and shoot him if there are any more disturbances. He also says that he escaped the attempt to kidnap him.

Lanser orders the arrest of Orden and Winter, although he knows that this will not end the rebellion.

Chapter 8

Orden and Winter are under guard in the palace. Orden says he could not stop the rebellion even if he wanted to, and Winter agrees that the cause of the townspeople will grow stronger. Both men know they will be shot. Orden quotes the last speech of Socrates, from Plato's *Apology* which he remembers from many years ago. Socrates said that what mattered was not living or dying but doing the right thing. Orden continues to recite the speech, prompted by Winter. Lanser enters and listens. Prackle enters and reports that they have found some men with dynamite.

Orden refuses to tell the people not to use the dynamite. There is the sound of an explosion, and then another explosion blows out one of the doors. Orden moves toward the door, knowing that he is about to be taken out and shot.

CHARACTERS

Will Anders

Will Anders is a fisherman. When his brother commits an act of sabotage, the invaders come looking for him. He therefore escapes by sea to England and conveys the message to send explosives.

Tom Anders

Like his brother Will, Tom Anders is a fisherman. He escapes to England with Will.

Annie

Annie is the cook in the mayor's palace. She is a truculent woman who does not take kindly to the presence of soldiers. Soon after the invasion, she throws boiling water at them. This makes her something of a heroine in the town, and as the occupation continues, she grows more and more angry.

Captain Bentick

Captain Bentick is a member of the invading army. He is described as "a family man, a lover of dogs and pink children and Christmas." He admires the English and likes to take his vacations in England. He is not an ambitious man and has therefore not risen beyond the rank of captain. Bentick is killed by Alex Morden at the mine.

George Corell

A short, bald man, George Corell is a traitor who betrays his countrymen to the enemy. He is a popular shopkeeper and has lived in the town for years. But unbeknownst to anyone, he secretly prepares the way for the invasion. He makes a list of all the firearms in the town and makes sure that all the town's troops are six miles away at a shooting competition on the morning of the invasion. After the invasion he wants Colonel Lanser to make him mayor, but Lanser refuses. Lanser warns him that his life is in danger, and the local people shun him and plot to kill him. He manages to survive, however.

Major Hunter

Major Hunter is one of the invaders. He is an engineer and spends most of his time working at his drawing board designing building projects, such as a new railroad siding. He is kept busy because the British keep bombing whatever he has built. He is described as "a haunted little man of figures, a little man who, being a dependable unit, considered all other men either as degradable units or as unfit to live."

Joseph

Joseph is the servant in the mayor's palace. He is described as "elderly and lean and serious, and his life was so complicated that only a profound man would know him to be simple." Like the other people in the town, Joseph obeys the instructions of the invaders but finds ways of resisting them in his manner and bearing.

Colonel Lanser

Colonel Lanser is the commander of the invading and occupying army. He is a veteran of a previous war (obviously World War I), having served in Belgium and France. Unlike his young officers, he has no illusions about what war is really like. He knows he will be compelled to take repressive measures against the local people, and he knows also that this will only increase the level of resistance. Lanser is presented as a civilized, humane man who goes about his duties reluctantly. He is lenient with Annie, for example, when she scalds a soldier with boiling water. He does not even order her arrest. However, he does not allow his own thoughts about the stupidity of war to stop him from carrying out his duty.

Captain Loft

Captain Loft is a young man who has become a captain as a result of his driving ambition. He loves being in the army; it is his whole life, and he is expected to rise quickly to higher ranks. He insists on always following military regulations, and he irritates other people because he is always so certain he is right. Loft is in charge of operations at the mine. It is he who sparks the incident in which Bentick is killed, when Loft orders Alex to work. Loft also thinks up the scheme to withhold food from the families of any of the men who refuse to work.

Alex Morden

Alex Morden is a quick-tempered young miner. He objects to being told by Captain Loft to go to work and tries to strike him. Bentick intervenes and Alex hits him instead. Bentick is killed, and

Alex is tried and convicted of murder. He says at the trial that he is not sorry for what he did. He is sentenced to death and taken out and shot immediately.

Molly Morden

Molly Morden is the pretty wife of Alex Morden. She is about thirty years old. In revenge for the execution of Alex for murder, she murders Lieutenant Tonder with a pair of scissors when he comes to visit her.

Madame Orden

Madame Orden is the mayor's wife. She is a small, strong-willed, intense woman. She and the mayor have been married a long time, and she likes to take a lot of the credit for making the mayor the man he is.

Mayor Orden

Mayor Orden is the mayor of the conquered town. He is old and white-haired and has been mayor for a very long time. He is calm after the invasion, but his refusal to speak while Corell is in the room shows the depths of his feelings about what has happened. He does not at first proclaim that the people must resist; rather, he waits to see what they will do, since he sees himself as the embodiment of the will of the people. As the story unfolds, Mayor Orden shows his admirable character in small acts of defiance against the invader and in his solidarity with the people. He congratulates Alex on the answer he gives at his trial, and he insists that Alex be allowed to sit rather than stand. He also refuses to issue the death sentence himself, saying he has no authority to do so. As the resistance grows, Mayor Orden gives it all the support he can, telling Tom and Will Anders to ask the English to send them explosives. Finally, he shows his courage when he is arrested and asked to tell the townspeople to stop the rebellion. He refuses, knowing full well that he will be shot, but also knowing that the resistance will continue whether he is alive or dead.

Lieutenant Prackle

Lieutenant Prackle, like Tonder, is a sentimental young man, and he is also moody. He likes to dance, and he has some artistic talent. He talks a lot with Tonder about girls. Prackle believes completely in the virtue of the political system he represents, but the strain of the occupation soon weighs him down. He becomes nervous and gloomy. He is wounded in the shoulder in an attack on the palace.

Lieutenant Tonder

Lieutenant Tonder is a romantic, sentimental young man who likes poetry and has dreams of glory on the battlefield. However, he has little real understanding of war. He thinks it will all be easy and will be over very quickly. He has no idea of how a conquered people is likely to behave. At first, he likes the country and the people and has a fanciful notion that, when the war is over, he will settle there. Later, however, as the occupation drags on and the people resist, he gets restless and lonely and wants to return home. He now hates the people he formerly professed to like. His fatal error is to take a liking to a blond girl he has seen in the town and to visit her one evening. This is Molly Morden, whose husband was murdered by the invaders. Tonder has no idea of her identity, however. When he visits her, he says he wants to look after her. When he returns later the same evening, she kills him by stabbing him with a pair of scissors.

Doctor Winter

Doctor Winter is the town physician and also the local historian. Like Mayor Orden, he is old. He and Orden are friends, and they have frequent discussions about the situation in the town. Like Orden, Winter does what he can to resist the occupation. He accompanies Orden to Molly Morden's house to meet Tom and Will and tell them of their plan. It is Winter who explains that, if they have dynamite, the invader will never be able to rest. Winter is later arrested along with Orden. Orden is the first to be shot, but Winter knows this will be his fate too, and he accepts it with equanimity.

THEMES

Leadership

Two different forms of leadership are contrasted in *The Moon Is Down*, along with two different ways of organizing a society or conducting a war. The invaders simply follow a leader; they are described as "herd men" by Mayor Orden. If their leader is defeated, they are beaten, too. They cannot fight on because they have only ever learned to follow the leader. They have no other principle by which they live. In contrast,

TOPICS FOR FURTHER STUDY

- With your classmates, stage one scene of the novel as a play. The descriptive passages can be read by a narrator. Have the narrator comment on the reason that scene was chosen by your group.

- Create an interactive online World War II timeline for the war in Europe that shows which countries were under German occupation and when they were liberated. Remember to include the dates of the Allied invasion of Europe and the major battles that followed to liberate them. Provide links to Web sites that explain more about each date.

- Why does Mayor Orden recall the Greek philosopher Socrates and quote lines from Plato's *Apology*? Using online and print sources, find out the significance of Mayor Orden's words to Winter just before he is taken out to be shot, "Crito, I owe a cock to Asclepius." What is the significance of those words in the context of the novel? Write an essay in which you discuss your findings.

- When the invaders speak of the Leader, they are referring to Adolf Hitler, the German dictator during World War II. Create a multimedia presentation about Hitler's leadership style. How did he get the German people to follow him? How did he make decisions? Consult *Adolf Hitler* (2006), a biography for young-adult readers by Katie Daynes, for more information.

- Read one of the twelve fictionalized accounts of teenage war heroes in Sally M. Rogow's *Faces of Courage: Young Heroes of World War II* (2003). Write an essay that illuminates the leadership qualities exhibited by the hero in the face of adversity.

Orden describes "free men," who detest being conquered and will fight on whatever happens to their leaders. This represents a democratic form of leadership, in which leaders respond to what the people want. Such leaders are replaceable; the people who live in this kind of society cannot be defeated even if their leaders are killed.

Mayor Orden makes it clear at the beginning that he is not a dictator who gives his people orders. He does not show his hand during the initial interview with Lanser. He says he does not know how his people will react to the situation, and he makes no statements about his own attitude. He tells Lanser that, in the town where he holds office, the form of government has grown up over a period of four hundred years. In other words, it has evolved gradually in an organic kind of way rather than being shaped by someone who seizes authority and imposes it on everyone. Orden tells Lanser,

> Some people accept appointed leaders and obey them. But my people have elected me. They made me and they can unmake me. Perhaps they will if they think I have gone over to you. I just don't know.

When Lanser presses him to compel his people to continue to work the coal mine, he says, "My people don't like to have others think for them." This is why the mayor often says he does not know what will happen or what the people will do. It is not that he lacks leadership but that his leadership style is to defer to the people, and in the early stages of the conflict, the people have not shown they will react. Lanser is impatient with the mayor's cagey attitude, which he does not understand: "Always the people! The people are disarmed. The people have no say."

Orden elaborates on the same point in the final chapter, when he once more speaks to Lanser. Whereas Lanser can order his men to do or not to do something, it is not so with Orden. He is simply the embodiment of the will of the people at any moment. He cannot tell them what to do. As he explains to Lanser, the people in the town will fight back against the invaders regardless of whether he tells them to do so or asks them to stop. It is useless for Lanser to try to keep order by telling the mayor to give his people instructions not to fight. They will not listen to him. Leadership is thus in a sense spread out over everyone, unlike the hierarchical structure of the society of "herd men." As Orden tries to explain to Lanser, even the mayor himself cannot be arrested, because "the Mayor is an idea conceived by free men. It will escape arrest." The invaders do not understand this concept.

Norwegian coal mine *(Tyler Olson | Shutterstock.com)*

This is shown by the words of the traitor Corell, who urges Lanser to arrest Orden and Winter and shoot them if the rebellion continues. He says, "Then we have authority. Then rebellion will be broken. When we have killed the leaders, the rebellion will be broken." Lanser may doubt that Corell is right, but he follows his advice nonetheless.

Freedom

Freedom is unquenchable, whatever the odds it faces. At the beginning of *The Moon Is Down*, it looks as if the town is completely defeated. The townspeople have been caught by surprise and disarmed. Their situation appears hopeless. But because they have had a long tradition of freedom, the desire for it is built into the way they think and act. They can be kept under by an invading army for only so long, and then the will for freedom reasserts itself. As the mayor puts it just before he is taken out to be shot: "The people don't like to be conquered, sir, and so they will not be." So it is that the people find the courage they need and take action against the invaders in any way they can.

STYLE

Metaphor

When Tonder reports that he dreamed that the Leader was crazy, he shouts out, "Maybe the Leader is crazy. Flies conquer the flypaper. Flies capture two hundred miles of new flypaper!" He is using a metaphor to describe the paradoxical situation of the invaders. They have conquered the town, and yet they feel afraid; they are ostensibly in charge, yet they feel surrounded. In the metaphor, the invaders are the flies and the townspeople are the flypaper. Tonder implies that the Leader is crazy and will present as a victory what in fact is, or soon will be, a defeat. The townspeople hear about Tonder's words and make a song about it, called "The flies have conquered the flypaper."

Setting

The small-town setting is emphasized by the frequent use of the word "little" to describe it. The mayor's palace is "little," too. The word "little" is also used to describe the people in the town. This

COMPARE & CONTRAST

- **1942:** Nazi collaborator Vidkun Quisling becomes head of state in Norway. Norway is occupied by Germany.

  Today: Norway is a constitutional monarchy. The head of state is King Harald V. The political system is democratic. Elections to the parliament are held every four years under a system of proportional representation.

- **1942:** The British army defeats the Germans at the Battle of El Alamein in North Africa; U.S. forces engage in the Guadalcanal Campaign in the Pacific to protect trade routes; the German Sixth Army is surrounded at Stalingrad in Russia and will soon be forced to surrender. These victories signal turning points in the war in favor of the Allies.

Today: Most of the major belligerents in World War II are allies: Britain, France, and Germany are members of the European Community and of NATO, the Western military alliance. The United States is also a member of NATO, and Japan is a U.S. ally. Russia, after the cold war ended in the late 1980s, has improved relations with the United States and Western Europe.

- **1942:** In World War II, the Japanese make sweeping conquests in East and Southeast Asia. However, the U.S. Navy defeats the Japanese navy at the Battle of Midway, which becomes a turning point in the war in the Pacific.

  Today: The United States and Japan are political allies and important trading partners.

---

does not mean that they are small in physical stature but that they are, on the face of it, helpless against the military might of the invaders. However, appearances may be deceptive, as Mayor Orden's words to Doctor Winter near the end of the novel convey, "I am a little man and this is a little town, but there must be a spark in little men that can burst into flame."

Most of the novel takes place in winter. By the end of chapter 3, snow begins to fall, and for the remainder of the novel, there is deep, packed snow on the ground. The coldness of the weather reflects the coldness with which the townspeople treat the invaders. The environment is inhospitable to them, as suggested by their "miserable, cold patrol" on the streets. There are also frequent references to darkness and night, which suggest the idea that a dark power has descended on the town. During the first snowstorm, for example, "over the town there hung a blackness that was deeper than the cloud." The title of the novel also suggests the extinguishing of light.

HISTORICAL CONTEXT

The German Invasion of Norway

When World War II broke out in 1939, Norway declared its neutrality. Germany needed access to Norway because its economy depended on obtaining iron ore from Sweden. In the winter, when the Baltic Sea was icebound, the iron ore had to be taken by rail to the Norwegian port of Narvik, and then in German ships down the entire Norwegian coast.

Aware of the importance of Norway to the Germans, Britain and France were planning a military expedition to take control of Narvik, but their plans were preempted by the surprise German invasion of Norway on the night of April 8–9, 1940. The Germans landed at many points on the Norwegian coast and launched air attacks on the Norwegian cities of Narvik, Trondheim, Bergen, Stavanger, Oslo, and Kristiansund. The Germans demanded that the Norwegians surrender, saying that they were saving Norway, as well as Denmark, which they also

Machinery frequently froze. (Iculig / Shutterstock.com)

occupied, from attack by Britain and France. The Norwegians resisted but, within one day, all the major Norwegian cities and ports, as well as its airfield, were under German control. The conquest had been accomplished with only ten thousand troops.

Small pockets of resistance, did, however, continue, and Britain and France promised Norway assistance. In mid-April, a British force landed near Narvik and a combined British and French force at Namso. Narvik was captured by the end of May, but within ten days, events elsewhere in Western Europe compelled the Allies to withdraw from Norway. King Haakon VII and the Norwegian government escaped to Britain and set up a government-in-exile.

A Norwegian politician and Nazi sympathizer named Vidkun Quisling offered to form a government that would collaborate with the Germans. The Germans initially wanted the existing government to remain in place, but when the Norwegians failed to cooperate, the Germans recognized Quisling as the new prime minister. However, they soon found that Quisling had little support. The Germans thus ruled Norway directly until Quisling was installed as a puppet head of state in February 1942. After the war, Quisling was tried and executed. Since then, his name has become synonymous with traitor.

Despite the military defeat, the Norwegian resistance (known as Milorg) emerged to continue the fight against the Germans. Armed resistance grew during the years of the occupation. By 1944, Milorg numbered 32,000. Much of its work took the form (as in the novel) of sabotage of trains and railroads. Milorg also provided the intelligence that helped Norwegian troops destroy a heavy water factory in Rjukan, Norway, in 1943. Heavy water (water containing a high proportion of molecules with deuterium atoms, used in nuclear reactors) was essential to Germany's atomic energy program; the program was struck another severe blow when the Norwegian resistance sank a ferry boat that was carrying about 1,300 pounds of heavy water to Germany.

In addition to armed resistance, many Norwegians practiced civil disobedience and passive resistance. Like the inhabitants of the town in *The Moon Is Down*, they refused, wherever possible, to speak to Germans.

The German occupation of Norway continued until the end of the war. The Germans surrendered in Norway on May 8, 1945.

CRITICAL OVERVIEW

The Moon Is Down was received with great controversy when published in 1942. The book was attacked by some critics as being too easy on the invading forces, who were obviously the German Nazis. To these critics, Steinbeck had made the mistake of presenting the Nazis in a too human and civilized light; in real life, occupation by the Nazis was a much more brutal thing. Among the chief detractors was Clifton Fadiman, who, reviewing the book for the *New Yorker*, writes that Steinbeck's "message is inadequate" and that the novel is "a melodramatic simplification of the issues involved." James Thurber, in the *New Republic*, was also unconvinced of the novel's merit, declaring that it "needs more guts and less moon."

Others defended the novel. For Norman Cousins, writing in the *Saturday Review*, the novel has "simplicity, force, dignity, and even beauty" and conveys "vital suspense" and a "strong . . . feeling of reality." The controversy raged for several months in newspapers and periodicals. Whatever its mixed reception in the United States, *The Moon Is Down* circulated widely in occupied Europe and was read with enthusiasm. By 1944, almost every occupied country had its own translation of the book. Not surprisingly, the Germans banned it. After the war, in 1946, Steinbeck was awarded the Haakon VII Cross by the Norwegian king in recognition of the contribution the novel made to Norwegian resistance.

CRITICISM

Bryan Aubrey

Aubrey holds a Ph.D. in English. In the following essay, he discusses the fact that The Moon Is Down *resembles a play and also considers Steinbeck's presentation of the humanity rather than the brutality of the invaders.*

> LANSER MAY NOT POSSESS THE COURAGE TO REBEL AGAINST HIS FATE; HE IS A RELUCTANT COG IN THE MILITARY MACHINE THAT GRINDS ON REGARDLESS, BUT HE DOES HAVE THE INTELLIGENCE AND THE WISDOM TO SEE A LITTLE FURTHER THAN THE AVERAGE MAN."

Although *The Moon Is Down* is now regarded as one of Steinbeck's minor works, it caused quite a stir at the time of publication. As a work of propaganda, trumpeting the ability of the small countries of Europe to resist Nazi occupation, it was enormously successful. It was even read with approval by British wartime prime minister Winston Churchill. Roy Simmonds, in his biography *John Steinbeck: The War Years, 1939–1945*, points out that Churchill even wrote a memorandum to the British minister of economic warfare, commenting on how the book emphasized the importance of getting weapons and explosives to those in the occupied countries who were resisting German occupation. In March 1942, when the novel was published, these countries included Norway, Denmark, Belgium, the Netherlands, Poland, and France. Steinbeck was well pleased with the reception of the book in Europe, since he was anxious to do everything he could to help the war effort. Like many others, he had long believed it inevitable that the United States would be drawn into World War II, and he had actually completed the first draft of *The Moon Is Down* on December 7, 1941—the very day the Japanese bombed Pearl Harbor, bringing the United States into the war.

The alert reader of *The Moon Is Down* will quickly notice that it reads not quite like a normal novel but, in large sections, more like a play. Steinbeck intended it to be both, and the theatrical version was produced on Broadway at the Martin Beck Theater on April 7, 1942. From the beginning, he also had in mind a movie version—which was released by Twentieth-Century Fox in 1943—so as he conceived the work it was to do triple duty as novel, play, and film, a

WHAT DO I READ NEXT?

- Noted historian Stephen E. Ambrose tells the story of World War II especially for young adults in *The Good Fight: How World War II Was Won* (2001). The book is illustrated with color and black-and-white photographs, as well as many maps. Every chapter highlights the main facts in an easy-to-read box format. The clearly written narrative emphasizes the main events from the rise of Hitler in the 1930s to the atomic bombs dropped on Japan in 1945 and the postwar war crimes trials.

- *Night of Flames: A Novel of World War II* (2008), by Douglas W. Jacobson, is a well-researched war story with plenty of excitement and suspense. Set in Europe in World War II, the story follows the fortunes of Jan and Anna, a husband and wife who are forced to flee Poland. They become separated, and Anna ends up supporting the Belgian Resistance while Jan works for British Intelligence and searches for his lost wife.

- In *Folklore Fights the Nazis: Humor in Occupied Norway, 1940–1945* (1997), Kathleen Stokker describes how the Norwegians fought back against the Nazis by using humor. Stokker argues that the anti-Nazi jokes helped the Norwegians to develop a sense of solidarity. The humor was conveyed through methods that included anecdotes, posters, cartoons, children's stories, Christmas cards, personal ads, and fake postage stamps. The book informs as well as amuses.

- Steinbeck's novel *The Grapes of Wrath* is usually considered his masterpiece. First published in 1939, it tells the story of how farmers in the Plains States in the 1930s were unable to make a living and trekked to California in search of work. The narrative concentrates on one family, the Joads, and the hardship they endure. A modern edition of the novel is available, published in the Penguin Classics series in 2006.

- *Code Talker: A Novel about the Navajo Marines of World War Two* (2005), by Native American writer Joseph Bruchac, is a novel for young adults about the Navajos who joined the military and helped the Allied war effort in World War II. The Navajos sent radio messages conveying vital information in their native language. The story is told by a Navajo grandfather who tells his grandchildren about his experiences as a Marine during the war.

- *Norway 1940* (1991), by François Kersaudy, is an account of the German invasion of Norway in 1940 and its aftermath, including the sending and quick withdrawal of the British and French expeditionary force. Kersaudy emphasizes the failure to recognize the early warnings signs of the impending invasion, and the betrayal of the Norwegians by the weak Allied response.

remarkably ambitious goal. He described it as a "hybrid form of prose writing" (quoted by Simmonds in his biography of Steinbeck) that he had first attempted in *Of Mice and Men* (1937), and he admitted to the possibility that, in aiming to satisfy the demands of three different genres, *The Moon Is Down* might well fail in all of them.

This triple focus can be seen in several ways in the novel. The resemblance of the novel to a play script is particularly noticeable at the beginning of chapter 2, which introduces the five members of Colonel Lanser's staff as if they were characters in a play and the descriptions meant to guide the actor in how to interpret the role. Each is given a paragraph in which the author presents the salient points about the age, appearance, behavior, and personality of the character. After that, most of the chapter unfolds through dialogue, exactly as it would in a play, with a minimum of descriptive passages by the third-person omniscient narrator. This sets the pattern for the remainder of the novel. All of the chapters are set either in the mayor's palace or in Molly Morden's house, which are the two stage settings for the play. When each setting is mentioned for the first time (the palace in chapter 1, Molly's house in chapter 6), the interior of the room is described as it might appear in the text of a stage play as a guide to how the set should appear. The descriptions with which most of the chapters begin read cinematically, as if the author had in mind the way in which the sequences of the film he envisioned might show the passage of time and alteration of place.

The play-like nature of the novel did not sit well with some reviewers when it was first published. Noting that Steinbeck had a play version in mind, James Thurber, in *New Republic*, complained,

> This has had the unfortunate effect of giving the interiors in the novel the feel of sets. I could not believe that the people who enter Mayor Orden's living room come from the streets and houses of a little town. They come from their dressing rooms.

This hybrid nature of the work has not found favor among literary critics since, and in general, the novel has not fared well over the passage of time. Few today would argue that it is entirely successful, and many regard it as a failure, whatever success it might have enjoyed as propaganda for the war effort. John H. Timmerman, in *John Steinbeck's Fiction: The Aesthetics of the Road Taken*, calls the writing of the book "hasty and superficial, at best a mechanical hack work, and the weaknesses show everywhere." Timmerman argues that the setting and characters are unconvincing and that the work exhibits "a failure of language and stylistic technique." He points to "repetitively short sentences ... [and] a routine sameness of rhetorical method," which produce "the dullness and inefficiency of the prose to move the story along." This may sound harsh, but it is by no means an unfair portrayal of the novel. The unadorned style is indeed monotonous, and the dialogue sometimes sounds stilted and unnatural. The characters do not quite come to life as real people, and the overall result is that the novel does not achieve the emotional charge needed to

move the reader. It seems too simple and contrived, more fable than war story.

This being said, however, *The Moon Is Down* is not without interest. Many reviewers at the time claimed that Steinbeck had created far too sympathetic a portrait of the invaders, who were, after all, only thinly veiled German Nazis. Among the reviewers who expressed this view was Thurber, who in a response to those who criticized him, wrote a letter to the editor of the *New Republic* in which he contrasted "Steinbeck's view of Nazi conquest" with "its true story of hell, horror, and hopelessness" (quoted by Simmonds in *John Steinbeck: The War Years, 1939–1945*). Be that as it may—and letters on both sides of the issue poured into the *New Republic* in 1942—Steinbeck knew exactly what he was doing in this respect. He had no more interest in the stock figure of the brutal Nazi than in Hitler's stock figure of the Jew. His intention was to present the Germans not as monsters but as men.

A case in point is Colonel Lanser. Even given the facts that the characters are not fully lifelike and that Lanser does not exhibit any growth in character from beginning to end, he is nonetheless an interesting example of what Steinbeck was trying to do. If Mayor Orden and, to a lesser extent, Doctor Winter emerge as heroes (as do all the anonymous "little people" who do the work of sabotage), Lanser is an intriguing figure: he has greater self-awareness than the other invaders and knows better than they do how things are likely to end up. Yet he must play the part that has been allotted to him.

The first impression given by the colonel when he arrives at the palace immediately following the successful invasion is of a courteous man who thinks of himself as being considerate. When the mayor inquires whether there was any resistance, Lanser "looked at him compassionately." He prefers to think of the invasion as an engineering project rather than the conquest of a people. He needs to ensure that the mine continues to produce coal. This impression of a civilized, humane man is expanded in the character sketch provided in chapter 2. Unlike the other members of his staff, he fought in World War I (referred to simply as a war twenty years before), so he knows what war is really like: "War is treachery and hatred, the muddling of incompetent generals, the torture and killing and sickness and tiredness, until at last it is over and nothing

Signs of Nazi occupation *(Dariush M | Shutterstock.com)*

has changed except for new weariness and new hatreds." He knows that he is there simply to carry out orders, and he tries to convince himself that this war will be different, but he knows in his heart that it will not be. When he speaks to Corell, he shows the shallowness of the collaborator's understanding of the situation. Corell thinks he is safe because the people are defeated, but Lanser knows better. He says, "Defeat is a momentary thing. A defeat doesn't last. We were defeated and now we attack. Defeat means nothing." To understand something so well, to see its bitter outcome in advance, and yet to be powerless to affect it—"what I think, sir, I, a man of a certain age and certain memories, is of no importance"—is a poignant fate for anyone to contemplate. Lanser may not possess the courage to rebel against his fate; he is a reluctant cog in the military machine that grinds on regardless, but he does have the intelligence and the wisdom to see a little further than the average man. This makes him, if not exactly a sympathetic figure, at least an interesting one. Whether any real-life German officers were actually like him is another matter, but readers of the novel may be

grateful that Steinbeck presented him and the other "German" characters with a degree of humanity rather than indulging in stereotypes of the evil enemy that are all too common when nations go to war.

Source: Bryan Aubrey, Critical Essay on *The Moon Is Down*, in *Novels for Students*, Gale, Cengage Learning, 2011.

Mark D. Bradbury

In the following review, Bradbury describes the book as a compelling fictionalized case study of public service ethics and leadership and the perseverance of free men.

Originally published in 1942 during the first months of America's entry into World War II, *The Moon Is Down* has been described as "a work of literature that served as propaganda," intended both to warn the nation of the perils of war and to celebrate the resilience of the democratic spirit (Coers 1995, xxiv). Although not generally considered one of John Steinbeck's stronger works, the book is a compelling fictionalized case study of public service ethics and leadership, and the perseverance of free men.

> BY FOCUSING ON THE REALITY OF HUMAN BEHAVIOR, RATHER THAN WHAT IT OUGHT TO BE, STEINBECK'S DEPICTIONS OF THE OCCUPIERS AND THE RESIDENTS ARE, ON A SUPERFICIAL LEVEL, MORALLY NEUTRAL."

The central story line focuses on the occupation of an unnamed northern European town by an unidentified invader. Although the explicit anonymity was designed to evoke the universality of the moral conundrums faced by the characters, the narrative contains many clues suggesting a Scandinavian town occupied by the German Nazis during the early part of World War II. The invaders occupy the town in order to access the nearby coal mines. Although a collaborationist resident aids the initial invasion, the masses wage a deliberate resistance of psychological and material sabotage, marked by critical incidents of violence.

One of the notable, and most controversial, characteristics of the drama is the "humanness" of the occupiers, whose obedient, servile, and virulent role is coupled with their individual hopes, fears, loneliness, and compassion. Indeed, Steinbeck was criticized for portraying the occupiers in too positive a light. Looking back at these criticisms, Steinbeck explained, "I had written of Germans as men, not supermen, and this was considered a very weak attitude to take. I couldn't make much sense out of this, and it seems absurd now that we know the Germans were men, and thus fallible, even defeatable" (1953, 29). The humanistic portrayal of both the protagonists and the antagonists heightens the utility of the book as a fictional case in the study of public administration.

The story of the occupation is told largely through the interactions of the democratically elected Mayor Orden and the commanding officer of the occupiers, Colonel Lanser. These two executives hold markedly different positions, and are expected to fulfill contrasting responsibilities. Reminiscent of Rosenbloom's managerial approach to public administration (1983),

Mayor Orden literally represents not only the people of the town, but also the democratic ideal. Described by Steinbeck as the "Idea-Mayor" of the town, Orden provides deviously restrained leadership to the resistance while insisting that he is but a public servant: "Some people accept appointed leaders and obey them. But my people have elected me. They made me and they can unmake me."

In contrast, Colonel Lanser exhibits a traditional, militaristic, and largely bureaucratic style of leadership (Rosenbloom 1983). Although Steinbeck's description of the character is a notable departure from the stereotypical Nazi commander, Lanser is nevertheless in charge of the occupying force and tempers his tolerance and diplomacy with stern fortitude. The contrast between the leadership styles and responsibilities of Mayor Orden and Colonel Lanser is most clear in the following exchange:

> "I'm sorry," the colonel said. "No. These are the orders of my leader."
> "The people will not like it," Orden said.
> "Always the people! The people are disarmed. The people have no say."
> Mayor Orden shook his head. "You do not know, sir."

With "its central conflict being one of ideas rather than of fully-drawn characters" (Ditsky 1989, 177), the pedagogical value of *The Moon Is Down* lies with the various ethical and moral themes imbedded in the story. Indeed, the story line and dialogue are replete with examples of core aspects of public service ethics. The principles embodied in the ASPA Code of Ethics are apparent in the book—notably, serving the public interest, respecting the law, and demonstrating personal integrity. Other important themes include the importance of the use of discretion, organizational change/adaptation, steadfast leadership, objectivity, decision-making under pressure, and the mastership of the public in a democracy.

The dominant perspective of the work is the triumph of morality and virtuous character, particularly of the town's residents and the mayor in their resistance efforts. There is also a focus on virtue, however, in the humane description of the occupiers: "They were, under pressure, capable of cowardice or courage, as everyone is." Consequently, the empathetic characterizations of the occupied and the occupier lead to a sort of right-vs.-right dilemma, such as personal integrity vs. responsibility (Brousseau 1998).

Applying the triangle approach to public service ethics (Svara 1997), one also finds evidence of deontological and teleological ethics in the novel. Deontological, or rules-based, ethics suggests a concern for fairness and justice. Rules-based ethics can also be applied too rigidly, as in the overly strict enforcement of orders or laws (Bowman et al. 2004, 72). Such a corruption of due process occurs in the story when one of the occupiers is killed in a scuffle with a miner. A show trial is held in the mayor's house, and the miner is sentenced and executed despite the mayor's insistence that a display of violent retribution will do little to affect the attitudes or actions of the residents. To this, Colonel Lanser replies: "You see, what I think, sir, I, a man of a certain age and certain memories, is of no importance. I might agree with you, but that would change nothing. The military, the political pattern I work in has certain tendencies and practices which are invariable." Similarly, in response to a challenge by Doctor Winter as to the inevitable failure of such orders, Lanser replies, "I will carry out my orders no matter what they are."

In contrast, teleological ethics is primarily focused on results, typically presented as the greatest good for the greatest number. A telling illustration of this occurs at the end of the novel with the impending execution of Mayor Orden and Doctor Winter, the mayor's confidant and adviser, for their role in the resistance. The mayor finds comfort in the words of Socrates: "a man who is good for anything ought not to calculate the chance of living or dying; he ought only to consider whether he is doing right or wrong."

Despite his explicit attempt at nonjudgmental objectivity (Ditsky 1989, 179), Steinbeck's bias for individualism shows through in the book. By focusing on the reality of human behavior, rather than what it ought to be, Steinbeck's depictions of the occupiers and the residents are, on a superficial level, morally neutral. By the end of the novel, however, the moral superiority of the residents, as exemplified by Mayor Orden, is laid bare. In his last statement to Colonel Lanser, the mayor observes that "Free men cannot start a war, but once it is started, they can fight on in defeat. Herd men, followers of a leader, cannot do that, and so it is always herd men who win battles and the free men who win wars."

The terms "herd men" and "free men" are obviously normative descriptions. Herd men are identified by their group and follow orders, surrendering their will and ethics to the dictates of a leader (Ditsky 1989, 189). Free men, conversely, are individuals guided by a "moral consciousness" when choosing leaders to speak for them and are inherently stronger and more worthy. In his introduction to the novel, Coers makes the point clear: "Steinbeck calmly reaffirmed ... the bedrock principles of democracy: the worth of the individual, and the power deriving from free citizens sharing common commitments" (1995, xxiv).

Whatever consequences this explicit bias has for *The Moon Is Down* in terms of literary merit, experience using the novel in public administration seminars suggests that the pro-democracy message is an asset. Students can be challenged to recognize and appreciate the numerous ethical angles of the story without being distracted by a controversial ideological overtone. The issues are apparent and complex, but ultimately reaffirming, and "less concerned with the strict logic of a political scientist than in the hopeful thinking of people directed by a strong-hearted moral consciousness" (Lewis and Britch 1989, 174).

On a practical level, the novel works as a fictional case study because of its relative brevity, requiring only a handful of hours to complete, but providing ample material for discussion. Steinbeck presents a host of public service themes that appeal to undergraduates and graduate students of all ages and levels of professional experience. Students, and instructors, also benefit from the break from the standard slate of academic materials that reading a novel provides. In sum, the moral and ethical challenges presented in *The Moon Is Down* remain vital and compelling, a full three generations removed from the geopolitics that inspired one of the giants of American literature.

Source: Mark D. Bradbury, Review of *The Moon is Down*, in *Public Integrity*, Spring 2007, pp. 201–04.

Christopher C. Sullivan

In the following excerpt, Sullivan examines the controversy surrounding the purpose of writing The Moon Is Down.

Before Pearl Harbor, John Steinbeck was content to look at the phenomenon of armed conflict in an abstract way. War, he wrote in the 1941 book *Sea of Cortez*, could be viewed as a "diagnostic trait of Homo sapiens," comparable

"

IF A WRITER STARTS WITH THE CONVICTION

THAT HIS JOB IS TO PRESENT THE TRUTH, AND IF

HE HAS THE GIFT AND COURAGE TO FOLLOW THAT

QUEST, THERE ARE MANY AVENUES TO THIS END

AND MANY DESTINATIONS THAT WE CAN

CORRECTLY CALL TRUTH."

to the instinct of crayfish to fight as soon as they meet. "And perhaps," he added, "our species is not likely to forgo war without some psychic mutation, which at present, at least, does not seem imminent." Steinbeck relished dissecting the psychology underlying large-scale movements of people, as he had demonstrated in 1939 in *The Grapes of Wrath*. Thus, the wartime military's esprit de corps might well be lumped together with characteristics of mobs and athletic teams; war with its alternating tension and excitement, killing one day and bivouacking in the rain the next, became to the writer "one great gray dream."

Nonetheless, when Franklin Roosevelt declared global war, Steinbeck could be detached no longer, nor did he desire to be. All Americans, including this novelist at the height of his powers with an international following, became part of the effort to bring victory. (Only later, looking back on newswriting he produced during that period, did he use the phrase "a huge and gassy thing called the War Effort.") Thus John Steinbeck, unlikely at age forty to be called up and, anyway, under attack by his local draft board in California, among others, as a "communist" or "disloyal" because of his writings, joined up the best way he could: He picked up his duffel bag and his portable typewriter (along with four quarts of scotch) and enlisted as a writer.

During World War II, the novelist who had won the Pulitzer Prize and would later win the Nobel Prize produced journalism, working as an accredited correspondent for the *New York Herald Tribune*. Datelines on Steinbeck's dispatches included pre-D-Day London, occupied North Africa, and other parts of the Mediterranean theater of war, where he joined U.S. commando raids that were part of the Allied assault on Italy.

He also wrote a government-commissioned book, *Bombs Away*, based on his experiences with American fliers in training.

At the same time, Steinbeck continued to produce fiction, notably the play-novel, *The Moon Is Down*, which appeared in 1942. It is about the occupation of a town, universalized in his description but presumably Scandinavian, by an army with much in common with the Nazis, and about the townspeople's quiet but deadly effective resistance. Near the end of that book, Steinbeck puts in the mouth of the town's mayor, facing execution if the citizens' sabotage continues, a statement of the author's sociology of war. The defiant mayor tells the commander of the invading force:

> The people don't like being conquered ...and so they will not be. Free men cannot start a war, but once it is started, they can fight on in defeat. Herd men, followers of a leader, cannot do that, and so it is always the herd men who win battles and the free men who win wars.

Throughout the war years, Steinbeck continued to produce work, including some in direct support of the war effort, and in this he contrasted with Faulkner and other great writers of the era, who declined the government harness.

Yet in war, the saying goes, the "first casualty" is truth, and the statement probably has as much validity as any that becomes a cliche. In re-examining the reportage and fiction of John Steinbeck during World War II, some critics have asserted that his work, too, became such a casualty. Indeed, Steinbeck himself called his own war correspondence "untrue" when he reread it fifteen years out of context. It is not that simple.

"Maybe the hardest thing in writing is simply to tell the truth about things as we see them," Steinbeck once observed. He is known to have discarded at least four completed manuscripts of novels because they did not meet an uncompromising standard of honesty. "Oh! the incidents all happened, but I'm not telling as much of the truth about them as I know," he explained in a letter to his publisher, referring to one of these books, a first, failed attempt to deal with the subject matter that later yielded *The Grapes of Wrath*. He went further: "I've written three books now that were dishonest because they were less than the best I could do." It is not surprising that a fourth book that he shelved was about war, produced while the fighting was still going on.

Those who knew Steinbeck say he was a personally conservative man, holding strictly to many old-fashioned values. His eagerness to pitch in on the war effort, for example, grew out of a straightforward patriotism. (This earned him considerable criticism when, during the Vietnam war, he scorned peace demonstrators. His writing during that war, in which is son was fighting, will not be addressed in this article.) Steinbeck, who had met FDR following publication of *The Grapes of Wrath*, made several suggestions to the president for defeating the Axis—from making better use of Japanese biologists' prewar maps of islands that the U.S. Navy might want to assault, to dropping tons of counterfeit marks behind German lines to drive up inflation. Ironically, Steinbeck was among those proposing creation of a wartime information service, which became the forerunner of intelligence agencies that later spied on the author himself.

In the mind of the traditionalist Steinbeck, then, honesty and duty stood out as beacons. Of the unique, ancient duty thrust upon a writer, Steinbeck said in his Nobel Prize acceptance speech:

> He is charged with exposing our many grievous faults and failures, with dredging up to the light our dark and dangerous dreams for the purpose of improvement. Furthermore, the writer is delegated to declare and to celebrate man's proven capacity for greatness of heart and spirit—for gallantry in defeat, for courage, compassion and love. In the endless war against weakness and despair, these are the bright rally flags of hope and emulation.

When deeply understood and sincerely accepted, the duties of citizen and of writer can come into wrenching conflict; this dilemma confronts journalists every day. What we see in John Steinbeck's World War II writing and his sometimes harsh self-assessment is often evidence of such conflict. At the same time, a close reading of his many kinds of writing in the crucible of war reveals types and degrees of truth that neither he nor his critics at the time were capable of seeing.

. . . The charge that hurt Steinbeck most, however, was a variant that came a year before he actually covered the war. It came in response to his war novel, which he turned into a Broadway play, *The Moon Is Down*, about a conquered

town's resistance. The charge: That Steinbeck's book gave comfort to the Fascist enemy.

James Thurber, reviewing the book only four months after Pearl Harbor, ridiculed it as a "fable of War in Wonderland." But then he noted that the war could be lost and that "nothing would help more toward that end than for Americans to believe Steinbeck's version of Nazi conquest instead of the true story of hell, horror and hopelessness." Rebuttals came from many who had endured Nazi occupation, and as time passed, the most telling reply came from resistance fighters themselves, who translated and reprinted the book almost as an instruction manual. Looking through magazines in which such critiques and equally strenuous defenses of the author appeared, one glimpses what an all-encompassing thing the "war effort" concept was; victory is the main or sub-theme of virtually every article, the justification for buying every ad's product. A full page for Lockheed, for example, shows a Luftwaffe bomber going down in flames, but more typical is an ad for Pepsi, showing a smiling, sweating factory worker taking a break for a patriotic drink: "American energy will win!" says the legend. Though the point of the ads and of Thurber's criticism is long moot, the context they reveal is most relevant.

Steinbeck thought he had written in *The Moon Is Down* "a kind of celebration of democracy." He had deliberately universalized the story, nowhere labeling the invaders as Germans; when the play went to Broadway the stage directions specified that the occupiers' uniforms not be identifiable as those "of any known nation." Although critics have faulted the novel-play on several grounds, some recognize that its truth could only blossom out of its own time. It is, said one, "a parable for the future."

This was another variety of truth, which Steinbeck recognized. "You can write anything in the morning paper so long as it happened," he wrote once to a friend, but added:

> The fiction writer wouldn't dare do this. What he writes must . . . not only have happened but must continue to happen. This makes it more difficult. . . . Ideally, fiction takes on a greater reality in the mind of the reader than nonfiction. Participation in *Crime and Punishment* has a greater reality to most people than anything that has or is likely to happen to them.

Steinbeck was tarred for making the invaders too human in *The Moon Is Down*. One by one, he describes the occupying officers, each a plausible portrait of one of war's ironies: the major, an engineer who sees life in terms as mechanical as the measurements in his plans to rebuild dynamited rail lines; the ambitious, spit-polished captain who has "no unmilitary moments"; the green lieutenants, including one romantic who "sometimes spoke blank verse under his breath to imaginary dark women. He longed for death on the battlefield."

The most sympathetic officer is the leader of the occupiers, Colonel Lanser, who doubted headquarters' orders but carried them out anyway, even executions. Only he, Steinbeck says, knew what war really is in the long run:

> Lanser had been in Belgium and France twenty years before and he tried not to think what he knew—that war is treachery and hatred, the muddling of incompetent generals, the torture and killing and sickness and tiredness, until at last it is over and nothing has changed except for a new weariness and new hatreds. Lanser told himself he was a soldier, given orders to carry out. He…tried to put aside the sick memories of the other war and the certainty that this would be the same. This one will be different, he said to himself fifty times a day; this one will be different."

In an extraordinary passage that follows, Steinbeck's irony about the elusiveness of war's meaning shines through:

> In marching, in mobs, in football games, and in war, outlines become vague; real things become unreal and a fog creeps over the mind. Tension and excitement, weariness, movement—all merge in one great gray dream, so that when it is over, it is hard to remember how it was when you killed men or ordered them to be killed. Then other people who were not there tell you what it was like and you say vaguely, 'Yes, I guess that's how it was.'

Laid beside Steinbeck's nonfiction of the war years, his novel-play clearly fills in many background truths. They almost need to be read side-by-side for the complementary perspectives and insights. To take one obvious example, he has said war correspondents could not write the truth about dubious officers. Yet Steinbeck knew better than most who those officers were: he had seen many in action during his work for the War Department on *Bombs Away* and other projects. Fiction allowed him to draw at least some of the portrait, leaving it to readers, then or in the future, to decide whether it applied to their time and nation.

Laid beside Steinbeck's war correspondence, *The Moon is Down* unquestionably lacks action and life. Indeed, the book's opening lines declare: "By ten-forty-five it was all over. The town was occupied, the defenders defeated, and the war finished." More than one critic has echoed the complaint that the story's characters are "qualities masquerading as human beings." But again, perhaps Steinbeck's creation of walking representations of ideas and themes (the mayor as Democracy and Hope, and so on) was a kind of intellectual complement, almost like a cloudy mirror, to the frantic action of history that people were living at that time. For a writer of Steinbeck's facility with rich, humane characterization (it is the thing he does best), isn't it likely that this was intentional—that these universalized characters, speaking often in phrases that could be carved on monuments, were meant to reveal the unspoken ideals and philosophical doubts that the wartime world was mostly too busy, and partly too afraid, to let walk about?

If this is questionable drama, then so are the dialogues of Plato, a few lines of which provide some of the most heartrending tension in *The Moon is Down*. When the mayor, facing execution, reminisces about a schoolboy oratory performance and tries to recall the condemned Socrates' last speech, a missing word is supplied by none other than the commander of the occupying force, who has given the execution order. If the ultimate truth of this fiction is that war is a cursedly human activity, carried out by fallible and complex humans, in part because of corrupted systems of leadership invented by humans and in part because of Homo sapiens' instinct for war, could that truth be stated more forcefully than with such a tragic, yet credible, irony?

If a writer starts with the conviction that his job is to present the truth, and if he has the gift and courage to follow that quest, there are many avenues to this end and many destinations that we can correctly call truth. Steinbeck was wrong to label his dispatches from the front "untrue"; although they failed to tell all, at a time when they could not ethically have done so, they contained much that was deeply revealing about the fighting and its costs. The critics were wrong to call his novel-play about an occupied town "untrue," regardless of his never having been there and regardless of the wartime atrocities elsewhere that he did not detail.

Shakespeare's great general, Othello, salutes "the neighing steed and the shrill trump, the spirit-stirring drum, the ear-piercing fife, the royal banner, and all quality, pride, pomp and circumstance of glorious war!" In these details lies a fictional truth. A nonfiction truth about war reflects in chiseled rows of names on the polished granite of the Vietnam Veterans Memorial in Washington: combat "journalism" gets no more stark or true than this, one might say.

"I've had a good, full, painful life," Steinbeck summed up in his last years. "I've tried to write the truth as I saw it and I have not held on to a truth when it becomes false." Sometimes that meant sending onto a stage unwelcome questions about humankind's darker nature. Sometimes it meant lying face-down in the sand of a landing beach, watching. Sometimes it meant doubting the whole exhausting effort. In writing about war, Steinbeck learned and shared the truths he could.

Source: Christopher C. Sullivan, "John Steinbeck, War Reporter: Fiction, Journalism and Types of Truth," in *Journalism History*, Vol. 23, No. 1, Spring 1997, pp. 16–23.

SOURCES

Astro, Richard, "John Steinbeck," in *Dictionary of Literary Biography*, Vol. 9, *American Novelists, 1910–1945*, edited by James J. Martine, Gale Research, 1981, pp. 43–68.

Cousins, Norman, "*The Will to Live and Resist*" in *John Steinbeck: The Contemporary Reviews*, edited by Joseph R. McElrath Jr., Jesse S. Crisler, and Susan Shillinglaw, Cambridge University Press, 1996, p. 224; originally published in *New Yorker*, March 7, 1942.

Fadiman, Clifton, "Two Ways to Win the War," in *John Steinbeck: The Contemporary Reviews*, edited by Joseph R. McElrath Jr., Jesse S. Crisler, and Susan Shillinglaw, Cambridge University Press, 1996, pp. 217–18; originally published in *Saturday Review*, March 14, 1942.

"Norway," *in CIA: The World Factbook*, https://www.cia.gov/library/publications/the-world-factbook/geos/no.html (accessed September 21, 2010).

Simmonds, Roy, *John Steinbeck: The War Years, 1939–1945*, Bucknell University Press, 1996, pp. 97, 114.

Steinbeck, John, *The Moon Is Down*, Viking Press, 1942.

Timmerman, John H., *John Steinbeck's Fiction: The Aesthetics of the Road Taken*, University of Oklahoma Press, 1986, pp. 183–86.

Thurber, James, "What Price Conquest?," in *John Steinbeck: The Contemporary Reviews*, edited by Joseph R. McElrath Jr., Jesse S. Crisler, and Susan Shillinglaw, Cambridge University Press, 1996, p. 225; originally published in *New Republic*, March 16, 1942.

Trueman, Chris, "The Norwegian Resistance," in *History Learning Site*, http://www.historylearningsite.co.uk/norwegian_resistance.htm (accessed September 20, 2010).

FURTHER READING

Benson, Jackson J., *John Steinbeck, Writer: A Biography*, Penguin Books, 1990.

> This definitive biography of Steinbeck won the PEN-USA West award for nonfiction. It presents an in-depth analysis of all aspects of Steinbeck's life.

Coers, Donald V., *John Steinbeck as Propagandist:* The Moon Is Down *Goes to War*, University of Alabama Press, 1991.

> Coers chronicles the whole story of the impact *The Moon Is Down* had in the countries under German occupation.

French, Warren, *John Steinbeck's Fiction Revisited*, Twayne's United States Author Series, No. 638, Twayne Publishers, 1994.

> French provides an examination of Steinbeck's fiction. He discusses Steinbeck's relationship to modernism and to the work of his contemporaries, and assesses Steinbeck's position in American literature several decades after his death.

Schultz, Jeffrey D., and Luchen Li, *Critical Companion to John Steinbeck: A Literary Reference to His Life and Work*, Facts on File/Checkmark Books, 2005.

> This reference book provides a review of Steinbeck's life and work. The authors provide information about all of Steinbeck's work—fiction and nonfiction, published and unpublished. There are synopses and character descriptions for each novel, along with other information including critical reception and film adaptations.

SUGGESTED SEARCH TERMS

John Steinbeck

The Moon Is Down

Quisling

German invasion AND Norway

World War II AND occupied Europe

Steinbeck AND war literature

Steinbeck AND World War II

Milorg

Nazis AND Steinbeck

World War II AND liberated Europe

Steinbeck AND The Moon is Down

Pudd'nhead Wilson

MARK TWAIN
1894

When Mark Twain published his novel *Pudd'nhead Wilson* in 1894, he had already gained immense popularity with the publication of *The Adventures of Tom Sawyer* in 1876 and the even more successful *The Adventures of Huckleberry Finn* in 1885. *Pudd'nhead Wilson* is typically regarded as darker in tone than its more lighthearted predecessors.

While it contains elements of humor, the work is laden with tragedy throughout. Set in the 1830s, in the slave-holding South, *Pudd'nhead Wilson* is a work in which the titular character does not figure prominently until the novel's conclusion. To a large degree, the novel is concerned with a slave, Chambers, who is switched by his slave mother into the cradle of the wealthy landowner's son, named Tom. The heir to the estate is thus raised as a slave, while the slave is raised with all the benefits of being rich and white lavished upon him. Raised as Tom, Chambers becomes insolent and mean-spirited, while Tom, raised as the slave child Chambers, becomes strong, yet meek.

Plagued with gambling debts as a young adult, the man known as Tom (Chambers) murders and robs the man whom he believes to be his uncle. Pudd'nhead Wilson, a lawyer by trade who was unfairly labeled a fool and dubbed "Pudd'nhead" on his first day in town, successfully navigates this mystery and solves the crime. Tom, who is really Chambers, is then sold down

Mark Twain *(© Pictorial Press Ltd / Alamy)*

the river, a fate underscored throughout the novel as the worst fate a slave could endure, while Chambers, who was born as Tom, is left to fend for himself. He is completely illiterate and, having been raised a slave, speaks only in the heavy dialect of slaves in that region.

The work highlights the cruelties of the slave-holding system and explores the nature of identity and morality. Twain originally wrote a shorter version of the story, called *Those Extraordinary Twins*, in which the Italian twins that figure in the plot of *Pudd'nhead Wilson* appear as conjoined twins. This version of the story was intended as farce, a humorous tale often featuring improbable elements. The shorter tale is typically printed as an addendum to the full-length novel along with Twain's explanation of his original intentions.

Originally published in 1894 by Chatto & Windus, *Pudd'nhead Wilson* is available in several modern editions, including the 1969 edition, published by Penguin and reprinted in 1986. The Penguin edition includes *Those Extraordinary Twins*. The title of the novel is sometimes rendered as *The Tragedy of Pudd'nhead Wilson*, as it was for the first American edition of the work.

AUTHOR BIOGRAPHY

When Twain was born in Florida, Missouri, on November 30, 1835, he was given the name Samuel Langhorne Clemens. His father was John Marshall Clemens, and his mother was Jane Lampton Clemens. At the age of four, Twain moved with his family to the town of Hannibal, Missouri, on the Mississippi River. Twain grew up in Hannibal, living there until he was eighteen years old. His formal education ceased when his father died in 1847, at which time Twain became apprenticed to a printer in order to help support his mother and his siblings. His older brother, Orion, worked as an editor for the *Courier*, and Twain worked under him for a time. In 1853, Twain set out, exploring both the East coast and the burgeoning Western frontier, working as a journeyman printer.

Securing a position on a steamboat, Twain became a licensed steamboat pilot in 1859. During the Civil War years, Twain served as a volunteer soldier before moving on to gold prospecting in Nevada. He also worked in the timber industry and as a speculator and began his writing career as a journalist at this time as well. For some of this time, Twain traveled with his brother Orion. In 1863, while working as a journalist for the Virginia City paper, the *Enterprise*, Twain adopted the pseudonym Mark Twain. The term refers to the call of boatmen along the river to indicate a water depth of two fathoms.

Twain published his first work of fiction, a humorous piece, "The Celebrated Jumping Frog of Calveras County," in 1865 in the *New York Saturday Press*. He then traveled extensively as a correspondent for *Alta California*, sailing from the West Coast to Nicaragua, then crossing the isthmus and sailing along the Atlantic Coast to New York. Twain then traveled to and through Europe, continuing to write.

In 1867, he met Olivia Langdon, the sister of a friend with whom he had traveled. Twain's journeys furnished him with material to publish what would become his first literary success, *Innocents Abroad*, published in 1869. In 1870, he and Olivia married, and they moved to Connecticut in 1871. They would eventually have four children; the first, a son, died at the age of nineteen months.

Twain entered an extremely productive and successful period, publishing *The Adventures of Tom Sawyer* in 1876, *Life on the Mississippi* in 1883, and *The Adventures of Huckleberry Finn* in 1884–1885. He traveled, wrote, and engaged in financial speculations in the next decade. In 1894, the year *Pudd'nhead Wilson* was published,

Twain's investments left him bankrupt. Two of his daughters died in their twenties, one in 1898 and the second in 1909. His wife died in 1904. The closing years of his life were marked by the grief generated by these losses. Twain died in Redding, Connecticut, on April 21, 1910.

PLOT SUMMARY

Chapters 1–3

As *Pudd'nhead Wilson* opens, the narrator offers an introduction to the town of Dawson's Landing, Missouri, as it existed in 1830, when the story takes place. The narrator further provides background information on several characters: the town's most prominent individuals. As the descriptions go on, the reader is informed that Percy Driscoll, the brother of the town's most notable citizen, York Driscoll, has recently become a father. On the same day that Percy Driscoll's son is born, another child is born to Roxana, a slave in the Driscoll home. Percy's wife dies shortly after giving birth.

The narrator turns his attention now to a new arrival in town, a young lawyer named David Wilson. Wilson makes a joke about a barking dog, commenting that he wished he owned half the dog so he could kill his half of it. The townsfolk who overhear this remark are perplexed, unable to find either sense or humor in it. They henceforth dub Wilson a fool and nickname him Pudd'nhead. As a consequence, Wilson is never taken seriously as a lawyer and must support himself as an accountant and land surveyor instead.

Wilson is interested in fingerprinting, and over the course of his time in Dawson's Landing, he takes the fingerprints of many of the town's residents. When the baby boys Tom and Chambers are five months old, he takes their fingerprints. When Roxana, also known as Roxy, is accused, along with two other slaves, of stealing, she fears for her son's life, knowing that he, like any slave, could be sold "down the river," as her master, Percy Driscoll, has threatened to do with her. The term "down the river" refers to the Deep South, where slaves endure a life in the cotton fields and are believed by slaves in more northern regions to be treated to more physical abuse than they themselves receive. To protect her son from the harshest of slave conditions, Roxy decides that, as her own son is as fair as the

MEDIA ADAPTATIONS

- Twain's *The Tragedy of Pudd'nhead Wilson* is available in an unabridged audio CD format released by Blackstone Audio in 2005. The work is read by a full cast of readers representing the narrator and the various characters in the novel.

- A full cast production of *Pudd'nhead Wilson* was released as an audio CD in 2004 by Alcazar Audioworks. It is narrated by Bobbie Frohman.

- The Tantor Unabridged Classics audio CD edition of *The Tragedy of Pudd'nhead Wilson* was released in 2009 and is narrated by Michael Prichard. This edition is accompanied by an online edition.

- Three unabridged audiocassette versions of Twain's novel are available, one read by Norman Dietz and released by Recorded Books in 1992, one read by Jim Roberts and released in 1982 by Jimcin Recordings, and one read by Flo Gibson and released by Audiobook Contractors in 2007.

- Twain's *Those Extraordinary Twins: Mark Twain's First Draft of Pudd'nhead Wilson* is available in an audio CD format read by Richard Henzel and released by Big Happy Family in 2008.

white child, being only one thirty-second black, she will swap the boys. She has Wilson fingerprint them again shortly after this exchange, a swap no one notices.

Chapters 4–6

As the fourth chapter opens, the narrator informs the reader that his story will now "accommodate itself to the change which Roxana has consummated" and call the white child by the slave name with which he is now bestowed, Chambers, and call the black child by his new white name, Tom. The narrator then highlights the way in which Roxy's deception begins to work even on Roxy herself, and she soon finds it natural to treat her own son as her master. The boys' childhoods are summarized by the narrator as a period in which Chambers grows strong, fighting Tom's battles for him. He is meek and obedient, where Tom is indolent and mean-spirited. At the end of this chapter, Percy Driscoll dies. His brother, Judge Driscoll, and his wife take custody of Tom and have recently purchased Chambers as well.

In the next chapter, the reader is informed that the judge's wife dies two years later, at which point the judge's childless sister, Mrs. Pratt, steps in to help raise the child. Tom goes to Yale and returns two years later "with his manners a good deal improved." The year is now 1853, and the boys are twenty-three years old. The town grows excited when it is learned that two foreigners, the Italians Angelo and Luigi Capello, will be boarding in the room for rent in the home of Patsy Cooper, who hosts an open house in which members of the town can gather to meet the new arrivals.

Chapters 7–9
In Chapter 7, the Italian twins are introduced to Wilson, and they enjoy an extensive conversation. Later, Wilson notices from his window what appears to be a young woman in Tom Driscoll's bedroom. (Judge Driscoll's house and Wilson's are only separated by a short distance.)

As the next chapter opens, the narrator returns to Roxy's story. She has procured employment on a riverboat, having been freed by Percy Driscoll just prior to his death. Although she saved money in order to retire from her work as a chambermaid, the bank "had gone to smash and carried her four hundred dollars with it." Roxy subsequently returns to Dawson's Landing and attempts to blackmail money from Tom, having first appealed to his sense of pity.

Roxy is no longer able to work due to the rheumatism in her arms. Tom, the reader has learned, has accrued quite a gambling debt and fears Roxy somehow has learned about this and will disclose the information to his uncle. Tom fears that his uncle will cut him out of his will, as he has done before. Having earned back his uncle's trust, he is loathe to be stricken from the will once again. When Tom meets Roxy in an abandoned cabin, Roxy informs Tom about his true identity. Tom confesses to Roxy that he has been stealing small valuable items from his neighbors' homes and selling them to pay off his

debts. Roxy insists that Tom continue his thefts, pay off his debts, and pay her half of the monthly allotment his uncle gives him.

Chapters 10–12
Tom is depressed and noticeably meeker in temperament after learning that he was born a slave, but he soon resorts to his former boorish behavior. Tom abides by Roxy's plan and continues his crime spree in order to pay off his debts. The reader learns that he has been dressing up as a woman in order to disguise himself during these escapades, and it was in fact Tom whom Wilson saw through his window.

As Chapter 11 opens, Wilson is entertaining Luigi and Angelo in his home when Tom arrives. In the course of the evening, Wilson's fingerprinting hobby is brought up, and Luigi, Angelo, and Tom are fingerprinted. Wilson also is an amateur palm reader and reveals that Luigi once killed a man. Luigi explains that this act was done in order to defend his brother and himself from would-be attackers. The men are invited to attend a meeting of a political organization, the "rum party." As the members of this gathering grow increasingly inebriated, Tom insults Luigi and Luigi kicks Tom. In Chapter 12, Tom's uncle learns that Tom has pressed legal charges against Luigi rather than challenging him to a duel. With the family's honor sullied, Judge Driscoll resolves to challenge Luigi himself and tears up his will.

Chapters 13–15
Tom begins to realize that his thefts are being reported and that Wilson is attempting to solve this mystery. Wilson reveals that the knife that had earlier been the topic of conversation at Wilson's, the very distinctive dagger with which Luigi has killed a man, has been stolen. Tom is well aware of this, as it is Tom himself who has taken it. He learns of Wilson's plan to catch the thief.

Judge Driscoll prepares for his duel. He redraws his will, once again including Tom. The judge fears dying in the duel and leaving Tom penniless. Tom discovers that his uncle has redrawn the will and vows to refrain from gambling and thievery in order to remain in his uncle's good graces. Roxy encourages Tom along this path and advises him to make arrangements with his creditors whereby he pays them monthly, with interest. Tom and Roxy are counting on the elderly Judge Driscoll not living much longer, at which point Tom can claim his inheritance.

In Chapter 15, Tom, having consulted with Roxy, discusses with Wilson his plan to catch the thief. Wilson confirms the particulars of the plan, which he had previously kept a secret, and is astounded that Tom has figured out the trick Wilson had intended to use to draw out the thief. As the reader and Tom both know, it was the clever Roxy who guessed the way Wilson intended to get the thief to reveal himself when he went to pawn the knife. As the thief, Tom is now no longer in danger of being discovered by Wilson, but he has also been unable to profit from his theft by selling the knife nearby. He consequently takes his loot, minus the knife, to St. Louis but is robbed on the boat.

Chapters 16–18

Because Tom's ability to pay the monthly interest on his debt has been thwarted by his having been robbed, Roxy devises another plan to save her son. She suggests to Tom that he sell her into slavery and use the money to pay his debt. He is then to save his monthly allotment from his uncle and buy Roxy back in a year. Her only stipulation is that she is sold to a northern farm rather than a downriver plantation. Tom stumbles upon an opportunity, however, to sell her to a cotton planter and proceeds to set into motion Roxy's worst fear. He has sold her down the river. Although the buyer insists that Roxy will not be aware which direction she is traveling, Roxy has worked on a riverboat and is quite aware that she is headed south.

In Chapter 17, the Italian twins and Wilson all enter the mayoral race. Judge Driscoll and Tom begin planting suspicions that the twins' knife was not, in fact, stolen, and the Judge makes reference to the knife having been used in an assassination. Wilson wins the election, and the twins go into hiding. Roxy finds Tom in a hotel room in St. Louis. She has escaped from the plantation after attacking the overseer in an effort to protect a child who was being beaten. Roxy tells Tom he must ask his uncle for money so that he may buy Roxy back; Tom resolves instead to rob his uncle.

Chapters 19–21

Luigi challenges Judge Driscoll to a duel for having impugned his honor, but Judge Driscoll refuses to duel an assassin. In preparation for his next robbery, Tom disguises himself as a woman and finds his uncle asleep. Money is spread out and in piles, as if the judge has been counting his money and attending to his bookkeeping. Tom has Luigi's knife with him. Just as he is about to begin pocketing money, his uncle wakes up. Tom stabs him, then escapes to the abandoned cabin, burns his women's clothing, and hops a riverboat back to St. Louis. Luigi and Angelo, who were out walking that night, hear Judge Driscoll's cry for help and run to his aid. They arrive to find Luigi's bloody knife and Judge Driscoll, dead. Luigi is charged with the crime, and Wilson vows to defend him as his lawyer. Seeing the bloody fingerprints on the knife, Wilson pursues his investigation of the crime.

Wilson, who has already compared the fingerprints on the knife with those of Luigi, is determined to find a female assailant, as he thinks back to the mysterious woman he saw in Tom's room. Luigi's trial progresses, but Wilson is granted a stay in the proceedings until the following morning. After Tom visits Wilson to mock him, he leaves his fingerprints on one of the glass fingerprint strips Wilson has been examining. Wilson begins to draw new conclusions and rushes Tom out the door. After studying Tom's fingerprints, he realizes not only that Tom is the killer but also that Tom is not Driscoll's son but Roxy's. The final chapter begins with Wilson's preparations for the trial. In court, Wilson patiently explains and reveals all he has discovered. Tom faints when his guilt is revealed, and Roxy falls to the floor sobbing.

Conclusion

In this final brief section of the novel, the narrator informs the reader that Wilson's reputation is now cleared; he is no longer regarded as a fool. The fate of illiterate Chambers, who is really Tom Driscoll, is left unexplained by the narrator. The reader learns solely that he feels at home only among slaves and that to tell of his fate would be too long a story. Tom, who is really Roxy's son, Chambers, is sold down the river.

CHARACTERS

Jim Blake

Jim Blake has a minor role in the novel. He serves as the town's constable and ineffectually investigates the series of thefts in Dawson's Landing as well as the murder of Judge Driscoll.

John Buckstone

John Buckstone is a local politician in Dawson's Landing and is leader of the so-called "rum party." He organizes a meeting of the party to which he invites the Capello twins.

Angelo Capello

Angelo Capello is one of the Italian twins who settles in Dawson's Landing. He is fairer of complexion and milder mannered than his brother Luigi. After Luigi is cleared of the murder charge against him, Angelo and Luigi depart for Europe.

Luigi Capello

Luigi Capello is Angelo's brother, the brunet twin. Luigi reveals without shame or guilt that he once killed a man. He explains that he was protecting Angelo, who was held at knifepoint by an assailant who sought to steal a unique knife, the very one with which Luigi kills the assailant. This fact, combined with his aggression against Tom Driscoll and his appearance at the scene of Judge Driscoll's murder, lead to Luigi's being charged with that murder. Luigi and Angelo depart for Europe at the novel's conclusion.

Chambers (also known as Tom Driscoll)

The infant given the name Chambers is the slave Roxana's son. He is originally dubbed "Valet de Chambre" (a term that refers to a personal servant). Roxy abbreviates and alters the name to be simply "Chambers." From his birth, his identity is associated with the role he will fulfill as a slave in the Driscoll household. While Chambers is still an infant, Roxy, in an effort to spare him the tragedy and hardship of one day being sold to a plantation, dresses Chambers as the rich, white infant Tom Driscoll, placing him in Tom's cradle. Tom is then transferred to Chambers's cradle, in Chambers's rough slave tunic.

After this switch, the narrator begins referring to each child by his new name. As Tom, Chambers grows up to assume the demeanor of a wealthy and privileged only child. Tom, as he is called for the remainder of the novel and as he will now be called here according to the narrator's convention, bullies his slave, Chambers (the real Tom Driscoll).

As an adult, Tom develops a gambling problem. His gambling debts motivate his actions and also shape the course of the novel. Even after his mother tells him his true identity, Tom feels nothing but disdain for the black individuals with whom he comes in contact and even sells his own mother, who has been freed, in order to pay off his debts. Out of concern for his wealth and his position, Tom murders Judge Driscoll, who raised Tom after Percy Driscoll's death. At the novel's conclusion, Tom is not only sold as a slave but sold into the worst kind of slavery; he is sold "down the river."

Patsy Cooper

Patsy Cooper, who is sometimes called "Aunt Patsy," becomes the center of the town's attention when her advertisement for a room for rent is answered by Italian twins Luigi and Angelo Capello. She fusses over the pair in a motherly fashion and hosts a gathering so that the residents of Dawson's Landing can visit with the newcomers.

Rowena Cooper

Rowena Cooper is the pretty, nineteen-year-old daughter of Patsy Cooper. Rowena, filled with romantic notions, is thrilled to have the Italians rooming in her home, and she envisions the way her own celebrity within the town will become elevated due to her close proximity to the foreigners.

Thomas à Becket Driscoll (also known as Chambers)

Thomas Driscoll is the son of Percy Driscoll and his wife. Mrs. Driscoll dies a week after the birth of her son. In the care of the slave Roxana, Thomas, or Tom, is raised alongside Roxana's own son, Chambers, who was born on the same day as Tom. When the infants are approximately seven months old, Roxy takes Tom out of his cradle and fine clothes, dresses him in the rough slave clothing her own son wears, and places Tom in her own son's cradle. Chambers is then dressed as Tom and laid in Tom's cradle and from this point on assumes the role of the Driscoll heir. Tom, who is now referred to by the narrator by his new name, Chambers, is raised as a slave and as a personal attendant to the new Tom.

Chambers, as he will now be called according to the narrator's convention, defends Tom in fights and grows up to be a physically strong individual, but Roxana teaches him to be meek and quiet, the expected behavior for a slave. Chambers is purchased by Percy Driscoll's brother, Judge Driscoll, just prior to Percy's death. At the novel's conclusion, when Chambers's true identity is revealed, Chambers finds he cannot simply step into the life of Tom Driscoll. He is illiterate, cannot speak in the fashion of his new social class, and is only at home in the kitchen among other slaves. The narrator does not further discuss Chambers's future.

Percy Northumberland Driscoll

Percy Driscoll is the father of Tom and the brother of Judge Driscoll. Until his death early in the novel, Percy Driscoll shows himself to be a harsh slave owner, threatening to sell three slaves "down the river." He believes one of them to be responsible for a theft and states that he will sell all three if the real thief does not step forward. When Tom and Chambers are fifteen years old, Percy Driscoll dies. He frees Roxana just before his death and asks his brother to become the guardian of Tom.

Mrs. Percy Driscoll

Mrs. Percy Driscoll is Tom Driscoll's mother. She dies a week after her son is born.

Judge York Leicester Driscoll

Judge Driscoll, Tom's uncle, is a prominent figure throughout the novel. After Tom returns from Yale, Judge Driscoll is on several occasions motivated to disinherit Tom, as when he learns of Tom's gambling debts or when he finds out that Tom has refused to duel Luigi Capello after Luigi has kicked Tom. Judge Driscoll has a strong sense of family honor and duels Luigi himself when Tom refuses to do so. He also demonstrates that he has a malicious streak: when Luigi and Angelo enter the mayoral race in Dawson's Landing, Judge Driscoll, who is backing Pudd'nhead Wilson, tries to discredit Luigi with a rumor that he has learned from Tom. In a speech, he makes reference to the knife that Luigi and Angelo insist has been stolen. Not only does he suggest that the young men have lied about the theft, Judge Driscoll states his certainty that the knife could be found if an assassination became necessary. This underhanded tactic proves successful, and Luigi and Angelo become the objects of scorn in the small town. The judge is murdered and robbed by Tom near the end of the novel.

Mrs. York Driscoll

Mrs. Driscoll is Judge Driscoll's wife. She dies two years after she and her husband become Tom Driscoll's guardian.

Pembroke Howard

Pembroke Howard is Judge Driscoll's friend. He is the public prosecutor and pursues the state's case against Luigi Capello in the murder of Judge Driscoll.

Rachel Pratt

Rachel Pratt is Judge Driscoll's widowed, childless sister. After the judge's wife dies, Mrs. Pratt steps in to help raise Tom Driscoll, the judge's nephew.

Justice Robinson

Justice Robinson presides over two cases in the novel: that of the assault and battery case against Luigi Capello, filed by Tom Driscoll, and that of the state versus Luigi Capello in the murder of Judge Driscoll. Justice Robinson also serves as coroner after Judge Driscoll's death.

Roxana

Roxana (also called Roxy) is one of Percy Driscoll's slaves. She is described as beautiful, intelligent, and very fair; she is one-sixteenth black. Roxana's greatest fear as a slave is being sold downriver to a cotton plantation, where conditions are far more brutal than what she endures as a house slave in the Driscoll home. She is threatened with such a fate when Percy Driscoll accuses Roxy and two other slaves of stealing from him. Fearing that one day her son might be sold in such a manner, Roxy commits herself to the idea that she must kill her infant son and then herself. Before she can act, she happens upon another idea and resolves instead to exchange her son for the heir of the Driscoll estate.

Roxana is freed by Percy Driscoll just before his death, and she embarks upon a new career as a chambermaid aboard a riverboat. When she loses her savings and returns to Dawson's Landing, Roxana initiates contact with her son, tells him of his real identity, and threatens to reveal the truth about his history if he does not help her. While Roxy initially sought to protect her son from the fate of being sold down the river out of maternal love and an instinct to protect her child, she now seeks to spare him from this fate largely because she requires financial assistance. Despite all of her manipulations, however, Roxana nevertheless creates a situation in which her son's identity is finally revealed, and he is, in fact, sold down the river.

David "Pudd'nhead" Wilson

David Wilson is nicknamed Pudd'nhead on his first day in town, when he jokes about how he wished a barking dog were half his, so he could kill his half. Listeners do not comprehend the fact that Wilson intends the comment as a joke; they take his words literally and assume he is a fool. Unable to work as a lawyer after this incident, Wilson supports himself with other endeavors, namely accounting and land surveying. He has an interest in fingerprinting and collects most of the townspeople's fingerprints. He befriends Luigi and Angelo Capello and defends Luigi in court. Wilson's intellect is displayed when he uses science and logic to unravel the mystery of Judge Driscoll's death. His reputation is restored by the novel's end.

THEMES

Identity

In *Pudd'nhead Wilson*, Twain explores the nature of identity and the forces that shape it. This study is primarily achieved through the characters of Chambers and Tom. (Here the boy who is born as Chambers but assumes Tom's identity shall be referred to as Tom, per the author's convention in the novel.) Tom, born a slave but raised as a wealthy white child, is bestowed with endless privileges. He is given everything he desires and is also given a slave, Chambers (the true Driscoll heir) as his personal attendant. Chambers essentially becomes a bodyguard for Tom, who grows up to be an insolent braggart. Twain takes pains to show that Chambers's physical strength can be attributed to his life as a slave and the labors he endures. His meek nature is cultivated by punishment doled out by Tom's father against him, in the instances where Chambers dared raised a hand to Tom in order to defend himself against Tom's bullying. Chambers becomes what he is based on how he is treated.

Similarly, Tom, because his station in life bestows on him the role of "master," becomes shaped by the established conventions of what this role entails, yet, as Roxy finds out, Tom is a distinctly ungentle master. Even before Tom knows that Roxy is his mother, she hopes that Tom will treat her decently as the only mother figure in his life. He never does. His nature as an unkind, unyielding bully, is, according to Twain's depiction, developed as a result of the slave-holding system; he has been taught to see blacks as beneath him, as something less than human. While Tom to some degree appears cruel and thoughtless by nature, Twain takes pains throughout the course of the novel to demonstrate the way Tom's identity is shaped by a culture in which whites are held to be superior to blacks. Similarly Chambers's identity is molded by this same system, but in a different way. At the novel's end, Chambers appears unable to dismantle the behavior he has cultivated as a slave.

Slavery

Twain's treatment of slavery in *Pudd'nhead Wilson* explores the ways in which slavery corrupts whites as much as it destroys blacks emotionally and spiritually. Through the character of Roxana, Twain depicts a young woman, described as beautiful and intelligent, who is willing to do anything to protect her son from the horrors of slavery. She justifies her action of swapping her son for the white heir to the Driscoll estate by measuring it against the actions of whites. Having heard of a situation where a white woman made a similar switch, Roxana insists to herself that it must not be a sin. Although a religious woman, the moral rules upon which she bases her actions are the ones that whites have created by virtue of their own actions.

Once freed, Roxy is hard working, and it is only after her return to Dawson's Landing that she sees what her son has truly become. She can no longer find any trace of a young man who could be her son in the person who treats her with contempt and cruelty, with no regard for her desperate state. In an environment where whites have enslaved blacks for so many years, Roxy sees nothing wrong with stealing from them, as she advises Tom to continue to do, and blackmailing Tom himself. To Roxy, Tom is both the slave child she saved by placing him in a white world and also the white man he has become. She manipulates him freely yet still attempts to save him by allowing herself to be sold into slavery once again to help him. Without a qualm, Tom agrees to this plan, even knowing that Roxy is his mother. Tom sees slaves as inhuman, but his own humanity is erased because he is raised as a slave owner. Slavery has destroyed Tom; his fears of being

TOPICS FOR FURTHER STUDY

- *Pudd'nhead Wilson* is a tragic novel that grew out of Twain's farcical novella *Those Extraordinary Twins*. Read *Those Extraordinary Twins*, and compare the shorter story with the novel. What are some of the major changes Twain made in transforming the work? Are the main characters more fully developed? What themes does Twain explore in the novel that he does not cover in the shorter work? Consider also the differences in tone and style. Write a comparative essay or create a Web page in which you diagram the similarities and differences in the two works.

- *Pudd'nhead Wilson* takes place in the American South in the 1830s. In 1831, the slave Nat Turner led a slave rebellion and was eventually captured. During his incarceration prior to his hanging, Turner discussed his motivations and actions. His confession to lawyer Thomas Gray has been preserved as a historical document and later inspired a novelistic interpretation. The confession itself, along with supporting historical materials, including newspaper articles and trial transcripts, have been collected and introduced by Kenneth S. Greenberg in *The Confessions of Nat Turner, and Related Documents*, published in 1996 by Bedford/St. Martins. Read Nat Turner's confession and survey the historical documents that accompany it in Greenberg's collection. With a small group, discuss these documents. How do the newspaper accounts of the event correspond with Turner's confession? Does Turner's confession itself appear to be genuine, or do you think that his confession was filtered by the prejudices of the white lawyer who took the confession? Create an online blog in which members of your group can post their comments, opinions, and questions about Turner's confession and the way Turner's rebellion and trial were covered by the newspapers at that time.

- The young-adult epistolary novel (an epistolary novel is a fictional narrative told through letters) *Letters from a Slave Girl: The Story of Harriet Jacobs* (2007) was written by Mary E. Lyons and is based on the autobiography of a slave who eventually attained her freedom. Read the novel, considering the fact that it reflects the real-life experience of the slave Harriet Jacobs. Write an essay discussing how the treatment of slavery in this novel compares with Twain's treatment of slavery in *Pudd'nhead Wilson*.

- Although *Pudd'nhead Wilson* takes place in the 1830s, Twain published it in 1894, in the aftermath of the Reconstruction era. Research this period in American history, from the close of the Civil War in 1865 through 1877. What were some of the laws that were passed during this time period? How were the economies of the North and the South shifting? How did race relations evolve during this time period, after slavery was abolished? Write a research paper or create a Wikispace in which you summarize key events during these years. Be sure to cite and/or link to all of your sources.

---

revealed as a slave compel him to sell his mother and to murder the man who has cared for him like a father for many years.

Although Chambers's story is explored much less thoroughly by Twain, at the novel's end, the white child raised as a slave is given back his life. However, he has been so schooled by both his fellow slaves and his white masters as to what it means to be a slave that he is utterly lost in his new world.

The "mighty" Mississippi River (Irene Pearcey / Shutterstock.com)

STYLE

Third-Person Narration

In *Pudd'nhead Wilson* Twain employs the use of a third-person narrator. Not a character in the story, the third-person narrator is omniscient in Twain's story, that is, aware of everything that is going on. The narrator reveals to the reader the thoughts of various characters and relates events from the perspectives of various characters. However, Twain's narrator does not always provide information, in terms of thoughts and perspectives, of characters who are arguably critical to the story. While Tom and Roxana are the focus of the narrator, the narrator offers little of the perspective of the title character, Pudd'nhead Wilson, or that of the true Tom Driscoll, who takes the role of Chambers in the novel. The omniscience of Twain's third-person narrator is therefore selective or limited. Twain's use of the third-person narrator furthermore has the effect of making the story appear as though it is being told to the reader, conveyed orally.

Local Color (Regionalism)

Twain employs the use of a technique that came to be known as regionalism, using "local color" as a means of establishing a sense of realism. In *Pudd'nhead Wilson*, this effect is seen in Twain's use of the distinct slave dialect with which the slaves in his story speak. He also explores the South in general as a distinct region, with Dawson's Landing reflecting the riverside towns along the Mississippi. The term "local color" is sometimes associated with literature in which the particularities of a region are generalized into stereotypes. As a realistic tool, then, local color can be seen as diminishing the aims of realism through such over-generalization. Twain's work is sometimes regarded as an effort to transcend the more superficial aims of local color and to explore deeper concerns with individualized human nature.

HISTORICAL CONTEXT

The American South in the Mid- to Late-Nineteenth Century

The American South, the setting for many of Twain's novels, underwent dramatic upheavals during the nineteenth century. In the 1830s, the

COMPARE & CONTRAST

- **1830s:** The United States is fractured by an array of divisive issues, including the question of the morality or immorality of slavery, the removal of Native Americans from U.S. lands east of the Mississippi, and an economy plagued by unemployment and bank failures. The economic distress culminates in a financial crisis: the Panic of 1837.

  1890s: As a result of industrialization, labor strikes and disputes erupt across the country, and some strikes lead to riots. A financial crisis, the Panic of 1893, hits early in the decade. Despite the constitutional amendments designed to ensure freedom for African Americans, a deep racial divide exists in the country, and segregation and violence are prominent issues.

  Today: The United States' economic crisis of the late first decade of the twenty-first century is mirrored globally. The causes and effects of the current financial troubles are compared with the Great Depression of the 1930s. The country is divided on issues such as gay rights, abortion, and immigration.

- **1830s:** The institution of slavery is legal in the United States, and slaves endure horrific conditions, including physical abuse, torture, rape, and murder. Abolitionist movements attempt to change public opinion and governmental policy concerning slavery.

  1890s: Slavery has been abolished by the Thirteenth Amendment to the Constitution, but the violence perpetrated by whites against blacks continues unchecked in the South after the end of Reconstruction under a set of laws and social norms that come to be known as Jim Crow laws.

  Today: Racism continues to be an issue in the United States in the twenty-first century. A 2009 Gallup poll finds that many African Americans are optimistic about the possibility that race relations will improve under President Barack Obama. At the same time, the NAACP has criticized the Tea Party movement, a growing, conservative political movement, for what the NAACP sees as "continued tolerance for bigotry and bigoted statements," according to Shannon Travis in a 2010 article for *CNN News*.

- **1830s:** As the United States expands its borders, frontier literature becomes popular. James Kirke Paulding, for example, writes a play titled *The Lion of the West* in 1831 that features a Davey Crockett-like character. American writers, such as Edgar Allan Poe and Emily Dickinson, straddle two movements in American literature, romanticism and realism, and explore the individual psyche in poetry and short fiction.

  1890s: American realism is the dominant mode of fiction. Some authors, such as Mark Twain and Kate Chopin, focus on the American South in particular and, through various techniques, emphasize the specific nature of the society and culture of that region.

  Today: Twenty-first century American fiction is not dominated by a particular movement but is influenced by both history and contemporary society. Some authors focus on the American South, slavery, or racial injustice. Novelists writing in this vein include Valerie Martin, author of *Property* (2004); Delores Phillips, author of *The Darkest Child* (2005); and Daniel Black, author of *They Tell Me of a Home* (2005).

time period in which Twain's novel *Pudd'nhead Wilson*, is set, the Southern economy is dominated by plantation-grown cotton, an agricultural industry powered by slavery. Fears of slave revolts were common, particularly after the revolt lead by Nat Turner in 1831, which resulted in the deaths of both blacks and whites. Turner, an educated slave, led a group of fellow slaves on a killing spree of whites in Southampton County, Virginia. In retaliation, slaves were beaten or killed without cause across the region. Turner was incarcerated and then hanged. At the same time, some southern states attempted to gradually abolish slavery, but such efforts were unsuccessful. In 1832, for example, the state of Virginia debated the topic of gradual emancipation (freeing of slaves), but such measures were voted down.

During this time period, the United States was expanding its borders and pushing Native Americans further west in the process. New states admitted to the United States during the 1830s and 1840s included Arkansas in 1836 and Florida and Texas in 1845. All three states entered the union as slave-holding states. Under President Jackson's administration, the Indian Removal Act was passed in 1830, authorizing the president to engage in negotiations with all tribes east of the Mississippi and to move them west of the Mississippi. In 1838, President Van Buren had federal troops forcibly march thousands of Cherokees west from Georgia and surrounding states to Oklahoma, following the Choctaws and the Creeks, who had been removed several years earlier.

As these tensions built, the Civil War was also brewing. Fought over the issue of slavery but also that of the rights of states to form their own laws, the Civil War began in 1861. A number of Southern states declared their secession (withdrawal) from the United States in January of 1861, following the election of President Lincoln, who was known to oppose slavery. The Southern states collectively identified themselves as the Confederacy. The first shots of the war were fired over Fort Sumter in April of 1861. The war lasted until 1865.

In the decades that followed, the Confederate states were reintegrated into the United States, and an era known as Reconstruction began. From 1865 through 1870, a series of constitutional amendments were passed that abolished slavery, redefined citizenship to include blacks and former slaves, and allowed black men the right to vote. The American South was forced to adapt to an economic model not based on slave labor. Black workers, along with poor white workers, were nevertheless exploited as sharecroppers as former plantation owners sought to rebuild some of their fortune. Increasing industrialization, in both the North and the South, drew workers to city factories and away from farmlands. As the economy adjusted to these transformations, a severe depression hit in 1893. Industrialists, however, were making money, and this period saw increases in both monopolies and labor organizations, and consequently in labor disputes as well.

Race Relations in the 1890s

In the 1890s, race relations were dominated by what came to be known as Jim Crow laws. These laws, passed after the end of Reconstruction in 1877, undercut the legal rights won by blacks with the passage of the Thirteenth, Fourteenth, and Fifteenth Amendments to the Constitution and created an environment dominated by legal segregation of the races based on racial fears, suspicion, and hatred. According to David Pilgrim, writing for Ferris State University's Jim Crow Museum of Racist Memorabilia Web sote, the name Jim Crow derives from a stereotypical black character played by a white man, Thomas Rice, in a traveling show. The term Jim Crow became a common derogatory name for African Americans, essentially a racial slur. Gradually the term began to be applied to the segregationist laws designed to limit the rights and freedoms of African Americans.

In addition to actual legislation passed, Jim Crow came to be associated with an understood system of segregation, in which, for example, blacks and whites did not eat together, and whites always had the right of way in an intersection. In 1891, Homer Plessy [who was seven-eighths white and one-eighth black] tested Louisiana's legislation whereby blacks and whites were required to sit in separate railroad cars. He was arrested. In the famous case *Plessy v. Ferguson*, the Supreme Court upheld the Louisiana state law, stating that separate facilities for blacks and whites did not imply that said facilities were not equal. Violation of Jim Crow laws often resulted in brutality against blacks, and lynchings (execution-style hangings meant to intimidate other blacks) were common during this time period.

Roxy worked on a riverboat. *(0750978987 | Shutterstock.com)*

CRITICAL OVERVIEW

Not surprisingly, Twain's treatment of slavery is commonly the focus of modern critical studies of *Pudd'nhead Wilson*. Contemporary reviews of the work, however, viewed this topic somewhat differently than the way it is regarded by more recent critics. An early contributor to the *Hartford Times* in 1895 notes that the work is a "mixed mess" and that it would be an easy feat "to criticise some of the features of the main story, but whoever feels like criticizing Mark Twain?" The critic then states that for "the worthless Tom Driscoll," it is his drop of slave blood that "proves, in spite of his octoroon mother's strong character, his bane and his downfall."

Unlike the often ambiguous commentators of Twain's day, modern critics are quicker to underscore Twain's anti-slavery intentions in this novel and in other works. R. D. Gooder, in his 1992 introduction to *Pudd'nhead Wilson, Those Extraordinary Twins; the Man that Corrupted Hadleyburg*, states that, through the character of Roxy, Twain conveys his "loathing of human oppression in general, of slavery in particular, and . . . of the complacency and false gentility that allowed the institution of slavery to survive." Gooder additionally observes that Roxy, enmeshed as she is in the psychology of the slave-holding system of the South, "accepts the white man's analysis of the character of her own child" and identifies Tom's failings as a by-product of his slave blood.

Other critics found Twain's treatment of these issues well-intentioned but somewhat flawed. In *Nobody's Home: Speech, Self, and Place in American Fiction from Hawthorne to DeLillo*, Arnold Weinstein explores the ways in which Twain depicts Tom and Chambers and their ultimate fates. As Weinstein points out, Chambers is a victim of the slave environment in which he was nurtured, while Tom was given all the privileges white society could offer. However, Tom nevertheless could not escape what was inherent in him, namely, his slave blood. Weinstein argues that Twain appears to be contending that either way, "We lose." Weinstein states that the novel "is Twain's most remarkable effort to tell it both ways, to treat the damning forces of his culture in such a fashion as to see past them without ignoring their authority."

CRITICISM

Catherine Dominic

Dominic is a novelist and a freelance writer and editor. In the following essay, she explores the Shakespearean allusions in Pudd'nhead Wilson *and investigates the relevance of these correspondences to Twain's treatment of the themes of identity, nobility, and honor.*

Twain's novel *Pudd'nhead Wilson* was originally titled *The Tragedy of Pudd'nhead Wilson*, according to Malcolm Bradbury in the 1969 introduction to *Pudd'nhead Wilson and Those Extraordinary Twins*. Bradbury further notes that Wilson is "the one person for whom the action clearly *isn't* a tragedy." Paul A. Escholz, in a 1973 essay for the *Explicator*, disagrees. Wilson, Escholz states, is a "rational, moral, man" who elects to remain in Dawson's Landing despite the fact that, due to a joke, the people label him a fool and prevent him from practicing as an attorney. Escholz goes on to observe that, at the novel's end, Wilson wins the approval of the people at long last but that this victory is nothing short of "a moral disaster." Wilson is now accepted and embraced by a town that condones the evil of slaveholding, becoming one of the town's most prominent citizens by virtue of proving that Tom is really a slave. Not only is Wilson now a hero among slave holders, his actions result in Tom being sold down the river.

One must ask, then, considering these differences in opinion, wherein does the tragedy lie? Is it in Wilson's being thought a fool for over twenty years, or is it, as Escholz contends, in his being crowned a hero amongst people who fail to see the evil in slavery? The more obvious tragedy is that of Roxana. Compelled by maternal love and the instinct to protect her son, she places him in a role in which he will be able to avoid the curse of slavery. At the same time, she knowingly condemns another child to that horrific fate. Her plan works so well, however, that Roxana seems at times unable to recognize that Tom is in fact her son. His contemptuous treatment of her sparks in Roxana the malice to blackmail him, and in the end, in large part due to Roxana's actions, Tom's true identity is

> REPEATEDLY, TWAIN SEEMS TO HINT AT A SHAKESPEAREAN PARALLEL IN *PUDD'NHEAD WILSON*, ONLY TO ADAPT OR SUBVERT THE SHAKESPEAREAN ELEMENT TO A DIFFERENT PURPOSE IN HIS OWN WORK."

discovered, and he is sold as a slave. That Tom, despite all the advantages given to him, could not avoid his fate—life as a slave—is another of the novel's tragedies. With these multiple layers of tragedy, Twain explores the nature of tragedy itself, both as a human experience and as a literary construct.

In the course of this exploration, Twain inserts a number of references to Shakespearean plays. These allusions do not yield direct correspondences between elements in Twain's novel and in Shakespeare's plays. Repeatedly, Twain seems to hint at a Shakespearean parallel in *Pudd'nhead Wilson*, only to adapt or subvert the Shakespearean element to a different purpose in his own work. Although Twain's intentions cannot be known, his interest in Shakespeare is documented by critics and by his own work, *Is Shakespeare Dead?*, published in 1909, in which Twain speculates on the controversy concerning the authorship of Shakespeare's plays. Exploring these Shakespearean allusions draws us back to the notion of tragedy, and understanding this link can aid the reader in understanding Twain's treatment of the serious themes, the themes of tragedy, such as the nature of identity, nobility, and honor, in his novel *Pudd'nhead Wilson*. There are a number of categories of Shakespearean allusion in *Pudd'nhead Wilson*, but Twain's naming conventions and the use of twins will be the two areas explored in this essay.

In *Pudd'nhead Wilson*, as in Shakespeare's *The Comedy of Errors*, there seem to be two sets of twins. Luigi and Angelo Capello are identified specifically as twins. Tom and Chambers, on the other hand, are not technically twins but are twinned characters. As infants, they closely resemble one another, so much so that they can only be told apart by their clothes. Both children

WHAT DO I READ NEXT?

- Twain's *The Adventures of Huckleberry Finn*, first published in 1884–1885, is considered his masterpiece. It explores the experiences of a youth traveling the Mississippi with an escaped slave. A modern edition, published in 2008, is available through Brandywine Studio Press.

- *The Best Short Stories of Mark Twain*, selected by Lawrence I. Berkove and introduced by Pete Hamill, is a collection featuring short fiction by Twain, selected from the entire span of his career. Humorous earlier pieces, as well as the darker works of Twain's later years, are included. The volume was published in 2004 by Modern Library.

- *Mark Twain: A Life*, by Ron Powers, was published by Free Press in 2005. The highly acclaimed work provides a detailed discussion of Twain's life and career.

- Frederick Douglass, an escaped slave who went on to become a statesman and abolitionist leader, published an autobiographical account of his life as a slave and his subsequent escape. The work was originally published in 1845. A modern edition of *Narrative of the Life of Frederick Douglass: An American Slave, Written by Himself*, was published in 2002 by Bedford/St. Martins.

- *Glory Field*, by African American novelist Walter Dean Myers, is a young-adult novel that traces the history of one African American family through several generations. The work begins in Africa, where a man, Muhammad, is abducted and sold as a slave in America, and concludes with a reunion of family members on the plantation where Muhammad was a slave. Myers explores the racism, brutality, and discrimination endured by the family through the Civil War, Reconstruction, and the Civil Rights era. The novel was published by Point in 1995 and reissued by Scholastic in 2008.

- *The Reckless Decade: America in the 1890s*, by H. W. Brands, details the social, political, and cultural developments that occurred during this decade. The volume was published by the University of Chicago Press in 2002.

---

have blue eyes and blond hair. It is this strong resemblance that inspires in Roxy the plan to swap the children. These are the points that suggest to a reader familiar with Shakespeare and with Twain's known interest in Shakespeare a correspondence between the two authors. Shakespeare used twins in plays like *The Comedy of Errors*, capitalizing on their identical nature in order to incorporate the humor of mistaken identities into his more lighthearted plays. *The Comedy of Errors* is the only play of Shakespeare's that features two sets of twins.

Some critics, such as John Carlos Rowe in the 1990 *Mark Twain's Pudd'nhead Wilson: Race, Conflict, and Culture*, have suggested that Tom and Chambers are actually half brothers,

both fathered by Percy Driscoll, despite Roxana's claim that Colonel Essex is her son's father. Such a connection further underscores their similarities in appearance. The twins Luigi and Angelo, unlike Shakespeare's twins, are not identical, although Twain, as many critics have noted, originally intended the twins to be conjoined. One is blond, the other brunet, and they are never mistaken for one another in the course of the novel. Tom and Chambers, who may or may not be biologically related, are not actually twins but, as infants, bear such a close resemblance to one another that a change in clothing and cradles is enough to convince everyone, including one child's father, that the slave child is the white heir.

While the twins in *The Comedy of Errors* are, in many ways, interchangeable, Twain takes pains to show in his novel that each individual is molded by his circumstances but also possesses unique, innate personal traits. With Tom and Chambers, Twain demonstrates the way the slavery shapes one child's life, while being schooled in the ways of being superior, a master of slaves, shapes the other child. With Luigi and Angelo, Twain shows that, despite their shared personal history, Luigi and Angelo have always had distinct personalities, with Luigi being more outgoing and prone to action, while Angelo is the more quiet and calm twin. In examining the argument regarding whether one's nature or one's environment is the key to identity, Twain appears to argue, through these four individuals, that both factors are determinants.

Unlike Shakespeare in *The Comedy of Errors*, Twain does not use a light, comic approach with his use of twins. While Shakespeare explores the humor in the instances of mistaken identity, Twain studies the effects of Roxy's intentionally switching the identities of the two boys. Her desire to mislead, to manipulate, even if motivated by good intentions for her son, has disastrous consequences for both children. As Twain makes plain, it is the institution of slavery that is to be blamed rather than Roxy herself. Shakespeare's comic use of twins in *The Comedy of Errors* serves as a contrast, allowing Twain to demonstrate the serious issues concerned with the nature of personal identity.

Just as Twain's use of the double set of twins or twin-like characters calls to mind Shakespeare's employment of a similar group of characters, so does Twain's naming of particular characters underscore another connection between his novel and the works of Shakespeare. Percy, Northumberland, York, Pembroke, and Essex are all names that appear in Shakespeare's history plays and in Twain's *Pudd'nhead Wilson*. A survey of Shakespeare's historical characters reveals few direct correspondences between them and the Twain characters, however. For example, the role played by Northumberland in *Richard II*, for example, does not resemble Percy Northumberland Driscoll's function in Twain's novel. However, the preponderance of Shakespearean names cannot be ignored.

In Shakespeare's plays, this group of characters is associated with English nobility and aristocracy. These are the men vying for the throne of England. They are members of a privileged, ruling class. By bestowing on his own characters some of these same names, Twain suggests the prominence and prestige of the white, ruling, landowning class in the South by likening them to English nobility. In doing so, he emphasizes their sense of honor, their respected role in their community, and their status as gentlemen. At the same time, Twain points to another status-related affiliation his Shakespearean-named characters possess: they are descendants of the First Families of Virginia, those members of the English aristocratic families who helped colonize the American South. As Twain explains in the novel, the F.F.V. designation implies "aristocracy." In the eyes of the F.F.V. families, the Howards and the Driscolls, "it was a nobility."

In two ways, then, through the Shakespearean names and through the reference to the F.F.V., Twain underscores the noble lineage or characteristics of these men. This nobility is complicated, however, by the fact that the F.F.V. as a group is associated with the white supremacist movement. As several critics have pointed out, Twain's work exhibits a conflict between his opposition to slavery and his affinity for the notion of an aristocratic South.

As R. D. Gooder states in his introduction to *Pudd'nhead Wilson; Those Extraordinary Twins; The Main that Corrupted Hadleyburg*, "Mark Twain did believe that there was such a thing as a 'natural aristocracy.'" Similarly, in *Nobody's Home: Speech, Self, and Place in American Fiction from Hawthorne to DeLillo*, Arnold Weinstein touches on Twain's ambiguous attitude as well as the white-supremacist nature of the F.F.V., stating that while Twain explored the notion of one's environment being the factor that determined or explained human behavior, he "had to contend with some powerful rival theories, notably the white-supremacy views held by the general populace and brought to their finest flower in the code of the F.F.V."

The notion of gentlemanly honor is advocated not only by the F.F.V. families of Howard and Driscoll in Twain's novel but by the typically fair-minded and even-tempered Wilson as well, who admonishes Tom for not dueling Luigi. Wilson vehemently scolds Tom, calling him a "degenerate remnant of an honourable line." In this way, Twain suggests that, despite the fact that the Southern gentleman is typically

David Wilson, aka "Pudd'nhead," collected fingerprints. (*Undergroundarts.co.uk | Shutterstock.com*)

a slave-owner, there is some value in the aristocratic notion of gentlemanly honor.

In his treatment of the themes of identity and honor, Twain employs Shakespearean elements to underscore his own argument. In examining the theme of identity development, Twain invokes Shakespeare's double set of twins from *The Comedy of Errors* in order to highlight, through contrast, the tragedy involved when a case of mistaken identity is engineered. This stands in opposition to the humor Shakespeare creates when the mistakes are accidental. Exploring the notion of honor and nobility, Twain draws comparisons between his privileged characters and key players in Shakespeare's historical dramas. In doing so, Twain emphasizes a strength of character in his Southern men, a nobility that stands in sharp contrast to the evil of slavery embraced by the same individuals.

Source: Catherine Dominic, Critical Essay on *Pudd'nhead Wilson*, in *Novels for Students*, Gale, Cengage Learning, 2011.

Derek Parker Royal

In the following excerpt, Royal examines the centrality of Twain's tendency to use twinning themes in the novel in terms of individual and societal identity.

Perhaps no other work better reveals the double-minded impulse in Mark Twain than does *Pudd'nhead Wilson*. Not only do twins make up the structural core of the tale, but the composition history of the novel is a case study in Twain's narrative double-play. Beginning as *Those Extraordinary Twins*, a short piece centered around Italian-born Siamese twins, the project quickly developed into something more than Twain thought he could handle. What had originally started as a farce soon turned into a tragedy—"a most embarrassing circumstance," according to its author (*Pudd'nhead*). It was not one separate story, but two intertwined tales that "obstructed and interrupted each other at every turn and created no end of confusion and annoyance," leaving Twain with a literary task of surgical proportions: "I pulled one of the stories out by the roots, and left the other one—a kind of

> HIS LARGER INTENTIONS ARE NEVER ENTIRELY CLEAR IN THE NOVEL, AND THE READER IS RARELY CERTAIN AT ANY POINT WHETHER WILSON IS AN INGENUOUS FOOL OR A SHREWD OPERATOR COGNIZANT OF HIS EVERY MOVE."

literary Caesarean operation." Twain concludes his history of "jack-leg" composition by stating that the twins' "story was one story, the new people's story was another story, and there was no connection between them, no interdependence, no kinship."

This last remark appears too emphatically dismissive to be dismissed, and if we were to take the author at his word, our reading of *Pudd'nhead Wilson* would be tragically abortive. If the tales of the twins—the Capellos in the farce as well as Tom Driscoll and Valet de Chambers in the tragedy—suggest anything, it is the impossibility of an autonomous identity. The two individual stories may have progressed along separate trajectories, but they nonetheless share a favorite Twain theme: twinning. The literal twins in *Those Extraordinary Twins* evolved into a series of thematic twins in *Pudd'nhead Wilson*, including Luigi and Angelo, Tom and Chambers, Tom and Roxy, Roxy and Wilson, Wilson and Judge Driscoll, and Wilson and Tom. But one of the most significant acts of twinning in the novel occurs within the single character of David Wilson. He embodies the two conflicting impulses of power that seem to permeate Twain's later writings: the will to emancipate and the will to manipulate. As the primary figure of authority in the text, David Wilson functions as the "extraordinary twin" of Twain's revised tale and works as the philopena of power in Dawson's Landing.

Many critics of *Pudd'nhead Wilson* have acknowledged the centrality of the twinning theme in the novel in terms of individual and societal identity in general. Arnold Weinstein, for instance, looking at society and identity within the novel argues that "the twinning principle is a way of making elastic what would be rigid, of spoofing what would be solemn, of

annexing more space and having more fun in quarters that are pretty cramped and dull" (73). And of those critics who have acknowledged the centrality of David Wilson in the novel, there is disagreement as to how he should be read. Most view Wilson in terms of either his intelligence or else the degree to which he lives up to the name pudd'nhead. However insightful these studies may be, the ambiguous nature of Wilson's power in Dawson's Landing has been by and large neglected. Yet whether as Columbo or as Barney Fife, Wilson unquestionably possesses some form of power, and it is this authority that best reveals Twain's textual double-mindedness.

Some of the criticism concerning David Wilson suggests an innocent or benevolent character who functions as a figure of enlightenment and emancipation. Other readings of Wilson, however, suggest a more sinister or self-serving figure. But if doubleness or twinning lies at the heart of *Pudd'nhead Wilson*'s structure, then one would expect its title character to embody this in some way. However, some critics deny David Wilson the central focus that the novel's title suggests. For instance, James M. Cox has stated that Wilson is an incomplete character, "little more than a massive plot device" who only functions as a part "of the plot machinery" (Mark Twain). His "incompleteness," for Cox, is also responsible for disrupting the "nature vs. nurture" dialectic that the novel sets out to explore ("Revisited"). Likewise, Marvin Fisher and Michael Elliott point to Wilson's inconsistencies as a reason to discount him as any type of hero. They argue, "It would be too much to insist that the bifurcated character of Pudd'nhead Wilson is thematically appropriate to the novel, but it is even less justifiable to view Wilson as a largely sympathetic character reflecting the author's own opinions" (541–42). Both of these criticisms rest by and large on a letter that Twain wrote to Livy in January 1894 in which he recounts a Professor Powell telling him:

> Pudd'nhead was clearly & powerfully drawn & would live & take his place as one of the great creations of American fiction. Isn't that pleasant—& unexpected! For I have never thought of Pudd'nhead as a character, but only as a piece of machinery—a button or a crank or a lever, with a useful function to perform in a machine, but with no dignity above that.... Well, oddly enough, other people have spoken of him to me much as Prof. Powell has spoken. (*Love Letters*)

Elsewhere, in his remarks on the novel's construction, Twain says that Wilson "had to be brought in to help work the machinery" (*Pudd'nhead*).

If we are to take at face value Twain's account, the question becomes whose acuity to trust: Powell's (and the "other people's") or Twain's? The answer, it would seem, is both. The professor is correct to have noticed in the character of Wilson an embodiment of the force or forces at work in the novel. A telltale sign of this, after all, lies in the fact that the title of the novel bears his name. Twain may have been, in his own words, a "jack-leg" novelist, but he probably knew what he was doing—consciously or unconsciously—in choosing a title for the finished work. Also, Twain is strikingly honest in his characterization of Wilson as a "piece of machinery." On the level of plot, Wilson is a motivating force that drives the mystery underlying the novel. Yet he is at the same time a presence that reflects the greater workings of the text. Here Wilson functions as the symbolic microcosm of the entire narrative. His duplicity, the contradictory impulses of emancipator and enslaver, is not only at work within his character, but also serves to highlight the duplicity or twinness at work within the larger text. What many Twain critics have failed to acknowledge is that the problem of Wilson as a "full" character is one and the same with Wilson as a figure of authority, or, put another way, of authority as it functions in the novel as a whole.

Twain's fascination with authority and authority figures manifests itself in some of his earliest writings. The narrators of *The Innocents Abroad, Roughing It,* and *Life on the Mississippi* are all taken by—and at times in complete awe of—rulers of nations, stage drivers, and riverboat pilots, respectively. In his boyhood novels, Twain locates power and authority in major figures like Tom Sawyer (whose showmanship both playfully entertains and selfishly manipulates) as well as in minor characters such as Colonel Sherburn (whose commanding power over his fellow citizens impresses Huckleberry Finn, yet who at the same shoots a man in cold blood). Yet it is in his later fiction that Twain most fully confronts the dynamics of authority and its relationship to the culture of his time. In *A Connecticut Yankee in King Arthur's Court, Pudd'nhead Wilson,* and the *Mysterious Stranger* manuscripts, he explores the darker side of power,

not only the ways that it can be used to liberate and benefit society, but more disturbingly the ways in which it is handled in a duplicitous and Machiavellian manner. David Wilson stands out as perhaps one of Twain's most mysterious of manipulative strangers in that throughout most of the text, he strikes the people of Dawson's Landing (and the reader) as a quiet, bumbling—and perhaps even gentle—citizen of the town. However, it is his most striking hobby, the seemingly innocent art of fingerprinting, that best defines him and helps legitimate a culture of injustice and oppression. Writing in a time that privileged individual industry and scientific inquiry, Twain suggests in *Pudd'nhead Wilson* that intentional or not, enlightened rational endeavors can have a subtle yet potentially devastating effect.

Mapping the character of David Wilson is a labyrinthine project filled with false leads and blind alleys, all of which frustrate the reader at every turn. Like Hank Morgan before him, he embodies contradictory impulses that never negotiate a synthesis and refuse to interpenetrate. Much like young Satan in the *Mysterious Stranger* manuscripts, he is of an indeterminate ethical character that combines justice and selflessness with an equal amount of ego-centered deviousness. He resembles, in other words, the Siamese twins in *Those Extraordinary Twins.* But whereas in the finished novel Twain was able to take the twins apart and make them into separate men, he augmented the duality of Wilson. Indeed, as one set of twins was divided into minor individual parts, another rose up through all the "confusion and annoyance" to take the center stage. In the case of *Pudd'nhead Wilson,* the study of the unlikely twins goes from being a humorous look at individual identity to a more solemn investigation into the fragmented and often duplicitous nature of authority.

For Twain, there is something both beautiful and sinister about fragmented identities. In *A Connecticut Yankee in King Arthur's Court,* Sir Kay is quick to notice in Hank something of a "horrible sky-towering monster" and a "man-devouring ogre." The Capello twins are not only a farcical vehicle of amusement, but perhaps more significantly, an unnatural phenomenon that inspires both awe and trepidation. Twain describes "it" (in the singular, which rhetorically enhances the sense of abnormal otherness) as "the twin-monster" and he had planned in the original work "to exhibit that monstrous 'freak' in all sorts of grotesque lights" (*Pudd'nhead*). In *Those Extraordinary Twins* when Luigi is acquitted for having kicked Tom at the anti-temperance meeting, Judge Robinson, an impartial man who "usually made up in good sense what he lacked in technique," notices the dangers inherent in the town's embrace of the twins. Coming as they do immediately after an otherwise comic courtroom scene, the judge's solemn words take on a particularly striking resonance:

> You have set adrift, unadmonished, in this community, two men endowed with an awful and mysterious gift, a hidden and grisly power for evil—a power by which each in his turn may commit crime after crime of the most heinous character, and no man be able to tell which is the guilty or which the innocent party in any case of them all. Look to your homes—look to your property—look to your lives—for you have need!

This disjunctive "evil" is nonetheless coupled with a facade of harmonious beauty and civility, something that commands admiration as it woos its audience. In *Pudd'nhead Wilson*, the twins are the toast of the town, and their manners and talents win over almost all of Dawson's Landing. Their piano playing, for instance, enchants the guests at the Cooper's party, leading them to feel that "all the music that they had ever heard before seemed spiritless prentice-work and barren of grace or charm when compared with these intoxicating floods of melodious sound. They realized that for once in their lives they were hearing masters." This combination of artful performance and ethical indeterminacy, so much a part of *A Connecticut Yankee*, again comes up in the *Mysterious Stranger* writings. When Satan plays the piano in *The Chronicle of Young Satan*, Marget and Wilhelm feel that it was

> no music such as they had ever heard before. It was not one instrument talking, it was a whole vague, dreamy, far-off orchestra—flutes, and violins, and silver horns, and drums, and cymbals, and all manner of other instruments, blending their soft tones in one rich stream of harmony. (*Mysterious*)

As Theodor describes, "it feels like music" being around Satan.

David Wilson is also a double-edged figure, a "monstrous" twin whose threatening qualities are not outwardly expressed in freakish or violent behavior, but subtly wrapped within an enigmatic demeanor. He simultaneously assumes two positions within the Dawson's Landing community:

as an outsider relegated to the margins and as an insider giving company to the most respected citizens within the society. His "half a dog" remark banishes him to the outskirts of professional respectability, where the citizens strip him of any prior identity and inscribe upon him the mark of a societal outcast: "Within a week he had lost his first name; Pudd'nhead took its place." What is more, Wilson literally lives on the margins of the community. His house is just three hundred yards from the haunted house, "the last house in the town at that end." With the haunted house being the location where the ex-slave Roxy takes refuge, Wilson's position is just one step removed from both legal and cultural marginalization. Conversely, Tom, although a spoiled fruit of the local aristocracy, is nonetheless a member of the town's cultural elite who holds Wilson in high esteem. Wilson also enjoys the company and the respectability of Judge Driscoll, "the person of most consequence in the community." A member of the First Families of Virginia, the judge symbolizes the aristocratic elite of the region, the icon of leisured privilege, the moral center of his society, and the foundation upon which law and respectability rest. His adherence to the chivalric code notwithstanding, Judge Driscoll also represents the intellectual elite of Dawson's Landing. The Freethinker's Society, "the old lawyer's main interest in life," is composed only of him and Wilson, and he is the only one in the town to appreciate Wilson's ironic style. At the same time as he flounders along the periphery, Wilson's association and friendship with Driscoll and Tom clearly place him within the social center of Dawson's Landing.

The descriptions of Pudd'nhead Wilson likewise raise questions as to the determinacy of his character. Throughout the text he is defined in terms that are noncomplementary and at times downright contradictory. His larger intentions are never entirely clear in the novel, and the reader is rarely certain at any point whether Wilson is an ingenuous fool or a shrewd operator cognizant of his every move. Upon first entering Dawson's Landing, he is described as possessing "an intelligent blue eye" whose twinkle reveals both a "frankness" and a "covert" quality. Wilson is a text incapable of being accurately read, a sphinx-like presence whose ambiguity disturbs and even threatens the tranquil order of the town. After he utters his ironic and highly enigmatic remark on owning and killing half of the barking dog, the townspeople "searched his face with curiosity, with anxiety even, but found no light there, no expression that they could read. They fell away from him as from something uncanny, and went into privacy to discuss him." Roxy, one of the most discerning, conniving, and outright formidable characters in the novel, states with much apprehension, "Dey ain't but one man dat I's afeared of, en dat's Pudd'nhead Wilson." She is "afeared" because of her inability to read Wilson with any accuracy, and she is forced to conclude that he is nothing less than a witch. The mystery breeds a feeling of monstrousness. Twain tells us that Wilson was "a cipher in the estimation of the public, and nobody attached any importance to what he thought or did." This is not because he falls within the understanding of the town and comes up wanting, but rather, as with Roxy, he inhabits a realm entirely beyond the comprehension of everyone else . . . .

Source: Derek Parker Royal, "The Clinician as Enslaver: *Pudd'nhead Wilson* and the Rationalization of Identity," in *Texas Studies in Literature and Language*, Vol. 44, No. 4, Winter 2002, pp. 414–31.

Linda A. Morris
In the following excerpt, Morris explores how Twain used clothing, race, and gender in his work.

> And thus in the land of the Color-line I saw, as it fell across my baby, the shadow of the Veil.
>
> —W. E. B. Du Bois, *The Souls of Black Folk*

> Now who would b'lieve clo'es could do de like o' dat?
>
> —Mark Twain, *Pudd'nhead Wilson*

The idyllic opening of *Pudd'nhead Wilson*, with its description of Dawson's Landing's modest dwellings with whitewashed exteriors and a cat asleep in a flower box, concludes with the description of the village bounded on the front by the Mississippi River and on the back by a row of high hills that, Mark Twain writes, were "clothed with forests from foot to summit." Thus, unobtrusively and in the context of a tranquil landscape, he introduces what is to become one of the major subtexts of the novel: namely, clothes as markers of identity, race, and gender. The text is rich with masquerading, with layering of clothing, with cross-dressing and misleading gender markers, with foppery, veiling and unveiling, and with clothing as cues (and mis-cues) to sexual and racial identity. Yet across the novel's critical history, Twain's preoccupation with clothing in the text has been all but invisible.

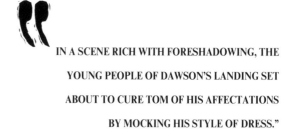

IN A SCENE RICH WITH FORESHADOWING, THE YOUNG PEOPLE OF DAWSON'S LANDING SET ABOUT TO CURE TOM OF HIS AFFECTATIONS BY MOCKING HIS STYLE OF DRESS."

For the first generation of critics and reviewers of *Pudd'nhead Wilson*, even the multiple acts of cross-dressing performed by both the slave heroine, Roxana, and her son escaped public notice. The reviewer for *Cosmopolitan*, for instance, called attention to a host of melodramatic elements in the novel, but made no mention of cross-dressing:

> exchanges of infants in the cradle, a hero with negro taint in his blood substituted for the legitimate white heir, midnight encounters in a haunted house between the false heir and his colored mother, murder by the villain of his supposed uncle and benefactor, accusation of an innocent foreigner, and final sensational acquittal and general unraveling of the tangled skein . . . .

This reviewer goes on in familiar nineteenth-century terms to extol the virtue of the text's black language: "How deliciously rich, racy, and copious is, for instance, his negro talk. The very gurgling laugh and cooing cadence seems, somehow, implied in the text." The reviewer for *the Spectator*, responding to the wry humor of the novel, wondered if Twain had "found Missouri audiences or readers slow to appreciate his jokes," while the *Bookman* focused on the novelty of fingerprint records that ultimately reveal the true identity of the false heir who murders his purported uncle. These reviewers, as others across the work's critical history, responded to *Pudd'nhead Wilson*'s deeply disturbing critique of racial categories, but none of them perceived how metaphors of clothing and cross-dressed performances complicate and complement the racial issues at the core of the novel.

More recently, *Pudd'nhead Wilson* criticism has taken two distinct directions. Scholars such as Hershel Parker have taken pains to understand how Twain composed *Pudd'nhead Wilson*, not being content to accept the author's flippant description of how he simply removed the

Siamese twins from his original manuscript by Cesarean surgery once the slave Roxana and her son "took over" the text. By delicate surgical procedures of their own, these scholars have reconstructed Twain's composing and revising processes that led to the ultimate creation of two texts, *Pudd'nhead Wilson* and *Those Extraordinary Twins*. They note, for example, that in the original manuscript, now known as the Morgan Manuscript, there were no changelings; Tom Driscoll was white, not black; and the Italian twins were Siamese twins who were ultimately hanged by the good citizens of Dawson's Landing. (More accurately, only one of the twins was hanged; but as the citizenry deduced about Wilson's dog at the beginning of the story, killing one half of the animal would for all practical purposes also kill the other.)

A second strand of modern scholarship, as represented in Susan Gilman and Forrest Robinson's collection of essays, *Mark Twain's Pudd'nhead Wilson: Race, Conflict, and Culture*, reads the text historically and interprets late nineteenth-century culture through the text. Critics such as Eric Sundquist and Shelley Fisher Fishkin recontextualize the novel in ways that emphasize the relationship between *Pudd'nhead Wilson* and the racial politics of the day, while Carolyn Porter and Myra Jehlen read the racial and gendered subtexts of the novel. Susan Gilman explores the relationship between twins, duality, and identity in the novel, and positions the novel in relationship to Twain's late dream narratives. Most of these critics, especially those exploring the intersections of race and gender, note that cross-dressing occurs at key crisis points in the novel and that it contributes to and highlights crises of race and identity, but none pursues this subject in depth. Nor has anyone yet noticed how relentlessly the text enacts more conventionally defined issues of dress and clothing.

This essay will focus in particular upon dress and clothing as markers of identity, race, and gender as played out in relation to two of the primary characters in the novel, Roxana and her son Chambers, also known as Tom. Representations of their clothing simultaneously confound the already problematic categories of race and make problematic the categories of gender. Such confounding, we will see, further destabilizes the precarious social order of Dawson's Landing and the post-Reconstruction South of Twain's own time.

. . . In the early pages of *Pudd'nhead Wilson*, then, Twain establishes that clothing and dress will carry the weight of race as it is performed (and deconstructed) in the novel. The expected, indeed purportedly "indelible" stamps of race, both black and white—facial features, hair, skin color—are unreliable from the beginning. Moreover, clothing codes, which we would expect to be the more mutable markers of race, are unfailingly enforced by social dictate. The supposedly "natural" boundaries between the races were disappearing through racial mixing at the time of the novel's writing, leading to demands that they be reinforced by new boundaries and powerful markers. Yet Roxana's action demonstrates that these, too, are unreliable, even deceptive. Dawson's Landing, unbeknownst to its principal citizens, is in the midst of a cultural crisis; its socially constructed codes are unraveling before its very eyes.

As a young boy, the changeling Tom, who knows nothing of his identity as a changeling, is the master of Chambers, and he is spoiled by both Roxana and the white families with whom he resides. Pampered, undisciplined, indulged, he tyrannizes over Chambers and treats Roxana with contempt. Chambers, in contrast, is quickly taught his place as a slave. The relationship between the two boys is expressed in part through metaphors of clothing. Tom, who is cowardly and a bully, makes Chambers do all his fighting for him; consequently, Chambers earns a reputation as an accomplished fighter, until "by and by . . . Tom could have changed clothes with him, and 'ridden in peace,' like Sir Kay in Launcelot's armor." There is no hint of irony in this passage, no sense that Twain is making a conscious joke about the exchange of identities that has already taken place, although the passage evokes in its readers that ever-present knowledge. The literal "armor" that Chambers wears is Tom's cast-off, worn-out clothes that are described ironically by Twain as "holy": "'holy' red mittens, and 'holy' shoes, and pants 'holy' at the knees and seat."

Twain's exploration of the childhood relationship between Tom and Chambers comes to an end when Chambers saves Tom from drowning, which earns him only insults for his trouble. Their playmates tease Tom that Chambers is his "Nigger-pappy—to signify that he had had a second birth into this life, and that Chambers was the author of his new being." Infuriated by the taunting, Tom orders Chambers to attack the boys; when he fails to do so, Tom "drove his pocket knife into him two or three times before the boys could snatch him away and give the wounded lad a chance to escape." And escape he does. After this scene, Twain has no more interest in Chambers until the end of the story; he slips out of sight while Tom takes center stage as the (wrongful) heir to the Driscoll name and fortune.

When he is nineteen, Tom is sent off to Yale, where he learns to "tipple," gamble, and affect "eastern fashion." Upon returning to Dawson's Landing, he particularly offends the young people of his social set by wearing gloves. He also "brought home with him a suit of clothes of such exquisite style and cut and fashion—eastern fashion, city fashion—that it filled everybody with anguish and was regarded as a peculiarly wanton affront." In a scene rich with foreshadowing, the young people of Dawson's Landing set about to cure Tom of his affectations by mocking his style of dress. They tailor a suit that burlesques Tom's and fit it to the town's "old deformed negro bellringer." He follows Tom through the streets, "tricked out in a flamboyant curtain-calico exaggeration of his finery, and imitating his fancy eastern graces as well as he could." The mockery works: "Tom surrendered, and after that clothed himself in the local fashion."

In commenting on this scene, Myra Jehlen rather enigmatically asserts that "it is unclear just what is being satirized: is it simply foppish pretensions, or rather some absurdity of black foppery? Because the characters are unaware that their parody of Tom possesses this additional dimension, it becomes a joke shared by the narrator and the reader, a joke with a new target." Eric Lott reads the incident as "a sort of minstrel gag in reverse; the black man burlesques Tom's acquired graces, and does so at the behest of an audience of village white boys ... it also suggests that Tom's whiteness is itself an act, a suggestion that is truer than either the bell ringer or Tom can know since Tom's identity is precisely a black man's whiteface performance." Both Jehlen and Lott raise important points, but both critics quickly slip past the specific image of the "flamboyant curtain-calico exaggeration of his finery." Jehlen's focus is on who is the target of the joke, while Lott's is on the performance of race. More fundamentally, we

might wonder why this scene has such a haunting quality about it. We are left with the image of the black bellringer shadowing Tom through the streets of Dawson's Landing, mirroring Tom in a distorted mirror that reflects both his costume and his manners. Tom has been perceived by his contemporaries as feminized, as suggested by reference to his "fancy eastern graces." Later, as we shall see, when Tom cross-dresses as a young girl and like Huck Finn practices being a girl, this same language is echoed in the text. By then he will know that by society's definitions, he is really a black man, and he will assume a series of masquerades only to deceive. The bellringer, by contrast, is a figure used to re-establish, at least temporarily, Dawson's Landing's social order, which its young male citizens believe has been disrupted by Tom's putting on airs. In Bakhtinian terms, the scene is carnivalesque, with the most lowly member of the community, the deformed Negro bellringer, dressed in clothing intended to mock a member of the town's most privileged class. While the black bellringer is not protected by the customs of a festival as he would be in Bakhtin's ceremonial world, he is protected by the cover of the white youths on whose behalf he performs. Nothing in the text suggests that the black bellringer is himself foolish or absurd, and to assume the joke is somehow on Tom because he is "really" black but does not know it misses the point. Lott's notion that Tom's whiteness is itself a performance comes much closer to the mark; nonetheless, his analysis stops with this observation, thereby missing the opportunity to investigate the convergence of a racialized and gendered performance.

Cured of his worst pretensions, Tom nonetheless continues to commit offenses against the social order. He accrues a sizable gambling debt that will, if revealed, cause him to be disinherited, so he resorts to theft and deceit to pay off his creditors. In order to steal from the villagers of Dawson's Landing, he assumes a series of disguises to mask his identity. Most powerfully and most successfully, he cross-dresses as both a young girl and an old woman. The first time we see him cross-dressed as a girl, we watch him through Pudd'nhead Wilson's eyes, although neither the reader nor Wilson knows at that moment that the "girl" we are watching is Tom. The scene is in fact represented twice in the text, first from David Wilson's perspective and then from Tom's.

In the first instance, Wilson chances to look out of his window across a vacant lot into Tom's bedroom window in Judge Driscoll's house. There he sees a girl in a pink and white striped dress "practicing steps, gaits and attitudes, apparently; she was doing the thing gracefully, and was very much absorbed in her work." Wilson wonders what a girl is doing in Tom's bedroom, and for some time tries unsuccessfully to discover her identity. Three chapters later, Twain repeats the same scene, but this time from Tom's point of view. This second time the scene is dramatized much more fully and more elaborately, and we do not know at first we are witnessing what we have seen before. Until close to the end there is no mention at all of David Wilson.

> He [Tom] arrived at the haunted house in disguise on the Wednesday before the advent of the Twins,—after writing his Aunt Pratt that he would not arrive until two days later—and lay in hiding there with his mother until toward daylight Friday morning, when he went to his uncle's house and entered by the back way with his own key and slipped up to his room, where he could have the use of mirror and toilet articles. He had a suit of girl's clothes with him in a bundle as a disguise for his raid, and was wearing a suit of his mother's clothing, with black gloves and veil. By dawn he was tricked out for his raid.

While Wilson had seen only a girl in a striped summer dress in Tom's room, we now see Tom cross-dressed not once but twice, first in his mother's clothing, then as the young girl Wilson sees. The added detail of the second female identity assumed by Tom is further intensified by the new information that he had slipped into his own room at his uncle's house so that "he could have the use of [a] mirror." While David Wilson is watching Tom, not knowing who he is, Tom is gazing at one of his female selves in the mirror. He is in the act of performing a gender as surely as his life has become an act of performing a race. Further, the scene and imagery recall his mother's act of looking at herself in the mirror just before she chances upon the scheme to exchange the babies, turning the "black" Chambers into the "white" Tom. That is to say, Tom's identity as a "white" man began with his mother's glance in the mirror, just as one of his identities as a woman is likewise reflected in a mirror.

The scene is filled with images of performing, posturing, mirroring. Just after this passage, Tom notices that Wilson is watching him from his house. The two men, in Twain's words, "caught a glimpse"

of each other peering through their respective windows. Far from being upset by his discovery that Wilson is watching him, Tom "entertained Wilson with some airs and graces and attitudes for a while." Tom deliberately performs for Wilson as a girl, and as a girl he is apparently wholly convincing. Only after Wilson is confronted with other, overwhelming evidence that Tom is an impostor does he "see" beyond the female masquerade: "Idiot that I was! Nothing but a girl would do me—a man in girl's clothes never occurred to me." This is the admission of one of the two founders of the Society of Free Thinkers in the town; in spite of his reputation as being a Pudd'nhead, David Wilson is a shrewd and discerning man. If he is unable to see beyond Tom's cross-gendered disguise, who can?

After his performance, however, Tom is not entirely confident that he has thrown Wilson off track and so changes back into his mother's clothes before leaving the house. Just as Twain had repeated the performance scene twice, he now repeats twice in three sentences the same information about Tom's changing into his mother's clothing, under scoring the intensity of his preoccupation with cross-dressing in this text:

> Then [Tom] stepped out of sight and resumed the other disguise, and by and by went down and out the back way and started downtown to reconnoitre the scene of his intended labors.

> But he was ill at ease. He had changed back to Roxy's dress, with the stoop of age added to the disguise, so that Wilson would not bother himself about a humble old woman leaving a neighbor's house by the back way in the early morning, in case he was still spying.

Tom's cross-dressing in order to commit burglaries sets the scene for even more complex gendered and racial crossing that follows. It is both a symptom and a cause of the category crisis that is at the heart of the novel . . . .

Source: Linda A. Morris, "Beneath the Veil: Clothing, Race, and Gender in Mark Twain's *Pudd'nhead Wilson*," in *Studies in American Fiction*, Vol. 27, No. 1, Spring 1999, p. 37.

SOURCES

Bradbury, Malcolm, Introduction to *Pudd'nhead Wilson*, Penguin, 1969, pp. 9–46.

Campbell, Donna, "Brief Timeline of American Literature and Events: Pre-1620 to 1920," in *Washington State University's American Literature Web Site*, http://www.wsu.edu/~campbelld/amlit/timefram.html (accessed October 10, 2010).

Cashman, Sean Dennis, "Industrial Spring," in *America in the Gilded Age: From the Death of Lincoln to the Rise of Theodore Roosevelt*, 3rd ed., New York University Press, 1993, pp. 1–35.

Escholz, Paul A., "Twain's *The Tragedy of Pudd'nhead Wilson*," in *Explicator*, Vol. 31, No. 8, 1973, pp. 129–31.

Goldman, Russell, and Jake Tapper, "Islamic Center 'Ground Zero Mosque' Controversy Heats Up," in *ABC News/Politics*, August 19, 2010, http://abcnews.go.com/Politics/islamic-center-ground-mosque-controversy-heats/story?id=11435030 (accessed October 10, 2010).

Gooder, R. D., Introduction to *Pudd'nhead Wilson; Those Extraordinary Twins; The Man That Corrupted Hadleyburg*, Oxford University Press, 1992, pp. vii–xxviii.

Hill, Hamlin, "Samuel Langhorne Clemens," in *Dictionary of Literary Biography*, Vol. 12, *American Realists and Naturalists*, edited by Donald Pizer, The Gale Group, 1982, pp. 71–94.

"New Books," in *Hartford Times*, Vol. 18, February 1895, p. 8; reprinted in *Mark Twain: The Contemporary Reviews*, edited by Louis J. Budd, Cambridge University Press, 1999, pp. 370–71.

Norton, Mary Beth, Carol Sheriff, David M. Katzman, David W. Blight, and Howard Chudacoff, "The Rise of the South: 1815–1860," in *A People and a Nation: A History of the United States*, Wadsworth, 2010, pp. 230–60.

Pilgrim, David, "Who Was Jim Crow," and "What Was Jim Crow," in *Ferris State University's Jim Crow Museum of Racist Memorabilia*, http://www.ferris.edu/jimcrow/menu.htm (accessed October 10, 2010).

"Reconstruction Amendments," in *The Black Past: Remembered and Reclaimed*, http://www.blackpast.org/?q=primary/reconstruction-amendments (accessed October 20, 2010).

Rowe, John Carlos, "Fatal Speculations: Murder, Money, and Manners in *Pudd'nhead Wilson*," in *Mark Twain's Pudd'nhead Wilson: Race, Conflict, and Culture*, edited by Susan Gillman and Forrest G. Robinson, Duke University Press, 1990, pp. 137–54.

Saad, Lydia, "U.S. Waiting for Race Relations to Improve under Obama," in *Gallup*, November 9, 2009, http://www.gallup.com/poll/124181/U.S.-Waiting-Race-Relations-Improve-Obama.aspx (accessed October 20, 2010).

Travis, Shannon, "NAACP Passes Resolution Blasting Tea Party 'Racism,'" in *CNN/Politics*, July 14, 2010, http://articles.cnn.com/2010-07-14/politics/naacp.tea.party_1_tea-party-hilary-shelton-rampant-racism?_s=PM:POLITICS (accessed October 20, 2010).

Twain, Mark, *Pudd'nhead Wilson*, Penguin, 1969, pp. 51–226.

Weinstein, Arnold, "Twain: The Twinning Principle in *Pudd'nhead Wilson*," in *Nobody's Home: Speech, Self, and Place in American Fiction from Hawthorne to DeLillo*, Oxford University Press, 1993, pp. 65–90.

Zevin, Robert, "Been Down So Long," in *Huffington Post*, October 14, 2010, http://www.huffingtonpost.com/robert-zevin/been-down-so-long-_b_761693.html (accessed October 20, 2010).

FURTHER READING

Berret, Anthony J., *Mark Twain and Shakespeare: A Cultural Legacy*, University Press of America, 1993.
> Inspired by Twain's work *Is Shakespeare Dead?*, Berret explores the impact of Shakespeare on Twain and the development of this influence in Twain's writings. Berret studies in some detail a number of Twain's writings, although *Pudd'nhead Wilson* is not included in his analysis.

Fitzgerald, Michael W., *Splendid Failure: Postwar Reconstruction in the American South*, Ivan R. Dee, 2008.
> Fitzgerald offers a comprehensive overview of the Reconstruction era, detailing the social, political, cultural, and economic elements of this time period.

Lathbury, Roger, and Karen Myers, *Realism and Regionalism: 1860–1910*, 2nd ed., Chelsea House, 2010.
> This survey of realist and regionalist movements in American literature is geared toward a young-adult audience. The authors focus on the ways in which the historical, cultural, and political events of this time period influenced the literature produced during these years.

Twain, Mark, *The Autobiography of Mark Twain*, Vol. 1, University of California Press, 2010.
> Twain originally published chapters of his autobiography in serial form in 1906 and 1907, and edited versions have been published since then. This edition represents the first time the complete, unabridged manuscript has been published, with volumes 2 and 3 to follow.

SUGGESTED SEARCH TERMS

Twain AND Pudd'nhead Wilson

Twain AND regionalism

Twain AND local color

Twain AND slavery

Twain AND American South

Twain AND realism

Twain AND humorist

Twain AND satire

Twain AND biography

Twain AND Mississippi River

Tar Baby

TONI MORRISON

1981

Tar Baby, by Toni Morrison, was published in 1981. It is Morrison's fourth novel and is frequently overlooked in favor of her more widely read novels such as *The Bluest Eye* (1970), *Song of Solomon* (1977), and the Pulitzer Prize-winning *Beloved* (1987). Although it is not one of Morrison's more famous novels, it has received significant critical attention over the years, and Morrison has been lauded for her implementation of folklore in the work. Morrison has stated that she used folk takes to recall the importance of storytelling in her childhood. Like many of Morrison's other novels, *Tar Baby* showcases minorities and women, though it is one of her few works that feature major Caucasian characters as well. The work deals with themes of ethnic identity and gender roles, as the main character, Jadine, attempts to define herself between two cultures. The novel includes several graphic scenes involving sex, violence, and strong language. It is available in a 2004 paperback edition by Vintage.

AUTHOR BIOGRAPHY

Morrison was born Chloe Anthony Wofford on February 18, 1931, in Lorain, Ohio, to Ella Ramah Willis and George Wofford. She did not become known as Toni Morrison until the publication of her first novel, *The Bluest Eye*, which she published under that pseudonym. As

Toni Morrison (*AP Images*)

Morrison grew up, her family had a profound influence on her. Her maternal grandparents relocated from the South to Ohio in search of greater opportunities in a time when racism against African Americans was still rampant. Both Morrison's grandparents and her parents stressed the importance of education. Morrison excelled throughout her early education and spent time working as a helper in the Lorain Public Library when she was a teenager.

Although Morrison had aspirations to become a dancer when she graduated from high school, she ended up majoring in English and minoring in the classics at Howard University. She continued her studies in English literature at Cornell University, graduating with a master's degree in 1955. She wrote her master's thesis on suicide as a literary construct in the work of Virginia Woolf and William Faulkner.

Following the completion of her master's degree, Morrison accepted a position as a professor at Texas Southern University. After just two years at Texas Southern, Morrison returned to Howard University as an English Instructor. There she met Harold Morrison, a Jamaican architect, whom she married in 1958. In 1961, Morrison gave birth to her first child, a son

named Harold. Morrison's marriage was an unhappy one, and in 1963, she left Howard University and took her son to Europe to travel. In 1964, Morrison returned to the United States, divorced her husband, and gave birth to her second son, Slade. The following year Morrison moved her family to Syracuse, New York, to work as an editor for a subsidiary of Random House that published textbooks. In 1967, she was transferred to New York to work as a senior editor at Random House.

While working at Random House, Morrison published her first novel, *The Bluest Eye*, in 1970. The book received positive reviews, but it was not commercially successful. Her next novel, *Sula*, was nominated for an American Book Award. In 1976 and 1977, Morrison worked as a visiting lecturer at Yale University and published her third novel, *Song of Solomon*, which won several literary awards and was a factor in her appointment to the National Council on the Arts by President Jimmy Carter in 1980. The following year, *Tar Baby*, was published. Unfortunately, Morrison's early novels are frequently overshadowed by the success of her 1988 Pulitzer Prize-winning novel, *Beloved*.

From 1983 to 1987, Morrison continued to write while serving as the Albert Schweitzer Professor of the Humanities at the State University of New York in Albany. In 1987, Morrison received the honor of becoming the first African American woman to become a named chairperson at an Ivy-League university when she was appointed the Robert F. Goheen Professor in the Council of Humanities at Princeton University. At Princeton, Morrison continued to teach and write and developed a special workshop for writers and performers. In 1993, Morrison became the first African American to ever receive a Nobel Prize in literature. Beginning in 1999, Morrison collaborated on a series of children's books with her son Slade while continuing to write and publish novels.

In 2006, Morrison retired from Princeton. She continues to write and serves as a member of the editorial board for the *Nation* magazine. In addition to her accomplishments as a novelist, Morrison has written plays, an opera, and countless nonfiction pieces. She has been awarded an honorary degree from Oxford University and has appeared at literary conferences around the world. She has played a significant role in shaping the genre of African American literature and continues to be a major force in the field of American literature in general.

PLOT SUMMARY

Prologue

Tar Baby is set in a variety of locations, including the Caribbean, New York, and Eloe, Florida, in the late 1970s. The novel opens in the middle of the night as a nameless young black man stands on the edge of a ship called the H.M.S. *Stor Konigsgaarten* near the coast of the island of Dominique in the Caribbean sea. After observing his surroundings and ensuring that the coast is clear, he jumps overboard.

As he swims, the pressure of the warm water is described as the hand of a woman, pressing at his chest. Realizing that it would take too much effort to swim to shore, he decides to climb aboard a nearby boat labeled the *Seabird II*, which has a ladder hanging over the side. Once aboard the ship, he quietly crawls into a closet and falls asleep.

The man soon wakes up to the voices of women talking, and catches a glimpse of a well-manicured hand. Later it is revealed that the women are Margaret Street and Jadine Childs, two of the main characters of the novel. He listens to the noises of the boat, which indicate that the women are docking at a pier for the night. Once the boat is quiet, he goes up to the deck and looks at the moon and the stars. As the prologue closes, the omniscient narrator references an African American folktale.

Chapter 1

Chapter 1 begins with a description of the Caribbean island called Isle des Chevaliers, where most of the novel takes place. Three hundred years ago, slaves were brought from Haiti to clear the land. The oldest and largest house on the island is called L'Arbe de la Croix, which is described as a "wonderful house," filled with quirks. The current owner, Valerian Street, has owned the house for a long while as a vacation home, but only started living there year round roughly three and a half years before the novel opens.

The narrator remarks that the only things that Valerian misses from his old home in Philadelphia are the hydrangeas and the postman. He brought with him his wife Margaret, a former beauty queen once known as the Principal Beauty of Maine, and his two lifelong servants, Sydney and Ondine, who are married to each other. His wife very badly wants to move back to the United States, and Valerian makes comments indicating that they will to placate her, although he has no real intention of leaving the island.

One morning in December, Valerian sits at the breakfast table while his butler, Sydney, serves him breakfast. Sydney and Ondine, who cooks for the family, have lived with the Streets for decades and are almost like members of the family. The two men converse, and Sydney reveals to Valerian that Margaret is expecting their son, Michael Street, to come for Christmas. Valerian does not believe he will come.

Margaret joins the breakfast table, and she and Valerian almost immediately begin to bicker about whether or not Michael will actually show up for Christmas. When Margaret and Valerian tease, it is difficult to tell whether they are being malicious or playful. The couple moves on to the topic of whether or not Sydney and Ondine will leave if their niece, Jadine, moves back to Paris.

Later, Sydney and Ondine discuss Margaret, whom they sarcastically call the "Principal Beauty," and whether or not Michael will make it home for Christmas. Sydney states that Ondine and Margaret spoiled Michael when he was a child. Ondine speaks about Margaret with hostility and claims that she was a bad mother. Jadine enters the kitchen, and Sydney and Ondine lavish her with affection. It is clear that the couple adores Jadine.

Chapter 2

The narrator describes the activity at L'Arbe de la Croix in the middle of the night. Sydney and Ondine sleep peacefully with their backs touching each other. Valerian is restless. He has trouble sleeping because he frequently takes naps during the day. Margaret sleeps in a separate bedroom, after going through her elaborate nighttime ritual. Jadine is wide awake in her room, after waking up startled from a dream.

In her dream, she recalls a beautiful African woman wearing a yellow dress that she once encountered in a grocery store in Paris. As she was leaving the store, the African woman looked at Jadine and spat on the ground, a gesture that hurts Jadine's feelings because she wanted the woman to respect her. Jadine also thinks about Ryk, the white Frenchman who proposed to her in Paris. She is worried that Ryk only wants to marry her because he likes the idea of marrying a black woman.

As Jadine drifts off, Valerian awakens and reflects on the past. Valerian inherited the Street Brothers Candy Company from his uncles. When he was growing up, it was understood that he would inherit the company, as he was the only male child that any of the brothers had. At thirty-nine, he noticed Margaret on a trip to Maine. The two of them got married and had their son Michael. Valerian remembers how he had hoped to have a relationship with Michael, but he never did, much to his disappointment.

In her own room, Margaret is somewhere between asleep and awake. She thinks about her increasing forgetfulness. The narrator reveals the details of Margaret's past. Margaret fell in love with and married Valerian when she was just seventeen. Early on in the marriage, she felt uncomfortable and out of place when Valerian would host large parties with sophisticated guests. She preferred to spend time in the kitchen with Ondine. However, Valerian disapproved of her spending so much time with Ondine and put a stop to it. When Michael was born, Margaret felt overwhelmed by how much he needed her. She feels that no one believed that she loved him, even though she did.

Chapter 3

The Streets are once again seated around the table. Valerian chastises Margaret for eating her dinner so slowly, not aware that Margaret is taking a long time because she is experiencing one of her moments of confusion and forgetfulness, and the couple begins to argue. Jadine tries to change the subject and lighten the mood by bringing up Christmas, unaware that this is a sore spot for Valerian, who is still upset that Margaret has invited guests. As the argument between the couple escalates, Jadine considers the nature of their fighting. The couple continues to argue until Margaret becomes so upset that she leaves the table in a huff, before dinner is finished.

After an awkward pause, Valerian apologizes to Jadine for the argument and says that both he and Margaret are tense. He begins to chat with her about Michael. Valerian believes Margaret has raised Michael to be an impractical idealist and expresses his disappointment with the way Michael turned out. As Valerian continues to talk about his son, Jadine listens quietly, unsure of what to say.

All of a sudden, Margaret enters the room, screaming hysterically. Sydney and Ondine, hearing her screams, also run into the room, and everyone tries to get Margaret to explain what is wrong,

but she is speechless. Finally she stutters that there is something black in her closet. Valerian thinks that Margaret is drunk, but Ondine instructs Sydney to take a gun and look in Margaret's closet. In a moment, Sydney returns, holding a black man with dreadlocked hair at gunpoint. Sydney and Ondine want to call the police immediately, but Valerian simply invites the strange man to sit down for a drink.

The man is the same man who snuck onto the boat with Margaret and Jadine at the beginning of the novel. He followed them back to the house and has been secretly living there and stealing food from the pantry ever since.

Chapter 4

The next morning, Margaret contemplates the previous evening. Meanwhile, in her own room, Jadine is showing Ondine the sealskin coat that her French boyfriend, Ryk, sent her for Christmas.

Later, Ondine is cooking in the kitchen when Sydney enters. Sydney and Ondine discuss the events of the previous evening; both are upset that Valerian let the man stay. Sydney is particularly upset that the man is staying in the guest room next to Jadine's bedroom, but Ondine tells him that they must put up with Valerian's antics since they are both too old to find new jobs.

In her room, Jadine continues to fawn over her coat and then takes a shower. When she gets out of the shower, wrapped in a towel, she sees the reflection of the dreadlocked man in her mirror. She chastises him for not knocking before he entered the room and then asks his name, which she will later find out is Son.

They begin to discuss Jadine and her background as a model, and Jadine shows him some of her modeling photographs. The two talk about her career for a while, until Son suddenly asks her how many sexual favors she had to perform to attain nice things and become a model. Jadine, shocked and offended, spits in his face and tells him he smells. She says that, if he rapes her, he will be killed like an animal. He responds by saying that he would never rape a white girl. Jadine resolves to tell Valerian about the encounter. However, when she goes to talk to Valerian, she finds him laughing with Son.

Chapter 5

Jadine and Margaret conspire about what they should do about Valerian's interest in the man. They decide to call the police but change their minds when they see the man showered, shaved, and cleaned up. While Jadine and Margaret have been talking, Son has been showering in Jadine's bathroom. He reflects on the fact that everyone in the house, except Valerian, is afraid of him. It is revealed that, for the past eight years, Son has been on the run and has had seven different identities. Son watches Gideon, the man who tends the Streets' property, working in the back-yard and admires how hard he works.

In the greenhouse, Valerian watches Thérèse working in the washing shed. It reminds him of the washing shed outside his childhood home. Valerian thinks about all of the things he said to Jadine the previous night, regretting some of them. His thoughts drift to his first wife and then to the ghostly image he saw of his son Michael at the dinner table the night before. Soon he is interrupted by Son entering the greenhouse. The two men begin to talk, and Son asks Valerian if he is going to turn him in. Valerian says he will not.

Valerian instructs Gideon and Thérèse to take Son into town and get him cleaned up. Thérèse asks Son if it is true that American women kill their own children and about other horrific things that she believes occur in America. Gideon tells Son to ignore her.

The next morning, Son asks Jadine to go on a picnic with him. Jadine makes fun of Son for being uneducated and unmotivated, and the two talk about the town that he is from, Eloe, Florida. Son reveals that he had to leave Eloe after accidentally killing his wife, Cheyenne. After discovering that she was committing adultery with a thirteen-year-old boy, Son ran a car into their house, and she died. He has been on the run ever since. Son tells her that she should not be afraid of him though, because he would never harm her, and then begins to talk about how much he loves her feet. After Son strokes her foot, Jadine suddenly exclaims that she needs to go back to the house.

On the way back to the house, they run out of gas, and Son walks to get some while Jadine waits with the car. As she is waiting, she decides to walk around. She accidentally walks too far onto swamp land though and begins to sink in. After much struggle, she manages to climb out but is covered all over in mud.

When they get back to the house, Jadine explains to Margaret what happened, and Margaret declares that Son is bad luck. Margaret continues to talk about how Son makes her feel

uneasy, and Jadine teases her, asking if Margaret thinks Son is sexually attracted to her. Jadine is disgusted by the idea that Margaret would think Son would be sexually attracted to an old white woman instead of herself.

Chapter 6

On the day before Christmas eve, Valerian and Margaret are in high spirits. Valerian has apologized for being insensitive to Margaret's fright upon finding Son in her closet, and the two have slept together the night before for the first time in a long time.

On Christmas Eve, none of the invited guests show up for dinner. Valerian attempts to cheer Margaret up by encouraging a family dinner. On Christmas morning, the Streets have still received no word from Michael. Distraught, Margaret stops cooking halfway through the day.

That night, the Streets, the Childs, and Son all sit down to eat. Everyone compliments Margaret on the meal she only half prepared. Son mentions that he is sad that Gideon could not join them, and everyone at the table is surprised to learn that "Yardman" and "Mary" are actually "Gideon" and "Thérèse." At that point, Valerian mentions that he fired them earlier that day for stealing some of the apples Margaret requested for the apple pie.

Ondine is outraged that Valerian did not even bother to inform her or Sydney that he had fired them. Son too is upset at how easily Valerian let them go. The tension begins to escalate after Son insults Margaret, and Valerian tells him to leave the house. Jadine tries to calm everyone down, but when Ondine also insults Margaret, a shouting match breaks loose.

As insults are exchanged, Margaret throws a glass of water in Ondine's face and Ondine slaps Margaret across the cheek. The two women begin to fight with one another and, even after they are separated, continue to scream insults at each other. Ondine accuses Margaret of being a "baby killer" and claims that, when Michael was a toddler, Margaret used to abuse him by sticking pins in him and putting out cigarettes on him. As everyone sits silently, shocked by this revelation, Margaret simply states that she has always loved her son.

Son and Jadine go upstairs together, shocked by the night's events. Jadine says she wants Son to stay and sleep with her but that she does not want to have sex. Once they are in bed together, they both state several times that they do not want to have sex with each other, although it is evident that they have a mutual attraction.

Chapter 7

Chapter 7 opens in New York City, where Son awaits Jadine's arrival. In the two days following the disastrous Christmas dinner, the two have been inseparable, although it was obvious that Son needed to leave the house as soon as possible. Son used Jadine's plane ticket and Gideon's passport and left for New York immediately. However, once he was there, he worried about whether Jadine had really fallen in love with him or not. When Jadine arrives in the city, she is excited to be back and to see Son again.

The couple moves into Jadine's friend Dawn's apartment while Dawn is out of the city. Jadine and Son have a carefree time in the city getting to know each other better, although Son keeps insisting that he wants to go back to his hometown of Eloe, Florida. Jadine feels slightly guilty for leaving Sydney and Ondine, who do not know that she is with Son.

Son and Jadine do not seem to worry about money, despite the fact that Jadine does not have much in savings and Son has practically nothing. Jadine considers finding a steady modeling job but does not. The two become increasingly wrapped up in each other, until they hardly leave the apartment. At the end of the chapter, Son and Jadine leave for Eloe.

Chapter 8

Back on the Isle des Chevaliers, Valerian is wrought with the memory of Michael singing a sad song under the sink and is devastated to realize that Margaret's years of strange behavior were not a result of secret alcoholism as he thought but an effect of her abuse of Michael. Margaret tried to explain her actions to Valerian at the dinner table on Christmas night, but he refused to listen to her.

The next morning, Margaret wakes up feeling relieved that her secret is finally out. Sydney and Ondine are still worried about losing their jobs, and Valerian is still in shock. Margaret continues to try and explain her abusive behavior to Valerian.

On January first, Margaret asks Ondine why she did not tell her secret before. Ondine explains that she was afraid that, if she told, she and Sydney would lose their jobs. When Margaret tells Ondine that she should have stopped her, Ondine explains that she was only a young girl, just like Margaret. Margaret expresses her

wish that she and Ondine get along and become friends again, to which Ondine does not react one way or another.

Chapter 9

Son and Jadine have to find a ride to Eloe, because it is such a small town that no buses go there. After catching a ride, the couple stops to visit a friend of Son's from the army, called Soldier. Jadine is shocked by how small and rural Eloe is. Son asks Jadine if she will stay with Soldier while he goes to visit his father, to which she reluctantly agrees. Son goes to see his father, Old Man, who is shocked by his arrival. Son is shocked to learn that his father has cashed very few of the money orders he has sent. He tells Son that he and Jadine cannot stay in the same house because they are not married. He tells Son that he should see whether Jadine could stay with his Aunt Rosa.

When Son returns to Soldier's house, he is angry to learn that Jadine has been taking pictures of people with her camera. Jadine is offended that Son grabbed her camera away and upset by the fact that she has to stay at his Aunt's house. That night, Jadine falls asleep quickly at Rosa's house but wakes up in the middle of the night. Rosa hears Jadine moving around in her room and comes in. When Rosa sees Jadine naked, she makes Jadine feel ashamed. Jadine says that she has forgotten her nightclothes, instead of admitting that she always sleeps naked, and Rosa gets her a nightgown.

On Sunday, Jadine and Soldier talk while Son drives Aunt Rosa to church. Soldier asks who is in control of Son and Jadine's relationship and whether they will get married. Jadine is annoyed with Soldier's insistent questioning. She begins to feel increasingly uncomfortable in Eloe and imagines that the women of the town are judging her. She decides to leave immediately.

Back in New York, Jadine waits for Son, but he does not arrive when he is supposed to. When he finally does show up, he and Jadine fight regularly. Jadine wants to ask Valerian for financial help, but Son rejects the idea. The fights between the two of them become physical. Jadine accuses Son of being lazy and not ambitious enough, and Son accuses Jadine of being oblivious to the cruel realities of the world.

Despite all of their arguments, Jadine agrees to marry Son on the condition that he goes to school. He agrees. However, one night, after a particularly bad argument, Son returns to their apartment to find that Jadine has left. She left

behind an envelope of the pictures that she had took in Eloe. Son looks at the pictures and thinks that the people in them look rural and stupid. He resolves to find Jadine.

Chapter 10
After leaving New York, Jadine goes back to L'Arbe de la Croix. She finds the house in a much different state of affairs than she left it. Valerian has grown feeble, and Margaret and Sydney have to take care of him, which has changed the power dynamics in the house. Jadine tries to explain her relationship with Son to Ondine, but Ondine does not want to hear about it. She is angry that Jadine will not stay and take care of her and Sydney in their old age. She believes that Jadine has an obligation to them, because she is practically their daughter. Sydney also feels that Jadine is acting inappropriately. Jadine instructs them not to reveal her whereabouts to Son if he asks. The next day she boards a plane for Paris. On the plane she resolves to forget Son.

Epilogue
Son returns to Queen of France searching for Jadine. He encounters Gideon and Thérèse there and discovers that they are working as cab drivers. They are both happy to see him. Gideon refuses to take Son to the Isle des Chevaliers, but Thérèse says that she will. Because her vision is so poor, she has to navigate the boat by the feel of the water. Thérèse drops Son off at the back side of the island, far away from the main house. Thérèse urges Son to stop pursuing Jadine and tells him that the mythical horsemen of the island are waiting for him. At the novel's cryptic end, Son is running through the trees, metaphorically riding off with the horsemen.

CHARACTERS

Aunt Rosa
Aunt Rosa is Son's aunt, with whom Jadine stays in Eloe. She makes Jadine feel ashamed for sleeping naked.

Cheyenne
Cheyenne is Son's first wife, whom he accidentally killed by running a car into their house after discovering that she was having an affair with a thirteen-year-old boy.

Jadine Childs
Jadine is one of the main characters of the novel. She is the niece of Ondine and Sydney, although they have raised her as if she were their own child. Jadine is a young, beautiful, educated black woman who has worked as a runway model in Paris. Valerian paid for her college education at the Sorbonne in Paris, where she studied art history. Throughout the novel, Jadine struggles with her identity.

As a beautiful, light-skinned African American who has been readily accepted by Caucasians and idealized as a fashion model, she sometimes has difficulty identifying with black culture. She values high art (Ave Maria over gospel music and Picasso over African masks) and cosmopolitan city living. She hopes to eventually open up her own clothing boutique in Paris. At the dinner table, Jadine sits down to eat with Margaret and Valerian while her aunt and uncle serve her, along with their employers.

Jadine is very different from the other black characters in the book, and she is not fully comfortable with the place she has carved out for herself. She is drawn to Son, who is rough, uneducated, and intimately connected with black culture: her complete opposite in almost every way.

Ondine Childs
Ondine is Sydney's wife and has served as a cook for the Street family for many years. Ondine, unlike her quiet husband, is not shy about voicing her opinion, which sometimes causes chaos. Ondine and Margaret used to be close friends when the Streets were first married, but Valerian put a stop to it. Around the same time, Ondine discovered a dark secret about Margaret, which she kept to herself for many years. However, keeping the secret caused her to resent Margaret deeply. Ondine adores her niece Jadine, whom she treats as a daughter, and is disgusted with her at the end of the novel, feeling that Jadine has abandoned her.

Sydney Childs
Sydney is the Streets' long time butler and Ondine's husband. He has an uncanny ability to anticipate Valerian's needs. Sydney and his wife consider themselves to be superior to the black people on the island because they are from America. Sydney is very protective of his wife and only speaks out against the Streets one time in the novel, in her defense. At the end of the novel, Valerian becomes almost entirely dependent on Sydney.

Like Ondine, Sydney feels abandoned by his niece Jadine.

Dawn
Dawn is a friend of Jadine's in New York who lets Jadine and Son stay in her apartment.

Gideon
Gideon, also known as Yardman, is an islander who does work around the Streets' house. He befriends Son and even lets Son stay with him the first night that Son is discovered in the house. Gideon lends Son his passport when Son and Jade want to go to America. Gideon lives with Thérèse, whom the Streets and Ondine and Sydney call Mary. Valerian fires Gideon and Thérèse when it is discovered that they stole apples from him.

Franklin G. Green
See Old Man

William Green
See Son

Jade
See Jadine Childs

Joseph Lordi
Joseph Lordi is Margaret's father.

Leonora Lordi
Leonora Lordi is Margaret's mother.

Mary
See Thérèse

Dr. Robert Michelin
Dr. Michelin is a French dentist who has been exiled from Algeria and lives on Queen of France, an island near the Isle des Chevaliers. Valerian first meets him when he treats his abscessed tooth in the middle of the night, and the two become good friends.

Old Man
Son's father is referred to as Old Man. Son and Jadine visit him in Florida, and he refuses to let them sleep in his house together because they are not married.

Ryk
Ryk is a wealthy, white Frenchmen who proposes to Jadine in Paris before the start of the novel. He sends Jadine an elegant sealskin coat that she prizes. Ryk and Son are juxtaposed as polar opposites.

Soldier
Soldier is a friend of Son's from the army. Jadine and Son visit him in Eloe.

Son
Son is Jadine's lover, a poor black man on the run, attempting to escape a crime he committed long ago. Son accidentally killed his wife Cheyenne by running his car into their house after discovering that she was having an affair. Son and Jadine are fundamentally different. Son comes from a rural town and does not feel comfortable with city life. He believes that black people and white people are fundamentally different and should not try to interact with one another.

Margaret Street
Margaret is Valerian's wife, a great beauty who was once crowned Miss Maine. Valerian first saw her atop a float in a parade when she was seventeen and fell in love with her instantly. Valerian seems to have very little respect for Margaret; he constantly taunts her and does not take her seriously. Valerian also thinks that Margaret has a drinking problem because she suffers bouts of confusion during which she will forget the proper use for everyday items, such as a fork or a tube of lipstick.

Margaret is lonely on the island, with no real friends or company and a distant husband. She dreams of moving back to America, and living near her son Michael, whom she seems to adore. Toward the end of the novel, Ondine reveals that Margaret was abusive towards Michael when he was a baby. Margaret changes after her secret comes out, suddenly feeling more free.

Michael Street
Michael is Valerian and Margaret's son who is mysteriously absent for most of the novel. At the time the novel takes place, he is around thirty years old.

Valerian Street
Valerian is a wealthy white man who used to run his family's candy factory. He is living out his retirement on the Isle des Chevaliers and is quite determined to enjoy it by relaxing and gardening in his greenhouse. Valerian is roughly seventy years old. He regrets the fact that his relationship with his son Michael is distant and strained and

thinks of his greenhouse as something to fill the void left by the lack of any true connection with Michael. Valerian is stubborn and teases his wife constantly. As the novel progresses, he becomes increasingly feeble and depends on others to take care of him.

Thérèse

Thérèse is the black woman who does the Streets' laundry. She lives with Gideon. She is fired every now and again by the Streets or the Childs, but Gideon simply waits awhile and brings her back again. The Streets and Childs do not pay enough attention to her to realize that it is the same woman every time and instead think that Gideon continues to bring new women. The Streets and Childs call her "Mary." They believe they cannot be wrong in calling her that, because all the women on the island have Mary among their names. Thérèse is resentful towards all people who are not native to the island, particularly Americans. Thérèse worked as a wet nurse for white women for many years, because her breasts never stopped producing milk. The invention of baby formula put her out of business. Thérèse has problems with her eyes and cannot see well. She and Gideon are fired when it is revealed that they stole Valerian's apples.

Yardman

See Gideon

THEMES

Ethnic Identity

Although the majority of Morrison's novels feature black women, *Tar Baby* is the first of her works to specifically portray in depth the interactions between black and white characters. The conflict between black culture and white culture in the novel is demonstrated through the contrast of the stereotypical white couple, Margaret and Valerian, with the stereotypical black couple, Ondine and Sydney. The conflict comes to a head in the relationship of Son and Jadine.

While Son is entirely comfortable with and embraces his ethnic identity, Jadine's identity is more fluid. At times, she seems to transcend the racial barriers that separate black and white, and at other times, she seems ashamed of certain aspects of black culture. She tells Valerian that she prefers the artwork of Picasso to traditional African masks and that she prefers Ave Maria to gospel songs. She has studied at the Sorbonne in Paris, worked as a runway model, and graced the cover of *Elle*. In Paris, her white boyfriend proposes to her and lavishes her with expensive gifts, a prospect that makes her Aunt Ondine uncomfortable. She eats dinner in the dining room with her aunt and uncle's white employers, while her aunt and uncle serve her. Even her skin is symbolically lighter than that of the other African American characters in the novel.

Her ethnic confusion does not go unnoticed. At one point, Son tells Jadine that he would not sleep with her because he would never sleep with a white woman. The theme of ethnic identity is continually highlighted in the novel by way of Jadine's contrast with the other black characters, particularly Thérèse. Thérèse, a native of the island, is superstitious, mystical, and skeptical of white people. Jadine blindly dismisses Thérèse and does not even bother to learn her name. Jadine's conflicted identity is also symbolically represented by the fact that she leaves her wealthy, sophisticated, European boyfriend Ryk for Son, a man who believes that blacks and whites should not sit down to dinner together.

Gender Roles

Another central theme of the work is complicated gender roles. All of the women in the novel, in some way, fail to meet the expectations of gender that were prevalent at the time the novel is set and was written. Margaret, perhaps most obviously, fails by any standard past or present to be a good mother. Although she claims she always loved her son, she habitually abused him by sticking him with pins and burning him with cigarettes when Michael was a toddler. Margaret was clearly unprepared and unfit to be a mother, because the only way she was able to deal with what she describes as Michael's overwhelming need for her was through abuse.

Jadine, on the other hand, failed to be a daughter. She was removed from the daughter role quite literally at a young age when she was orphaned. The closest thing Jadine has to a mother is her Aunt Ondine, but by abandoning Ondine and Sydney at the end of the novel, she completely fails at fulfilling the daughter role.

Ondine, the primary caretaker of the household and the most motherly figure in the novel, failed at being a mother in the literal sense because she and Sydney were not able to have

TOPICS FOR FURTHER STUDY

- In *Tar Baby*, the protagonist Jadine identifies with other cultures and ethnicities better than her own. Are there any aspects (music, art, film, language, food, etc.) of other cultures that you admire and enjoy or with which you identify? What aspects of your own culture are most important to you? Using a graphics program such as Microsoft Paint, create an image that represents the cultural aspects with which you identify. The representation can be more abstract, such as a picture, graphic, or web chart. Explain your representation to your classmates.

- Read the young-adult novel *Call Me Maria* by Judith Ortiz Cofer. Like Jadine in *Tar Baby*, Maria struggles to define her identity in the space between the two environments in which she was raised: Puerto Rico and New York. Using a spreadsheet application such as Microsoft Excel, create a chart in which you compare and contrast Jadine and Maria. What are each character's struggles?

How do they resolve their identities? Do you think one is more successful than the other?

- Morrison is one of the most influential writers in the genre of African American literature. Using the Internet, research the history of the genre, including its most significant works and writers. With a classmate, make a digitally-created poster designed to teach about the genre to someone who knows nothing about it. Present your poster to the class.

- In *Tar Baby*, many of the female characters do not live up to the expectations that defined womanhood in the late 1970s. How do you think expectations of women and men have evolved in the past decade? Do you believe that gender roles are divided by strict qualifications today, or do you view gender as a more malleable concept? Write a paper explaining your beliefs. Substantiate your claims with examples from history, the news, literature, or your own life.

---

children. Though she views Jadine as her own child and tells Sydney that she does not regret not having her own children so long as she has Jadine, Jadine's abandonment of Ondine and Sydney at the end of the novel demonstrates that the feeling was not reciprocal and, to some extent, invalidates Ondine and Jadine's mother-daughter relationship.

STYLE

Romantic Novel

The term romantic novel has been used to define a myriad of different types of literature in the past. By the twentieth century, the term evolved to include any type of novel that portrays bizarre, unusual, or supernatural events, a quest, or intense love. *Tar Baby* is a romantic novel on the basis of all of these characteristics. Son and Jadine's

passionate love affair that takes them from the Caribbean, to New York, to Eloe is emblematic of the romance genre. The supernatural and mythical elements of the novel, particularly the ending, in which Son seems to ride off with the wild horsemen of the island, is also indicative of the romance genre.

Use of Folktales

In *Tar Baby*, Morrison uses traditional African folktales to provide a narrative framework. The title itself, tar baby, is an archetypal character in African folklore. In many folktales, a tar baby was some sort of sticky material such as gum or wax that was used specifically for the purpose of trapping someone. The term was popularized in the nineteenth century by Joel Chandler Harris, the author of the Uncle Remus tales. In one tale, the character Br'er fox makes a doll out of tar in an attempt to catch his enemy, Br'er Rabbit. Other folktales and legends are woven

The novel tells a troubled love story. (*Kudryashka /*
Shutterstock.com)

throughout the novel such as the myth of the
blinding of the slaves mentioned in the prologue
and Thérèse's insistence that a race of blind
horsemen live on the island. These tales add a
sense of antiquity, grandeur, and permanence to
the novel.

Dialogue

Compared with Morrison's other novels, a great
deal of the plot of *Tar Baby* unfolds through
dialogue between the characters, as opposed to
narrative exposition. Morrison's dialogue is highly
stylized, and many of her characters, particularly
Son, Ondine, and Sydney, speak in African American vernacular. Morrison's gift for dialogue brings
a heightened sense of realism and immediacy to the
novel. The fact that Morrison supplies her characters with strong, distinctive voices is also the main
reason that the characters in *Tar Baby* come to life
for the reader.

HISTORICAL CONTEXT

"Everyday Racism" in the 1980s

One of the central themes of *Tar Baby* involves
black-white race relations and the stereotypes
that each group uses to label the other. When
Morrison was writing the novel in the late 1970s
and 1980s, a new perspective on race relations
emerged in the wake of the civil-rights movement,

the concept of "everyday racism." While what
people generally think of as racist acts, such as
lynch mobs and hate crimes, are easily recognizable, everyday racism involves acts that are more
subtle, such as a white worker choosing to sit at a
table of only other white workers at lunch time.
Everyday racism is so embedded in culture that it
can be inflicted accidentally or unintentionally by
almost anyone.

Everyday racism shows that, although the
dominant ideology concerning race in the United
States shifted after the civil rights movement, many
people, whether consciously or unconsciously, still
make instantaneous judgments based on race
alone. The concept of everyday racism contradicts
the notion that racism is a thing of the past
and calls attention to acts that on the surface
may not seem to be blatantly racist. This phenomenon began to be heavily documented and scrutinized in the 1980s.

In the book *Double Burden: Black Women and
Everyday Racism*, authors Joe R. Feagin and
Yanick St. Jean describe a heavily documented
instance of everyday racism that occurred during
the 1988 presidential race. Candidate George H.
W. Bush repeatedly used the image of William R.
"Willie" Horton, an African American convicted
felon, in his ad campaigns and brought him up in
speeches. According to Feagin and Yanick, Horton's image was used as a scare tactic to dissuade
white voters from supporting democratic candidate Michael Dukakis, who had supported a weekend furlough program, of which Horton was a
beneficiary. On his furlough, Horton went on a
crime spree and did not return to jail, prompting
Bush representatives to heavily implement frightening images of Horton in their attacks on
Dukakis.

The Education System and Women

In *Tar Baby*, Jadine, the only woman who does not
fill a motherly role, is also the only woman who has
received a college degree. Unlike today, a woman
who, in 1980, had completed three or more years of
graduate school was significantly less likely to be
married and have a family than a woman who had
only completed high school. Pursuing education
sometimes came at the expense of a marriage
and family for women. Additionally, there was a
marked tendency for women to marry men who
were better educated than themselves (as exhibited
by Margaret and Valerian in the novel). Elaina
Rose defined the decreased tendency of women

COMPARE
&
CONTRAST

- **1980s:** On June 22, 1982, Willie Turks, an African American subway maintenance worker, is beaten to death in Brooklyn, New York, by a group of Caucasian men on his way home from work. His death is the first of three race-related killings of African Americans (the second and third being the murders of Michael Griffith and Yusuf Hawkins) carried out by white mobs in New York in the 1980s.

  Today: The New York City Commission on Human Rights, an organization that documents and works to prevent racial discrimination and attacks like the brutal murder of Willie Turks, celebrates its fiftieth anniversary. To commemorate the anniversary, the commission releases a report documenting the past fifty years of discrimination and race relations in New York.

- **1980s:** 1985 is a triumphant year for women, because for the first time in history, the majority of college students in America (52 percent) are women. The previous year, 49 percent of college students in America were women.

- **Today:** For the first time in history, more doctoral degrees are awarded to women than to men in the United States. In 2008–2009, women account for 50.4 percent of the doctoral degrees awarded. Although women have a steadily increasing presence in higher education, until recently men dominate the realm of higher degrees.

- **1980s:** In 1978, the Schomburg Center for Research in Black Culture, part of the New York Public Library, is added to the National Registry of Historic Places. The Schomburg Center houses a myriad of work by black artists, including films, manuscripts, and visual art pieces. It also showcases readings, plays, and other types of performances. Its addition to the National Registry further validates the importance of documenting black artwork.

  Today: Since the 1980s, visitation to the Schomburg center triples to over 120,000 people each year.

---

with more education to marry as the "success gap" in her essay "Education and Hypergamy, and the 'Success Gap.'" Although Jadine stands out in the novel as a strong, educated, and independent young black woman, today she would be fairly commonplace. According to the African American Education Data Book, the number of black women earning bachelor's degrees has increased 55 percent since the mid-1970s.

CRITICAL OVERVIEW

Critical reviews of *Tar Baby* at the time of its publication were mixed. However, over time, numerous critics have confirmed its value as an important part of Morrison's oeuvre.

In his essay "Tar Baby, She Don' Say Nothin'," Robert G. O'Meally claims that, although the novel exhibits many technical feats, the main characters Jade and Son are uninspiring and uninteresting. O'Meally comments that "the novel is selling well, and I believe it will teach well, but for sheer storytelling that seems uncontrived and lively, one must go to Morrison's better novels: *Sula* and the masterful *Song of Solomon*."

Later reviews of the work were more favorable. In Jan Furman's 1996 essay on the work, "Community and Cultural Identity: *Tar Baby*," published in the book *Toni Morrison's Fiction*, Furman praises the work, describing it as an "examination of the intricacies of inter- and intraracial relationships." Furman particularly commends

The Caribbean home of the Street family is an important setting in the novel. *(Karen Hadley / Shutterstock.com)*

Morrison as a novelist with the capability to effectively invoke a moral lesson. She states that "*Tar Baby* is a fable for these modern times when old stories are unfamiliar to a recent generation that needs to learn its lessons as much, if not more, than the previous generations."

Some critics have provided nuanced readings of the work. Critic Terry Otten points out ways that *Tar Baby* resembles biblical stories in the essay, "The Crime of Innocence in Toni Morrison's *Tar Baby*." According to Otten,

> *Tar Baby* describes the passage from innocence to experience with biblical and theological elements: garden images, references to the 'snake,' expression of guilt and lost innocence, a yearning for the garden. In all this [Morrison] incorporates the black search for identity.

Criticism of *Tar Baby* has been abundant since its publication. The reviews of the work have been both positive and negative and are representative of almost all of the popular critical literary theories. One thing almost all critics agree on, however, is that the novel, as a whole, is provocative.

CRITICISM

Rachel Porter

Porter is a freelance writer and editor who holds a bachelor of arts degree in English literature. In the following essay, she argues that it is Jadine's encounters with the black women in Tar Baby, *rather than her relationship with Son, that lead her to question her identity but also aid her in resolving it.*

Much of the contemporary criticism regarding Toni Morrison's novel *Tar Baby* revolves around Jadine's relationship with Son. In his 2000 essay on the novel, "The 'Romance' Novels: *Song of Solomon* and *Tar Baby*," Linden Peach states,

> The complexity of the novel derives from the way in which Jadine and Son are attracted to each other at the same time as each is repelled by the other. They each undergo a process of transformation, initiated by the other.

However, although Jadine and Son's relationship is indisputably central to the action of the novel, Son's effect on Jadine is only marginally consequential to her struggle with identity.

WHAT DO I READ NEXT?

- *Let the Circle Be Unbroken* is a young-adult novel by Mildred Taylor, published in 1981, the same year as *Tar Baby*. This tale of a young black man being falsely convicted of murdering a white man by an all-white jury in the depression era focuses heavily on race relations.

- *What Moves at the Margin* is a collection of Toni Morrison's nonfiction work that was compiled and edited by Carolyn C. Denard and published in 2008. This collection includes speeches, essays, and reviews written by Morrison between 1971 and 2002 that reveals her views on subjects such as racism and the feminist movement.

- *African American Literature* by Keith Gilyard and Anissa Wardi, published in 2004, is a comprehensive survey of the genre organized by theme. The thematic approach is useful in demonstrating how relevant African American works are related to one another.

- *Tracks*, by Louise Erdrich, was published in 1989. This novel, the story of two conflicting Chippewa families, includes many elements that are central to *Tar Baby*, such as race relations, culture, romance, and sexuality.

- *The Bluest Eye* is Morrison's first novel, published in 1970. Like Jadine in *Tar Baby*, the novel's eleven-year-old protagonist Pecola struggles with her African American identity. Because Pecola is abused by her parents and constantly told that she is an ugly girl, she deeply longs to be a Caucasian girl with blue eyes. Racist ideology has become so ingrained in Pecola that she associates whiteness with everything that is beautiful and with being loved and finds her own race to be a source of self-loathing. Eventually, her obsession with becoming a white girl with blue eyes, coupled with the horrifying abuse inflicted upon her by her father, causes Pecola to lose her grip on reality.

- *The House on Mango Street* is a novel published in 1984 by Sandra Cisneros. This coming-of-age tale is the story of Esperanza Cordero, a young girl who feels conflicted about her Latina identity and also wishes to escape confining gender roles.

In actuality, the crux of Jadine's identity crisis, the central point of tension in the novel, is brought on by her perception of and relationships with the other black women in the novel. Moreover, Jadine's identity at the end of the novel is not, as many readings would suggest, solidified by her rejection of Son, who embodies black culture, but rather by her ultimate refusal to assume the role of a daughter to her black women elders. Jadine's relationship with Son is merely a symptom of her more consequential relations with black women. Jadine and Son's turbulent love affair is emblematic of her identity struggle; her quiet rejection of him is emblematic of her identity resolution.

Jadine's struggle to accept her role as a black daughter is perhaps initiated by her literal lack of a black mother. Despite the fact that Jadine's last name is "Childs," she is no longer anyone's child, having been orphaned at a young age. Jadine's lack of a mother is obviously a point of contention for her. At the end of the novel, when her Aunt Ondine acknowledges it, "blood rushed to Jadine's skin the way it always did when her motherlessness was mentioned." Blood rushing to her skin could represent several different emotions, such as shame, anger, or despair; it is an indicator of her intense feelings.

Jadine's second, more symbolic abandonment is recounted to the reader through a flashback in chapter 2. Jadine wakes up from a nightmare and recalls an incident that occurred two months before in Paris. Jadine had received the news that she had been chosen for the cover of *Elle* magazine and also that she had passed her oral exams at the Sorbonne, and she decided to throw a fancy dinner

> **JADINE'S IDENTITY AT THE END OF THE NOVEL IS NOT, AS MANY READINGS WOULD SUGGEST, SOLIDIFIED BY HER REJECTION OF SON, WHO EMBODIES BLACK CULTURE, BUT RATHER BY HER ULTIMATE REFUSAL TO ASSUME THE ROLE OF A DAUGHTER TO HER BLACK WOMEN ELDERS."**

party to celebrate. While at the grocery store buying expensive ingredients for her party, Jadine witnessed a beautiful and distinctive-looking African woman buy three loose eggs.

Many of the store patrons, including Jadine, noticed the woman, who was unusually tall, had no eyelashes, tribal markings on her cheeks, and was attired in a long yellow dress, a yellow head scarf, and multicolored sandals. Jadine was fascinated by the woman and watched her in awe as she moved through the store, made her purchase, and left. However, once the woman was on the street outside the store, she turned back, looked directly at Jadine through the windowpane, and spit on the ground.

Jadine was distraught by the incident: "She couldn't figure out why the woman's insulting gesture had derailed her—shaken her out of proportion to the incident. Why she had wanted that woman to like and respect her." This African woman's rejection of Jadine, who longed for acceptance from her, is the inverse of Jadine's refusal of other black women in the novel who try to claim her as a daughter. It is also indicative of the fact that she does not feel completely comfortable with the identity she has created for herself in Paris as a sophisticated, highly educated fashion model who throws elaborate parties and dates wealthy white men.

The narrator further explains, "The woman had made her feel lonely in a way. Lonely and inauthentic." Jadine muses that perhaps the woman made such an impact on her because she appeared when Jadine was in the midst of deciding whether or not to accept a proposal from a white man. Jadine leaves Paris "because Ryk is white and the woman had spit at her and she had to come see her aunt and uncle to see what they would feel, think, say." It was the simple gesture of a black woman spitting at her that caused Jadine to question the entire life she had built for herself in Paris and travel to the Isle des Chevaliers to visit her aunt and uncle.

Ironically, though it is the disapproval of an older black woman that ignited her fleeing from Paris, once she is at L'Arbe de la Croix she does not spend her time with her Aunt Ondine, the closest thing she has to a black mother, but rather with Ondine's white employer Margaret, the least motherly character in the book. In fact, Margaret's habitual physical abuse of her son when he was a young boy proves that she is an outright failure as a mother, just as Jadine fails to be a daughter. Jadine and Margaret take comfort in one another's company, probably because their relationship does not remotely resemble that of a mother and a daughter. They spend their time gossiping, discussing fashion, and participating in other activities that close girlfriends engage in.

Jadine's plan to sort out her future at L'Arbe de la Croixis is derailed by the arrival of Son. Son seems to fill the exact void that Jadine first noticed while still in Paris. From the moment he presses himself against her in her bedroom, he awakens something in her that she has not experienced before. She feels that "with him she was in strange waters. She had not seen a Black like him in ten years." As Jadine's relationship with Son intensifies, it is constantly stimulating, exciting, and passionate. They run away to New York together and live a carefree, easygoing life. Son is not a crisis for Jadine, he is an adventure.

Son and Jadine's relationship does not become troubled until they travel to Son's home town of Eloe, Florida. Eloe is the apex of everything that is unfamiliar to and uncomfortable for Jadine. It is full of rural, uneducated blacks who value strong family ties. Jadine finds them crude and unsophisticated. It is Jadine's encounters with the black women of Eloe in particular that push her to the point of crisis.

Because the people of Eloe frown on unmarried couples staying in the same house, Jadine has to stay with Son's Aunt Rosa. The first night she stays in Aunt Rosa's house, she wakes suddenly in the middle of the night. She opens the door in her room that leads to the backyard and observes the symbolic blackness outside. When Aunt Rosa enters the room to check on Jadine, she is startled to find Jadine completely naked and assumes she must have forgotten her nightclothes. Rather than explain to Rosa that she never wears nightclothes,

Jadine, ashamed, accepts a slip to wear. As Rosa hands her the slip, she asks Jadine, "You all right, daughter?" implying a family relationship between them. This encounter with Rosa leaves Jadine feeling upset and "like a slut."

The next night, she experiences an even more upsetting encounter, in which it is not shame inflicted by one woman that plagues Jadine but shame inflicted by several imagined women. As she lies awake in bed, she feels as if all the black women of the novel, dead or alive, are coming in through her open bedroom door and crowding around her. She imagines that the women look down upon her and bare their breasts to her insistently. The vision of the black women displaying their womanhood frightens Jadine, and she begins to sob. In the morning, she is determined to leave Eloe immediately: "The women in the night had killed the whole weekend. Eloe was rotten and more boring than ever. A burnt-out place. There was no life there."

Prompted by the crisis of the night before, Jadine leaves for New York that very day, and from that point, her relationship with Son is not the same. When he rejoins her in New York, they fight constantly and become abusive to one another. Somehow, the shame and terror that Jadine feels during her experience with the night women of Eloe change her profoundly and put an end to the new way of living and thinking that she has experienced with Son.

Jadine leaves Son and returns to the Isle des Chevaliers to collect her things before flying back to Paris to resume her old life. There, Ondine expresses her disappointment in Jadine for not saying goodbye before running away with Son. Ondine also feels deeply betrayed by the fact that Jadine refuses to stay and care for her and Sydney in their old age. She says,

> Jadine, a girl has got to be a daughter first. She have to learn that. And if she never learns to be a daughter, she can't never learn how to be a woman. I mean a real woman: a woman good enough for a child; good enough for a man—good enough even for the respect of other women.

Indeed, what Jadine lacks is the respect of other woman, yet when Ondine urges Jadine to learn how to be a daughter, she doesn't just mean it in the literal sense, she is also alluding to the fact that Jadine has largely rejected her heritage. Ondine adds, "A daughter is a woman that cares about where she come from and takes care of them that took care of her."

Beautiful African American model (*Jason Stiti | Shutterstock.com*)

Jadine's quest for identity is ultimately a failure because she refuses to accept any of the black women in the novel as mother figures, and she rejects her role as a daughter. By refusing to be a daughter, Jadine pushes away her ancestry and culture and is left to return to her soulless shell of a life as a high-fashion runway model in Paris. By abandoning Ondine and Sydney at the end of the novel, she literally abandons her ancestry, the only family she has, as she continually pushed it away throughout the course of the novel by refusing to accept a daughterly role. It is Jadine's encounters with the women of the novel, not with Son, that bring her to the realization that she wishes to completely sever herself from her lineage.

Source: Rachel Porter, Critical Essay on *Tar Baby*, in *Novels For Students*, Gale, Cengage Learning, 2011.

Malin Walther Pereira

In the following essay, Pereira examines the description of the life of a queen of soldier ants in African American female author Toni Morrison's

REREADING MORRISON THROUGH PLATH
BROADENS THE DISCOURSE TO INCLUDE AN AFRICAN
AMERICAN PERSPECTIVE ON FEMALE SELFHOOD AND
TRUTH."

work Tar Baby *and its comparison to the description of a bee queen from female author Sylvia Plath's bee poetry sequence in her poem "Ariel" and reveals some interesting insights.*

In *Playing in the Dark: Whiteness and the Literary Imagination,* Toni Morrison outlines a critical reading practice by which we might study "America Africanism" in canonical (usually white male, sometimes white female) texts. As she defines it, *Playing in the Dark* investigates "the ways in which a non-white, Africanlike (or Africanist) presence or persona was constructed in the United States, and the imaginative uses this fabricated presence served." Morrison's readings of works by Cather, Melville, Twain, Poe, and Hemingway convincingly illustrate how an Africanist presence is used in their works. Ultimately, whatever literary strategies the writers employ, Morrison argues that the "always choked representation of an Africanist presence" in their work is a reflection of the effects of a racialized society on nonblacks; the misreadings, distortions, erasures, and caricatures marking the Africanist presence in nonblack texts say more about the writer's fears, desires, and ambivalences than they state any truth about African Americans. Some critical works have already begun the project Morrison suggests, such as Alan Nadel's *Invisible Criticism: Ralph Ellison and the American Canon,* Dana D. Nelson's *The Word in Black and White: Reading "Race" in American Literature, 1638–1876,* and Eric J. Sundquist's *To Wake the Nations: Race in the Making of American Literature.* Such work needs to expand into exploring the Africanist presence in twentieth-century canonical literature.

The rereadings Morrison calls for can clarify both the racial substructures of texts by significant precursors and the ways Morrison's own fiction responds to the call of her theory. In this essay, I would like to focus on one such response: Morrison's signifying repetition and revision in *Tar Baby* of the bee queen from Sylvia Plath's bee poem sequence in *Ariel,* an intertextual relation

which reveals an unacknowledged racial (and racist) dimension in Plath's poetry. Near the end of *Tar Baby,* Morrison describes in some detail the life of the queen of the soldier ants on Isle des Chevaliers. Following directly on the departure of Jadine, the description of the ant queen appears as a commentary on Jadine's quest for self, thereby recalling—in both the image of an insect queen and the theme of female selfhood—Plath's bee sequence. This is of particular significance because many critics have interpreted Plath's bee queen as the emblem for a female self. Rereading through Morrison reveals this self to be a white self, constructed in part by the fear and repression of blackness.

Morrison's repetition and revision of Plath's bee queen in *Tar Baby* uncovers an Africanist presence in Plath's bee poems, a presence unnoticed by Plath critics. Furthermore, fiction, unlike criticism, allows Morrison a space for a corrective revision to such distorted representations of Africanism, a place in which the truth of African American being can be told. Reading Plath through Morrison thus reveals the American Africanism in Plath's bee poem sequence and the limitations of Plath's (white) feminist vision; reading Morrison through Plath tells us the other side of the story and expands our understanding of the limitations of Jadine's choice at the end of the novel. Furthermore, Morrison's novel self-reflexively comments on the power relations at work when discourses make competing claims of epistemological and ontological truth.

The ant queen parable in *Tar Baby* occurs immediately after Jadine's plane takes off for France, thus suggesting its role as commentary on Jadine's quest for self. Morrison details the lives of the soldier ants, who "have no time for dreaming." Almost all of them are women because, as Morrison writes, "the life of their world requires organization so tight and sacrifice so complete there is little need for males and they are seldom produced." However, the queen of the soldier ants vividly remembers her bridal flight with a male, her "one, first and last copulation." Morrison writes:

> Once in life, this little Amazon trembled in the air waiting for a male to mount her. And when he did, . . . he knew at last what his wings were for. Frenzied, he flies into the humming cloud to fight gravity and time in order to do, just once, the single thing he was born for. Then he drops dead, having emptied his sperm into his lady love. . . . Once the lady has collected the sperm, she too falls to the ground [and sheds]

the wings she will never need again. Then she begins her journey searching for a suitable place to build her kingdom.

The ant queen leads a hard life, "bearing, hunting, eating, fighting, burying." Although the passage repeatedly insists the "soldier ants have no time for dreaming," the queen of the soldier ants dreams of her bridal flight, remembering "the rush of wind on her belly—the stretch of fresh wings, the blinding anticipation and herself, there, air-borne, suspended, open, trusting, frightened, deter-mined, vulnerable—girlish, even, for an entire second and then another and another." The para-ble closes with the ant queen wondering about the male's last moments, then thinking: "But soldier ants have no time for dreaming. They are women and have much to do. Still it would be hard. So very hard to forget the man who [. . .] like a star."

Morrison's use of an ant queen to comment on Jadine's flight from the island signifies on Plath's use of a bee queen as a metaphor for the female self in her bee poems. Plath's bee poems consist of a series of five poems written in October 1962, occasioned by Plath's acquisition of a bee colony after her separation from her husband, Ted Hughes. Read through the lens of Morrison's text, Plath's use of the bees and the bee colony as a metaphor for a female escape from patriarchal colonization reveals an uncritical participation in Western racialized discourse, a point missed by Plath critics. While many critics have discussed the black/white color imagery of the sequence (and in Plath's poetry generally), and several have focused on the poems' treatment of issues of power, hierarchy, and the master/slave relation-ship, no critic has interrogated the texts as racial discourse.

The first poem in the series, "The Bee Meet-ing," sets up the black/white imagery running throughout the series. The speaker is clothed in white from her neck to her knees, which she hopes will prevent the bees from smelling her "fear." Her whiteness is starkly opposed to the bees' blackness throughout the poems, culminat-ing in the final poem, "Wintering," where they are depicted as a "Black / Mind against all that white." Such a dichotomous representation of race perpetuates the oppositionalism that critics such as Patricia Hill Collins have argued is foun-dational to Western discourse. Furthermore, black and white are not merely opposed in this depiction: the poem ultimately reaffirms white supremacy by insisting on black stupidity in the

representation of the bees as "Black asininity" (Collins 218).

In the second poem of the series, "The Arrival of the Bee Box," Plath moves beyond simple color imagery to specifically introduce race. Within the bee box

> It is dark, dark, With the swarmy feeling of African hands Minute and shrunk for export, Black on black, angrily clambering.
>
> How can I let them out? It is the noise that appalls me most of all, The unintelligible syllables.

Plath's image of the bees as Africans sold to the slave trade draws on the horrors of the middle passage and ultimately appropriates it as a meta-phor for female colonization throughout the bee poems. The imagery, furthermore, seems racially stereotypical in its representation of African hands as "swarmy" and the echoes of shrunken heads, both of which connote savagery. Although Plath appropriates slavery as an emblem of her female speaker's colonization within patriarchy, the text fails to critique the speaker's own position as a white colonizer. The speaker, in fact, so fears the bees that she exults in her power over them: "They can be sent back. / They can die, I need feed them nothing, I am the owner." She paints herself a benevolent master in the hope they won't turn on her, promising "Tomorrow I will be sweet God, I will set them free." That the speaker's relationship to the bees is represented through the figures of enslavement and ownership reflects the defining racial discourse informing the poems' epistemology.

The enslaved bees appall the speaker with their communication "noise" that appears to her as "unintelligible syllables." That she cannot per-ceive their discourse as intelligible recalls Cornel West's observation in *Prophesy Deliverance!* that Western discourse renders African American expression "incomprehensible and unintelligible" (47). West argues that "the idea of white suprem-acy was constituted as an object of modern dis-course in the West," whose underlying logic is manifest in the way in which the controlling meta-phors, notions, and categories of modern discourse produce and prohibit, develop and delimit, specific conceptions of truth and knowledge, beauty and character, so that certain ideas are rendered incom-prehensible and unintelligible. (47)

Modern Western discourse creates and per-petuates white supremacy in its blindness to alternative ways of knowing. By rendering those alternative conceptions incomprehensible, it effectively delegitimates them and reifies its own discourse. Plath's representation of the bees as unintelligible to the speaker thus disables her from depicting the truth of their be(e)ing. Morrison's parable of the ant queen critiques appropriations like Plath's as limited in their understanding of the racial dimension of Western discourse, and responds by representing the ant queen's point of view as comprehensible and intelligible. In the passage, the repeated insistence that there's "no time for dreaming" in the lives of the soldier ants, a view that a colonizer of the island might take, is undercut by the ant queen's very full description of her dream.

Morrison also images the ant queen as an alternative to Plath's hierarchical and isolationist conception of escape from colonization. In Plath's bee poems, the queen's escape is symbolized by her flight from the hive, a flight that recovers the self. In "Stings," the speaker rejects identifying with the "honey-drudgers" of the hive, asserting instead, "I have a self to recover, a queen." The queen is imaged as "flying / More terrible than she ever was, red / Scar in the sky, red comet / Over the engine that killed her— / The mausoleum, the wax house." Morrison's ant queen, too, has a moment of flight, after which, however, she sheds "the wings she will never need again." Morrison rejects an escape that abandons the community. The ant queen has her flight and her dream and returns to the community to bear her eggs, the next generation of the hive. In using soldier ants rather than bees, Morrison literally grounds her symbolic figure: while Plath's queen escapes, rejecting her community, Morrison's queen flies only once, in the nuptial flight. That Jadine's flight from the island immediately precedes the ant parable delineates the limitations of the escape Jadine has chosen and links her with the Western discourse shaping the escape of Plath's queen from the hive. Signifying on Plath's bee queen in order to comment on Jadine's quest for self, Morrison implicitly links Jadine with the Western discourse shaping Plath's bee queen's idea of selfhood and underlines Jadine's departure from African American notions of female selfhood.

Morrison's representation of the ant queen directly rebuts Plath's virginal imagery as participating in the virgin/whore dichotomy common in Western discourse. Repeatedly in the bee poems, Plath figures the hive as, for example, "as snug as a virgin" ("The Bee Meeting"). Morrison critiques

Plath's erasure of sex and reproduction by emphasizing the ant queen's enduring memory of "the man who [...] like a star" and her subsequent bearing of generations for the hive's continuation. While the (white) feminist escape from patriarchal colonization of Plath's queen can only be figured within an epistemology that constructs her as celibate and alone, the ontology of Morrison's queen allows her selfhood, sexuality, and progeny. Thus Morrison's revision offers on alternative truth, depicting an insect queen who, unlike Plath's, can have self without giving up sexuality or children. Morrison's version emphasizes an African-derived ontology in which self is relational, in contrast to a European-derived solipsistic focus on the individual self.

Morrison's signifying on Plath's bee queen in *Tar Baby* reveals two discourses jockeying over the truth of African American female being. Power, however, is not equally distributed between the discourses, as Morrison well knows. Beyond the ant queen passage, *Tar Baby* generally explores the power dynamics behind which discourses get adopted as "truth." Placing the novel mainly on a fictive Caribbean island allows Morrison to explore the intersecting and divergent discourses resulting from the African diaspora and European colonialism. Central to Morrison's voicing of competing discourses in *Tar Baby* is a nuanced understanding of the power and legitimacy some cultural discourses have over others within modern discourse as a whole.

The differing stories attempting to explain Son's presence in the house enact this struggle over "truth." Characters in the novel repeatedly engage in constructing stories about one another, stories that reflect the epistemologies of their particular cultural discourse as well as the limitations of one discourse's ability to account for the whole truth. Consider, for example, the scene in which Son is found in Margaret's closet. Morrison provides three plausible accounts to explain his presence—"plausible" within each speaker's knowledge system, yet each contradicting the other two accounts.

Ironically recalling Plath's version of the white female self, Margaret constructs an American black male rapist narrative to account for Son's presence. Her construction reflects more than Margaret's individual racial fears: it draws on the white American discourse about black men. Morrison underlines the inability of this one cultural discourse to capture, or even come close to, the whole truth by juxtaposing Margaret's narrative with various others, including Son's own. Son's version is inherently doubly conscious, for it accounts for both his own point of view while rebutting the white American view of him. Son's narrative not only details his escape from the ship and subsequent efforts to survive; it also insists he is not there to rape the women by repeating seven times within five pages, "He had not followed the women."

Tar Baby offers yet a third point of view explaining Son's presence in the house in the form of Therese's construction of a romance story that draws on the cultural discourse of the island, depicting Son as one of the horsemen from the island hills come down to get Jadine. Yet Gideon's critique of her story points out how each of these accounts is circumscribed by its cultural discourse—even Therese's. Her story cannot get at the whole truth either, for it leaves "out the white bosses."

Therese's response to Gideon's critique further amplifies the inherent epistemological limitations of all cultural discourses, a point Morrison understands but Plath uncritically enacts: the insight that each discourse's point of view provides is counterpointed by a blindness to alternative discourses' conceptions of truth and knowledge. Therese thinks, "It was true. She had forgotten the white Americans. How would they fit into the story? She could not imagine them." The discourse that shapes Therese's story renders the white Americans incomprehensible. She cannot imagine them. In trying to imagine them, Therese realizes "that all her life she thought they felt nothing at all." Therese recognizes that incorporating their point of view would fundamentally alter her story. Morrison writes:

> Therese resented the problem and the necessity for solving it to get on with the story. "What difference does it make," she murmured. "I don't know what they would think about him, but I know for certain what they would do about him. Kill him. Kill the chocolate-eating black man. Kill him dead. Ah. Poor thing. Poor, poor thing. He dies and the fast-ass is brought low at last. Too late bitch—too late you discover how wonderful he really was."

Ultimately, Therese cannot rewrite the cultural discourse shaping her story. She cannot incorporate the white American point of view because it would shift the point of view of her story away from the island romance plot between the blind horsemen and the swamp women which she sees Son and Jadine enacting. The white Americans remain simply types in the drama whose actions serve only to further the main romance plot.

Morrison's text reveals an understanding of the varying degrees of authority accorded competing discourses, an understanding Plath's text lacks. *Tar Baby* emphasizes that these three versions of reality do not carry equal weight. Of the three stories explaining Son's presence in the house, Margaret's carries the most power because she is white and the wife of the white man in power, Valerian. Even Margaret's version of reality is delegitimated by Valerian, however, when he views her within the frame of a cultural discourse that situates her by gender as an hysterical woman. Nonetheless, as history has shown, even "hysterical" white women's perceptions of black men as sexual threats have carried a great deal of power, often resulting in the lynching death of the black man. In this scenario, then, the white man, Valerian, carries the power to authorize or delegitimate others' constructions of reality; he validates Son's, not because he inherently believes it, but because it suits his own purposes at the time. Therese's story, notably, is not even heard by Valerian, reflecting his ignorance and erasure of her cultural discourse from his Eurocentric dominion. Even if she were heard, her story would be dismissed as myth. Yet her version contains the insight the others lack, or perhaps suppress: the white Americans have the power to kill Son. Therese's representation of the white Americans forces attention to their power to silence alternative discourses and their messengers.

Rereading Plath's bee queen sequence through Morrison's parable of the soldier ant queen in *Tar Baby* allows us to see how Plath's text silences alternative discourses and their messengers and reveals limitations in the white female vision of a self. Rereading Morrison through Plath broadens the discourse to include an African American perspective on female selfhood and truth. Creating such a dialogue between texts and their discourses is a critical project we might profitably extend to other texts to gain insight into multiple "truths" and ways of be(e)ing.

Source: Malin Walther Pereira, "Be(e)ing and 'Truth': *Tar Baby's* Signifying on Sylvia Plath's Bee Poems," in *Twentieth Century Literature*, Vol. 42, No. 4, Winter 1996, pp. 526–35.

SOURCES

"Black Women Bridging the Economic Gap," in *Louisiana Weekly*, June 22, 2009, http://www.louisianaweekly.com/news.php?viewStory = 1471 (accessed November 21, 2010).

Coates, Ta-Nehisi Paul, "Why 'Tar Baby' Is Such a Sticky Phrase," in *Time*, August 1, 2006, http://www.time.com/time/nation/article/0,8599,1221764,00.html (accessed October 5, 2010).

Collins, Patricia Hill, Review of *Everyday Racism: An Interdisciplinary Theory* in *Contemporary Sociology*, Vol. 1, No. 6, November 1992, pp. 790–91.

"Discrimination and Race Relations: Selected Reports," in *New York City Web site*, http://www.nyc.gov/html/cchr/html/anniversary.html (accessed October 5, 2010).

"Educated Women Less Likely to Skip Marriage and Motherhood, Study Shows," in *Science Blog*, http://scienceblog.com/community/older/2004/10/20049512.shtml (accessed October 5, 2010).

"Everyday Racism," in *Online Encyclopedia*http://encyclopedia.jrank.org/articles/pages/6205/Everyday-Racism.html (accessed October 5, 2010).

Feagin, Joe R., and Yanick St. Jean, "White Manipulation," in *Double Burden: Black Women and Everyday Racism*, M. E. Sharpe, 1998, pp. 52–61.

Furman, Jan, "Community and Cultural Identity: *Tar Baby*," in *Toni Morrison's Fiction*, University of South Carolina Press, 1996, pp. 49–66.

Gillespie, Carmen, "Part 1: Biography," and "Part 2: Tar Baby," in *The Critical Companion to Toni Morrison*, Facts on File, 2008, pp. 208–28.

Heinert, Jennifer Lee Jordan, "(Re)Defining Race: Folktale and Stereotypes in *Tar Baby*," in *Narrative Conventions and Race in the Novels of Toni Morrison*, Routledge, 2009, pp. 36–55.

Jaschik, Scott, "For First Time, More Women Than Men Earn PhD," in *USA Today*, http://www.usatoday.com/news/education/2010-09-15-womenphd14_st_N.htm (accessed October 5, 2010).

Lee, Felicia R., "Harlem Center's Director to Retire in Early 2011," in *New York Times*, http://www.nytimes.com/2010/04/19/arts/19library.html?_r = 1&scp = 1&sq = Schomburg&st = cse (accessed October 5, 2010).

Morrison, Toni, *Tar Baby*, Vintage, 2004.

Murfin, Ross, and Supryia M. Ray, "Romance," in *The Bedford Glossary of Critical and Literary Terms*, Bedford/St. Martin's Press, 2003, pp. 414–15.

O'Meally, Robert G., "Tar Baby, She Don' Say Nothin'," in *Callaloo*, Vol. 11, No. 13, 1981, pp. 193–98.

Otten, Terry, "The Crime of Innocence in Toni Morrison's *Tar Baby*," in *Toni Morrison*, edited by Harold Bloom, Chelsea House Publishers, 1999, pp. 101–15.

Peach, Linden, "The 'Romance' Novels: *Song of Solomon* and *Tar Baby*," in *Toni Morrison*, St. Martin's Press, 2000, pp. 64–101.

Rose, Elaina, "Education and Hypergamy, and the 'Success Gap,'" in *University of Washington Center for Statistics and the Social Sciences*, www.csss.washington.edu/Papers/wp53.pdf (accessed October 5, 2010).

"Toni Morrison Biography," in *Biography.com*, http://www.biography.com/articles/Toni-Morrison-9415590 (accessed October 7, 2010).

"Women's History in America," in *Women's International Center*, http://www.wic.org/misc/history.htm (accessed October 5, 2010).

FURTHER READING

Andrews, William L., Francis Smith Foster, and Trudier Harris, eds., *The Concise Oxford Companion to African American Literature*, Oxford University Press, 2001.
    This sourcebook is essential to anyone wishing to contextualize Morrison's work within the broad scope of African American literature. It contains biographies of over four hundred writers, as well as essays on topics related to this increasingly inclusive genre.

Bloom, Harold, ed., *Toni Morrison*, "Bloom's Modern Critical Views" series, Chelsea House Publications, 2004.
    This biography of Morrison not only details the author's life but also includes critical essays on some of her more famous works.

Tally, Justine, ed., *The Cambridge Companion to Toni Morrison*, Cambridge University Press, 2007.
    The authors of this work scrutinize not only Morrison's literary fiction but also her artwork in other genres and her career as an editor and an educator.

Thomas, Gail E., *U.S. Race Relations in the 1980s and 1990s: Challenges and Alternatives*, Hemisphere Publishing, 1990.
    This study examines race relations in the United States from educational, social, and economical perspectives with regard to African Americans, Hispanics, and Native Americans.

SUGGESTED SEARCH TERMS

Toni Morrison

Toni Morrison AND Tar Baby

Toni Morrison AND novel

Toni Morrison AND identity

Toni Morrison AND race issues

Toni Morrison AND romance novels

Toni Morrison AND African American literature

Tar Baby AND race issues

Tar Baby AND controversy

Tar Baby AND African folktales

Glossary of Literary Terms

A

Abstract: As an adjective applied to writing or literary works, abstract refers to words or phrases that name things not knowable through the five senses.

Aestheticism: A literary and artistic movement of the nineteenth century. Followers of the movement believed that art should not be mixed with social, political, or moral teaching. The statement "art for art's sake" is a good summary of aestheticism. The movement had its roots in France, but it gained widespread importance in England in the last half of the nineteenth century, where it helped change the Victorian practice of including moral lessons in literature.

Allegory: A narrative technique in which characters representing things or abstract ideas are used to convey a message or teach a lesson. Allegory is typically used to teach moral, ethical, or religious lessons but is sometimes used for satiric or political purposes.

Allusion: A reference to a familiar literary or historical person or event, used to make an idea more easily understood.

Analogy: A comparison of two things made to explain something unfamiliar through its similarities to something familiar, or to prove one point based on the acceptedness of another. Similes and metaphors are types of analogies.

Antagonist: The major character in a narrative or drama who works against the hero or protagonist.

Anthropomorphism: The presentation of animals or objects in human shape or with human characteristics. The term is derived from the Greek word for "human form."

Anti-hero: A central character in a work of literature who lacks traditional heroic qualities such as courage, physical prowess, and fortitude. Anti-heroes typically distrust conventional values and are unable to commit themselves to any ideals. They generally feel helpless in a world over which they have no control. Anti-heroes usually accept, and often celebrate, their positions as social outcasts.

Apprenticeship Novel: See *Bildungsroman*

Archetype: The word archetype is commonly used to describe an original pattern or model from which all other things of the same kind are made. This term was introduced to literary criticism from the psychology of Carl Jung. It expresses Jung's theory that behind every person's "unconscious," or repressed memories of the past, lies the "collective unconscious" of the human race: memories of the countless typical experiences of our ancestors. These memories are said to prompt illogical associations that trigger powerful emotions in the reader. Often, the emotional process is primitive, even primordial. Archetypes are the literary images that grow out of the "collective unconscious." They appear in literature as incidents and plots that repeat basic patterns of life. They may also appear as stereotyped characters.

Avant-garde: French term meaning "vanguard." It is used in literary criticism to describe new writing that rejects traditional approaches to literature in favor of innovations in style or content.

B

Beat Movement: A period featuring a group of American poets and novelists of the 1950s and 1960s—including Jack Kerouac, Allen Ginsberg, Gregory Corso, William S. Burroughs, and Lawrence Ferlinghetti—who rejected established social and literary values. Using such techniques as stream of consciousness writing and jazz-influenced free verse and focusing on unusual or abnormal states of mind—generated by religious ecstasy or the use of drugs—the Beat writers aimed to create works that were unconventional in both form and subject matter.

Bildungsroman: A German word meaning "novel of development." The *bildungsroman* is a study of the maturation of a youthful character, typically brought about through a series of social or sexual encounters that lead to self-awareness. *Bildungsroman* is used interchangeably with *erziehungsroman*, a novel of initiation and education. When a *bildungsroman* is concerned with the development of an artist (as in James Joyce's *A Portrait of the Artist as a Young Man*), it is often termed a *kunstlerroman*.

Black Aesthetic Movement: A period of artistic and literary development among African Americans in the 1960s and early 1970s. This was the first major African-American artistic movement since the Harlem Renaissance and was closely paralleled by the civil rights and black power movements. The black aesthetic writers attempted to produce works of art that would be meaningful to the black masses. Key figures in black aesthetics included one of its founders, poet and playwright Amiri Baraka, formerly known as LeRoi Jones; poet and essayist Haki R. Madhubuti, formerly Don L. Lee; poet and playwright Sonia Sanchez; and dramatist Ed Bullins.

Black Humor: Writing that places grotesque elements side by side with humorous ones in an attempt to shock the reader, forcing him or her to laugh at the horrifying reality of a disordered world.

Burlesque: Any literary work that uses exaggeration to make its subject appear ridiculous, either by treating a trivial subject with profound seriousness or by treating a dignified subject frivolously. The word "burlesque" may also be used as an adjective, as in "burlesque show," to mean "striptease act."

C

Character: Broadly speaking, a person in a literary work. The actions of characters are what constitute the plot of a story, novel, or poem. There are numerous types of characters, ranging from simple, stereotypical figures to intricate, multifaceted ones. In the techniques of anthropomorphism and personification, animals—and even places or things—can assume aspects of character. "Characterization" is the process by which an author creates vivid, believable characters in a work of art. This may be done in a variety of ways, including (1) direct description of the character by the narrator; (2) the direct presentation of the speech, thoughts, or actions of the character; and (3) the responses of other characters to the character. The term "character" also refers to a form originated by the ancient Greek writer Theophrastus that later became popular in the seventeenth and eighteenth centuries. It is a short essay or sketch of a person who prominently displays a specific attribute or quality, such as miserliness or ambition.

Climax: The turning point in a narrative, the moment when the conflict is at its most intense. Typically, the structure of stories, novels, and plays is one of rising action, in which tension builds to the climax, followed by falling action, in which tension lessens as the story moves to its conclusion.

Colloquialism: A word, phrase, or form of pronunciation that is acceptable in casual conversation but not in formal, written communication. It is considered more acceptable than slang.

Coming of Age Novel: See *Bildungsroman*

Concrete: Concrete is the opposite of abstract, and refers to a thing that actually exists or a description that allows the reader to experience an object or concept with the senses.

Connotation: The impression that a word gives beyond its defined meaning. Connotations may be universally understood or may be significant only to a certain group.

Convention: Any widely accepted literary device, style, or form.

D

Denotation: The definition of a word, apart from the impressions or feelings it creates (connotations) in the reader.

Denouement: A French word meaning "the unknotting." In literary criticism, it denotes the resolution of conflict in fiction or drama. The *denouement* follows the climax and provides an outcome to the primary plot situation as well as an explanation of secondary plot complications. The *denouement* often involves a character's recognition of his or her state of mind or moral condition.

Description: Descriptive writing is intended to allow a reader to picture the scene or setting in which the action of a story takes place. The form this description takes often evokes an intended emotional response—a dark, spooky graveyard will evoke fear, and a peaceful, sunny meadow will evoke calmness.

Dialogue: In its widest sense, dialogue is simply conversation between people in a literary work; in its most restricted sense, it refers specifically to the speech of characters in a drama. As a specific literary genre, a "dialogue" is a composition in which characters debate an issue or idea.

Diction: The selection and arrangement of words in a literary work. Either or both may vary depending on the desired effect. There are four general types of diction: "formal," used in scholarly or lofty writing; "informal," used in relaxed but educated conversation; "colloquial," used in everyday speech; and "slang," containing newly coined words and other terms not accepted in formal usage.

Didactic: A term used to describe works of literature that aim to teach some moral, religious, political, or practical lesson. Although didactic elements are often found in artistically pleasing works, the term "didactic" usually refers to literature in which the message is more important than the form. The term may also be used to criticize a work that the critic finds "overly didactic," that is, heavy-handed in its delivery of a lesson.

Doppelganger: A literary technique by which a character is duplicated (usually in the form of an alter ego, though sometimes as a ghostly counterpart) or divided into two distinct, usually opposite personalities. The use of this character device is widespread in nineteenth- and twentieth-century literature, and indicates a growing awareness among authors that the "self" is really a composite of many "selves."

Double Entendre: A corruption of a French phrase meaning "double meaning." The term is used to indicate a word or phrase that is deliberately ambiguous, especially when one of the meanings is risqué or improper.

Dramatic Irony: Occurs when the audience of a play or the reader of a work of literature knows something that a character in the work itself does not know. The irony is in the contrast between the intended meaning of the statements or actions of a character and the additional information understood by the audience.

Dystopia: An imaginary place in a work of fiction where the characters lead dehumanized, fearful lives.

E

Edwardian: Describes cultural conventions identified with the period of the reign of Edward VII of England (1901-1910). Writers of the Edwardian Age typically displayed a strong reaction against the propriety and conservatism of the Victorian Age. Their work often exhibits distrust of authority in religion, politics, and art and expresses strong doubts about the soundness of conventional values.

Empathy: A sense of shared experience, including emotional and physical feelings, with someone or something other than oneself. Empathy is often used to describe the response of a reader to a literary character.

Enlightenment, The: An eighteenth-century philosophical movement. It began in France but had a wide impact throughout Europe and America. Thinkers of the Enlightenment valued reason and believed that both the individual and society could achieve a state of perfection. Corresponding to this essentially humanist vision was a resistance to religious authority.

Epigram: A saying that makes the speaker's point quickly and concisely. Often used to preface a novel.

Epilogue: A concluding statement or section of a literary work. In dramas, particularly those of the seventeenth and eighteenth centuries, the epilogue is a closing speech, often in verse, delivered by an actor at the end of a play and spoken directly to the audience.

Epiphany: A sudden revelation of truth inspired by a seemingly trivial incident.

Episode: An incident that forms part of a story and is significantly related to it. Episodes may be either self-contained narratives or events that depend on a larger context for their sense and importance.

Epistolary Novel: A novel in the form of letters. The form was particularly popular in the eighteenth century.

Epithet: A word or phrase, often disparaging or abusive, that expresses a character trait of someone or something.

Existentialism: A predominantly twentieth-century philosophy concerned with the nature and perception of human existence. There are two major strains of existentialist thought: atheistic and Christian. Followers of atheistic existentialism believe that the individual is alone in a godless universe and that the basic human condition is one of suffering and loneliness. Nevertheless, because there are no fixed values, individuals can create their own characters— indeed, they can shape themselves—through the exercise of free will. The atheistic strain culminates in and is popularly associated with the works of Jean-Paul Sartre. The Christian existentialists, on the other hand, believe that only in God may people find freedom from life's anguish. The two strains hold certain beliefs in common: that existence cannot be fully understood or described through empirical effort; that anguish is a universal element of life; that individuals must bear responsibility for their actions; and that there is no common standard of behavior or perception for religious and ethical matters.

Expatriates: See *Expatriatism*

Expatriatism: The practice of leaving one's country to live for an extended period in another country.

Exposition: Writing intended to explain the nature of an idea, thing, or theme. Expository writing is often combined with description, narration, or argument. In dramatic writing, the exposition is the introductory material which presents the characters, setting, and tone of the play.

Expressionism: An indistinct literary term, originally used to describe an early twentieth-century school of German painting. The term applies to almost any mode of unconventional, highly subjective writing that distorts reality in some way.

F

Fable: A prose or verse narrative intended to convey a moral. Animals or inanimate objects with human characteristics often serve as characters in fables.

Falling Action: See *Denouement*

Fantasy: A literary form related to mythology and folklore. Fantasy literature is typically set in non-existent realms and features supernatural beings.

Farce: A type of comedy characterized by broad humor, outlandish incidents, and often vulgar subject matter.

Femme fatale: A French phrase with the literal translation "fatal woman." A *femme fatale* is a sensuous, alluring woman who often leads men into danger or trouble.

Fiction: Any story that is the product of imagination rather than a documentation of fact. characters and events in such narratives may be based in real life but their ultimate form and configuration is a creation of the author.

Figurative Language: A technique in writing in which the author temporarily interrupts the order, construction, or meaning of the writing for a particular effect. This interruption takes the form of one or more figures of speech such as hyperbole, irony, or simile. Figurative language is the opposite of literal language, in which every word is truthful, accurate, and free of exaggeration or embellishment.

Figures of Speech: Writing that differs from customary conventions for construction, meaning, order, or significance for the purpose of a special meaning or effect. There are two major types of figures of speech: rhetorical figures, which do not make changes in the meaning of the words, and tropes, which do.

Fin de siecle: A French term meaning "end of the century." The term is used to denote the last decade of the nineteenth century, a transition period when writers and other artists abandoned old conventions and looked for new techniques and objectives.

First Person: See *Point of View*

Flashback: A device used in literature to present action that occurred before the beginning of the story. Flashbacks are often introduced as the dreams or recollections of one or more characters.

Foil: A character in a work of literature whose physical or psychological qualities contrast strongly with, and therefore highlight, the corresponding qualities of another character.

Folklore: Traditions and myths preserved in a culture or group of people. Typically, these are passed on by word of mouth in various forms—such as legends, songs, and proverbs—or preserved in customs and ceremonies. This term was first used by W. J. Thoms in 1846.

Folktale: A story originating in oral tradition. Folktales fall into a variety of categories, including legends, ghost stories, fairy tales, fables, and anecdotes based on historical figures and events.

Foreshadowing: A device used in literature to create expectation or to set up an explanation of later developments.

Form: The pattern or construction of a work which identifies its genre and distinguishes it from other genres.

G

Genre: A category of literary work. In critical theory, genre may refer to both the content of a given work—tragedy, comedy, pastoral—and to its form, such as poetry, novel, or drama.

Gilded Age: A period in American history during the 1870s characterized by political corruption and materialism. A number of important novels of social and political criticism were written during this time.

Gothicism: In literary criticism, works characterized by a taste for the medieval or morbidly attractive. A gothic novel prominently features elements of horror, the supernatural, gloom, and violence: clanking chains, terror, charnel houses, ghosts, medieval castles, and mysteriously slamming doors. The term "gothic novel" is also applied to novels that lack elements of the traditional Gothic setting but that create a similar atmosphere of terror or dread.

Grotesque: In literary criticism, the subject matter of a work or a style of expression characterized by exaggeration, deformity, freakishness, and disorder. The grotesque often includes an element of comic absurdity.

H

Harlem Renaissance: The Harlem Renaissance of the 1920s is generally considered the first significant movement of black writers and artists in the United States. During this period, new and established black writers published more fiction and poetry than ever before, the first influential black literary journals were established, and black authors and artists received their first widespread recognition and serious critical appraisal. Among the major writers associated with this period are Claude McKay, Jean Toomer, Countee Cullen, Langston Hughes, Arna Bontemps, Nella Larsen, and Zora Neale Hurston.

Hero/Heroine: The principal sympathetic character (male or female) in a literary work. Heroes and heroines typically exhibit admirable traits: idealism, courage, and integrity, for example.

Holocaust Literature: Literature influenced by or written about the Holocaust of World War II. Such literature includes true stories of survival in concentration camps, escape, and life after the war, as well as fictional works and poetry.

Humanism: A philosophy that places faith in the dignity of humankind and rejects the medieval perception of the individual as a weak, fallen creature. "Humanists" typically believe in the perfectibility of human nature and view reason and education as the means to that end.

Hyperbole: In literary criticism, deliberate exaggeration used to achieve an effect.

I

Idiom: A word construction or verbal expression closely associated with a given language.

Image: A concrete representation of an object or sensory experience. Typically, such a representation helps evoke the feelings associated with the object or experience itself. Images are either "literal" or "figurative." Literal images are especially concrete and involve little or no extension of the obvious meaning of the words used to express them. Figurative images do not follow the literal meaning of the words exactly. Images in literature are usually visual, but the term "image" can also refer to the representation of any sensory experience.

Imagery: The array of images in a literary work. Also, figurative language.

In medias res: A Latin term meaning "in the middle of things." It refers to the technique of beginning a story at its midpoint and then using various flashback devices to reveal previous action.

Interior Monologue: A narrative technique in which characters' thoughts are revealed in a way that appears to be uncontrolled by the author. The interior monologue typically aims to reveal the inner self of a character. It portrays emotional experiences as they occur at both a conscious and unconscious level. images are often used to represent sensations or emotions.

Irony: In literary criticism, the effect of language in which the intended meaning is the opposite of what is stated.

J

Jargon: Language that is used or understood only by a select group of people. Jargon may refer to terminology used in a certain profession, such as computer jargon, or it may refer to any nonsensical language that is not understood by most people.

L

Leitmotiv: See *Motif*

Literal Language: An author uses literal language when he or she writes without exaggerating or embellishing the subject matter and without any tools of figurative language.

Lost Generation: A term first used by Gertrude Stein to describe the post-World War I generation of American writers: men and women haunted by a sense of betrayal and emptiness brought about by the destructiveness of the war.

M

Mannerism: Exaggerated, artificial adherence to a literary manner or style. Also, a popular style of the visual arts of late sixteenth-century

Europe that was marked by elongation of the human form and by intentional spatial distortion. Literary works that are self-consciously high-toned and artistic are often said to be "mannered."

Metaphor: A figure of speech that expresses an idea through the image of another object. Metaphors suggest the essence of the first object by identifying it with certain qualities of the second object.

Modernism: Modern literary practices. Also, the principles of a literary school that lasted from roughly the beginning of the twentieth century until the end of World War II. Modernism is defined by its rejection of the literary conventions of the nineteenth century and by its opposition to conventional morality, taste, traditions, and economic values.

Mood: The prevailing emotions of a work or of the author in his or her creation of the work. The mood of a work is not always what might be expected based on its subject matter.

Motif: A theme, character type, image, metaphor, or other verbal element that recurs throughout a single work of literature or occurs in a number of different works over a period of time.

Myth: An anonymous tale emerging from the traditional beliefs of a culture or social unit. Myths use supernatural explanations for natural phenomena. They may also explain cosmic issues like creation and death. Collections of myths, known as mythologies, are common to all cultures and nations, but the best-known myths belong to the Norse, Roman, and Greek mythologies.

N

Narration: The telling of a series of events, real or invented. A narration may be either a simple narrative, in which the events are recounted chronologically, or a narrative with a plot, in which the account is given in a style reflecting the author's artistic concept of the story. Narration is sometimes used as a synonym for "storyline."

Narrative: A verse or prose accounting of an event or sequence of events, real or invented. The term is also used as an adjective in the sense "method of narration." For example, in literary criticism, the expression "narrative technique" usually refers to the way the author structures and presents his or her story.

Narrator: The teller of a story. The narrator may be the author or a character in the story through whom the author speaks.

Naturalism: A literary movement of the late nineteenth and early twentieth centuries. The movement's major theorist, French novelist Emile Zola, envisioned a type of fiction that would examine human life with the objectivity of scientific inquiry. The Naturalists typically viewed human beings as either the products of "biological determinism," ruled by hereditary instincts and engaged in an endless struggle for survival, or as the products of "socioeconomic determinism," ruled by social and economic forces beyond their control. In their works, the Naturalists generally ignored the highest levels of society and focused on degradation: poverty, alcoholism, prostitution, insanity, and disease.

Noble Savage: The idea that primitive man is noble and good but becomes evil and corrupted as he becomes civilized. The concept of the noble savage originated in the Renaissance period but is more closely identified with such later writers as Jean-Jacques Rousseau and Aphra Behn.

Novel: A long fictional narrative written in prose, which developed from the novella and other early forms of narrative. A novel is usually organized under a plot or theme with a focus on character development and action.

Novel of Ideas: A novel in which the examination of intellectual issues and concepts takes precedence over characterization or a traditional storyline.

Novel of Manners: A novel that examines the customs and mores of a cultural group.

Novella: An Italian term meaning "story." This term has been especially used to describe fourteenth-century Italian tales, but it also refers to modern short novels.

O

Objective Correlative: An outward set of objects, a situation, or a chain of events corresponding to an inward experience and evoking this experience in the reader. The term frequently appears in modern criticism in discussions of authors' intended effects on the emotional responses of readers.

Objectivity: A quality in writing characterized by the absence of the author's opinion or feeling about the subject matter. Objectivity is an important factor in criticism.

Oedipus Complex: A son's amorous obsession with his mother. The phrase is derived from the story of the ancient Theban hero Oedipus, who unknowingly killed his father and married his mother.

Omniscience: See *Point of View*

Onomatopoeia: The use of words whose sounds express or suggest their meaning. In its simplest sense, onomatopoeia may be represented by words that mimic the sounds they denote such as "hiss" or "meow." At a more subtle level, the pattern and rhythm of sounds and rhymes of a line or poem may be onomatopoeic.

Oxymoron: A phrase combining two contradictory terms. Oxymorons may be intentional or unintentional.

P

Parable: A story intended to teach a moral lesson or answer an ethical question.

Paradox: A statement that appears illogical or contradictory at first, but may actually point to an underlying truth.

Parallelism: A method of comparison of two ideas in which each is developed in the same grammatical structure.

Parody: In literary criticism, this term refers to an imitation of a serious literary work or the signature style of a particular author in a ridiculous manner. A typical parody adopts the style of the original and applies it to an inappropriate subject for humorous effect. Parody is a form of satire and could be considered the literary equivalent of a caricature or cartoon.

Pastoral: A term derived from the Latin word "pastor," meaning shepherd. A pastoral is a literary composition on a rural theme. The conventions of the pastoral were originated by the third-century Greek poet Theocritus, who wrote about the experiences, love affairs, and pastimes of Sicilian shepherds. In a pastoral, characters and language of a courtly nature are often placed in a simple setting. The term pastoral is also used to classify dramas, elegies, and lyrics that exhibit the use of country settings and shepherd characters.

Pen Name: See *Pseudonym*

Persona: A Latin term meaning "mask." *Personae* are the characters in a fictional work of literature. The *persona* generally functions as a mask through which the author tells a story in a voice other than his or her own. A *persona* is usually either a character in a story who acts as a narrator or an "implied author," a voice created by the author to act as the narrator for himself or herself.

Personification: A figure of speech that gives human qualities to abstract ideas, animals, and inanimate objects.

Picaresque Novel: Episodic fiction depicting the adventures of a roguish central character ("picaro" is Spanish for "rogue"). The picaresque hero is commonly a low-born but clever individual who wanders into and out of various affairs of love, danger, and farcical intrigue. These involvements may take place at all social levels and typically present a humorous and wide-ranging satire of a given society.

Plagiarism: Claiming another person's written material as one's own. Plagiarism can take the form of direct, word-for-word copying or the theft of the substance or idea of the work.

Plot: In literary criticism, this term refers to the pattern of events in a narrative or drama. In its simplest sense, the plot guides the author in composing the work and helps the reader follow the work. Typically, plots exhibit causality and unity and have a beginning, a middle, and an end. Sometimes, however, a plot may consist of a series of disconnected events, in which case it is known as an "episodic plot."

Poetic Justice: An outcome in a literary work, not necessarily a poem, in which the good are rewarded and the evil are punished, especially in ways that particularly fit their virtues or crimes.

Poetic License: Distortions of fact and literary convention made by a writer—not always a poet—for the sake of the effect gained. Poetic license is closely related to the concept of "artistic freedom."

Poetics: This term has two closely related meanings. It denotes (1) an aesthetic theory in literary criticism about the essence of poetry or (2) rules prescribing the proper methods, content, style, or diction of poetry. The term poetics may also refer to theories about literature in general, not just poetry.

Point of View: The narrative perspective from which a literary work is presented to the reader. There are four traditional points of view. The "third person omniscient" gives the reader a "godlike" perspective, unrestricted by time or place, from which to see actions and look into the minds of characters. This allows the author to comment openly on characters and events in the work. The "third person" point of view presents the events of the story from outside of any single character's perception, much like the omniscient point of view, but the reader must understand the action as it takes place and without any special insight into characters' minds or motivations. The "first person" or "personal" point of view relates events as they are perceived by a single character. The main character "tells" the story and may offer opinions about the action and characters which differ from those of the author. Much less common than omniscient, third person, and first person is the "second person" point of view, wherein the author tells the story as if it is happening to the reader.

Polemic: A work in which the author takes a stand on a controversial subject, such as abortion or religion. Such works are often extremely argumentative or provocative.

Pornography: Writing intended to provoke feelings of lust in the reader. Such works are often condemned by critics and teachers, but those which can be shown to have literary value are viewed less harshly.

Post-Aesthetic Movement: An artistic response made by African Americans to the black aesthetic movement of the 1960s and early '70s. Writers since that time have adopted a somewhat different tone in their work, with less emphasis placed on the disparity between black and white in the United States. In the words of post-aesthetic authors such as Toni Morrison, John Edgar Wideman, and Kristin Hunter, African Americans are portrayed as looking inward for answers to their own questions, rather than always looking to the outside world.

Postmodernism: Writing from the 1960s forward characterized by experimentation and continuing to apply some of the fundamentals of modernism, which included existentialism and alienation. Postmodernists have gone a step further in the rejection of tradition begun with the modernists by also rejecting traditional forms, preferring the anti-novel over the novel and the anti-hero over the hero.

Primitivism: The belief that primitive peoples were nobler and less flawed than civilized peoples because they had not been subjected to the tainting influence of society.

Prologue: An introductory section of a literary work. It often contains information establishing the situation of the characters or presents information about the setting, time period, or action. In drama, the prologue is spoken by a chorus or by one of the principal characters.

Prose: A literary medium that attempts to mirror the language of everyday speech. It is distinguished from poetry by its use of unmetered, unrhymed language consisting of logically related sentences. Prose is usually grouped into paragraphs that form a cohesive whole such as an essay or a novel.

Prosopopoeia: See *Personification*

Protagonist: The central character of a story who serves as a focus for its themes and incidents and as the principal rationale for its development. The protagonist is sometimes referred to in discussions of modern literature as the hero or anti-hero.

Protest Fiction: Protest fiction has as its primary purpose the protesting of some social injustice, such as racism or discrimination.

Proverb: A brief, sage saying that expresses a truth about life in a striking manner.

Pseudonym: A name assumed by a writer, most often intended to prevent his or her identification as the author of a work. Two or more authors may work together under one pseudonym, or an author may use a different name for each genre he or she publishes in. Some publishing companies maintain "house pseudonyms," under which any number of authors may write installations in a series. Some authors also choose a pseudonym over their real names the way an actor may use a stage name.

Pun: A play on words that have similar sounds but different meanings.

R

Realism: A nineteenth-century European literary movement that sought to portray familiar characters, situations, and settings in a realistic manner. This was done primarily by using an objective narrative point of view and through the buildup of accurate detail. The standard for success of any realistic work depends on how faithfully it transfers common experience into fictional forms. The realistic method may be altered or extended, as in stream of consciousness writing, to record highly subjective experience.

Repartee: Conversation featuring snappy retorts and witticisms.

Resolution: The portion of a story following the climax, in which the conflict is resolved.

Rhetoric: In literary criticism, this term denotes the art of ethical persuasion. In its strictest sense, rhetoric adheres to various principles developed since classical times for arranging facts and ideas in a clear, persuasive, appealing manner. The term is also used to refer to effective prose in general and theories of or methods for composing effective prose.

Rhetorical Question: A question intended to provoke thought, but not an expressed answer, in the reader. It is most commonly used in oratory and other persuasive genres.

Rising Action: The part of a drama where the plot becomes increasingly complicated. Rising action leads up to the climax, or turning point, of a drama.

Roman à clef: A French phrase meaning "novel with a key." It refers to a narrative in which real persons are portrayed under fictitious names.

Romance: A broad term, usually denoting a narrative with exotic, exaggerated, often idealized characters, scenes, and themes.

Romanticism: This term has two widely accepted meanings. In historical criticism, it refers to a European intellectual and artistic movement of the late eighteenth and early nineteenth centuries that sought greater freedom of personal expression than that allowed by the strict rules of literary form and logic of the eighteenth-century neoclassicists. The Romantics preferred emotional and imaginative expression to rational analysis. They considered the individual to be at the center of all experience and so placed him or her at the center of their art. The Romantics believed that the creative imagination reveals nobler truths—unique feelings and attitudes—than those that could be discovered by logic or by scientific examination. Both the natural world and the state of childhood were important sources for revelations of "eternal truths." "Romanticism" is also used as a general term to refer to a type of sensibility found in all periods of literary history and usually considered to be in opposition to the principles of classicism. In this sense, Romanticism signifies any work or philosophy in which the exotic or dreamlike figure strongly, or that is devoted to individualistic expression, self-analysis, or a pursuit of a higher realm of knowledge than can be discovered by human reason.

Romantics: See *Romanticism*

S

Satire: A work that uses ridicule, humor, and wit to criticize and provoke change in human nature and institutions. There are two major types of satire: "formal" or "direct" satire speaks directly to the reader or to a character in the work; "indirect" satire relies upon the ridiculous behavior of its characters to make its point. Formal satire is further divided into two manners: the "Horatian," which ridicules gently, and the "Juvenalian," which derides its subjects harshly and bitterly.

Science Fiction: A type of narrative about or based upon real or imagined scientific theories and technology. Science fiction is often peopled with alien creatures and set on other planets or in different dimensions.

Second Person: See *Point of View*

Setting: The time, place, and culture in which the action of a narrative takes place. The elements of setting may include geographic location, characters' physical and mental environments, prevailing cultural attitudes, or the historical time in which the action takes place.

Simile: A comparison, usually using "like" or "as," of two essentially dissimilar things, as in "coffee as cold as ice" or "He sounded like a broken record."

Slang: A type of informal verbal communication that is generally unacceptable for formal writing. Slang words and phrases are often colorful exaggerations used to emphasize the speaker's point; they may also be shortened versions of an often-used word or phrase.

Slave Narrative: Autobiographical accounts of American slave life as told by escaped slaves. These works first appeared during the abolition movement of the 1830s through the 1850s.

Socialist Realism: The Socialist Realism school of literary theory was proposed by Maxim Gorky and established as a dogma by the first Soviet Congress of Writers. It demanded adherence to a communist worldview in works of literature. Its doctrines required an objective viewpoint comprehensible to the working classes and themes of social struggle featuring strong proletarian heroes.

Stereotype: A stereotype was originally the name for a duplication made during the printing process; this led to its modern definition as a person or thing that is (or is assumed to be) the same as all others of its type.

Stream of Consciousness: A narrative technique for rendering the inward experience of a character. This technique is designed to give the impression of an ever-changing series of thoughts, emotions, images, and memories in the spontaneous and seemingly illogical order that they occur in life.

Structure: The form taken by a piece of literature. The structure may be made obvious for ease of understanding, as in nonfiction works, or may obscured for artistic purposes, as in some poetry or seemingly "unstructured" prose.

Sturm und Drang: A German term meaning "storm and stress." It refers to a German literary movement of the 1770s and 1780s that reacted against the order and rationalism of the enlightenment, focusing instead on the intense experience of extraordinary individuals.

Style: A writer's distinctive manner of arranging words to suit his or her ideas and purpose in writing. The unique imprint of the author's personality upon his or her writing, style is the product of an author's way of arranging ideas and his or her use of diction, different sentence structures, rhythm, figures of speech, rhetorical principles, and other elements of composition.

Subjectivity: Writing that expresses the author's personal feelings about his subject, and which may or may not include factual information about the subject.

Subplot: A secondary story in a narrative. A subplot may serve as a motivating or complicating force for the main plot of the work, or it may provide emphasis for, or relief from, the main plot.

Surrealism: A term introduced to criticism by Guillaume Apollinaire and later adopted by Andre Breton. It refers to a French literary and artistic movement founded in the 1920s. The Surrealists sought to express unconscious thoughts and feelings in their works. The best-known technique used for achieving this aim was automatic writing—transcriptions of spontaneous outpourings from the unconscious. The Surrealists proposed to unify the contrary levels of conscious and unconscious, dream and reality, objectivity and subjectivity into a new level of "super-realism."

Suspense: A literary device in which the author maintains the audience's attention through the buildup of events, the outcome of which will soon be revealed.

Symbol: Something that suggests or stands for something else without losing its original identity. In literature, symbols combine their literal meaning with the suggestion of an abstract concept. Literary symbols are of two types: those that carry complex associations of meaning no matter what their contexts, and those that derive their suggestive meaning from their functions in specific literary works.

Symbolism: This term has two widely accepted meanings. In historical criticism, it denotes an early modernist literary movement initiated in France during the nineteenth century that reacted against the prevailing standards of realism. Writers in this movement aimed to evoke, indirectly and symbolically, an order of being beyond the material world of the five senses. Poetic expression of personal emotion figured strongly in the movement, typically by means of a private set of symbols uniquely identifiable with the individual poet. The principal aim of the Symbolists was to express in words the highly complex feelings that grew out of everyday contact with the world. In a broader sense, the term "symbolism" refers to the use of one object to represent another.

T

Tall Tale: A humorous tale told in a straightforward, credible tone but relating absolutely impossible events or feats of the characters. Such tales were commonly told of frontier adventures during the settlement of the west in the United States.

Theme: The main point of a work of literature. The term is used interchangeably with thesis.

Thesis: A thesis is both an essay and the point argued in the essay. Thesis novels and thesis plays share the quality of containing a thesis which is supported through the action of the story.

Third Person: See *Point of View*

Tone: The author's attitude toward his or her audience may be deduced from the tone of the work. A formal tone may create distance or convey politeness, while an informal tone may encourage a friendly, intimate, or intrusive feeling in the reader. The author's attitude toward his or her subject matter may also be deduced from the tone of the words he or she uses in discussing it.

Transcendentalism: An American philosophical and religious movement, based in New England from around 1835 until the Civil War. Transcendentalism was a form of American romanticism that had its roots abroad in the works of Thomas Carlyle, Samuel Coleridge, and Johann Wolfgang von Goethe. The Transcendentalists stressed the importance of intuition and subjective experience in communication with God. They rejected religious dogma and texts in favor of mysticism and scientific naturalism. They pursued truths that lie beyond the "colorless" realms perceived by reason and the senses and were active social reformers in public education, women's rights, and the abolition of slavery.

U

Urban Realism: A branch of realist writing that attempts to accurately reflect the often harsh facts of modern urban existence.

Utopia: A fictional perfect place, such as "paradise" or "heaven."

V

Verisimilitude: Literally, the appearance of truth. In literary criticism, the term refers to aspects of a work of literature that seem true to the reader.

Victorian: Refers broadly to the reign of Queen Victoria of England (1837-1901) and to anything with qualities typical of that era. For example, the qualities of smug narrowmindedness, bourgeois materialism, faith in social progress, and priggish morality are often considered Victorian. This stereotype is contradicted by such dramatic intellectual developments as the theories of Charles Darwin, Karl Marx, and Sigmund Freud (which stirred strong debates in England) and the critical attitudes of serious Victorian writers like Charles Dickens and George Eliot. In literature, the Victorian Period was the great age of the English novel, and the latter part of the era saw the rise of movements such as decadence and symbolism.

W

Weltanschauung: A German term referring to a person's worldview or philosophy.

Weltschmerz: A German term meaning "world pain." It describes a sense of anguish about the nature of existence, usually associated with a melancholy, pessimistic attitude.

Z

Zeitgeist: A German term meaning "spirit of the time." It refers to the moral and intellectual trends of a given era.

Cumulative
Author/Title Index

Cumulative Nationality/Ethnicity Index

Subject/Theme Index

Oedipus complex
  The Haunting of Hill House: 218
Oppression (Politics)
  A Bend in the River: 62, 75
  Breath, Eyes, Memory: 148
  Jasmine: 268
Optimism
  Holes: 240, 248, 249
Outsiders
  The Age of Innocence: 6, 7, 16

P

Pain
  Breath, Eyes, Memory: 137–139, 141, 149
Paradoxes
  Bone: 100
  The Haunting of Hill House: 198
  The Moon Is Down: 285
Past
  A Bend in the River: 55, 78
  Bone: 88, 95
  The Bostonians: 115–116
Pathos
  The Beet Queen: 39
Patience
  The Bostonians: 121
Patriarchy
  Jasmine: 271, 273
  Tar Baby: 340
Patriotism
  The Moon Is Down: 295
Perseverance
  Going after Cacciato: 195
  The Moon Is Down: 291–293
Pessimism
  A Bend in the River: 78
Philosophy
  Frankenstein: 164
Point of view (Literature)
  The Beet Queen: 36
  A Bend in the River: 66, 67
  Breath, Eyes, Memory: 141
Politics
  A Bend in the River: 63, 71–77
  The Bostonians: 132, 133
Postcolonial Africa
  A Bend in the River: 53, 63, 66, 68, 69, 78
Postcolonialism
  Jasmine: 251, 269–270, 273, 274
Postmodernism
  The Haunting of Hill House: 211
Power (Philosophy)
  A Bend in the River: 58
  Jasmine: 257, 261–262, 276
  Pudd'nhead Wilson: 316
  Tar Baby: 341
Predestination
  Frankenstein: 160
  Jasmine: 260, 265

Private and public
  The Bostonians: 126
Progress
  A Bend in the River: 56, 74, 75
Psychoanalysis
  The Bostonians: 127
  The Haunting of Hill House: 217–220
Public and private
  The Bostonians: 133
Punishment
  Frankenstein: 165
  The Haunting of Hill House: 203
Purity
  The Bostonians: 113
  Breath, Eyes, Memory: 149

R

Race relations
  The Beet Queen: 40
  A Bend in the River: 66, 74, 75–76
  Holes: 237–238
  Pudd'nhead Wilson: 309, 319, 320
  Tar Baby: 330
Racism
  Pudd'nhead Wilson: 309
  Tar Baby: 333
Rape
  Breath, Eyes, Memory: 137, 138, 147, 149
  Jasmine: 254, 262, 263, 273
Realism (Cultural movement)
  The Bostonians: 116–117
Reality
  Bone: 102
  Going after Cacciato: 191, 194, 195
  The Haunting of Hill House: 202, 204–205
Rebellion
  The Age of Innocence: 5, 16
  The Beet Queen: 30
  A Bend in the River: 59
Rebirth
  Jasmine: 254, 269
Reconciliation
  Breath, Eyes, Memory: 149
Redemption
  The Haunting of Hill House: 204
Refugees
  Jasmine: 272
Regionalism
  The Bostonians: 118–120
  Pudd'nhead Wilson: 307
Rejection
  The Beet Queen: 47
  Bone: 101
Resentment
  Frankenstein: 160
  The Haunting of Hill House: 219
  Jasmine: 257

Resilience
  Breath, Eyes, Memory: 142
  Holes: 249
Resistance
  A Bend in the River: 56
  Jasmine: 270
  The Moon Is Down: 282, 283, 287–288
Responsibility
  Jasmine: 268, 274
Restlessness
  The Moon Is Down: 283
Revenge
  The Bostonians: 131
  The Moon Is Down: 283
Rituals
  The Age of Innocence: 1
  Breath, Eyes, Memory: 147, 149
  Jasmine: 268
Rivalry
  The Bostonians: 127
Romantic love
  The Age of Innocence: 23
  The Bostonians: 110
Romanticism
  Tar Baby: 332
Rural life
  The Beet Queen: 23

S

Sacrifice
  The Age of Innocence: 21
  The Bostonians: 123, 124
  The Moon Is Down: 278
Sadness
  Breath, Eyes, Memory: 149
Sainthood
  The Bostonians: 123–125
Satire
  The Bostonians: 117, 120, 128–129
  The Haunting of Hill House: 198, 204, 206–207
Science
  Frankenstein: 157
  The Haunting of Hill House: 203, 214
Security
  The Beet Queen: 46
  Holes: 235, 245
Self destruction
  A Bend in the River: 67
Self identity
  A Bend in the River: 60–61
  Jasmine: 253
  Tar Baby: 329, 341
Self image
  The Age of Innocence: 5
  The Haunting of Hill House: 220
  Holes: 234
Self love
  The Haunting of Hill House: 218

Verisimilitude
    Going after Cacciato: 183–184
Vietnam War, 1959-1975
    Going after Cacciato: 171,
        173–177, 182–184, 186–187,
        191–196
Violence
    A Bend in the River: 56, 57, 59, 71,
        74, 75
    Frankenstein: 160
    Holes: 248
    Jasmine: 262, 272
Virginity
    Breath, Eyes, Memory: 137–139,
        144, 147

Virtue
    The Moon Is Down: 292–293
Vulnerability
    The Haunting of Hill House: 220
    Jasmine: 273

W

Wars
    Going after Cacciato: 171,
        173–177, 184, 186–193,
        195–196
    The Moon Is Down: 278, 279–283,
        290–291, 293–297

Western culture
    A Bend in the River: 58, 62, 67–68,
        74–77, 79
    Jasmine: 272
    Tar Baby: 340
Widowhood
    Jasmine: 258, 260, 272
Women's rights
    The Bostonians: 104, 110, 113–115,
        117–118, 122–123, 130–133
Working class
    Bone: 102
World War II, 1939-1945
    The Moon Is Down: 278, 279–283,
        286–288, 294–295